Today's Moral Problems

Today's Moral Problems

EDITED BY
Richard Wasserstrom
University of California, Los Angeles

MACMILLAN PUBLISHING CO., INC.
New York

COLLIER MACMILLAN PUBLISHERS
London

Macmillan Publishing Co., Inc.
866 Third Avenue, New York, New York 10022

Collier-Macmillan Canada, Ltd.

Library of Congress Cataloging in Publication Data

Wasserstrom, Richard A,   comp.
  Today's moral problems.
  Includes bibliographical references.
  1. United States—Moral conditions. I. Title.
HN90.M6W37   301.41'7973   74–86
ISBN 0–02–424790–1

Printing: 1 2 3 4 5 6 7 8   Year: 5 6 7 8 9 0

PREFACE

The writings in this collection deal with moral issues that have been of special concern to people living in the United States during the past five or ten years. In addition, almost all of the selections were written during the past decade. It is worth asking why this latter fact is so. Part of the explanation, of course, is the problems selected for inclusion. Because such things as war, abortion, and sexual morality have been among the particular worries of this generation, it is not surprising that contemporary moral philosophers have turned their attention to issues such as these.

But this is not the whole answer. The problems considered in this collection are hardly new problems, or even problems that have only acquired a particular urgency in our own time. Nor have philosophers just become aware of moral issues such as these; morality has been a concern of philosophers for as long as there has been philosophy. So, the recent vintage of most of these pieces does not reflect either a new-found philosophical concern for morality or the rise to prominence of new moral problems. What it does reflect, at least, is a change of sorts in Anglo-American academic philosophy.

For some time philosophers who were interested in moral philosophy were interested primarily in what have been called the problems of metaethics. They were concerned with such things as the analysis and examination of the way moral concepts and moral arguments worked and, sometimes, the development of general theories about the meaning and characteristics of fundamental moral ideas. Their philosophical inquiries were about ethical statements and judgments.

Many of the writings found in this collection are not metaethics but rather normative ethics. That is to say, they are philosophical attempts to elucidate and assess what is to be said for and against particular ways of behaving in respect to particular moral problems. The distinction between metaethics and normative ethics is anything but precise. And even if it were, no philosophical inquiry worthy of respect could help engaging in substantial metaethical activity. Nonetheless, what distinguishes these writings from the writings in moral philosophy of the recent past is this immersion in specific moral issues and this willingness to move to the presentation of more particular moral assessments.

I think that the inquiries collected here are exciting both because of what they teach about the moral problems they examine and because of what they show about this additional aspect of philosophical activity. I hope that those who read these philosophical writings will find them exhilarating. I hope that they will serve to introduce people to some of the important, but less traditional, types of philosophical explorations that can take place in respect to morality. And I hope, as well, that these writings reveal to them some of the ways in which philosophy can make an important contribution to an adequate and informed understanding of serious, live moral issues.

R. W.

CONTENTS

4 SEXUAL MORALITY

5 PUNISHMENT

PRIVACY 1

STANLEY I. BENN
Privacy, Freedom, and Respect for Persons

When your mind is set on mating
It is highly irritating
To see an ornithologist below:
Though it may be nature-study,
To a bird it's merely bloody
Awful manners. Can't he see that he's de trop!*

Introduction

If two people retire to the privacy of the bushes, they go where they expect to be unobserved. What they do is done *privately,* or *in private,* if they are not actually seen doing it. Should they later advertise or publish what they were about, what *was* private would then become public knowledge. Or they may have been mistaken in thinking their retreat private—they may have been in full view of passersby all the time. One's *private affairs,* however, are private in a different sense. It is not that

Reprinted from *Privacy,* Nomos, Vol. 13 (1971), 1–26, ed. J. Roland Pennock and John W. Chapman. (New York: Atherton Press, 1971). Reprinted by Permission of the Author and the Publishers, Lieber-Atherton, Inc. Copyright © 1971 by Atherton Press, Inc. All Rights Reserved.

I wish to acknowledge my indebtedness to my colleague Geoffrey Mortimore for his many helpful suggestions and no less for his trenchant criticism of this paper.
* From "Bird-watching—The Song of the Redstart," in A. N. L. Munby, *Lyra Catenata* (printed privately 1948). Quoted in John Buxton, *The Redstart* (London: Collins, 1950).

they are kept out of sight or from the knowledge of others that makes them private. Rather, they are matters that it would be inappropriate for others to try to find out about, much less report on, without one's consent; one complains if they are publicized precisely because they are private. Similarly, a private room remains private in spite of uninvited intruders, for, unlike the case of the couple in the bushes, falsifying the expectation that no one will intrude is not a logically sufficient ground for saying that something private in this sense is not private after all.

"Private" used in this second, *immunity-claiming*[1] way is both norm-dependent and norm-invoking. It is norm-dependent because *private affairs* and *private rooms* cannot be identified without some reference to norms. So any definition of the concept "private affairs" must presuppose the existence of *some* norms restricting unlicensed observation, reporting, or entry, even though no norm in particular is necessary to the concept. It is norm-invoking in that one need say no more than "This is a private matter" to claim that anyone not invited to concern himself with it ought to stay out of it. That is why the normative implications of "Private" on a letter or a notice board do not need to be spelled out.[2]

The norms invoked by the concept are not necessarily immunity-conferring, however; one can imagine cultures, for instance, in which they would be prohibitive, where to say that someone had done something in private would be to accuse him of acting inappropriately—perhaps cutting himself off from a collective experience and cheating others of their right to share in it. Or again, "privacy" might apply mandatorily; that is, anything private *ought* to be kept from the knowledge of others. This is rather the sense of the somewhat old-fashioned phrase "private parts," referring not to parts of the body that one might keep unseen if one chose, but to parts that one had a duty to keep out of sight. In our culture, sexual and excretory acts are private not merely in the sense that performers are immune from observation but also in the sense that some care ought to be taken that they are not generally observed. Thus, liberty to publicize, that is, to license scrutiny and publicity, whether generally or to a select public, is commonly but by no means necessarily associated with the right to immunity from observation.

The norms invoked by the concept of privacy are diverse, therefore, not only in substance but also in logical form; some grant immunities,

---

[1] I do not use "immunity" in this paper in the technical Hohfeldian sense. Where it is not used in a simple descriptive sense, I intend that a person shall be understood to be immune from observation if he has grounds for complaint should anyone watch him; an activity is immune if it is not appropriate for unauthorized persons to watch it.

[2] Of course, though "Someone has been reading my private letters" is enough to state a protest, it need not be well founded; the letters may not really qualify as private, or even if they are, there may be other conditions overriding the implicit claim to immunity.

some are prohibitive, some are mandatory. There may be cultures, indeed, with no norm-invoking concept of privacy at all, where *nothing* is thought properly immune from observation and anything may be generally displayed. It might still be possible, of course, to seek out private situations where one would not be observed, but it would never be a ground of grievance either that an action was or was not open for all to see or that someone was watching. But whatever the possible diversity, some privacy claims seem to rest on something a bit more solid than mere cultural contingency. The first objective of this paper is to explore the possibility that some minimal right to immunity from uninvited observation and reporting is required by certain basic features of our conception of a person.

The General Principle of Privacy and Respect for Persons

The umbrella "right to privacy" extends, no doubt, to other claims besides the claims not to be watched, listened to, or reported upon without leave, and not to have public attention focused upon one uninvited. It is these particular claims, however, that I have primarily in mind in this paper. It deals, therefore, with a cluster of immunities which, if acknowledged, curb the freedom of others to do things that are generally quite innocent if done to objects other than persons, and even to persons, if done with their permission. There is nothing intrinsically objectionable in observing the world, including its inhabitants, and in sharing one's discoveries with anyone who finds them interesting; and this is not on account of any special claims, for instance, for scientific curiosity, or for a public interest in the discovery of truth. For I take as a fundamental principle in morals a general liberty to do whatever one chooses unless someone else has good reasons for interfering to prevent it, reasons grounded either on the freedom of others or on some other moral principle such as justice or respect for persons or the avoidance of needless pain. The onus of justification, in brief, lies on the advocate of restraint, not on the person restrained. The present question, then, is whether any moral principle will provide a quite general ground for a prima facie claim that B should not observe and report on A unless A agrees to it. Is there a principle of privacy extending immunity to inquiry to all human activities, to be overridden only by special considerations, like those suggested? Or is it rather that there is a general freedom to inquire, observe, and report on human affairs as on other things, unless a special case can be made out for denying it with respect to certain activities that are *specifically* private?

My strategy, then, is to inquire, first, whether anyone is entitled, prima facie, to be private if he chooses, irrespective of what he is about: would the couple in the bushes have grounds for complaint if they discovered

3

someone eavesdropping on their discussion of, say, relativity theory? Second, whether or not such grounds exist, can any rational account be given (that is, an account not wholly dependent on conventional norms) of "private affairs," the area in which uninvited intrusions are judged *particularly* inappropriate?

The former, more sweeping claim may appear at first sight extravagant, even as only a prima facie claim. Anyone who wants to remain unobserved and unidentified, it might be said, should stay at home or go out only in disguise. Yet there is a difference between happening to be seen and having someone closely observe, and perhaps record, what one is doing, even in a public place. Nor is the resentment that some people feel at being watched necessarily connected with fears of damaging disclosures in the Sunday papers or in a graduate thesis in social science. How reasonable is it, then, for a person to resent being treated much in the way that a birdwatcher might treat a redstart?

Putting the case initially at this rather trivial level has the advantage of excluding two complicating considerations. In the first place, I have postulated a kind of intrusion (if that is what it is) which does no obvious damage. It is not like publishing details of someone's sex life and ruining his career. Furthermore, what is resented is not being watched *tout court,* but being watched without leave. If observation as such were intrinsically or even consequentially damaging, it might be objectionable even if done with consent. In the present instance, consent removes all ground for objection. In the second place, by concentrating on simple unlicensed observation, I can leave aside the kind of interference with which Mill was mainly concerned in the essay *On Liberty,* namely, anything that prevents people doing, in their private lives, something they want to do, or that requires them to do what they do not want to do.[3] Threatening a man with penalties, or taking away his stick, are ways of preventing his beating his donkey; but if he stops simply because he is watched, the interference is of a different kind. He could continue if he chose; being observed affects his action only by changing his perception of it. The observer makes the act impossible only in the sense that the actor now sees it in a different light. The intrusion is not therefore obviously objectionable as an interference with freedom of action. It is true that there are special kinds of action—any that depend upon surprise, for example—that could be made objectively impossible merely by watching and reporting on them; but my present purpose is to ask whether a *general* case can be made out, not one that depends on special conditions of that kind.

Of course, there is always a danger that information may be used to

---

[3] W. L. Weinstein's illuminating contribution to this volume, "The Private and the Free: A Conceptual Inquiry," is mainly concerned with Mill's questions; I shall touch on them only indirectly.

harm a man in some way. The usual arguments against wiretapping, bugging, a National Data Center, and private investigators rest heavily on the contingent possibility that a tyrannical government or unscrupulous individuals might misuse them for blackmail or victimization. The more one knows about a person, the greater one's power to damage him. Now it may be that fears like this are the only reasonable ground for objecting *in general* to being watched. I might suspect a man who watches my house of "casing the joint." But if he can show me he intends no such thing, and if there is no possibility of his observations being used against me in any other way, it would seem to follow that I could have no further reasonable ground for objecting. Eliza Doolittle resents Professor Higgins's recording her speech in Covent Garden because she believes that a girl of her class subject to so close a scrutiny is in danger of police persecution: "You dunno what it means to me. Theyll take away my character and drive me on the streets for speaking to gentlemen."[4] But the resentment of the bystanders is excited by something else, something intrinsic in Higgins's performance, not merely some possible consequence of his ability to spot their origins by their accents: "See here: what call have you to know about people what never offered to meddle with you? . . . You take us for dirt under your feet, dont you? Catch you taking liberties with a gentleman!" What this man resents is surely that Higgins fails to show a proper respect for persons; he is treating people as objects or specimens—like "dirt"—and not as subjects with sensibilities, ends, and aspirations of their own, morally responsible for their own decisions, and capable, as mere specimens are not, of reciprocal relations with the observer. This failure is, of course, precisely what Eliza, in her later incarnation as Higgins's Galatea, complains of too. These resentments suggest a possible ground for a prima facie claim not to be watched, at any rate in the same manner as one watches a thing or an animal. For this is "to take liberties," to act impudently, to show less than a proper regard for human dignity.

Finding oneself an object of scrutiny, as the focus of another's attention, brings one to a new consciousness of oneself, as something seen through another's eyes. According to Sartre, indeed, it is a necessary condition for knowing oneself *as* anything at all that one should conceive oneself as an object of scrutiny.[5] It is only through the regard of the other that the observed becomes aware of himself as an object, knowable, having a determinate character, in principle predictable. His consciousness of pure freedom as subject, or originator and chooser, is at once assailed by it; he is fixed *as something*—with limited probabilities rather than infinite, indeterminate possibilities. Sartre's account of human relations is of an obsessional need to master an unbearable alien freedom

4 G. B. Shaw, *Pygmalion*, Act I.

5 See J.-P. Sartre: *L'être et le néant* (Paris, 1953), Part 3, "Le pour-autrui."

that undermines one's belief in one's own; for Ego is aware of Alter not only as a fact, an object in his world, but also as the subject of a quite independent world of Alter's own, wherein Ego himself is mere object. The relationship between the two is essentially hostile. Each, doubting his own freedom, is driven to assert the primacy of his own subjectivity. But the struggle for mastery, as Sartre readily admits, is a self-frustrating response; Alter's reassurance would be worthless to Ego unless it were freely given, yet the freedom to give it would at once refute it.

What Sartre conceived as a phenomenologically necessary dilemma, however, reappears in R. D. Laing's *The Divided Self*[6] as a characteristically schizoid perception of the world, the response of a personality denied free development, trying to preserve itself from domination by hiding away a "real self" where it cannot be absorbed or overwhelmed. The schizoid's problem arises because he cannot believe fully in his own existence as a person. He may *need* to be observed in order to be convinced that he exists, if only in the world of another; yet, resenting the necessity to be what the other perceives him as, he may try at the same time to hide. His predicament, like Sartre's, may seem to him to arise not from the *manner* of his being observed, but to be implicit in the very relation of observer and observed.

Sartre, however, does not show why the awareness of others as subjects must evoke so hostile a response. Even if it were true that my consciousness of my own infinite freedom is shaken by my being made aware that in the eyes of another I have only limited possibilities, still if I am not free, it is not his regard that confines me; it only draws my attention to what I was able formerly to disregard. And if I *am* free, then his regard makes no real difference. And if there is a dilemma here, may I not infer from it that the Other sees me too as a subject, and has the same problem? Could this not be a bond between us rather than a source of resentment, each according the other the same dignity as subject?

It is because the schizoid cannot believe in himself as a person, that he cannot form such a bond, or accept the respectful regard of another. So every look is a threat or an insult. Still, without question, there are ways of looking at a man that do diminish him, that provide cause for offense as real as any physical assault. But, of course, that cannot be a reason either for hiding or for going around with one's eyes shut. Yet it does suggest that if, like a doctor, one has occasion to make someone an object of scrutiny and study, or like a clinician the topic for a lecture, the patient will have grounds for resentment if the examiner appears insensible to the fact that it is a person he is examining, a subject to whom it makes a difference that he is observed, who will also have a

[6] Harmondsworth, England, 1965.

view about what is discovered or demonstrated, and will put his own value upon it.

It would be a mistake to think that the only objection to such examination is that an incautious observer could cause damage to a sensitive person's mental state, for that could be avoided by watching him secretly. To treat a man without respect is not to injure him—at least, not in *that* sense; it is more like insulting him. Nor is it the fact of scrutiny as such that is offensive, but only unlicensed scrutiny, which may in fact do no damage at all, yet still be properly resented as an impertinence.

I am suggesting that a general principle of privacy might be grounded on the more general principle of respect for persons. By a *person* I understand a subject with a consciousness of himself as agent, one who is capable of having projects, and assessing his achievements in relation to them. To *conceive* someone as a person is to see him as actually or potentially a chooser, as one attempting to steer his own course through the world, adjusting his behavior as his apperception of the world changes, and correcting course as he perceives his errors. It is to understand that his life is for him a kind of enterprise like one's own, not merely a succession of more or less fortunate happenings, but a record of achievements and failures; and just as one cannot describe one's own life in these terms without claiming that what happens is important, so to see another's in the same light is to see that for him at least this must be important. Professor Higgins's offense was to be insensitive to this fact about other people. Of course, one may have a clinical interest in people as project-makers without oneself attaching any importance to their projects. Still, if one fails to see how their aims and activities could be important for them, one has not properly understood what they are about. Even so, it requires a further step to see that recognizing another as engaged on such an enterprise makes a claim on oneself. To *respect* someone as a person is to concede that one ought to take account of the way in which his enterprise might be affected by one's own decisions. By the principle of respect for persons, then, I mean the principle that every human being, insofar as he is qualified as a person, is entitled to this minimal degree of consideration.

I do not mean, of course, that someone's having some attitude toward *anything* I propose to do is alone sufficient for his wishes to be a relevant consideration, for he will certainly have attitudes and wishes about actions of mine that do not affect his enterprise at all. B's dislike of cruelty to animals is not in itself a reason why A should stop beating his donkey. It is not enough that B will be gratified if he can approve A's action, and disappointed if not; it is the conception of B as a chooser, as engaged in an active, creative enterprise, that lays an obligation of respect upon A, not the conception of him as *suffering* gratifications and disappointments. This can be a ground for sympathetic joy or pity, but not respect. B's

7

attitudes are considerations relevant for A's decisions only if what A does will make a difference to the conditions under which B makes *his* choices, either denying him an otherwise available option (which would be to interfere with his freedom of action) or changing the significance or meaning for B of acts still open to him. B may disapprove of A's watching C or listening to his conversation with D, but B's own conditions of action—what I have called B's enterprise—remain unaffected. On the other hand, if C knows that A is listening, A's intrusion alters C's consciousness of himself, and his experienced relation to his world. Formerly self-forgetful, perhaps, he may now be conscious of his opinions as candidates for A's approval or contempt. But even without self-consciousness of this kind, his immediate enterprise—the conversation with D—may be changed for him merely by the fact of A's presence. I am not postulating a private conversation in the sense of one about personal matters; what is at issue is the change in the way C apprehends his own performance—the topic makes no difference to this argument. A's uninvited intrusion is an impertinence because he treats it as of no consequence that he may have effected an alteration in C's perception of himself and of the nature of his performance.[7] Of course, no *damage* may have been done; C may actually enjoy performing before an enlarged audience. But C's wishes in the matter must surely be a relevant consideration (as B's are not), and in the absence of some overriding reason to the contrary, if C were inclined to complain, he has legitimate grounds.

The underpinning of a claim not to be watched without leave will be more general if it can be grounded in this way on the principle of respect for persons than on a utilitarian duty to avoid inflicting suffering. That duty may, of course, reinforce the claim in particular instances. But respect for persons will sustain an objection even to secret watching, which may do no actual harm at all. Covert observation—spying—is objectionable because it deliberately deceives a person about his world, thwarting, for reasons that *cannot* be his reasons, his attempts to make a rational choice. One cannot be said to respect a man as engaged on an enterprise worthy of consideration if one knowingly and deliberately alters his conditions of action, concealing the fact from him. The offense is different in this instance, of course, from A's open intrusion on C's conversation. In that case, A's attentions were liable to affect C's enterprise by changing C's perception of it; he may have felt differently about his conversation with D, even to the extent of not being able to see it as any longer the same activity, knowing that A was now listening. In the present instance, C is unaware of A. Nevertheless, he is wronged because the sig-

---

[7] Of course, there are situations, such as in university common rooms, where there is a kind of conventional general license to join an ongoing conversation. A railway compartment confers a similar license in Italy, but not in England. In such situations, if one does not wish to be listened to, one stays silent.

nificance to him of his enterprise, assumed unobserved, is deliberately falsified by A. He may be in a fool's paradise or a fool's hell; either way, A is making a fool of him. Suppose that in a situation in which he might be observed, there is no reason why he should not choose to act privately (for instance, he is doing nothing wrong); then for anyone to watch without his knowledge is to show disrespect not only for the privacy that may have been his choice, but, by implication, for him, as a chooser. I can well imagine myself freely consenting to someone's watching me at work, but deeply resenting anyone's doing so without my knowledge—as though it didn't matter whether I liked it or not. So a policeman may treat suspected criminals like this only if there are good grounds for believing that there is an overriding need to frustrate what they are about, not because they have no rights as persons to privacy. Psychiatrists may be entitled to treat lunatics like this—but only to the extent that being incapable of rational choice, they are defective as persons. (Even so, their interests, if not their wishes, will be limiting considerations.)

The close connection between the general principle of privacy and respect for persons may account for much of the resentment evoked by the idea of a National Data Center, collating all that is known about an individual from his past contacts with government agencies. Much has been made, of course—and no doubt rightly—of the dangers of computerized data banks, governmental or otherwise. The information supplied to and by them may be false; or if true, may still put a man in a false light, by drawing attention, say, to delinquencies in his distant past that he has now lived down. And even the most conforming of citizens would have reason for dread if officials came to regard their computers as both omniscient and infallible. A good deal of legislative invention has been exercised, accordingly, in seeking safeguards against the abuse of information power. Yet for some objectors at least it altogether misses the point. It is not just a matter of a fear to be allayed by reassurances, but of a resentment that anyone—even a thoroughly trustworthy official—should be able at will to satisfy any curiosity, without the knowledge let alone the consent of the subject. For since what others know about him can radically affect a man's view of himself, to treat the collation of personal information about him as if it raised purely technical problems of safeguards against abuse is to disregard his claim to consideration and respect as a person.

I have argued so far as though the principle of respect for persons clearly indicated what a man might reasonably resent. This needs some qualification. If someone stares at my face, I cannot help seeing his gaze as focused on me. I am no less self-conscious if I catch him scrutinizing the clothes I am wearing. But would it be reasonable to resent scrutiny of a suit I am not wearing—one I have just given, perhaps, to an old

9

folks' home? Or of my car outside my home? Or in the service station? Granted that I can reasonably claim immunity from the uninvited attentions of observers and reporters, what is to count for this purpose as *me?* As I suggested above, it cannot be sufficient that I do not *want* you to observe something; for the principle of respect to be relevant, it must be something about my own person that is in question, otherwise the principle would be so wide that a mere wish of mine would be a prima facie reason for everyone to refrain from observing and reporting on anything at all. I do not make something a part of me merely by having feelings about it. The principle of privacy proposed here is, rather, that any man who desires that he *himself* should not be an object of scrutiny has a reasonable prima facie claim to immunity. But the ground is not in the mere fact of his desiring, but in the relation between himself as an object of scrutiny and as a conscious and experiencing subject. And it is clearly not enough for a man to *say* that something pertains to him as a person and therefore shares his immunity; there must be reasons for saying so.

What could count as a reason? The very intimate connection between the concepts of *oneself* and *one's body* (about which philosophers have written at length) would seem to put that much beyond question (though some schizoids' perception of the world would suggest that dissociation even of these concepts is possible). Beyond that point, however, cultural norms cannot be ignored. In a possessive individualist culture, in which a man's property is seen as an extension of his personality, as an index to his social standing, a measure of his achievements, or an expression of his taste, to look critically on his clothes or his car is to look critically on him. In other cultures, the standards might well be different. The notion we have of our own extension, of the outer limits of our personalities—those events or situations in respect of which we feel pride or shame—is unquestionably culture-variant; consequently, the application even of a quite general principle of privacy will be affected by culturally variant norms—those regarding family, say, or property.

Applying the General Principle

Allow that the principle of respect for persons will underpin a general principle of privacy; even so, it would amount only to a prima facie ground for limiting the freedom of others to observe and report at will. It would place on them a burden of justification but it would not override any special justification. The principle might be thought quite inadequate, for instance, to sustain on its own a case for legal restraints; the protection of privacy is less important, perhaps, than the danger to political freedom from legal restrictions on reporting. It might be argued that in every case it is for the press to show what reasonable public interest publicity would serve. But so uncertain a criterion could result in an overtimorous press. The courts have been properly wary of recognizing rights that might discourage if not disable the press from publicizing what *ought* to be exposed.

General principles do not *determine* solutions to moral problems of this kind. They indicate what needs to be justified, where the onus of justification lies, and what can count as a justification. So to count as an overriding consideration, an argument must refer to some further principle. Consider the difficult case of the privacy of celebrities. According to a learned American judge, the law "recognizes a legitimate public curiosity about the personalities of celebrities, and about a great deal of otherwise private and personal information about them."[8] But is all curiosity equally legitimate, or must there be something about the kind of celebrity that legitimizes special kinds of curiosity? Is there no difference between, say, a serious historian's curiosity about what (and who) prompted President Johnson's decision not to run a second time and that to which the Sunday gossip columnists appeal? If a person is in the public eye for some performance that he intends to be public or that is in its nature public—like conducting an orchestra—this may, as a matter of fact, make "human interest stories" about him more entertaining and exciting than similar stories about an unknown. But the fact that many people enjoy that kind of entertainment is no reason at all for overriding the principle of privacy; for though there is a presumptive liberty to do whatever there is no reason for not doing, there is no general claim to have whatever one enjoys. To treat even an entertainer's life simply as material for entertainment is to pay no more regard to him as a person than to an animal in a menagerie. Of course, anyone who indiscriminately courts publicity, as some entertainers do, can hardly complain if they are understood to be offering a general license. But merely to be a celebrity—even a willing celebrity—does not disable someone from claiming the consideration due to a person. Admittedly, it opens up a range of special claims to information about him, to override his general claim to privacy. Candidates for appointment to the Supreme Court must expect some public concern with their business integrity. Or —a rather different case—because an eminent conductor participates in a public activity with a public tradition, anyone choosing conducting as a profession must expect that his musical experience, where he was trained, who has influenced his interpretations, will be matters of legitimate interest to others concerned as he is with music. But this is not a warrant for prying into other facts about him that have nothing to do with his music: his taste in wines, perhaps, or women. The principle of privacy would properly give way in one area, but it would stand in any other to which the special overriding grounds were irrelevant. For the principle

8 See W. L. Prosser, "Privacy," *California Law Review,* 48 (1960), 416–417.   11

itself is not limited in its application; it constitutes a prima facie claim in respect to *anything* a man does.

"Private Affairs" and Personal Ideals

To claim immunity on the ground that an inquiry is an intrusion into one's *private affairs* is to make an argumentative move of a quite different kind. For this concept entrenches the privacy of certain special areas far more strongly than the mere presumptive immunity of the general principle. To justify such an intrusion, one has to have not merely a reason, but one strong enough to override special reasons for *not* intruding. So while the interests of phonetic science might justify Professor Higgins's impertinence in Covent Garden, they would not be good enough reasons for bugging Eliza's bedroom.

The activities and experiences commonly thought to fall within this special private area are diverse and largely culture-dependent. Some seem to have no rational grounds at all. For instance, why should the bodily functions that in our culture are appropriately performed in solitude include defecation but not eating? Of course, so long as certain acts are assigned to this category anyone who has internalized the social norms will experience a painful embarrassment if seen doing them; embarrassment, indeed, is the culturally appropriate response in a society with the concept of *pudenda,* and anyone not showing it may be censured as brazen or insensitive. But though this furnishes a kind of rational interest in privacy of this kind, its rationale depends on a conventional norm that may itself be wholly irrational.

Not all areas of privacy are like this, however; others are closely related to ideals of life and character which would be difficult, perhaps impossible, to achieve were privacy not safeguarded. The liberal individualist tradition has stressed, in particular, three personal ideals, to each of which corresponds a range of "private affairs." The first is the ideal of personal relations; the second, the Lockian ideal of the politically free man in a minimally regulated society; the third, the Kantian ideal of the morally autonomous man, acting on principles that he accepts as rational.

THE PRIVACY OF PERSONAL RELATIONS

By personal relations, I mean relations between persons that are considered valuable and important at least as much because of the quality of each person's attitude to another as for what each does to, or for, another.

All characteristically human relations—I mean relations of a kind that could not exist between stones or wombats—involve some element, however small, of role-expectancy. We structure our relations with others according to an understanding of *what* they are and what accordingly is

12

due to them and from them. That may exhaust some relations: if the railway booking clerk gives me the correct ticket in exchange for my fare, he has fulfilled his function. Moreover, the point of the relationship calls for no more than this; the grating that separates us, with just space enough to push through a ticket or a coin, appropriately symbolizes it. One cannot be indifferent to his performance, but one need not attend to his personality.

The relation between father and son, or husband and wife, is necessarily more than this, or if in a given instance it is not, then that instance is defective. Here, too, there are role-expectancies, but each particular set of related persons will fulfill them in a different way. There is room for being a father in this or in that manner. Moreover, only a part of what it is to be a father has been met when the specified duties of the role have been fulfilled. Beyond that, the value of the relation depends on a personal understanding between the parties, and on whether, and how, they care about one another. Father and son might be meticulous in the performance of the formal duties of their roles, but if they are quite indifferent to each other, the relationship is missing its point. The relationship between friends or lovers is still less role-structured than family relations, though even here there are conventional patterns and rituals—gifts on ritual occasions, forms of wooing, etc. But they are primarily symbols: their main point is to communicate a feeling or an attitude, to reassure, perhaps, or make a proposal. And though they could be gone through even if the feeling did not really exist, such a performance would surely be a pretense or a deception, and therefore parasitic on the primary point.

Personal relations can of course be of public concern; children may need to be protected, for instance, from certain kinds of corrupting relations with adults. But while it may be possible and desirable to prevent such relations altogether, there is little that third parties can do to regulate or reshape them. By inducing the booking clerk to do his job more efficiently, or passengers to state their destinations more clearly, the railway staff controller can improve the relation between them. But this is because he can keep them up to the mark—they are all interested exclusively in role-performance, and each can have a clear notion of the standard that the other's performance should reach. But friends can be kept up to the mark only by one another. There is no "mark" that anyone outside could use to assess them, for friendship is not confined by role requirements.[9]

9 "According to the newspaper *Szabad Nép,* some members of the Communist Party in Hungary have not a single working man among their friends, and they are censured in a way that implies that they had better quickly make a friend of a worker or it will be the worse for them" (*The Times* [London], July 20, 1949, quoted by P. Halmos, *Solitude and Privacy* [London, 1952], p. 167).

To intrude on personal relations of this kind may be very much worse than useless. Of course, people do take their troubles to others, to friends or marriage counselors for guidance and advice. But this is to invite the counselor to become, in a small way perhaps, a party to the relationship —or rather, to enter into a relationship with him, the success of which depends on his resolve to keep it a purely second-order relationship, demanding of him a sensitive and reticent understanding of the first. Personal relations are exploratory and creative; they survive and develop if they are given care and attention; they require continuous adjustment as the personalities of the parties are modified by experience, both of one another and of their external environment. Such relationships are, in their nature, private. They could not exist if it were not possible to create excluding conditions. One cannot have a personal relation with all comers, nor carry on personal conversations under the same conditions as an open seminar.[10]

If we value personal relations, then, we must recognize these at least as specifically private areas. And since the family and the family home are the focal points of important and very generally significant personal relations, these must be immune from intrusion, at least beyond the point at which minimal public role requirements are satisfied. A father who regularly beats the children insensible cannot claim, of course, that intrusion could only spoil his personal relations. But while the public is properly concerned that there should be no cruelty, exploitation, or neglect, these are only the minimal conditions for personal relations. The rest are the private business of the parties.

Preoccupation with privacy—in particular with the privacy of family relations—has been criticized by some writers, however, as an unhealthy feature of post-Renaissance bourgeois society. Consider Edmund Leach's strictures:

In the past, kinsfolk and neighbors gave the individual continuous moral support throughout his life. Today the domestic household is isolated. The family looks inward upon itself; there is an intensification of emotional stress between husband and wife, and parents and children. The strain is greater than most of us can bear. Far from being the basis of the good society, the family, with its narrow privacy and tawdry secrets, is the source of all our discontents.[11]

---

[10] Charles Fried has argued that privacy is logically prior to love and friendship, since a necessary feature of these concepts is a "sharing of information about one's actions, beliefs, or emotions which one does not share with all, and which one has the right not to share with anyone. By conferring this right, privacy creates the moral capital which we spend in friendship and love" ("Privacy," in G. Hughes, ed., *Law, Reason, and Justice* [New York, 1969], p. 56).

[11] E. Leach, *A Runaway World,* The 1967 Reith Lectures (London, 1968), p. 44.

Paul Halmos, too, speaks of "a hypertrophied family devotion and family insularity," arising from the attempt by contemporary man "to transcend his solitude. . . ."

[He] may finally negate his apartness in an obsessional affirmation of
family ties. . . . Friendship and companionship, when manifestly present
in the marital couple, is regarded as an instance of great virtue
even when it is equally manifestly absent in all other relationships.
Furthermore, the nepotistic solidarity of the family is another symptom of
the contemporary attitude according to which the world is hostile
and dangerous and the family is the only solid rock which is to be protected
against all comers.[12]

The insistence on the private area is, in this view, either a symptom or a contributory cause of a pathological condition. But to concede this diagnosis need not weaken the argument I am advancing for the right of exclusion, for it may imply only that in modern society we seek personal relations with too few people, the ones we succeed in forming being overtaxed in consequence by the emotional weight they are forced to bear.

Halmos concedes the value and importance of the personal relations between lovers and "the composed intimacy and companionship of man and wife," admitting these as properly and necessarily exclusive: "Such retreat and privacy may vary according to cultural standards but they are on the whole universal among mankind and not infrequent among animals."[13] It is not clear, however, how much value Halmos attaches to personal relations in general. It may be that men suffer least from neurotic maladjustments in communities like the kibbutz, where everyone feels the security and comfortable warmth of acceptance by a peer group, without the tensions of too-personalized individual attachments. But the children of the kibbutz have been found by some observers defective as persons, precisely because their emotional stability has been purchased at the cost of an incapacity to establish deep personal relations. Perhaps we have to choose between the sensitive, human understanding that we achieve only by the cultivation of our relations within a confined circle and the extrovert assurance and adjustment that a *Gemeinschaft* can confer. However this may be, to the extent that we value the former, we shall be committed to valuing the right of privacy.

Though personal relations need some freedom from interference, different kinds of interference would affect them differently. An extreme

---

[12] P. Halmos; *Solitude and Privacy* (London, 1952), pp. 121–122.

[13] Halmos, *Solitude and Privacy*, p. 121. The standpoint Halmos adopts may be inferred from the following passage: "While . . . the material needs of man . . . have been increasingly satisfied, since the Industrial Revolution, the bio-social needs have been more and more neglected. Culture, a fortuitous expression of the basic principia of life, rarely favoured man's pacific, creative gregariousness . . ." p. 51.

kind is to attempt to participate—to turn, for instance, a relation *à deux* into one *à trois*. It is not evident, however, that the attentions of the observer and reporter are necessarily so objectionable. A strong-minded couple might pursue their own course undisturbed under the eyes of a reasonably tactful and self-effacing paying guest. Of course, the uncommitted observer makes most of us self-conscious and inhibited—we do not find it as easy to express our feelings for one another spontaneously, to produce the same kind of mutually sensitive and responsive relations, in full view of a nonparticipant third party, as we do in private. I do not know, however, whether this is a psychologically necessary fact about human beings, or only a culturally conditioned one. Certainly, personal relations are not impossible in places where people live perforce on top of one another. But they call for a good deal of tact and goodwill from the bystanders; there is some evidence that in such conditions, people develop psychological avoidance arrangements—a capacity for not noticing, and a corresponding confidence in not being noticed—that substitute for physical seclusion.[14]

The importance of personal relations suggests a limit to what can be done by antidiscrimination laws. Whatever the justification for interfering with the freedom to discriminate in, say, hiring workers, there are some kinds of choice where a man's reasons for his preferences and antipathies are less important than that he has them. If the personal relations of a home are valued, its constituent members must be left free to decide who can be accepted into it, for example, as a lodger. Club membership might be different. True, we join clubs to cultivate personal relations, like friendships; but we do not expect to enter into such relations with every member. The mere presence in the clubroom of people whom one would not invite to join one's circle of intimates need not endanger the relations within that circle. Nevertheless, if the club's members are, in general, antipathetic to a particular group, to deny them the right of exclusion may create tensions defeating the end for which the club exists.

Of course, merely having prejudices gives no man a right to discriminate unfairly and irrationally in all his relations at whatever cost to the personal dignity of the outsider; insofar as the relations can be specified in terms of role-performances, it is reasonable to demand that discriminations be based only on relevant differences. But to the degree that the point of the relationship has built into it a quality of life depending on reciprocal caring, it qualifies as an area of privacy, and therefore as immune from regulation. (There may be overriding reasons, in times of racial tension and hostility, for discouraging the formation of exclusive clubs, whose rules can only appear inflammatory. But this is to adduce

---

[14] See A. F. Westin; *Privacy and Freedom* (New York, 1967), p. 18, for references to evidence of this point.

further special reasons against privacy, overriding reasons for it based on the value of personal relations.)

THE PRIVACY OF THE FREE CITIZEN

The second personal ideal to which privacy is closely related is that of the free man in a minimally regulated society, a way of life where, first, the average individual is subject only within reasonable and legally safe-guarded limits to the power of others, and, second, where the require-ments of his social roles still leave him considerable breadth of choice in the way he lives. The first of these considerations, the one that has received most attention in the polemical literature on privacy, I have re-ferred to already. The dossier and the computer bank threaten us with victimization and persecution by unscrupulous, intolerant, or merely mis-understanding officials. But these misgivings might be set at rest, at least in principle, by institutional safeguards and assurances. More fundamen-tal is the second consideration, which depends on a conceptual distinction between the private and the official.

The judge's pronouncements on the bench have public significance; though he may not be easily called to account, still there is an important sense in which he has a public responsibility. What he says in his home or in his club—even on matters of law—is another matter; it has no official standing and no official consequences. Of course, if he happens also to be club secretary, what he says about members in *this* official capacity is not "his own private affair"; but conversely, the members might resist a police inquiry into its secretary's statements as an interference with the club's private affairs. What is official and what is private depends, there-fore, on the frame of reference. But for there to be privacy of this kind at all the distinction between official and nonofficial must be intelligible. Admittedly, we may all have some public (that is, official) roles as voters, taxpayers, jurymen, and so on. But we distinguish what we do as family men, shopkeepers, and club treasurers from such public functions. A private citizen, unlike a public official, has no *special* official roles, just as a private member of parliament, not being a minister, has no special official function in Parliament.

This conception of privacy is closely bound up with the liberal ideal. The totalitarian claims that everything a man is and does has significance for society at large. He sees the state as the self-conscious organization of society for the well-being of society; the social significance of our actions and relations overrides any other. Consequently, the public or political universe is all inclusive, *all* roles are public, and every function, whether political, economic, or artistic, can be interpreted as involving a public responsibility.

The liberal, on the other hand, claims not merely a private capacity—an area of action in which he is not responsible to the state for what he does   17 so long as he respects certain minimal rights of others; he claims further that this is the residual category, that the onus is on anyone who claims he is accountable. How he does his job may affect the gross national product, and not only his own slice of it. But he will grant that this is socially significant only in the same way that a drought is, for that too can have serious economic consequences. He may consent to public manipulation of the environment of private choices, by subsidies or customs duties, for instance, as he may agree to cloud-seeding to break a drought, but he resists the suggestion that every citizen should be held publicly responsible for his economic choices as though he were a public servant or the governor of the central bank.

This ideal of the private citizen provides no very precise criteria for distinguishing the private realm; it is rather that no citizen other than actual employees of the administration can be held culpable—even morally culpable—for any action as a failure in public duty unless special grounds can be shown why this is a matter in which he may not merely please himself. Of course, there will be duties associated with roles he has voluntarily assumed—as husband, employee, and so on—but such responsibilities are of his own choosing, not thrust upon him, like his public roles of juror, or taxpayer.

Just as the privacy of personal relations may be invoked to rationalize an obsessive preoccupation with the restricted family, to the exclusion of all other human concern, so the privacy of the free citizen may be invoked to rationalize a selfish economic individualism. One critic, H. W. Arndt, has written that

The cult of privacy seems specifically designed as a defence mechanism
for the protection of anti-social behaviour. . . . The cult of privacy
rests on an individualist conception of society, not merely in the innocent
and beneficial sense of a society in which the welfare of individuals
is conceived as the end of all social organisation, but in the more specific
sense of "each for himself and the devil take the hindmost." . . .
An individualist of this sort sees "the Government" where we might see
"the public interest," and this Government will appear to him often
as no more than one antagonist in the battle of wits which is life—or
business.[15]

There is room for a good deal of disagreement about the extent to which considerations like those of general economic well-being, social equality, or national security justify pressing back the frontiers of the private, to hold men responsible for the way they conduct their daily business. For the liberal, however, every step he is forced to take in that direction counts as a retreat from an otherwise desirable state of affairs, in

[15] H. W. Arndt, "The Cult of Privacy," *Australian Quarterly*, XXI: 3 (September 1949), 69, 70–71.

which because men may please themselves what they are about is no one's business but their own.

PRIVACY AND PERSONAL AUTONOMY

The third personal ideal is that of the independently minded individual, whose actions are governed by principles that are his own. This does not mean, of course, that he has concocted them out of nothing, but that he subjects his principles to critical review, rather than taking them over unexamined from his social environment. He is the man who resists social pressures to conform if he has grounds for uneasiness in doing the conformist thing.

Much has been made of the need for privacy, as a safeguard aganist conformism. Hubert Humphrey has written:

We act differently if we believe we are being observed. If we can never be sure whether or not we are being watched and listened to, all our actions will be altered and our very character will change.[16]

Senator Edward V. Long deplores the decline in spontaneity attendant on a situation where "because of this diligent accumulation of facts about each of us, it is difficult to speak or act today without wondering if the words or actions will reappear 'on the record.' "[17]

It is not only the authorities we fear. We are all under strong pressure from our friends and neighbors to live up to the roles in which they cast us. If we disappoint them, we risk their disapproval, and what may be worse, their ridicule. For many of us, we are free to be ourselves only within that area from which observers can legitimately be excluded. We need a sanctuary or retreat, in which we can drop the mask, desist for a while from projecting on the world the image we want to be accepted as ourselves, an image that may reflect the values of our peers rather than the realities of our natures. To remain sane, we need a closed environment, open only to those we trust, with whom we have an unspoken understanding that whatever is revealed goes no farther.

Put in this way, however, the case for privacy begins to look like a claim to the conditions of life necessary only for second-grade men in a second-grade society. For the man who is truly independent—the autonomous man—is the one who has the strength of mind to resist the pressure to believe with the rest, and has the courage to act on his convictions. He is the man who despises bad faith, and refuses to be anything or to pretend to be anything merely because the world casts him for the part. He is the man who does not hesitate to stand and be counted. That sort of man can be greatly inconvenienced by the world's clamor—but he *does* what

[16] Foreword to Edward V. Long, *The Intruders* (New York, 1967), p. viii.
[17] *Ibid.*, p. 55.

lesser men claim that they are not free to do. "There is no reason," writes Senator Long, "why conformity must be made an inescapable part of the American dream. Excessive pressures can and must be prevented: there must be preserved in each individual a sphere of privacy that will allow his personality to bloom and thrive."[18] One wonders, however, whether the Senator has drawn the right moral. Excessive pressures can be prevented not merely by allowing an individual to hide, but by tolerating the heresy he is not afraid to publish. Socrates did not ask to be allowed to teach philosophy in private. Senator Long quotes a speech of Judge Learned Hand, with apparent approval: "I believe that community is already in process of dissolution . . . when faith in the eventual supremacy of reason has become so timid that we dare not enter our convictions in the open lists to win or lose."[19] But the moral of that sentiment is that preoccupation with the need for a private retreat is a symptom of social sickness.

Of course, there are not many like Socrates in any society; not many have the knowledge of what they are, the virtue to be content with what they know, and the courage to pretend to be nothing else. For the rest of us, the freedom we need is the freedom to be something else—to be ourselves, to do what we think best, in a small, protected sea, where the winds of opinion cannot blow us off course. We cannot learn to be autonomous save by practicing independent judgment. It is important for the moral education of children that at a certain stage they should find the rules porous—that sometimes they should be left to decide what is best to do. Not many of us perhaps have gone so far along the road to moral maturity that we can bear unrelenting exposure to criticism without flinching.

This last stage of my argument brings me back to the grounds for the general principle of privacy, to which I devoted the first half of this paper. I argued that respect for someone as a person, as a chooser, implied respect for him as one engaged on a kind of self-creative enterprise, which could be disrupted, distorted, or frustrated even by so limited an intrusion as watching. A man's view of what he does may be radically altered by having to see it, as it were, through another man's eyes. Now a man has attained a measure of success in his enterprise to the degree that he has achieved autonomy. To the same degree, the importance to him of protection from eavesdropping and Peeping Toms diminishes as he becomes less vulnerable to the judgments of others, more reliant on his own (though he will still need privacy for personal relations, and protection from the grosser kinds of persecution).

This does not weaken the ground for the general principle, however, for this was not a consequentialist ground. It was not that allowing men privacy would give them a better chance to be autonomous. It was rather

[18] *Ibid.*, p. 62.

[19] *Ibid.*, p. 63.

that a person—anyone potentially autonomous—was worthy of respect on that account; and that if such a person wanted to pursue his enterprise unobserved, he was entitled, unless there were overriding reasons against it, to do as he wished. The argument there was, in terms of respect for the enterprise as such, irrespective of the chances of success or failure in any particular instance. In this last section, I have suggested a further, reinforcing argument for privacy as a condition necessary, though to a progressively diminishing degree, if that enterprise is to succeed.

CHARLES FRIED
Privacy: A Rational Context

In this chapter I analyze the concept of privacy and attempt to show why it assumes such high significance in our system of values. There is a puzzle here, since we do not feel comfortable about asserting that privacy is intrinsically valuable, an end in itself—privacy is always for or in relation to something or someone. On the other hand, to view privacy as simply instrumental, as one way of getting other goods, seems unsatisfactory too. For we feel that there is a necessary quality, after all, to the importance we ascribe to privacy. This perplexity is displayed when we ask how privacy might be traded off against other values. We wish to ascribe to privacy more than an ordinary priority. My analysis attempts to show why we value privacy highly and why also we do not treat it as an end in itself. Briefly, my argument is that privacy provides the rational context for a number of our most significant ends, such as love, trust and friendship, respect and self-respect. Since it is a necessary element of those ends, it draws its significance from them. And yet since privacy is only an element of those ends, not the whole, we have not felt inclined to attribute to privacy ultimate significance. In general this analysis of privacy illustrates how the concepts in this essay can provide a rational account for deeply held moral values.

An Immodest Proposal: Electronic Monitoring

There are available today electronic devices to be worn on one's person which emit signals permitting one's exact location to be determined by a monitor some distance away. These devices are so small as to be entirely

Reprinted by permission of the author and the publishers from Charles Fried, *An Anatomy of Values: Problems of Personal and Social Choice,* chap. IX. Cambridge, Mass.: Harvard University Press, Copyright 1970 by the President and Fellows of Harvard College.

unobtrusive: other persons cannot tell that a subject is "wired," and even the subject himself—if he could forget the initial installation—need be no more aware of the device than of a small bandage. Moreover, existing technology can produce devices capable of monitoring not only a person's location, but other significant facts about him: his temperature, pulse rate, blood pressure, the alcoholic content of his blood, the sounds in his immediate environment—for example, what he says and what is said to him —and perhaps in the not too distant future even the pattern of his brain waves. The suggestion has been made, and is being actively investigated, that such devices might be employed in the surveillance of persons on probation or parole.

Probation leaves an offender at large in the community as an alternative to imprisonment, and parole is the release of an imprisoned person prior to the time that all justification for supervising him and limiting his liberty has expired. Typically, both probation and parole are granted subject to various restrictions. Most usually the probationer or parolee is not allowed to leave a prescribed area. Also common are restrictions on the kinds of places he may visit—bars, pool halls, brothels, and the like may be forbidden—the persons he may associate with, and the activities he may engage in. The most common restriction on activities is a prohibition on drinking, but sometimes probation and parole have been revoked for "immorality"—that is, intercourse with a person other than a spouse. There are also affirmative conditions, such as a requirement that the subject work regularly in an approved employment, maintain an approved residence, report regularly to correctional, social, or psychiatric personnel. Failure to abide by such conditions is thought to endanger the rehabilitation of the subject and to identify him as a poor risk.

Now the application of personal monitoring to probation and parole is obvious. Violations of any one of the conditions and restrictions could be uncovered immediately by devices using present technology or developments of it; by the same token, a wired subject assured of detection would be much more likely to obey. Although monitoring is admitted to be unusually intrusive, it is argued that this particular use of monitoring is entirely proper, since it justifies the release of persons who would otherwise remain in prison, and since surely there is little that is more intrusive and unprivate than a prison regime. Moreover, no one is obliged to submit to monitoring: an offender may decline and wait in prison until his sentence has expired or until he is judged a proper risk for parole even without monitoring. Proponents of monitoring suggest that seen in this way monitoring of offenders subject to supervision is no more offensive than the monitoring of an entirely voluntary basis of epileptics, diabetics, cardiac patients, and the like.

Much of the discussion about this and similar (though perhaps less futuristic) measures has proceeded in a fragmentary way to catalog the disadvantages they entail: the danger of the information falling into the wrong hands, the opportunity presented for harassment, the inevitable involvement of persons as to whom no basis for supervision exists, the use of the material monitored by the government for unauthorized purposes, the danger to political expression and association, and so on.

Such arguments are often sufficiently compelling, but situations may be envisaged where they are overridden. The monitoring case in some of its aspects is such a situation. And yet one often wants to say the invasion of privacy is wrong, intolerable, although each discrete objection can be met. The reason for this, I submit, is that privacy is much more than just a possible social technique for assuring this or that substantive interest. Such analyses of the value of privacy often lead to the conclusion that the various substantive interests may after all be protected as well by some other means, or that if they cannot be protected quite as well, still those other means will do, given the importance of our reasons for violating privacy. It is just because this instrumental analysis makes privacy so vulnerable that we feel impelled to assign to privacy some intrinsic significance. But to translate privacy to the level of an intrinsic value might seem more a way of cutting off analysis than of carrying it forward.

It is my thesis that privacy is not just one possible means among others to insure some other value, but that it is necessarily related to ends and relations of the most fundamental sort: respect, love, friendship, and trust. Privacy is not merely a good technique for furthering these fundamental relations; rather without privacy they are simply inconceivable. They require a context of privacy or the possibility of privacy for their existence. To make clear the necessity of privacy as a context for respect, love, friendship, and trust is to bring out also why a threat to privacy seems to threaten our very integrity as persons. To respect, love, trust, or feel affection for others and to regard ourselves as the objects of love, trust, and affection is at the heart of our notion of ourselves as persons among persons, and privacy is the necessary atmosphere for these attitudes and actions, as oxygen is for combustion.

Privacy and Personal Relations

Before going further, it is necessary to sharpen the intuitive concept of privacy. As a first approximation, privacy seems to be related to secrecy, to limiting the knowledge of others about oneself. This notion must be refined. It is not true, for instance, that the less that is known about us the more privacy we have. Privacy is not simply an absence of information about us in the minds of others; rather it is the control we have over information about ourselves.

To refer, for instance, to the privacy of a lonely man on a desert island would be to engage in irony. The person who enjoys privacy is able to   23 grant or deny access to others. Even when one considers private situations into which outsiders could not possibly intrude, the context implies some alternative situation where the intrusion is possible. A man's house may be private, for instance, but that is because it is constructed—with doors, windows, window shades—to allow it to be made private, and because the law entitles a man to exclude unauthorized persons. And even the remote vacation hideaway is private just because one resorts to it in order—in part —to preclude access to unauthorized persons.

Privacy, thus, is control over knowledge about oneself. But it is not simply control over the quality of information abroad; there are modulations in the quality of the knowledge as well. We may not mind that a person knows a general fact about us, and yet feel our privacy invaded if he knows the details. For instance, a casual acquaintance may comfortably know that I am sick, but it would violate my privacy if he knew the nature of the illness. Or a good friend may know what particular illness I am suffering from, but it would violate my privacy if he were actually to witness my suffering from some symptom which he must know is associated with the disease.

Privacy in its dimension of control over information is an aspect of personal liberty. Acts derive their meaning partly from their social context —from how many people know about them and what the knowledge consists of. For instance, a reproof administered out of the hearing of third persons may be an act of kindness, but if administered in public it becomes cruel and degrading. Thus if a man cannot be sure that third persons are not listening—if his privacy is not secure—he is denied the freedom to do what he regards as an act of kindness.

Besides giving us control over the context in which we act, privacy has a more defensive role in protecting our liberty. We may wish to do or say things not forbidden by the restraints of morality but nevertheless unpopular or unconventional. If we thought that our every word and deed were public, fear of disapproval or more tangible retaliation might keep us from doing or saying things which we would do or say if we could be sure of keeping them to ourselves or within a circle of those who we know approve or tolerate our tastes.

These reasons support the familiar arguments for the right of privacy. Yet they leave privacy with less security than we feel it deserves; they leave it vulnerable to arguments that a particular invasion of privacy will secure to us other kinds of liberty which more than compensate for what is lost. To present privacy, then, only as an aspect of or an aid to general liberty is to miss some of its most significant differentiating features. The value of control over information about ourselves is more nearly absolute than that. For privacy is the necessary context for relationships which we would hardly be human if we had to do without—the relationships of love, 24 friendship, and trust.

Love and friendship, as analyzed in Chapter Five, involve the initial respect for the rights of others which morality requires of everyone. They further involve the voluntary and spontaneous relinquishment of something between friend and friend, lover and lover. The title to information about oneself conferred by privacy provides the necessary something. To be friends or lovers persons must be intimate to some degree with each other. Intimacy is the sharing of information about one's actions, beliefs or emotions which one does not share with all, and which one has the right not to share with anyone. By conferring this right, privacy creates the moral capital which we spend in friendship and love.

The entitlements of privacy are not just one kind of entitlement among many which a lover can surrender to show his love. Love or friendship can be partially expressed by the gift of other rights—gifts of property or of service. But these gifts, without the intimacy of shared private information, cannot alone constitute love or friendship. The man who is generous with his possessions, but not with himself, can hardly be a friend, nor—and this more clearly shows the necessity of privacy for love —can the man who, voluntarily or involuntarily, shares everything about himself with the world indiscriminately.

Privacy is essential to friendship and love in another respect besides providing what I call moral capital. The rights of privacy are among those basic entitlements which men must respect in each other; and mutual respect is the minimal precondition for love and friendship.

Privacy also provides the means for modulating those degrees of friendship which fall short of love. Few persons have the emotional resources to be on the most intimate terms with all their friends. Privacy grants the control over information which enables us to maintain degrees of intimacy. Thus even between friends the restraints of privacy apply; since friendship implies a voluntary relinquishment of private information, one will not wish to know what his friend or lover has not chosen to share with him. The rupture of this balance by a third party—the state perhaps— thrusting information concerning one friend upon another might well destroy the limited degree of intimacy the two have achieved.

Finally, there is a more extreme case where privacy serves not to save something which will be "spent" on a friend, but to keep it from all the world. There are thoughts whose expression to a friend or lover would be a hostile act, though the entertaining of them is completely consistent with friendship or love. That is because these thoughts, prior to being given expression, are mere unratified possibilities for action. Only by expressing them do we adopt them, choose them as part of ourselves, and draw them into our relations with others. Now a sophisticated person knows that a friend or lover must entertain thoughts which if expressed would be wounding, and so—it might be objected—why should he attach any significance to their actual expression? In a sense the objection is well 25 taken. If it were possible to give expression to these thoughts and yet make clear to ourselves and to others that we do not thereby ratify them, adopt them as our own, it might be that in some relations, at least, another could be allowed complete access to us. But this possibility is not a very likely one. Thus the most complete form of privacy is perhaps also the most basic, since it is necessary not only to our freedom to define our relations with others but also to our freedom to define ourselves. To be deprived of this control over what we do and who we are is the ultimate assault on liberty, personality, and self-respect.

Trust is the attitude of expectation that another will behave according to the constraints of morality. Insofar as trust is only instrumental to the more convenient conduct of life, its purposes could be as well served by cheap and efficient surveillance of the person upon whom one depends. One does not trust machines or animals; one takes the fullest economically feasible precautions against their going wrong. Often, however, we choose to trust people where it would be safer to take precautions—to watch them or require a bond from them. This must be because, as I have already argued, we value the relation of trust for its own sake. It is one of those relations, less inspiring than love or friendship but also less tiring, through which we express our humanity.

There can be no trust where there is no possibility of error. More specifically, man cannot know that he is trusted unless he has a right to act without constant surveillance so that he knows he can betray the trust. Privacy confers that essential right. And since, as I have argued, trust in its fullest sense is reciprocal, the man who cannot be trusted cannot himself trust or learn to trust. Without privacy and the possibility of error which it protects that aspect of his humanity is denied to him.

The Concrete Recognition of Privacy

In concrete situations and actual societies, control over information about oneself, like control over one's bodily security or property, can only be relative and qualified. As is true for property or bodily security, the control over privacy must be limited by the rights of others. And as in the cases of property and bodily security, so too with privacy, the more one ventures into the outside, the more one pursues one's other interests with the aid of, in competition with, or even in the presence of others, the more one must risk invasions. As with property and personal security, it is the business of legal and social institutions to define and protect the right of privacy which emerges intact from the hurly-burly of social interactions. Now it would be absurd to argue that these concrete definitions and protections, differing as they do from society to society, are or should be strict derivations from general principles, the only legitimate variables being differing empirical circumstances (such as differing technologies or climatic conditions). The delineation of standards must be left to a political and social process the results of which will accord with justice if two conditions are met: (1) the process itself is just, that is, the interests of all are fairly represented; and (2) the outcome of the process protects basic dignity and provides moral capital for personal relations in the form of absolute title to at least some information about oneself.

The particular areas of life which are protected by privacy will be conventional at least in part, not only because they are the products of political processes, but also because of one of the reasons we value privacy. Insofar as privacy is regarded as moral capital for relations of love, friendship, and trust, there are situations where what kinds of information one is entitled to keep to oneself is not of the first importance. The important thing is that there be *some* information which is protected. Convention may quite properly rule in determining the particular areas which are private.

Convention plays another more important role in fostering privacy and the respect and esteem which it protects; it designates certain areas, intrinsically no more private than other areas, as symbolic of the whole institution of privacy, and thus deserving of protection beyond their particular importance. This apparently exaggerated respect for conventionally protected areas compensates for the inevitable fact that privacy is gravely compromised in any concrete social system: it is compromised by the inevitably and utterly just exercise of rights by others, it is compromised by the questionable but politically sanctioned exercise of rights by others, it is compromised by conduct which society does not condone but which it is unable or unwilling to forbid, and it is compromised by plainly wrongful invasions and aggressions. In all this there is a real danger that privacy might be crushed altogether, or, what would be as bad, that any venture outside the most limited area of activity would mean risking an almost total compromise of privacy.

Given these threats to privacy in general, social systems have given symbolic importance to certain conventionally designated areas of privacy. Thus in our culture the excretory functions are so shielded that situations in which this privacy is violated are experienced as extremely distressing, as detracting from one's dignity and self-esteem. Yet there does not seem to be any reason connected with the principles of respect, esteem, and the like why this would have to be so, and one can imagine other cultures in which it was not so, but where the same symbolic privacy was attached to, say, eating and drinking. There are other more subtly modulated symbolic areas of privacy, some of which merge into what I call substantive privacy (that is, areas where privacy does protect substantial interests). The very complex norms of privacy about matters of sex and health are good examples.

An excellent, very different sort of example of a contingent, symbolic recognition of an area of privacy as an expression of respect for personal integrity is the privilege against self-incrimination and the associated doctrines denying officials the power to compel other kinds of information 27 without some explicit warrant. By according the privilege as fully as it does, our society affirms the extreme value of the individual's control over information about himself. To be sure, prying into a man's personal affairs by asking questions of others or by observing him is not prevented. Rather it is the point of the privilege that a man cannot be forced to make public information about himself. Thereby his sense of control over what others know of him is significantly enhanced, even if other sources of the same information exist. Without his cooperation, the other sources are necessarily incomplete, since he himself is the only ineluctable witness to his own present life, public or private, internal or manifest. And information about himself which others have to give out is in one sense information over which he has already relinquished control.

The privilege is contingent and symbolic. It is part of a whole structure of rules by which there is created an institution of privacy sufficient to the sense of respect, trust, and intimacy. It is contingent in that it cannot, I believe, be shown that some particular set of rules is necessary to the existence of such an institution of privacy. It is symbolic because the exercise of the privilege provides a striking expression of society's willingness to accept constraints on the pursuit of valid, perhaps vital, interests in order to recognize the right of privacy and the respect for the individual that privacy entails. Conversely, a proceeding in which compulsion is brought to bear on an individual to force him to make revelations about himself provides a striking and dramatic instance of a denial of title to control information about oneself, to control the picture we would have others have of us. In this sense such a procedure quite rightly seems profoundly humiliating. Nevertheless it is not clear to me that a system is unjust which sometimes allows such an imposition.

In calling attention to the symbolic aspect of some areas of privacy I do not mean to minimize their importance. On the contrary, they are highly significant as expressions of respect for others in a general situation where much of what we do to each other may signify a lack of respect or at least presents no occasion for expressing respect. That this is so is shown not so much on the occasions where these symbolic constraints are observed, for they are part of our system of expectations, but where they are violated. Not only does a person feel his standing is gravely compromised by such symbolic violations, but also those who wish to degrade and humiliate others often choose just such symbolic aggressions and invasions on the assumed though conventional area of privacy.

The Concept of Privacy Applied to the Problem of Monitoring

Let us return now to the concrete problem of electronic monitoring to see whether the foregoing elucidation of the concept of privacy will help to establish on firmer ground the intuitive objection that monitoring is an
28 intolerable violation of privacy. Let us consider the more intrusive forms

of monitoring where not only location but conversations and perhaps other data are monitored.

Obviously such a system of monitoring drastically curtails or eliminates altogether the power to control information about oneself. But, it might be said, this is not a significant objection if we assumed the monitored data will go only to authorized persons—probation or parole officers—and cannot be prejudicial so long as the subject of the monitoring is not violating the conditions under which he is allowed to be at liberty. This retort misses the importance of privacy as a context for all kinds of relations, from the most intense to the most casual. For all of these may require a context of some degree of intimacy, and intimacy is made impossible by monitoring.

It is worth being more precise about this notion of intimacy. Monitoring obviously presents vast opportunities for malice and misunderstanding on the part of authorized personnel. For that reason the subject has reason to be constantly apprehensive and inhibited in what he does. There is always an unseen audience, which is the more threatening because of the possibility that one may forget about it and let down his guard, as one would not with a visible audience. Even assuming the benevolence and understanding of the official audience, there are serious consequences to the fact that no degree of true intimacy is possible for the subject. Privacy is not, as we have seen, just a defensive right. It forms the necessary context for the intimate relations of love and friendship which give our lives much of whatever affirmative value they have. In the role of citizen or fellow worker, one need reveal himself to no greater extent than is necessary to display the attributes of competence and morality appropriate to those roles. In order to be a friend or lover one must reveal far more of himself. Yet where any intimate revelation may be heard by monitoring officials, it loses the quality of exclusive intimacy required of a gesture of love or friendship. Thus monitoring, in depriving one of privacy, destroys the possibility of bestowing the gift of intimacy, and makes impossible the essential dimension of love and friendship.

Monitoring similarly undermines the subject's capacity to enter into relations of trust. As I analyzed trust, it required the possibility of error on the part of the person trusted. The negation of trust is constant surveillance—such as monitoring—which minimizes the possibility of undetected default. The monitored parolee is denied the sense of self-respect inherent in being trusted by the government which has released him. More important, monitoring prevents the parolee from entering into true *relations* of trust with persons in the outside world. An employer, unaware of the monitoring, who entrusts a sum of money to the parolee cannot thereby grant him the sense of responsibility and autonomy which an unmonitored person in the same position would have. The parolee in a real—if special and ironical—sense, cannot be trusted.

Now let us consider the argument that however intrusive monitoring   29 may seem, surely prison life is more so. In part, of course, this will be a matter of fact. It may be that a reasonably secure and well-run prison will allow prisoners occasions for conversation among themselves, with guards, or with visitors, which are quite private. Such a prison regime would in this respect be less intrusive than monitoring. Often prison regimes do not allow even this, and go far toward depriving a prisoner of any sense of privacy: if the cells have doors, these may be equipped with peepholes. But there is still an important difference between this kind of prison and monitoring: the prison environment is overtly, even punitively unprivate. The contexts for relations to others are obviously and drastically different from what they are on the "outside." This itself, it seems to me, protects the prisoner's human orientation where monitoring only assails it. If the prisoner has a reasonably developed capacity for love, trust, and friendship and has in fact experienced ties of this sort, he is likely to be strongly aware (at least for a time) that prison life is a drastically different context from the one in which he enjoyed those relations, and this awareness will militate against his confusing the kinds of relations that can obtain in a "total institution" like a prison with those of freer social settings on the outside.

Monitoring, by contrast, alters only in a subtle and unobtrusive way —though a significant one—the context for relations. The subject appears free to perform the same actions as others and to enter the same relations, but in fact an important element of autonomy, of control over one's environment, is missing: he cannot be private. A prisoner can adopt a stance of withdrawal, of hibernation as it were, and thus preserve his sense of privacy intact to a degree. A person subject to monitoring by virtue of being in a free environment, dealing with people who expect him to have certain responses, capacities, and dispositions, is forced to make at least a show of intimacy to the persons he works closely with, those who would be his friends, and so on. They expect these things of him, because he is assumed to have the capacity and disposition to enter into ordinary relations with them. Yet if he does—if, for instance, he enters into light banter with slight sexual overtones with the waitress at the diner where he eats regularly—he has been forced to violate his own integrity by revealing to his official monitors even so small an aspect of his private personality, the personality he wishes to reserve for persons toward whom he will make some gestures of intimacy and friendship. Theoretically, of course, a monitored parolee might adopt the same attitude of withdrawal that a prisoner does, but in fact that too would be a costly and degrading experience. He would be tempted, as in prison he would not be, to "give himself away" and to act like everyone else, since in every outward respect he seems like everyone else. Moreover, by withdrawing, the person subject to monitoring would risk seeming cold, unnatural, odd, inhuman, to the very people whose esteem and affection he craves. In prison the circum-

30

stances dictating a reserved and tentative facade are so apparent to all that adopting such a facade is no reflection on the prisoner's humanity.

The insidiousness of a technique which forces a man to betray himself in this humiliating way or else seem inhuman is compounded when one considers that the subject is also forced to betray others who may become intimate with him. Even persons in the overt oppressiveness of a prison do not labor under the burden of this double betrayal.

As against all of these considerations, there remains the argument that so long as monitoring depends on the consent of the subject, who feels it is preferable to prison, to close off this alternative in the name of a morality so intimately concerned with liberty is absurd. This argument may be decisive; I am not at all confident that the alternative of monitored release should be closed off. My analysis does show, I think, that it involves costs to the prisoner which are easily overlooked, that on inspection it is a less desirable alternative than might at first appear. Moreover, monitoring presents systematic dangers to potential subjects as a class. Its availability as a compromise between conditional release and continued imprisonment may lead officials who are an any doubt whether or not to trust a man on parole or probation to assuage their doubts by resorting to monitoring.

The seductions of monitored release disguise not only a cost to the subject but to society as well. The discussion of trust should make clear that unmonitored release is a very different experience from monitored release, and so the educational and rehabilitative effect of unmonitored release is also different. Unmonitored release affirms in a far more significant way the relations of trust between the convicted criminal and the society which he violated by his crime and which we should now be seeking to re-establish. But trust can only arise, as any parent knows, through the experience of being trusted.

Finally, it must be recognized that more limited monitoring—for instance where only the approximate location of the subject is revealed—lacks the offensive features of total monitoring, and is obviously preferable to prison.

The Role of Law

This evaluation of the proposal for electronic monitoring has depended on the general theoretical framework of this whole essay. It is worth noting the kind of evaluation that framework has permitted. Rather than inviting a fragmentation of the proposal into various pleasant and unpleasant elements and comparing the "net utility" of the proposal with its alternatives, we have been able to evaluate the total situation created by the proposal in another way. We have been able to see it as a system in which certain actions and relations, the pursuit of certain ends, are possible or   31 impossible. Certain systems of actions, ends, and relations are possible or impossible in different social contexts. Moreover, the social context itself is a system of actions and relations. The social contexts created by monitoring and its alternatives, liberty or imprisonment, are thus evaluated by their conformity to a model system in which are instantiated the principles of morality, justice, friendship, and love. Such a model, which is used as a standard, is of course partially unspecified in that there is perhaps an infinite number of specific systems which conform to those principles. Now actual systems, as we have seen, may vary in respect to how other ends— for example, beauty, knowledge—may be pursued in them, and they may be extremely deficient in allowing for the pursuit of such ends. But those who design, propose, and administer social systems are first of all bound to make them conform to the model of morality and injustice, for in so doing they express respect and even friendship—what might be called civic friendship—toward those implicated in the system. If designers and administrators fail to conform to this model, they fail to express that aspect of their humanity which makes them in turn fit subjects for the respect, friendship, and love of others.

Finally, a point should be noted about the relation between legal structures and other social structures in establishing a rational context such as privacy. This context is established in part by rules which guarantee to a person the claim to control certain areas, his home, perhaps his telephone communications, and so forth, and back this guarantee with enforceable sanctions. These norms are, of course, legal norms. Now these legal norms are incomprehensible without some understanding of what kind of a situation one seeks to establish with their aid. Without this understanding we cannot grasp their importance, the vector of development from them in changing circumstances (such as new technology), the consequences of abandoning them, and so on.[1] What is less obvious is that law is not just an instrument for bringing about a separately identifiable and significant social result: it is a part of the very situation that it helps to bring about. The concept of privacy requires, as we have seen, a sense of control and a justified, acknowledged power to control aspects of one's environment. In most developed societies the only way to give a person the full measure of both the sense and the fact of control is to give him a legal title to control. A legal right to control is control which is the least

---

[1] It is a tenet of some forms of positivism that this statement is wrong insofar as it suggests that without appreciation of the context we have no understanding of the meaning of legal norms. This tenet seems wrong for a number of reasons. Legal norms are necessarily phrased in open-ended language, and their specification in actual circumstances needs the aid of the context—that is, the reason for the norm— to determine the appropriate application. This is obviously so when there are changed circumstances and recourse must be had to the principle of the norm. It is less obvious in so-called "central" or "paradigm" cases, but I suggest this is less obvious only because the context is so unproblematic as to require no explicit attention.

open to question and argument, it is the kind of control we are most serious about. Consider the analogy of the power of testamentary disposition. A testator is subject to all sorts of obligations, pressures, and arguments; certain things are so outrageous that he would scarcely dare to do them. Yet, within very broad limits, in the last analysis he is after all free to do the outrageous. And both the fact that certain dispositions are outrageous, immoral, wrong, and the fact that the testator is nevertheless free to make them are *together* important to define the autonomy and personality of a person in the particular situation. In the same way the public and ultimate character of law is part of the definition of the rational context of privacy.

JOEL FEINBERG
Legal Paternalism

The principle of legal paternalism justifies state coercion to protect individuals from self-inflicted harm, or in its extreme version, to guide them, whether they like it or not, toward their own good. Parents can be expected to justify their interference in the lives of their children (e.g., telling them what they must eat and when they must sleep) on the ground that "daddy knows best." Legal paternalism seems to imply that since the state often can know the interests of individual citizens better than the citizens know them themselves, it stands as a permanent guardian of those interests *in loco parentis*. Put in this blunt way, paternalism seems a preposterous doctrine. If adults are treated as children they will come in time to be like children. Deprived of the right to choose for themselves, they will soon lose the power of rational judgment and decision. Even children, after a certain point, had better not be "treated as children," else they will never acquire the outlook and capability of responsible adults.

Yet if we reject paternalism entirely, and deny that a person's own good is *ever* a valid ground for coercing him, we seem to fly in the face both of common sense and our long established customs and laws. In the criminal law, for example, a prospective victim's freely granted consent is no defense to the charge of mayhem or homicide. The state simply refuses to permit anyone to agree to his own disablement or killing. The law of contracts, similarly, refuses to recognize as valid, contracts to sell oneself into slavery, or to become a mistress, or a second wife. Any ordinary citizen is legally justified in using reasonable force to prevent another from

This material is here reprinted from Volume 1, Number 1 of the *Canadian Journal of Philosophy* (1971), 105–124, by permission of the author and the Canadian Association for Publishing in Philosophy.

mutilating himself or committing suicide. No one is allowed to purchase certain drugs even for therapeutic purposes without a physician's prescription (Doctor knows best). The use of other drugs, such as heroin, for pleasure merely, is permitted under no circumstances whatever. It is hard to find any plausible rationale for all such restrictions apart from the argument that beatings, mutilations, and death, concubinage, slavery, and bigamy are always bad for a person whether he or she knows it or not, and that antibiotics are too dangerous for any non-expert, and heroin for anyone at all, to take on his own initiative.

The trick is stopping short once we undertake this path, unless we wish to ban whiskey, cigarettes, and fried foods, which tend to be bad for people too, whether they know it or not. The problem is to reconcile somehow our general repugnance for paternalism with the apparent necessity, or at least reasonableness, of some paternalistic regulations. My method of dealing with this problem will not be particularly ideological. Rather, I shall try to organize our elementary intuitions by finding a principle that will render them consistent. Let us begin, then, by rejecting the views both that the protection of a person from himself is *always* a valid ground for interference in his affairs, and that it is *never* a valid ground. It follows that it is a valid ground only under certain conditions, and we must now try to state those conditions.[1]

I

It will be useful to make some preliminary distinctions. The first distinction is between harms or likely harms that are produced directly by a person upon himself and those produced by the actions of another person to which the first party has consented. Committing suicide would be an example of self-inflicted harm; arranging for a person to put one out of one's misery would be an example of a "harm" inflicted by the action of another to which one has consented. There is a venerable legal maxim traceable to the Roman Law that "*Volenti non fit inuria*," sometimes translated, misleadingly, as: "To one who consents no harm is done." Now, I suppose that the notion of consent applies, strictly speaking, only to the actions of another person that affect oneself. If so, then, consent to

---

[1] The discussion that follows has two important unstated and undefended presuppositions. The first is that in some societies, at least, and at some times, a line can be drawn (as Mill claimed it could in Victorian England) between other-regarding behaviour and behaviour that is primarily and directly self-regarding and only indirectly and remotely, therefore trivially, other-regarding. If this assumption is false, there is no interesting problem concerning legal paternalism since all "paternalistic" restrictions, in that case, could be defended as necessary to protect persons other than those restricted, and hence would not be (wholly) paternalistic. The second presupposition is that the spontaneous repugnance toward paternalism (which I assume the reader shares with me) is well-grounded and supportable.

one's *own* actions is a kind of metaphor. Indeed, to say that I consented to my own actions, seems just a colorful way to saying that I acted voluntarily. My involuntary actions, after all, are, from the moral point of view, no different from the actions of someone else to which I have not had an opportunity to consent. In any case, it seems plainly false to say that a person cannot be *harmed* by actions, whether his own or those of another, to which he has consented. People who quite voluntarily eat an amount that is in fact too much cause themselves to suffer from indigestion; and girls who consent to advances sometimes become pregnant.

One way of interpreting the *Volenti* maxim is to take it as a kind of presumptive principle. A person does not generally consent to what he believes will be, on balance, harmful to himself, and by and large, an individual is in a better position to appraise risks to himself than are outsiders. Given these data, and considerations of convenience in the administration of the law, the *Volenti* maxim might be understood to say that for the purposes of the law (whatever the actual facts might be) nothing is to count as harm to a given person that he has freely consented to. If this presumption is held to be conclusive, then the *Volenti* maxim becomes a kind of "legal fiction" when applied to cases of undeniable harm resulting from behavior to which the harmed one freely consented. A much more likely interpretation, however, takes the *Volenti* maxim to say nothing at all, literal or fictional, about *harms*. Rather, it is about what used to be called "injuries," that is, injustices or wrongs. To one who freely consents to a thing no *wrong* is done, no matter how harmful to him the consequences may be. "He cannot waive his right," says Salmond, "and then complain of its infringement."[2] If the *Volenti* maxim is simply an expression of Salmond's insight, it is not a presumptive or fictional principle about harms, but rather an absolute principle about wrongs.

The *Volenti* maxim (or something very like it) plays a key role in the argument for John Stuart Mill's doctrine about liberty. Characteristically, Mill seems to employ the maxim in both of its interpretations, as it suits his purposes, without noticing the distinction between them. On the one hand, Mill's argument purports to be an elaborate application of the calculus of harms and benefits to the problem of political liberty. The state can rightly restrain a man to prevent harm to others. Why then can it not restrain a man to prevent him from harming himself? After all, a harm is a harm whatever its cause, and if our sole concern is to minimize harms all round, why should we distinguish between origins of harm? One way Mill answers this question is to employ the *Volenti* maxim in its first interpretation. For the purposes of his argument, he will presume conclusively that "to one who consents no *harm* is done." Self-inflicted or consented-to harm simply

[2] See Glanville Williams (ed.), *Salmond on Jurisprudence,* Eleventh Edition (London: Sweet & Maxwell, 1957), p. 531.

is not to count as harm at all; and the reasons for this are that the coercion required to prevent such harm is itself a harm of such gravity that it is likely in the overwhelming proportion of cases to outweigh any good it can produce for the one coerced; and moreover, individuals themselves, in the overwhelming proportion of cases, can know their own true interests better than any outsiders can, so that outside coercion is almost certain to be self-defeating.

But as Gerald Dworkin has pointed out,[3] arguments of this merely statistical kind at best create a strong but rebuttable presumption against coercion of a man in his own interest. Yet Mill purports to be arguing for an absolute prohibition. Absolute prohibitions are hard to defend on purely utilitarian grounds, so Mill, when his confidence wanes, tends to move to the second interpretation of the *Volenti* maxim. To what a man consents he may be harmed, but he cannot be wronged; and Mill's "harm principle," reinterpreted accordingly, is designed to protect him and others only from wrongful invasions of their interest. Moreover, when the state intervenes on any other ground, its *own* intervention is a wrongful invasion. What justifies the absolute prohibition of interference in primarily self-regarding affairs is *not* that such interference is self-defeating and likely (merely likely) to cause more harm than it prevents, but rather that it would itself be an injustice, a wrong, a violation of the private sanctuary which is every person's self; and this is so whatever the calculus of harms and benefits might show.[4]

The second distinction is between those cases where a person directly produces harm to himself, where the harm is the certain upshot of his conduct and its desired end, on the one hand, and those cases where a person simply creates a *risk* of harm to himself in the course of activities directed toward other ends. The man who knowingly swallows a lethal

---

[3] See his excellent article, "Paternalism" in *Morality and the Law,* ed. by R. A. Wasserstrom (Belmont, Calif: Wadsworth Publishing Co., 1971).

[4] Mill's rhetoric often supports this second interpretation of his argument. He is especially fond of such political metaphors as independence, legitimate rule, dominion, and sovereignty. The state must respect the status of the individual as an independent entity whose "*sovereignty* over himself" (in Mill's phrase), like Britain's over its territory, is absolute. In self-regarding affairs, a person's individuality ought to "*reign uncontrolled from the outside*" (another phrase of Mill's). Interference in those affairs, whether successful or self-defeating, is a violation of *legitimate boundaries,* like trespass in law, or aggression between states. Even self-mutilation and suicide are permissible if the individual truly chooses them, and other interests are not directly affected. The individual person has an absolute right to choose for himself, to be wrong, to go to hell on his own, and it is nobody else's proper *business* or *office* to interfere. The individual *owns* (not merely possesses) his life; he has *title* to it. He alone is *arbiter* of his own life and death. See how legalistic and un-utilitarian these terms are! The great wonder is that Mill could claim to have foregone any benefit in argument from the notion of an abstract right. Mill's intentions aside, however, I can not conceal my own preference for this second interpretation of his argument.

dose of arsenic will certainly die, and death must be imputed to him as his goal in acting. Another man is offended by the sight of his left hand, so he grasps an ax in his right hand and chops his left hand off. He does not thereby "endanger" his interest in the physical integrity of his limbs or "risk" the loss of his hand. He brings about the loss directly and deliberately. On the other hand, to smoke cigarettes or to drive at excessive speeds is not directly to harm oneself, but rather to increase beyond a normal level the probability that harm to oneself will result.

The third distinction is that between reasonable and unreasonable risks. There is no form of activity (or inactivity either for that matter) that does not involve some risks. On some occasions we have a choice between more and less risky actions and prudence dictates that we take the less dangerous course; but what is called "prudence" is not always reasonable. Sometimes it is more reasonable to assume a great risk for a great gain than to play it safe and forfeit a unique opportunity. Thus it is not necessarily more reasonable for a coronary patient to increase his life expectancy by living a life of quiet inactivity than to continue working hard at his career in the hope of achieving something important even at the risk of a sudden fatal heart attack at any moment. There is no simple mathematical formula to guide one in making such decisions or for judging them "reasonable" or "unreasonable." On the other hand, there are other decisions that are manifestly unreasonable. It is unreasonable to drive at sixty miles an hour through a twenty mile an hour zone in order to arrive at a party on time, but it may be reasonable to drive fifty miles an hour to get a pregnant wife to the maternity ward. It is foolish to resist an armed robber in an effort to protect one's wallet, but it may be worth a desperate lunge to protect one's very life, or the life of a loved one.

In all of these cases a number of district considerations are involved.[5] If there is time to deliberate one should consider: (1) the degree of probability that harm to oneself will result from a given course of action, (2) the seriousness of the harm being risked, i.e. "the value or importance of that which is exposed to the risk," (3) the degree of probability that the goal inclining one to shoulder the risk will in fact result from the course of action, (4) the value or importance of achieving that goal, that is, just how worthwhile it is to one (this is the intimately personal factor, requiring a decision about one's own preferences, that makes the reasonableness of a risk-assessment on the whole so difficult for the *outsider* to make), and (5) the necessity of the risk, that is, the availability or absence of alternative, less risky, means to the desired goal. Certain judgments about the reasonableness of risk-assumptions are quite uncontroversial. We can say, for example, that the greater are considerations (1) the probability of harm to

[5] The distinctions in this paragraph are borrowed from: Henry T. Terry, "Negligence," *Harvard Law Review,* Vol. 29 (1915).

self, and (2) the magnitude of the harm risked, the *less* reasonable the risk; and the greater considerations (3) the probability the desired goal will result, (4) the importance of that goal to the actor, and (5) the necessity of the means, the *more* reasonable the risk. But in a given difficult case, even where questions of "probability" are meaningful and beyond dispute, and where all the relevant facts are known, the risk-decision may defy objective assessment because of its component personal value judgments. In any case, if the state is to be given the right to prevent a person from risking harm to himself (and only himself) this must not be on the ground that the prohibited action is risky, or even that it is extremely risky, but rather on the ground that the risk is extreme and, in respect to its objectively assessable components, manifestly *unreasonable*. There are very good reasons, sometimes, for regarding even a person's judgment of personal worthwhileness (consideration 4) to be "manifestly unreasonable," but it remains to be seen whether (or when) that kind of unreasonableness can be sufficient grounds for interference.

The fourth and final distinction is between fully voluntary and not fully voluntary assumptions of a risk. One assumes a risk in a fully voluntary way when one shoulders it while fully informed of all relevant facts and contingencies, with one's eyes wide open, so to speak, and in the absence of all coercive pressure of compulsion. There must be calmness and deliberateness, no distracting or unsettling emotions, no neurotic compulsion, no misunderstanding. To whatever extent there is compulsion, misinformation, excitement or impetuousness, clouded judgment (as e.g. from alcohol), or immature or defective faculties of reasoning, to that extent the choice falls short of perfect voluntariness. Voluntariness then is a matter of degree. One's "choice" is *completely involuntary* either when it is no choice at all, properly speaking—when one lacks all muscular control of one's movements, or when one is knocked down, or pushed, or sent reeling by a blow, or a wind, or an explosion—or when through ignorance one chooses something other than what one means to choose, as when one thinks the arsenic powder is table salt, and thus chooses to sprinkle it on one's scrambled eggs. Most harmful choices, as most choices generally, fall somewhere in between the extremes of perfect voluntariness and complete involuntariness.

Now, the terms "voluntary" and "involuntary" have a variety of disparate but overlapping uses in philosophy, law, and ordinary life, and some of them are not altogether clear. I should point out here that my usage does not correspond with that of Aristotle, who allowed that infants, animals, drunkards, and men in a towering rage might yet act voluntarily if only they are undeceived and not overwhelmed by external physical force. What I call a voluntary assumption of risk corresponds more closely to what Aristotle called "deliberate choice." Impulsive and emotional actions, and those of animals and infants are voluntary in Aristotle's sense, but they are not *chosen*. Chosen actions are those that are decided upon by *deliberation,* and that is a process that requires time, information, a clear head, and highly developed rational faculties. When I use such phrases then as "voluntary act," "free and genuine consent," and so on, I refer to acts that are more than "voluntary" in the Aristotelian sense, acts that Aristotle himself would call "deliberately chosen." Such acts not only have their origin "in the agent," they also represent him faithfully in some important way: they express his settled values and preferences. In the fullest sense, therefore, they are actions for which he can take responsibility.

II

The central thesis of John Stuart Mill and other individualists about paternalism is that the fully voluntary choice or consent of a mature and rational human being concerning matters that affect only his own interests is such a precious thing that no one else (and certainly not the state) has a right to interfere with it simply for the person's "own good." No doubt this thesis was also meant to apply to almost-but-not-quite fully voluntary choices as well, and probably also even to some substantially non-voluntary ones (e.g. a neurotic person's choice of a wife who will satisfy his neurotic needs but only at the price of great unhappiness, eventual divorce, and exacerbated guilt); but it is not probable that the individualist thesis was meant to apply to choices near the bottom of the scale of voluntariness, and Mill himself left no doubt that he did *not* intend it to apply to completely involuntary "choices." Nor should we *expect* anti-paternalistic individualism to deny protection to a person from his own nonvoluntary choices, for insofar as the choices are not voluntary they are just as alien to him as the choices of someone else.

Thus Mill would permit the state to protect a man from his own ignorance at least in circumstances that create a strong presumption that his uninformed or misinformed choice would not correspond to his eventual one.

If either a public officer or anyone else saw a person attempting to cross a bridge which had been ascertained to be unsafe, and there were no time to warn him of his danger, they might seize him and turn him back, without any real infringement of his liberty; for liberty consists in doing what one desires, and he does not desire to fall into the river.[6]

Of course, for all the public officer may know, the man on the bridge does desire to fall into the river, or to take the risk of falling for other purposes. If the person is then fully warned of the danger and wishes to proceed anyway, then, Mill argues, that is his business alone; but because most

[6] J. S. Mill, *On Liberty* (New York: Liberal Arts Press, 1956), p. 117.

people do *not* wish to run such risks, there was a solid presumption, in advance of checking, that this person did not wish to run the risk either. Hence the officer was justified, Mill would argue, in his original interference.

On other occasions a person may need to be protected not from his ignorance but from some other condition that may render his informed choice substantially less than voluntary. He may be "a child, or delirious, or in some state of excitement or absorption incompatible with the full use of the reflecting faculty."[7] Mill would not permit any such person to cross an objectively unsafe bridge. On the other hand, there is no reason why a child, or an excited person, or a drunkard, or a mentally ill person should not be allowed to proceed on his way home across a perfectly safe thoroughfare. Even substantially nonvoluntary choices deserve protection unless there is good reason to judge them dangerous.

Now it may be the case, for all we can know, that the behaviour of a drunk or an emotionally upset person would be exactly the same even if he were sober and calm; but when the behaviour seems patently self-damaging and is of a sort that most calm and normal persons would not engage in, then there are strong grounds, if only a statistical sort, for inferring the opposite; and these grounds, on Mill's principle, would justify interference. It may be that there is no kind of action of which it can be said "No mentally competent adult in a calm, attentive mood, fully informed, etc. would *ever* choose (or consent to) *that*." Nevertheless, there are actions of a kind that create a powerful *presumption* that any given actor, if he were in his right mind, would not choose them. The point of calling this hypothesis a "presumption" is to require that it be completely overridden before legal permission be given to a person, who has already been interfered with, to go on as before. So, for example, if a policeman (or anyone else) sees John Doe about to chop off his hand with an ax, he is perfectly justified in using force to prevent him, because of the presumption that no one could voluntarily choose to do such a thing. The presumption, however, should always be taken as rebuttable in principle; and now it will be up to Doe to prove before an official tribunal that he is calm, competent, and free, and that he still wishes to chop off his hand. Perhaps this is too great a burden to expect Doe himself to "prove," but the tribunal should require that the presumption against voluntariness be overturned by evidence from some source or other. The existence of the presumption should require that an objective determination be made, whether by the usual adversary procedures of law courts, or simply by a collective investigation by the tribunal into the available facts. The greater the presumption to be overridden, the more elaborate and fastidious should be the legal paraphernalia required, and the stricter the standards of evidence. (The

[7] *Loc. cit.*

law of wills might prove a model for this.) The point of the procedure would not be to evaluate the wisdom or worthiness of a person's choice, but rather to determine whether the choice really is his.

This seems to lead us to a form of paternalism that is so weak and innocuous that it could be accepted even by Mill, namely, that the state has the right to prevent self-regarding harmful conduct only when it is substantially nonvoluntary or when temporary intervention is necessary to establish whether it is voluntary or not. When there is a strong presumption that no normal person would voluntarily choose or consent to the kind of conduct in question, that should be a proper ground for detaining the person until the voluntary character of his choice can be established. We can use the phrase "the standard of voluntariness" as a label for the considerations that mediate the application of the principle that a person may properly be protected from his own folly. (Still another ground for forcible delay and inquiry that is perfectly compatible with Mill's individualism is the possibility that important third party interests might be involved. Perhaps a man's wife and family should have some say before he is permitted to commit suicide—or even to chop off his hand.)

III

Working out the details of the voluntariness standard is far too difficult to undertake here, but some of the complexities, at least, can be illustrated by a consideration of some typical hard cases. Consider first of all the problem of harmful drugs. Suppose Richard Roe requests a prescription of drug X from Dr. Doe, and the following discussion ensues:

Dr. Doe: I cannot prescribe drug X to you because it will do you physical harm.

Mr. Roe: But you are mistaken. It will not cause me physical harm.

In a case like this, the state, of course, backs the doctor. The state deems medical questions to be technical matters subject to expert opinions. This entails that a non-expert layman is not the best judge of his own medical interests. If a layman disagrees with a physician on a question of medical fact the layman can be presumed wrong, and if nevertheless he chooses to act on his factually mistaken belief, his action will be substantially less than fully voluntary in the sense explained above. That is to say that the action of *ingesting a substance which will in fact harm him* is not the action he voluntarily chooses to do. Hence the state intervenes to protect him not from his own free and voluntary choices, but from his own ignorance.

Suppose however that the exchange goes as follows:

Dr. Doe: I cannot prescribe drug X to you because it will do you physical harm.

Mr. Roe: Exactly. That's just what I want. I want to harm myself.

In this case Roe *is* properly apprised of the facts. He suffers from no de-   41 lusions or misconceptions. Yet his choice is so odd that there exists a reasonable presumption that he has been deprived somehow of the "full use of his reflecting faculty." It is because we know that the overwhelming majority of choices to inflict injury for its own sake on oneself are not fully voluntary that we are entitled to presume that the present choice too is not fully voluntary. If no further evidence of derangement, or illness, or severe depression, or unsettling excitation can be discovered, however, and the patient can convince an objective panel that his choice is voluntary (unlikely event!) and further if there are no third party interests, for example those of wife or family, that require protection, then our "voluntariness standard" would permit no further state constraint.

Now consider the third possibility:

Dr. Doe: I cannot prescribe drug X to you because it is very likely to do you physical harm.

Mr. Roe: I don't care if it causes me physical harm. I'll get a lot of pleasure first, so much pleasure in fact, that it is well worth running the risk of physical harm. If I must pay a price for my pleasure I am willing to do so.

This is perhaps the most troublesome case. Roe's choice is not patently irrational on its face. He may have a well thought-out philosophical hedonism as one of his profoundest convictions. He may have made a fundamental decision of principle committing himself to the intensely pleasurable, even if brief life. If no third party interests are directly involved, the state can hardly be permitted to declare his philosophical convictions unsound or "sick" and prevent him from practicing them, without assuming powers that it will inevitably misuse disastrously.

On the other hand, this case may be very little different from the preceding one, depending of course on what the exact facts are. If the drug is known to give only an hour's mild euphoria and then cause an immediate violently painful death, then the risks incurred appear so unreasonable as to create a powerful presumption of nonvoluntariness. The desire to commit suicide must always be presumed to be both nonvoluntary and harmful to others until shown otherwise. (Of course in some cases it *can* be shown otherwise.) On the other hand, drug X may be harmful in the way nicotine is now known to be harmful; twenty or thirty years of heavy use may create a grave risk of lung cancer or heart disease. Using the drug for pleasure merely, when the risks are of this kind, may be to run unreasonable risks, but that is no strong evidence of nonvoluntariness. Many perfectly normal, rational persons voluntarily choose to run precisely these risks for whatever pleasures they find in smoking.[8] The way for the state

---

[8] Perfectly rational men can have "unreasonable desires" as judged by other perfectly rational men, just as perfectly rational men (e.g. great philosophers) can hold "unreasonable beliefs" or doctrines as judged by other perfectly rational men. Particular unreasonableness, then, can hardly be strong evidence of general irrationality.

to assure itself that such practices are truly voluntary is continually to confront smokers with the ugly medical facts so that there is no escaping the knowledge of what the medical risks to health exactly are. Constant reminders of the hazards should be at every hand and with no softening of the gory details. The state might even be justified in using its taxing, regulatory, and persuasive powers to make smoking (and similar drug usage) more difficult or less attractive; but to prohibit it outright for everyone would be to tell the voluntary risk-taker that even his informed judgments of what is worthwhile are less reasonable than those of the state, and that therefore, he may not act on them. This is paternalism of the strong kind, unmediated by the voluntariness standard. As a principle of public policy, it has an acrid moral flavour, and creates serious risks of governmental tyranny.

IV

Another class of hard cases are those involving contracts in which one party agrees to restrict his own liberty in some respect. The most extreme case is that in which one party freely sells himself into slavery to another, perhaps in exchange for some benefit that is to be consumed before the period of slavery begins, perhaps for some reward to be bestowed upon some third party. Our point of departure will be Mill's classic treatment of the subject:

In this and most other civilized countries . . . an engagement by which a person should sell himself, or allow himself to be sold, as a slave would be null and void, neither enforced by law nor by opinion. The ground for *thus limiting his power of voluntarily disposing of his own lot in life* is apparent, and is very clearly seen in this extreme case. The reason for not interfering, unless for the sake of others, with a person's voluntary acts is consideration for his liberty. His voluntary choice is evidence that what he so chooses is desirable, or at least endurable to him, and his good is on the whole best provided for by allowing him to take his own means of pursuing it. But by selling himself for a slave, he abdicates his liberty; he foregoes any future use of it beyond that single act. He therefore defeats, in his own case, the very purpose which is the justification of allowing him to dispose of himself. He is no longer free, but is thenceforth in a position which has no longer the presumption in its favour that would be afforded by his voluntarily remaining in it. The principle of freedom cannot require that he should be free not to be free.[9] [my italics]

It seems plain to me that Mill, in this one extreme case, has been driven to embrace the principle of paternalism. The "harm-to-others principle,"

[9] Mill, *op. cit.*, p. 125.

as mediated by the *Volenti* maxim[10] would permit a competent, fully informed adult, who is capable of rational reflection and free of undue pressure, to be himself the judge of his own interests, no matter how queer or perverse his judgment may seem to others. There is, of course, always the presumption, and a very strong one indeed, that a person who elects to "sell" himself into slavery is either incompetent, unfree, or misinformed. Hence the state should require very strong evidence of voluntariness—elaborate tests, swearings, psychiatric testifying, waiting periods, public witnessing, and the like—before validating such contracts. Similar forms of official "making sure" are involved in marriages and wills, and slavery is even more serious a thing, not to be rashly undertaken. Undoubtedly, very few slavery contracts would survive such procedures, perhaps even none at all. It may be literally true that "no one in his right mind would sell himself into slavery," but if this is a truth it is not an *a priori* one but rather one that must be tested anew in each case by the application of independent, non-circular criteria of mental illness.

The supposition is at least intelligible, therefore, that every now and then a normal person in full possession of his faculties would voluntarily consent to permanent slavery. We can imagine any number of intelligible (if not attractive) motives for doing such a thing. A person might agree to become a slave in exchange for a million dollars to be delivered in advance to a loved one or to a worthy cause, or out of a religious conviction requiring a life of humility or penitence, or in payment for the prior enjoyment of some supreme benefit, as in the *Faust* legend. Mill, in the passage quoted above, would disallow such a contract no matter how certain it is that the agreement is fully voluntary, apparently on the ground that the permanent and irrevocable loss of freedom is such a great evil, and slavery so harmful a condition, that no one ought ever to be allowed to choose it, even voluntarily. Any person who thinks that he can be a gainer, in the end, from such an agreement, Mill implies, is simply wrong whatever his reasons, and can be known *a priori* to be wrong. Mill's earlier argument, if I understand it correctly, implies that a man should be permitted to mutilate his body, take harmful drugs, or commit suicide, provided only that his decision to do these things is voluntary and no other person will be directly and seriously harmed. But voluntarily acceding to slavery is too much for Mill to stomach. Here is an evil of another order, he seems to say; so the "harm to others" principle and the *Volenti* maxim come to their limiting point here, and paternalism in the strong sense (unmediated by the voluntariness test) must be invoked, if only for this one kind of case.

There are, of course, other ways of justifying the refusal to enforce slavery contracts. Some of these are derived from principles not acknowl-

---

[10] That is, the principle that prevention of harm to others is the sole ground for legal coercion, *and* that what is freely consented to is not to count as harm. These are Mill's primary normative principles in *On Liberty*.

edged in Mill's moral philosophy but which at least have the merit of being non-paternalistic. One might argue that what is odious in "harsh and unconscionable" contracts, even when they are voluntary on both sides, is not that a man should suffer the harm he freely risked, but rather that another party should "exploit" or take advantage of him. What is to be prevented, according to this line of argument, is one man exploiting the weakness, or foolishness, or recklessness of another. If a weak, foolish, or reckless man freely chooses to harm or risk harm to himself, that is all right, but that is no reason why another should be a party to it, or be permitted to benefit himself at the other's expense. (This principle, however, can only apply to extreme cases, else it will ban all competition.) Applied to voluntary slavery, the principle of non-exploitation might say that it isn't aimed at preventing one man from being a slave so much as preventing the other from being a slave-owner. The basic principle of argument here is a form of legal moralism. To own another human being, as one might own a table or a horse, is to be in a relation to him that is inherently immoral, and therefore properly forbidden by law. That, of course, is a line of argument that would be uncongenial to Mill, as would also be the Kantian argument that there is something in every man that is not his to alienate or dispose of, *viz.,* the "humanity" that we are enjoined to "respect, whether in our own person or that of another." (It is worth noting, in passing, that Kant was an uncompromising foe of legal paternalism.)

There are still other ways of arguing against the recognition of slavery contracts, however, that are neither paternalistic (in the strong sense) nor inconsistent with Mill's primary principles. One might argue, for example, that weakening respect for human dignity (which is weak enough to begin with) can lead in the long run to harm of the most serious kind to nonconsenting parties. Or one might use a variant of the "public charge" argument commonly used in the nineteenth century against permitting even those without dependents to assume the risk of penury, illness, and starvation. We could let men gamble recklessly with their own lives, and then adopt inflexibly unsympathetic attitudes toward the losers. "They made their beds," we might say in the manner of some proper Victorians, "now let them sleep in them." But this would be to render the whole national character cold and hard. It would encourage insensitivity generally and impose an unfair economic penalty on those who possess the socially useful virtue of benevolence. Realistically, we just can't let men wither and die right in front our eyes; and if we intervene to help, as we inevitably must, it will cost us a lot of money. There are certain risks then of an *apparently* self-regarding kind that men cannot be permitted to run, if only for the sake of others who must either pay the bill or turn their backs on intolerable misery. This kind of argument, which can be applied equally well to the slavery case, is at least not *very* paternalistic.

45

   Finally, a non-paternalistic opponent of voluntary slavery might argue (and this the argument to which I wish to give the most emphasis) that while exclusively self-regarding and fully voluntary "slavery contracts" are unobjectionable in principle, the legal machinery for testing voluntariness would be so cumbersome and expensive as to be impractical. Such procedures, after all, would have to be paid for out of tax revenues, the payment of which is mandatory for taxpayers. (And psychiatric consultant fees, among other things, are very high.) Even expensive legal machinery might be so highly fallible that there could be no sure way of determining voluntariness, so that some mentally ill people, for example, might become enslaved. Given the uncertain quality of evidence on these matters, and the enormous general presumption of nonvoluntariness, the state might be justified simply in *presuming nonvoluntariness conclusively in every case as the least risky course.* Some rational bargain-makers might be unfairly restrained under this policy, but on the alternative policy, even more people, perhaps, would become unjustly (mistakenly) enslaved, so that the evil prevented by the absolute prohibition would be greater than the occasional evil permitted. The principles involved in this argument are of the following two kinds: (1) It is better (say) that one hundred people be wrongly denied permission to be enslaved than that one be wrongly permitted, and (2) If we allow the institution of "voluntary slavery" at all, then no matter how stringent our tests of voluntariness are, it is likely that a good many persons *will* be wrongly permitted.

V

Mill's argument that leads to a (strong) paternalistic conclusion in this one case (slavery) employs only calculations of harms and benefits and the presumptive interpretation of *Volenti non fit inuria.* The notion of the inviolable sovereignty of the individual person over his own life does not appear in the argument. Liberty, he seems to tell us, is one good or benefit (though an extremely important one) among many, and its loss, one evil or harm (though an extremely serious one) among many types of harm. The aim of the law being to prevent harms of all kinds and from all sources, the law must take a very negative attitude toward forfeitures of liberty. Still, by and large, legal paternalism is an unacceptable policy because in attempting to impose upon a man an external conception of his own good, it is very likely to be self-defeating. "His voluntary choice is *evidence* (emphasis added) that what he so chooses is desirable, or at least endurable to him, and his good is *on the whole* (more emphasis added) best provided for by allowing him to take his own means of pursuing it." On the whole, then, the harm of coercion will outweigh any good it can produce for the person coerced. But when the person chooses slavery, the scales are clearly and necessarily tipped the other way, and the normal

46

case against intervention is defeated. The ultimate appeal in this argument of Mill's is to the prevention of personal harms, so that permitting a person voluntarily to sell all his freedom would be to permit him to be "free not to be free," that is, free to inflict an *undeniable* harm upon himself, and this (Mill would say) is as paradoxical as permitting a legislature to vote by a majority to abolish majority rule. If, on the other hand, our ultimate principle expresses respect for a person's voluntary choice as *such,* even when it is the choice of a loss of freedom, we can remain adamantly opposed to paternalism even in the most extreme cases of self-harm, for we shall be committed to the view that there is something more important (even) than the avoidance of harm. The principle that shuts and locks the door leading to strong paternalism is that every man has a human right to "voluntarily dispose of his own lot in life" whatever the effect on his own net balance of benefits (including "freedom") and harms.

What does Mill say about less extreme cases of contracting away liberty? His next sentence (but one) is revealing: "These reasons, the force of which is so conspicuous in this particular case [slavery], are evidently of far wider application, yet a limit is everywhere set to them by the necessities of life, which continually require, not indeed that we should resign our freedom, but that we should consent to this and the other limitation of it."[11] Mill seems to say here that the same reasons that justify preventing the total and irrevocable relinquishment of freedom also militate against agreements to relinquish lesser amounts for lesser periods, but that unfortunately such agreements are sometimes rendered necessary by practical considerations. I would prefer to argue in the very opposite way, from the obvious permissibility of limited resignations of freedom to the permissibility in principle even of extreme forfeitures, except that in the latter case (slavery) the "necessities of life"—administrative complications in determining voluntariness, high expenses, and so on—forbid it.

Many perfectly reasonable employment contracts involve an agreement by the employee virtually to abandon his liberty to do as he pleases for a daily period, and even to do (within obvious limits) whatever his boss tells him, in exchange for a salary that the employer, in turn, is not at liberty to withhold. Sometimes, of course, the terms of such agreements are quite unfavourable to one of the parties, but when the agreements have been fairly bargained, with no undue pressure or deception (i.e. when they are fully voluntary) the courts enforce them even though lopsided in their distribution of benefits. Employment contracts, of course, are relatively easily broken; so in that respect they are altogether different from "slavery contracts." Perhaps better examples for our purposes, therefore, are contractual forfeitures of some extensive liberty for long periods of time or even forever. Certain contracts "in restraint of trade" are good examples. Consider contracts for the sale of the "good will" of a business:

[11] *Loc. cit.*

47

Manifestly, the buyer of a shop or of a practice will not be satisfied with what he buys unless he can persuade the seller to contract that he will not immediately set up a competing business next door and draw back most of his old clients or customers. Hence the buyer will usually request the seller to agree not to enter into competition with him . . . . Clauses of this kind are [also] often found in written contracts of employment, the employer requiring his employee to agree that he will not work for a competing employer after he leaves his present work.[12]

There are limits, both spatial and temporal, to the amount of liberty the courts will permit to be relinquished in such contracts. In general, it is considered reasonable for a seller to agree not to reopen a business in the same neighborhood or even the same city for several years, but not reasonable to agree not to re-enter the trade in a distant city, or for a period (say) of fifty years. The courts insist that the agreed-to-self-restraint be no wider "than is reasonably necessary to protect the buyer's purchase;"[13] but where the buyer's interests are very large the restraints may cover a great deal of space and time:

For instance, in the leading case on the subject, a company which bought an armaments business for the colossal sum of £287,000 was held justified in taking a contract from the seller that he would not enter into competition with this business anywhere in the world for a period of twenty-five years. In view of the fact that the business was world-wide in its operations, and that its customers were mainly governments, any attempt by the seller to re-enter the armament business anywhere in the world might easily have affected the value of the buyer's purchase.[14]

The courts then do permit people to contract away extensive liberties for extensive periods of time in exchange for other benefits in reasonable bargains. Persons are even permitted to forfeit their future liberties in exchange for cash. Sometimes such transactions are perfectly reasonable, promoting the interests of both parties. Hence there would appear to be no good reason why they should be prohibited. Selling oneself into slavery is forfeiting *all* one's liberty for the rest of one's life in exchange for some prized benefit, and thus is only the extreme limiting case of contracting away liberty, but not altogether different in principle. Mill's argument that liberty is not the sort of good that by its very nature can properly be traded, then, does not seem a convincing way of arguing against voluntary slavery.

On the other hand, a court does not permit the seller of a business freely

---

[12] P. S. Atiyah, *An Introduction to the Law of Contracts* (Oxford: Clarendon Press, 1961), p. 176.

[13] *Ibid.*, pp. 176–77.

[14] *Ibid.*, p. 177.

to forfeit any more liberty than is reasonable or necessary, and reserves to *itself* the right to determine the question of reasonableness. This restrictive policy *could* be an expression of paternalism designed to protect contracters from their own foolishness; but in fact it is based on an entirely different ground—the public interest in maintaining a competitive system of free trade. The consumer's interests in having prices determined by a competitive marketplace rather than by uncontrolled monopolies requires that the state make it difficult for wealthy businessmen to buy off their competitors. Reasonable contracts "in restraint of trade" are a limited class of exceptions to a general policy designed to protect the economic interests of third parties (consumers) rather than the expression of an independent paternalistic policy of protecting free bargainers from their own mistakes.

There is still a final class of cases that deserve mention. These too are instances of persons voluntarily relinquishing liberties for other benefits; but they occur under such circumstances that prohibitions against them could not plausibly be justified except on paternalistic grounds, and usually not even on those grounds. I have in mind examples of persons who voluntarily "put themselves under the protection of rules" that deprive them and others too of liberties, when those liberties are unrewarding and burdensome. Suppose all upperclass undergraduates are given the option by their college to live either in private apartment buildings entirely unrestricted or else in college dormitories subject to the usual curfew and parietal rules. If one chooses the latter, he or she must be in after a certain hour, be quiet after a certain time, and so on, subject to certain sanctions. In "exchange" for these forfeitures, of course, one is assured that the other students too must be predictable in their habits, orderly, and quiet. The net gain for one's interests as a student over the "freer" private life could be considerable. Moreover, the curfew rule can be a great convenience for a girl who wishes to "date" boys very often, but who also wishes: (a) to get enough sleep for good health, (b) to remain efficient in her work, and (c) to be free of tension and quarrels when on dates over the question of when it is time to return home. If the rule requires a return at a certain time then neither the girl nor the boy has any choice in the matter, and what a boon that can be! To invoke these considerations is *not* to resort to paternalism unless they are employed in support of a prohibition. It is paternalism to *forbid* a student to live in a private apartment "for his own good" or "his own safety." It is not paternalism to *permit* him to live under the governance of coercive rules when he freely chooses to do so, and the other alternative is kept open to him. In fact it would be paternalism to deny a person the liberty of trading liberties for other benefits when he voluntarily chooses to do so.

VI

In summary: There are weak and strong versions of legal paternalism. The weak version is hardly an independent principle and can be entirely acceptable to the philosopher who, like Mill, is committed only to the "harm to others" principle as mediated by the *Volenti* maxim, where the latter is more than a mere presumption derived from generalizations about the causes of harm. According to the strong version of legal paternalism, the state is justified in protecting a person, against his will, from the harmful consequences even of his fully voluntary choices and undertakings. Strong paternalism is a departure from the "harm to others" principle and the strictly interpreted *Volenti* maxim that Mill should not, or need not, have taken in his discussion of contractual forfeitures of liberty. According to the weaker version of legal paternalism, a man can rightly be prevented from harming himself (when other interests are not directly involved) only if his intended action is substantially non voluntary or can be presumed to be so in the absence of evidence to the contrary. The "harm to others" principle, after all, permits us to protect a man from the choices of other people; weak paternalism would permit us to protect him from "nonvoluntary choices," which, being the choices of no one at all, are no less foreign to him.

Griswold v. State of Connecticut 381 U.S. 479, 85 S.Ct. 1678 (1965)

MR. JUSTICE DOUGLAS delivered the opinion of the Court.

Appellant Griswold is Executive Director of the Planned Parenthood League of Connecticut. Appellant Buxton is a licensed physician and a professor at the Yale Medical School who served as Medical Director for the League at its Center in New Haven—a center open and operating from November 1 to November 10, 1961, when appellants were arrested.

They gave information, instruction, and medical advice to *married persons* as to the means of preventing conception. They examined the wife and prescribed the best contraceptive device or material for her use. Fees were usually charged, although some couples were serviced free.

The statutes whose constitutionality is involved in this appeal are §§ 53–

Editor's Note: The opinions have been edited. In addition the concurring opinions of Justices Goldberg and Harlan, the dissenting opinion of Justice Black, and a number of case citations and footnotes have been omitted.

32 and 54–196 of the General Statutes of Connecticut (1958 rev.). The former provides:

Any person who uses any drug, medicinal article or instrument for the purpose of preventing conception shall be fined not less than fifty dollars or imprisoned not less than sixty days nor more than one year or be both fined and imprisoned.

Section 54–196 provides:

Any person who assists, abets, counsels, causes, hires or commands another to commit any offense may be prosecuted and punished as if he were the principal offender.

The appellants were found guilty as accessories and fined $100 each, against the claim that the accessory statute as so applied violated the Fourteenth Amendment. The Appellate Division of the Circuit Court affirmed. The Supreme Court of Errors affirmed that judgment. 151 Conn. 544, 200 A. 2d 479. We noted probable jurisdiction. 379 U.S. 926.

. . .

Coming to the merits, we are met with a wide range of questions that implicate the Due Process Clause of the Fourteenth Amendment. . . .

The association of people is not mentioned in the Constitution nor in the Bill of Rights. The right to educate a child in a school of the parents' choice—whether public or private or parochial—is also not mentioned. Nor is the right to study any particular subject or any foreign language. Yet the First Amendment has been construed to include certain of those rights.

By Pierce v. Society of Sisters, supra, the right to educate one's children as one chooses is made applicable to the States by the force of the First and Fourteenth Amendments. By Meyer v. State of Nebraska, supra, the same dignity is given the right to study the German language in a private school. In other words, the State may not, consistently with the spirit of the First Amendment, contract the spectrum of available knowledge. The right of freedom of speech and press includes not only the right to utter or to print, but the right to distribute, the right to receive, the right to read . . . and freedom of inquiry, freedom of thought, and freedom to teach . . . indeed the freedom of the entire university community. . . . Without those peripheral rights the specific rights would be less secure. And so we reaffirm the principle of the Pierce and the Meyer cases.

In NAACP v. State of Alabama, 357 U.S. 449, 462, 78 S.Ct. 1163, 1172, we protected the "freedom to associate and privacy in one's associations," noting that freedom of association was a peripheral First Amendment right. Disclosure of membership lists of a constitutionally valid association, we held, was invalid "as entailing the likelihood of a substantial 51 restraint upon the exercise by petitioner's members of their right to freedom of association." Ibid. In other words, the First Amendment has a penumbra where privacy is protected from governmental intrusion. In like context, we have protected forms of "association" that are not political in the customary sense but pertain to the social, legal, and economic benefit of the members. NAACP v. Button, 371 U.S. 415, 430–431, 83 S.Ct. 328, 336–337. In Schware v. Board of Bar Examiners, 353 U.S. 232, 77 S.Ct. 752, 1 L.Ed.2d 796, we held it not permissible to bar a lawyer from practice, because he had once been a member of the Communist Party. The man's "association with that Party" was not shown to be "anything more than a political faith in a political party" (id., at 244, 77 S.Ct. at 759) and was not action of a kind proving bad moral character. Id., at 245–246, 77 S.Ct. at 759–760.

Those cases involved more than the "right of assembly"—a right that extends to all irrespective of their race or idealogy.... The right of "association," like the right of belief ... is more than the right to attend a meeting; it includes the right to express one's attitudes or philosophies by membership in a group or by affiliation with it or by other lawful means. Association in that context is a form of expression of opinion; and while it is not expressly included in the First Amendment its existence is necessary in making the express guarantees fully meaningful.

The foregoing cases suggest that specific guarantees in the Bill of Rights have penumbras, formed by emanations from those guarantees that help give them life and substance. See Poe v. Ullman, 367 U.S. 497, 516–522, 81 S.Ct. 1752, 6 L.Ed.2d 989 (dissenting opinion). Various guarantees create zones of privacy. The right of association contained in the penumbra of the First Amendment is one, as we have seen. The Third Amendment in its prohibition against the quartering of soldiers "in any house" in time of peace without the consent of the owner is another facet of that privacy. The Fourth Amendment explicitly affirms the "right of the people to be secure in their persons, houses, papers, and effects, against unreasonable searches and seizures." The Fifth Amendment in its Self-Incrimination Clause enables the citizen to create a zone of privacy which government may not force him to surrender to his detriment. The Ninth Amendment provides: "The enumeration in the Constitution, of certain rights, shall not be construed to deny or disparage others retained by the people."

The Fourth and Fifth Amendments were described in Boyd v. United States, 116 U.S. 616, 630, 6 S.Ct. 524, 532, 29 L.Ed. 746, as protection against all governmental invasions "of the sanctity of a man's home and the privacies of life."[1] We recently referred in Mapp v. Ohio, 367 U.S.

---

[1] The Court said in full about this right of privacy:

"The principles laid down in this opinion [by Lord Camden in Entick v. Carrington, 19 How.St.Tr. 1029] affect the very essence of constitutional liberty and security. They reach further than the concrete form of the case then before the court, with its adventitious circumstances; they apply to all invasions on the part of the govern-

643, 656, 81 S.Ct. 1684, 1692, 6 L.Ed.2d 1081, to the Fourth Amendment as creating a "right to privacy, no less important than any other right carefully and particularly reserved to the people." See Beaney, The Constitutional Right to Privacy, 1962 Sup.Ct.Rev. 212; Griswold, The Right to be Let Alone, 55 Nw.U.L.Rev. 216 (1960).

. . .

The present case, then, concerns a relationship lying within the zone of privacy created by several fundamental constitutional guarantees. And it concerns a law which, in forbidding the *use* of contraceptives rather than regulating their manufacture or sale, seeks to achieve its goals by means having a maximum destructive impact upon that relationship. Such a law cannot stand in light of the familiar principle, so often applied by this Court, that a "governmental purpose to control or prevent activities constitutionally subject to state regulation may not be achieved by means which sweep unnecessarily broadly and thereby invade the area of protected freedoms." NAACP v. Alabama, 377 U.S. 288, 307, 84 S.Ct. 1302, 1314, 12 L.Ed.2d 325. Would we allow the police to search the sacred precincts of marital bedrooms for telltale signs of the use of contraceptives? The very idea is repulsive to the notions of privacy surrounding the marriage relationship.

We deal with a right of privacy older than the Bill of Rights—older than our political parties, older than our school system. Marriage is a coming together for better or for worse, hopefully enduring, and intimate to the degree of being sacred. It is an association that promotes a way of life, not causes; a harmony in living, not political faiths; a bilateral loyalty, not commercial or social projects. Yet it is an association for as noble a purpose as any involved in our prior decisions.

Reversed.

. . .

MR. JUSTICE WHITE, concurring in the judgment.

In my view this Connecticut law as applied to married couples deprives them of "liberty" without due process of law, as that concept is used in the Fourteenth Amendment. I therefore concur in the judgment

---

ment and its employes of the sanctity of a man's home and the privacies of life. It is not the breaking of his doors, and the rummaging of his drawers, that constitutes the essence of the offense; but it is the invasion of his indefeasible right of personal security, personal liberty and private property, where that right has never been forfeited by his conviction of some public offense,—it is the invasion of this sacred right which underlies and constitutes the essence of Lord Camden's judgment. Breaking into a house and opening boxes and drawers are circumstances of aggravation; but any forcible and compulsory extortion of a man's own testimony, or of his private papers to be used as evidence to convict him of crime, or to forfeit his goods, is within the condemnation of that judgment. In this regard the fourth and fifth amendments run almost into each other." 116 U.S., at 630, 6 S.Ct., at 532.

of the Court reversing these convictions under Connecticut's aiding and abetting statute.

It would be unduly repetitious, and belaboring the obvious, to expound on the impact of this statute on the liberty guaranteed by the Fourteenth Amendment against arbitrary or capricious denials or on the nature of this liberty. Suffice it to say that this is not the first time this Court has had occasion to articulate that the liberty entitled to protection under the Fourteenth Amendment includes the right "to marry, establish a home and bring up children," Meyer v. State of Nebraska, 262 U.S. 390, 399, 43 S.Ct. 625, 626, 67 L.Ed.2d 1042 and "the liberty * * * to direct the upbringing and education of children," Pierce v. Society of Sisters, 268 U.S. 510, 534–535, 45 S.Ct. 571, 573, 69 L.Ed. 1070, and that these are among "the basic civil rights of man." Skinner v. State of Oklahoma, 316 U.S. 535, 541, 62 S.Ct. 1110, 1113, 86 L.Ed. 1655. These decisions affirm that there is a "realm of family life which the state cannot enter" without substantial justification. Prince v. Com. of Massachusetts, 321 U.S. 158, 166, 64 S.Ct. 438, 442, 88 L.Ed. 645.

Surely the right invoked in this case, to be free of regulation of the intimacies of the marriage relationship, "come[s] to this Court with a momentum for respect lacking when appeal is made to liberties which derive merely from shifting economic arrangements." Kovacs v. Cooper, 336 U.S. 77, 95, 69 S.Ct. 448, 458, 93 L.Ed. 513 (opinion of Frankfurter, J.).

The Connecticut anti-contraceptive statute deals rather substantially with this relationship. For it forbids all married persons the right to use birth-control devices, regardless of whether their use is dictated by considerations of family planning, . . . health, or indeed even of life itself. . . . The anti-use statute, together with the general aiding and abetting statute, prohibits doctors from affording advice to married persons on proper and effective methods of birth control. . . . And the clear effect of these statutes, as enforced, is to deny disadvantaged citizens of Connecticut, those without either adequate knowledge or resources to obtain private counseling, access to medical assistance and up-to-date information in respect to proper methods of birth control. . . . In my view, a statute with these effects bears a substantial burden of justification when attacked under the Fourteenth Amendment. . . .

An examination of the justification offered, however, cannot be avoided by saying that the Connecticut anti-use statute invades a protected area of privacy and association or that it demeans the marriage relationship. The nature of the right invaded is pertinent, to be sure, for statutes regulating sensitive areas of liberty do, under the cases of this Court, require "strict scrutiny," Skinner v. State of Oklahoma, 316 U.S. 535, 541, 62

S.Ct. 1110, and "must be viewed in the light of less drastic means for achieving the same basic purpose." Shelton v. Tucker, 364 U.S. 479, 488, 81 S.Ct. 247, 252, 5 L.Ed.2d 231. "Where there is a significant encroachment upon personal liberty, the State may prevail only upon showing a subordinating interest which is compelling." Bates v. City of Little Rock, 361 U.S. 516, 524, 80 S.Ct. 412, 417. See also McLaughlin v. State of Florida, 379 U.S. 184, 85 S.Ct. 283. But such statutes, if reasonably necessary for the effectuation of a legitimate and substantial state interest, and not arbitrary or capricious in application, are not invalid under the Due Process Clause. . . .

As I read the opinions of the Connecticut courts and the argument of Connecticut in this Court, the State claims but one justification for its anti-use statute. . . . There is no serious contention that Connecticut thinks the use of artificial or external methods of contraception immoral or unwise in itself, or that the anti-use statute is founded upon any policy of promoting population expansion. Rather, the statute is said to serve the State's policy against all forms of promiscuous or illicit sexual relationships, be they premarital or extramarital, concededly a permissible and legitimate legislative goal.

Without taking issue with the premise that the fear of conception operates as a deterrent to such relationships in addition to the criminal proscriptions Connecticut has against such conduct, I wholly fail to see how the ban on the use of contraceptives by married couples in any way reinforces the State's ban on illicit sexual relationships. . . . Connecticut does not bar the importation or possession of contraceptive devices; they are not considered contraband material under state law, . . . and their availability in that State is not seriously disputed. The only way Connecticut seeks to limit or control the availability of such devices is through its general aiding and abetting statute whose operation in this context has been quite obviously ineffective and whose most serious use has been against birth-control clinics rendering advice to married, rather than unmarried, persons. . . . Indeed, after over 80 years of the State's proscription of use, the legality of the sale of such devices to prevent disease has never been expressly passed upon, although it appears that sales have long occurred and have only infrequently been challenged. This "undeviating policy * * * throughout all the long years * * * bespeaks more than prosecutorial paralysis." Poe v. Ullman, 367 U.S. 497, 502, 81 S.Ct. 1752, 1755. Moreover, it would appear that the sale of contraceptives to prevent disease is plainly legal under Connecticut law.

In these circumstances one is rather hard pressed to explain how the ban on use by married persons in any way prevents use of such devices by persons engaging in illicit sexual relations and thereby contributes to the State's policy against such relationships. Neither the state courts nor the State before the bar of this Court has tendered such an explanation. 55

It is purely fanciful to believe that the broad proscription on use facilitates discovery of use by persons engaging in a prohibited relationship or for some other reason makes such use more unlikely and thus can be supported by any sort of administrative consideration. Perhaps the theory is that the flat ban on use prevents married people from possessing contraceptives and without the ready availability of such devices for use in the marital relationship, there will be no or less temptation to use them in extramarital ones. This reasoning rests on the premise that married people will comply with the ban in regard to their marital relationship, notwithstanding total nonenforcement in this context and apparent nonenforcibility, but will not comply with criminal statutes prohibiting extramarital affairs and the anti-use statute in respect to illicit sexual relationships, a premise whose validity has not been demonstrated and whose intrinsic validity is not very evident. At most the broad ban is of marginal utility to the declared objective. A statute limiting its prohibition on use to persons engaging in the prohibited relationship would serve the end posited by Connecticut in the same way, and with the same effectiveness, or ineffectiveness, as the broad anti-use statute under attack in this case. I find nothing in this record justifying the sweeping scope of this statute, with its telling effect on the freedoms of married persons, and therefore conclude that it deprives such persons of liberty without due process of law.

. . . .

MR. JUSTICE STEWART, whom MR. JUSTICE BLACK joins, dissenting.

Since 1879 Connecticut has had on its books a law which forbids the use of contraceptives by anyone. I think this is an uncommonly silly law. As a practical matter, the law is obviously unenforceable, except in the oblique context of the present case. As a philosophical matter, I believe the use of contraceptives in the relationship of marriage should be left to personal and private choice, based upon each individual's moral, ethical, and religious beliefs. As a matter of social policy, I think professional counsel about methods of birth control should be available to all, so that each individual's choice can be meaningfully made. But we are not asked in this case to say whether we think this law is unwise, or even asinine. We are asked to hold that it violates the United States Constitution. And that I cannot do.

In the course of its opinion the Court refers to no less than six Amendments to the Constitution: the First, the Third, the Fourth, the Fifth, the Ninth, and the Fourteenth.

But the Court does not say which of these Amendments, if any, it thinks is infringed by this Connecticut law.

56   We *are* told that the Due Process Clause of the Fourteenth Amend-

ment is not, as such, the "guide" in this case. With that much I agree. There is no claim that this law, duly enacted by the Connecticut Legislature, is unconstitutionally vague. There is no claim that the appellants were denied any of the elements of procedural due process at their trial, so as to make their convictions constitutionally invalid. And, as the Court says, the day has long passed since the Due Process Clause was regarded as a proper instrument for determining "the wisdom, need, and propriety" of state laws. . . . My Brothers HARLAN and WHITE to the contrary, "[w]e have returned to the original constitutional proposition that courts do not substitute their social and economic beliefs for the judgment of legislative bodies, who are elected to pass laws." Ferguson v. Skrupa, supra, 372 U.S. at 730, 83 S.Ct. at 1031.

As to the First, Third, Fourth, and Fifth Amendments, I can find nothing in any of them to invalidate this Connecticut law, even assuming that all those Amendments are fully applicable against the States.[2] It has not even been argued that this is a law "respecting an establishment of religion, or prohibiting the free exercise thereof."[3] And surely, unless the solemn process of constitutional adjudication is to descend to the level of a play on words, there is not involved here any abridgment of "the freedom of speech, or of the press; or the right of the people peaceably to assemble, and to petition the Government for a redress of grievances."[4] No soldier has been quartered in any house.[5] There has been no search, and no seizure.[6] Nobody has been compelled to be a witness against himself.[7]

[2] The Amendments in question were, as everyone knows, originally adopted as limitations upon the power of the newly created Federal Government, not as limitations upon the powers of the individual States. But the Court has held that many of the provisions of the first eight amendments are fully embraced by the Fourteenth Amendment as limitations upon state action, and some members of the Court have held the view that the adoption of the Fourteenth Amendment made every provision of the first eight amendments fully applicable against the States. See Adamson v. People of State of California, 332 U.S. 46, 68, 67 S.Ct. 1672, 1684 (dissenting opinion of Mr. Justice Black).

[3] U.S.Constitution, Amendment I. To be sure, the injunction contained in the Connecticut statute coincides with the doctrine of certain religious faiths. But if that were enough to invalidate a law under the provisions of the First Amendment relating to religion, then most criminal laws would be invalidated. See, e.g., the Ten Commandments. The Bible, Exodus 20:2–17 (King James).

[4] U.S.Constitution, Amendment I. If all the appellants had done was to advise people that they thought the use of contraceptives was desirable, or even to counsel their use, the appellants would, of course, have a substantial First Amendment claim. But their activities went far beyond mere advocacy. They prescribed specific contraceptive devices and furnished patients with the prescribed contraceptive materials.

[5] U.S.Constitution, Amendment III.

[6] U.S.Constitution, Amendment IV.

[7] U.S.Constitution, Amendment V.

The Court also quotes the Ninth Amendment, and my Brother GOLD-BERG's concurring opinion relies heavily upon it. But to say that the Ninth Amendment has anything to do with this case is to turn somersaults with history. The Ninth Amendment, like its companion the Tenth, which this Court held "states but a truism that all is retained which has not been surrendered," United States v. Darby, 312 U.S. 100, 124, 61 S.Ct. 451, 462, 85 L.Ed. 609, was framed by James Madison and adopted by the States simply to make clear that the adoption of the Bill of Rights did not alter the plan that the *Federal* Government was to be a government of express and limited powers, and that all rights and powers not delegated to it were retained by the people and the individual States. Until today no member of this Court has ever suggested that the Ninth Amendment meant anything else, and the idea that a federal court could ever use the Ninth Amendment to annul a law passed by the elected representatives of the people of the State of Connecticut would have caused James Madison no little wonder.

What provision of the Constitution, then, does make this state law invalid? The Court says it is the right of privacy "created by several fundamental constitutional guarantees." With all deference, I can find no such general right of privacy in the Bill of Rights, in any other part of the Constitution, or in any case ever before decided by this Court.[8]

At the oral argument in this case we were told that the Connecticut law does not "conform to current community standards." But it is not the function of this Court to decide cases on the basis of community standards. We are here to decide cases "agreeably to the Constitution and laws of the United States." It is the essence of judicial duty to subordinate our own personal views, our own ideas of what legislation is wise and what is not. If, as I should surely hope, the law before us does not reflect the standards of the people of Connecticut, the people of Connecticut can freely exercise their true Ninth and Tenth Amendment rights to persuade their elected representatives to repeal it. That is the constitutional way to take this law off the books.

---

[8] . . . The Court does not say how far the new constitutional right of privacy announced today extends. See, e.g., Mueller, Legal Regulation of Sexual Conduct, at 127; Ploscowe, Sex and the Law, at 189. I suppose, however, that even after today a State can constitutionally still punish at least some offenses which are not committed in public.

Katz v. United States 389 U.S. 349, 88 S.Ct. 507 (1967)

MR. JUSTICE STEWART delivered the opinion of the Court.

The petitioner was convicted in the District Court for the Southern District of California under an eight-count indictment charging him with transmitting wagering information by telephone from Los Angeles to Miami and Boston in violation of a federal statute.[1] At trial the Government was permitted, over the petitioner's objection, to introduce evidence of the petitioner's end of telephone conversations, overheard by FBI agents who had attached an electronic listening and recording device to the outside of the public telephone booth from which he had placed his calls. In affirming his conviction, the Court of Appeals rejected the contention that the recordings had been obtained in violation of the Fourth Amendment, because "[t]here was no physical entrance into the area occupied by, [the petitioner]."[2] We granted certiorari in order to consider the constitutional questions thus presented.

The petitioner has phrased those questions as follows:

"A.   Whether a public telephone booth is a constitutionally protected area so that evidence obtained by attaching an electronic listening recording device to the top of such a booth is obtained in violation of the right to privacy of the user of the booth.

"B.   Whether physical penetration of a constitutionally protected area is necessary before a search and seizure can be said to be violative of the Fourth Amendment to the United States Constitution."

Editor's Note: Reprinted with some footnotes omitted; footnotes remaining have been renumbered.

[1] 18 U.S.C. § 1084. That statute provides in pertinent part:

"(a) Whoever being engaged in the business of betting or wagering knowingly uses a wire communication facility for the transmission in interstate or foreign commerce of bets or wagers or information assisting in the placing of bets or wagers on any sporting event or contest, or for the transmission of a wire communication which entitles the recipient to receive money or credit as a result of bets or wagers, or for information assisting in the placing of bets or wagers, shall be fined not more than $10,000 or imprisoned not more than two years, or both.

"(b) Nothing in this section shall be construed to prevent the transmission in interstate or foreign commerce of information for use in news reporting of sporting events or contests, or for the transmission of information assisting in the placing of bets or wagers on a sporting event or contest from a State where betting on that sporting event or contest is legal into a State in which such betting is legal."

[2] 9 Cir., 369 F.2d 130, 134.

We decline to adopt this formulation of the issues. In the first place the correct solution of Fourth Amendment problems is not necessarily promoted by incantation of the phrase "constitutionally protected area." Secondly, the Fourth Amendment cannot be translated into a general constitutional "right to privacy." That Amendment protects individual privacy against certain kinds of governmental intrusion, but its protections go further, and often have nothing to do with privacy at all.[3] Other provisions of the Constitution protect personal privacy from other forms of governmental invasion. But the protection of a person's *general* right to privacy—his right to be let alone by other people[4]—is, like the protection of his property and of his very life, left largely to the law of the individual States.

Because of the misleading way the issues have been formulated, the parties have attached great significance to the characterization of the telephone booth from which the petitioner placed his calls. The petitioner has strenuously argued that the booth was a "constitutionally protected area." The Government has maintained with equal vigor that it was not.[5] But this effort to decide whether or not a given "area," viewed in the abstract, is "constitutionally protected" deflects attention from the problem presented by this case. For the Fourth Amendment protects people, not places. What a person knowingly exposes to the public, even in his own home or office, is not a subject of Fourth Amendment protection. But what he seeks to preserve as private, even in an area accessible to the public, may be constitutionally protected. . . .

The Government stresses the fact that the telephone booth from which the petitioner made his calls was constructed partly of glass, so that he was as visible after he entered it as he would have been if he had remained outside. But what he sought to exclude when he entered the booth was not the intruding eye—it was the uninvited ear. He did not shed his right to do so simply because he made his calls from a place where he might be seen. No less than an individual in a business office,

[3] "The average man would very likely not have his feelings soothed any more by having his property seized openly than by having it seized privately and by stealth. . . . And a person can be just as much, if not more, irritated, annoyed and injured by an unceremonious public arrest by a policeman as he is by a seizure in the privacy of his office or home." Griswold v. State of Connecticut, 381 U.S. 479, 509, 85 S.Ct. 1678, 1695, 14 L.Ed.2d 510 (dissenting opinion of MR. JUSTICE BLACK).

[4] See Warren & Brandeis, The Right to Privacy, 4 Harv.L.Rev. 193 (1890).

[5] In support of their respective claims, the parties have compiled competing lists of "protected areas" for our consideration. It appears to be common ground that a private home is such an area, . . . but that an open field is not. . . . Defending the inclusion of a telephone booth in his list the petitioner cites United States v. Stone, D.C., 232 F.Supp. 396, and United States v. Madison, 32 L.W. 2243 (D.C.Ct.Gen. Sess.). Urging that the telephone booth should be excluded, the Government finds support in United States v. Borgese, D.C., 235 F.Supp. 286.

in a friend's apartment, or in a taxicab, a person in a telephone booth may rely upon the protection of the Fourth Amendment. One who occupies it, shuts the door behind him, and pays the toll that permits him to place a call is surely entitled to assume that the words he utters into the mouthpiece will not be broadcast to the world. To read the Constitution more narrowly is to ignore the vital role that the public telephone has come to play in private communication.

The Government contends, however, that the activities of its agents in this case should not be tested by Fourth Amendment requirements, for the surveillance technique they employed involved no physical penetration of the telephone booth from which the petitioner placed his calls. It is true that the absence of such penetration was at one time thought to foreclose further Fourth Amendment inquiry, ... for that Amendment was thought to limit only searches and seizures of tangible property.[6] But "[t]he premise that property interests control the right of the Government to search and seize has been discredited." Warden, Md. Penitentiary v. Hayden, 387 U.S. 294, 304, 87 S.Ct. 1642, 1648, 18 L.Ed.2d 782. Thus, although a closely divided Court supposed in *Olmstead* that surveillance without any trespass and without the seizure of any material object fell outside the ambit of the Constitution, we have since departed from the narrow view on which that decision rested. Indeed, we have expressly held that the Fourth Amendment governs not only the seizure of tangible items, but extends as well to the recording of oral statements overheard without any "technical trespass under * * * local property law." Silverman v. United States, 365 U.S. 505, 511, 81 S.Ct. 679, 682, 5 L.Ed.2d 734. Once this much is acknowledged, and once it is recognized that the Fourth Amendment protects people—and not simply "areas"—against unreasonable searches and seizures it becomes clear that the reach of that Amendment cannot turn upon the presence or absence of a physical intrusion into any given enclosure.

We conclude that the underpinnings of *Olmstead* and *Goldman* have been so eroded by our subsequent decisions that the "trespass" doctrine there enunciated can no longer be regarded as controlling. The Government's activities in electronically listening to and recording the petitioner's words violated the privacy upon which he justifiably relied while using the telephone booth and thus constituted a "search and seizure" within the meaning of the Fourth Amendment. The fact that the electronic device employed to achieve that end did not happen to penetrate the wall of the booth can have no constitutional significance.

The question remaining for decision, then, is whether the search and seizure conducted in this case complied with constitutional standards. In

[6] See Olmstead v. United States, 277 U.S. 438, 464–466, 48 S.Ct. 564, 567–569, 72 L.Ed. 944. We do not deal in this case with the law of detention or arrest under the Fourth Amendment.

that regard, the Government's position is that its agents acted in an entirely defensible manner: They did not begin their electronic surveillance until investigation of the petitioner's activities had established a strong probability that he was using the telephone in question to transmit gambling information to persons in other States, in violation of federal law. Moreover, the surveillance was limited, both in scope and in duration, to the specific purpose of establishing the contents of the petitioner's unlawful telephonic communications. The agents confined their surveillance to the brief periods during which he used the telephone booth,[7] and they took great care to overhear only the conversations of the petitioner himself.[8]

Accepting this account of the Government's actions as accurate, it is clear that this surveillance was so narrowly circumscribed that a duly authorized magistrate, properly notified of the need for such investigation, specifically informed of the basis on which it was to proceed, and clearly apprised of the precise intrusion it would entail, could constitutionally have authorized, with appropriate safeguards, the very limited search and seizure that the Government asserts in fact took place. Only last Term we sustained the validity of such an authorization, holding that, under sufficiently "precise and discriminate circumstances," a federal court may empower government agents to employ a concealed electronic device "for the narrow and particularized purpose of ascertaining the truth of the * * * allegations" of a "detailed factual affidavit alleging the commission of a specific criminal offense." Osborn v. United States, 385 U.S. 323, 329–330, 87 S.Ct. 429, 433, 17 L.Ed.2d 394. Discussing that holding, the Court in Berger v. State of New York, 388 U.S. 41, 87 S.Ct. 1873, 18 L.Ed.2d 1040, said that "the order authorizing the use of the electronic device" in *Osborn* "afforded similar protections to those * * * of conventional warrants authorizing the seizure of tangible evidence." Through those protections, "no greater invasion of privacy was permitted than was necessary under the circumstances." Id., at 57, 87 S.Ct. at 1882. Here, too, a similar judicial order could have accommodated "the legitimate needs of law enforcement" by authorizing the carefully limited use of electronic surveillance.

The Government urges that, because its agents relied upon the decisions in *Olmstead* and *Goldman,* and because they did no more here than they might properly have done with prior judicial sanction, we should

---

[7] Based upon their previous visual observations of the petitioner, the agents correctly predicted that he would use the telephone booth for several minutes at approximately the same time each morning. The petitioner was subjected to electronic surveillance only during this predetermined period. Six recordings, averaging some three minutes each, were obtained and admitted in evidence. They preserved the petitioner's end of conversations concerning the placing of bets and the receipt of wagering information.

[8] On the single occasion when the statements of another person were inadvertently intercepted, the agents refrained from listening to them.

retroactively validate their conduct. That we cannot do. It is apparent that the agents in this case acted with restraint. Yet the inescapable fact is that this restraint was imposed by the agents themselves, not by a judicial officer. They were not required, before commencing the search, to present their estimate of probable cause for detached scrutiny by a neutral magistrate. They were not compelled, during the conduct of the search itself, to observe precise limits established in advance by a specific court order. Nor were they directed, after the search had been completed, to notify the authorizing magistrate in detail of all that had been seized. In the absence of such safeguards, this Court has never sustained a search upon the sole ground that officers reasonably expected to find evidence of a particular crime and voluntarily confined their activities to the least intrusive means consistent with that end. Searches conducted without warrants have been held unlawful "notwithstanding facts unquestionably showing probable cause," Agnello v. United States, 269 U.S. 20, 33, 46 S.Ct. 4, 6, 70 L.Ed. 145, for the Constitution requires "that the deliberate, impartial judgment of a judicial officer * * * be interposed between the citizen and the police * * *." Wong Sun v. United States, 371 U.S. 471, 481–482, 83 S.Ct. 407, 414, 9 L.Ed.2d 441. "Over and again this Court has emphasized that the mandate of the [Fourth] Amendment requires adherence to judicial processes," United States v. Jeffers, 342 U.S. 48, 51, 72 S.Ct. 93, 95, 96 L.Ed. 59, and that searches conducted outside the judicial process, without prior approval by judge or magistrate, are *per se* unreasonable under the Fourth Amendment—subject only to a few specifically established and well-delineated exceptions.

It is difficult to imagine how any of those exceptions could ever apply to the sort of search and seizure involved in this case. Even electronic surveillance substantially contemporaneous with an individual's arrest could hardly be deemed an "incident" of that arrest. Nor could the use of electronic surveillance without prior authorization be justified on grounds of "hot pursuit."[9] And, of course, the very nature of electronic surveillance precludes its use pursuant to the suspect's consent.

The Government does not question these basic principles. Rather, it urges the creation of a new exception to cover this case.[10] It argues that surveillance of a telephone booth should be exempted from the usual requirement of advance authorization by a magistrate upon a showing of probable cause. We cannot agree. Omission of such authorization

[9] Although "[t]he Fourth Amendment does not require police officers to delay in the course of an investigation if to do so would gravely endanger their lives or the lives of others," Warden Md. Penitentiary v. Hayden, 387 U.S. 294, 298–299, 87 S.Ct. 1642, 1646, 18 L.Ed.2d 782, there seems little likelihood that electronic surveillance would be a realistic possibility in a situation so fraught with urgency.

[10] Whether safeguards other than prior authorization by a magistrate would satisfy the Fourth Amendment in a situation involving the national security is a question not presented by this case.

bypasses the safeguards provided by an objective predetermination of probable cause, and substitutes instead the far less reliable procedure of an after-the-event justification for the * * * search, too likely to be subtly influenced by the familiar shortcomings of hindsight judgment. Beck v. State of Ohio, 379 U.S. 89, 96, 85 S.Ct. 223, 228, 13 L.Ed.2d 142.

And bypassing a neutral predetermination of the *scope* of a search leaves individuals secure from Fourth Amendment violations "only in the discretion of the police." Id., at 97, 85 S.Ct. at 229.

These considerations do not vanish when the search in question is transferred from the setting of a home, an office, or a hotel room to that of a telephone booth. Wherever a man may be, he is entitled to know that he will remain free from unreasonable searches and seizures. The government agents here ignored "the procedure of antecedent justification * * * that is central to the Fourth Amendment,"[11] a procedure that we hold to be a constitutional precondition of the kind of electronic surveillance involved in this case. Because the surveillance here failed to meet that condition, and because it led to the petitioner's conviction, the judgment must be reversed.

It is so ordered.

Judgment reversed.

[11] See Osborn v. United States, 385 U.S. 323, 330, 87 S.Ct. 429, 433, 17 L.Ed.2d 394.

Selected Bibliography

Brandeis, Louis D., and Charles Warren. "The Right to Privacy," 4 *Harv. Law Review* (1890), 193.

Gerstein, Robert. "Privacy and Self-Incrimination," *Ethics,* Vol. 80 (1970), 87.

Mill, John Stuart. *On Liberty.*

Pennock, J. Roland, and John W. Chapman (eds.). *Privacy* (Nomos, Vol. XIII). New York: Atherton Press, 1971.

Wasserstrom, Richard. *Morality and the Law.* Belmont, Calif.: Wadsworth Publishing Co., 1970.

Westin, Alan. *Privacy and Freedom.* New York: Athenium Publishers, 1967.

Roe v. Wade
410 U.S. 113, 93 S.Ct. 705 (1973)

**One of the plaintiffs in this case was a pregnant single woman
who sued under the fictitious name of Jane Roe to challenge
the constitutionality of various Texas criminal statutes relating
to abortion. The sections of the Texas Penal Code under attack
read as follows:**

1. "Article 1191. Abortion
    "If any person shall designedly administer to a pregnant woman
or knowingly procure to be administered with her consent any
drug or medicine, or shall use towards her any violence or means
whatever externally or internally applied, and thereby procure an
abortion, he shall be confined in the penitentiary not less than two
nor more than five years; if it be done without her consent, the
punishment shall be doubled. By 'abortion' is meant that the life
of the fetus or embryo shall be destroyed in the woman's womb
or that a premature birth thereof be caused.
"Art. 1192. Furnishing the means
    "Whoever furnishes the means for procuring an abortion
knowing the purpose intended is guilty as an accomplice.
"Art. 1193. Attempt at abortion
    "If the means used shall fail to produce an abortion, the offender
is nevertheless guilty of an attempt to produce abortion, provided
it be shown that such means were calculated to produce that
result, and shall be fined not less than one hundred nor more
than one thousand dollars.
"Art. 1194. Murder in producing abortion
    "If the death of the mother is occasioned by an abortion so
produced or by an attempt to effect the same it is murder.
"Art. 1196. By medical advice,
    "Nothing in this chapter applies to an abortion procured or
attempted by medical advice for the purpose of saving the life of
the mother."

In addition, Article 1195, not challenged in the lawsuit read:

"Art. 1195.   Destroying unborn child
"Whoever shall during parturition of the mother destroy the vitality or life
in a child in a state of being born and before actual birth, which
child would otherwise have been born alive, shall be confined in the penitentiary for life or for not less than five years."

**In her lawsuit Jane Roe asked the federal district court for a declaratory
judgment that the statutes were unconstitutional and for an injunction
against their enforcement. She claimed that she was unable to secure a
safe abortion performed by a competent physician under clinical conditions
because her life was not threatened by the pregnancy. She also claimed
that she lacked the funds to travel to any other state where safe abortions
for persons such as herself were legal.**

**What follows are portions of the majority opinion by Justice Blackmun,
the concurring opinion of Justice Douglas, and the dissenting opinion of
Justice White. The concurring opinion of Justice Stewart and the dissenting
opinion of Justice Rehnquist have been omitted and the remaining footnotes
have been renumbered.**

.   .   .

MR. JUSTICE BLACKMUN delivered the opinion of the Court.

Three reasons have been advanced to explain historically the enactment
of criminal abortion laws in the 19th century and to justify their continued existence.

It has been argued occasionally that these laws were the product of
a Victorian social concern to discourage illicit sexual conduct. Texas,
however, does not advance this justification in the present case, and it
appears that no court or commentator has taken the argument seriously.
The appellants and *amici* contend, moreover, that this is not a proper
state purpose at all and suggest that, if it were, the Texas statutes are
overbroad in protecting it since the law fails to distinguish between married and unwed mothers.

A second reason is concerned with abortion as a medical procedure.
When most criminal abortion laws were first enacted, the procedure was
a hazardous one for the woman.[1] This was particularly true prior to the
development of antisepsis. Antiseptic techniques, of course, were based
on discoveries by Lister, Pasteur, and others first announced in 1867,
but were not generally accepted and employed until about the turn of
the century. Abortion mortality was high. Even after 1900, and perhaps
until as late as the development of antibiotics in the 1940's, standard
modern techniques such as dilation and curettage were not nearly so safe
as they are today. Thus it has been argued that a State's real concern

[1] See C. Haagensen & W. Lloyd, A Hundred Years of Medicine 19 (1943).

in enacting a criminal abortion law was to protect the pregnant woman, that is, to restrain her from submitting to a procedure that placed her life in serious jeopardy.

Modern medical techniques have altered this situation. Appellants and various *amici* refer to medical data indicating that abortion in early pregnancy, that is, prior to the end of first trimester, although not without its risk, is now relatively safe. Mortality rates for women undergoing early abortions, where the procedure is legal, appear to be as low as or lower than the rates for normal childbirth.[2] Consequently, any interest of the State in protecting the woman from an inherently hazardous procedure, except when it would be equally dangerous for her to forgo it, has largely disappeared. Of course, important state interests in the area of health and medical standards do remain. The State has a legitimate interest in seeing to it that abortion, like any other medical procedure, is performed under circumstances that insure maximum safety for the patient. This interest obviously extends at least to the performing physician and his staff, to the facilities involved, to the availability of aftercare, and to adequate provision for any complication or emergency that might arise. The prevalence of high mortality rates at illegal "abortion mills" strengthens, rather than weakens, the State's interest in regulating the conditions under which abortions are performed. Moreover, the risk to the woman increases as her pregnancy continues. Thus the State retains a definite interest in protecting the woman's own health and safety when an abortion is proposed at a late stage of pregnancy.

The third reason is the State's interest—some phrase it in terms of duty —in protecting prenatal life. Some of the argument for this justification rests on the theory that a new human life is present from the moment of conception.[3] The State's interest and general obligation to protect life then extends, it is argued, to prenatal life. Only when the life of the pregnant mother herself is at stake, balanced against the life she carries within her, should the interest of the embryo or fetus not prevail. Logically, of course, a legitimate state interest in this area need not stand or fall on acceptance of the belief that life begins at conception or at

[2] Potts, Postconception Control of Fertility, 8 Int'l J. of G. & O. 957, 967 (1970) (England and Wales); Abortion Mortality, 20 Morbidity and Morality, 208, 209 (July 12, 1971) (U.S. Dept. of HEW, Public Health Service) (New York City); Tietze, United States: Therapeutic Abortions, 1963–1968, 59 Studies in Family Planning 5, 7 (1970); Tietze, Mortality with Contraception and Induced Abortion, 45 Studies in Family Planning 6 (1969) (Japan, Czechoslovakia, Hungary); Tietze & Lehfeldt, Legal Abortion in Eastern Europe, 175 J.A.M.A. 1149, 1152 (April 1961). Other sources are discussed in Lader 17–23[L. Lader, Abortion, 1966].

[3] See Brief of Amicus National Right to Life Foundation; R. Drinan, The Inviolability of the Right to Be Born, in Abortion and the Law 107 (D. Smith, editor, 1967); Louisell, Abortion, The Practice of Medicine, and the Due Process of Law, 16 UCLA L.Rev. 233 (1969); Noonan 1[J. Noonan, ed. The Morality of Abortion, 1970].

some other point prior to live birth. In assessing the State's interest, recognition may be given to the less rigid claim that as long as at least *potential* life is involved, the State may assert interests beyond the protection of the pregnant woman alone.

Parties challenging state abortion laws have sharply disputed in some courts the contention that a purpose of these laws, when enacted, was to protect prenatal life. Pointing to the absence of legislative history to support the contention, they claim that most state laws were designed solely to protect the woman. Because medical advances have lessened this concern, at least with respect to abortion in early pregnancy, they argue that with respect to such abortions the laws can no longer be justified by any state interest. There is some scholarly support for this view of original purpose. The few state courts called upon to interpret their laws in the late 19th and early 20th centuries did focus on the State's interest in protecting the woman's health rather than in preserving the embryo and fetus. Proponents of this view point out that in many States, including Texas, by statute or judicial interpretation, the pregnant woman herself could not be prosecuted for self-abortion or for cooperating in an abortion performed upon her by another. They claim that adoption of the "quickening" distinction through received common law and state statutes tacitly recognizes the greater health hazards inherent in late abortion and impliedly repudiates the theory that life begins at conception.

It is with these interests, and the weight to be attached to them, that this case is concerned.

The Constitution does not explicitly mention any right of privacy. In a line of decisions, however, going back perhaps as far as Union Pacific R. Co. v. Botsford, 141 U.S. 250, 251, 11 S.Ct. 1000, 1001, 35 L.Ed. 734 (1891), the Court has recognized that a right of personal privacy, or a guarantee of certain areas or zones of privacy, does exist under the Constitution. In varying contexts the Court or individual Justices have indeed found at least the roots of that right in the First Amendment . . .; in the Fourth and Fifth Amendments, . . . in the penumbras of the Bill of Rights, . . . in the Ninth Amendment, or in the concept of liberty guaranteed by the first section of the Fourteenth Amendment, . . . These decisions make it clear that only personal rights that can be deemed "fundamental" or "implicit in the concept of ordered liberty," . . . are included in this guarantee of personal privacy. They also make it clear that the right has some extension to activities relating to marriage, . . . procreation, . . . contraception, . . . family relationships, . . . and child rearing and education, . . .

This right of privacy, whether it be founded in the Fourteenth Amendment's concept of personal liberty and restrictions upon state action, as we feel it is, or, as the District Court determined, in the Ninth Amendment's reservation of rights to the people, is broad enough to encompass a woman's decision whether or not to terminate her pregnancy. The detriment that the State would impose upon the pregnant woman by denying this choice altogether is apparent. Specific and direct harm medically diagnosable even in early pregnancy may be involved. Maternity, or additional offspring, may force upon the woman a distressful life and future. Psychological harm may be imminent. Mental and physical health may be taxed by child care. There is also the distress, for all concerned, associated with the unwanted child, and there is the problem of bringing a child into a family already unable, psychologically and otherwise, to care for it. In other cases, as in this one, the additional difficulties and continuing stigma of unwed motherhood may be involved. All these are factors the woman and her responsible physician necessarily will consider in consultation.

On the basis of elements such as these, appellants and some *amici* argue that the woman's right is absolute and that she is entitled to terminate her pregnancy at whatever time, in whatever way, and for whatever reason she alone chooses. With this we do not agree. Appellants' arguments that Texas either has no valid interest at all in regulating the abortion decision, or no interest strong enough to support any limitation upon the woman's sole determination, is unpersuasive. The Court's decisions recognizing a right of privacy also acknowledge that some state regulation in areas protected by that right is appropriate. As noted above, a state may properly assert important interests in safeguarding health, in maintaining medical standards, and in protecting potential life. At some point in pregnancy, these respective interests become sufficiently compelling to sustain regulation of the factors that govern the abortion decision. The privacy right involved, therefore, cannot be said to be absolute. In fact, it is not clear to us that the claim asserted by some *amici* that one has an unlimited right to do with one's body as one pleases bears a close relationship to the right of privacy previously articulated in the Court's decisions. The Court has refused to recognize an unlimited right of this kind in the past. Jacobson v. Massachusetts, 197 U.S. 11, 25 S.Ct. 358, 49 L.Ed. 643 (1905) (vaccination); Buck v. Bell, 274 U.S. 200, 47 S.Ct. 584, 71 L.Ed. 1000 (1927) (sterilization).

We therefore conclude that the right of personal privacy includes the abortion decision, but that this right is not unqualified and must be considered against important state interests in regulation.

We note that those federal and state courts that have recently considered abortion law challenges have reached the same conclusion. A majority, in addition to the District Court in the present case, have held state laws unconstitutional, at least in part, because of vagueness or because of overbreadth and abridgement of rights. . . .

Although the results are divided, most of these courts have agreed that 69 the right of privacy, however based, is broad enough to cover the abortion decision; that the right, nonetheless, is not absolute and is subject to some limitations; and that at some point the state interests as to protection of health, medical standards, and prenatal life, become dominant. We agree with this approach.

Where certain "fundamental rights" are involved, the Court has held that regulation limiting these rights may be justified only by a "compelling state interest," . . . and that legislative enactments must be narrowly drawn to express only the legitimate state interests at stake. . . .

In the recent abortion cases, cited above, courts have recognized these principles. Those striking down state laws have generally scrutinized the State's interest in protecting health and potential life and have concluded that neither interest justified broad limitations on the reasons for which a physician and his pregnant patient might decide that she should have an abortion in the early stages of pregnancy. Courts sustaining state laws have held that the State's determinations to protect health or prenatal life are dominant and constitutionally justifiable.

The District Court held that the appellee failed to meet his burden of demonstrating that the Texas statute's infringement upon Roe's rights was necessary to support a compelling state interest, and that, although the defendant presented "several compelling justifications for state presence in the area of abortions," the statutes outstripped these justifications and swept "far beyond any areas of compelling state interest." . . . Appellant and appellee both contest that holding. Appellant, as has been indicated, claims an absolute right that bars any state imposition of criminal penalties in the area. Appellee argues that the State's determination to recognize and protect prenatal life from and after conception constitutes a compelling state interest. As noted above, we do not agree fully with either formulation.

A.   The appellee and certain *amici* argue that the fetus is a "person" within the language and meaning of the Fourteenth Amendment. In support of this they outline at length and in detail the well-known facts of fetal development. If this suggestion of personhood is established, the appellant's case, of course, collapses, for the fetus' right to life is then guaranteed specifically by the Amendment. The appellant conceded as much on reargument. On the other hand, the appellee conceded on reargument that no case could be cited that holds that a fetus is a person within the meaning of the Fourteenth Amendment.

The Constitution does not define "person" in so many words. Section 1 of the Fourteenth Amendment contains three references to "person." The first, in defining "citizens," speaks of "persons born or naturalized in the United States." The word also appears both in the Due Process Clause and in the Equal Protection Clause. "Person" is used in other places in the Constitution: in the listing of qualifications for representatives and senators, Art. I, § 2, cl. 2, and § 3, cl. 3; in the Apportionment Clause, Art. I, § 2, cl. 3;[4] in the Migration and Importation provision, Art. I, § 9, cl. 1; in the Emolument Clause, Art. I, § 9, cl. 8; in the Electors provisions, Art. II, § 1, cl. 2, and the superseded cl. 3; in the provision outlining qualifications for the office of President, Art. II, § 1, cl. 5; in the Extradition provisions, Art. IV, § 2, cl. 2, and the superseded Fugitive Slave cl. 3; and in the Fifth, Twelfth, and Twenty-second Amendments as well as in §§ 2 and 3 of the Fourteenth Amendment. But in nearly all these instances, the use of the word is such that it has application only postnatally. None indicates, with any assurance, that it has any possible pre-natal application.[5]

[12] All this, together with our observation, *supra,* that throughout the major portion of the 19th century prevailing legal abortion practices were far freer than they are today, persuades us that the word "person," as used in the Fourteenth Amendment, does not include the unborn.[6] This is in accord with the results reached in those few cases where the issue has been squarely presented. . . . Indeed, our decision in United States v. Vuitch, 402 U.S. 62, 91 S.Ct. 1294, 28 L.Ed.2d 601 (1971), inferentially is to the same effect, for we there would not have indulged in statutory interpretation favorable to abortion in specified circumstances if the necessary consequence was the termination of life entitled to Fourteenth Amendment protection.

This conclusion, however, does not of itself fully answer the contentions raised by Texas, and we pass on to other considerations.

B. The pregnant woman cannot be isolated in her privacy. She car-

---

[4] We are not aware that in the taking of any census under this clause, a fetus has ever been counted.

[5] When Texas urges that a fetus is entitled to Fourteenth Amendment protection as a person, it faces a dilemma. Neither in Texas nor in any other State are all abortions prohibited. Despite broad proscription, an exception always exists. The exception contained in Art. 1196, for an abortion procured or attempted by medical advice for the purpose of saving the life of the mother, is typical. But if the fetus is a person who is not to be deprived of life without due process of law, and if the mother's condition is the sole determinant, does not the Texas exception appear to be out of line with the Amendment's command?

There are other inconsistencies between Fourteenth Amendment status and the typical abortion statute. It has already been pointed out, n. 49, *supra,* that in Texas the woman is not a principal or an accomplice with respect to an abortion upon her. If the fetus is a person, why is the woman not a principal or an accomplice? Further, the penalty for criminal abortion specified by Art. 1195 is significantly less than the maximum penalty for murder prescribed by Art. 1257 of the Texas Penal Code. If the fetus is a person, may the penalties be different?

[6] Cf. the Wisconsin abortion statute, defining "unborn child" to mean "a human being from the time of conception until it is born alive," Wis.Stat. § 940.04(6) (1969), and the new Connecticut statute, Public Act No. 1, May 1972 Special Session, declaring it to be the public policy of the State and the legislative intent "to protect and preserve human life from the moment of conception."

ries an embryo and, later, a fetus, if one accepts the medical definitions of the developing young in the human uterus. See Dorland's Illustrated Medical Dictionary, 478–479, 547 (24th ed. 1965). The situation therefore is inherently different from marital intimacy, or bedroom possession of obscene material, or marriage, or procreation, or education, with which *Eisenstadt, Griswold, Stanley, Loving, Skinner, Pierce,* and *Meyer* were respectively concerned. As we have intimated above, it is reasonable and appropriate for a State to decide that at some point in time another interest, that of health of the mother or that of potential human life, becomes significantly involved. The woman's privacy is no longer sole and any right of privacy she possesses must be measured accordingly.

Texas urges that, apart from the Fourteenth Amendment, life begins at conception and is present throughout pregnancy, and that, therefore, the State has a compelling interest in protecting that life from and after conception. We need not resolve the difficult question of when life begins. When those trained in the respective disciplines of medicine, philosophy, and theology are unable to arrive at any consensus, the judiciary, at this point in the development of man's knowledge, is not in a position to speculate as to the answer.

It should be sufficient to note briefly the wide divergence of thinking on this most sensitive and difficult question. There has always been strong support for the view that life does not begin until live birth. This was the belief of the Stoics. It appears to be the predominant, though not the unanimous, attitude of the Jewish faith.[7] It may be taken to represent also the position of a large segment of the Protestant community, insofar as that can be ascertained; organized groups that have taken a formal position on the abortion issue have generally regarded abortion as a matter for the conscience of the individual and her family. As we have noted, the common law found greater significance in quickening. Physicians and their scientific colleagues have regarded that event with less interest and have tended to focus either upon conception or upon live birth or upon the interim point at which the fetus becomes "viable," that is, potentially able to live outside the mother's womb, albeit with artificial aid.[8] Viability is usually placed at about seven months (28 weeks) but may occur earlier, even at 24 weeks.[9] The Aristotelian theory of "mediate animation," that held sway throughout the Middle Ages and the Renaissance in Europe, continued to be official Roman Catholic dogma until the 19th century, despite oppositon to this "ensoulment" theory

[7] Lader 97–99; D. Feldman, Birth Control in Jewish Law 251–294 (1968). For a stricter view, see I. Jakobovits, Jewish Views on Abortion, in Abortion and the Law 124 (D. Smith ed. 1967).

[8] L. Hellman & J. Pritchard, Williams Obstetrics 493 (14th ed. 1971); Dorland's Illustrated Medical Dictionary 1689 (24th ed. 1965).

[9] Hellman & Pritchard, *supra,* n. 58, at 493.

from those in the Church who would recognize the existence of life from the moment of conception.[10] The latter is now, of course, the official belief of the Catholic Church. As one of the briefs *amicus* discloses, this is a view strongly held by many non-Catholics as well, and by many physicians. Substantial problems for precise definition of this view are posed, however, by new embryological data that purport to indicate that conception is a "process" over time, rather than an event, and by new medical techniques such as menstrual extraction, the "morning-after" pill, implantation of embryos, artificial insemination, and even artificial wombs.[11]

In areas other than criminal abortion the law has been reluctant to endorse any theory that life, as we recognize it, begins before live birth or to accord legal rights to the unborn except in narrowly defined situations and except when the rights are contingent upon live birth. For example, the traditional rule of tort law had denied recovery for prenatal injuries even though the child was born alive.[12] That rule has been changed in almost every jurisdiction. In most States recovery is said to be permitted only if the fetus was viable, or at least quick, when the injuries were sustained, though few courts have squarely so held. In a recent development, generally opposed by the commentators, some States permit the parents of a stillborn child to maintain an action for wrongful death because of prenatal injuries. Such an action, however, would appear to be one to vindicate the parents' interest and is thus consistent with the view that the fetus, at most, represents only the potentiality of life. Similarly, unborn children have been recognized as acquiring rights or interests by way of inheritance or other devolution of property, and have been represented by guardians *ad litem*.[13] Perfection of the interests involved, again, has generally been contingent upon live birth. In short, the unborn have never been recognized in the law as persons in the whole sense.

[10] For discussions of the development of the Roman Catholic position, see D. Callahan, Abortion: Law, Choice and Morality 409–447 (1970); Noonan 1.

[11] See D. Brodie, The New Biology and the Prenatal Child, 9 J.Fam.L. 391, 397 (1970); R. Gorney, The New Biology and the Future of Man, 15 UCLA L.Rev. 273 (1968); Note, Criminal Law—Abortion—The "Morning-After" Pill and Other Pre-Implantation Birth-Control Methods and the Law, 46 Ore.L.Rev. 211 (1967); G. Taylor, The Biological Time Bomb 32 (1968); A. Rosenfeld, The Second Genesis 138–139 (1969); G. Smith, Through a Test Tube Darkly: Artificial Insemination and the Law, 67 Mich.L.Rev. 127 (1968); Note, Artificial Insemination and the Law, U.Ill.L.F. 203 (1968).

[12] Prosser, Handbook of the Law of Torts 335–338 (1971); 2 Harper & James, The Law of Torts 1028–1031 (1956); Note, 63 Harv.L.Rev. 173 (1949).

[13] D. Louisell, Abortion, The Practice of Medicine, and the Due Process of Law, 16 UCLA L.Rev. 233, 235–238 (1969); Note, 56 Iowa L.Rev. 994, 999–1000 (1971); Note, The Law and the Unborn Child, 46 Notre Dame Law, 349, 351–354 (1971).

In view of all this, we do not agree that, by adopting one theory of life, Texas may override the rights of the pregnant woman that are at stake. We repeat, however, that the State does have an important and legitimate interest in preserving and protecting the health of the pregnant woman, whether she be a resident of the State or a non-resident who seeks medical consultation and treatment there, and that it has still *another* important and legitimate interest in protecting the potentiality of human life. These interests are separate and distinct. Each grows in substantiality as the woman approaches term and, at a point during pregnancy, each becomes "compelling."

With respect to the State's important and legitimate interest in the health of the mother, the "compelling" point, in the light of present medical knowledge, is at approximately the end of the first trimester. This is so because of the now established medical fact, referred to above . . . that until the end of the first trimester mortality in abortion is less than mortality in normal childbirth. It follows that, from and after this point, a State may regulate the abortion procedure to the extent that the regulation reasonably relates to the preservation and protection of maternal health. Examples of permissible state regulation in this area are requirements as to the qualifications of the person who is to perform the abortion; as to the licensure of that person; as to the facility in which the procedure is to be performed, that is, whether it must be a hospital or may be a clinic or some other place of less-than-hospital status; as to the licensing of the facility; and the like.

This means, on the other hand, that, for the period of pregnancy prior to this "compelling" point, the attending physician, in consultation with his patient, is free to determine, without regulation by the State, that in his medical judgment the patient's pregnancy should be terminated. If that decision is reached, the judgment may be effectuated by an abortion free of interference by the State.

With respect to the State's important and legitimate interest in potential life, the "compelling" point is at viability. This is so because the fetus then presumably has the capability of meaningful life outside the mother's womb. State regulation protective of fetal life after viability thus has both logical and biological justifications. If the State is interested in protecting fetal life after viability, it may go so far as to proscribe abortion during that period except when it is necessary to preserve the life or health of the mother.

Measured against these standards, Art. 1196 of the Texas Penal Code, in restricting legal abortions to those "procured or attempted by medical advice for the purpose of saving the life of the mother," sweeps too broadly. The statute makes no distinction between abortions performed early in pregnancy and those performed later, and it limits to a single reason, "saving" the mother's life, the legal justification for the procedure.

The statute, therefore, cannot survive the constitutional attack made upon it here.

This conclusion makes it unnecessary for us to consider the additional challenge to the Texas statute asserted on grounds of vagueness. . . .

. . .

MR. JUSTICE DOUGLAS, concurring. [Mr. Justice Douglas' concurrence applied both to this case and to the companion case from Georgia, Doe v. Bolton, 410 U.S. 179.]

While I join the opinion of the Court, I add a few words.

The questions presented in the present cases go far beyond the issues of vagueness, which we considered in United States v. Vuitch, 402 U.S. 62, 91 S.Ct. 1294, 28 L.Ed.2d 601. They involve the right of privacy, one aspect of which we considered in Griswold v. Connecticut, 381 U.S. 479, 484, 85 S.Ct. 1678, 1681, 14 L.Ed.2d 510, when we held that various guarantees in the Bill of Rights create zones of privacy.[14]

The *Griswold* case involved a law forbidding the use of contraceptives. We held that law as applied to married people unconstitutional:

We deal with a right of privacy older than the Bill of Rights—older than our political parties, older than our school system. Marriage is a coming together for better or for worse, hopefully enduring, and intimate to the degree of being sacred. *Id.*, 486, 85 S.Ct., 1682.

The District Court in *Doe* held that *Griswold* and related cases "establish a Constitutional right to privacy broad enough to encompass the

---

[14] There is no mention of privacy in our Bill of Rights but our decisions have recognized it as one of the fundamental values those amendments were designed to protect. The fountainhead case is Boyd v. United States, 116 U.S. 616, 6 S.Ct. 524, 29 L.Ed. 746, holding that a federal statute which authorized a court in tax cases to require a taxpayer to produce his records or to concede the Government's allegations offended the Fourth and Fifth Amendments. Justice Bradley, for the Court, found that the measure unduly intruded into the "sanctity of a man's home and the privacies of life." *Id.*, 630, 6 S.Ct., 532. Prior to *Boyd,* in Kilbourn v. Thompson, 103 U.S. 168, 195, 26 L.Ed. 377, Mr. Justice Miller held for the Court that neither House of Congress "possesses the general power of making inquiry into the private affairs of the citizen." Of *Kilbourn* Mr. Justice Field later said, "This case will stand for all time as a bulwark against the invasion of the right of the citizen to protection in his private affairs against the unlimited scrutiny of investigation by a congressional committee." In re Pacific Ry. Comm'n, C.C., 32 F. 241, 253 (cited with approval in Sinclair v. United States, 279 U.S. 263, 293, 49 S.Ct. 268, 271, 73 L.Ed. 692). Mr. Justice Harlan, also speaking for the Court, in Interstate Commerce Comm'n v. Brimson, 154 U.S. 447, 478, 14 S.Ct. 1125, 1134, 38 L.Ed. 1047, thought the same was true of administrative inquiries, saying the Constitution did not permit a "general power of making inquiry into the private affairs of the citizen." . . .

right of a woman to terminate an unwanted pregnancy in its early stages, by obtaining an abortion." ...

The Supreme Court of California expressed the same view in People v. Belous,[15] 71 Cal.2d 954, 963, 80 Cal.Rptr. 354, 458 P.2d 194.

The Ninth Amendment obviously does not create federally enforceable rights. It merely says, "The enumeration in the Constitution of certain rights, shall not be construed to deny or disparage others retained by the people." But a catalogue of these rights includes customary, traditional, and time-honored rights, amenities, privileges, and immunities that come within the sweep of "the Blessings of Liberty" mentioned in the preamble to the Constitution. Many of them in my view come within the meaning of the term "liberty" as used in the Fourteenth Amendment.

First is the autonomous control over the development and expression on one's intellect, interests, tastes, and personality.

These are rights protected by the First Amendment and in my view they are absolute, permitting of no exceptions. ... The Free Exercise Clause of the First Amendment is one facet of this constitutional right. The right to remain silent as respects one's own beliefs, ... is protected by the First and the Fifth. The First Amendment grants the privacy of first-class mail, ... All of these aspects of the right of privacy are "rights retained by the people" in the meaning of the Ninth Amendment.

Second is freedom of choice in the basic decisions of one's life respecting marriage, divorce, procreation, contraception, and the education and upbringing of children.

These rights, unlike those protected by the First Amendment, are subject to some control by the police power. Thus the Fourth Amendment speaks only of "unreasonable searches and seizures" and of "probable cause." These rights are "fundamental" and we have held that in order to support legislative action the statute must be narrowly and precisely drawn and that a "compelling state interest" must be shown in support of the limitation. ...

The liberty to marry a person of one's own choosing, ... the right of procreation, ... the liberty to direct the education of one's children, ... and the privacy of the marital relation, ... are in this category. Only last Term in Eisenstadt v. Baird, 405 U.S. 438, 92 S.Ct. 1029, 31 L.Ed.2d 349, another contraceptive case, we expanded the concept of *Griswold* by saying:

[15] The California abortion statute, held unconstitutional in the *Belous* case made it a crime to perform or help perform an abortion "unless the same is necessary to preserve [the mother's] life." ...

It is true that in Griswold the right of privacy in question inhered in the marital relationship. Yet the marital couple is not an independent entity with a mind and heart of its own, but an association of two individuals each with a separate intellectual and emotional make up. If the right of privacy means anything, it is the right of the *individual*, married or single, to be free from unwarranted governmental intrusion into matters so fundamentally affecting a person as the decision whether to bear or beget a child.

This right of privacy was called by Mr. Justice Brandeis the right "to be let alone." Olmstead v. United States, 277 U.S. 438, 478, 48 S.Ct. 564, 572, 72 L.Ed. 944. That right includes the privilege of an individual to plan his own affairs, for, "outside areas of plainly harmful conduct, every American is left to shape his own life as he thinks best, do what he pleases, go where he pleases." Kent v. Dulles, 357 U.S. 116, 126, 78 S.Ct. 1113, 1118, 2 L.Ed.2d 1204.

Third is the freedom to care for one's health and person, freedom from bodily restraint or compulsion, freedom to walk, stroll, or loaf.

These rights, though fundamental, are likewise subject to regulation on a showing of "compelling state interest." We stated in Papachristou v. City of Jacksonville, 405 U.S. 156, 164, 92 S.Ct. 839, 844, 31 L.Ed.2d 110, that walking, strolling, and wandering "are historically part of the amenities of life as we have known [them]." As stated in Jacobson v. Massachusetts, 197 U.S. 11, 29, 25 S.Ct. 358, 362, 49 L.Ed. 643:

There is, of course, a sphere within which the individual may assert the supremacy of his own will and rightfully dispute the authority of any human government,—especially of any free government existing under a written constitution, to interfere with the exercise of that will.

In Union Pac. Ry. Co. v. Botsford, 141 U.S. 250, 252, 11 S.Ct. 1000, 1001, 35 L.Ed. 734, the Court said,

The inviolability of the person is as much invaded by a compulsory stripping and exposure as by a blow.

In Terry v. Ohio, 392 U.S. 1, 8–9, 88 S.Ct. 1868, 1873, 20 L.Ed.2d 889, the Court in speaking of the Fourth Amendment stated

This inestimable right of personal security belongs as much to the citizen on the streets of our cities as to the [Governor] closeted in his study to dispose of his secret affairs.

Katz v. United States, 389 U.S. 347, 350, 88 S.Ct. 507, 510, 19 L.Ed.2d 576, emphasizes that the Fourth Amendment protects individual privacy against certain kinds of governmental intrusion.

In Meyer v. Nebraska, 262 U.S. 390, 399, 43 S.Ct. 625, 626, 67 L.Ed. 1042, the Court said:

Without doubt, it [liberty] denotes not merely freedom from bodily restraint but also the right of the individual to contract, to engage in any of the common occupations of life, to acquire useful knowledge, to marry, establish a home and bring up children, to worship God according to the dictates of his own conscience, and generally to enjoy those privileges long recognized at common law as essential to the orderly pursuit of happiness by free men.

The Georgia statute is at war with the clear message of these cases— that a woman is free to make the basic decision whether to bear an unwanted child. Elaborate argument is hardly necessary to demonstrate that childbirth may deprive a woman of her preferred life style and force upon her a radically different and undesired future. For example, rejected applicants under the Georgia statute are required to endure the discomforts of pregnancy; to incur the pain, higher mortality rate, and aftereffects of childbirth; to abandon educational plans; to sustain loss of income; to forgo the satisfactions of careers; to tax further mental and physical health in providing childcare; and, in some cases, to bear the lifelong stigma of unwed motherhood, a badge which may haunt, if not deter, later legitimate family relationships.

Such a holding is, however, only the beginning of the problem. The State has interests to protect. Vaccinations to prevent epidemics are one example, as *Jacobson* holds. The Court held that compulsory sterilization of imbeciles afflicted with hereditary forms of insanity or imbecility is another. . . . Abortion affects another. While childbirth endangers the lives of some women, voluntary abortion at any time and place regardless of medical standards would impinge on a rightful concern of society. The woman's health is part of that concern; as is the life of the fetus after quickening. These concerns justify the State in treating the procedure as a medical one.

One difficulty is that this statute as construed and applied apparently does not give full sweep to the "psychological as well as physical well-being" of women patients which saved the concept "health" from being void for vagueness in United States v. Vuitch, *supra,* 402 U.S. at 72, 91 S.Ct. at 1299. But apart from that, Georgia's enactment has a constitutional infirmity because, as stated by the District Court, it "limits the number of reasons for which an abortion may be sought." I agree with the holding of the District Court, "This the State may not do, because such action unduly restricts a decision sheltered by the Constitutional right to privacy.". . .

The vicissitudes of life produce pregnancies which may be unwanted, or which may impair "health" in the broad *Vuitch* sense of the term, or which may imperil the life of the mother, or which in the full setting of the case may create such suffering, dislocations, misery, or tragedy as to make an early abortion the only civilized step to take. These hardships may be properly embraced in the "health" factor of the mother as appraised by a person of insight. Or they may be part of a broader medical judgment based on what is "appropriate" in a given case, though perhaps not "necessary" in a strict sense.

The "liberty" of the mother, though rooted as it is in the Constitution, may be qualified by the State for the reasons we have stated. But where fundamental personal rights and liberties are involved, the corrective legislation must be "narrowly drawn to prevent the supposed evil,". . . and not be dealt with in an "unlimited and indiscriminate" manner. . . . Unless regulatory measures are so confined and are addressed to the specific areas of compelling legislative concern, the police power would become the great leveller of constitutional rights and liberties.

There is no doubt that the State may require abortions to be performed by qualified medical personnel. The legitimate objective of preserving the mother's health clearly supports such laws. Their impact upon the woman's privacy is minimal. But the Georgia statute outlaws virtually all such operations—even in the earliest stages of pregnancy. In light of modern medical evidence suggesting that an early abortion is safer healthwise than childbirth itself,[16] it cannot be seriously urged that so comprehensive a ban is aimed at protecting the woman's health. Rather, this expansive proscription of all abortions along the temporal spectrum can rest only on a public goal of preserving both embryonic and fetal life.

The present statute has struck the balance between the woman and the State's interests wholly in favor of the latter. I am not prepared to hold that a State may equate, as Georgia has done, all phases of maturation preceding birth. We held in *Griswold* that the States may not preclude spouses from attempting to avoid the joinder of sperm and egg. If this is true, it is difficult to perceive any overriding public necessity which might

[16] Many studies show that it is safer for a woman to have a medically induced abortion than to bear a child. In the first 11 months of operation of the New York abortion law, the mortality rate associated with such operations was six per 100,000 operations. Abortion Mortality, 20 Morbidity and Mortality 208, 209 (1971) (U.S. Department of Health, Education, and Welfare, Public Health Service). On the other hand, the maternal mortality rate associated with childbirths other than abortions was 18 per 100,000 live births. Tietze, Mortality with Contraception and Induced Abortion, 45 Studies in Family Planning 6 (1969). See also C. Tietze & H. Lehfeldt, Legal Abortion in Eastern Europe 175 J.A.M.A. 1149, 1152 (1961); V. Kolblova, Legal Abortion in Czechoslovakia, 196 J.A.M.A. 371 (1966); Mehland, Combating Illegal Abortion in the Socialist Countries of Europe, 13 World Med.J. 84 (1966).

attach precisely at the moment of conception. As Mr. Justice Clark has said:[17]

To say that life is present at conception is to give recognition to the potential, rather than the actual. The unfertilized egg has life, and if fertilized, it takes on human proportions. But the law deals in reality, not obscurity— the known rather than the unknown. When sperm meets egg, life may eventually form, but quite often it does not. The law does not deal in specula- tion. The phenomenon of life takes time to develop, and until it is actually present, it cannot be destroyed. Its interruption prior to formation would hardly be homicide, and as we have seen, society does not regard it as such. The rites of Baptism are not performed and death certificates are not required when a miscarriage occurs. No prosecutor has ever returned a murder indictment charging the taking of the life of a fetus.[18] This would not be the case if the fetus constituted human life.

In summary, the enactment is overbroad. It is not closely correlated to the aim of preserving pre-natal life. In fact, it permits its destruction in several cases, including pregnancies resulting from sex acts in which un- married females are below the statutory age of consent. At the same time, however, the measure broadly proscribes aborting other pregnancies which may cause severe mental disorders. Additionally, the statute is overbroad because it equates the value of embryonic life immediately after conception with the worth of life immediately before birth.

Under the Georgia Act the mother's physician is not the sole judge as to whether the abortion should be performed. Two other licensed physicians must concur in his judgment. Moreover, the abortion must be performed in a licensed hospital; and the abortion must be approved in advance by a committee of the medical staff of that hospital.

Physicians, who speak to us in *Doe* through an *amicus* brief, complain of the Georgia Act's interference with their practice of their profession.

The right of privacy has no more conspicuous place than in the physi- cian-patient relationship, unless it be in the priest-penitent relation.

It is one thing for a patient to agree that her physician may consult with another physician about her case. It is quite a different matter for the

[17] Religion, Morality and Abortion: A Constitutional Appraisal, 2 Loy.U. (L.A.) L.Rev. 1, 10 (1969).

[18] In Keeler v. Superior Court of Amador County, 2 Cal.3d 619, 87 Cal.Rptr. 481, 470 P.2d 617, the California Supreme Court held in 1970 that the California mur- der statute did not cover the killing of an unborn fetus, even though the fetus be "viable" and that it was beyond judicial power to extend the statute to the killing of an unborn. It held that the child must be "born alive before a charge of homicide can be sustained." 2 Cal.3d, at 639, 87 Cal.Rptr., at 494, 470 P.2d, at 630.

State compulsorily to impose on that physician-patient relationship another layer or, as in this case, still a third layer of physicians. The right of privacy—the right to care for one's health and person and to seek out a physician of one's own choice protected by the Fourteenth Amendment— becomes only a matter of theory not a reality, when a multiple physician approval system is mandated by the State.

The State licenses a physician. If he is derelict or faithless, the procedures available to punish him or to deprive him of his license are well known. He is entitled to procedural due process before professional disciplinary sanctions may be imposed. . . . Crucial here, however, is state-imposed control over the medical decision whether pregnancy should be interrupted. The good-faith decision of the patient's chosen physician is overriden and the final decision passed on to others in whose selection the patient has no part. This is a total destruction of the right of privacy between physician and patient and the intimacy of relation which that entails.

The right to seek advice on one's health and the right to place his reliance on the physician of his choice are basic to Fourteenth Amendment values. We deal with fundamental rights and liberties, which, as already noted, can be contained or controlled only by discretely drawn legislation that preserves the "liberty" and regulates only those phases of the problem of compelling legislative concern. The imposition by the State of group controls over the physician-patient relation is not made on any medical procedure apart from abortion, no matter how dangerous the medical step may be. The oversight imposed on the physician and patient in abortion cases denies them their "liberty," *viz.,* their right of privacy, without any compelling, discernable state interest.

Georgia has constitutional warrant in treating abortion as a medical problem. To protect the woman's right of privacy, however, the control must be through the physician of her choice and the standards set for his performance.

The protection of the fetus when it has acquired life is a legitimate concern of the State. Georgia's law makes no rational, discernible decision on that score.[19] For under the Act the developmental stage of the fetus is irrelevant when pregnancy is the result of rape or when the fetus will very likely be born with a permanent defect or when a continuation of the pregnancy will endanger the life of the mother or permanently injure her health. When life is present is a question we do not try to resolve. While basically a question for medical experts, as stated by Mr. Justice Clark,[20] it is, of course, caught up in matters of religion and morality.

In short, I agree with the Court that endangering the life of the woman

[19] See Rochat, Tyler, and Schoenbucher, An Epidemiological Analysis of Abortion in Georgia, 61 Am.J. of Public Health 541 (1971).

[20] Religion, Morality and Abortion: A Constitutional Appraisal, 2 Loy.U. (L.A.) L.Rev. 1, 10 (1969).

or seriously and permanently injuring her health are standards too narrow for the right of privacy that are at stake.

I also agree that the superstructure of medical supervision which Georgia has erected violates the patient's right of privacy inherent in her choice of her own physician.

. . .

Mr. Justice White, with whom Mr. Justice Rehnquist joins, dissenting.

At the heart of the controversy in these cases are those recurring pregnancies that pose no danger whatsoever to the life or health of the mother but are nevertheless unwanted for any one or more of a variety of reasons —convenience, family planning, economics, dislike of children, the embarrassment of illegitimacy, etc., The common claim before us is that for any one of such reasons, or for no reason at all, and without asserting or claiming any threat to life or health, any woman is entitled to an abortion at her request if she is able to find a medical advisor willing to undertake the procedure.

The Court for the most part sustains this position: During the period prior to the time the fetus becomes viable, the Constitution of the United States values the convenience, whim or caprice of the putative mother more than the life or potential life of the fetus; the Constitution, therefore, guarantees the right to an abortion as against any state law or policy seeking to protect the fetus from an abortion not prompted by more compelling reasons of the mother.

With all due respect, I dissent. I find nothing in the language or history of the Constitution to support the Court's judgment. The Court simply fashions and announces a new constitutional right for pregnant mothers and, with scarcely any reason or authority for its action, invests that right with sufficient substance to override most existing state abortion statutes. The upshot is that the people and the legislatures of the 50 States are constitutionally disentitled to weigh the relative importance of the continued existence and development of the fetus on the one hand against a spectrum of possible impacts on the mother on the other hand. As an exercise of raw judicial power, the Court perhaps has authority to do what it does today; but in my view its judgment is an improvident and extravagant exercise of the power of judicial review which the Constitution extends to this Court.

The Court apparently values the convenience of the pregnant mother more than the continued existence and development of the life or potential life which she carries. Whether or not I might agree with that marshalling of values, I can in no event join the Court's judgment because I find no constitutional warrant for imposing such an order of priorities on the people and legislatures of the States. In a sensitive area such as this, involving as it does issues over which reasonable men may easily and heatedly differ,

I cannot accept the Court's exercise of its clear power of choice by inter-posing a constitutional barrier to state efforts to protect human life and by investing mothers and doctors with the constitutionally protected right to exterminate it. This issue, for the most part, should be left with the people and to the political processes the people have devised to govern their affairs.

It is my view, therefore, that the Texas statute is not constitutionally infirm because it denies abortions to those who seek to serve only their convenience rather than to protect their life or health. Nor is this plaintiff, who claims no threat to her mental or physical health, entitled to assert the possible rights of those women whose pregnancy assertedly implicates their health. This, together with United States v. Vuitch, 402 U.S. 62, 91 S.Ct. 1294, 28 L.Ed.2d 601 (1971), dictates reversal of the judgment of the District Court.

Likewise, because Georgia may constitutionally forbid abortions to puta-tive mothers who, like the plaintiff in this case, do not fall within the reach of § 26–1202(a) of its criminal code, I have no occasion, and the District Court had none, to consider the constitutionality of the procedural re-quirements of the Georgia statute as applied to those pregnancies posing substantial hazards to either life or health. I would reverse the judgment of the District Court in the Georgia case.

GERMAIN GRISEZ
Abortion: Ethical Arguments

Utilitarianism—the New Morality

If we set aside the personhood of the unborn, arguments against abortion are arguments against contraception. Since I have treated this point at length elsewhere, I will not deal with it here.

However, if we accept the position that the aborted *are* persons, the ethical issues are far from settled. What is excluded is any extreme position that would in effect equate abortion with contraception.

Thus the view that abortion is justified whenever the woman wants it, because she has a right to control her own reproductive capacity, is ruled out as soon as one grants that the fetus also is a person with rights. For if this is true, the fetus' right to life obviously is more important than the woman's right to dispose of her own reproductive capacity. Clearly, an obligation on a pregnant woman to forego abortion no more infringes on

Reprinted, with notes omitted, from Germain Grisez, *Abortion: The Myths, The Realities, and the Arguments* (New York: Corpus Books, 1970), pp. 287–290, 304–307, 315–321, 333–334, 340–346, by permission of the publisher.

her rights than an obligation to forego infanticide infringes on parental rights.

We have responsibilities to those who are dependent on us, and we can hardly claim a right to kill merely to free ourselves of the burden of putting up with and caring for our dependents. If they are *ours,* they are not ours to dispose of as we will; that is the difference between our property and our relatives. The former is an extension of ourselves, but the latter, being other persons, have some importance in themselves.

Arguments that no unwanted child should be permitted to be born and that we must value quality of life more than mere quantity of life also have been introduced into the abortion controversy after having been used to defend the morality of contraception. However, a utilitarian theory of morality can use these arguments even on the supposition that the unborn are persons. And a utilitarian theory would be even more likely to argue the justifiability of abortion in particularly difficult cases—for example, when the mother's health is seriously endangered, when the child will be seriously defective, when the circumstances of the child's conception render its prospects very dim, or when the birth of the child would seriously lessen the chances of several brothers and sisters for a good life.

How would a utilitarian ethics defend abortion in such cases?

Utilitarianism holds that the moral good or evil of human acts is determined by the results of the acts. If an act has good consequences then that act will be good; if it has bad consequences, it will be bad. Of course, most acts have consequences that are partly good and partly bad. Therefore, utilitarianism holds that the morally good act will be the one that on the whole gives the best results. Whenever we act there are alternatives, including not acting or delaying action. If we can add up the good results expected from each alternative and subtract in each case the expected bad results from the good, then according to utilitarian ethics we should choose the act that carries the prospect of the *greatest net good.* Only that act will be a morally good and right one to choose. Other possibilities will be more or less immoral depending upon how far their net value falls short of the single morally good act.

Of course, this theory of morality immediately raises two questions. One question is whether the person acting must consider the good of others, or only his own good, or both. The other question is what will count as good consequences.

The answer of classical utilitarianism to the first of these questions is that one should consider the good of all indiscriminately when counting up good and bad results. We should seek "the greatest good of the greatest number"—so the maxim goes. Thus the agent himself, his friends and family, his enemies and those he has never met would all deserve equal consideration. This position is somewhat unclear, since it does not settle what to do if greater total good can be done to fewer persons by one act and a somewhat lesser total good to a much larger number of persons by the alternative. I think that this and other like ambiguities must be settled on the side of greatest net value, if the simple theory is to be maintained.

The other question—what will count as good consequences?—also has a classic answer. The good is pleasure and the absence of pain. Utilitarians have been criticized for the narrowness of this conception of good, but what they mean by "pleasure" includes every sort of enjoyment, felt satisfaction, and desirable experience. On this theory, the only thing good for its own sake is that conscious experience be as one would wish: rich, intense, and without pain, anguish, or boredom.

An issue often debated among those who espouse utilitarianism is whether each individual act must be judged immediately by the standard of good consequences or whether particular acts should be judged by moral norms which, in turn, would be submitted to the utilitarian test. The first position is called "act-utilitarianism" and the second "rule-utilitarianism." Rule-utilitarianism may seem more plausible, because it leaves room for the ordinary belief that there are some moral norms that should be respected.

However, the two positions actually amount to the same thing. For act-utilitarianism admits that the judgment that is right in any given case should be followed by anyone who faces a similar set of alternatives having a like balance of good and bad consequences. Thus the judgment of the individual act really is universal, and amounts to a rule. And rule-utilitarians, for their part, do not hold that the rules should be maintained even if on the whole and in the long run a change would be for the better. Thus the rules are subject to revisions which admit all reasonable exceptions, and reasonableness is judged by the criterion of utility.

Rule-utilitarians often argue that their position takes account of situations in which it is harmless to the community and advantageous for each individual to act in a certain way but disastrous for all if everyone acts in that way—e.g., the contamination of a public waterway by private sewage systems. However, act-utilitarianism can justify making and enforcing rules to restrain everyone from contributing to a situation when cumulative action would result in common disadvantage. Among the bad consequences of an individual act are the implications it has for the action of others and together with the action of others. Thus if utilitarianism were a usable method of moral judgment, act and rule utilitarianism would yield the same results.

Utilitarianism is a secular ethic in the sense that it has developed as a "new morality" in conscious reaction to traditional religious ethics. The origins of the theory are in modern humanism, which especially in the nineteenth century sought to reform society and to change established customs, many of which rationalized grievous inequalities on the ground that the advantages of the upper classes were theirs by rights founded in "traditional" morality. Since religious morality had been perverted to defend social injustices, humanistic reformers sought a non-religious ethics to serve as the ideology of needed reform. The utilitarian theory was one candidate for this function; Marxism was another. But utilitarianism was compatible with the political outlook of Britain and America, while Marxism was not.

Utilitarianism and Marxism are both this-worldly. Both locate the good in people themselves. Both consider any act good if it has sufficiently good consequences. But Marxism locates the good in an ideal society—a kind of Kingdom of God without God—while utilitarianism locates the good in the experience of individuals—a kind of heavenly bliss without heaven.

Not surprisingly, therefore, utilitarian and Marxist ethics agree in justifying the killing of some people when such killing has sufficiently good consequences. The Marxist will justify killing if it promotes the revolution and the coming into being of the communist society. The utilitarian does not expect any such ideal society and he does not subordinate individual happiness to the community. But the utilitarian can justify killing some to save more, killing those whose lives are more miserable than satisfying, and the like.

Thus we can understand most common arguments in favor of abortion, for most of these arguments simply assume without proof (or even question) a utilitarian type of ethics. Surely, the argument will begin, it is right to induce abortion if it is necessary to save the mother's life, since otherwise both she and the baby would die together, and it is better to save one than to lose both lives. Then, of course, even if it is a case of *either/or,* it usually will be better to kill the baby, since the mother's life will normally mean more to herself and others than the unborn's life means to it and to others. Next, the lack of advanced awareness and susceptibility to mental anguish in the unborn (or even in the young child) will justify killing it if its continued existence will spoil someone else's life (the mother's health; the well being of existing children; the protection of society from the population explosion). Then too, if the child's own life will likely be more a misery than a joy, it may be killed (defects of a serious sort; perhaps the burden of being illegitimate; perhaps even the sad condition of being unwanted).

Everyone is familiar by now with the utilitarian sort of argument. It is usually, and most effectively, presented by detailing some actual, horrible case which appeals strongly to humane sensibility. We identify with the mother and feel acutely the weight of net value for and in her on the side of abortion. We neglect the embryo, even if we admit it to be human, because we have no memory of being in its condition, because it looks odd (perhaps, even, repulsive), because we do not know it, because it has no role in our society.

86 Those who argue for abortion on utilitarian grounds have adopted an

effective rhetoric that does little justice to their opponents. The two chief elements in this rhetoric are an appeal to contemporary prejudice against the authority of traditional religion and an appeal to humane sympathy for the plight of persons in the face of objective, "impersonal" moral standards. Proponents of abortion may be fully sincere in this rhetoric. The prevailing rejection of abortion as immoral undoubtedly arose from the religious tradition, and many opponents argue on the basis of religious faith rather than develop a rational alternative to utilitarianism. Also the depersonalization of modern life in technological and bureaucratic society often pits the person against cold, "objective" requirements, and opponents of utilitarianism have not shown sufficiently that utilitarianism itself reflects modern depersonalization. Most important of all, opponents of utilitarianism have not effectively shown why mere good consequences cannot be an adequate criterion of moral goodness.

· · ·

A Reformulation of the Ethical Issue

In denying that there is any kind of act so evil that good consequences might not sometimes justify it, utilitarianism excluded the notion that we have any duties that we must always fulfill, regardless of consequences. But if we have no such duties, then neither do we have any unexceptionable rights. Rights and duties are correlative. If I have an unalienable right to life, then it is always wrong for others to kill me. If it is sometimes justified for them to kill me, then my right to life is not unalienable—rather, it all depends on circumstances.

In general, we tend to believe that all men are equal in their right to life and that all men have an equal duty to respect the lives of others. We make exceptions in regard to capital punishment and justified killing in war. But in such cases we think that the criminal or the enemy has somehow surrendered the common, equal right to respect for life.

Obviously, our belief in equality in the right to life is incompatible with utilitarianism. Also, though less obviously, any approach that tries to justify any killing of one human being by another on the basis of factual differences between the two is slipping into a utilitarian attitude toward the good of human life. For, in fact, it is of course true that all of us differ from one another in many ways and all of us are unequal on the basis of each and every difference. No one is superior in every respect; there is some way in which each of us is definitely inferior to others.

To decide that some of these differences, some of these inequalities, some of these ways of being inferior can so detract from the basic worth of a person as to warrant his destruction by another is essentially to decide that all persons have a certain definite and limited worth and that certain facts characterizing persons can lessen that worth in a definite and calculable   87 way. Now, this is precisely the mistake of utilitarianism. It understands human worth not in terms of what is intrinsic to the person and his life—dignity—but in terms of what is extrinsic—value *for something*. Human goods can then be appraised and weighed, and the right to kill will depend upon computation.

In effect, utilitarianism puts a price on every man's head. Every person is transformed into an object. On the model of technological reasoning, the price of one is compared with the price of another. Those whose lives, if continued, would detract from rather than add to the sum total of human value must be eliminated, just as an employer gets rid of an unproductive employee by firing him.

We may feel safe enough, personally, in using the factual inequality and inferiority of the embryo as a ground for treating its life as expendable. After all, we are not now and never again will be unequal and inferior in just the way that the embryo is. But in reasoning thus we are being arbitrary, for we are selecting as decisive the characteristics we prefer among all the differences of human beings. And we must always remember that there is no common denominator of the importance of these differences.

Thus, we may suppose that the embryo's right to life must give way because it is undeveloped, because its specifically human abilities are latent in potentiality. If the embryo could argue with us, however, he might contend that the life of an adult is of less worth than his. After all, the adult has less time left to live, and all that he has gained in actualization he has lost in possibility. Most of what he could have been has been sacrificed in his becoming what he is, and much that he has been can never be recaptured.

"Isn't it part of the *wonder* you feel when you hold an infant," the embryo might ask us, "that he can still be anything, that all of life lies open before him? And isn't it part of the *sadness* you feel as you grow older that possibilities are closing off for you, like so many gates slamming shut in the maze of life, until there remains only one gate open—the one that leads into the darkness of death? If death is not better than life," the embryo might conclude his case against the mature adult, "then my life is far better than yours, for my life is a process of development and ever increasing vitality, while yours is a process of deterioration and waning vitality as you decline toward death."

I do not suggest that the embryo's argument would be sound; obviously it is fallacious to suppose that the dignity of a person is measured by his degree of vitality. But the embryo's argument would be no more fallacious than ours, if we measure his worth by his degree of development. And our argument would certainly sound fallacious to him, if he were able to hear and comprehend it.

The ethical issue regarding abortion, therefore, is not precisely stated when it is put in terms of whether it is ever morally right to kill the unborn and, if so, under what conditions. Rather, the question is whether it is ever morally right for any human person to kill another one and, if so, under what conditions. To question the absoluteness of the right to life of the unborn is to question the absoluteness of everyone's right to life. Since, as persons, we are incomparable with one another in dignity and equal in our right to life, the principle that protects the lives of all of us also protects the lives of those unborn, while any reasonable ground for morally approving the killing of those unborn also is a reasonable ground for morally approving the killing of persons in any other period or condition of their lives.

Since, in fact, we do believe that on the whole it is wrong to kill human beings but that in certain cases such killing is justifiable, our problem is reduced to investigating whether this belief is correct and, if so, why. Then we must apply to the special case of the unborn any ground that justifies killing, to see which justifications for abortion, if any, are valid.

It might be objected that our examination of the question whether the aborted are human beings did not demonstrate absolutely that they are, in fact, persons. But this objection would miss the point of that consideration in two ways.

In the first place, we saw that beyond doubt the *facts* show the embryo at every stage to be a *living, human individual*. To go beyond this is not a question of fact but a question of metaphysics. We should not expect and will never get a factual answer to the ulterior question. What our arguments revealed is that there is no compelling reason to deny that the embryo is a person. As the Anglican committee frankly stated, to deny personality to the embryo is merely a postulate necessary to leave room for killing it. If ethics is to be anything better than rationalization, such an approach will not do. We must admit, at the very least, that the embryo can as well be considered a person as not.

And therefore, in the second place, ethics must proceed on the supposition that abortion does kill a person. For ethics is concerned with moral responsibility for doing what is right and wrong, and right and wrong are in one's willingness, not in what is beyond our knowledge, actual or even possible. We do not consider ourselves immoral if we discover that some action of ours seriously harmed another, though we did not know and could not have known it would have that effect. Similarly, we cannot consider ourselves blameless if we are willing to kill what may or may not be a person, even if it is not.

In being willing to kill the embryo, we accept responsibility for killing what we must admit *may* be a person. There is some reason to believe it is—namely the *fact* that it is a living, human individual and the inconclusiveness of arguments that try to exclude it from the protected circle of personhood.

To be willing to kill what for all we know could be a person is to be 89 *willing to kill it if it is a person.* And since we cannot absolutely settle if it is a person except by a metaphysical postulate, for all practical purposes we must hold that to be willing to kill the embryo is to be willing to kill a person.

Consequently, we may not evade moral responsibility for killing a person if we take responsibility for an abortion. This is not yet to say that the responsibility is always *guilt,* that will be true only if killing such persons is always *wrong.*

The important point to realize is that ethical consideration of abortion must not treat it as an isolated case, as if it had nothing to do with the whole question of the ethics of killing human beings. Certainly, the literature we have reviewed also shows that abortion is connected with other forms of killing such an infanticide, and euthanasia. If a utilitarian theory is accepted, not only the personhood of the unborn, but the personhood of all of us is put in jeopardy. Anyone with sufficient ingenuity in metaphysical argument should be able to construct some sort of plausible theory of personality according to which any one of us will turn out to be a non-person.

It is also important to notice that in locating the ethical issue in the way I do, the following discussion does not become completely separated from serious ethical reflection with which I do not wholly agree. The Protestant situationists (as distinguished from those who hold a form of utilitarianism) examine the issue of abortion in the context of a firm conviction that the real issue is the justifiability of taking the lives of persons. Moreover, not only theological moral reflection but also secular medical and jurisprudential consideration, until the last few years, proceeded generally on the same basis, . . .

. . . . .

. . . What divides moral good from moral evil? The answer is that moral goodness and evil depend upon the attitude with which we choose. Not that any and every choice would be good if only it were made with the proper attitude, for some choices cannot be made with the right attitude. But if we have the right attitude, we make good choices; if we have the wrong attitude, we make evil ones.

But what is the right attitude? It is realistic, in the sense that it conforms fully with reality. To choose a particular good with an appreciation of its genuine but limited possibility and its objectively human character is to choose it with an attitude of realism. Such choice does not attempt to transform and belittle the goodness of what is not chosen, but only to realize what is chosen.

The attitude which leads to immoral choices, by contrast, narrows the good to the possibilities one chooses to realize. The good is not appreciated in its objectively human character, simply as a good, but as *this* good of *such* a sort to be achieved *by me*. Instead of conforming to the real amplitude of human possibility, such an attitude transforms that possibility by restriction. Immoral choice forecloses possibilities merely because they are not chosen; rather than merely realizing some goods while leaving others unrealized, such choice presumes to negate what it does not embrace in order to exalt what it chooses. Goods equally ultimate are reduced to the status of mere means for maximizing preferred possibilities; principles of practical reason as fundamental as those that make the choice possible are brushed aside as if they wholly lacked validity.

No single good, nothing that can be embraced in the object of any single choice, is sufficient to exhaust human good, to fulfill all of the possibilities open before man. If we choose with an attitude of openness to goods not chosen, the good is not restricted. We respect the possibility we cannot realize through this choice. But if we restrict our perspective by redefining what is good according to our particular choice, we are attempting to negate the meaningfulness of what we reject and to absolutize what we prefer.

A proper attitude respects equally all of the basic goods and listens equally to all of the appeals they express through principles of practical reason. Because of the incompatibility of actual alternatives, a choice is necessary. But a right attitude does not seek to subvert some principles of practical reason by an appeal to others. An immoral attitude involves such irrationality, for while the evil choice depends upon the principles of practical reason, it seeks to invalidate the claims of those principles which would have grounded an alternate choice.

If the principle that distinguishes moral good from evil is an attitude such as we have just described, still two serious questions must be considered. First, is not moral evil something more interpersonal than the unrealistic and narrow attitude just described? Does not moral evil involve the violation of the good of others? From a religious viewpoint, must it not be seen as alienation from God—a rejection of his love? Second, how does an open attitude such as we have described shape itself into concrete moral obligations to do or avoid specific acts?

The answer to the first question is easy. The principle of moral evil can be located in the unrealistic attitude described, but the impact or significance of such evil is by no means limited to oneself.

If I choose with the attitude that my commitment defines and delimits the good, I shall lack the detachment to appreciate the possibilities of others' lives, which could complement my own by realizing the values I cannot. Their good, which I do not choose, will become for me at best a non-good, something to which I shall remain indifferent. Egoism can decrease only to the extent that I am open to the embrace of all goods, those as well as these, yours as well as mine. The attitude of immorality is an irrational attempt to reorganize the moral universe, so that the center is not the whole range of human possibilities in which we can all share, but the goods I can actually pursue through my actions. Instead of community, immorality generates alienation, and the conflict of competing immoralities is reflected by incompatible personal rationalizations and social ideologies, each of which seeks to remake the entire moral universe in conformity with its own fundamental bias.

Those who understand immorality in religious terms of course cannot be expected to find any merely philosophic account entirely satisfactory. But the philosophic account proposed here might coincide with a religious view. It certainly is impossible to maintain a fully open attitude toward all human goods, irreducibly diverse and incommensurable as they are, unless we accept the reference of our conception of goodness to a reality we do not yet understand.

For if the goods we do know—which constitute a *unified* field for our choices—are not diverse participations in a unity beyond all of them, they must be unified by reference to one another. In that case, what we choose will appropriate the priority of an absolute to which what we reject will be subordinated—if it is regarded as good in any sense at all. However, if we accept the reference of our conception of goodness to a reality we do not yet understand, our openness to that goodness may count as love of it, although it is not an intelligible objective of any particular action.

Such love of the good can be interpreted in a religious context as at least compatible with a response of love to God's love. And if the goodness in question is identified with God, respect and openness to all human goods may be interpreted as man's fulfillment by participation in a good which first belongs to God. An immoral attitude, by contrast, would exclude a real goodness beyond the goods we know and choose; immorality would refuse to seek human fulfillment as a realization by participation in God's own goodness. From a religious viewpoint, any morally evil act, in which the good chosen is made to define goodness itself, really is an instance of covert idolatry.

The second question—how a morally right attitude can shape itself into specific obligations—is extremely important for ethical theory.

The solution almost automatically taken for granted in most contemporary discussions is that openness to all human goods requires a moral judgment in accord with the utilitarian maxim: the greatest good for the greatest number. However, as we have seen, utilitarianism is incoherent, because the goods are many and incommensurable, and there is no single standard or least common denominator by which the "greatest good" could be measured. In fact, self-determination is possible only because the "greatest good" cannot be determined by calculation; utilitarianism is actually incompatible with freedom.

Of course, once a definite goal has been determined, it is possible for us to calculate the efficient means to it. If we take an immoral attitude toward the goods we choose, utilitarianism may seem a suitable method for rationalizing our prejudice. (Not everyone who theorizes as if utilitarianism were a moral system practices what he teaches.)

Ideally, the discernment of specific moral obligations would require neither calculation nor even reflection. If one's moral attitude were right and his whole personality were perfectly integrated with that moral attitude, then his own sense of appropriateness, his own spontaneous judgments, would be the surest index of moral good and evil. This is what St. Augustine meant when he said (in religious terms): "Love God, and then do what you wish."

However, when we have a moral question, obviously our moral sensibility has failed us. At this point it is useless to say: "Act by your own right will," because the question would never have arisen but for the conflict within ourselves. "What we wish" is not decisive because we wish one thing with one part of ourself and another thing with another part.

Then too, when it comes to explaining our moral evaluation to others, our moral sensibility is not helpful, because it is incommunicable. At such a juncture, articulate reasons are essential. We must ask what our moral judgments would be if we were perfectly integrated in accord with a right moral attitude.

First, if we were open to all of the goods, we would at least take them into account in our deliberations. We would never make a choice by which one of the goods was seriously affected without considering our action in that light. Thus, we would never choose to act in a way that caused anyone's death without being aware of the impact of what we were doing. In this respect, Protestant situationism reveals moral sensitivity that seems missing from some utilitarian theories.

Second, if we had a right moral attitude we would avoid ways of acting that inhibit the realization of any one of the goods and prefer ways of acting that contribute to each one, other things being equal. One who has a positive attitude toward human life certainly makes a presumption in its favor and does not gratuitously negate this good (or any other).

Third, if we had a truly realistic appreciation of the entire ambit of human goods, we would not hesitate to contribute our effort to their realization in others, when our help is needed urgently, merely because no particular benefit accrued to ourselves. True enough, we have primary obligations to realize human goods in ourselves and in those near us, for we can do in ourselves what no one else can. But we should be more interested in *the good* than in *our* good. Therefore, we reveal an immoral attitude if we prefer our own good merely because it is ours, when our help is urgently needed by others. For this reason, one who had a morally right attitude certainly would prefer another's life to his own comfort, or to other goods to which he would prefer his own life.

Fourth, if we had a right moral attitude, we would fulfill our role in any cooperative venture into which we enter not only to the extent necessary to get out of it what we seek for ourselves but to the full extent needed to achieve the good whose concrete possibility depends on the common effort. This principle does not preclude the criticism of institutions or the reformation of structures, but it does rule out attempts to revise social relationships simply to make them more favorable to ourselves, even at the expense of the common good. Thus we cannot rightly seek to preserve and protect our own lives by institutions, such as criminal law, which we refuse to apply equally to the rights of others. Equality before the law is a moral principle as well as a legal one.

Fifth, if we were fully integrated toward the goods, we would carry out our engagements with them. As our life progresses, we make commitments, such as choice of career, which preclude the pursuit of many other possibilities. If these commitments are made in view of the real good we can achieve, we will not set them aside merely because we encounter difficulties. A genuine respect for the goods we do not choose to pursue will make us doubly dedicated to the realization of those on which we concentrate our efforts.

The teacher who is cynical about education, the corrupt politician, the careless physician, the slipshod craftsman—all show a lack of faithful dedication to what they have chosen as their own share of man's effort to achieve the goods open to us. Parents and physicians both are especially engaged in the good of human life in the helpless and dependent. Therefore, failure on their part to protect and promote this good is an abdication of responsibility that reveals an improper moral attitude.

All of the preceding ways in which concrete moral obligations take shape reveal something about the reason why human life, which is one of the basic goods, must be respected. Yet none of these forms of obligation would require an unexceptionable respect for life. Not even the parent and physician need always act to preserve and promote life, for sometimes other goods also are very pressing. A proper moral attitude is compatible with the omission of action that would realize a good, provided that omission itself is essential to realize another good (or the same generic good in another instance).

However, there is still another mode of moral obligation which binds us with greater strictness. If we had a right moral attitude, which means a truly realistic appreciation of each human good, we would never act directly against the realization of any basic good and we would never act in a way directly destructive of a realization of any of the basic goods. To act directly against a good is to subordinate that good to whatever leads us to choose such a course of action. We treat an end as if it were a mere means; we treat an aspect of the person as if it were an object of measurable and calculable worth. Yet each of the principles of practical reason is as basic as the others and each of them must be respected by us equally if we are not to narrow and foreshorten human goodness to conform to our choices.

Of course, each of the basic human goods may be inhibited or interfered with when we act for any good. But it is one thing for inhibition or interference with other goods to occur as unsought but unavoidable side-effects of an effort to pursue a good, and it is quite another thing directly to choose to inhibit or destroy a realization of a basic human good. To reluctantly accept the adverse aspects of one's action is one thing; to purposely determine ourselves to an action that is of its very character against a basic good is quite another matter.

It is only possible for us to do this insofar as a direct attack on a good can be useful to some ulterior good consequence—the end rationalizes the means. But, against utilitarian theories, I think we must maintain that the end which rationalizes the means cannot justify the means when the means in question involves turning against a good equally basic, equally an end, equally a principle of rational action as the good consequence sought to be achieved.

Here, I believe, we arrive at the reason why we consider actions which kill human beings to be generally immoral. Human life is a basic good and it is intrinsic to the person, not extrinsic as property is. To choose directly to destroy a human life is to turn against this fundamental human good. We can make such a choice only by regarding life as a measurable value, one that can be compared to other values and calculated to be of less worth. To attempt such a rationalization is to reduce an end to the status of mere means. Whatever good is achieved by such a means could not have been chosen except by a pretense that the good of the life which is destroyed is not really an irreplaceable human possibility. Undoubtedly, it is for this reason that those who seek to justify direct abortion and other direct attacks on human life strive to deny the humanity and/or personality of the intended victims.

Two sorts of objections are likely to be raised against this conclusion. First, it will be argued that a single act of killing—for example, the single choice to abort an infant—should not be isolated from the whole context of a person's life. Second, it will be objected that almost every moral system has recognized some cases in which killing is justifiable: for example, in self defense, as capital punishment, in warfare, and, in the case of abortion, to save the mother's life. This second objection demands a careful treatment, and the next section will be devoted to it. But the first objection can be disposed of at once.

Each single act is an engagement of one's freedom, a determination of one's self by one's self. A particular choice against human life therefore has a moral significance in itself, for that choice either squares or not with a right moral orientation. Of course, one who performs an isolated immoral act is not damaged in moral character so badly as one who habitually chooses or approves such acts. But a little immorality is still immorality.

Actually, I think, those who ask us to consider the act of killing within 95 the whole context of a person's life are assuming that "circumstances" or "other values" that are present "in the situation" will offset the disvalue of the act and so justify it. Such an argument really amounts to a covert form of utilitarianism.

Situations do not present themselves to us ready made. They take their shape and find their limits because of our interests. Once we have chosen, a situation has been finally settled. Before choice we always are able to extend our reflection so as to enlarge the situation and even to transform it by taking into account what our initial interest did not require us to notice. Moral judgments, good or bad, delimit human situations; potentially our human situation is unlimited. For this reason it is a mistake to look to the situation for the meaning of the act.

Nevertheless, Protestant situation ethics is not pointless. There are cases in which there seems to be a genuine conflict of obligations, so that one would appear unable to avoid falling into some moral evil. Undoubtedly, the number of such apparent conflict cases would be greatly reduced if all the possible courses of action were considered instead of some being excluded in advance because they would involve difficulty or hardship which we all too easily decide is "impossibility." Again, apparent conflict cases would be lessened if we kept clearly in mind that there is no moral obligation to choose all possible goods, including incompatible ones. It is not immoral to leave some good undone providing that good is appreciated and respected and some other good is done.

Yet there remain conflict cases such as those in which most moral systems have admitted the justifiability of killing human beings. To such cases we must now turn our attention.

．　　・　　．

One need neither confuse the moral reality of the act with its behavioral aspect nor divide the *meaningfulness* of the behavior from the *enactment* of the purpose to observe that human acts sometimes are means to ends extrinsic to themselves: for example, the work of a person who is only interested in pay. If the work is that of a gunman who will kill anyone for a price, then the psychological intention by which he sets himself directly against human life is morally significant, for this intention orients the self in a manner that is incompatible with openness to the basic good of human life and respect for it. Whatever his ulterior purpose might be, his acts are morally evil, for one basic human good is treated as expendable for the sake of another (or of the same in another realization). . . .

Nevertheless, it seems to me that the principle of double effect in its modern formulation is too restrictive insofar as it demands that even in the order of physical causality the evil aspect of the act not precede the good. The critics are right, I believe, in their insistence that the behavioral aspect of the act is not morally determinate apart from the meaning that shapes the human act. In this respect, Aquinas' formulation seems to me to have been more accurate, for he did not make an issue of which effect (aspect of the act) is prior in physical causality, but he did insist that when a single human act has a good and a bad aspect the latter could not rightly fall within the scope of intention, even as a means to a good end.

From the point of view of human moral activity, the initiation of an indivisible process through one's own causality renders all that is involved in that process equally immediate. So long as no other human act intervenes or could intervene, the meaning (intention) of the behavior which initiates such a process is no less immediate to what is, from the point of view of physical causality, a proximate effect or a secondary or remote consequence. For on the hypothesis that no other human act intervenes or could intervene, the moral agent who posits a natural cause *simultaneously* (morally speaking) posits its foreseen effects. The fact that not everything in the behavior which is relevant to basic human goods equally affects the agent's moral standing arises not from the diverse physical dispositions of the elements of the behavioral aspect of the act, but from the diverse dispositions of the agent's intention with regard to the intelligible aspects of the act.

But it is the intelligible aspects of the indivisible human act that count, not purposes sought and values hoped for in ulterior human acts, whether of the agent himself or of another. For otherwise the end will justify the means, and some sort of utilitarianism or inadequate consistency-criterion will replace the true standard of moral value.

Moreover, even if the particular process initiated by one's behavior is in fact indivisible, he obviously does not escape full moral responsibility for significant aspects of it that could have been avoided by the choice of an alternative behavior having the same determining intention but a diverse mode of accomplishment. Then too, if the unity of the process is merely *de facto,* arising from the agent's failure to divide and limit his behavior, then the act is not truly indivisible and the determining intention will not exclude moral responsibility for aspects of the act that could have been excluded, but were not.

This theoretical formulation will be considerably clarified by application to some examples. Obviously, cases generally approved by application of the principle of double effect as it is conventionally formulated also will be approved if the modification I am suggesting is correct, since the modification broadens the strict condition about the order of the effects as it is usually expressed. For this reason, we need not review many examples usually used to illustrate the principle, but we must consider some where the proposed modification leads to a result different from the usual formulation. Also, it will be worth noting how the proposed modification would deal more restrictively with some of the types of cases mentioned by critics of the traditional principle.

97

. . .

According to the present theory, then, in which cases would it be permissible to do the deadly deed involving the unborn? We must bear in mind from the previous argument that they must be treated as persons whose lives are inviolable to any direct attack. The question therefore becomes a matter of trying to apply the revised version of the principle of double effect to these cases.

In the chapter on medical aspects, we saw that there are relatively few cases in which the life or physical health of the mother seems to require abortion. Two types of cases of this sort are those involving ectopic pregnancy (implantation of the embryo outside the uterus) and certain cases involving impaired heart and/or kidney function.

Ectopic pregnancy, we have seen in dealing with religious aspects, has been dealt with by Catholic moralists by the argument that the condition itself is pathological, and that the pathology, even apart from the developing embryo, presents a threat to the mother. It must be removed, and in the process the embryo is incidentally removed.

Assuming the soundness of the position, I think a simpler justification is possible. This justification will also apply to abortions previously considered direct having strict medical indications such as those mentioned involving impaired heart and/or kidney function.

The justification is simply that the very same act, indivisible as to its behavioral process, has both the good effect of protecting human life and the bad effect of destroying it. The fact that the good effect is subsequent in time and in physical process to the evil one is irrelevant, because the entire process is indivisible by human choice and hence all aspects of it are equally present to the agent at the moment he makes his choice.

It will be helpful, perhaps, in gaining acceptance for this view—although it is not theoretically essential to the argument—if we note that it is not precisely the infant's death that benefits the mother but its removal from her. From this point of view, even if the abortion were intended (which I do not think it has to be), the killing of the infant would not have to be intended. The distinction is clearly illustrated if we imagine a probable future development—an artificial womb. Embryos aborted in such cases could conceivably be saved and brought to birth by such a device. Thus, the very meaning of *abortion* need not be *feticide,* for even if the two cannot now be separated in fact, they could be, and what could be separate in fact obviously cannot be identical in meaning.

If the threat to the mother's life or health can be obviated without the removal of the unborn child, then the aspects of the human act which involves abortion are, in fact, separable. In such a case one cannot argue that the alternative to abortion is difficult, inconvenient, and costly. For that is to make these factors of cost equal in value to the dignity of human life. If one does not take an alternative in which the good effect is achieved without the deadly deed, then killing falls within the scope of one's intention.

What if there is no alternative to abortion, in some sort of case, if the mother's health is to be protected, although the risk to her does not involve the probability of accelerated death? In principle, if the good effect is attained in and through the same indivisible process which is initiated by the abortifacient procedure, then the abortion need not be intended. However, one does not sacrifice life for health, since the latter is only a partial aspect of the former.

To subordinate life to health is something I could not do in my own case —I would never be healthier dead. Nor can one reasonably prefer health to life, the part of life (health) to the whole of life. To act on such a preference involving another's life and my health indicates that it is not the basic human good itself, but a particular realization of it, that concerns me. This is a limiting attitude, not compatible with moral uprightness.

This conclusion that abortion is not morally permitted when only health is at stake also applies to the entire area of the psychiatric indication. Moreover, the good effects presumably justifying such cases of abortion are not achieved through a physical process that is unified and morally indivisible, but rather in ulterior effects of distinct human acts.

For this reason, even if a threat of suicide is serious and abortion would prevent it (something hardly likely as we saw in chapter three), abortion would not be justified in such a case. The good effect would be achieved only by preventing another act, and the abortion itself would be a means, intentionally chosen, to this ulterior end.

In times past complications of delivery raised serious problems. Now where medical facilities are available such difficulties are rare, most difficult cases being prevented by timely surgery. However, if it were impossible to prevent the mother's death (or, worse, the death of both) except by cutting up and removing the child piecemeal, it seems to me that this death-dealing deed could be done without the killing itself coming within the scope of intention. The very deed which deals death also (by hypothesis) initiates a unified and humanly indivisible physical process which saves life. But if it is possible to save the mother without the death-dealing deed, then the intent to kill would enter the agent's act as its determining meaning.

The attempt to justify abortion in cases involving prospective birth defects obviously is unsatisfactory. If the goods sought are in others, then the deadly deed does not itself achieve them, and it becomes an intended means to an ulterior end. On the other hand, if life is a human good, even a defective life is better than no life at all—some value is better than no value. In any case, defects cannot touch many central values of the human person, as we saw earlier in this chapter. The real reasons underlying this 99 "indication" are utilitarian—the supposition that an infant is like a product, and that imperfect specimens should be scrapped.

A sound appraisal of the moral significance of abortion as a method of eliminating the defective was given by Martin Ginsberg, a New York state Assemblyman, in the 1969 New York legislative debate. The proposed bill would have permitted abortion

when there is medical evidence of a substantial risk that the foetus, if born, would be so grossly malformed, or would have such serious physical or mental abnormalities, as to be permanently incapable of caring for himself.

Mr. Ginsberg, a thirty-eight-year-old lawyer who was crippled by polio at the age of thirteen months, walks only with difficulty, using metal crutches and leg braces.

He began his speech by mentioning a number of persons who achieved greatness despite handicaps—Toulouse Lautrec, Alec Templeton, Charles Steinmetz, Lord Byron, and Helen Keller. Then he went on:

What this bill says is that those who are malformed or abnormal have no reason to be part of our society. If we are prepared to say that a life should not come into this world malformed or abnormal, then tomorrow we should be prepared to say that a life already in this world which becomes malformed or abnormal should not be permitted to live.

Ginsberg, who did not oppose abortion law relaxation in general, was given a standing ovation by the Assembly.

The bill's sponsor, Albert H. Blumenthal, attacked Ginsberg, accusing him of telling women they could not protect themselves from harm:

That's what you're telling my wife, Marty. You're telling her she has no right to protect herself from harm. You don't have that right, Marty. Nobody gave you that right. Not God. Not man.

However, Blumenthal did not explain how eliminating possible defective children would protect mothers from harm. Although before the debate there were six votes more than the number needed for passage pledged in favor of the bill, the *New York Times,* which has promoted abortion law relaxation for years, was forced to headline: "Assembly Blocks Abortion Reform in Sudden Switch—14 Legislators Pledged to Bill Defect After Polio Victim Urges Defeat."

Abortion used as a form of birth prevention—whether in cases of illegitimate children, or in cases of economic hardship, or in cases of simple reluctance to have a child—clearly cannot be justified. Here the whole point of the operation is to get rid of the baby, to end its life, because its continued existence is simply rejected. This is not to say that in some such

100

cases there is not a genuinely good ulterior motive—e.g., avoiding future hardship for already existing children in an impoverished family. However, these good motives—while they may well win our sympathy and deserve our compassion—do not ethically justify the abortifacient procedure, for it achieves none of these goods. They are present only in future human actions.

Moreover, the goods sought in all such cases are achievable otherwise. The unmarried girl should be helped and arrangements made for the child's care, whether or not she wishes to bring it up. The problems of poverty and social stress would yield to our compassion if it were real and active enough, not merely a weak sympathy. Those who do not want children need not conceive them; they do so by their own free acts.

But what about the rare case in which a woman is raped and conceives a child of her attacker? She has not had a choice; the child has come to be through no act of hers. Moreover, it is not clear that her precise concern is to kill the child. She simply does not wish to bear it. If the artificial uterus were available, she might be happy to have the baby removed and placed in such a device, later to be born and cared for as any infant that becomes a social charge. Now, clearly, one could not object if that were done. May the death of the child that is in fact brought about by aborting it actually be unintended in this case? I believe that the answer must be yes.

But this answer does not mean that abortion in such a case would be ethically right. I fail to see what basic human good is achieved if the developing baby is aborted. The victim of rape has been violated and has a good reason to resent it. Yet the unborn infant is not the attacker. It is hers as much as his. She does not wish to bear it—an understandable emotional reaction. But really at stake is only such trouble, risk and inconvenience as is attendant on any pregnancy. To kill the baby for the sake of such goods reveals an attitude toward human life that is not in keeping with its inherently immeasurable dignity. One of the simpler modes of obligation is violated—that which requires us to do good to another when we can and there is no serious reason not to do it.

Even psychologically, I doubt the wisdom of a woman who has been raped disposing of a child conceived of the attack. Her problem is largely to accept herself, to realize that she is not inherently tainted and damaged by her unfortunate experience. The unborn child is partly hers, and she must accept herself in it if she is really to overcome her sense of self-rejection. To get rid of the child is to evade this issue, not to solve it. A woman who uses such an evasion may feel temporary relief but may be permanently blocked from achieving the peace with herself she seeks.

Incest presents no special problem. Clearly here abortion is a method of disposing of an unwanted baby. I see no reason why incest often is coupled with rape in discussions of abortion, except for the fact that 101 both arouse in most people an emotion of revulsion which proponents of abortion seek to divert from parties who are guilty to individuals who are innocent—the nameless unborn.

If abortion is justified, then it should be performed in a way that gives the child a chance of survival, if there is any chance at all. The effort to save the aborted child and to find ways of saving all who are justifiably aborted would be a token of sincerity that the death of the child really was not in the scope of the intention.

If abortion is intended, how it is done is ethically irrelevant except to the extent that some methods might unnecessarily endanger the mother as well. Certainly, abortion is no less immoral if it is done with an abortion pill near the beginning of pregnancy than if it is done with a curette later on, or by delivering the child at or after viability and putting it down an incinerator, as has happened in England under the new abortion law.

One might wonder about the moral status of birth control methods that are probably or possibly abortifacient, as we saw in the latter part of chapter three is the case with the IUD and the "pill." If one recognizes that human life is at stake if these methods do indeed work in an abortifacient manner, then it is clear that the willingness to use them is a willingness to kill human beings directly. The effect of killing the already conceived individual, if it occurs, is no accident, but the precise thing sought in committing oneself to birth prevention. *If one is willing to get a desired result by killing, and does not know whether he is killing or not, he might as well know that he is killing,* for he is willing to accept that as the meaning of his act: Everyone who knows the facts and who prescribes or uses birth control methods that might be abortifacient is an abortionist at heart.

The judgment may be seen more clearly by considering it from the point of view of someone who sincerely believes conception-prevention to be legitimate and any interference after conception to be unjustifiably killing a person. On these assumptions, it clearly is insufficient to know that a given method prevents *births,* such a person would be willing to prevent conception but absolutely unwilling to interfere once conception had occurred. The abortifacient character of a technique, even if certainly known to occur in only a small percentage of cases, could not be viewed as incidental to the intended conception prevention, since in those cases there would be no conception prevention. Nor could the abortions which might occur be outside the scope of the intention defined as *birth prevention,* since if conception were not prevented, the only meaning of "birth prevention" would be *abortion.* Uncertainty about a method's mode of action would perhaps be tolerable if the uncertainty regarded side effects. However, here the uncertainty is concerned with the very meaning of the *intended* birth prevention: whether it is conception prevention or abortion.

102

It is often said that one should not becloud the ethical issues regarding abortion by referring to it as *murder*. Certainly the word has a legal sense, and it would prejudice the jurisprudential discussion of abortion in the next chapter to classify abortion with the crime of murder. On the other hand, "murder" also has an ethical sense: it is the wrongful and purposeful taking of human life. It would be question-begging to call abortion "murder" before examining its morality. Now that we have completed such an examination, however, it is accurate and appropriate to say that abortion, whenever it involves the direct attack on human life (which is almost always) is *murder*. To reject this classification of the act is itself a merely emotional reaction, an attempt to sanctify evil by removing its bad name.

To say this, however, is not to assert that everyone who has an abortion or who performs an abortion incurs the full moral responsibility for murder. Many who do the evil deed do not know, or do not fully appreciate, what they do—this is true of all murder, not only of abortion. Some act through fear, through anxiety, through shame. They are less guilty than those who act through cool and brutal calculation, such as a utilitarian, if he were true to his principles, should applaud. Still, if one's lack of appreciation of what the deadly deed really means or if one's weakness to resist is a product of one's own habit of treating the good of life lightly or of one's unwillingness to see and feel the wrong one does, then responsibility is not lessened, but increased.

Granting that someone has done his best to see what is right and to be ready to do the right as he sees it, he is of course free of moral guilt. In this sense, one who follows steadfastly the direction of a firm and honest conscience is doing as he ought. Still, conscience must be shaped according to ethical truth. A sincere conscience can be mistaken, and such a mistake does not make the deed good, although it does not make the doer guilty.

Roman Catholic readers may notice that my conclusions about abortion diverge from common theological teachings, and also diverge from the official teaching of the Church as it was laid down by the Holy Office in the nineteenth century. I am aware of the divergence, but would point out that my theory is consonant with the more important and more formally definite teaching that direct killing of the unborn is wrong. I reach conclusions that are not traditional by broadening the meaning of "unintended" in a revision of the principle of double effect, not by accepting the rightness of direct killing or the violability of unborn life because of any ulterior purpose or indication.

Most important, I cannot as a philosopher limit my conclusions by theological principles. However, I can as a Catholic propose my philosophic conclusions as suggestions for consideration in the light of faith, while not proposing anything contrary to the Church's teaching as a 103

practical norm of conduct for my fellow believers. Those who really
believe that there exists on this earth a community whose leaders are
appointed and continuously assisted by God to guide those who accept
their authority safely through time to eternity would be foolish to direct
their lives by some frail fabrication of mere reason instead of by conforming to a guidance system designed and maintained by divine wisdom.

I do not doubt that the survivors of a nuclear holocaust, when they
look back upon our time, will clearly discern a common thread uniting
our deterrent strategy, our increasing resort to violence in place of orderly civil process, and our relaxed attitude toward the killing of the
unborn. If we want freedom and progress together with law and order,
we must begin by recommitting ourselves to the basic good of human
life, a good that is fundamental to all the others. If we do not respect
human life, what human good will we any longer respect?

JUDITH JARVIS THOMSON
A Defense of Abortion[1]

Most opposition to abortion relies on the premise that the fetus is a
human being, a person, from the moment of conception. The premise
is argued for, but, as I think, not well. Take, for example, the most
common argument. We are asked to notice that the development of a
human being from conception through birth into childhood is continuous; then it is said that to draw a line, to choose a point in this development and say "before this point the thing is not a person, after this
point it is a person" is to make an arbitrary choice, a choice for which
in the nature of things no good reason can be given. It is concluded that
the fetus is, or anyway that we had better say it is, a person from the
moment of conception. But this conclusion does not follow. Similar
things might be said about the development of an acorn into an oak
tree, and it does not follow that acorns are oak trees, or that we had
better say they are. Arguments of this form are sometimes called "slip-
pery slope arguments"—the phrase is perhaps self-explanatory—and it
is dismaying that opponents of abortion rely on them so heavily and
uncritically.

Reprinted from *Philosophy and Public Affairs,* Vol. 1, No. 1 (1971), 47–66. Copyright © 1971 by Princeton University Press. Reprinted by permission of the author
and Princeton University Press.

[1] I am very much indebted to James Thomson for discussion, criticism, and many
helpful suggestions.

I am inclined to agree, however, that the prospects for "drawing a line" in the development of the fetus look dim. I am inclined to think also that we shall probably have to agree that the fetus has already become a human person well before birth. Indeed, it comes as a surprise when one first learns how early in its life it begins to acquire human characteristics. By the tenth week, for example, it already has a face, arms and legs, fingers and toes; it has internal organs, and brain activity is detectable.[2] On the other hand, I think that the premise is false, that the fetus is not a person from the moment of conception. A newly fertilized ovum, a newly implanted clump of cells, is no more a person than an acorn is an oak tree. But I shall not discuss any of this. For it seems to me to be of great interest to ask what happens if, for the sake of argument, we allow the premise. How, precisely, are we supposed to get from there to the conclusion that abortion is morally impermissible? Opponents of abortion commonly spend most of their time establishing that the fetus is a person, and hardly any time explaining the step from there to the impermissibility of abortion. Perhaps they think the step too simple and obvious to require much comment. Or perhaps instead they are simply being economical in argument. Many of those who defend abortion rely on the premise that the fetus is not a person, but only a bit of tissue that will become a person at birth; and why pay out more arguments than you have to? Whatever the explanation, I suggest that the step they take is neither easy nor obvious, that it calls for closer examination than it is commonly given, and that when we do give it this closer examination we shall feel inclined to reject it.

I propose, then, that we grant that the fetus is a person from the moment of conception. How does the argument go from here? Something like this, I take it. Every person has a right to life. So the fetus has a right to life. No doubt the mother has a right to decide what shall happen in and to her body; everyone would grant that. But surely a person's right to life is stronger and more stringent than the mother's right to decide what happens in and to her body, and so outweighs it. So the fetus may not be killed; an abortion may not be performed.

It sounds plausible. But now let me ask you to imagine this. You wake up in the morning and find yourself back to back in bed with an unconscious violinist. A famous unconscious violinist. He has been found to have a fatal kidney ailment, and the Society of Music Lovers has canvassed all the available medical records and found that you alone have

---

[2] Daniel Callahan, *Abortion: Law, Choice and Morality* (New York, 1970), p. 373. This book gives a fascinating survey of the available information on abortion. The Jewish tradition is surveyed in David M. Feldman, *Birth Control in Jewish Law* (New York, 1968), Part 5, the Catholic tradition in John T. Noonan, Jr., "An Almost Absolute Value in History," in *The Morality of Abortion,* ed. John T. Noonan, Jr. (Cambridge, Mass., 1970).

the right blood type to help. They have therefore kidnapped you, and last night the violinist's circulatory system was plugged into yours, so that your kidneys can be used to extract poisons from his blood as well as your own. The director of the hospital now tells you, "Look, we're sorry the Society of Music Lovers did this to you—we would never have permitted it if we had known. But still, they did it, and the violinist now is plugged into you. To unplug you would be to kill him. But never mind, it's only for nine months. By then he will have recovered from his ailment, and can safely be unplugged from you." Is it morally incumbent on you to accede to this situation? No doubt it would be very nice of you if you did, a great kindness. But do you *have* to accede to it? What if it were not nine months, but nine years? Or longer still? What if the director of the hospital says, "Tough luck, I agree, but you've now got to stay in bed, with the violinist plugged into you, for the rest of your life. Because remember this. All persons have a right to life, and violinists are persons. Granted you have a right to decide what happens in and to your body, but a person's right to life outweighs your right to decide what happens in and to your body. So you cannot ever be unplugged from him." I imagine you would regard this as outrageous, which suggests that something really is wrong with that plausible-sounding argument I mentioned a moment ago.

In this case, of course, you were kidnapped; you didn't volunteer for the operation that plugged the violinist into your kidneys. Can those who oppose abortion on the ground I mentioned make an exception for a pregnancy due to rape? Certainly. They can say that persons have a right to life only if they didn't come into existence because of rape; or they can say that all persons have a right to life, but that some have less of a right to life than others, in particular, that those who came into existence because of rape have less. But these statements have a rather unpleasant sound. Surely the question of whether you have a right to life at all, or how much of it you have, shouldn't turn on the question of whether or not you are the product of a rape. And in fact the people who oppose abortion on the ground I mentioned do not make this distinction, and hence do not make an exception in case of rape.

Nor do they make an exception for a case in which the mother has to spend the nine months of her pregnancy in bed. They would agree that would be a great pity, and hard on the mother; but all the same, all persons have a right to life, the fetus is a person, and so on. I suspect, in fact, that they would not make an exception for a case in which, miraculously enough, the pregnancy went on for nine years, or even the rest of the mother's life.

Some won't even make an exception for a case in which continuation of the pregnancy is likely to shorten the mother's life; they regard abortion as impermissible even to save the mother's life. Such cases are 106 nowadays very rare, and many opponents of abortion do not accept this extreme view. All the same, it is a good place to begin: a number of points of interest come out in respect to it.

1. Let us call the view that abortion is impermissible even to save the mother's life "the extreme view." I want to suggest first that it does not issue from the argument I mentioned earlier without the addition of some fairly powerful premises. Suppose a woman has become pregnant, and now learns that she has a cardiac condition such that she will die if she carries the baby to term. What may be done for her? The fetus, being a person, has a right to life, but as the mother is a person too, so has she a right to life. Presumably they have an equal right to life. How is it supposed to come out that an abortion may not be performed? If mother and child have an equal right to life, shouldn't we perhaps flip a coin? Or should we add to the mother's right to life her right to decide what happens in and to her body, which everybody seems to be ready to grant—the sum of her rights now outweighing the fetus' right to life?

The most familiar argument here is the following. We are told that performing the abortion would be directly killing[3] the child, whereas doing nothing would not be killing the mother, but only letting her die. Moreover, in killing the child, one would be killing an innocent person, for the child has committed no crime, and is not aiming at his mother's death. And then there are a variety of ways in which this might be continued. (1) But as directly killing an innocent person is always and absolutely impermissible, an abortion may not be performed. Or, (2) as directly killing an innocent person is murder, and murder is always and absolutely impermissible, an abortion may not be performed.[4] Or, (3) as one's duty to refrain from directly killing an innocent person is more stringent than one's duty to keep a person from dying, an abortion may not be performed. Or, (4) if one's only options are directly killing an innocent person or letting a person die, one must prefer letting the person die, and thus an abortion may not be performed.[5]

[3] The term "direct" in the arguments I refer to is a technical one. Roughly, what is meant by "direct killing" is either killing as an end in itself, or killing as a means to some end, for example, the end of saving someone else's life. See note 6, below, for an example of its use.

[4] Cf. *Encyclical Letter of Pope Pius XI on Christian Marriage,* St. Paul Editions (Boston, n.d.), p. 32: "however much we may pity the mother whose health and even life is gravely imperiled in the performance of the duty allotted to her by nature, nevertheless what could ever be a sufficient reason for excusing in any way the direct murder of the innocent? This is precisely what we are dealing with here." Noonan (*The Morality of Abortion,* p. 43) reads this as follows: "What cause can ever avail to excuse in any way the direct killing of the innocent? For it is a question of that."

[5] The thesis in (4) is in an interesting way weaker than those in (1), (2), and (3): they rule out abortion even in cases in which both mother *and* child will die if the abortion is not performed. By contrast, one who held the view expressed in (4) could consistently say that one needn't prefer letting two persons die to killing one.

Some people seem to have thought that these are not further premises which must be added if the conclusion is to be reached, but that
they follow from the very fact that an innocent person has a right to
life.[6] But this seems to me to be a mistake, and perhaps the simplest
way to show this is to bring out that while we must certainly grant that
innocent persons have a right to life, the theses in (1) through (4)
are all false. Take (2), for example. If directly killing an innocent person is murder, and thus is impermissible, then the mother's directly killing
the innocent person inside her is murder, and thus is impermissible. But
it cannot seriously be thought to be murder if the mother performs an
abortion on herself to save her life. It cannot seriously be said that she
must refrain, that she *must* sit passively by and wait for her death. Let
us look again at the case of you and the violinist. There you are, in bed
with the violinist, and the director of the hospital says to you, "It's all
most distressing, and I deeply sympathize, but you see this is putting an
additional strain on your kidneys, and you'll be dead within the month.
But you *have* to stay where you are all the same. Because unplugging
you would be directly killing an innocent violinist, and that's murder,
and that's impermissible." If anything in the world is true, it is that you
do not commit murder, you do not do what is impermissible, if you
reach around to your back and unplug yourself from that violinist to
save your life.

The main focus of attention in writings on abortion has been on what
a third party may or may not do in answer to a request from a woman
for an abortion. This is in a way understandable. Things being as they
are, there isn't much a woman can safely do to abort herself. So the
question asked is what a third party may do, and what the mother may
do, if it is mentioned at all, is deduced, almost as an afterthought, from
what it is concluded that third parties may do. But it seems to me that
to treat the matter in this way is to refuse to grant to the mother that
very status of person which is so firmly insisted on for the fetus. For
we cannot simply read off what a person may do from what a third party
may do. Suppose you find yourself trapped in a tiny house with a growing child. I mean a very tiny house, and a rapidly growing child—you
are already up against the wall of the house and in a few mintues you'll

[6] Cf. the following passage from Pius XII, *Address to the Italian Catholic Society
of Midwives:* "The baby in the maternal breast has the right to life immediately
from God.—Hence there is no man, no human authority, no science, no medical,
eugenic, social, economic or moral 'indication' which can establish or grant a valid
juridical ground for a direct deliberate disposition of an innocent human life,
that is a disposition which looks to its destruction either as an end or as a means
to another end perhaps in itself not illicit.—The baby, still not born, is a man
in the same degree and for the same reason as the mother" (quoted in Noonan,
The Morality of Abortion, p. 45).

be crushed to death. The child on the other hand won't be crushed to death; if nothing is done to stop him from growing he'll be hurt, but in the end he'll simply burst open the house and walk out a free man. Now I could well understand it if a bystander were to say, "There's nothing we can do for you. We cannot choose between your life and his, we cannot be the ones to decide who is to live, we cannot intervene." But it cannot be concluded that you too can do nothing, that you cannot attack it to save your life. However innocent the child may be, you do not have to wait passively while it crushes you to death. Perhaps a pregnant woman is vaguely felt to have the status of house, to which we don't allow the right of self-defense. But if the woman houses the child, it should be remembered that she is a person who houses it.

I should perhaps stop to say explicitly that I am not claiming that people have a right to do anything whatever to save their lives. I think, rather, that there are drastic limits to the right of self-defense. If someone threatens you with death unless you torture someone else to death, I think you have not the right, even to save your life, to do so. But the case under consideration here is very different. In our case there are only two people involved, one whose life is threatened, and one who threatens it. Both are innocent: the one who is threatened is not threatened because of any fault, the one who threatens does not threaten because of any fault. For this reason we may feel that we bystanders cannot intervene. But the person threatened can.

In sum, a woman surely can defend her life against the threat to it posed by the unborn child, even if doing so involves its death. And this shows not merely that the theses in (1) through (4) are false; it shows also that the extreme view of abortion is false, and so we need not canvass any other possible ways of arriving at it from the argument I mentioned at the outset.

2. The extreme view could of course be weakened to say that while abortion is permissible to save the mother's life, it may not be performed by a third party, but only by the mother herself. But this cannot be right either. For what we have to keep in mind is that the mother and the unborn child are not like two tenants in a small house which has, by an unfortunate mistake, been rented to both: the mother *owns* the house. The fact that she does adds to the offensiveness of deducing that the mother can do nothing from the supposition that third parties can do nothing. But it does more than this: it casts a bright light on the supposition that third parties can do nothing. Certainly it lets us see that a third party who says "I cannot choose between you" is fooling himself if he thinks this is impartiality. If Jones has found and fastened on a certain coat, which he needs to keep him from freezing, but which Smith also needs to keep him from freezing, then it is not impartiality that says "I cannot choose between you" when Smith owns the coat. Women have 109

said again and again "This body is *my* body!" and they have reason to feel angry, reason to feel that it has been like shouting into the wind. Smith, after all, is hardly likely to bless us if we say to him, "Of course it's your coat, anybody would grant that it is. But no one may choose between you and Jones who is to have it."

We should really ask what it is that says "no one may choose" in the face of the fact that the body that houses the child is the mother's body. It may be simply a failure to appreciate this fact. But it may be something more interesting, namely the sense that one has a right to refuse to lay hands on people, even where it would be just and fair to do so, even where justice seems to require that somebody do so. Thus justice might call for somebody to get Smith's coat back from Jones, and yet you have a right to refuse to be the one to lay hands on Jones, a right to refuse to do physical violence to him. This, I think, must be granted. But then what should be said is not "no one may choose," but only "*I* cannot choose," and indeed not even this, but "*I* will not *act*," leaving it open that somebody else can or should, and in particular that anyone in a position of authority, with the job of securing people's rights, both can and should. So this is no difficulty. I have not been arguing that any given third party must accede to the mother's request that he perform an abortion to save her life, but only that he may.

I suppose that in some views of human life the mother's body is only on loan to her, the loan not being one which gives her any prior claim to it. One who held this view might well think it impartiality to say "I cannot choose." But I shall simply ignore this possibility. My own view is that if a human being has any just, prior claim to anything at all, he has a just, prior claim to his own body. And perhaps this needn't be argued for here anyway, since, as I mentioned, the arguments against abortion we are looking at do grant that the woman has a right to decide what happens in and to her body.

But although they do grant it, I have tried to show that they do not take seriously what is done in granting it. I suggest the same thing will reappear even more clearly when we turn away from cases in which the mother's life is at stake, and attend, as I propose we now do, to the vasty more common cases in which a woman wants an abortion for some less weighty reason than preserving her own life.

3. Where the mother's life is not at stake, the argument I mentioned at the outset seems to have a much stronger pull. "Everyone has a right to life, so the unborn person has a right to life." And isn't the child's right to life weightier than anything other than the mother's own right to life, which she might put forward as ground for an abortion?

This argument treats the right to life as if it were unproblematic. It is not, and this seems to me to be precisely the source of the mistake.

For we should now, at long last, ask what it comes to, to have a right to life. In some views having a right to life includes having a right to be given at least the bare minimum one needs for continued life. But suppose that what in fact *is* the bare minimum a man needs for continued life is something he has no right at all to be given? If I am sick unto death, and the only thing that will save my life is the touch of Henry Fonda's cool hand on my fevered brow, then all the same, I have no right to be given the touch of Henry Fonda's cool hand on my fevered brow. It would be frightfully nice of him to fly in from the West Coast to provide it. It would be less nice, though no doubt well meant, if my friends flew out to the West Coast and carried Henry Fonda back with them. But I have no right at all against anybody that he should do this for me. Or again, to return to the story I told earlier, the fact that for continued life that violinist needs the continued use of your kidneys does not establish that he has a right to be given the continued use of your kidneys. He certainly has no right against you that *you* should give him continued use of your kidneys. For nobody has any right to use your kidneys unless you give him such a right; and nobody has the right against you that you shall give him this right—if you do allow him to go on using your kidneys, this is a kindness on your part, and not something he can claim from you as his due. Nor has he any right against anybody else that *they* should give him continued use of your kidneys. Certainly he had no right against the Society of Music Lovers that they should plug him into you in the first place. And if you now start to unplug yourself, having learned that you will otherwise have to spend nine years in bed with him, there is nobody in the world who must try to prevent you, in order to see to it that he is given something he has a right to be given.

Some people are rather stricter about the right to life. In their view, it does not include the right to be given anything, but amounts to, and only to, the right not to be killed by anybody. But here a related difficulty arises. If everybody is to refrain from killing that violinist, then everybody must refrain from doing a great many different sorts of things. Everybody must refrain from slitting his throat, everybody must refrain from shooting him—and everybody must refrain from unplugging you from him. But does he have a right against everybody that they shall refrain from unplugging you from him? To refrain from doing this is to allow him to continue to use your kidneys. It could be argued that he has a right against us that *we* should allow him to continue to use your kidneys. That is, while he had no right against us that we should give him the use of your kidneys, it might be argued that he anyway has a right against us that we shall not now intervene and deprive him of the use of your kidneys. I shall come back to third-party interventions later. But certainly the violinist has no right against you that *you* shall allow him to continue to use your kidneys. As I said, if you do allow 111 him to use them, it is a kindness on your part, and not something you owe him.

The difficulty I point to here is not peculiar to the right to life. It reappears in connection with all the other natural rights; and it is something which an adequate account of rights must deal with. For present purposes it is enough just to draw attention to it. But I would stress that I am not arguing that people do not have a right to life—quite to the contrary, it seems to me that the primary control we must place on the acceptability of an account of rights is that it should turn out in that account to be a truth that all persons have a right to life. I am arguing only that having a right to life does not guarantee having either a right to be given the use of or a right to be allowed continued use of another person's body—even if one needs it for life itself. So the right to life will not serve the opponents of abortion in the very simple and clear way in which they seem to have thought it would.

4. There is another way to bring out the difficulty. In the most ordinary sort of case, to deprive someone of what he has a right to is to treat him unjustly. Suppose a boy and his small brother are jointly given a box of chocolates for Christmas. If the older boy takes the box and refuses to give his brother any of the chocolates, he is unjust to him, for the brother has been given a right to half of them. But suppose that, having learned that otherwise it means nine years in bed with that violinist, you unplug yourself from him. You surely are not being unjust to him, for you gave him no right to use your kidneys, and no one else can have given him any such right. But we have to notice that in unplugging yourself, you are killing him; and violinists, like everybody else, have a right to life, and thus in the view we were considering just now, the right not to be killed. So here you do what he supposedly has a right you shall not do, but you do not act unjustly to him in doing it.

The emendation which may be made at this point is this: the right to life consists not in the right not to be killed, but rather in the right not to be killed unjustly. This runs a risk of circularity, but never mind: it would enable us to square the fact that the violinist has a right to life with the fact that you do not act unjustly toward him in unplugging yourself, thereby killing him. For if you do not kill him unjustly, you do not violate his right to life, and so it is no wonder you do him no injustice.

But if this emendation is accepted, the gap in the argument against abortion stares us plainly in the face: it is by no means enough to show that the fetus is a person, and to remind us that all persons have a right to life —we need to be shown also that killing the fetus violates its right to life, i.e., that abortion is unjust killing. And is it?

I suppose we may take it as a datum that in a case of pregnancy due to rape the mother has not given the unborn person a right to the use of her body for food and shelter. Indeed, in what pregnancy could it be supposed that the mother has given the unborn person such a right? It is not as if there were unborn persons drifting about the world, to whom a woman who wants a child says "I invite you in."

But it might be argued that there are other ways one can have acquired a right to the use of another person's body than by having been invited to use it by that person. Suppose a woman voluntarily indulges in intercourse, knowing of the chance it will issue in pregnancy, and then she does become pregnant; is she not in part responsible for the presence, in fact the very existence, of the unborn person inside her? No doubt she did not invite it in. But doesn't her partial responsibility for its being there itself give it a right to the use of her body?[7] If so, then her aborting it would be more like the boy's taking away the chocolates, and less like your unplugging yourself from the violinist—doing so would be depriving it of what it does have a right to, and thus would be doing it an injustice.

And then, too, it might be asked whether or not she can kill it even to save her own life: If she voluntarily called it into existence, how can she now kill it, even in self-defense?

The first thing to be said about this is that it is something new. Opponents of abortion have been so concerned to make out the independence of the fetus, in order to establish that it has a right to life, just as its mother does, that they have tended to overlook the possible support they might gain from making out that the fetus is *dependent* on the mother, in order to establish that she has a special kind of responsibility for it, a responsibility that gives it rights against her which are not possessed by any independent person—such as an ailing violinist who is a stranger to her.

On the other hand, this argument would give the unborn person a right to its mother's body only if her pregnancy resulted from a voluntary act, undertaken in full knowledge of the chance a pregnancy might result from it. It would leave out entirely the unborn person whose existence is due to rape. Pending the availability of some further argument, then, we would be left with the conclusion that unborn persons whose existence is due to rape have no right to the use of their mothers' bodies, and thus that aborting them is not depriving them of anything they have a right to and hence is not unjust killing.

And we should also notice that it is not at all plain that this argument really does go even as far as it purports to. For there are cases and cases, and the details make a difference. If the room is stuffy, and I therefore open a window to air it, and a burglar climbs in, it would be absurd to say, "Ah, now he can stay, she's given him a right to the use of her house

---

[7] The need for a discussion of this argument was brought home to me by members of the Society for Ethical and Legal Philosophy, to whom this paper was originally presented.

—for she is partially responsible for his presence there, having voluntarily done what enabled him to get in, in full knowledge that there are such things as burglars, and that burglars burgle." It would be still more absurd to say this if I had had bars installed outside my windows, precisely to prevent burglars from getting in, and a burglar got in only because of a defect in the bars. It remains equally absurd if we imagine it is not a burglar who climbs in, but an innocent person who blunders or falls in. Again, suppose it were like this: people-seeds drift about in the air like pollen, and if you open your windows, one may drift in and take root in your carpets or upholstery. You don't want children, so you fix up your windows with fine mesh screens, the very best you can buy. As can happen, however, and on very, very rare occasions does happen, one of the screens is defective; and a seed drifts in and takes root. Does the person-plant who now develops have a right to the use of your house? Surely not —despite the fact that you voluntarily opened your windows, you knowingly kept carpets and upholstered furniture, and you knew that screens were sometimes defective. Someone may argue that you are responsible for its rooting, that it does have a right to your house, because after all you *could* have lived out your life with bare floors and furniture, or with sealed windows and doors. But this won't do—for by the same token anyone can avoid a pregnancy due to rape by having a hysterectomy, or anyway by never leaving home without a (reliable!) army.

It seems to me that the argument we are looking at can establish at most that there are *some* cases in which the unborn person has a right to the use of its mother's body, and therefore *some* cases in which abortion is unjust killing. There is room for much discussion and argument as to precisely which, if any. But I think we should sidestep this issue and leave it open, for at any rate the argument certainly does not establish that all abortion is unjust killing.

5. There is room for yet another argument here, however. We surely must all grant that there may be cases in which it would be morally indecent to detach a person from your body at the cost of his life. Suppose you learn that what the violinist needs is not nine years of your life, but only one hour: all you need do to save his life is to spend one hour in that bed with him. Suppose also that letting him use your kidneys for that one hour would not affect your health in the slightest. Admittedly you were kidnapped. Admittedly you did not give anyone permission to plug him into you. Nevertheless it seems to me plain you *ought* to allow him to use your kidneys for that hour—it would be indecent to refuse.

Again, suppose pregnancy lasted only an hour, and constituted no threat to life or health. And suppose that a woman becomes pregnant as a result of rape. Admittedly she did not voluntarily do anything to bring about the existence of a child. Admittedly she did nothing at all which would give
114 the unborn person a right to the use of her body. All the same it might well

be said, as in the newly emended violinist story, that she *ought* to allow it to remain for that hour—that it would be indecent in her to refuse.

Now some people are inclined to use the term "right" in such a way that it follows from the fact that you ought to allow a person to use your body for the hour he needs, that he has a right to use your body for the hour he needs, even though he has not been given that right by any person or act. They may say that it follows also that if you refuse, you act unjustly toward him. This use of the term is perhaps so common that it cannot be called wrong; nevertheless it seems to me to be an unfortunate loosening of what we would do better to keep a tight rein on. Suppose that box of chocolates I mentioned earlier had not been given to both boys jointly, but was given only to the older boy. There he sits, stolidly eating his way through the box, his small brother watching enviously. Here we are likely to say "You ought not to be so mean. You ought to give your brother some of those chocolates." My own view is that it just does not follow from the truth of this that the brother has any right to any of the chocolates. If the boy refuses to give his brother any, he is greedy, stingy, callous —but not unjust. I suppose that the people I have in mind will say it does follow that the brother has a right to some of the chocolates, and thus that the boy does act unjustly if he refuses to give his brother any. But the effect of saying this is to obscure what we should keep distinct, namely the difference between the boy's refusal in this case and the boy's refusal in the earlier case, in which the box was given to both boys jointly, and in which the small brother thus had what was from any point of view clear title to half.

A further objection to so using the term "right" that from the fact that A ought to do a thing for B, it follows that B has a right against A that A do it for him, is that it is going to make the question of whether or not a man has a right to a thing turn on how easy it is to provide him with it; and this seems not merely unfortunate, but morally unacceptable. Take the case of Henry Fonda again. I said earlier that I had no right to the touch of his cool hand on my fevered brow, even though I needed it to save my life. I said it would be frightfully nice of him to fly in from the West Coast to provide me with it, but that I had no right against him that he should do so. But suppose he isn't on the West Coast. Suppose he has only to walk across the room, place a hand briefly on my brow—and lo, my life is saved. Then surely he ought to do it, it would be indecent to refuse. Is it to be said "Ah, well, it follows that in this case she has a right to the touch of his hand on her brow, and so it would be an injustice in him to refuse"? So that I have a right to it when it is easy for him to provide it, though no right when it's hard? It's rather a shocking idea that anyone's rights should fade away and disappear as it gets harder and harder to accord them to him.

So my own view is that even though you ought to let the violinist use 115 your kidneys for the one hour he needs, we should not conclude that he has a right to do so—we would say that if you refuse, you are, like the boy who owns all the chocolates and will give none away, self-centered and callous, indecent in fact, but not unjust. And similarly, that even supposing a case in which a woman pregnant due to rape ought to allow the unborn person to use her body for the hour he needs, we should not conclude that he has a right to do so; we should conclude that she is self-centered, callous, indecent, but not unjust, if she refuses. The complaints are no less grave; they are just different. However, there is no need to insist on this point. If anyone does wish to deduce "he has a right" from "you ought," then all the same he must surely grant that there are cases in which it is not morally required of you that you allow that violinist to use your kidneys, and in which he does not have a right to use them, and in which you do not do him an injustice if you refuse. And so also for mother and unborn child. Except in such cases as the unborn person has a right to demand it—and we were leaving open the possibility that there may be such cases—nobody is morally *required* to make large sacrifices, of health, of all other interests and concerns, of all other duties and commitments, for nine years, or even for nine months, in order to keep another person alive.

6. We have in fact to distinguish between two kinds of Samaritan: the Good Samaritan and what we might call the Minimally Decent Samaritan. The story of the Good Samaritan, you will remember, goes like this:

A certain man went down from Jerusalem to Jericho, and fell among thieves, which stripped him of his raiment, and wounded him, and departed, leaving him half dead.

And by chance there came down a certain priest that way; and when he saw him, he passed by on the other side.

And likewise a Levite, when he was at the place, came and looked on him, and passed by on the other side.

But a certain Samaritan, as he journeyed, came where he was; and when he saw him he had compassion on him.

And went to him, and bound up his wounds, pouring in oil and wine, and set him on his own beast, and brought him to an inn, and took care of him.

And on the morrow, when he departed, he took out two pence, and gave them to the host, and said unto him, "Take care of him; and whatsoever thou spendest more, when I come again, I will repay thee."

(Luke 10:30–35)

The Good Samaritan went out of his way, at some cost to himself, to help one in need of it. We are not told what the options were, that is, whether or not the priest and the Levite could have helped by doing less than the Good Samaritan did, but assuming they could have, then the fact they did

116

nothing at all shows they were not even Minimally Decent Samaritans, not because they were not Samaritans, but because they were not even minimally decent.

These things are a matter of degree, of course, but there is a difference, and it comes out perhaps most clearly in the story of Kitty Genovese, who, as you will remember, was murdered while thirty-eight people watched or listened, and did nothing at all to help her. A Good Samaritan would have rushed out to give direct assistance against the murderer. Or perhaps we had better allow that it would have been a Splendid Samaritan who did this, on the ground that it would have involved a risk of death for himself. But the thirty-eight not only did not do this, they did not even trouble to pick up a phone to call the police. Minimally Decent Samaritanism would call for doing at least that, and their not having done it was monstrous.

After telling the story of the Good Samaritan, Jesus said "Go, and do thou likewise." Perhaps he meant that we are morally required to act as the Good Samaritan did. Perhaps he was urging people to do more than is morally required of them. At all events it seems plain that it was not morally required of any of the thirty-eight that he rush out to give direct assistance at the risk of his own life, and that it is not morally required of anyone that he give long stretches of his life—nine years or nine months— to sustaining the life of a person who has no special right (we were leaving open the possibility of this) to demand it.

Indeed, with one rather striking class of exceptions, no one in any country in the world is *legally* required to do anywhere near as much as this for anyone else. The class of exceptions is obvious. My main concern here is not the state of the law in respect to abortion, but it is worth drawing attention to the fact that in no state in this country is any man compelled by law to be even a Minimally Decent Samaritan to any person; there is no law under which charges could be brought against the thirty-eight who stood by while Kitty Genovese died. By contrast, in most states in this country women are compelled by law to be not merely Minimally Decent Samaritans, but Good Samaritans to unborn persons inside them. This doesn't by itself settle anything one way or the other, because it may well be argued that there should be laws in this country—as there are in many European countries—compelling at least Minimally Decent Samaritanism.[8] But it does show that there is a gross injustice in the existing state of the law. And it shows also that the groups currently working against liberalization of abortion laws, in fact working toward having it declared unconstitutional for a state to permit abortion, had better start working for the adoption of Good Samaritan laws generally, or earn the charge that they are acting in bad faith.

[8] For a discussion of the difficulties involved, and a survey of the European experience with such laws, see *The Good Samaritan and the Law,* ed. James M. Ratcliffe (New York, 1966).

I should think, myself, that Minimally Decent Samaritan laws would be one thing, Good Samaritan laws quite another, and in fact highly improper. But we are not here concerned with the law. What we should ask is not whether anybody should be compelled by law to be a Good Samaritan, but whether we must accede to a situation in which somebody is being compelled—by nature, perhaps—to be a Good Samaritan. We have, in other words, to look now at third-party interventions. I have been arguing that no person is morally required to make large sacrifices to sustain the life of another who has no right to demand them, and this even where the sacrifices do not include life itself; we are not morally required to be Good Samaritans or anyway Very Good Samaritans to one another. But what if a man cannot extricate himself from such a situation? What if he appeals to us to extricate him? It seems to me plain that there are cases in which we can, cases in which a Good Samaritan would extricate him. There you are, you were kidnapped, and nine years in bed with that violinist lie ahead of you. You have your own life to lead. You are sorry, but you simply cannot see giving up so much of your life to the sustaining of his. You cannot extricate yourself, and ask us to do so. I should have thought that—in light of his having no right to the use of your body—it was obvious that we do not have to accede to your being forced to give up so much. We can do what you ask. There is no injustice to the violinist in our doing so.

7. Following the lead of the opponents of abortion, I have throughout been speaking of the fetus merely as a person, and what I have been asking is whether or not the argument we began with, which proceeds only from the fetus' being a person, really does establish its conclusion. I have argued that it does not.

But of course there are arguments and arguments, and it may be said that I have simply fastened on the wrong one. It may be said that what is important is not merely the fact that the fetus is a person, but that it is a person for whom the woman has a special kind of responsibility issuing from the fact that she is its mother. And it might be argued that all my analogies are therefore irrelevant—for you do not have that special kind of responsibility for that violinist, Henry Fonda does not have that special kind of responsibility for me. And our attention might be drawn to the fact that men and women both *are* compelled by law to provide support for their children.

I have in effect dealt (briefly) with this argument in section 4 above; but a (still briefer) recapitulation now may be in order. Surely we do not have any such "special responsibility" for a person unless we have assumed it, explicitly or implicitly. If a set of parents do not try to prevent pregnancy, do not obtain an abortion, and then at the time of birth of the child do not put it out for adoption, but rather take it home with them, then they have assumed responsibility for it, they have given it rights, and they cannot *now* withdraw support from it at the cost of its life because they now find it difficult to go on providing for it. But if they have taken all reasonable precautions against having a child, they do not simply by virtue of their biological relationship to the child who comes into existence have a special responsibility for it. They may wish to assume responsibility for it, or they may not wish to. And I am suggesting that if assuming responsibility for it would require large sacrifices, then they may refuse. A Good Samaritan would not refuse—or anyway, a Splendid Samaritan, if the sacrifices that had to be made were enormous. But then so would a Good Samaritan assume responsibility for that violinist; so would Henry Fonda, if he is a Good Samaritan, fly in from the West Coast and assume responsibility for me.

8. My argument will be found unsatisfactory on two counts by many of those who want to regard abortion as morally permissible. First, while I do argue that abortion is not impermissible, I do not argue that it is always permissible. There may well be cases in which carrying the child to term requires only Minimally Decent Samaritanism of the mother, and this is a standard we must not fall below. I am inclined to think it a merit of my account precisely that it does *not* give a general yes or a general no. It allows for and supports our sense that, for example, a sick and desperately frightened fourteen-year-old schoolgirl, pregnant due to rape, may *of course* choose abortion, and that any law which rules this out is an insane law. And it also allows for and supports our sense that in other cases resort to abortion is even positively indecent. It would be indecent in the woman to request an abortion, and indecent in a doctor to perform it, if she is in her seventh month, and wants the abortion just to avoid the nuisance of postponing a trip abroad. The very fact that the arguments I have been drawing attention to treat all cases of abortion, or even all cases of abortion in which the mother's life is not at stake, as morally on a par ought to have made them suspect at the outset.

Secondly, while I am arguing for the permissibility of abortion in some cases, I am not arguing for the right to secure the death of the unborn child. It is easy to confuse these two things in that up to a certain point in the life of the fetus it is not able to survive outside the mother's body; hence removing it from her body guarantees its death. But they are importantly different. I have argued that you are not morally required to spend nine months in bed, sustaining the life of that violinist; but to say this is by no means to say that if, when you unplug yourself, there is a miracle and he survives, you then have a right to turn round and slit his throat. You may detach yourself even if this costs him his life; you have no right to be guaranteed his death, by some other means, if unplugging yourself does not kill him. There are some people who will feel dissatisfied by this feature of my argument. A woman may be utterly devastated by the thought of a child, a bit of herself, put out for adoption and never seen or heard of again. She may therefore want not merely that the child be   119 detached from her, but more, that it die. Some opponents of abortion are inclined to regard this as beneath contempt—thereby showing insensitivity to what is surely a powerful source of despair. All the same, I agree that the desire for the child's death is not one which anybody may gratify, should it turn out to be possible to detach the child alive.

At this place, however, it should be remembered that we have only been pretending throughout that the fetus is a human being from the moment of conception. A very early abortion is surely not the killing of a person, and so is not dealt with by anything I have said here.

MARY ANNE WARREN
On the Moral and Legal Status of Abortion

We will be concerned with both the moral status of abortion, which for our purposes we may define as the act which a woman performs in voluntarily terminating, or allowing another person to terminate, her pregnancy, and the legal status which is appropriate for this act. I will argue that, while it is not possible to produce a satisfactory defense of a woman's right to obtain an abortion without showing that a fetus is not a human being, in the morally relevant sense of that term, we ought not to conclude that the difficulties involved in determining whether or not a fetus is human make it impossible to produce any satisfactory solution to the problem of the moral status of abortion. For it is possible to show that, on the basis of intuitions which we may expect even the opponents of abortion to share, a fetus is not a person, and hence not the sort of entity to which it is proper to ascribe full moral rights.

Of course, while some philosophers would deny the possibility of any such proof,[1] others will deny that there is any need for it, since the moral permissibility of abortion appears to them to be too obvious to require proof. But the inadequacy of this attitude should be evident from the fact

Reprinted from *The Monist*, Volume 57, No. 1 (January 1973), 43–61, La Salle, Illinois, with the permission of the publisher and the author. The "Postscript on Infanticide" by Mary Anne Warren was added especially for this volume.

[1] For example, Roger Wertheimer, who in "Understanding the Abortion Argument" (*Philosophy and Public Affairs*, 1, No. 1 [Fall, 1971], 67–95), argues that the problem of the moral status of abortion is insoluble, in that the dispute over the status of the fetus is not a question of fact at all, but only a question of how one responds to the facts.

that both the friends and the foes of abortion consider their position to be morally self-evident. Because pro-abortionists have never adequately come to grips with the conceptual issues surrounding abortion, most if not all, of the arguments which they advance in opposition to laws restricting access to abortion fail to refute or even weaken the traditional antiabortion argument, i.e., that a fetus is a human being, and therefore abortion is murder.

These arguments are typically of one of two sorts. Either they point to the terrible side effects of the restrictive laws, e.g., the deaths due to illegal abortions, and the fact that it is poor women who suffer the most as a result of these laws, or else they state that to deny a woman access to abortion is to deprive her of her right to control her own body. Unfortunately, however, the fact that restricting access to abortion has tragic side effects does not, in itself, show that the restrictions are unjustified, since murder is wrong regardless of the consequences of prohibiting it; and the appeal to the right to control one's body, which is generally construed as a property right, is at best a rather feeble argument for the permissibility of abortion. Mere ownership does not give me the right to kill innocent people whom I find on my property, and indeed I am apt to be held responsible if such people injure themselves while on my property. It is equally unclear that I have any moral right to expel an innocent person from my property when I know that doing so will result in his death.

Furthermore, it is probably inappropriate to describe a woman's body as her property, since it seems natural to hold that a person is something distinct from her property, but not from her body. Even those who would object to the identification of a person with his body, or with the conjunction of his body and his mind, must admit that it would be very odd to describe, say, breaking a leg, as damaging one's property, and much more appropriate to describe it as injuring one*self*. Thus it is probably a mistake to argue that the right to obtain an abortion is in any way derived from the right to own and regulate property.

But however we wish to construe the right to abortion, we cannot hope to convince those who consider abortion a form of murder of the existence of any such right unless we are able to produce a clear and convincing refutation of the traditional antiabortion argument, and this has not, to my knowledge, been done. With respect to the two most vital issues which that argument involves, i.e., the humanity of the fetus and its implication for the moral status of abortion, confusion has prevailed on both sides of the dispute.

Thus, both proabortionists and antiabortionists have tended to abstract the question of whether abortion is wrong to that of whether it is wrong to destroy a fetus, just as though the rights of another person were not necessarily involved. This mistaken abstraction has led to the almost universal assumption that if a fetus is a human being, with a right to life, then it follows immediately that abortion is wrong (except perhaps when neces- 121 sary to save the woman's life), and that it ought to be prohibited. It has also been generally assumed that unless the question about the status of the fetus is answered, the moral status of abortion cannot possibly be determined.

Two recent papers, one by B. A. Brody,[2] and one by Judith Thomson,[3] have attempted to settle the question of whether abortion ought to be prohibited apart from the question of whether or not the fetus is human. Brody examines the possibility that the following two statements are compatible: (1) that abortion is the taking of innocent human life, and therefore wrong; and (2) that nevertheless it ought not to be prohibited by law, at least under the present circumstances.[4] Not surprisingly, Brody finds it impossible to reconcile these two statements, since, as he rightly argues, none of the unfortunate side effects of the prohibition of abortion is bad enough to justify legalizing the *wrongful* taking of human life. He is mistaken, however, in concluding that the incompatibility of (1) and (2), in itself, shows that "the legal problem about abortion cannot be resolved independently of the status of the fetus problem" (p. 369).

What Brody fails to realize is that (1) embodies the questionable assumption that if a fetus is a human being, then of course abortion is morally wrong, and that an attack on *this* assumption is more promising, as a way of reconciling the humanity of the fetus with the claim that laws prohibiting abortion are unjustified, than is an attack on the assumption that if abortion is the wrongful killing of innocent human beings then it ought to be prohibited. He thus overlooks the possibility that a fetus may have a right to life and abortion still be morally permissible, in that the right of a woman to terminate an unwanted pregnancy might override the right of the fetus to be kept alive. The immorality of abortion is no more demonstrated by the humanity of the fetus, in itself, than the immorality of killing in self-defense is demonstrated by the fact that the assailant is a human being. Neither is it demonstrated by the *innocence* of the fetus, since there may be situations in which the killing of innocent human beings is justified.

It is perhaps not surprising that Brody fails to spot this assumption, since it has been accepted with little or no argument by nearly everyone who has written on the morality of abortion. John Noonan is correct in saying that "the fundamental question in the long history of abortion is, How do you determine the humanity of a being?"[5] He summarizes his own

[2] B. A. Brody, "Abortion and the Law," *The Journal of Philosophy,* 68, No. 12 (June 17, 1971), 357–69.

[3] Judith Thomson, "A Defense of Abortion," *Philosophy and Public Affairs,* 1, No. 1 (Fall, 1971), 47–66.

[4] I have abbreviated these statements somewhat, but not in a way which affects the argument.

[5] John Noonan, "Abortion and the Catholic Church: A Summary History," *Natural Law Forum,* 12 (1967), 125.

antiabortion argument, which is a version of the official position of the Catholic Church, as follows:

... it is wrong to kill humans, however poor, weak, defenseless, and lacking in opportunity to develop their potential they may be. It is therefore morally wrong to kill Biafrans. Similarly, it is morally wrong to kill embryos.[6]

Noonan bases his claim that fetuses are human upon what he calls the theologians' criterion of humanity: that whoever is conceived of human beings is human. But although he argues at length for the appropriateness of this criterion, he never questions the assumption that if a fetus is human then abortion is wrong for exactly the same reason that murder is wrong.

Judith Thomson is, in fact, the only writer I am aware of who has seriously questioned this assumption; she has argued that, even if we grant the antiabortionist his claim that a fetus is a human being, with the same right to life as any other human being, we can still demonstrate that, in at least some and perhaps most cases, a woman is under no moral obligation to complete an unwanted pregnancy.[7] Her argument is worth examining, since if it holds up it may enable us to establish the moral permissibility of abortion without becoming involved in problems about what entitles an entity to be considered human, and accorded full moral rights. To be able to do this would be a great gain in the power and simplicity of the pro-abortion position, since, although I will argue that these problems can be solved at least as decisively as can any other moral problem, we should certainly be pleased to be able to avoid having to solve them as part of the justification of abortion.

On the other hand, even if Thomson's argument dose not hold up, her insight, i.e., that it requires *argument* to show that if fetuses are human then abortion is properly classified as murder, is an extremely valuable one. The assumption she attacks is particularly invidious, for it amounts to the decision that it is appropriate, in deciding the moral status of abortion, to leave the rights of the pregnant woman out of consideration entirely, except possibly when her life is threatened. Obviously, this will not do; determining what moral rights, if any, a fetus possesses is only the first step in determining the moral status of abortion. Step two, which is at least equally essential, is finding a just solution to the conflict between whatever rights the fetus may have, and the rights of the woman who is unwillingly pregnant. While the historical error has been to pay far too little attention to the second step, Ms. Thomson's suggestion is that if we look at the second step first we may find that a woman has a right to obtain an abortion *regardless* of what rights the fetus has.

Our own inquiry will also have two stages. In Section I, we will con-

---

[6] John Noonan, "Deciding Who is Human," *Natural Law Forum,* 13 (1968), 134.
[7] "A Defense of Abortion."

sider whether or not it is possible to establish that abortion is morally permissible even on the assumption that a fetus is an entity with a full-fledged right to life. I will argue that in fact this cannot be established, at least not with the conclusiveness which is essential to our hopes of convincing those who are skeptical about the morality of abortion, and that we therefore cannot avoid dealing with the question of whether or not a fetus really does have the same right to life as a (more fully developed) human being.

In Section II, I will propose an answer to this question, namely, that a fetus cannot be considered a member of the moral community, the set of beings with full and equal moral rights, for the simple reason that it is not a person, and that it is personhood, and not genetic humanity, i.e., humanity as defined by Noonan, which is the basis for membership in this community. I will argue that a fetus, whatever its stage of development, satisfies none of the basic criteria of personhood, and is not even enough *like* a person to be accorded even some of the same rights on the basis of this resemblance. Nor, as we will see, is a fetus's *potential* personhood a threat to the morality of abortion, since, whatever the rights of potential people may be, they are invariably overridden in any conflict with the moral rights of actual people.

I

We turn now to Professor Thomson's case for the claim that even if a fetus has full moral rights, abortion is still morally permissible, at least sometimes, and for some reasons other than to save the woman's life. Her argument is based upon a clever, but I think faulty, analogy. She asks us to picture ourselves waking up one day, in bed with a famous violinist. Imagine that you have been kidnapped, and your bloodstream hooked up to that of the violinist, who happens to have an ailment which will certainly kill him unless he is permitted to share your kidneys for a period of nine months. No one else can save him, since you alone have the right type of blood. He will be unconscious all that time, and you will have to stay in bed with him, but after the nine months are over he may be unplugged, completely cured, that is provided that you have cooperated.

Now then, she continues, what are your obligations in this situation? The antiabortionist, if he is consistent, will have to say that you are obligated to stay in bed with the violinist: for all people have a right to life, and violinists are people, and therefore it would be murder for you to disconnect yourself from him and let him die (p. 49). But this is outrageous, and so there must be something wrong with the same argument when it is applied to abortion. It would certainly be commendable of you to agree to save the violinist, but it is absurd to suggest that your refusal to do so would be murder. His right to life does not obligate you to do whatever is

124 required to keep him alive; nor does it justify anyone else in forcing you

to do so. A law which required you to stay in bed with the violinist would clearly be an unjust law, since it is no proper function of the law to force unwilling people to make huge sacrifices for the sake of other people toward whom they have no such prior obligation.

Thomson concludes that, if this analogy is an apt one, then we can grant the antiabortionist his claim that a fetus is a human being, and still hold that it is at least sometimes the case that a pregnant woman has the right to refuse to be a Good Samaritan towards the fetus, i.e., to obtain an abortion. For there is a great gap between the claim that x has a right to life, and the claim that y is obligated to do whatever is necessary to keep x alive, let alone that he ought to be forced to do so. It is y's duty to keep x alive only if he has somehow contracted a *special* obligation to do so; and a woman who is unwillingly pregnant, e.g., who was raped, has done nothing which obligates her to make the enormous sacrifice which is necessary to preserve the conceptus.

This argument is initially quite plausible, and in the extreme case of pregnancy due to rape it is probably conclusive. Difficulties arise, however, when we try to specify more exactly the range of cases in which abortion is clearly justifiable even on the assumption that the fetus is human. Professor Thomson considers it a virtue of her argument that it does not enable us to conclude that abortion is *always* permissible. It would, she says, be "indecent" for a woman in her seventh month to obtain an abortion just to avoid having to postpone a trip to Europe. On the other hand, her argument enables us to see that "a sick and desperately frightened schoolgirl pregnant due to rape may *of course* choose abortion, and that any law which rules this out is an insane law" (p. 65). So far, so good; but what are we to say about the woman who becomes pregnant not through rape but as a result of her own carelessness, or because of contraceptive failure, or who gets pregnant intentionally and then changes her mind about wanting a child? With respect to such cases, the violinist analogy is of much less use to the defender of the woman's right to obtain an abortion.

Indeed, the choice of a pregnancy due to rape, as an example of a case in which abortion is permissible even if a fetus is considered a human being, is extremely significant; for it is only in the case of pregnancy due to rape that the woman's situation is adequately analogous to the violinist case for our intuitions about the latter to transfer convincingly. The crucial difference between a pregnancy due to rape and the *normal* case of an unwanted pregnancy is that in the normal case we cannot claim that the woman is in no way responsible for her predicament; she could have remained chaste, or taken her pills more faithfully, or abstained on dangerous days, and so on. If, on the other hand, you are kidnapped by strangers, and hooked up to a strange violinist, then you are free of any shred of responsibility for the situation, on the basis of which it could be argued that you are obligated to keep the violinist alive. Only when 125 her pregnancy is due to rape is a woman clearly just as nonresponsible.[8]

Consequently, there is room for the antiabortionist to argue that in the normal case of unwanted pregnancy a woman has, by her own actions, assumed responsibility for the fetus. For if x behaves in a way which he could have avoided, and which he knows involves, let us say, a 1 percent chance of bringing into existence a human being, with a right to life, and does so knowing that if this should happen then that human being will perish unless x does certain things to keep him alive, then it is by no means clear that when it does happen x is free of any obligation to what he knew in advance would be required to keep that human being alive.

The plausibility of such an argument is enough to show that the Thomson analogy can provide a clear and persuasive defense of a woman's right to obtain an abortion only with respect to those cases in which the woman is in no way responsible for her pregnancy, e.g., where it is due to rape. In all other cases, we would almost certainly conclude that it was necessary to look carefully at the particular circumstances in order to determine the extent of the woman's responsibility, and hence the extent of her obligation. This is an extremely unsatisfactory outcome, from the viewpoint of the opponents of restrictive abortion laws, most of whom are convinced that a woman has a right to obtain an abortion regardless of how and why she got pregnant.

Of course a supporter of the violinist analogy might point out that it is absurd to suggest that forgetting her pill one day might be sufficient to obligate a woman to complete an unwanted pregnancy. And indeed it *is* absurd to suggest this. As we will see, the moral right to obtain an abortion is not in the least dependent upon the extent to which the woman is responsible for her pregnancy. But unfortunately, once we allow the assumption that a fetus has full moral rights, we cannot avoid taking this absurd suggestion seriously. Perhaps we can make this point more clear by altering the violinist story just enough to make it more analogous to a normal unwanted pregnancy and less to a pregnancy due to rape, and then seeing whether it is still obvious that you are not obligated to stay in bed with the fellow.

Suppose, then, that violinists are peculiarly prone to the sort of illness the only cure for which is the use of someone else's bloodstream for nine months, and that because of this there has been formed a society of music lovers who agree that whenever a violinist is stricken they will draw lots and the loser will, by some means, be made the one and only

[8] We may safely ignore the fact that she might have avoided getting raped, e.g., by carrying a gun, since by similar means you might likewise have avoided getting kidnapped, and in neither case does the victim's failure to take all possible precautions against a highly unlikely event (as opposed to reasonable precautions against a rather likely event) mean that he is morally responsible for what happens.

person capable of saving him. Now then, would you be obligated to cooperate in curing the violinist if you had voluntarily joined this society, knowing the possible consequences, and then your name had been drawn and you had been kidnapped? Admittedly, you did not promise ahead of time that you would, but you did deliberately place yourself in a position in which it might happen that a human life would be lost if you did not. Surely this is at least a prima facie reason for supposing that you have an obligation to stay in bed with the violinist. Suppose that you had gotten your name drawn deliberately; surely *that* would be quite a strong reason for thinking that you had such an obligation.

It might be suggested that there is one important disanalogy between the modified violinist case and the case of an unwanted pregnancy, which makes the woman's responsibility significantly less, namely, the fact that the fetus *comes into existence* as the result of the result of the woman's actions. This fact might give her a right to refuse to keep it alive, whereas she would not have had this right had it existed previously, independently, and then as a result of her actions become dependent upon her for its survival.

My own intuition, however, is that x has no more right to bring into existence, either deliberately or as a foreseeable result of actions he could have avoided, a being with full moral rights (y), and then refuse to do what he knew beforehand would be required to keep that being alive, than he has to enter into an agreement with an existing person, whereby he may be called upon to save that person's life, and then refuse to do so when so called upon. Thus, x's responsibility for y's existence does not seem to lessen his obligation to keep y alive, if he is also responsible for y's being in a situation in which only he can save him.

Whether or not this intuition is entirely correct, it brings us back once again to the conclusion that once we allow the assumption that a fetus has full moral rights it becomes an extremely complex and difficult question whether and when abortion is justifiable. Thus the Thomson analogy cannot help us produce a clear and persuasive proof of the moral permissibility of abortion. Nor will the opponents of the restrictive laws thank us for anything less; for their conviction (for the most part) is that abortion is obviously *not* a morally serious and extremely unfortunate, even though sometimes justified act, comparable to killing in self-defense or to letting the violinist die, but rather is closer to being a morally neutral act, like cutting one's hair.

The basis of this conviction, I believe, is the realization that a fetus is not a person, and thus does not have a full-fledged right to life. Perhaps the reason why this claim has been so inadequately defended is that it seems self-evident to those who accept it. And so it is, insofar as it follows from what I take to be perfectly obvious claims about the nature of personhood, and about the proper grounds for ascribing moral 127 rights, claims which ought, indeed, to be obvious to both the friends and foes of abortion. Nevertheless, it is worth examining these claims, and showing how they demonstrate the moral innocuousness of abortion, since this apparently has not been adequately done before.

II

The question which we must answer in order to produce a satisfactory solution to the problem of the moral status of abortion is this: How are we to define the moral community, the set of beings with full and equal moral rights, such that we can decide whether a human fetus is a member of this community or not? What sort of entity, exactly, has the inalienable rights to life, liberty, and the pursuit of happiness? Jefferson attributed these rights to all *men,* and it may or may not be fair to suggest that he intended to attribute them *only* to men. Perhaps he ought to have attributed them to all human beings. If so, then we arrive, first, at Noonan's problem of defining what makes a being human, and, second, at the equally vital question which Noonan does not consider, namely, What reason is there for identifying the moral community with the set of all human beings, in whatever way we have chosen to define that term?

1. ON THE DEFINITION OF 'HUMAN'

One reason why this vital second question is so frequently overlooked in the debate over the moral status of abortion is that the term 'human' has two distinct, but not often distinguished, senses. This fact results in a slide of meaning, which serves to conceal the fallaciousness of the traditional argument that since (1) it is wrong to kill innocent human beings, and (2) fetuses are innocent human beings, then (3) it is wrong to kill fetuses. For if 'human' is used in the same sense in both (1) and (2) then, whichever of the two senses is meant, one of these premises is question-begging. And if it is used in two different senses then of course the conclusion doesn't follow.

Thus, (1) is a self-evident moral truth,[9] and avoids begging the question about abortion, only if 'human being' is used to mean something like 'a full-fledged member of the moral community.' (It may or may not also be meant to refer exclusively to members of the species *Homo sapiens.*) We may call this the *moral* sense of 'human.' It is not to be confused with what we will call the *genetic* sense, i.e., the sense in which *any* member of the species is a human being, and no member of any other species could be. If (1) is acceptable only if the moral sense is

---

[9] Of course, the principle that it is (always) wrong to kill innocent human beings is in need of many other modifications, e.g., that it may be permissible to do so to save a greater number of other innocent human beings, but we may safely ignore these complications here.

intended, (2) is non-question-begging only if what is intended is the genetic sense.

In "Deciding Who is Human," Noonan argues for the classification of fetuses with human beings by pointing to the presence of the full genetic code, and the potential capacity for rational thought (p. 135). It is clear that what he needs to show, for his version of the traditional argument to be valid, is that fetuses are human in the moral sense, the sense in which it is analytically true that all human beings have full moral rights. But, in the absence of any argument showing that whatever is genetically human is also morally human, and he gives none, nothing more than genetic humanity can be demonstrated by the presence of the human genetic code. And, as we will see, the *potential* capacity for rational thought can at most show that an entity has the potential for *becoming* human in the moral sense.

2. DEFINING THE MORAL COMMUNITY

Can it be established that genetic humanity is sufficient for moral humanity? I think that there are very good reasons for not defining the moral community in this way. I would like to suggest an alternative way of defining the moral community, which I will argue for only to the extent of explaining why it is, or should be, self-evident. The suggestion is simply that the moral community consists of all and only *people,* rather than all and only human beings;[10] and probably the best way of demonstrating its self-evidence is by considering the concept of personhood, to see what sorts of entity are and are not persons, and what the decision that a being is or is not a person implies about its moral rights.

What characteristics entitle an entity to be considered a person? This is obviously not the place to attempt a complete analysis of the concept of personhood, but we do not need such a fully adequate analysis just to determine whether and why a fetus is or isn't a person. All we need is a rough and approximate list of the most basic criteria of personhood, and some idea of which, or how many, of these an entity must satisfy in order to properly be considered a person.

In searching for such criteria, it is useful to look beyond the set of people with whom we are acquainted, and ask how we would decide whether a totally alien being was a person or not. (For we have no right to assume that genetic humanity is necessary for personhood.) Imagine a space traveler who lands on an unknown planet and encounters a race of beings utterly unlike any he has ever seen or heard of. If he wants to be sure of behaving morally toward these beings, he has to somehow decide whether they are people, and hence have full moral

10 From here on, we will use 'human' to mean genetically human, since the moral sense seems closely connected to, and perhaps derived from, the assumption that genetic humanity is sufficient for membership in the moral community.

129

rights, or whether they are the sort of thing which he need not feel guilty about treating as, for example, a source of food.

How should he go about making this decision? If he has some anthropological background, he might look for such things as religion, art, and the manufacturing of tools, weapons, or shelters, since these factors have been used to distinguish our human from our prehuman ancestors, in what seems to be closer to the moral than the genetic sense of 'human.' And no doubt he would be right to consider the presence of such factors as good evidence that the alien beings were people, and morally human. It would, however, be overly anthropocentric of him to take the absence of these things as adequate evidence that they were not, since we can imagine people who have progressed beyond, or evolved without ever developing, these cultural characteristics.

I suggest that the traits which are most central to the concept of personhood, or humanity in the moral sense, are, very roughly, the following:

1. consciousness (of objects and events external and/or internal to the being), and in particular the capacity to feel pain;
2. reasoning (the *developed* capacity to solve new and relatively complex problems);
3. self-motivated activity (activity which is relatively independent of either genetic or direct external control);
4. the capacity to communicate, by whatever means, messages of an indefinite variety of types, that is, not just with an indefinite number of possible contents, but on indefinitely many possible topics;
5. the presence of self-concepts, and self-awareness, either individual or racial, or both.

Admittedly, there are apt to be a great many problems involved in formulating precise definitions of these criteria, let alone in developing universally valid behavioral criteria for deciding when they apply. But I will assume that both we and our explorer know approximately what (1)–(5) mean, and that he is also able to determine whether or not they apply. How, then, should he use his findings to decide whether or not the alien beings are people? We needn't suppose that an entity must have *all* of these attributes to be properly considered a person; (1) and (2) alone may well be sufficient for personhood, and quite probably (1)–(3) are sufficient. Neither do we need to insist that any one of these criteria is *necessary* for personhood, although once again (1) and (2) look like fairly good candidates for necessary conditions, as does (3), if 'activity' is construed so as to include the activity of reasoning.

All we need to claim, to demonstrate that a fetus is not a person, is that any being which satisfies *none* of (1)–(5) is certainly not a person. I consider this claim to be so obvious that I think anyone who 130 denied it, and claimed that a being which satisfied none of (1)–(5)

was a person all the same, would thereby demonstrate that he had no notion at all of what a person is—perhaps because he had confused the concept of a person with that of genetic humanity. If the opponents of abortion were to deny the appropriateness of these five criteria, I do not know what further arguments would convince them. We would probably have to admit that our conceptual schemes were indeed irreconcilably different, and that our dispute could not be settled objectively.

I do not expect this to happen, however, since I think that the concept of a person is one which is very nearly universal (to people), and that it is common to both proabortionists and antiabortionists, even though neither group has fully realized the relevance of this concept to the resolution of their dispute. Furthermore, I think that on reflection even the antiabortionists ought to agree not only that (1)–(5) are central to the concept of personhood, but also that it is a part of this concept that all and only people have full moral rights. The concept of a person is in part a moral concept; once we have admitted that *x* is a person we have recognized, even if we have not agreed to respect, *x*'s right to be treated as a member of the moral community. It is true that the claim that *x* is a *human being* is more commonly voiced as part of an appeal to treat *x* decently than is the claim that *x* is a person, but this is either because 'human being' is here used in the sense which implies personhood, or because the genetic and moral senses of 'human' have been confused.

Now if (1)–(5) are indeed the primary criteria of personhood, then it is clear that genetic humanity is neither necessary nor sufficient for establishing that an entity is a person. Some human beings are not people, and there may well be people who are not human beings. A man or woman whose consciousness has been permanently obliterated but who remains alive is a human being which is no longer a person; defective human beings, with no appreciable mental capacity, are not and presumably never will be people; and a fetus is a human being which is not yet a person, and which therefore cannot coherently be said to have full moral rights. Citizens of the next century should be prepared to recognize highly advanced, self-aware robots or computers, should such be developed, and intelligent inhabitants of other worlds, should such be found, as people in the fullest sense, and to respect their moral rights. But to ascribe full moral rights to an entity which is not a person is as absurd as to ascribe moral obligations and responsibilities to such an entity.

3. FETAL DEVELOPMENT AND THE RIGHT TO LIFE

Two problems arise in the application of these suggestions for the definition of the moral community to the determination of the precise moral status of a human fetus. Given that the paradigm example of a person   131 is a normal adult human being, then (1) How like this paradigm, in particular how far advanced since conception, does a human being need to be before it begins to have a right to life by virtue, not of being fully a person as of yet, but of being *like* a person? and (2) To what extent, if any, does the fact that a fetus has the *potential* for becoming a person endow it with some of the same rights? Each of these questions requires some comment.

In answering the first question, we need not attempt a detailed consideration of the moral rights of organisms which are not developed enough, aware enough, intelligent enough, etc., to be considered people, but which resemble people in some respects. It does seem reasonable to suggest that the more like a person, in the relevant respects, a being is, the stronger is the case for regarding it as having a right to life, and indeed the stronger its right to life is. Thus we ought to take seriously the suggestion that, insofar as "the human individual develops biologically in a continuous fashion . . . the rights of a human person might develop in the same way."[11] But we must keep in mind that the attributes which are relevant in determining whether or not an entity is enough like a person to be regarded as having some of the same moral rights are no different from those which are relevant to determining whether or not it is fully a person—i.e., are no different from (1)–(5)—and that being genetically human, or having recognizably human facial and other physical features, or detectable brain activity, or the capacity to survive outside the uterus, are simply not among these relevant attributes.

Thus it is clear that even though a seven- or eight-month fetus has features which make it apt to arouse in us almost the same powerful protective instinct as is commonly aroused by a small infant, nevertheless it is not significantly more personlike than is a very small embryo. It is *somewhat* more personlike; it can apparently feel and respond to pain, and it may even have a rudimentary form of consciousness, insofar as its brain is quite active. Nevertheless, it seems safe to say that it is not fully conscious, in the way that an infant of a few months is, and that it cannot reason, or communicate messages of indefinitely many sorts, does not engage in self-motivated activity, and has no self-awareness. Thus, in the *relevant* respects, a fetus, even a fully developed one, is considerably less personlike than is the average mature mammal, indeed the average fish. And I think that a rational person must conclude that if the right to life of a fetus is to be based upon its resemblance to a person, then it cannot be said to have any more right to life than, let us say, a newborn guppy (which also seems to be capable of feeling

[11] Thomas L. Hayes, "A Biological View," *Commonweal*, 85 (March 17, 1967), 677–78; quoted by Daniel Callahan, in *Abortion, Law, Choice, and Morality* (London: Macmillan & Co., 1970).

pain), and that a right of that magnitude could never override a woman's right to obtain an abortion, at any stage of her pregnancy.

There may, of course, be other arguments in favor of placing legal limits upon the stage of pregnancy in which an abortion may be performed. Given the relative safety of the new techniques of artificially inducing labor during the third trimester, the danger to the woman's life or health is no longer such an argument. Neither is the fact that people tend to respond to the thought of abortion in the later stages of pregnancy with emotional repulsion, since mere emotional responses cannot take the place of moral reasoning in determining what ought to be permitted. Nor, finally, is the frequently heard argument that legalizing abortion, especially late in the pregnancy, may erode the level of respect for human life, leading, perhaps, to an increase in unjustified euthanasia and other crimes. For this threat, if it is a threat, can be better met by educating people to the kinds of moral distinctions which we are making here than by limiting access to abortion (which limitation may, in its disregard for the rights of women, be just as damaging to the level of respect for human rights).

Thus, since the fact that even a fully developed fetus is not personlike enough to have any significant right to life on the basis of its personlikeness shows that no legal restrictions upon the stage of pregnancy in which an abortion may be performed can be justified on the grounds that we should protect the rights of the older fetus; and since there is no other apparent justification for such restrictions, we may conclude that they are entirely unjustified. Whether or not it would be *indecent* (whatever that means) for a woman in her seventh month to obtain an abortion just to avoid having to postpone a trip to Europe, it would not, in itself, be *immoral,* and therefore it ought to be permitted.

4. POTENTIAL PERSONHOOD AND THE RIGHT TO LIFE

We have seen that a fetus does not resemble a person in any way which can support the claim that it has even some of the same rights. But what about its *potential,* the fact that if nurtured and allowed to develop naturally it will very probably become a person? Doesn't that alone give it at least some right to life? It is hard to deny that the fact that an entity is a potential person is a strong prima facie reason for not destroying it; but we need not conclude from this that a potential person has a right to life, by virtue of that potential. It may be that our feeling that it is better, other things being equal, not to destroy a potential person is better explained by the fact that potential people are still (felt to be) an invaluable resource, not to be lightly squandered. Surely, if every speck of dust were a potential person, we would be much less apt to conclude that every potential person has a right to become actual.

Still, we do not need to insist that a potential person has no right to 133 life whatever. There may well be something immoral, and not just imprudent, about wantonly destroying potential people, when doing so isn't necessary to protect anyone's rights. But even if a potential person does have some prima facie right to life, such a right could not possibly outweigh the right of a woman to obtain an abortion, since the rights of any actual person invariably outweigh those of any potential person, whenever the two conflict. Since this may not be immediately obvious in the case of a human fetus, let us look at another case.

Suppose that our space explorer falls into the hands of an alien culture, whose scientists decide to create a few hundred thousand or more human beings, by breaking his body into its component cells, and using these to create fully developed human beings, with, of course, his genetic code. We may imagine that each of these newly created men will have all of the original man's abilities, skills, knowledge, and so on, and also have an individual self-concept, in short that each of them will be a bona fide (though hardly unique) person. Imagine that the whole project will take only seconds, and that its chances of success are extremely high, and that our explorer knows all of this, and also knows that these people will be treated fairly. I maintain that in such a situation he would have every right to escape if he could, and thus to deprive all of these potential people of their potential lives; for his right to life outweighs all of theirs together, in spite of the fact that they are all genetically human, all innocent, and all have a very high probability of becoming people very soon, if only he refrains from acting.

Indeed, I think he would have a right to escape even if it were not his life which the alien scientists planned to take, but only a year of his freedom, or, indeed, only a day. Nor would he be obligated to stay if he had gotten captured (thus bringing all these people-potentials into existence) because of his own carelessness, or even if he had done so deliberately, knowing the consequences. Regardless of how he got captured, he is not morally obligated to remain in captivity for *any* period of time for the sake of permitting any number of potential people to come into actuality, so great is the margin by which one actual person's right to liberty outweighs whatever right to life even a hundred thousand potential people have. And it seems reasonable to conclude that the rights of a woman will outweigh by a similar margin whatever right to life a fetus may have by virtue of its potential personhood.

Thus, neither a fetus's resemblance to a person, nor its potential for becoming a person provides any basis whatever for the claim that it has any significant right to life. Consequently, a woman's right to protect her health, happiness, freedom, and even her life,[12] by terminating an

---

[12] That is, insofar as the death rate, for the woman, is higher for childbirth than 134 for early abortion.

unwanted pregnancy, will always override whatever right to life it may be appropriate to ascribe to a fetus, even a fully developed one. And thus, in the absence of any overwhelming social need for every possible child, the laws which restrict the right to obtain an abortion, or limit the period of pregnancy during which an abortion may be performed, are a wholly unjustified violation of a woman's most basic moral and constitutional rights.[13]

Postscript on Infanticide

Since the publication of this article, many people have written to point out that my argument appears to justify not only abortion, but infanticide as well. For a new-born infant is not significantly more person-like than an advanced fetus, and consequently it would seem that if the destruction of the latter is permissible so too must be that of the former. Inasmuch as most people, regardless of how they feel about the morality of abortion, consider infanticide a form of murder, this might appear to represent a serious flaw in my argument.

Now, if I am right in holding that it is only people who have a full-fledged right to life, and who can be murdered, and if the criteria of personhood are as I have described them, then it obviously follows that killing a new-born infant isn't murder. It does *not* follow, however, that infanticide is permissible, for two reasons. In the first place, it would be wrong, at least in this country and in this period of history, and other things being equal, to kill a new-born infant, because even if its parents do not want it and would not suffer from its destruction, there are other people who would like to have it, and would, in all probability, be deprived of a great deal of pleasure by its destruction. Thus, infanticide is wrong for reasons analogous to those which make it wrong to wantonly destroy natural resources, or great works of art.

Secondly, most people, at least in this country, value infants and would much prefer that they be preserved, even if foster parents are not immediately available. Most of us would rather be taxed to support orphanages than allow unwanted infants to be destroyed. So long as there are people who want an infant preserved, and who are willing and able to provide the means of caring for it, under reasonably humane conditions, it is, *ceteris parabis,* wrong to destroy it.

But, it might be replied, if this argument shows that infanticide is wrong, at least at this time and in this country, doesn't it also show that abortion is wrong? After all, many people value fetuses, are disturbed by their destruction, and would much prefer that they be preserved, even

[13] My thanks to the following people, who were kind enough to read and criticize an earlier version of this paper: Herbert Gold, Gene Glass, Anne Lauterbach, Judith Thomson, Mary Mothersill, and Timothy Binkley.

at some cost to themselves. Furthermore, as a potential source of pleasure to some foster family, a fetus is just as valuable as an infant. There is, however, a crucial difference between the two cases: so long as the fetus is unborn, its preservation, contrary to the wishes of the pregnant woman, violates her rights to freedom, happiness, and self-determination. Her rights override the rights of those who would like the fetus preserved, just as if someone's life or limb is threatened by a wild animal, his right to protect himself by destroying the animal overrides the rights of those who would prefer that the animal not be harmed.

The minute the infant is born, however, its preservation no longer violates any of its mother's rights, even if she wants it destroyed, because she is free to put it up for adoption. Consequently, while the moment of birth does not mark any sharp discontinuity in the degree to which an infant possesses the right to life, it does mark the end of its mother's right to determine its fate. Indeed, if abortion could be performed without killing the fetus, she would never possess the right to have the fetus destroyed, for the same reasons that she has no right to have an infant destroyed.

On the other hand, it follows from my argument that when an unwanted or defective infant is born into a society which cannot afford and/or is not willing to care for it, then its destruction is permissible. This conclusion will, no doubt, strike many people as heartless and immoral; but remember that the very existence of people who feel this way, and who are willing and able to provide care for unwanted infants, is reason enough to conclude that they should be preserved.

Selected Bibliography

Callahan, Daniel. *Abortion: Law, Choice and Morality.* New York: Macmillan, 1970.

Feinberg, Joel (ed.). *The Problem of Abortion.* Belmont, Calif.: Wadsworth Publishing Co., 1973.

Foot, Philippa. "The Problem of Abortion and the Doctrine of Double Effect," *Oxford Review,* **5** (1967). Reprinted in James Rachel (ed.), *Moral Problems,* p. 28. New York: Harper & Row, 1971.

Noonan, John T., Jr. (ed.). *The Morality of Abortion: Legal and Historical Perspectives.* Cambridge, Mass.: Harvard University Press, 1970.

Tooley, Michael. "Abortion and Infanticide," *Philosophy and Public Affairs,* Vol. 2, No. 1 (1972), 37.

Wertheimer, Roger. "Understanding the Abortion Argument," *Philosophy and Public Affairs,* Vol. 1, No. 1 (1971), 67.

RACISM AND SEXISM 3

THOMAS E. HILL, JR.
Servility and Self-Respect

Several motives underlie this paper.[1] In the first place, I am curious to see if there is a legitimate source for the increasingly common feeling that servility can be as much a vice as arrogance. There seems to be something morally defective about the Uncle Tom and the submissive housewife; and yet, on the other hand, if the only interests they sacrifice are their own, it seems that we should have no right to complain. Secondly, I have some sympathy for the now unfashionable view that each person has duties to himself as well as to others. It does seem absurd to say that a person could literally violate his own rights or owe himself a debt of gratitude, but I suspect that the classic defenders of duties to oneself had something different in mind. If there are duties to oneself, it is natural to expect that a duty to avoid being servile would have a prominent place among them. Thirdly, I am interested in making sense of Kant's puzzling, but suggestive, remarks about respect for persons and respect for the moral law. On the usual reading, these remarks seem unduly moralistic; but, viewed in another way, they suggest an argument for a kind of self-respect which is incompatible with a servile attitude.

My procedure will not be to explicate Kant directly. Instead I shall try to isolate the defect of servility and sketch an argu-

Reprinted from *The Monist,* Vol. 57, No. 1 (January 1973), 87–104, La Salle, Illinois, with the permission of the publisher and the author.

[1] An earlier version of this paper was presented at the meetings of the American Philosophical Association, Pacific Division. A number of revisions have been made as a result of the helpful comments of others, especially Norman Dahl, Sharon Hill, Herbert Morris, and Mary Mothersill.

ment to show why it is objectionable, noting only in passing how this relates to Kant and the controversy about duties to oneself. What I say about self-respect is far from the whole story. In particular, it is not concerned with esteem for one's special abilities and achievements or with the self-confidence which characterizes the especially autonomous person. Nor is my concern with the psychological antecedents and effects of self-respect. Nevertheless, my conclusions, if correct, should be of interest; for they imply that, given a common view of morality, there are nonutilitarian moral reasons for each person, regardless of his merits, to respect himself. To avoid servility to the extent that one can is not simply a right but a duty, not simply a duty to others but a duty to oneself.

I

Three examples may give a preliminary idea of what I mean by *servility*. Consider, first, an extremely deferential black, whom I shall call the *Uncle Tom*. He always steps aside for white men; he does not complain when less qualified whites take over his job; he gratefully accepts whatever benefits his all-white government and employers allot him, and he would not think of protesting its insufficiency. He displays the symbols of deference to whites, and of contempt towards blacks; he faces the former with bowed stance and a ready 'sir' and 'Ma'am'; he reserves his strongest obscenities for the latter. Imagine, too, that he is not playing a game. He is not the shrewdly prudent calculator, who knows how to make the best of a bad lot and mocks his masters behind their backs. He accepts without question the idea that, as a black, he is owed less than whites. He may believe that blacks are mentally inferior and of less social utility, but that is not the crucial point. The attitude which he displays is that what he values, aspires for, and can demand is of less importance than what whites value, aspire for, and can demand. He is far from the picture book's carefree, happy servant, but he does not feel that he has a right to expect anything better.

Another pattern of servility is illustrated by a person I shall call the *Self-Deprecator*. Like the Uncle Tom, he is reluctant to make demands. He says nothing when others take unfair advantage of him. When asked for his preferences or opinions, he tends to shrink away as if what he said should make no difference. His problem, however, is not a sense of racial inferiority but rather an acute awareness of his own inadequacies and failures as an individual. These defects are not imaginary: he has in fact done poorly by his own standards and others'. But, unlike many of us in the same situation, he acts as if his failings warrant quite unrelated maltreatment even by strangers. His sense of shame and self-contempt make him content to be the instrument of others. He feels that nothing is owed him until he has earned it and that he has earned very little. He is not simply playing a masochist's game of winning sympathy by disparaging himself. On the contrary, he assesses his individual merits with painful accuracy.

A rather different case is that of the *Deferential Wife*. This is a woman who is utterly devoted to serving her husband. She buys the clothes *he* prefers, invites the guests *he* wants to entertain, and makes love whenever *he* is in the mood. She willingly moves to a new city in order for him to have a more attractive job, counting her own friendships and geographical preferences insignificant by comparison. She loves her husband, but her conduct is not simply an expression of love. She is happy, but she does not subordinate herself as a means to happiness. She does not simply defer to her husband in certain spheres as a trade-off for his deference in other spheres. On the contrary, she tends not to form her own interests, values, and ideals; and, when she does, she counts them as less important than her husband's. She readily responds to appeals from Women's Liberation that she agrees that women are mentally and physically equal, if not superior, to men. She just believes that the proper role for a woman is to serve her family. As a matter of fact, much of her happiness derives from her belief that she fulfills this role very well. No one is trampling on her rights, she says; for she is quite glad, and proud, to serve her husband as she does.

Each one of these cases reflects the attitude which I call servility.[2] It betrays the absence of a certain kind of self-respect. What I take this attitude to be, more specifically, will become clearer later on. It is important at the outset, however, not to confuse the three cases sketched above with other, superficially similar cases. In particular, the cases I have sketched are not simply cases in which someone refuses to press his rights, speaks disparagingly of himself, or devotes himself to another. A black, for example, is not necessarily servile because he does not demand a just wage; for, seeing that such a demand would result in his being fired, he might forbear for the sake of his children. A self-critical person is not necessarily servile by virtue of bemoaning his faults in public; for his behavior may be merely a complex way of satisfying his own inner needs quite independent of a willingness to accept abuse from others. A woman need not be servile whenever she works to make her

---

[2] Each of the cases is intended to represent only one possible pattern of servility. I make no claims about how often these patterns are exemplified, nor do I mean to imply that only these patterns could warrant the labels "Deferential Wife," "Uncle Tom," etc. All the more, I do not mean to imply any comparative judgments about the causes or relative magnitude of the problems of racial and sexual discrimination. One person, e.g. a self-contemptuous woman with a sense of racial inferiority, might exemplify features of several patterns at once; and, of course, a person might view her being a woman the way an Uncle Tom views his being black, etc.

husband happy and prosperous; for she might freely and knowingly choose to do so from love or from a desire to share the rewards of his success. If the effort did not require her to submit to humiliation or maltreatment, her choice would not mark her as servile. There may, of course, be grounds for objecting to the attitudes in these cases; but the defect is not servility of the sort I want to consider. It should also be noted that my cases of servility are not simply instances of deference to superior knowledge or judgment. To defer to an expert's judgment on matters of fact is not to be servile; to defer to his every wish and whim is. Similarly, the belief that one's talents and achievements are comparatively low does not, by itself, make one servile. It is no vice to acknowledge the truth, and one may in fact have achieved less, and have less ability, than others. To be servile is not simply to hold certain empirical beliefs but to have a certain attitude concerning one's rightful place in a moral community.

II

Are there grounds for regarding the attitudes of the Uncle Tom, the Self-Deprecator, and the Deferential Wife as morally objectionable? Are there moral arguments we could give them to show that they ought to have more self-respect? None of the more obvious replies is entirely satisfactory.

One might, in the first place, adduce utilitarian considerations. Typically the servile person will be less happy than he might be. Moreover, he may be less prone to make the best of his own socially useful abilities. He may become a nuisance to others by being overly dependent. He will, in any case, lose the special contentment that comes from standing up for one's rights. A submissive attitude encourages exploitation, and exploitation spreads misery in a variety of ways. These considerations provide a prima facie case against the attitudes of the Uncle Tom, the Deferential Wife, and the Self-Deprecator, but they are hardly conclusive. Other utilities tend to counterbalance the ones just mentioned. When people refuse to press their rights, there are usually others who profit. There are undeniable pleasures in associating with those who are devoted, understanding, and grateful for whatever we see fit to give them —as our fondness for dogs attests. Even the servile person may find his attitude a source of happiness, as the case of the Deferential Wife illustrates. There may be comfort and security in thinking that the hard choices must be made by others, that what I would say has little to do with what ought to be done. Self-condemnation may bring relief from the pangs of guilt even if it is not deliberately used for that purpose. On balance, then, utilitarian considerations may turn out to favor servility as much as they oppose it.

For those who share my moral intuitions, there is another sort of reason for not trying to rest a case against servility on utilitarian considerations. Certain utilities seem irrelevant to the issue. The utilitarian must weigh them along with others, but to do so seems morally inappropriate. Suppose, for example, that the submissive attitudes of the Uncle Tom and the Deferential Wife result in positive utilities for those who dominate and exploit them. Do we need to tabulate *these* utilities before conceding that servility is objectionable? The Uncle Tom, it seems, is making an error, a moral error, quite apart from consideration of how much others in fact profit from his attitude. The Deferential Wife may be quite happy; but if her happiness turns out to be contingent on her distorted view of her own rights and worth as a person, then it carries little moral weight against the contention that she ought to change that view. Suppose I could cause a woman to find her happiness in denying all her rights and serving my every wish. No doubt I could do so only by nonrational manipulative techniques, which I ought not to use. But is this the only objection? My efforts would be wrong, it seems, not only because of the techniques they require but also because the resultant attitude is itself objectionable. When a person's happiness stems from a morally objectionable attitude, it ought to be discounted. That a sadist gets pleasure from seeing others suffer should not count even as a partial justification for his attitude. That a servile person derives pleasure from denying her moral status, for similar reasons, cannot make her attitude acceptable. These brief intuitive remarks are not intended as a refutation of utilitarianism, with all its many varieties; but they do suggest that it is well to look elsewhere for adequate grounds for rejecting the attitudes of the Uncle Tom, the Self-Deprecator, and the Deferential Wife.

One might try to appeal to meritarian considerations. That is, one might argue that the servile person *deserves* more than he allows himself. This line of argument, however, is no more adequate than the utilitarian one. It may be wrong to deny others what they deserve, but it is not so obviously wrong to demand less for oneself than one deserves. In any case, the Self-Deprecator's problem is not that he underestimates his merits. By hypothesis, he assesses his merits quite accurately. We cannot reasonably tell him to have more respect for himself because he *deserves* more respect; he knows that he has not *earned* better treatment. His problem, in fact, is that he thinks of his moral status with regard to others as entirely dependent upon his merits. His interests and choices are important, he feels, only if he has earned the right to make demands; or if he had rights by birth, they were forfeited by his subsequent failures and misdeeds. My Self-Deprecator is no doubt an atypical person, but nevertheless he illustrates an important point. Normally when we find a self-contemptuous person, we can plausibly argue that he is not so bad as 141 he thinks, that his self-contempt is an overreaction prompted more by inner needs than by objective assessment of his merits. Because this argument cannot work with the Self-Deprecator, his case draws attention to a distinction, applicable in other cases as well, between saying that someone deserves respect for his merits and saying that he is owed respect as a person. On meritarian grounds we can only say 'You deserve better than this,' but the defect of the servile person is not merely failure to recognize his merits.

Other common arguments against the Uncle Tom, et al., may have some force but seem not to strike to the heart of the problem. For example, philosophers sometimes appeal to the value of human potentialities. As a human being, it is said, one at least has a capacity for rationality, morality, excellence, or autonomy, and this capacity is worthy of respect. Although such arguments have the merit of making respect independent of a person's actual deserts, they seem quite misplaced in some cases. There comes a time when we have sufficient evidence that a person is not ever going to *be* rational, moral, excellent, or autonomous even if he still has a capacity, in some sense, for being so. As a person approaches death with an atrocious record so far, the chances of his realizing his diminishing capacities become increasingly slim. To make these capacities the basis of his self-respect is to rest it on a shifting and unstable ground. We do, of course, respect persons for capacities which they are not exercising at the moment; for example, I might respect a person as a good philosopher even though he is just now blundering into gross confusion. In these cases, however, we respect the person for an active capacity, a ready disposition, which he has displayed on many occasions. On this analogy, a person should have respect for himself only when his capacities are developed and ready, needing only to be triggered by an appropriate occasion or the removal of some temporary obstacle. The Uncle Tom and the Deferential Wife, however, may in fact have quite limited capacities of this sort, and, since the Self-Deprecator is already overly concerned with his own inadequacies, drawing attention to his capacities seems a poor way to increase his self-respect. In any case, setting aside the Kantian nonempirical capacity for autonomy, the capacities of different persons vary widely; but what the servile person seems to overlook is something by virtue of which he is equal with every other person.

III

Why, then, is servility a moral defect? There is, I think, another sort of answer which is worth exploring. The first part of this answer must be an attempt to isolate the objectionable features of the servile person; later we can ask why these features are objectionable. As a step in this direction, let us examine again our three paradigm cases. The moral defect in each case, I suggest, is a failure to understand and acknowledge one's own moral rights. I assume, without argument here, that each person has moral rights.[3] Some of these rights may be basic human rights; that is, rights for which a person needs only to be human to qualify. Other rights will be derivative and contingent upon his special commitments, institutional affiliations, etc. Most rights will be prima facie ones; some may be absolute. Most can be waived under appropriate conditions; perhaps some cannot. Many rights can be forfeited; but some, presumably, cannot. The servile person does not, strictly speaking, violate his own rights. At least in our paradigm cases he fails to acknowledge fully his own moral status because he does not fully understand what his rights are, how they can be waived, and when they can be forfeited.

The defect of the Uncle Tom, for example, is that he displays an attitude that denies his moral equality with whites. He does not realize, or apprehend in an effective way, that he has as much right to a decent wage and a share of political power as any comparable white. His gratitude is misplaced; he accepts benefits which are his by right as if they were gifts. The Self-Deprecator is servile in a more complex way. He acts as if he has forfeited many important rights which in fact he has not. He does not understand, or fully realize in his own case, that certain rights to fair and decent treatment do not have to be earned. He sees his merits clearly enough, but he fails to see that what he can expect from others is not merely a function of his merits. The Deferential Wife *says* that she understands her rights vis-à-vis her husband, but what she fails to appreciate is that her consent to serve him is a valid waiver of her rights only under certain conditions. If her consent is coerced, say, by the lack of viable options for women in her society, then her consent is worth little. If socially fostered ignorance of her own talents and alternatives is responsible for her consent, then her consent should not count as a fully legitimate waiver of her right to equal consideration within the marriage. All the more, her consent to defer constantly to her husband is not a legitimate setting aside of her rights if it results from her mistaken belief that she has a moral duty to do so. (Recall: "The *proper* role for a woman is to serve her family.") If she believes that she has a *duty* to defer to her husband, then, whatever she may say, she cannot fully understand that she has a *right* not to defer to him. When she says that she freely gives up such a right, she is confused. Her confusion is rather like that of a person who has been persuaded by an unscrupulous

---

[3] As will become evident, I am also presupposing some form of cognitive or "naturalistic" interpretation of rights. If, to accommodate an emotivist or prescriptivist, we set aside talk of moral knowledge and ignorance, we might construct a somewhat analogous case against servility from the point of view of those who adopt principles ascribing rights to all; but the argument, I suspect, would be more complex and less persuasive.

lawyer that it is legally incumbent on him to refuse a jury trial but who nevertheless tells the judge that he understands that he has a right to a jury trial and freely waives it. He does not really understand what it is to have and freely give up the right if he thinks that it would be an offense for him to exercise it.

Insofar as servility results from moral ignorance or confusion, it need not be something for which a person is to blame. Even self-reproach may be inappropriate; for at the time a person is in ignorance he cannot feel guilty about his servility, and later he may conclude that his ignorance was unavoidable. In some cases, however, a person might reasonably believe that he should have known better. If, for example, the Deferential Wife's confusion about her rights resulted from a motivated resistance to drawing the implications of her own basic moral principles, then later she might find some ground for self-reproach. Whether blameworthy or not, servility could still be morally objectionable at least in the sense that it ought to be discouraged, that social conditions which nourish it should be reformed, and the like. Not all morally undesirable features of a person are ones for which he is responsible, but that does not mean that they are defects merely from an esthetic or prudential point of view.

In our paradigm cases, I have suggested, servility is a kind of deferential attitude towards others resulting from ignorance or misunderstanding of one's moral rights. A sufficient remedy, one might think, would be moral enlightenment. Suppose, however, that our servile persons come to know their rights but do not substantially alter their behavior. Are they not still servile in an objectionable way? One might even think that reproach is more appropriate now because they know what they are doing.

The problem, unfortunately, is not as simple as it may appear. Much depends on what they tolerate and why. Let us set aside cases in which a person merely refuses to *fight* for his rights, chooses not to exercise certain rights, or freely waives many rights which he might have insisted upon. Our problem concerns the previously servile person who continues to display the same marks of deference even after he fully knows his rights. Imagine, for example, that even after enlightenment our Uncle Tom persists in his old pattern of behavior, giving all the typical signs of believing that the injustices done to him are not really wrong. Suppose, too, that the newly enlightened Deferential Wife continues to defer to her husband, refusing to disturb the old way of life by introducing her new ideas. She acts as if she accepts the idea that she is merely doing her duty though actually she no longer believes it. Let us suppose, further, that the Uncle Tom and the Deferential Wife are not merely generous with their time and property; they also accept without protest, and even appear to sanction, treatment which is humiliating and degrading. That is, they do not simply consent to waive mutually acknowledged rights; they tolerate violations of their rights with apparent approval. They pre-

144

tend to give their permission for subtle humiliations which they really believe no permission can make legitimate. Are such persons still servile despite their moral knowledge?

The answer, I think, should depend upon why the deferential role is played. If the motive is a morally commendable one, or a desire to avert dire consequences to oneself, or even an ambition to set an oppressor up for a later fall, then I would not count the role player as servile. The Uncle Tom, for instance, is not servile in my sense if he shuffles and bows to keep the Klan from killing his children, to save his own skin, or even to buy time while he plans the revolution. Similarly, the Deferential Wife is not servile if she tolerates an abusive husband because he is so ill that further strain would kill him, because protesting would deprive her of her only means of survival, or because she is collecting atrocity stories for her book against marriage. If there is fault in these situations, it seems inappropriate to call it *servility*. The story is quite different, however, if a person continues in his deferential role just from laziness, timidity, or a desire for some minor advantage. He shows too little concern for his moral status as a person, one is tempted to say, if he is willing to deny it for a small profit or simply because it requires some effort and courage to affirm it openly. A black who plays the Uncle Tom merely to gain an advantage over other blacks is harming them, of course; but he is also displaying disregard for his own moral position as an equal among human beings. Similarly, a woman throws away her rights too lightly if she continues to play the subservient role because she is used to it or is too timid to risk a change. A Self-Deprecator who readily accepts what he knows are violations of his rights may be indulging his peculiar need for punishment at the expense of denying something more valuable. In these cases, I suggest, we have a kind of servility independent of any ignorance or confusion about one's rights. The person who has it may or may not be blameworthy, depending on many factors; and the line between servile and nonservile role playing will often be hard to draw. Nevertheless, the objectionable feature is perhaps clear enough for present purposes: it is a willingness to disavow one's moral status, publicly and systematically, in the absence of any strong reason to do so.

My proposal, then, is that there are at least two types of servility: one resulting from misunderstanding of one's rights and the other from placing a comparatively low value on them. In either case, servility manifests the absence of a certain kind of self-respect. The respect which is missing is not respect for one's merits but respect for one's rights. The servile person displays this absence of respect not directly by acting contrary to his own rights but indirectly by acting as if his rights were nonexistent or insignificant. An arrogant person ignores the rights of others, thereby arrogating for himself a higher status than he is entitled to; a servile person denies his own rights, thereby assuming a lower position than he is 145 entitled to. Whether rooted in ignorance or simply lack of concern for moral rights, the attitudes in both cases may be incompatible with a proper regard for morality. That this is so obvious in the case of arrogance; but to see it in the case of servility requires some further argument.

IV

The objectionable feature of the servile person, as I have described him, is his tendency to disavow his own moral rights either because he misunderstands them or because he cares little for them. The question remains: why should anyone regard this as a moral defect? After all, the rights which he denies are his own. He may be unfortunate, foolish, or even distasteful; but why *morally* deficient? One sort of answer, quite different from those reviewed earlier, is suggested by some of Kant's remarks. Kant held that servility is contrary to a perfect nonjuridical duty to oneself.[4] To say that the duty is perfect is roughly to say that it is stringent, never overridden by other considerations (e.g. beneficence). To say that the duty is nonjuridical is to say that a person cannot legitimately be coerced to comply. Although Kant did not develop an explicit argument for this view, an argument can easily be constructed from materials which reflect the spirit, if not the letter, of his moral theory. The argument which I have in mind is prompted by Kant's contention that respect for persons, strictly speaking, is respect for moral law.[5] If taken as a claim about all sorts of respect, this seems quite implausible. If it means that we respect persons only for their moral character, their capacity for moral conduct, or their status as "authors" of the moral law, then it seems unduly moralistic. My strategy is to construe the remark as saying that at least one sort of respect for persons is respect for the rights which the moral law accords them. If one respects the moral law, then one must respect one's own moral rights; and this amounts to having a kind of self-respect incompatible with servility.

The premises for the Kantian argument, which are all admittedly vague, can be sketched as follows:

First, let us assume, as Kant did, that all human beings have equal basic human rights. Specific rights vary with different conditions, but all must be

[4] See Immanuel Kant, *The Doctrine of Virtue,* Part II of *The Metaphysics of Morals,* ed. by M. J. Gregor (New York: Harper & Row, 1964), pp. 99–103; Prussian Academy edition, Vol. VI, pp. 434–37.

[5] Immanuel Kant, *Groundwork of the Metaphysics of Morals,* ed. by H. J. Paton (New York: Harper & Row, 1964), p. 69; Prussian Academy edition, Vol. IV, p. 401; *The Critique of Practical Reason,* ed. by Lewis W. Beck (New York: Bobbs-Merrill, 1956), pp. 81, 84; Prussian Academy edition, Vol. V, pp. 78, 81. My purpose here is not to interpret what Kant meant but to give a sense to his remark.

justified from a point of view under which all are equal. Not all rights need to be earned, and some cannot be forfeited. Many rights can be waived but only under certain conditions of knowledge and freedom. These conditions are complex and difficult to state; but they include something like the condition that a person's consent releases others from obligation only if it is autonomously given, and consent resulting from underestimation of one's moral status is not autonomously given. Rights can be objects of knowledge, but also of ignorance, misunderstanding, deception, and the like.

Second, let us assume that my account of servility is correct; or, if one prefers, we can take it as a definition. That is, in brief, a servile person is one who tends to deny or disavow his own moral rights because he does not understand them or has little concern for the status they give him.

Third, we need one formal premise concerning moral duty, namely, that each person ought, as far as possible, to respect the moral law. In less Kantian language, the point is that everyone should approximate, to the extent that he can, the ideal of a person who fully adopts the moral point of view. Roughly, this means not only that each person ought to do what is morally required and refrain from what is morally wrong but also that each person should treat all the provisions of morality as valuable—worth preserving and prizing as well as obeying. One must, so to speak, take up the spirit of morality as well as meet the letter of its requirements. To keep one's promises, avoid hurting others, and the like, is not sufficient; one should also take an attitude of respect towards the principles, ideals, and goals of morality. A respectful attitude towards a system of rights and duties consists of more than a disposition to conform to its definite rules of behavior; it also involves holding the system in esteem, being unwilling to ridicule it, and being reluctant to give up one's place in it. The essentially Kantian idea here is that morality, as a system of equal fundamental rights and duties, is worthy of respect, and hence a completely moral person would respect it in word and manner as well as in deed. And what a completely moral person would do, in Kant's view, is our duty to do so far as we can.

The assumptions here are, of course, strong ones, and I make no attempt to justify them. They are, I suspect, widely held though rarely articulated. In any case, my present purpose is not to evaluate them but to see how, if granted, they constitute a case against servility. The objection to the servile person; given our premises, is that he does not satisfy the basic requirement to respect morality. A person who fully respected a system of moral rights would be disposed to learn his proper place in it, to affirm it proudly, and not to tolerate abuses of it lightly. This is just the sort of disposition that the servile person lacks. If he does not understand the system, he is in no position to respect it adequately. This lack of respect may be no fault of his own, but it is still a way in which he falls short of a moral ideal. If, on the other hand, the servile person knowingly disavows his 147 moral rights by pretending to approve of violations of them, then, barring special explanations, he shows an indifference to whether the provisions of morality are honored and publicly acknowledged. This avoidable display of indifference, by our Kantian premises, is contrary to the duty to respect morality. The disrespect in this second case is somewhat like the disrespect a religious believer might show towards his religion if, to avoid embarrassment, he laughed congenially while nonbelievers were mocking the beliefs which he secretly held. In any case, the servile person, as such, does not express disrespect for the system of moral rights in the obvious way by violating the rights of others. His lack of respect is more subtly manifested by his acting before others as if he did not know or care about his position of equality under that system.

The central idea may be illustrated by an analogy. Imagine a club, say, an old German dueling fraternity. By the rules of the club, each member has certain rights and responsibilities. These are the same for each member regardless of what titles he may hold outside the club. Each has, for example, a right to be heard at meetings, a right not to be shouted down by the others. Some rights cannot be forfeited: for example, each may vote regardless of whether he has paid his dues and satisfied other rules. Some rights cannot be waived: for example, the right to be defended when attacked by several members of the rival fraternity. The members show respect for each other by respecting the status which the rules confer on each member. Now one new member is careful always to allow the others to speak at meetings; but when they shout him down, he does nothing. He just shrugs as if to say, 'Who am I to complain?' When he fails to stand up in defense of a fellow member, he feels ashamed and refuses to vote. He does not deserve to vote, he says. As the only commoner among illustrious barons, he feels that it is his place to serve them and defer to their decisions. When attackers from the rival fraternity come at him with swords drawn, he tells his companions to run and save themselves. When they defend him, he expresses immense gratitude—as if they had done him a gratuitous favor. Now one might argue that our new member fails to show respect for the fraternity and its rules. He does not actually violate any of the rules by refusing to vote, asking others not to defend him, and deferring to the barons, but he symbolically disavows the equal status which the rules confer on him. If he ought to have respect for the fraternity, he ought to change his attitude. Our servile person, then, is like the new member of the dueling fraternity in having insufficient respect for a system of rules and ideals. The difference is that everyone ought to respect morality whereas there is no comparable moral requirement to respect the fraternity.

The conclusion here is, of course, a limited one. Self-sacrifice is not always a sign of servility. It is not a duty always to press one's rights. Whether a given act is evidence of servility will depend not only on the attitude of the agent but also on the specific nature of his moral rights, a 148 matter not considered here. Moreover, the extent to which a person is responsible, or blameworthy, for his defect remains an open question. Nevertheless, the conclusion should not be minimized. In order to avoid servility, a person who gives up his rights must do so with a full appreciation for what they are. A woman, for example, may devote herself to her husband if she is uncoerced, knows what she is doing, and does not pretend that she has no decent alternative. A self-contemptuous person may decide not to press various unforfeited rights but only if he does not take the attitude that he is too rotten to deserve them. A black may demand less than is due to him provided he is prepared to acknowledge that no one has a right to expect this of him. Sacrifices of this sort, I suspect, are extremely rare. Most people, if they fully acknowledged their rights, would not autonomously refuse to press them.

An even stronger conclusion would emerge if we could assume that some basic rights cannot be waived. This is, if there are some rights that others are bound to respect regardless of what we say, then, barring special explanation, we would be obliged not only to acknowledge these rights but also to avoid any appearance of consenting to give them up. To act as if we could release others from their obligation to grant these rights, apart from special circumstances, would be to fail to respect morality. Rousseau, held, for example, that at least a minimal right to liberty cannot be waived. A man who consents to be enslaved, giving up liberty without *quid pro quo,* thereby displays a conditioned slavish mentality that renders his consent worthless. Similarly, a Kantian might argue that a person cannot release others from the obligation to refrain from killing him: consent is no defense against the charge of murder. To accept principles of this sort is to hold that rights to life and liberty are, as Kant believed, rather like a trustee's rights to preserve something valuable entrusted to him: he has not only a right but a duty to preserve it.

Even if there are no specific rights which cannot be waived, there might be at least one formal right of this sort. This is the right to some minimum degree of respect from others. No matter how willing a person is to submit to humiliation by others, they ought to show him some respect as a person. By analogy with self-respect, as presented here, this respect owed by others would consist of a willingness to acknowledge fully, in word as well as action, the person's basically equal moral status as defined by his other rights. To the extent that a person gives even tacit consent to humiliations incompatible with this respect, he will be acting as if he waives a right which he cannot in fact give up. To do this, barring special explanations, would mark one as servile.

V

Kant held that the avoidance of servility is a duty to oneself rather than a duty to others. Recent philosophers, however, tend to discard the idea of a duty to oneself as a conceptual confusion. Although admittedly the 149 analogy between a duty to oneself and a duty to others is not perfect, I suggest that something important is reflected in Kant's contention.

Let us consider briefly the function of saying that a duty is *to* someone. *First,* to say that a duty is *to* a given person sometimes merely indicates who is the object of that duty. That is, to tell us that the duty is concerned with how that person is to be treated, how his interests and wishes are to be taken into account, and the like. Here we might as well say that we have a duty *towards,* or *regarding* that person. Typically the person in question is the beneficiary of the fulfillment of the duty. For example, in this sense I have a duty to my children and even a duty to a distant stranger if I promised a third party that I would help that stranger. Clearly a duty to avoid servility would be a duty to oneself at least in this minimal sense, for it is a duty to avoid, so far as possible, the denial of one's own moral status. The duty is concerned with understanding and affirming one's rights, which are, at least as a rule, for one's own benefit.

Second, when we say that a duty is *to* a certain person, we often indicate thereby the person especially entitled to complain in case the duty is not fulfilled. For example, if I fail in my duty to my colleagues, then it is they who can most appropriately reproach me. Others may sometimes speak up on their behalf, but, for the most part, it is not the business of strangers to set me straight. Analogously, to say that the duty to avoid servility is a duty to onself would indicate that, though sometimes a person may justifiably reproach himself for being servile, others are not generally in the appropriate position to complain. Outside encouragement is sometimes necessary, but, if any blame is called for, it is primarily self-recrimination and not the censure of others.

Third, mention of the person to whom a duty is owed often tells us something about the source of that duty. For example, to say that I have a duty to another person may indicate that the argument to show that I have such a duty turns upon a promise to that person, his authority over me, my having accepted special benefits from him, or, more generally, his rights. Accordingly, to say that the duty to avoid servility is a duty to oneself would at least imply that it is not entirely based upon promises to others, their authority, their beneficence, or an obligation to respect their rights. More positively, the assertion might serve to indicate that the source of the duty is one's own rights rather than the rights of others, etc. That is, one ought not to be servile because, in some broad sense, one ought to respect one's own rights as a person. There is, to be sure, an asymmetry: one has certain duties to others because one ought not to violate their rights, and one has a duty to oneself because one ought to affirm one's own rights. Nevertheless, to dismiss duties to oneself out of hand is to overlook significant similarities.

Some familiar objections to duties to oneself, moreover, seem irrelevant 150 in the case of servility. For example, some place much stock in the idea that a person would have no duties if alone on a desert island. This can be doubted, but in any case is irrelevant here. The duty to avoid servility is a duty to take a certain stance towards others and hence would be inapplicable if one were isolated on a desert island. Again, some suggest that if there were duties to oneself then one could make promises to oneself or owe oneself a debt of gratitude. Their paradigms are familiar ones. Someone remarks, 'I promised myself a vacation this year' or 'I have been such a good boy I owe myself a treat'. Concentration on these facetious cases tends to confuse the issue. In any case the duty to avoid servility, as presented here, does not presuppose promises to oneself or debts of gratitude to oneself. Other objections stem from the intuition that a person has no duty to promote his own happiness. A duty to oneself, it is sometimes assumed, must be a duty to promote one's own happiness. From a utilitarian point of view, in fact, this is what a duty to oneself would most likely be. The problems with such alleged duties, however, are irrelevant to the duty to avoid servility. This is a duty to understand and affirm one's rights, not to promote one's own welfare. While it is usually in the interest of a person to affirm his rights, our Kantian argument against servility was not based upon this premise. Finally, a more subtle line of objection turns on the idea that, given that rights and duties are correlative, a person who acted contrary to a duty to oneself would have to be violating his own rights, which seems absurd.[6] This objection raises issues too complex to examine here. One should note, however, that I have tried to give a sense to saying that servility is contrary to a duty to oneself without presupposing that the servile person violates his own rights. If acts contrary to duties to others are always violations of their rights, then duties to oneself are not parallel with duties to others to that extent. But this does not mean that it is empty or pointless to say that a duty is to oneself.

My argument against servility may prompt some to say that the duty is "to morality" rather than "to oneself". All this means, however, is that the duty is derived from a basic requirement to respect the provisions of morality; and in this sense every duty is a duty "to morality". My duties to my children are also derivative from a general requirement to respect moral principles, but they are still duties *to* them.

Kant suggests that duties to oneself are a precondition of duties to others. On our account of servility, there is at least one sense in which this is so. Insofar as the servile person is ignorant of his own rights, he is not in an adequate position to appreciate the rights of others. Misunderstanding the moral basis for his equal status with others, he is necessarily liable to underestimate the rights of those with whom he classifies himself. On the other hand, if he plays the servile role knowingly, then, barring special

[6] This, I take it, is part of M. G. Singer's objection to duties to oneself in *Generalization in Ethics* (New York: Alfred A. Knopf, 1961), pp. 311–18. I have attempted to examine Singer's arguments in detail elsewhere.

explanation, he displays a lack of concern to see the principles of morality acknowledged and respected and thus the absence of one motive which can move a moral person to respect the rights of others. In either case, the servile person's lack of self-respect necessarily puts him in a less than ideal position to respect others. Failure to fulfill one duty to oneself, then, renders a person liable to violate duties to others. This, however, is a consequence of our argument against servility, not a presupposition of it.

ROBERT BAKER
"Pricks" and "Chicks":
A Plea for "Persons"

I. Talking About Women

There is a school of philosophers who believe that one starts philosophizing not by examining whatever it is one is philosophizing about, but by examining the words we use to designate the subject examined. I must confess my allegiance to this school. The import of this confession is that this is an essay on women's liberation.

There seems to be a curious malady that affects those philosophers who, in order, to analyze anything, must examine the way we talk about it; they seem to be incapable of talking about anything without talking about their talk about it—and, once again, I must confess to being typical. Thus I shall argue, first, that the way in which we identify something reflects our conception of it; second, that the conception of women embedded in our language is male chauvinistic; third, that the conceptual revisions proposed by the feminist movement are confused; and finally, that at the root of the problem is both our conception of sex, and the very structure of sexual identification.

II. Identification and Conception

I am not going to defend the position that the terms we utilize to identify something reflect our conception of it; I shall simply explain and illustrate a simplified version of this thesis. Let us assume that any term which can be (meaningfully) substituted for x in the following statements is a term used to identify something: "Where is the x?" "Who is the x?" Some of the terms that can be substituted for x in the above expressions are metaphors; I shall refer to such metaphors as metaphorical identifications. For example, Southerners frequently say such things as "Where did that girl get to?" and "Who is the new boy that Lou hired to help out at the filling station?" If the persons the terms are applied to are adult Afro-Americans then "girl" and "boy" are metaphorical identifications. The fact that the metaphorical identification in question is standard in the language reflects the fact that certain characteristics of the objects properly classified as boys or girls (e.g., immaturity, inability to take care of themselves, need for guidance, etc.) are generally held by those who use identifications, to be properly attributable to Afro-Americans. One might say that the whole theory of Southern white paternalism is implicit in the metaphorical identification "boy." (Just as the rejection of paternalism is implicit in the standardized Afro-American forms of address "Man" and "Woman"— e.g., "Hey Man, how are you?")

Most of what I am going to say in the rest of this essay is only significant if the way we metaphorically identify something is not a superficial bit of conceptually irrelevant happenstance, but rather a reflection of our conceptual structure. Thus if my reader is to accept my analysis, he must understand the significance of metaphorical identifications. The Southerner who identifies adult Afro-American males as "boys" may feel that this identification is "just the way people talk"; but for a group to talk that way, it must think that way. In the next few paragraphs I shall adduce what I hope is a persuasive example; an example of how, in one clear case, the change in the way we identify something paralleled the change in the way we think.

Until the 1960s Afro-Americans were identified by such terms as "Negro" and "colored" (the respectable terms) and by the more disreputable "nigger," "spook," "kink," etc. Recently there has been an unsuccessful attempt to replace the respectable identifications with such terms as "African," "Afro-American," and a more successful attempt to replace them with "black." The most outspoken champions of this linguistic reform were those who argued that nonviolence must be abandoned for Black Power (Stokely Carmichael, H. Rap Brown); that integration must be abandoned in favor of separation (the Black Muslims: Malcolm X, Muhammad Ali, etc.), and that Afro-Americans were an internal colony in the alien world of Babylon who must arm themselves against the possibility of extermination (the Black Panthers: Eldridge Cleaver, Huey Newton, etc.). All these movements and their partisans wished to stress that Afro-Americans were different from other Americans and could not be merged with them because the difference between the two was as great as that between black and white. Linguistically, of course, "black" and "white" are antonyms; and it is precisely this sense of oppositeness that those who see the Afro-American as alienated, separated, and nonintegratable wish to 153 capture with the term "black." Moreover, as any good dictionary makes clear, in some contexts, "black" is synonymous with "deadly," "sinister," "wicked," "evil," etc. The new militants were trying to create just this picture of the black man—civil rights and Uncle Tomism were dead, the ghost of Nat Turner was to be resurrected, Freedom Now or pay the price, the ballot or the bullet, "Violence is as American as Cherry Pie"—the new strategy was that the white man would either give the black man his due or pay the price in violence. Since, conceptually, a "black man" was an object to be feared, ("black" can be synonymous with "deadly," etc.) while a "colored man" or a "Negro" was not, the new strategy required that the "Negro" be supplanted by the "black" man. White America resisted the proposed linguistic reform quite vehemently until hundreds of riots forced the admission that the Afro-American was indeed black.

Now to the point. I have suggested that the word "black" replaced the word "Negro" because there was a change in our conceptual structure. One is likely to reply that while all that I have said above is well and good, one had, after all, no choice about the matter. White people are identified in terms of their skin color as whites; clearly if we are to recognize what is in reality nothing but the truth that in this society people are conscious of skin color, to treat blacks as equals is merely to identify them by their skin color, which is black. That is, one might argue that while there was a change in verbiage, we have not reason to think that there was a parallel conceptual change. If the term "black" has all the associations I talked about above, that is unfortunate; but in the context the use of the term "black" to identify the people formerly identified as "Negroes" is natural, inevitable, and in and of itself, neutral; black is, after all, the skin color of the people in question. (Notice that this defense of the natural-inevitable-and-neutral conception of identification quite nicely circumvents the possible use of such seemingly innocuous terms as "Afro-American" and "African," by suggesting that in this society it is *skin color* which is the relevant variable.)

The great flaw in this analysis is that the actual skin color of virtually all of the people whom we call "black" is not black at all. The color tones range from light yellow to a deep umber which occasionally is literally black. The skin color of most Afro-Americans is best designated by the word "brown." Yet "brown" is not a term which is standard for identifying Afro-Americans. For example, if someone asked "Who was the brown who designed Washington, D.C.?" we would not know how to construe the question. We might attempt to read "brown" as the proper name "Brown" —(Do you mean Arthur Brown, the designer?) We would have no trouble understanding the sentence "Who was the black (Negro, colored guy, etc.) who designed Washington, D.C.?"—("Oh, you mean Benjamin Banneker"). Clearly "brown" is not a standard term of identification for Afro-Americans. I hope that it is equally clear that "black" has become the

154

standard way of identifying Afro-Americans not because the term was natural, inevitable, and in the context, neutral, but because of its occasional synonymy with "sinister" and because as an antonym to "white" it best fitted the conceptual needs of those who saw race relations in terms of intensifying and insurmountable antonymies. If one accepts this point, then one must admit that there is a close connection between the way in which we identify things, and the way in which we conceive them—and thus it should be also clear why I wish to talk about the way in which women are identified in English. (Thus, for example, one would expect Black Muslims, who continually use the term "black *man*"—viz., "the black *man's* rights"—to be more chauvinistic than Afro-Americans who use the term "black *people*" or "black *folk*.")

III.   Ways of Identifying Women[1]

It may at first seem trivial to note that women (and men) are identified sexually; but, conceptually, this is extremely significant. To appreciate the significance of this fact, it is helpful to imagine a language in which proper names and personal pronouns do not reflect the sex of the person designated by them (as they do in our language). I have been told that in some oriental languages pronouns and proper names reflect social status rather than sex; but whether or not there actually exists such a language is irrelevant, for it is easy enough to imagine what one would be like. Let us then imagine a language where the proper names were sexually neutral (e.g., "Xanthe") so that one cannot tell from hearing a name whether the person so named is male or female—; a language in which the personal pronouns were "under" and "over." "Under" would be the personal pronoun appropriate for all those who were younger than thirty, while "over" would be appropriate to persons older than thirty. In such a language, instead of saying such things as "Where do you think *he* is living now?" one would say such things as "Where do you think *under* is living now?"

What would one be tempted to say about a cultural community which employed such a language? Clearly, one would wish to say that they thought that for purposes of intelligible communication it was more important to know a person's age grouping than the person's height, sex, race,

---

[1] The underlying techniques used in this essay were all developed (primarily by Austin and Strawson) to deal with the problems of metaphysics and epistemology. All I have done is attempt to apply them to other areas; I should note, however, that I rely rather heavily on metaphorical identifications, and that first philosophy tends not to require the analysis of such superficial aspects of language. Note also that it is an empirical matter whether or not people do use words in a certain way. In this essay I am just going to assume that the reader uses words more or less as my students do; for I gathered the data on which words we use to identify women, etc., simply by asking students. If the reader doesn't use terms as my students do, then what I say may be totally inapplicable to him.

hair coloring, or parentage. (There are many actual cultures, of course, in which people are identified by names that reflect their parentage; viz. Abu ben Adam—Abu son of Adam.) I think that one would also want to claim that this people would not have reflected these differences in the pronominal structure of their language if they did not believe that the differences between "unders" and "overs" was such that a statement would frequently have one meaning if it were about an "under" and a different meaning if it were about an "over." Once again, I shall illustrate what I have in mind with an example. In feudal times if a serf said "My Lord said to do this" that assertion was radically different from "Freeman John said to do this" since (presumably) the former had the status of a command, while the latter did not. Hence the conventions of Middle English required that one refer to people in such a way as to indicate their social status. Analogously, one would not distinguish between pronominal references according to the age differences in the persons referred to were there no shift in meaning involved.

If we apply the lesson illustrated by this imaginary language to our own, I think that it should be clear that in our language—since proper nouns and pronouns reflect sex rather than age, race, parentage, social status, religion, etc.—we believe that one of the most important things one can know about a person is that person's sex. (And, indeed, this is the first thing one seeks to determine about a newborn babe—our first question is almost invariably "Is it a boy or a girl?".) Moreover, we would not reflect this important difference pronominally did we not also believe that statements frequently mean one thing when applied to males, and something else when applied to females. Perhaps the most striking aspect of the conceptual discrimination reflected in our language is that man is, as it were, essentially human, whereas woman is only accidentally so.

This charge may seem rather extreme, but consider the following synonyms (which are readily confirmed by any dictionary). "Humanity" is synonymous with "mankind" but not with "womankind." "Man" can be substituted for "humanity" or "mankind" in any sentence in which the terms "mankind" or "humanity" occur without changing the meaning of the sentence, but significantly, "woman" cannot. Thus, the following expressions are all synonymous with each other: "humanity's great achievements"; "mankind's great achievements"; "man's great achievements." "Women's great achievements" is not synonymous with any of these. To highlight the degree to which women are excluded from humanity, let me point out that it is something of a truism to say that "man is a rational animal," whereas "woman is a rational animal" is quite debatable. Clearly, if "man" in the first assertion embraced both men and women, the second assertion would be just as much a truism as the first.[2]

[2] It is also interesting to talk about the technical terms that philosophers use. One fairly standard bit of technical terminology is "trouser word." J. L. Austin

Humanity, it would seem, is a male prerogative. Women are not (and, indeed, until recently, were not legally) human, but only biological mechanisms by which mankind reproduced itself. (And hence, just as one of the political goals of feminism is the removal of the legal barriers which impose upon women a less than human status, one of the conceptual goals of women's liberation is to alter our conceptual structure so that some day "mankind" will be regarded as an improper and vestigial ellipsis for "humankind" and "man" will have no special privileges in relation to "human being" that "woman" does not have.[3])

The major question before us is "How are women conceived of in our culture?" I have been trying to answer this question by talking about how they are identified. I first considered pronominal identification; now I wish to turn to identification through other types of noun phrases. Methods of nonpronominal identification can be discovered by determining which terms could be substituted for "woman" in such sentences as "Who is that woman over there?" without changing the meaning of the sentence. Virtually no term is interchangeable with "woman" in this sentence for all speakers on all occasions. Even "lady," which most speakers would accept as synonymous with "woman" in that sentence, will not do for a speaker who applies the term "lady" only to those women who display manners, poise, and sensitivity. In most contexts, some large group of students in one or more of my classes will accept the following types of terms as more

---

invented this bit of jargon to indicate which term in a pair of antonyms is important. Austin called the important term a "trouser word" because "it is the use which wears the trousers." Even in the language of philosophy, to be important is to play the male role. Of course, the antifeminism implicit in the language of technical philosophy is hardly comparable to the male chauvinism embedded in commonplaces of ordinary discourse.

[3] Although I thought it inappropriate to dwell on these matters in the text, it is quite clear that we do *not* associate many positions with females—as the following story brings out. I related this conundrum both to students in my regular courses and to students I teach in some experimental courses at a nearby community college. Among those students who had not previously heard the story, only native Swedes invariably resolved the problem; less than half of the students from an upper-class background would get it (eventually), while lower class and black students virtually never figured it out. Radical students, women, even members of women's liberation groups, fared no better than anyone else with their same class background. The story goes as follows: A little boy is wheeled into the emergency room of a hospital. The surgeon on emergency call looks at the boy and says, "I'm sorry I cannot operate on this child, he is my son." The surgeon was not the boy's father. In what relation did the surgeon stand to the child? Most students did not give any answer. The most frequent answer given was that the surgeon had fathered the boy illegitimately. (Others suggested that the surgeon had divorced the boy's mother and remarried and hence was not legally the boy's father.) Even though the story was related as a part of a lecture on women's liberation, at best only twenty percent of the written answers gave the correct and obvious answer—the surgeon was the boy's mother.

157

or less interchangeable with "woman." (An asterisk [*] will indicate inter-changes acceptable to both males and females; a plus, [+], terms restricted to black students only; terms with neither an asterisk nor a plus before them are accepted by all males but are not normally used by women.)

A. Neutral Terms
*lady
*gal
*girl (especially re. co-worker in office or factory.)
* +sister
*broad (Originally in the animal category, but most people do not think of the term as meaning pregnant cow.)

B. Animal
*chick
bird
fox
vixen
filly
bitch (Many do not know the literal meaning of the term; some men and most women construe this use as a pejorative; they think of "bitch" in the context of "bitchy," i.e., snappy, nasty, etc.; but a large group of men claim that it is a standard, nonpejorative term of identification —which may indicate that women have come to be thought of, by a large subclass of men, as shrews.)

C. Plaything
babe
doll
cuddly

D. Gender (Association with articles of clothing typically worn by those in the female gender role.)
skirt
hem

E. Sexual
snatch
cunt
ass
twat
piece (of ass, etc.)
lay

pussy (Could be put in the animal category, but most users associated it
    with slang expression indicating the female pubic region.)
+ hammer (Relates to anatomical analogy between hammer and breasts)
    There are many other usages (e.g., "bunny," "sweat hog") but these
    were not recognized as standard by as much as 10 percent of any
    given class.

The students in my classes reported that the most frequently used terms
of identification are in the neutral and animal classifications (although men
in their forties claim to use the gender classifications quite a bit) and that
the least frequently used terms of identification are sexual. Fortunately,
however, I am not interested in the frequency of such usages, only in
whether the use is standard enough to be recognized as an identification
among some group or other. (Recall that "brown" was not a standardized
term of identification and hence we could not make sense out of "Who was
the brown who planned Washington, D.C.?" Similarly, one has trouble
with "Who was the breasts who planned Washington, D.C.?" but not with
"Who was the babe [doll, chick, skirt, etc.] who planned D.C.?")

Except for two of the animal terms ("chick" and "broad"—but note
that "broad" is probably neutral today), women do not typically identify
themselves in sexual terms, nor in gender terms, as playthings or as animals; *only males use nonneutral terms to identify women.* Hence, it would
seem that there is a male conception of women and a female conception.
Only males identify women as foxes, babes, skirts, or cunts (and since all
the other nonneutral identifications are male, it is reasonable to assume that
the identification of a woman as a chick is primarily a male conception that
some women have adopted).

What kind of conception do men have of women? Clearly they think
that women share certain properties with certain types of animals, toys,
and playthings; they conceive of them in terms of the clothes associated
with the female gender role; and lastly (and, if my classes are any indication, least frequently) they conceive of women in terms of those parts of
their anatomy associated with sexual intercourse (i.e., as the identification
"lay" indicated quite clearly, as sexual partners).

The first two nonneutral male classifications—B, animal, and C, plaything—are *prima facie* denigrating (and I mean this in the literal sense of
"making one like a 'nigger' "). Consider the animal classification. All of
the terms listed, with the possible exception of "bird," refer to animals that
are either domesticated for servitude (to *man*) or hunted for sport. First,
let's consider the term "bird." When I asked my students what sort of birds
might be indicated they suggested: chick, canary, chicken (one member
in his forties had suggested "canary" as a term of identification), pigeon,
dove, parakeet, and hummingbird (only one member). With the exception
of the hummingbird (which like all the birds suggested is generally thought 159

to be diminutive and pretty), all of the birds are domesticated, usually as pets (which reminds one that "my pet" is an expression of endearment); none of the birds were predators, or symbols of intelligence or nobility (as are the owl, the eagle, the hawk, and the falcon) nor did large but beautiful birds seem appropriate (e.g., pheasants, peacocks, and swans). If one construes the bird terms (and, for that matter, "filly") as applicable to women because they are thought of as beautiful, or at least, pretty, *there is nothing denigrating about them.* If, on the other hand, the common properties which underlie the metaphorical identification are domesticity and servitude, then, they are indeed, denigrating (for myself I think that both domesticity and prettiness underlie the identification). "Broad," of course, is, or at least was, clearly denigrating, since nothing renders more service to the farmer than a pregnant cow, and such animals are not commonly thought of as the paradigms of beauty.

With one exception, all of the animal terms reflect a male conception of women as either domesticated servants or as pets (or both). Indeed, some of the terms reflect a conception of women first as pets and then as servants. Thus, when a pretty, cuddly little chick grows older, she becomes a very useful servant—the egg-laying hen.

"Vixen" and "fox" (two variants of the same term) are the one clear exception. None of the other animals with whom women are metaphorically identified are generally thought to be intelligent, aggressive, or independent—but the fox is. A chick is a soft, cuddly, entertaining, pretty, diminutive, domesticated, and dumb, animal. A fox too is soft, cuddly, entertaining, pretty, and diminutive, but it is neither dependent nor dumb. It is aggressive, intelligent, and a minor predator (indeed, it preys on chicks) and frequently outsmarts (i.e., outfoxes) men.

Thus the term "fox" or "vixen" is generally taken to be a compliment by both men and women, and, compared to any of the animal or plaything terms, it is indeed a compliment. Yet, considered in and of itself, the conception of a woman as a fox is not really complimentary at all; for the major connection between *man* and fox is that of predator and prey. The fox is an animal which men chase, and hunt and kill for sport. If women are conceived of as foxes, then they are conceived of as prey that is fun to hunt.

Let me now consider the plaything identifications. Only one sentence is necessary. *All the plaything identifications are clearly denigrating, since they assimilate women to the status of mindless or dependent objects.* "Doll" is to male paternalism what "boy" is to white paternalism.

At this point in our survey of male conceptions of women, without exception, every male identification discussed is clearly antithetical to the conception of women as human beings. (Recall that "man" was synonymous with "human" whereas "woman" was not.) Since the way we talk, and especially the way we identify, is the way in which we conceive of things, any movement dedicated to breaking the bonds of female servitude must destroy these ways of identifying and hence of conceiving of women. Only when both sexes find the terms "babe," "doll," "chick," "broad," etc., as objectionable as "boy" and "nigger" will women come to be conceived of as independent *human beings*.

The two remaining unexamined male identifications are gender and sex. There seems to be nothing objectionable about gender identifications *per se*. That is, women are metaphorically identified as skirts because, in this culture, skirts, like women, are peculiarly female. Indeed, if one accepts the view that the slogan *female and proud* should play the same role for women's liberation that the slogan *black and beautiful* plays for the black liberation movement, then female clothes should be worn with the same pride as Afro clothes. (Of course, one can argue that the skirt, like the cropped-down Afro, is a sign of bondage and hence both the item of clothing and the identification with it are to be rejected—i.e., cropped-down Afros are to Uncle Tom what skirts are to Uncle Mom.)

The last category, the sexual identifications, are obviously sexual, and frequently vulgar—for a variety of reasons I shall consider the import and nature of these identifications in a separate section.

IV. Men Ought Not to Think of Women as Sex Objects

The feminists have proposed many reforms, and most of them are clearly desirable: e.g. equal opportunity of self-development, equal pay for equal work, free day-care centers, etc. One feminist proposal, however, is peculiarly conceptual and enormously perplexing. I call this proposal peculiarly conceptual because, unlike the other reforms, it is directed at getting people to think differently. The proposal is that *men should not think of women (and women should not think of themselves) as sex objects*. In the rest of this essay I shall explore this nostrum, and I shall do so for two reasons. First, because the process of exploration should reveal the depth of the problem confronting the feminists; and second, because the feminists themselves seem to be entangled in the very concepts that obstruct their liberation.

To see why I find this proposal puzzling, one has to ask what it is to think of something as a sex object.

If a known object is an object we know, and an unidentified object is an object we have not identified, while a desired object is an object we desire, what then is a sex object? Clearly, a sex object is an object we have sex with. Hence to think of a woman as a sex object is to think of her as someone to have sexual relations with, and when the feminist proposes that men refrain from thinking of women in this way, *she is proposing that men not think of women as persons with whom one has sexual relations*.

161

What are we to make of this proposal? Is the feminist suggesting that women should not be conceived of in this way because such a conception is "dirty"? To conceive of sex and sex organs as dirty, is simply to be a prude. "Shit" is the paradigm case of a dirty word. It is a dirty word because the item it designates is taboo; it is literally unclean and untouchable (as opposed to something designated by what I call a curse-word, which is not untouchable but rather something to be feared—"damn" and "hell" are curse words; "piss" is a dirty word). If one claims that "cunt" (or "fuck") is a dirty word, then one holds that what this term designates is unclean and taboo—thus if one holds that the terms for sexual intercourse or sexual organs are dirty, one has accepted puritanism. If one is a puritan and a feminist, then indeed one ought to subscribe to the slogan *men should not conceive of women as sexual objects*. What is hard to understand is why anyone but a puritan (or, perhaps, a homosexual) would promulgate this slogan; yet most feminists, who are neither lesbians nor puritans, accept this slogan. Why?

A word about slogans. Philosophical slogans have been the subject of considerable analysis. They have the peculiar property (given a certain seemingly sound background story) of being obviously true, yet obviously false. "Men should not conceive of women as sex objects" is, I suggest, like a philosophical slogan in this respect. The immediate reaction of any humanistically oriented person on first hearing the slogan is to agree with it—yet the more one probes the meaning of the slogan the less likely one is to give one's assent. Philosophical analysts attempt to separate out the various elements involved in such slogans; to render the true-false slogan into a series of statements, some of which are true, some false, and others, perhaps, only probable—and this is what I am trying to do with the slogan in question. I have argued so far that one of the elements that seems to be implicit in the slogan is a rejection of women as the sexual partners for men, and that although this position might be proper for a homosexual or puritanical movement, it seems inappropriate to feminism. I am going to proceed to show that at least two other interpretations of the slogan lead to inappropriate results; but I shall argue that there are at least two respects in which the slogan is profoundly correct—even if misleadingly stated.

One plausible, but inappropriate, interpretation of "men ought not to conceive of women as sex objects" is that men ought not to conceive of women *exclusively* as sexual partners. The problem with this interpretation is that everyone can agree with it. Women are conceived of as companions, toys, servants, and even sisters, wives, and mothers—and hence not exclusively as sexual partners. Thus this slogan loses its revisionary impact since even a male chauvinist could accept the slogan without changing his conceptual structure in any way—which is only to say that men do not usually identify or conceive of woman as sexual partners (recall that the sexual method of identification of women (as "lays" etc., clearly indicates sexual partnership) was the *least* frequently used.

Yet another interpretation—what might be called the Kantian interpretation—is suggested by the term "object" in "sex object." This interpretation too has a certain amount of plausibility. The idea is that men should not treat woman as animate machines designed to masturbate men, or as conquests that allow men to "score" for purposes of building their egos. Both of these variations rest on the view that to be treated as an object is to be treated as less than human (i.e., to be treated as a machine or a score). Such relations between men and women are indeed immoral and there are, no doubt, men who believe in "scoring." Unfortunately, however, this interpretation—although it would render the slogan quite apt—also fails because of its restricted scope. When the feminists argue that men should not treat women as sex objects they are talking not *only* about fraternity boys and members of the Playboy club, they are talking about all males in our society. The charge is that in our society men treat women as sex objects rather than as persons—and it is this universality of scope that the present interpretation fails to secure. *Nonetheless, one of the reasons that we are prone to assent to the unrestricted charge that men treat women as sex objects is that the restricted charge is entirely correct.*

One might be tempted to argue that the charge that men treat women as sex objects is correct since such a conception underlies the most frequently used animal and plaything identifications; that is, these identifications indicate a sexual context in which the female is used as an object. Thus, it might be argued that the female fox is chased and slayed if she is four-legged, but, chased and layed if she is two-legged. Even if one admits the sexual context is *implicit* in *some* animal and plaything identifications, one will not have the generality required because, for the most part, the plaything and animal identifications themselves are nonsexual—most of them do not involve a sexual context. A pregnant cow, a toy doll, and a filly are hardly what one would call erotic objects. Babies do not normally excite sexual passion; and anyone whose erotic interests are directed toward chicks, canaries, parakeets, or other birds is clearly perverse. The animals and playthings to whom women are assimilated in the standard metaphorical identifications are not symbols of desire, eroticism, or passion (as, for example, a bull might be).

What is objectionable in the animal and plaything identifications is not the fact that some of these identifications reflect a sexual context, but rather that—regardless of the context—these identifications reflect a conception of women as mindless servants (whether animate or inanimate is irrelevant). The point is not that men ought not to think of women in sexual terms, but that they ought to think of them as human beings; and the slogan *Men should not think of women as sex objects,* is only appropriate when a man thinking of a woman as a sexual partner automatically 163 conceives of her as something less than human. It is precisely this anti-humanism implicit in the male concept of sex that we have as yet, failed to uncover—but then, of course, we have not yet examined the language we use to identify sexual acts.

V. Our Conception of Sexual Intercourse

Two profound insights underlie the slogan that "Men ought not conceive of women as sexual objects"; both have the generality of scope that justifies the universality with which the feminists apply the slogan; neither can be put as simply as the slogan. The first is that the conception of sexual intercourse that we have in this culture is antithetical to the conception of women as human beings—as persons rather than objects. (Recall that this is congruent with the fact that we noted earlier: "man" can be substituted for "humanity"; "woman" cannot.)

Many feminists have attempted to argue just this point, and perhaps the most famous defender of this view is Kate Millett (*Sexual Politics,* Doubleday 1971,—but see also *Sisterhood Is Powerful,* Robin Morgan, ed., Vintage Books, 1970). Millett unfortunately faces the problem of trying to make a point about our conceptual structure without having an adequate set of tools for analyzing conceptual structures. She is thus forced into the relatively weak position of analyzing the western-male conceptual structure on the basis of descriptions of sexual intercourse penned by three novelists: Henry Miller, Norman Mailer, and Jean Genet.

The following lines from Mailer are typical of the passages she quotes.

I had one of those splittings of a second where the senses fly out and there in
that instant the itch reached into me and drew me out and I jammed
up her ass and came as if I'd been flung across the room. She let out a cry
of rage.

The point for Millett is not the heterosexual sodomy, but the cry of rage. In sex, women are victimized, hurt, "contemptible female objects" who, to cite one of her quotes from Genet, "does not even have . . . the importance the sadist attaches to his victim."

Millett goes on to argue that the position of sexual ascendancy—man on top, woman on bottom—reflects the power relations in the society. She puts her point quite nicely in her introduction to her chapter on the theory of sexual politics.

The three instances of sexual description we have examined so far were
remarkable for the large part notions of ascendancy and power played within
them. Coitus can scarcely be said to take place in a vacuum; although
of itself it appears a biological and physical activity, it is set so deeply within

164

the larger context of human affairs that it serves as a charged
microcosm of the variety of attitudes and values to which the culture
subscribes. Among other things it may serve as a model of sexual politics on
an individual or personal plane.

Millett's book has been assailed by any number of reviewers, including
Irving Howe and Norman Mailer, and there are strong grounds for many
of the accusations against her.

The most serious charge is that she takes some passages from the supposedly autobiographical novels of three exceedingly atypical men: Miller,
Mailer, and Genet (if we are to accept the novels as autobiographical: a
sex-obsessed femcophilic womanizer, a sodomist, and a homosexual) and
argues that their conception of women (and especially Genet's conception
of the female role in homosexuality) is the *general* male conception of
women. Not only does she adduce very meager evidence for this rather
dubious conclusion—for example, one would not want to argue that all
men masturbate using cored apples, on the grounds that Miller's alter ego
does this in one of Miller's novels—but she goes on to argue that since
male chauvinism exists outside the bedroom, the Genet-Mailer-Miller description of the female sexual role *in* the bedroom is the major way men
conceive of women *outside* the context of the bedroom.

Although Millett's analysis has been justifiably castigated by critics, I
think that the analysis itself is fundamentally correct, and what I now
intend to do is develop a more substantial foundation for Millett's analysis.

The question Millett was dealing with was conceptual. Millett is, in
effect, asking about the nature of our conception of sexual roles. She tried
to answer this question by analyzing novels; I shall attempt to answer this
question by analyzing the terms we use to identify coitus; or more tech-
nically, the terms that function synonomously with "had sexual intercourse
with" in a sentence of the form "*A* had sexual intercourse with *B*." The
following is a list of some commonly used synonyms; numerous others
that are not as widely used have been omitted, for example, "diddled,"
"laid pipe with," etc.

screwed
layed
fucked
had
did it with (to)
banged
balled
humped
slept with
made love to

Now, for a select group of these verbs, names for males are the subjects of sentences with active constructions (i.e., where the subject is said to be doing the activity); and names for females require passive constructions (i.e., they are the recipients of the activity—whatever is done is done to them). Thus, we would not say "Jane did it to Dick," although we will say "Dick did it to Jane." Again, Dick bangs Jane, Jane does not bang Dick; Dick humps Jane, Jane does not hump Dick. In contrast, verbs like "did it with" do not require an active role for the male; thus, "Dick did it with Jane, and Jane with Dick." Again, Jane may make love to Dick, just as Dick makes love to Jane and Jane sleeps with Dick as easily as Dick sleeps with Jane. (My students were undecided about "layed"— most thought that it would be unusual indeed for Jane to lay Dick, unless she played the masculine role of seducer-aggressor.)

The sentences thus form the following pairs (those nonconjoined singular noun phrases where a female subject requires a passive construction are marked with the number sign [#]. The asterisk [*] indicates that the sentence in question is not a sentence of English if it is taken as synonymous with the sentence heading the column.[4])

Dick has sexual intercourse with Jane

Dick screwed Jane #	Dick humped Jane
Dick layed Jane #	Dick balled Jane
Dick fucked Jane #	Dick did it with Jane
Dick had Jane #	Dick slept with Jane
Dick did it to Jane #	Dick made love to Jane
Dick banged Jane #	

Jane had sexual intercourse with Dick

Jane was screwed by Dick	Jane slept with Dick
Jane was layed by Dick	Jane made love to Dick
Jane was fucked by Dick	*Jane screwed Dick
Jane was had by Dick	*Jane layed Dick (?)

4 For further analysis of verbs indicating copulation see "A Note on Conjoined Noun Phrases," *Journal of Philosophical Linguistics,* Vol. I, No. 2, Great Expectations, Evanston, Illinois. Reprinted with "English Sentences Without Overt Grammatical Subject" in Zwicky, Salus, Binnick, and Vanek (eds.), *Studies Out in Left Field: Defamatory Essays Presented to James D. McCawley* (Linguistic Research Inc., Edmonton, 1971). The puritanism in our society is such that both of these articles are pseudoanonymously published under the name of Quang Phuc Dong; Mr. Dong, however, has a fondness for citing and criticizing the articles and theories of Professor James McCawley, Department of Linguistics, University of Chicago. Professor McCawley himself was kind enough to criticize an earlier draft of this essay.

I should also like to thank G. E. M. Anscombe for some suggestions concerning this essay.

*Jane was done by Dick

Jane was banged by Dick

Jane was humped by Dick

Jane balled Dick (?)

Jane did it with Dick

*Jane fucked Dick

*Jane had Dick

*Jane did it to Dick

*Jane banged Dick

*Jane humped Dick

These lists make clear that within the standard view of sexual intercourse, males, or at least names for males, seem to play a different role than females, since male subjects play an active role in the language of screwing, fucking, having, doing it, and perhaps, laying, while female subjects play a passive role.

The asymmetrical nature of the relationship indicated by the sentences marked with a "#" is confirmed by the fact that the form "*xed with each other" is acceptable for the non# sentences, but not for those that require a male subject. Thus:

Dick and Jane had sexual intercourse with each other

Dick and Jane made love to each other

Dick and Jane slept with each other

Dick and Jane did it with each other

Dick and Jane balled with each other (*?)

*Dick and Jane banged with each other

*Dick and Jane did it to each other

*Dick and Jane had each other

*Dick and Jane fucked each other

*(?)Dick and Jane layed each other

*Dick and Jane screwed each other

It should be clear, therefore, that our language reflects a difference between the male and female sexual roles, and hence that we conceive of the male and female roles in different ways. The question that now arises is what difference in our conception of the male and female sexual roles requires active constructions for males and passive for females.

One way of explaining why the active construction is for males and the passive construction is for females is that this grammatical asymmetry merely reflects the natural physiological asymmetry between men and women: the asymmetry of to screw and to be screwed, to insert into and to be inserted into. That is, it might be argued that the difference between masculine and feminine grammatical roles merely reflects a difference naturally required by the anatomy of males and females. This explanation is inadequate. Anatomical differences do not determine how we are to conceptualize the relation between penis and vagina during intercourse. Thus one can easily imagine a society in which the female normally played the active role during intercourse; where female sub- 167 jects required active constructions with verbs indicating copulation; and where the standard metaphors were terms like "engulfing"—that is, instead of saying "he screwed her" they would say "she engulfed him." It follows that the use of passive constructions for female subjects of verbs indicating copulation does not reflect differences determined by human anatomy, but rather reflects those generated by human customs.

What I am going to argue next is that the passive construction of verbs indicating coitus (i.e., indicating the female position) can *also* be used to indicate that a person is being harmed. I am then going to argue that the metaphor involved would only make sense if we conceive of the female role in intercourse as that of a person being harmed (or being taken advantage of).

Passive constructions of "fucked," "screwed" and "had" indicate the female role. They also can be used to indicate being harmed. Thus, in all of the following sentences Marion plays the female role: "Bobbie fucked Marion," "Bobbie screwed Marion," "Bobbie had Marion," "Marion was fucked," "Marion was screwed," and "Marion was had." All of the statements are equivocal. They might literally mean that someone had sexual intercourse with Marion (who played the female role), or they might mean, metaphorically, that Marion was deceived, hurt, or taken advantage of. Thus, we say things as "I've been screwed" ("fucked," "had," "taken," etc.) when we have been treated unfairly, been sold shoddy merchandise, when someone cons us out of valuables, etc. Now throughout this essay, I have been arguing that metaphors are applied to things only if what the term actually applies to shares one or more properties with what the term metaphorically applies to. Thus, the female sexual role must have something in common with being conned or being sold shoddy merchandise. The only suitable property is that of being harmed, deceived, or taken advantage of. *Hence we conceive of a person who plays the female sexual role as someone who is being harmed* —(i.e., screwed, fucked, etc.).

It might be objected that this is clearly wrong, since, in the list preceding, the terms without the # sign do not indicate someone being harmed, and hence we do not conceive of having intercourse as being harmed. The point about the *unsignated terms,* however, is that the unsignated terms can take both females and males as subjects (in active constructions) and thus *do not pick out the female role.* This demonstrates that we conceive of sexual roles in such a way that only females are taken advantage of in intercourse.

The best part of solving a puzzle is when all of the pieces fall into place. If the subjects of the passive construction are being harmed, presumably the subjects of the active constructions ought to be doing harm, and, indeed, we do conceive of these subjects in precisely this way. Suppose you are angry at someone and wish to express your malevolence as forcefully as possible without actually committing an act of physical violence. If you are inclined to be vulgar, you can make the sign of the erect male cock by clenching your fist while raising your middle finger, or by clenching your fist and erecting your arm and shouting such things as "screw you," "up yours," or "fuck you." In other words, one of the strongest possible ways of telling someone that you wish to harm him is to tell him to assume the female sexual role relative to you. Again to say to someone "Go fuck yourself" is to order him to harm himself; while to call someone a "mother fucker" is not so much a play on his Oedipal fears, but rather to accuse him of being so low that he would inflict the greatest imaginable harm (fucking) upon that person who is most dear to him (his mother).

Clearly we conceive of the male sexual role as that of hurting the person in the female role—but lest my reader have any doubts, let me provide two further bits of confirming evidence: one linguistic, one non-linguistic.

One of the English terms for a person who hurts (and takes advantage of) others is the term "prick." This metaphorical identification would not make sense unless the bastard in question (i.e., the person outside the bonds of legitimacy) was thought to share some characteristics attributed to things that are literally pricks. As a verb, "prick" literally means to hurt—viz., "I pricked myself with a needle"; but the usage in question is as a noun. As a noun, "prick" is a colloquial term for "penis." Thus the question before us is what characteristic is shared by a penis and a person who harms others (or alternatively a penis and being stuck by a needle). Clearly, no physical characteristic is relevant; (physical characteristics might underlie the Yiddish metaphorical attribution "schmuck," but one would have to analyze Yiddish usage to determine this), hence the shared characteristic is nonphysical; the only relevant shared nonphysical characteristic is that both a literal prick and a figurative prick are agents that harm people.

Now for the nonlinguistic evidence. Imagine two doors; in front of each door a line of people; behind each door is a room; in each room is a bed; on each bed is a person. The line in front of one room consists of beautiful women, and on the bed in that room is a man having intercourse with each of these women in turn. Now one may think any number of things about this scene; the man may be in heaven, or enjoying himself at a bordello, or perhaps one only wonders at the oddness of it all. One doesn't think that he is being hurt, or violated or degraded —or at least the possibility does not immediately suggest itself, although one could conceive of situations where this was what was happening (especially, e.g., if the man was impotent). Now, consider the other line. Imagine that the figure on the bed is a woman, and that the line consists of handsome smiling men. The woman is having intercourse with 169 each of these men in turn. It immediately strikes one that the woman is being degraded, violated, etc.—"that poor woman."

When one man fucks many women, he is a playboy, etc., and gains status; when a woman is fucked by many men, she degrades herself and loses stature.

Our conceptual inventory is now complete enough for us to return to the task of analyzing the slogan that men ought not to think of women as sex objects.

I think that it is now plausible to argue that the appeal of the slogan "Men ought not to think of women as sex objects," and the thrust of much of the literature produced by contemporary feminists turns on something much deeper than a rejection of "scoring" (i.e., the utilization of sexual "conquests" to gain esteem) and yet is neither a call for homosexuality nor for puritanism.

The slogan is best understood as a call for a new conception of the male and female sexual roles. If the analysis developed above is correct our present conception of sexuality is such that to be a man is to be a person capable of brutalizing women (witness the slogans "The marines will make a man out of you!"; "The army builds *men!*" which are widely accepted and which simply state that learning how to kill people will make a person more manly). Such a conception of manhood not only bodes ill for a society led by such men but is clearly inimical to the best interests of women. It is only natural for women to reject such a sexual role, and it would seem the duty of any moral person to support their efforts, to redefine our conception not only of fucking, but of the fucker (man) and the fucked (woman).

This brings me to my final point. We are a society which is preoccupied with sex. As I noted previously, proper nouns and pronouns of our language are such that it is difficult to talk about someone without indicating that person's sex. This convention would not be part of the grammar of our language if we did not believe that knowledge of a person's sex was crucial to understanding what is said about that person. Another way of putting this point is that sexual discrimination permeates our conceptual structure. Such discrimination is clearly inimical to any movement toward sexual egalitarianism and virtually defeats its purpose at the outset. (Imagine, for example, that black people were always referred to as "them" and whites as "us," and that proper names for blacks always had an x suffix at the end. Clearly any movement for integration as equals would require the removal of these discriminatory indicators. Thus at the height of the melting pot era immigrants Americanized their names: "Bellinsky" became "Bell," "Burnstein" became "Burns," and "Lubitch" became "Baker".)

I should therefore like to close this essay by proposing that contemporary feminists should advocate: the use of neutral proper names; the elimination of gender from our language (as I have done in this paper); and should vigorously protest any use of third person pronouns "he" and "she" as examples of sexist discrimination (perhaps "person" would be a good third person pronoun); for, as one parent of linguistic analysis once said, "The limits of our language are the limits of our world."

SHARON HILL
Self-Determination and Autonomy

Some have spoken as if the sexual revolution amounts to greatly increased liberality about sex. Recently there is talk that it will not be accomplished until there is an end to sexual discrimination and women as well as men are liberated. Not a few are certain that they know what changes are required to liberate women. Many are content with things as they are, and some are merely complacent about this revolution. Others are perplexed though not unwilling to change, for those they love seem unhappy. In winding a way through an unreal but not unlikely dispute, I suggest a way of allaying these perplexities and justifying some of these demands. If what I say about how to set aside certain doubts about women's liberation is plausible, then I imagine radical changes are in order, not just about how we view and treat women, but also about how we view and treat men and children. What these changes are is difficult to say. In any case, my interest here is primarily in principles and arguments which might be used to explain and justify some of the demands now being made in the name of women's liberation. But to begin with, the dispute.

I. The Dispute

Over the years, John and Harriet have had long arguments about women's liberation. Both have come a long way. When Harriet first decided that she could not find self-fulfillment without a paying job, John felt threatened and protested that it would not be proper. But now he is reconciled and even insists that women get equal pay for equal work. He supports the Equal Rights Amendment and urges his company to give talented and well-trained women an equal chance at job opportuni-

Used with the permission of the author.

I wish to thank Thomas Hill, Jr., and Richard Wasserstrom who read earlier versions of this paper and made many helpful comments and suggestions. 171

ties. He has given up as muddled his old belief that women are naturally inferior to men in intelligence, objectivity, emotional stability and the like. He acknowledges that women have often been treated in degrading ways, and like many liberals, he has tried hard to purge his vocabulary of such words as "chick," "broad," and "piece." He even tries, not always successfully, to avoid references like "the girls in the office." Women, he says, have as much right to happiness as men, and so he is ready to oppose any social scheme which makes them, relative to men, systematically discontent or unhappy. But this is as far as he will go.

Harriet says that this is not far enough. And the dispute came to a head when she protested to the school principal and finally to the school board about their daughter's education. Harriet was distressed that girls were encouraged in numerous ways to accept the traditional feminine role. For example, the practice at most school dances was for girls to wait to be asked by boys. The school had well-developed and financed athletic programs for boys, but few for girls, and very little staff to help girls to develop their skills. The counselors were comparatively uninterested in advising girls about their futures. When they did, they assumed that, for the most part, appropriate careers for girls were as secretaries, decorators, teachers, nurses or medical assistants. Students' programs were then tailored for these vocations. These, in turn, were viewed as stop-gap or carry-over measures to enable girls to get through any periods in which they were not married or supported by someone. If they did marry, it was assumed that there would be children and a home to which the woman should devote herself.

Harriet gradually came to see that her objections to these practices arose as she faced her own feelings of resentment and betrayal at the kinds of opportunities and counseling she had early in life. Though she acknowledged the occasion of her objections, she also became convinced that her complaints were well founded. She was less clear how to support them, but her way of life seemed unnecessarily restrictive and she believed that she had interests and capacities which should have been developed but were not. She was irked, too, that she had never had a genuine opportunity to choose the way of life in which she and other women were so deeply involved. Whatever she might have chosen and whether or not she liked having a family and the feminine virtues, she felt that she had never really had any choice. She realized that part of the problem was that she herself had not regarded these as proper objects of her own choice. This failure she thought was the result of a complicated and overlapping set of teachings which had it that women were almost inevitably unfulfilled without having children, that normally they were better at raising children than men and men better suited for

172 earning a living. Consequently, as the story went, the current division

of labor is really most efficient, better for almost everyone and thus best. Both men and women were said to have duties associated with these roles. She now resents these teachings, justifiably she believes. She became especially anxious as she saw her daughter falling into the patterns of behavior and belief to which she now objects and so she complained to the school board.

John found Harriet less than convincing on these matters. It is important to oppose sex roles, he argued, if the roles function in a way which humiliates or degrades women or deprives them of political or economic rights. If these abuses could be avoided, he thinks the current standard division of labor and roles would not only be legitimate but quite a good way to arrange things. Someone, after all, needs to care for children and most women seem quite content. These arrangements seem natural to him. He suspects that women are naturally more sensitive and so make better parents for the very young; moreover, those he knows who have either not married or not had children seem to be weak and stunted characters or else hostile and aggressive. These observations suggest to him that most people, including women, are well off under something like the current division of labor and role. He acknowledges some, at least, of the difficulties about his belief that women are naturally suited for the domestic role. He does not, for example, rely on personality inventories of women versus men, because the traits they test for are bound to be influenced by the culture in which people grow up including, of course, some of the practices Harriet finds obnoxious. He does not appeal to the obvious physical differences between men and women, and he regards as irrelevant, at least in the modern world, appeals to differences in brute strength. Still he believes that some of the relevant differences are natural. He supports his suspicion by appeals to anthropological evidence about widely divergent groups in which women have almost invariably had the domestic role and quite often the traits which suit them for raising children and managing households. Were this not natural, he thinks it would not be so frequent. He has been known to remark that estrogen is associated with passive as opposed to aggressive personality traits, reminding Harriet that women maintain a higher level of this hormone than men. He suspects that the thwarted and hostile women he finds among the unmarried and childless result from frustration of the natural capacities of women for close emotional relations. There are, he admits, extraordinarily ambitious women who would be frustrated in following the traditional pattern; but a society which grants full political and economic rights to all adults can accommodate these exceptional people. Consequently, he resists the idea that there is something wrong with encouraging in young girls the feminine traits he so likes. He wants his daughter to be ladylike in figure and personality and hopes, for her sake, that she will never choose a career at the expense 173 of having a family. He communicates this to her in innumerable, sometimes subtle, sometimes direct ways.

It is at this point that Harriet becomes most exasperated and even despairing. By all the conventional criteria, John seems liberal enough. He believes in equal pay for equal work and equal opportunities for those of equal achievement, motivation and talent. He acknowledges that women have been deprived of income, opportunities, power and their associated satisfactions by unfair social practices of various sorts. What he envisages is a world in which these injustices are eradicated but one in which women remain sensitive, understanding and charming, and in which most take up a domestic life while most men take up a paying vocation. Since he thinks it only efficient to prepare people for these likely different but quite natural futures, he thinks sound educational policy calls for certain subtle differences in the training of males and females. Harriet, on the other hand, believes that her resentment is justified, that she has been wronged in some way and would continue to be wronged if the world were magically transformed to match John's dreams. She becomes most desperate when she thinks of her daughter who is being similarly wronged.

The perplexed, like John, may say, "But where is the difficulty?" They understand complaints about violations of political and economic rights, like the right to vote, hold office and receive equal pay for equal work. They admit that a person would be wronged if gratuitously insulted or deliberately injured. But none of these seem to fit the case of Harriet or her daughter at least in the world John wants. There is no reason to believe they will be insulted, and it is difficult to pick out any political or economic right which we could confidently claim would be violated. Even if we think that Harriet and her daughter have been injured by the workings of the social system in this world, it is not clear that the harm was deliberate. No definite person designed the social system for the purpose of keeping women down, much less for the purpose of harming Harriet; it, like Topsy, just growed. If that is the case, whatever harm they may have suffered seems in important respects like a natural misfortune and not a deliberate wrong. If Harriet's objections to John's views can be defended, it must be on some other pattern of reasoning.

In the following, I shall try to isolate and explain some principles which could be used to justify Harriet's feelings about her own life and her protests of school practices. Roughly, I shall argue that if adults are viewed as having a right of self-determination, then Harriet and other adult women do nothing inappropriate in eschewing a traditional role nor do they have duties directly associated with such a role. Moreover, if as adults, we are to have a right of self-determination which is meaningful, we ought not be treated in ways which distort or prevent the
174 development of the capacity for autonomous choice. I do not attempt

to justify the claim that adults have a right of self-determination nor the claim that viewing adults as having such a right is better than any of a variety of other ways of regarding them, for example, as potential contributors to the general welfare or to some social or economic ideal. I hope that some of what I say will make respect for a right of self-determination attractive, but here I only set out to explain something about the right.

I try this line of argument, first, because I think it a promising one to explain the depth and kind of feeling generated in women who begin thinking seriously about their lives and their daughters' prospects. In the end, it may help explain why such pervasive changes are required and why some of them must be changes in attitude. Secondly, it seems possible with this reasoning to avoid some philosophical and empirical difficulties involved in more familiar arguments. For example, a number of people argue for sweeping changes in the treatment of women on the grounds that the resulting system will be more efficient in turning out happy individuals or in using the available pool of natural abilities. One problem here, of course, is to determine what is to count as being happy and so what is to count as evidence that some new system will be more efficient producing it than the present one. Others suggest that there has been a deliberate male conspiracy to keep women in the kitchen and out of the most lucrative and satisfying jobs. There are innumerable problems about what could be meant by "deliberate conspiracy" in this case; there does not seem to have been a conspiratorial meeting attended by anyone much less by most men or by representative men. It does not even seem plausible that some rather large number of men have consciously intended to keep women out of the mainstream of social and economic life at least in recent history. Even if some clear sense can be given to the notion, successful completion of the argument would require complicated empirical inquiries. Although it is true that a deliberate conspiracy to do wrong makes things rather worse, what seems important here is rather the wrong that has been done. If questions about the deliberateness of the wrongs are important at all, they seem to belong rather with attempts to decide to whom the burdens of change may legitimately fall. Finally, the line of reasoning I propose directly undercuts two of the kinds of arguments John suggested against Harriet. In the end, he claimed that his views about women and educational policy could be supported by appeals to efficient ways of arranging for child rearing as well as the natural suitability of current sex roles and the division of labor. Once a right of self-determination is granted, however, it does not matter whether the complex facts John appeals to are true or not, that is, it does not matter whether current sex roles are efficient means of rearing children or whether women, on the average, are better at domestic affairs than men. There are other considerations having to 175 do with self-determination and autonomy which make these alleged facts irrelevant and which do justice to Harriet's response. She does not need to await empirical evidence about what is suitable for women and what makes women and children happy in order to know that something is wrong.

II. The Right of Self-Determination

To say that persons or states have a right of self-determination is to say minimally that they and only they have the authority to determine certain sorts of things. This does not necessarily mean that they have the power or capacity to determine these things, but rather that they have the title to. Sovereign states, for example, are widely regarded as having rather extensive authority to choose for themselves; they are said to have a right to determine how and who shall govern them, to have rights to determine for themselves what their ideals shall be, how they will allocate funds, what forms of culture they will support and devote themselves to, and the like. Having title to make these choices means that they have a right to expect others not to interfere with the legitimate exercise of their authority and a right to protect themselves from interference. It means, too, that they have a right to expect to carry on the processes of their government without foreign interest groups bribing their officials, and without being flooded with propaganda designed to influence the outcome of elections and the like. All this seems rather uncontroversial. More controversially, a small dependent state might claim that its right of self-determination was violated by threats of loss of essential support just because it failed to adopt the policies its larger, more affluent neighbor wanted. Withdrawal of such support makes it impossible to exercise its right of self-determination, consequently, threatening such withdrawal may be counted as incompatible with respecting the small nation's right. This may seem especially plausible where the support is well established, and where the threat is given for failure, say, to give up some local ritual or some trading policy mildly contrary to the interests of the affluent. Mature adults are often said to have a similar right, for example, to determine for themselves what their vocations shall be, whether to use their money for steaks or tennis balls, their leisure time for concerts or back-packing, and so on. Again, what is meant is that only they have the authority to make such choices, that others ought to refrain from interfering with the legitimate exercise of the title, and that they have the right to protect themselves from interference. Individuals may, if they wish, delegate parts of that authority. They give up some of it when they take a job, put themselves under the tutelage of an instructor or decide to let a friend choose the day's activities. Even in these cases, however, it is only they who may decide not

to exercise the right.

Like other rights, this one is limited. Sovereign states do not have a right to make war on their neighbors for profit. Individuals do not have the right to harm or restrain one another simply for the fun of it however much they may want to. The limitations on this right will be roughly what is prohibited by other moral principles. Although these limitations cannot be spelled out here, we could get agreement about a number of cases like injuring another for one's own pleasure. While this does not give us a satisfactory criterion for what morality forbids, it is enough to permit us to focus on the right of self-determination confident that it need not commit us to silly views about the rights of sadists.

Obviously the right is not in fact granted or guaranteed to everyone by the state or culture in which they live. Like the rights to life, liberty and security, it is a natural right, that is, it is thought of as belonging to everyone simply by virtue of their being human and so it is a right which everyone has equally. Society can and should protect us in exercising it in some ways, for example, in choosing a vocation. A state should not, however, enforce all the behavior and attitudes which might be appropriate in someone who believes in the right of self-determination. For example, I suspect that some committed to honoring the right of self-determination would regard themselves as bound not to influence those close to them by exploiting any emotional dependence they might have. If this is a reasonable attitude, it does not seem that it would be wise for a society to protect us from the influence of those on whom we are dependent emotionally. The right of self-determination does not, in general, determine a particular outcome as the just or only acceptable one. It rather outlines a range of considerations which should come into play whenever we are trying to adjust our behavior or attitudes to persons making permissible choices. I call it a right because it is thought of as a title and because the considerations it picks out as relevant mark off an area in which we do not allow conclusions about either the general good or an individual's good to be decisive. The point of the right of self-determination is to enable people to work out their own way of life in response to their own assessments of current conditions and their own interests, capacities and needs, rather than to secure the minimal conditions for living or to maximize a person's expectations for satisfaction. In respecting an individual's right of self-determination, one expresses a certain view about that person which is not a belief that one is acting for the good of that person (at least in some narrow sense of the person's good having to do with his or her welfare or happiness). The rough idea is that persons are, among other things, creatures who have title to select what they will do from among the permitted options. This establishes a presumption that other people should refrain from interfering with our selections whatever their content. They should refrain even if they do not like the particular choice or if they correctly believe that it is not in the chooser or society's long-term interests.

Applying the right of self-determination to questions about the treatment of women, John and Harriet readily agree on a number of conclusions. First, bending the will of a woman by force is wrong. Conquering nations violate the right of self-determination and so does the man who keeps a woman or harem in servitude however nice he may make their lives. The man who prevents his wife from attending her therapy session or sky-diving lessons by force also violates this right. He does not allow her to do what she has a right to do. He violates the right whether he prevents her because he fears the changes in her personality, or is jealous of her handsome teacher, or because he correctly and sincerely believes the group is harming her or that sky-diving is dangerous. So long as we are talking about a mature woman who is choosing nothing prohibited by morality, it does not matter whether he acts in her own interests or not, he will still have violated her right to determine on her own what she will do.

The husband who achieves similar results by threatening to divorce his wife who has no other means of support may also violate her right to self-determination. This would be like a powerful state that threatens to cut off aid whenever a dependent state acts contrary to its wishes. Some may feel more certain that the threatening husband makes a mistake than that the powerful state violates the right of self-determination of the smaller state. Someone may note that it is quite accepted that relations among nations proceed by threat and counter threat. Things do not go all that well when carried on in this manner, but they go on. When husband, wife, parents or friends resort to such tactics, the relation of friendship or love is effectively off. Someone who is prepared to use such tactics displays special callousness toward the friendship. If they care about maintaining it at all, they will have made a grave blunder. They will also have indicated that they are indifferent to the feelings of the individual they threaten. They show a willingness to harm them, and this may be considered a moral fault for which there is no analogue in the threatening state. These observations can be accepted, I think, without weakening the original claim. We began by saying that states and persons have a right to make certain sorts of choices for themselves without interference by force or threat of force or withdrawal of essential support. This implies in both the case of states and individuals that there is a special wrong in threatening those who are making perfectly permissible policy, namely the violation of this right; that other wrongs and blunders may also be involved is beside the point.

Finally, if a group of men were to conspire together to discourage their wives from taking jobs or joining groups where women work through their problems together, they would violate the women's right of self-determination. These conclusions are not a problem for a liberal like 178 John. He is not tempted to prevent his wife from going anywhere by force. Nor is he tempted to use the threat of loss of support in order to win a battle. He knows that would be to lose the war, and he wants her love and respect, not simply her presence and obedience. He knows, too, that his wife could find other means of support in this world. She is able, and this is not the nineteenth century where his support may well have been essential. Moreover, he has always been inclined to resist the temptation to adjust his relation to his wife in response to or in concert with others. So far the right of self-determination adds nothing startling to the list of legitimate complaints that women might have.

It does, however, add something to the reasons we may have for objecting to a variety of policies. For example, it means that some wrong is involved in the above cases apart from the objectionable techniques used to bring about the desired result. The wrong is not either simply that someone made a conscious attempt to interfere with someone's legitimate choice, but rather that someone's selections were blocked or interfered with. In addition, the right of self-determination takes us a good way toward directly undermining John's views about women. He seemed to think that it was perfectly all right to advise adult women to engage in and stick with traditional domestic life styles on the grounds that it was efficient and natural for women to have them. What appears to be the case now, is that, even if it is efficient and natural, enticing women to take this role for these reasons is likely to interfere with their right of self-determination. It is likely to do this because it encourages the false belief that these reasons are or should be decisive in determining an important lifetime commitment. Instead the right of self-determination establishes a presumption that within the range of permissible selections a person's uncoerced, unforced spontaneous responses to her own interests and circumstances are or should be decisive. It does not matter whether the interference is deliberate or non-deliberate or whether it is well-intended guidance. Once it is known that a practice, policy or teaching interferes, there is good reason to believe it should be revised. That is not to say that there is always sufficient reason, for this presumption like others can be rebutted. If the rebuttal is to work, however, it must give something like an equally important reason, for example, that revising the policy will cause perpetual or irremediable disaster, that it represents the only possible way for anyone to have a decent life, that some other natural right would be violated or that some particular person is not capable of exercising the right for some special reason. While this is not an adequate account of what will rebut the presumption established by the right of self-determination, it does suggest that John's arguments were simply beside the point if he was trying to justify policies which encourage a group of people to take up some lifetime role.

It is even difficult to see why the argument from efficiency should be 179 effective in persuading a particular person like Harriet to exercise her right of self-determination by choosing a traditional domestic role. It seemed to be an argument that society in general will run more efficiently under the current role division, and it is not obvious that it is wise to make important lifetime commitments on the grounds that society in general is likely to run more efficiently. If the argument is rather that Harriet's life would work more smoothly and efficiently if she has a domestic role, then the right of self-determination says that it is up to her whether to take these facts (supposing them to be determinate) as decisive. If she does not want to struggle or if she does not fancy some other definite way of life, she may prefer the so-called efficient way. At the same time, it should be noted that it is a little difficult to determine what is meant by saying that her life would be more efficient, for surely that will depend to some very great extent on what her ends are. If her ends are to develop some talents she has or even to remain a lively and developing person, this may not be an efficient route at all. Nor is the evidence clear that this is the most efficient way for her to raise healthy children; that will depend to some extent on whom she thinks of raising them with, how that is likely to work, and so on.

The argument that the current division of labor and role is in some deep and important sense natural is also beside the point. If these roles are "natural," then persons who are taught that they have a right of self-determination will tend to choose them. There is, then, no need to worry about what it might mean to say that the sex roles are natural, nor to await the empirical evidence about whether they are before we decide whether it is justifiable to encourage them or not. Moreover, taking the perspective of someone committed to the right of self-determination accords nicely with a reasonable suspicion that what is natural for persons is not determinate. Sometimes when people talk about a person being a natural in a role, they have in mind that given the person's background, achievement and current interests, he or she would do well at it and flourish in it. Sometimes, however, they attempt to tie success and satisfaction with a role more closely to a person's genetic heritage. In this sense, a role is natural for persons if because of their genetic endowment, they have certain special capacities which enable them to play the role well, the role does not frustrate some deep need and it provides opportunities for them to express their central interests. In the former sense, it is probably true that the domestic role is a natural for most women now, but it is the latter sense that plays a part in arguments that the current division of labor and role is natural and therefore justifiable. In a modern industrial community, however, there must be at the very least several life styles which could be natural in this sense for most any normal person. That is, there must be several ways of life in which their natural talents could be used and which would provide circumstances for the expression of a range of strong human interests without tending to frustrate deep needs. What the right of self-determination gives people is the title to let their own preferences put together a way of life. If these preferences are properly weighted by themselves and others, then the style they put together is very likely to be one which makes use of their special capacities, does not frustrate and provides opportunities for the expression of central interests.

Unfortunately, it is not clear that the right of self-determination will complete the job Harriet hoped it would; that is, adjudicate in her favor the dispute with John over their daughter's education. John, we may suppose, says that it will not do this because the right of self-determination is a right of adults and not of children. He says that it would be absurd if not impossible and immoral to treat young children as if they had the right to make major choices regarding their futures. Either we would give the children no guidance at all, in which case they may well feel lost and have too little discipline to gain what they will want as adults, or we would be required to use the techniques of rational persuasion that we use with adults. This, too, is likely to have disastrous consequences. At best it leads children to confuse the forms of reasoning with reasonable choosing and tends to make them overrate their capacities and status. Guidance must be given to children for their own sakes, and it will be guidance which inevitably will influence what they want later in life. The question is what kind of guidance to give. John wants to encourage in his daughter the feminine virtues. He wants her to be graceful in figure and movement, he is afraid that too much concentration on competitive athletic games will spoil her development. He thinks the modern dance and figure control programs the school has for girls are all that is important for them. He wants her to remain sweet and coy, affectionate and sensitive, and to develop feminine interests in cooking, sewing and children. Not only does he do what he can to encourage these traits in her, but he wants the school to. He thinks that Harriet and her friends have gone too far in complaining about the fact that only a few exceptionally talented or stubborn women are presented as professionals, and in demanding that the girls be taught the manual arts as well as home economics.

In the following section, I argue that even if the right of self-determination is reserved for adults, John's arguments about his daughter's education do not succeed. Even if the right of self-determination does not itself directly limit the kinds of guidance we may give our children, it does in an indirect way.

III.   The Importance of Autonomy

Let us say that parents have the authority to make certain decisions affecting the welfare of their offspring. They have this authority because children lack the know-how and the physical and psychological resources 181 to make it on their own. Typically parents are supposed to exercise this authority in the interests of their children though sometimes they may exercise it for their own peace of mind, especially after nine and on weekends. Even given this picture of legitimate parental authority, there is something wrong with John's educational policies. There are, I think, two objections to teaching girls the traditional feminine virtues and role. First (A), such teaching interferes subtly with their exercise of the right of self-determination as mature women. Second (B), anyone committed to the right of self-determination and its importance has reasons for attaching special significance to the development of the capacity to exercise it autonomously.

(A) To begin with, when we say that mature persons have a right of self-determination, we mean that they are entitled to decide for themselves which career they will attempt, whether or whom to marry, whether to have children, how to spend their leisure time and the like. We all know that deciding for oneself is incompatible with being coerced at the time of choice, but there are subtle influences which may occur earlier and which interfere with the exercise of the right of self-determination.

Let us imagine that a school system has the following practices. First, the system leads girls to take up domestic activities and keeps them from others like competitive games and mechanics. Then, when women reach the age to choose how to spend their time, they have already developed the skills to enjoy cooking and sewing at a high level and discover, not surprisingly, that they like domestic tasks, and not car repair, carpentry or basketball. Surely the possibility that these latter might have been the objects of their choice is virtually extinguished. By hypothesis, home economics training for the girls has been successful, that is, many of them really have learned to manage themselves in the kitchen or sewing room so that they are creative and effective, and they have not made similar progress in the workroom. People tend to prefer doing what they are good at, and so women will tend to prefer cooking.

It might be said that at the age of reason, women have the right of self-determination, to choose, for example, to learn carpentry or mechanics, but the right to choose these things will not be worth much if at that time they do not have the possibility of getting satisfaction from these activities at some fairly advanced level because whatever original interest they might have had was never exposed. Not, of course, that everyone should be forced to take home economics, mechanics, and so on, but adults would have a reason to complain if they were systematically deprived of the opportunity to develop some legitimate interest; whereas, if the opportunity had been there and they failed to take it, they would not.

182 Secondly, the schools do not provide girls with information about

women's capacities except for domestic affairs like mothering and cooking. If this occurs, then when the girls become women, they will be unlikely to imagine alternatives and choose intelligently between them. If this were to happen, then women could not even freely choose a domestic life, since they would be likely to see it as the only possibility instead of one among several. Alternatively, suppose that girls are presented with a few examples of women professionals, but these are always presented as rare, extraordinary persons who had to pay a high price for their aspirations. They either gave up the possibility of developing a marriage or they withstood criticism and ostracism for their strange ambitions or both. This makes the cost of choosing another way of life seem so high that most would be unwilling to select it.

Imagine next that girls are rewarded for being patient, sensitive, responsive and obedient, but that displays of ambition and curiosity are met with frowns or silence. The result is that the girls learn to be passive, understanding and sensitive, and not at the same time confident, interested and active. What has happened is that the pattern of traits they develop suit them for domestic life, and when they come to choose between being a housewife and a doctor, they may judge quite correctly that given their current wants and temperament, housewifery is a better prospect for them. If, however, they had been rewarded for curiosity and ambition, the pattern of their personalities would have been different, and it might have been worthwhile for them to develop interests they have in, say, some science, and so to choose another style of life. The difficulty with the training they in fact had is that it has made such a choice unreasonable and done so without attending to the spontaneous and quite legitimate preferences of girls as they developed.

Finally, suppose that certain styles of dress and standards of etiquette are insisted upon for girls and that boys are encouraged to expect girls to meet these and admire those who meet them well. Anyone who deviates from the norm is made to feel uneasy or embarrassed. Imagine, too, that style of dress, while insignificant in itself, is associated with certain career roles and basic life styles. Dress in such a world serves to symbolize the career role and set up important expectations. When the time comes for a woman to choose what she will do, her expectations tend to be fixed not just with regard to the otherwise insignificant matter of dress, but also with regard to what role she will take up. When this happens, it is difficult for her to choose any unexpected role, for any deviation from expectations about her will produce stress and recall the uneasiness she felt upon breaking the dress code.

If the above practices in fact have the effects I envisage, they interfere with the right of self-determination of mature women. To believe that mature persons have a right of self-determination and that such practices are justifiable is rather like believing that Southern Blacks have a right to vote, but that Whites may legitimately ostracize those who exercise it. It would be like believing that Blacks have a right to eat where Whites do and that it would be merely impolite for Whites to stare as if they did not. In some important respects, it would be like a government maintaining that its citizens have a right to travel wherever they choose, but confiscating the passports of those who go to Cuba. If these analogies are acceptable, then even though the educational policies described above do not violate the right of self-determination, they should be changed. Or rather they should be revised unless it can be argued reasonably that each proposed revision would cause disaster or violate some equally important right.

(B) So far Harriet's commitment to the right of self-determination inclines her to prevent and avoid violations and to minimize interferences like those described above. If, however, she is also committed to the importance of the right, she will want those she cares about to exercise it and to exercise it in a worthwhile way. It is not in general true that belief that one has a right means that one cares about having it or exercising it; for example, the right to travel or to marry do not seem to be rights that one need care about exercising or having. The right of self-determination, however, seems importantly different at least when it is accepted for the suggested rationale. The right was granted to persons to enable them to work out their own way of life in response to their own assessment of their situation, interests and capacities because it was thought appropriate and important that persons work out their own way of life believing that they have a right to. We may ask why this is important, but that is beyond the scope of the present inquiry. It would require explaining the advantages of regarding persons in part as creators of their own way of life rather than merely contributors to the general welfare or some other social ideal.

Assuming, then, that Harriet is also committed to the importance of the right of self-determination, she will want those she loves to exercise it and that its exercise be worthwhile for them. The right of self-determination tends to be worth less to mature persons the fewer opportunities and more interferences they are confronted with and the more they have been trained to have personality traits which make them suited for some definite life role. To say further what tends to make the right worth more, it helps to ask what one would want for persons one loves as they exercise the right of self-determination. Using this device, we are blocked from regarding ourselves as proper determiners of their life style. We do, however, want their good, but partly because we cannot properly determine it and partly because we do not know what will confront them, we do not know what in particular will be good or best for them. Still something can be said about what we want for them.

First, talking of our children and not knowing what they will face, we shall want them to develop the kind of personality which will enable them to respond well to their circumstances whatever they are. We shall want them to have what might be called broadly useful traits, that is, traits which will be helpful whatever their interests and circumstances, traits like confidence, intelligence and discipline. Self-confidence is, for example, a trait which it is good to have because it is useful in a wide variety of ways and inevitably satisfying. Broadly useful traits are the kinds which make a wider range of alternatives feasible for those who have them and so are important for exercising the right of self-determination. We should set about teaching these, then, rather than those associated with some culturally variable sex role.

Secondly, given that our children when mature will have a right of self-determination and given our ignorance of what they will face, it is not in general reasonable for us to aim for a particular outcome of our children's choices, but rather to develop their capacity to make choices in a certain way, namely, autonomously. That is, at least we want them to make the selections free from certain kinds of pressure. We do not want their selections to be coerced, threatened or bribed, and we do not want them to succumb easily to seductive advice or the bare weight of tradition. Neither do we want their preferences to be neurotic or self-destructive even though there are admittedly circumstances in which neurotic responses pay. In short, we want them to have certain psychological strengths which will enable them to make sensible use of the right of self-determination.

To want our children's choices to be autonomous is also to want their selections to express genuine interests of theirs which arise spontaneously under certain conditions. These are the circumstances in which they have the above psychological strengths and as they are making rational assessments of their capacities and situation. The selections should be spontaneous under these conditions because those are the choices we think of as expressive of us as individuals, and those in turn are the selections we tend to find most deeply satisfying and with which we feel most comfortable. Although we do not usually know what in particular these interests will be, we do know that there are certain basic human interests which anyone might have regardless of their sex or other peculiarities about them. Basic human interests are those taken in the kinds of activities which typically individuals find satisfying and which are potentially healthy. For example, people are capable of gaining satisfaction directly in their work or indirectly because it provides them with income, they find successful friendships and love relations satisfying, they enjoy play and developing their talents. The capacities to enjoy each of these interests, unlike other human capacities—for example, for self-destruction, enmity, hostility, envy and so on—are potentially healthy. They are potentially healthy in that they can be coordinated in one per- 185 son to produce a satisfying way of life and styles of life in which these capacities are exploited (and the others minimized) are styles which can be coordinated together in a smooth way. What we can legitimately want and hope that our children have, then, are the satisfactions associated with each of these kinds of interests, and more rather than less. These are legitimate aspirations for us to have for our children because they are the kinds they would want to build their lives around if they were mature and reasonable and if the background conditions of life were decent. Given that these are legitimate aspirations, we should set about helping children understand these potential satisfactions vividly and not to suiting them for some particular lifetime role. Then when people are of an age to warrant saying they have a right of self-determination, ideally they will have psychological strengths and a vivid appreciation of the range of enjoyments possible for them so that they are able to work out a satisfying way of life which is an expression of their spontaneous preferences. This does not require that each be equally capable of fitting in anywhere, but only that there is for everyone some array of feasible options.

According to the preceding argument, young persons should be treated in whatever ways give them the strength and imagination to make use of their right of self-determination autonomously when they reach maturity. Treating them in ways which are believed to do this is a way of respecting the right they will have when they reach maturity. In addition, if one is to respect someone's right of self-determination fully, one must be willing to allow its exercise even when one believes it is being done badly. This suggests that some importance should be attached to the choices of people simply because they are attempts to arrive at the available alternative most in line with their autonomous preferences. For the most part, this will probably amount to keeping out of others' business. In those we care about and love, however, it will mean valuing and appreciating what they choose simply because it is their choice. This is, perhaps, one way of expressing our love. If so, then Harriet may have taken John's reticence about some of her projects as signs that he did not love her. Equally, of course, he may have believed that Harriet was a bit wacky and irresponsible, or he may not be committed to the right of self-determination or its importance. None of these is likely to sit well with Harriet, who we might imagine really has reached a vision about the moral life which is incompatible with John's view and with which she feels quite comfortable.

IRVING THALBERG
Visceral Racism

At a meeting shortly before his death, Malcolm X was asked by a young white listener: "What contribution can youth, especially students who are disgusted with racism, make to the black struggle for freedom?" Malcolm X's reply has become a familiar one: "Whites who are sincere should organize among themselves and figure out some strategy to break down prejudice that exists in white communities. . . . This has never been done."[1]

I will not offer strategies, but I will do what I can with fairly standard philosophical techniques to delineate one target for action. I hope that the social phenomenon I analyze is what polemical writers had in view when they coined the term 'visceral racism.' At any rate the phenomenon is worth bringing into sharper focus; and therefore I will keep the emotively charged term 'racism' out of my discussion as much as possible. Nevertheless when I do for convenience use the expression 'visceral racism', I want it to be clear that I am not belaboring old-fashioned white supremacy doctrines and practices. Adherents of white supremacy are still both numerous and influential; but I doubt that further analysis is needed to understand or to attack their position. What I examine here is more protectively camouflaged and philosophically challenging.

1. *Not a 'latent' form of white supremacy.* The main components of the earlier tradition I take to be: (a) factual claims that, in various respects, black people are 'inferior'; (b) normative conclusions, drawn from such factual claims, about how others ought to treat black Americans; (c) regional and national customs of discriminatory treatment that are vindicated by these normative conclusions.[2] All three elements appear in Chief Justice Taney's account of the status of slaves and free Negroes under the U.S. Constitution. Writing immediately before the Civil War in the *Dred Scott* decision, Taney says:

Reprinted from *The Monist,* Vol. 56, No. 4 (Oct. 1972), 43–63, LaSalle, Illinois, with the permission of the publisher and the author.

[1] In G. Breitman, ed., *Malcolm X Speaks* (New York: Grove Press, 1966), p. 221.

[2] For general analyses of prejudice and discriminatory behavior, consult the following: G. W. Allport, *The Nature of Prejudice* (New York: Addison-Wesley, 1954); G. E. Simpson and J. M. Yinger, *Racial and Cultural Minorities* (New York: Harper & Row, 1965); B. Lindzey and E. Aronson, eds., *Prejudice and Ethnic Relations* (New York: Addison-Wesley, 1969); H. Tajfel, "Cognitive Aspects of Prejudice," *Journal of Social Issues,* 25, No. 4, (1969), 79–97.

> They had for more than a century . . . been regarded as beings of an inferior order, and altogether unfit to associate with the white race . . .; and so far inferior, that they had no rights which the white man was bound to respect (19 How. [60 U.S.] 392 [1857]).

An equally frank statement is Senator Tillman's apology for the discriminatory post-Reconstruction customs of his state:

> In 1876, . . . the people of South Carolina had been living under negro rule for eight years. There was a condition bordering upon anarchy. . . . There was no incentive to labor. . . .
>
> They were taxing us to death and confiscating our property. We felt the very foundations of our civilization crumbling beneath our feet, [sic] that we were sure to be engulfed by the black flood of barbarians . . . In desperation we determined to take the government away from the negroes.
>
> We reorganized the Democratic party with one plank, . . . namely that "this is a white man's country and white men must govern it."
> (*Congressional Record*, 59th Congress, 1907, pp. 1440–1.)

In more recent times, 'respectable' white supremacists have been less forthright about their intention to subjugate blacks. On the other hand, a few biologists and social scientists have plugged *lacunae* in the vague theory of racial inferiority. Their most interesting hypotheses are that Negroid *homo sapiens* evolved much later, and from different sub-*sapiens* ancestors, than Caucasoids; and that the resulting differences in Negroid and Caucasoid brain morphology still determine such things as school achievement and crime rates. Along with data from archeology and brain physiology, comparative psychometric studies of children in the Georgia public schools from 1954 to 1962 have been introduced as evidence for such 'inferiority' hypotheses.[3] This evidence, the leading theories, and especially the normative conclusions that have been drawn from scientific theories of racial inferiority, all have received thorough criticism in scientific and popular journals.[4] So I will turn to contrasts between white

[3] Psychometric studies are: Robert T. Osborne, *Racial Differences in School Achievement* (Monograph No. 3 in a series published by *Mankind Quarterly* [Edinburgh, Scotland], 1962); and Audrey M. Shuey, *The Testing of Negro Intelligence* (Lynchburg, Va., 1958). More general theories are put forth in Wesley C. George, *The Biology of the Race Problem*, a 1962 study commissioned by the Governor of Alabama; and in Carleton Putnam, *Evolution and Race: New Evidence* (New York: National Putnam Letters Committee, 1962). Both George and Putnam draw their conclusions from the theoretical work and archeological research of Carleton S. Coon, as published in such books as *The Origin of Races* (New York: Alfred A. Knopf, 1962).

[4] For example, Theodosius Dobzhansky's review of Coon: "A Debatable Account of the Origin of Races," *Scientific American* 208, No. 2 (1963), 169–172. See also the exchange of letters between Coon and Dobzhansky (*Ibid.*, 208, No. 4 [1963], 12–14).

supremacist and visceral racist attitudes. This calls for a preliminary characterization of the visceral syndrome, to which I will add all-important details later.

By visceral racism I will mean a set of unacknowledged attitudes that afflict me and most other 'unprejudiced' whites, especially middle-class liberals. These attitudes are mainly dispositions to perceive and to describe social events in which black people figure. Our most noticeable proclivities are, first, to structure and report such events in a manner that 'screens out' social inequalities which are glaringly evident to black observers; and secondly to represent black people as helplessly dependent upon the white majority. The overall tendency is for 'visceral' whites to regard themselves as doing just about as well as can be expected with 'the race problem'. Of course they never regard themselves as the problem! Examples will emphasize how the visceral racist does not want to think of himself as hostile toward blacks or indifferent to their individual and collective aspirations.

This sketch explains why the visceral inclinations that I shall analyze here are not dissimulated white supremacy attitudes. To recognize your viscerally racist dispositions is *not* to avow that deep down you think black people are all over-sexed savages, or that you really like the caste system we have. It is to notice the protective cocoon of ignorance and distortion that we have spun about ourselves.

Before I review the inequities that we thereby manage to ignore, I want to answer a natural objection from liberal white readers. Many will indignantly complain, "I've never had any hostile feelings toward black people, so how can you call me a visceral or any other kind of racist?"

2. *Not 'feelings'*. The visceral dispositions I'm analyzing do not consist in sensations or emotions. In this regard, white supremacist and viscerally racist inclinations are similar. Neither type of attitude—or any other attitude I can think of—is made up of twinges, glows, tingles, tugs, fantasy images, and similar 'inner sensations'. Perhaps feelings of tension come over a Southern sheriff when he sees a 'mixed' couple. But these feelings are never all, or even part, of what we mean when we say that the sheriff has a white supremacist outlook, and that he displays his attitude in his responses and conduct toward the couple. One proof is that it is not self-contradictory to assert that he displayed white supremacist reactions but was perfectly calm—felt serene or 'felt nothing'—inside. Another proof is that the couple are in no danger from his 'inner feelings'. The threat to their rights and dignity comes from his tendency to respond with insults and worse. As for the visceral racist, we have an even stronger reason for denying that his attitude consists in feelings. However confused our notion of inner sensations may be, one thing is 189

sure: they cannot occur while the person who has them is totally un-aware of them. Now the peculiarity of viscerally racist attitudes, ac-cording to the hypothesis I will develop, is that a person with these attitudes systematically ignores features of the social situation of black people in this country. If his attitudes were 'inner sensations', he would be aware of them, and presumably his tendency to misperceive would to that extent diminish. But, as I will illustrate, there are people who systematically distort things and yet seem totally unaware that they do. Therefore their disposition to distort things cannot consist in 'inner sen-sations'. The other two arguments also prove that viscerally racist atti-tudes cannot be 'inner sensation' feelings.

How about emotions? Aren't these kinds of 'feelings' part of what we mean when we talk of white supremacist and viscerally racist attitudes? Again, no. The sheriff may be agitated by surges of hatred and malevo-lence. Visceral racists might experience a rush of embarrassment when they meet the 'mixed' couple. More generally, they may be troubled by emotions ranging from 'guilt' to uneasiness whenever they deal with black people who do not occupy a subordinate role. But such emotions are only concomitants; they are not essential to, much less identical with, white supremacist and visceral attitudes.

The 'no contradiction' argument again suffices to prove this. If you have a female sibling, then you must have a sister. It is inconsistent for anyone to assert that you have a female sibling and deny that you have a sister. By contrast, it is never inconsistent to report that a white su-premacist, or a visceral racist, was free of emotion when he displayed his attitude. Indeed, one sinister aspect of both types of attitude is that people who have them go about their business in such an unemotional, matter-of-fact way.

Although this explains why you can be a visceral racist and have no 'feelings' of hostility toward black people, some philosophers may com-plain that I have made the case too easy by assimilating all emotion to episodes of turbulence and agitation. Aren't some emotions, such as resentment and hatred, long-term dispositions? No doubt we can classify a white supremacist's hatred as a settled disposition, which only comes to be displayed on certain occasions. For example, we could say that he began despising black people when he was a child, that he only ceased briefly during military service, because he was in a combat team with black soldiers, and that his hatred developed again when he returned to his old neighborhood. Perhaps you want to stretch the concept of an emotion to comprise such cases. But then what would it mean to insist that the attitudes of a white supremacist and a visceral racist are emo-tions? Surely not that, during all times when they have these dispositions they are constantly—or intermittently—stirred by hostility or uneasiness?

That is precisely the implication you avoided by broadening the concept of emotion. So you are left with an altogether vacuous account. Moreover, it sounds odd to characterize a man as having a particular *emotion* since childhood. To speak of attitudes in this way is standard.

These negative remarks, to the effect that viscerally racist attitudes are neither 'inner sensations' nor emotions, give us minimal insight. As soon as I explain briefly what we are disposed to ignore and to distort when we are afflicted by viscerally racist attitudes, I will offer a more positive analysis.

3. *What the visceral racist overlooks.* Militant readers will have lost patience by now. To them my investigation will appear worthlessly academic, because admittedly there is so little practical difference between the familiar old white supremacist and the 'well-meaning' people whose attitudes I'm analyzing. The visceral racist will not throw a brick through the window of a new black neighbor. He won't assault black children who are bussed to the neighborhood school. But what does he do to protect them? Doesn't he let the redneck do his dirty-work for him? In general, doesn't he support institutions that oppress black people in nearly every area of social life? Right; and that is why I want to diagnose his visceral inclinations to misperceive our society as progressing with all deliberate speed toward equality.

For the benefit of nonmilitants, I will explain briefly the claim that there is almost no practical difference for the majority of blacks under liberals and their 'reformed' institutions, in comparison with the old days. No doubt there are more lucky blacks who 'make it' nowadays. Certainly more vote. Fewer lynchings occur. Blacks are no longer obliged to display humility and gratitude. Otherwise the statistics on the vast *majority* of black people in America show little alteration. Except for temporary economic gains during World War II and the Korean War, most blacks have continued to enjoy a very small share of the nation's fabled prosperity. Typically, the 500 largest industrial corporations earn around 40% of the gross national product. About 7,000 companies with 100 or more employees do 90% of manufacturing and 80% of the sales. About 1.6% of the population owns more than 80% of the stock of these top corporations and others. As you would expect, members of this group control corporate and government policy. Blacks have not gotten into this 1.6% group that owns and runs the country. The few whites who belong to it are usually inheritors of wealth. Most stock ends up in the hands of white women, because of their longevity.[5]

Turning to black wage-earners, experts attribute to them between 55%

---

[5] For convenient and abundant documentation, largely based on government statistics and other 'respectable' sources, consult Ferdinand Lundberg, *The Rich and the Super Rich* (New York: Bantam Books, 1969), esp. pp. 12–20, 295–298, 354–355, 927–946.

and 70% of the salary that whites receive for equivalent work.[6] Incidentally, the percentage *declines* when we consider blacks with 'higher' positions and more formal education, thus refuting the myth that serious study and 'drive' will be differentially rewarded. Working-class blacks are twice as likely to be unemployed or laid off. In nearly every profession—including our own, academic philosophy—blacks are grossly under-represented. The same is true with skilled trades. Labor unions have driven blacks out of some fields. This happened with locomotive engineers and firemen in the South. Construction workers' unions have kept blacks out. And in automotive industry, unions have confined blacks to low-paying, no-seniority positions.[7]

Black consumers face similar hindrances. They pay more to buy or rent deteriorated housing. Mortgages are nearly unavailable to a black home-buyer. If he obtains one, he will pay higher interest than whites do. Neighborhood segregation is rising, and black children attend increasingly segregated schools, where considerably less is spent per pupil than in white areas. Barely 2% of elective offices at all levels of government are held by blacks—and this marks a relatively big step forward during the last few years. In their relations with government, notably police, most blacks have made no progress at all. Black citizens and property-owners are virtually without police protection, while harrassment from police has grown. Ten to seventeen times as many black people are arrested for major violent crimes.[8] Large numbers, including 'bystanders', fall victims of unprovoked attacks by police. Their property rights, and Fourth Amendment immunity to arbitrary search and seizure, are violated constantly by police. Blacks still constitute the majority of the more than 200,000 in-

[6] The lower figure is given by Thomas F. Mayer, on the basis of U.S. Bureau of Census figures for 1939 and 1947–62, in his useful résumé, "The Position and Progress of Black America," reprinted by Radical Education Project (Ann Arbor, 1967). *The Report of the National Advisory Commission on Civil Disorders* (Washington, D.C.: Government Printing Office, 1968) gives the higher figure for 23 cities it surveyed. Since Mayer draws upon a wide variety of official and scholarly sources, I generally paraphrase his summary of the situation in jobs, housing, and education.

[7] For typical railroad cases, see *Steele v. L. and N. R. Co.,* 323 U.S. 192 (1944), and *Railroad Trainmen v. Howard,* 343 U.S. 768 (1951). In Chicago during the summer of 1969, the Coalition for United Community Action established that of 87,783 union workers in 19 building trades, only 2,251 were black, Latin, or from a similar minority. On the automotive industry, my source is Robert Dudnick, *Black Workers in Revolt* (New York: Guardian Pamphlets, 1969). For broader background, see Ray Marshall, *The Negro and Organized Labor* (New York: John Wiley & Sons, Inc., 1965), and (with V. M. Briggs, Jr.) *The Negro and Apprenticeship* (Baltimore: Johns Hopkins, 1967).

[8] This last figure comes from a report by the National Commission on the Causes and Prevention of Violence, summarized in the *Chicago Sun-Times,* November 24, 1969, pp. 5, 18.

mates of federal and state prisons and reformatories, and are the least likely to have received an impartial trial.

All in all, this lack of progress since the passing of white supremacy appears to confirm Dr. King's foreboding. He wrote in 1963:

I have almost reached the regrettable conclusion that the Negro's great stumbling block in the stride toward freedom is not the White Citizen's Council-er or the Ku Klux Klanner, but the white moderate who is more devoted to "order" than to justice. . . . Shallow understanding from people of goodwill is more frustrating than absolute misunderstanding from people of ill will.[9]

It's hard to believe that the visceral racist manages to ignore all this. But as I shall illustrate, he sometimes even turns the situation upside down, and imagines that with all the current 'favoritism' toward blacks, there is discrimination against whites! In any case, my method is straightforward. Rather than suspect most 'well-meaning' whites of hypocrisy, I will look for patterns of selective and distorted perception of this background when they describe social occurrences involving black people. Since these epistemic and linguistic patterns have been stamped into me, and since I have lived for years among the whites whose attitudes I'm analyzing, I will not burden this part of my essay with much documentation. But presumably sociologists can verify whether the patterns are as widespread as this native thinks they are. Sociologists will also have to decide whether the attitudes I delineate are important causes of white complacency toward the grim situation I've reviewed.

4. *Visceral racism and language.* Whatever their causal role may be, the attitudes which concern me are manifest in reports that 'unprejudiced' whites spontaneously give of what blacks do and undergo. Reports of a black observer are likely to be at variance. The psychiatrist C. A. Pinderhughes expresses this neatly:

What most whites perceive as an orderly American social system most blacks experience as unresponsive, unremitting, dehumanized, well-rationalized, quiet, courteous, institutionalized violence not unlike colonialism.[10]

A visceral racist's description will also clash with his own account of similar events which feature whites. You will notice these disparities with respect to what is emphasized and neglected; what causes and effects of the occurrence are recorded; and what motives are ascribed to participants.

[9] "Letter from a Birmingham City Jail," reprinted in *Civil Disobedience,* ed. by H. A. Bedau (New York: Pegasus, 1969), p. 81.

[10] "Understanding Black Power: Processes and Proposals," *American Journal of Psychiatry,* 125, No. 11 (1969), 1555.

5. *A hackneyed illustration* of these discrepancies is easiest to start with. Consider the type of event that engulfed the Watts district of Los Angeles in August 1965; Detroit and Newark in July 1967; and Prague, Czechoslovakia, in August 1968. Why throw Prague into the same basket? Weren't the Czechs rising up against Soviet tyranny? Indeed they were. And the black commentators I've read are nearly unanimous in saying that the residents of Watts rebelled too. By the following summer, for example, Stokely Carmichael was interpreting such events as "rebellion" (*New York Times,* July 29, 1966, p. 13:1). Of course the inhabitants of Watts, and hundreds of other black communities since 1964, had little chance of overcoming police and National Guard firepower. But weren't the Czechs, the Hungarians in 1956, before them the East Berliners in 1953, and the Warsaw Jews in 1944, just as disorganized, just as unlikely to free themselves? So far, then, I find no reason for the visceral racist to withhold the laudatory term 'uprising' when he describes the behavior of Watts residents. Ironically enough, insurance companies tried to avoid compensating local property-owners by appealing to "insurrection" clauses in their policies! (*New York Times,* August 16, 1965, p. 16:5, 6, 8) The closest that white spokesmen came to this was when Los Angeles Police Chief Parker reported "guerrilla warfare" (*New York Times,* August 14, 1965, p. 1:8), and California Governor Brown admitted "guerrilla fighting with gangsters" in Watts (*New York Times,* August 17, 1965, p. 1:8).

Nowhere in the white media do you find echoes of the indignation that was expressed when Soviet troops and tanks "invaded" Prague. On that occasion, Senator Tower declared that the USSR had shown it could not maintain its "hegemony without military force" (*New York Times,* August 23, 1968, p. 8:3). Watts, Detroit and Newark surely illustrate the same point. In admiration of the Czechs, the *New York Times* said that the "populace openly voices its defiance and hostility" to the Russian occupiers (August 22, 1968, p. 1:3–7). It lamented that a mood of "sadness, fear and helplessness" was descending on Prague (August 30, 1968, p. 2:7). How about the mood of an occupied black community? The visceral racist seems to block out these aspects of such incidents. He focusses instead on ghetto dwellers removing the proverbial color television set from their local credit store.

6. *Disguising politically significant acts as 'ordinary crimes'.* Here you might ask: "Weren't the so-called 'rebels' of Watts, Detroit and Newark only interested in looting, and in destroying rather than liberating their ghettos? Weren't they simply criminals?" I won't attempt to devise general criteria for distinguishing between criminal and political acts. I assume that a single item of behavior might qualify as both. What I am trying to get at is the distortion that occurs when behavior is written off as *merely* a violation of the property rights of merchants and landlords by looters

and arsonists. Perhaps the simplest antidote would be to notice how these same acts appear in the context of ghetto life. Psychiatrists W. H. Grier and P. M. Cobbs take such a view:

> The goods of America, piled high in the neighborhood stores, had been offered to [black people] with a price tag that made work slavery and made balancing a budget a farce . . . The available jobs paid so poorly and the prices (plus interest) of goods were so high that if one made a purchase he was entering upon years of indebtedness. . . .
> . . . At bottom, America remains a slave country which happens to have removed the slave laws from the books. The question we must ask is: What held the slave rebellion in check for so long?[11]

Besides ignoring the exploitation of black community residents by merchants and landlords, the visceral racist 'filters out' crimes by police that have contributed to nearly all the hundreds of ghetto outbreaks since the 1964 Harlem 'riots'. This ingredient has been recognized by the National Advisory Commission on Civil Disorders, although the Commission did not talk of police 'crimes'. Well-known books on Watts, Detroit and Newark document the background of official lawlessness in those black communities.[12] I won't go over that material; but I will take a 'miniature' illustration from local newspaper reporting of a more limited clash between blacks and authorities.

7. *Police crimes 'screened out'.* The general background of this story is conflict between black youth 'gangs' and police in the South Chicago suburb of Robbins. The situation became newsworthy when the Mayor of Robbins was shot in the leg as he answered the doorbell Halloween evening, 1970. Naturally a search was on for the miscreants. An article in *Chicago Tribune* for November 7 begins: "Four street gang members were charged yesterday with last Saturday's shooting of Marion Smith, Robbins mayor." Further along, and altogether secondary to the wounding of Mayor Smith, we read that Smith had called in special sheriff's investigators

> to patrol the suburb after two persons were shot to death Monday [Nov. 2, 1970], in a shoot-out with [Robbins] police outside the Richard Flowers Housing Project. . . .
> According to sheriff's police one of the two, Ronald Lee, 29, . . . was shot by a Robbins policeman, Sgt. Melvin Jessup, as he stood outside a doorway from which Robbins police said shots were fired at them. Lee was found to be unarmed.

[11] *Black Rage* (New York: Bantam Books, 1969), pp. 58–59.

[12] Robert Conot, *Rivers of Blood, Years of Darkness* (New York: Bantam Books, 1967); John Hersey, *The Algiers Motel Incident* (New York: Alfred A. Knopf, 1968); Tom Hayden, *Rebellion in Newark* (New York: Random House, 1967).   195

However, sheriff's police still are investigating who fired the shot which killed Miss Barbara Franks, 18, as she was riding past in a car toward her home. . . .

Police Chief Porter McKamey of Robbins said no disciplinary action was planned against Jessup. (p. 5)

In an interview reported by *Chicago Today,* there is another priceless statement by Chief McKamey: "If a shot from a policeman killed the girl, it's one of those unfortunate incidents." (November 6, p. 5) The surprise ending is that Mayor Smith discharged Chief McKamey, Sergeant Jessup and two other patrolmen who were involved in the housing project gunplay.

This story recapitulates, in miniature, our perception of Watts-type incidents. We see black violence, and overlook the history of official lawlessness toward blacks. Next we subordinate the major consequences of official lawlessness, such as the death of black people, to comparatively minor results of black violence. Finally, when we cannot ignore a case of police violence, we agree with Chief McKamey to the extent that we *isolate* the case. Calling this an "unfortunate incident" is not enough for outraged liberals. They would rank it as 'tragic'. McKamey's choice of adjectives suggests that he may be either a disguised or an honest white supremacist.[13] However that may be, notice that McKamey and outraged liberals fail to mention the fact that this "incident" is typical rather than isolated. Liberals agree with McKamey in not recognizing that this sort of thing happens regularly to blacks of Robbins and other communities.

A similar distortion crops up when the liberal sees this 'tragic incident' as rectified when a few 'bad cops' like McKamey and Jessup are weeded out. More precisely, he distorts things when he believes that further incidents of this kind will not occur if enlightened 'professionals' replace hostile and trigger-happy policemen.

More generally, when the outraged liberal reads that these and other 'bad cops' have been discharged or 'transferred to less sensitive work', and concludes that 'real progress is being made in police-community relations', he misperceives things again. Mayor Smith's action against McKamey and

---

[13] In one of the few surveys ever made of policemen's social attitudes, fifty members of a Midwestern police department were asked what they thought of Negroes. Thirty-eight responded unfavorably. Twenty-two thought that Negroes were "biologically inferior." See the updated 1951 study of altogether eighty-five policemen, William A. Westley, *Violence and Police* (Cambridge: MIT Press, 1970). White supremacist attitudes toward black 'criminals' are epitomized by Eric Hoffer: "Our cities are packed with bushy-headed, brutalizing Negro hoodlums. . . . We cannot control these wilful savages, these beasts masquerading as men, who mug us, rob us . . ." (quoted by Richard Lemon, in a condensation of his then forthcoming book, *The Troubled American* [New York: Simon & Schuster, 1970], serialized in the Chicago *Daily News,* October 31–November 1, 1970, p. 10.

Jessup is far from typical. Crimes by authorities against black people almost never result in legal or disciplinary sanctions for official lawbreakers. Here is the more typical case. Three black students were killed, and 27 wounded, at the State College in Orangeburg, South Carolina, in February 1968. Nine State Highway patrolmen who were charged with shooting them have been promoted. But Cleveland Sellars, a young Student Non-Violent Coordinating Committee organizer, was sentenced to a year in jail for participating in a riot two nights before the killings.[14]

If the visceral response is, 'But that happened in the South', then more Northern 'incidents' are easy to find.[15] What I'm concerned to prove, however, is not the obvious point that violence against blacks is widespread and largely unpunished, but that most whites systematically overlook it, or subordinate it to black violence. These violent outbursts in turn are perceived as ordinary crimes, not rebellions. The epistemic pattern at least has the virtue of consistency. If you ignore conditions that provoke and justify it, you can more easily ignore an uprising.

Perhaps I have called too much attention to crimes by police against blacks. As I suggested earlier, policemen are not the only sources of oppression. Blacks must contend with other hostile and uncomprehending officials: welfare investigators, hospital admissions personnel, school administrators and teachers. Then there are various nongovernmental agents of white society: the neighborhood credit store owner; the loan shark; bill collectors; landlords. Even if some of these agents have dark skins, most are oppressing their brothers for the benefit of whites. The 'take' of black intermediaries is negligible. Anyway, the important point is that such official and nonofficial agents, both black and white, frequently behave lawlessly toward residents of the black community. Besides violating constitutional rights to due process, and immunities to arbitrary search and seizure, these agents of white society commit numerous 'ordinary' crimes against blacks. For instance, tenement owners commonly violate fire and safety regulations. Thus you realize why it is a distortion to perceive blacks as engaged in violent and criminal activities, such as looting. A more accurate description would be to say they are responding lawlessly toward the lawless agents of white society.

Maybe it sounds odd, in the cumulative setting of the 350 years that I evoked, to distinguish between legality and illegality. Is there enough contrast in the behavior of white Americans toward blacks to draw the distinction? If you don't think so, then you may find the terminology of insurrection more appropriate. In that case, you would *not* say that black community residents occasionally violate, *en masse,* a system of laws; for

[14] A full discussion will be found in Jack Nelson and Jack Bass, *The Orangeburg Massacre* (New York: World Publishing Co., 1970).

[15] See Eliot Asinof, *People v. Butcher* (New York: Viking Press, 1970); and Gene Marine, *The Black Panthers* (New York: Ramparts Books, 1969).

how can a system of laws be said to exist in the black community when officials deal as American officials do with blacks? Taking this perspective, you would report that black community residents are trying to overthrow, not a system of laws but a system of oppression. What is the goal of their uprising? Perhaps, among other things, some approximation to the system of law that was promised in the Constitution and its Amendments but not delivered. I won't pursue that inquiry, however, because we should be analyzing visceral racist attitudes *toward* black aspirations, not the goals themselves.

And here we must contend with white liberals and moderates who say: "I agree with their goals, and I admit that they are oppressed; but I just can't agree with their methods. Why are they so impatient?" We have already noticed distortions in the view that black people have used unlawful and violent methods. But the ascription of motives like impatience is revealing.

8. *The norm of submissiveness for blacks.* The visceral racist seems to be implying that black people should be more patient. Apparently he thinks that it would be both normal and right for black people to go on waiting and protesting "through legal channels." But why? Does he think that *people in general* do and ought to go on waiting, when for 350 years they have been systematically deprived of many basic constitutional rights, not to mention dignity and a sense of control over their collective destiny? Would he admit that the poor in America are oppressed, and then expect them to be patient? Would he say this of American women? He might describe the Catholics of Northern Ireland as 'angry' and 'violent', but never as 'impatient'. I do not want to pursue any of these overworked analogies. I'm attempting to track down our perceptual distortions of black people in America. And my suggestion now is that the visceral racist unconsciously imposes a norm of submissiveness upon black people alone. He both expects and requires them to be unusually passive, or else to have superhuman control over their frustrations. For when blacks deviate from this twofold standard of docility, the visceral racist perceives them as behaving abnormally—for blacks. The norm is his, not theirs.

9. *Confusion about threats to defend oneself.* The visceral racist will raise a further objection here which is equally revealing. He will deny that he is imposing a norm of submissiveness upon blacks. What bothers him now is that their reactions to frustration nowadays are becoming so aggressive. He is particularly apprehensive of black leaders, and organized groups like the Black Panther Party, who endorse violence. After all, don't they tell black people to arm themselves and to shoot down policemen? Next thing you know they will be invading the suburbs and attacking every white they see!

Aside from the strange reversal of National Guardsmen besieging Watts, Detroit and Newark, what is philosophically interesting about this visceral fantasy is the way it distorts black self-defense. Advocates of this policy have always been unequivocal. Malcolm X contended:

It is criminal to teach a man not to defend himself when he is the constant victim of brutal attacks. It is legal and lawful to own a shotgun or a rifle. . . .

In areas where our people are the constant victims of brutality, and the government seems unable or unwilling to protect them, we should form rifle clubs that can be used to defend our lives and property, in times of emergency, such as happened [in 1963] in Birmingham.[16]

He illustrated more poignantly at a meeting where Mrs. Fannie Lou Hamer spoke of the treatment she received as a result of her work for the Mississippi Freedom Democratic Party. Malcolm X said:

When I listen to Mrs. Hamer, a black woman—could be my mother, my sister, my daughter—describe what they had done to her in Mississippi, I ask myself: How in the world can we ever expect to be respected as *men* when we will allow something like that to be done to our women?[17]

The 'furthest' he went toward advocating attacks was in case authorities would not prosecute known murderers of black people. This was selective retaliation.[18] So far as I can tell, the Black Panther Party follows Malcolm X on these as well as many other points. As of mid-November 1970, their retaliatory attacks appear to have been limited to undercover policemen and informants in their midst; and at most one man may have died in this way. Scores of Party members have died in police attacks. How many have defended themselves? That is unclear. When police raiders killed Illinois Chairman Fred Hampton and Mark Clark in a 'shootout' December 4, 1969, one shot was fired from inside, while police riddled their apartment. A 'moderate' local newspaper quotes "Justice Department figures" to the effect that eleven Party members and nine policemen were killed between November 1968 and November 1970.

Exact figures are of less importance for my analysis than perceptual distortions. The profoundest one is that you are never legally entitled to use 'violence' to defend yourself against a policeman. Malcolm X remarked: "Nowadays, our people don't care who the oppressor is; whether he has on a sheet or whether he has on a uniform"; in other words, "a uniform does not give him the right to come and shoot up your neighborhood."[19] If the uniformed man is acting illegally, while you are not, and there is a

[16] In Breitman, ed., *Malcolm X Speaks*, p. 22.

[17] *Ibid.*, p. 107.

[18] *Ibid.*, pp. 7–8, 33, 43–44, 133–136, 160–165.

[19] *Ibid.*, pp. 67 and 164.

serious risk that he will kill you if you do not resist, you have a right to defend yourself. You may have difficulty proving your factual and legal claims; but the principle is obviously rooted in the Common Law regarding self-defense.

Other distortions are less profound but more evident in the visceral racist's account of self-defense: he confuses advocacy of self-defense with practicing it; then he confuses defensive violence with indiscriminately going on the warpath against policemen or whites generally. If this sounds too incredible, then I would say that at a minimum, the visceral racist either neglects the official violence which blacks say they will resist, or else he describes the situation so that it would appear to be the duty of black people, rather than their uniformed attackers, to restrain themselves. This last interpretation brings out the norm of submissiveness once again.

10. *Misperception of Black 'Demands'.* Before now the unacknowledged visceral racist will have asked, "What do they want anyhow? Will anything satisfy them?" One distortion here is the assumption that black people have to *ask* their oppressors for anything, as if it were a favor or privilege for them to have the same rights and opportunities that other groups do! A related distortion is to imagine that black people are 'demanding'—violently or nonviolently—deep alterations of American statutory and Common Law traditions. The changes they seem to be after are more changes in the behavior of officials and others who are covered by the laws we have. It is time civil rights laws and policies were obeyed! But what if we aren't legal experts? Then a minimal change would be that black people get at least the economic and other opportunities that 'poor whites' and working-class whites have.

In a minute I will analyze the troubling attitude of some of these whites to that suggestion. But first I want to correct one remaining visceral distortion that may have been encouraged by my analysis so far.

11. *Residual imagery of black victimization.* Suppose that we recognize and overcome the attitudes I have noted so far. We reject the norm of docility; we admit that policemen and other officials sometimes act lawlessly toward blacks; we recognize that blacks are already entitled by law to what they 'demand'. Unfortunately my own line of argumentation has nourished an attitude that meshes neatly with many of the attitudes I've been challenging, particularly the norm of submissiveness. For example, I began by calling attention to the ways they are oppressed and exploited in our society. In discussing the 'riot'-'insurrections' I highlighted police crimes against them. On the whole it may appear that, despite these outbursts of anger, black Americans are unwilling but helpless victims of white brutality and cunning: helpless, that is, unless their fellow citizens decide to let up.

Why are these descriptions viscerally racist? What specifically do they distort? Surely black Americans are victimized. Otherwise why bother to analyze our visceral inclinations to ignore their situation? I agree that they suffer unbearable injustices. But it is a distortion to cast them as merely victims. They have resisted too—and long before Watts. Instead of screening it out, one should underscore their determination to survive. Is that word-magic? No, I believe that this is an objective, empirical dispute. There are historical reasons to stress resistance instead of victimization. Many kidnapped Africans killed themselves and their children, rather than accept slavery. Slaves revolted on numerous occasions from 1529 onwards. Sabotage was practiced endlessly by slaves and later by oppressed black servants and laborers. From the earliest times, black freemen agitated for their rights and against slavery. Segregated schools were challenged by blacks as early as 1844 (*Sarah C. Roberts v. The City of Boston,* 59 Mass. 198 [1849]). Between 'Emancipation' and the full development of Jim Crow law in the South, blacks seized a fair amount of political power —although defenders of Jim Crow, like Senator Tillman, whom I quoted in Section 1, tend to exaggerate this. During the Jim Crow era, blacks courageously formed civil rights organizations. Most recently they have assumed fuller control of their own movements. And as we noticed, some groups have armed to repel official and unofficial attacks on their people. So while they can use aid from whites, they are not supine without it.

Along the same lines, it is a distortion to assume that every aspect of life among the majority of blacks is second-rate, so that their only hope rests in becoming 'integrated'. By way of illustration, notice how we often refer to black neighborhoods as 'ghettos'. Black children are said to be 'culturally deprived'; we describe their relatively matriarchal living groups as 'broken homes', not 'complete' families. But why assume that all blacks would prefer and be better off with the dominant society's culture and life styles? Taking that for granted is the visceral equivalent of a white supremacist's belief that his civilization is superior. Of course it is *not* visceral racism to insist that black Americans must have the same opportunities as others to choose between life styles, and to participate in all cultural activities.

No doubt there are other deposits of viscerally racist attitudes in myself and fellow liberals that I have failed to spot. But I think I have given a sufficiently detailed diagnosis so that the reader can 'go on by himself', and social scientists can investigate these attitudes and their linguistic manifestations. As a concluding exercise, however, I want to test out my account. I have been considering mainly the relatively verbalized and 'ideological' dispositions of white liberals. Now I want to see how we can use my analysis to characterize various well-known and deeply troubling attitudes of Northern white industrial laborers and craftsmen toward blacks who threaten them.

201

12. '*Why should white workers sacrifice the advantages they struggled for?*'
The exclusion of blacks from these sectors was documented earlier. The
test for my analysis is therefore simple. I will ask, of readily available
though relatively crude data, whether or not they qualify as evidence for
a viscerally racist outlook. Take this pungent interview:

Ray Walczak, 44, works as a gig grinder . . . in Milwaukee. As he walked
off his shift not long ago, he saw across the street the Rev. James
Groppi and a group of black militants picketing for more jobs.
  "Look at that," Ray Walczak said. "Bastards don't want jobs. If you offered
them jobs now, 90 per cent of them would run like hell. I tell you,
people on relief get better jobs, got better homes, than I've got. You're better
off now not working. The colored people are eating steak, and this
Polack bastard is eating chicken."
  "Damn right I'm bitter. The Polish race years ago didn't go out and riot
and ruin people's property. I've been in the shops since I was 16 . . .
if I live to be a hundred I'll probably be doing the same job.
  "The only raise I ever got was a union raise . . . never a merit raise
. . . We're peons, just numbers."[20]

That particular worker does not think himself privileged; but if you compare his situation with that of his potential black competitors, he is. There
is an interesting distortion in his claim that blacks do not really want the
meagre opportunities he has. There is even a slight contradiction between
his statement that they "don't want jobs" and his complaint that "people
on relief get better jobs"; but perhaps this indicates that he is candidly
expressing attitudes that conflict. Naturally he assumes that black pro-
testers are on relief!
  More explicit animosity toward blacks appears in another interview:

Ernest (Pee Wee) Hayes is 58, and for 37 years he has worked at
the Armco steel plant in Middleton, Ohio. . . .
  "We do all the work and the niggers have got it made. They keep closing
and closing in, working their way into everything. Last 3 or 4 months
you can't even turn on that damn TV without seeing a nigger. They're even
playing cowboys. We briarhoppers ain't gonna stand for it. And 90%
of Middletown is briarhoppers.
  "My man got beat, Wallace. We need someone to wake 'em up.
Shake 'em up. Kill 'em."[21]

This second worker is clearly a white supremacist, because in addition to
being hostile toward blacks, he recognizes that they do not presently have

[20] From Lemon, *The Troubled American,* as serialized in the Chicago *Daily News,*
October 29, 1970, p. 6.

[21] Lemon, *The Troubled American,* as serialized in the Chicago *Daily News,* October 30, 1970, p. 6.

the same opportunities he has, and he intends to keep things that way.

How about the first worker? I think that my analysis helps us notice distortions as well as white supremacist elements in his diatribe. One particular theme in that interview is worth examining further, because it is so common in discussions I've heard. The theme is that workers like this man have suffered to win the few advantages they have. They started working before they could complete high school, and they accepted miserable wages for long hours, under hazardous conditions. They joined the union movement, got fired and took beatings. How can you expect them to give up the few advantages they won, and step aside to benefit blacks? On this view, schemes for preferential recruitment of blacks, admission to apprenticeship programs, and promotion, all seem like 'favoritism' and 'discrimination in reverse'.

Why are these misdescriptions of economic reality? First, while it is true that white workers suffered, fought and took their knocks, it is a distortion to forget that black workers did also. Moreover, as we noticed in Section 3, labor unions regularly betrayed black workers, forcing companies to put them out of jobs they already had, and refusing to admit and represent them. Thus fatal ambiguities begin to appear in the claim that white workers gained the advantages they have by struggling. If you ask, "Struggling against whom, and advantages over whom?", the answer in each case is: "Employers *and* black workers." Now the struggle does not sound so much like 'the good fight' any more. And the privileges no longer appear to be *privileges for laborers in general*. We notice that they are to a considerable extent 'white-skin privileges', unfair advantages over potential black competitors. The case for white workers looks very twisted.

How about the 'sacrifice' and 'favoritism' themes? These are again gross distortions. In the first place, there is a confusion between actuality and possibility. So far, very few blacks have gotten into industrial and craft unions, apprenticeship programs and supervisory positions. Thus in actual fact, whites have made no sacrifices, and no favoritism has been shown to black workers. At most the complaint might be that *if* blacks eventually get what they demand, this *would be* the result. But the second point to raise here is: 'Would it be favoritism, and would there be sacrifices?' If you agree that white workers' advantages are unfair advantages, then how can you describe it as a 'sacrifice' when they must renounce them? Black workers have not called for the firing of whites. No renunciation of their legitimate privileges *as workers* is at issue: only their undeserved privileges as *white* workers. To end these privileges is no more a sacrifice than it is a sacrifice when you must return someone's property, whether you took it deliberately or by mistake, or whether you got it from your parents.

In connection with the 'favoritism' theme, what distorts things is the omission of all-important historical background. Consider preferential hiring programs in the setting of 350 years of gross favoritism toward 203 white laborers and craftsmen. Then it hardly sounds unfair when blacks announce: "Until we get our share, you will have to *wait longer* than usual for the new jobs, for promotions and for admission to apprenticeship programs." It is not favoritism toward blacks when whites lose their illegal monopoly.

White workers and their union representatives who describe economic circumstances in the manner I've been analyzing certainly display visceral racism. But the hitch is that when you expose these and similar distortions, many workers will become explicitly antagonistic towards blacks. How many? That is for trained interviewers to find out. At this stage of exploring a person's attitudes, does it make any difference whether you have a visceral racist or a white supremacist on your hands? Besides the ideological and theoretical differences I've noted, there might be a practical difference when someone is intellectually 'up against the wall'. The acknowledged white supremacist will want to preserve current inequalities. Visceral racists like ourselves, once we have stopped misperceiving things, have strong professed reasons to work for immediate and drastic change.[22]

LISA H. NEWTON
Reverse Discrimination
as Unjustified

I have heard it argued that "simple justice" requires that we favor women and blacks in employment and educational opportunities, since women and blacks were "unjustly" excluded from such opportunities for so many years in the not so distant past. It is a strange argument, an example of a possible implication of a true proposition advanced to dispute the proposition itself, like an octopus absent-mindedly slicing off his head with a stray

[22] For comments on an earlier draft of this paper, I am grateful to Kathryn Pyne Parsons, Ruth Barcan Marcus, George Favors and Robert Coburn and Peter Stone. The readings listed in n. 3 were suggested to me years ago by Charles Valentine, and Dr. Pinderhughes' essay (n. 11) was given to me by Dr. Alexander T. Smith. I thank Richard Lemon, Simon & Schuster and the Chicago *Daily News* for permission to quote from Lemon's book (see n. 13, n. 20 and n. 21). I first noticed the term "visceral racism" in Kenneth Clark, *Dark Ghetto* (Boston: Beacon Press, 1964), p. 20.

Reprinted from *Ethics*, Vol. 83, No. 4 (1973), 308–312. Copyright 1973 by The University of Chicago Press. Reprinted with the permission of the author and the publisher.

tentacle. A fatal confusion underlies this argument, a confusion fundamentally relevant to our understanding of the notion of the rule of law.

Two senses of justice and equality are involved in this confusion. The root notion of justice, progenitor of the other, is the one that Aristotle (*Nichomachean Ethics* 5. 6; *Politics* 1. 2; 3. 1) assumes to be the foundation and proper virtue of the political association. It is the condition which free men establish among themselves when they "share a common life in order that their association bring them self-sufficiency"—the regulation of their relationship by law, and the establishment, by law, of equality before the law. Rule of law is the name and pattern of this justice; its equality stands against the inequalities—of wealth, talent, etc.—otherwise obtaining among its participants, who by virtue of that equality are called "citizens." It is an achievement—complete, or, more frequently, partial—of certain people in certain concrete situations. It is fragile and easily disrupted by powerful individuals who discover that the blind equality of rule of law is inconvenient for their interests. Despite its obvious instability, Aristotle assumed that the establishment of justice in this sense, the creation of citizenship, was a permanent possibility for men and that the resultant association of citizens was the natural home of the species. At levels below the political association, this rule-governed equality is easily found; it is exemplified by any group of children agreeing together to play a game. At the level of the political association, the attainment of this justice is more difficult, simply because the stakes are so much higher for each participant. The equality of citizenship is not something that happens of its own accord, and without the expenditure of a fair amount of effort it will collapse into the rule of a powerful few over an apathetic many. But at least it has been achieved, at some times in some places; it is always worth trying to achieve, and eminently worth trying to maintain, wherever and to whatever degree it has been brought into being.

Aristotle's parochialism is notorious; he really did not imagine that persons other than Greeks could associate freely in justice, and the only form of association he had in mind was the Greek *polis*. With the decline of the *polis* and the shift in the center of political thought, his notion of justice underwent a sea change. To be exact, it ceased to represent a political type and became a moral ideal: the ideal of equality as we know it. This ideal demands that all men be included in citizenship—that one Law govern all equally, that all men regard all other men as fellow citizens, with the same guarantees, rights, and protections. Briefly, it demands that the circle of citizenship achieved by any group be extended to include the entire human race. Properly understood, its effect on our associations can be excellent: it congratulates us on our achievement of rule of law as a process of government but refuses to let us remain complacent until we have expanded the associations to include others within the ambit of the rules, as often and as far as possible. While one man is a slave, none of us may feel truly 205 free. We are constantly prodded by this ideal to look for possible unjustifiable discrimination, for inequalities not absolutely required for the functioning of the society and advantageous to all. And after twenty centuries of pressure, not at all constant, from this ideal, it might be said that some progress has been made. To take the cases in point for this problem, we are now prepared to assert, as Aristotle would never have been, the equality of sexes and of persons of different colors. The ambit of American citizenship, once restricted to white males of property, has been extended to include all adult free men, then all adult males including ex-slaves, then all women. The process of acquisition of full citizenship was for these groups a sporadic trail of half-measures, even now not complete; the steps on the road to full equality are marked by legislation and judicial decisions which are only recently concluded and still often not enforced. But the fact that we can now discuss the possibility of favoring such groups in hiring shows that over the area that concerns us, at least, full equality is presupposed as a basis for discussion. To that extent, they are full citizens, fully protected by the law of the land.

It is important for my argument that the moral ideal of equality be recognized as logically distinct from the condition (or virtue) of justice in the political sense. Justice in this sense exists *among* a citizenry, irrespective of the number of the populace included in that citizenry. Further, the moral ideal is parasitic upon the political virtue, for "equality" is unspecified—it means nothing until we are told in what respect that equality is to be realized. In a political context, "equality" is specified as "equal rights" —equal access to the public realm, public goods and offices, equal treatment under the law—in brief, the equality of citizenship. If citizenship is not a possibility, political equality is unintelligible. The ideal emerges as a generalization of the real condition and refers back to that condition for its content.

Now, if justice (Aristotle's justice in the political sense) is equal treatment under law for all citizens, what is injustice? Clearly, injustice is the violation of that equality, discriminating for or against a group of citizens, favoring them with special immunities and privileges or depriving them of those guaranteed to the others. When the southern employer refuses to hire blacks in white-collar jobs, when Wall Street will only hire women as secretaries with new titles, when Mississippi high schools routinely flunk all black boys above ninth grade, we have examples of injustice, and we work to restore the equality of the public realm by ensuring that equal opportunity will be provided in such cases in the future. But of course, when the employers and the schools *favor* women and blacks, the same injustice is done. Just as the previous discrimination did, this reverse discrimination violates the public equality which defines citizenship and destroys the rule of law for the areas in which these favors are granted. To the extent that we adopt a program of discrimination, reverse or otherwise, justice in the political sense is destroyed, and none of us, specifically affected or not, is a citizen, a bearer of rights—we are all petitioners for favors. And to the same extent, the ideal of equality is undermined, for it has content only where justice obtains, and by destroying justice we render the ideal meaningless. It is, then, an ironic paradox, if not a contradiction in terms, to assert that the ideal of equality justifies the violation of justice; it is as if one should argue, with William Buckley, that an ideal of humanity can justify the destruction of the human race.

Logically, the conclusion is simple enough: all discrimination is wrong prima facie because it violates justice, and that goes for reverse discrimination too. No violation of justice among the citizens may be justified (may overcome the prima facie objection) by appeal to the ideal of equality, for that ideal is logically dependent upon the notion of justice. Reverse discrimination, then, which attempts no other justification than an appeal to equality, is wrong. But let us try to make the conclusion more plausible by suggesting some of the implications of the suggested practice of reverse discrimination in employment and education. My argument will be that the problems raised there are insoluble, not only in practice but in principle.

We may argue, if we like, about what "discrimination" consists of. Do I discriminate against blacks if I admit none to my school when none of the black applicants are qualified by the tests I always give? How far must I go to root out cultural bias from my application forms and tests before I can say that I have not discriminated against those of different cultures? Can I assume that women are not strong enough to be roughnecks on my oil rigs, or must I test them individually? But this controversy, the most popular and well-argued aspect of the issue, is not as fatal as two others which cannot be avoided: if we are regarding the blacks as a "minority" victimized by discrimination, what is a "minority"? And for any group— blacks, women, whatever—that has been discriminated against, what amount of reverse discrimination wipes out the initial discrimination? Let us grant as true that women and blacks were discriminated against, even where laws forbade such discrimination, and grant for the sake of argument that a history of discrimination must be wiped out by reverse discrimination. What follows?

First, are there other groups which have been discriminated against? For they should have the same right of restitution. What about American Indians, Chicanos, Appalachian Mountain whites, Puerto Ricans, Jews, Cajuns, and Orientals? And if these are to be included, the principle according to which we specify a "minority" is simply the criterion of "ethnic (sub) group," and we're stuck with every hyphenated American in the lower-middle class clamoring for special privileges for *his* group—and with equal justification. For be it noted, when we run down the Harvard roster, we find not only a scarcity of blacks (in comparison with the proportion 207 in the population) but an even more striking scarcity of those second-, third-, and fourth-generation ethnics who make up the loudest voice of Middle America. Shouldn't they demand *their* share? And eventually, the WASPs will have to form their own lobby, for they too are a minority. The point is simply this: there is no "majority" in America who will not mind giving up just a bit of their rights to make room for a favored minority. There are only other minorities, each of which is discriminated against by the favoring. The initial injustice is then repeated dozens of times, and if each minority is granted the same right of restitution as the others, an entire area of rule governance is dissolved into a pushing and shoving match between self-interested groups. Each works to catch the public eye and political popularity by whatever means of advertising and power politics lend themselves to the effort, to capitalize as much as possible on temporary popularity until the restless mob picks another group to feel sorry for. Hardly an edifying spectacle, and in the long run no one can benefit: the pie is no larger—it's just that instead of setting up and enforcing rules for getting a piece, we've turned the contest into a free-for-all, requiring much more effort for no larger a reward. It would be in the interests of all the participants to reestablish an objective rule to govern the process, carefully enforced and the same for all.

Second, supposing that we do manage to agree in general that women and blacks (and all the others) have some right of restitution, some right to a privileged place in the structure of opportunities for a while, how will we know when that while is up? How much privilege is enough? When will the guilt be gone, the price paid, the balance restored? What recompense is right for centuries of exclusion? What criterion tells us when we are done? Our experience with the Civil Rights movement shows us that agreement on these terms cannot be presupposed: a process that appears to some to be going at a mad gallop into a black takeover appears to the rest of us to be at a standstill. Should a practice of reverse discrimination be adopted, we may safely predict that just as some of us begin to see "a satisfactory start toward righting the balance," others of us will see that we "have already gone too far in the other direction" and will suggest that the discrimination ought to be reversed again. And such disagreement is inevitable, for the point is that we could not *possibly* have any criteria for evaluating the kind of recompense we have in mind. The context presumed by any discussion of restitution is the context of rule of law: law sets the rights of men and simultaneously sets the method for remedying the violation of those rights. You may exact suffering from others and/or damage payments for yourself if and only if the others have violated your rights; the suffering you have endured is not sufficient reason for them to suffer. And remedial rights exist only where there is law: primary human rights are useful guides to legislation but cannot stand as reasons for awarding remedies for injuries sustained. But then, the context presupposed by any discussion of restitution is the context of preexistent full citizenship. No remedial rights could exist for the excluded; neither in law nor in logic does there exist a right to *sue* for a standing to sue.

From these two considerations, then, the difficulties with reverse discrimination become evident. Restitution for a disadvantaged group whose rights under the law have been violated is possible by legal means, but restitution for a disadvantaged group whose grievance is that there was no law to protect them simply is not. First, outside of the area of justice defined by the law, no sense can be made of "the group's rights," for no law recognizes that group or the individuals in it, qua members, as bearers of rights (hence *any* group can constitute itself as a disadvantaged minority in some sense and demand similar restitution). Second, outside of the area of protection of law, no sense can be made of the violation of rights (hence the amount of the recompense cannot be decided by any objective criterion). For both reasons, the practice of reverse discrimination undermines the foundation of the very ideal in whose name it is advocated; it destroys justice, law, equality, and citizenship itself, and replaces them with power struggles and popularity contests.

BERNARD R. BOXILL
The Morality of Reparation

In "Black Reparations—Two Views,"[1] Michael Harrington rejected and Arnold Kaufman endorsed James Forman's demand for $500 million in reparation from Christian churches and Jewish Synagogues for their part in the exploitation of black people. Harrington's position involves two different points; he argues that reparation is irrelevant and unwarranted because even if it were made, it would do little to "even up incomes"; and he maintains that the *demand* for reparation will be counterproductive, since it will "divert precious political energies from the actual struggle" to even up incomes. Now, though Kaufman seemed to show good reason that, contra Harrington, the demand for reparation could be productive, I shall in the ensuing, completely disregard that issue. Whether the demand for reparation is counterproductive or not is a question the answer to

Reprinted from *Social Theory and Practice*, Vol. 2, No. 1 (1972), 113–122, with the permission of the author and the publisher.

I am deeply indebted to Professor Thomas Hill, Jr., for helpful criticisms of earlier drafts of this paper.

[1] Michael Harrington and Arnold Kaufman, "Black Reparations—Two Views," *Dissent* 16 (July–Aug. 1969), 317–320.

which depends on the assessment of a large number of consequences which cannot be answered by philosophy alone.

In this paper I shall take issue with what I have distinguished as the first of Harrington's points, viz. that reparation is unwarranted and irrelevant because it would do little to even up incomes. I assume that, by implication, Harrington is not averse to special compensatory programs which will effectively raise the incomes of the poor; what he specifically opposes is reparation. By a discussion of the justification and aims of reparation and compensation, I shall now try to show that, though both are parts of justice, they have different aims, and hence compensation cannot replace reparation.

Let me begin with a discussion of how compensation may be justified. Because of the scarcity of positions and resources relative to aspiring individuals, every society that refuses to resort to paternalism or a strict regimentation of aspirations must incorporate competition among its members for scarce positions and resources. Given that freedom of choice necessitates at least the possibility of competition, I believe that justice requires that appropriate compensatory programs be instituted both to ensure that the competition is fair, and that the losers be protected.

If the minimum formal requirement of justice is that persons be given equal consideration, then it is clear that justice requires that compensatory programs be implemented in order to ensure that none of the participants suffers from a removable handicap. The same reasoning supports the contention that the losers in the competition be given, if necessary, sufficient compensation to enable them to reenter the competition on equal terms with the others. In other words, the losers can demand equal opportunity as well as can the beginners.

In addition to providing compensation in the above cases, the community has the duty to provide compensation to the victims of accident where no one was in the wrong, and to the victims of "acts of God" such as floods, hurricanes, and earthquakes. Here again, the justification is that such compensation is required if it is necessary to ensure equality of opportunity.

Now, it should be noted that, in all the cases I have stated as requiring compensation, no prior injustice need have occurred. This is clear, of course, in the case of accidents and "acts of God"; but it is also the case that in a competition, even if everyone abides by the rules and acts fairly and justly, some will necessarily be losers. In such a case, I maintain, if the losers are rendered so destitute as to be unable to compete equally, they can demand compensation from the community. Such a right to compensation does not render the competition nugatory; the losers cannot demand success—they can demand only the minimum necessary to reenter the competition. Neither is it the case that every failure has rights of compensation against the community. As we shall see, the right to compensation depends partly on the conviction that every individual has an equal right to pursue what he considers valuable; the wastrel or indolent man has signified what he values by what he has freely chosen to be. Thus, even if he seems a failure and considers himself a failure, he does not need or have a right of compensation. Finally, the case for compensation sketched is not necessarily paternalistic. It is not argued that society or government can decide what valuable things individuals should have and implement programs to see to it that they have them. Society must see to it that its members can pursue those things they consider valuable.

The justification of compensation rests on two premises: first, each individual is equal in dignity and worth to every other individual, and hence has a right, equal to that of any other, to arrange his life as he sees fit, and to pursue and acquire what he considers valuable; and second, the individuals involved must be members of a community. Both premises are necessary in order to show that compensation is both good and, in addition, mandatory or required by justice. One may, for example, concede that a man who is handicapped by some infirmity should receive compensation; but if the man is a member of no community, and if his infirmity is due to no injustice, then one would be hard put to find the party who could be legitimately forced to bear the cost of such compensation. Since persons can be legitimately compelled to do what justice dictates, then it would seem that in the absence of a community, and if the individual has suffered his handicap because of no injustice, that compensation cannot be part of justice. But given that the individual is a member of a community, then I maintain that he can legitimately demand compensation from that community. The members of a community are, in essential respects, members of a joint undertaking; the activities of the members of a community are interdependent and the community benefits from the efforts of its members even when such efforts do not bring the members what they individually aim at. It is legitimate to expect persons to follow the spirit and letter of rules and regulations, to work hard and honestly, to take calculated risks with their lives and fortunes, all of which helps society generally, only if such persons can demand compensation from society as a whole when necessary.

The case for rights of compensation depends, as I have argued above, on the fact that the individuals involved are members of a single community the very existence of which should imply a tacit agreement on the part of the whole to bear the costs of compensation. The case for reparation I shall try to show is more primitive in the sense that it depends only on the premise that every person has an equal right to pursue and acquire what he values. Recall that the crucial difference between compensation and reparation is that whereas the latter is due only after injustice, the former may be due when no one has acted unjustly to anyone else. It is this relative innocence of all the parties concerned which made it illegiti- 211 mate, in the absence of prior commitments, to compel anyone to bear the cost of compensation.

In the case of reparation, however, this difficulty does not exist. When reparation is due, it is not the case that no one is at fault, or that everyone is innocent; in such a case, necessarily, someone has infringed unjustly on another's right to pursue what he values. This could happen in several different ways, dispossession being perhaps the most obvious. When someone possesses something, he has signified by his choice that he values it. By taking it away from him one infringes on his equal right to pursue and possess what he values. On the other hand, if I thwart, unfairly, another's legitimate attempt to do or possess something, I have also acted unjustly; finally, an injustice has occurred when someone makes it impossible for others to pursue a legitimate goal, even if these others never actually attempt to achieve that goal. These examples of injustice differ in detail, but what they all have in common is that no supposition of prior commitment is necessary in order to be able to identify the parties who must bear the cost of reparation; it is simply and clearly the party who has acted unjustly.

The argument may, perhaps, be clarified by the ideas of a state of nature and a social contract. In the state of nature, as John Locke remarks, every man has the right to claim reparation from his injurer because of his right of self-preservation; if each man has a duty not to interfere in the rights of others, he has a duty to repair the results of his interference.[2] No social contract is required to legitimize compelling him to do so. But when compensation is due, i.e. when everyone has acted justly, and has done his duty, then a social contract or a prior agreement to help must be appealed to in order to legitimately compel an individual to help another.

The case for reparation thus requires for its justification less in the way of assumptions than the case for compensation. Examination of the justifications of reparation and compensation also reveals the difference in their aims.

The characteristic of compensatory programs is that they are essentially "forward looking"; by that I mean that such programs are intended to alleviate disabilities which stand in the way of some *future* good, *however* these disabilities may have come about. Thus, the history of injustices suffered by black and colonial people is quite irrelevant to their right to compensatory treatment. What is strictly relevant to this is that such compensatory treatment is necessary if some future goods such as increased happiness, equality of incomes, and so on, are to be secured. To put it another way, given the contingency of causal connections, the present condition of black and colonial people could have been produced in any

[2] John Locke, *Treatise of Civil Government and A Letter Concerning Toleration*, ed. Charles L. Sherman (New York: Appleton-Century Company, Inc., 1937), 9.

one of a very large set of different causal sequences. Compensation is concerned with the remedying of the present situation however it may have been produced; and to know the present situation, and how to remedy it, it is not, strictly speaking, necessary to know just how it was brought about, or whether it was brought about by injustice.

On the other hand, the justification of reparation is essentially "backward looking"; reparation is due only when a breach of justice *has* occurred. Thus, as opposed to the case of compensation, the case for reparation to black and colonial people depends precisely on the fact that such people have been reduced to their present condition by a history of injustice. In sum, while the aim of compensation is to procure some future good, that of reparation is to rectify past injustices; and rectifying past injustices may not insure equality of opportunity.

The fact that reparation aims precisely at correcting a prior injustice suggests one further important difference between reparation and compensation. Part of what is involved in rectifying an injustice is an acknowledgment on the part of the transgressor that what he is doing is required of him because of his prior error. This concession of error seems required by the premise that every person is equal in worth and dignity. Without the acknowledgment of error, the injurer implies that the injured has been treated in a manner that befits him; hence, he cannot feel that the injured party is his equal. In such a case, even if the unjust party repairs the damage he has caused, justice does not yet obtain between himself and his victim. For, if it is true that when someone has done his duty nothing can be demanded of him, it follows that if, in my estimation, I have acted dutifully even when someone is injured as a result, then I must feel that nothing can be demanded of me and that any repairs I may make are gratuitous. If justice can be demanded, it follows that I cannot think that what I am doing is part of justice.

It will be objected, of course, that I have not shown in this situation that, justice cannot obtain between injurer and victim, but only that the injurer does not *feel* that justice can hold between himself and the one he injures. The objection depends on the distinction between the objective transactions between the individuals and their subjective attitudes, and assumes that justice requires only the objective transactions. The model of justice presupposed by this objection is, no doubt, that justice requires equal treatment of equals, whereas the view I take is that justice requires equal consideration between equals; that is to say, justice requires not only that we *treat* people in a certain way, for whatever reason we please, but that we treat them as equals precisely because we believe they are our equals. In particular, justice requires that we acknowledge that our treatment of others can be required of us; thus, where an unjust injury has occurred, the injurer reaffirms his belief in the other's equality by conceding that repair can be demanded of him, 213 and the injured rejects the allegation of his inferiority contained in the other's behavior by demanding reparation.

Consequently, when injustice has reduced a people to indigency, compensatory programs alone cannot be all that justice requires. Since the avowed aim of compensatory programs is forward looking, such programs *necessarily* cannot affirm that the help they give is required because of a prior injustice. This must be the case even if it is the unjustly injuring party who makes compensation. Thus, since the acknowledgment of error is required by justice as part of what it means to give equal consideration, compensatory programs cannot take the place of reparation.

In sum, *compensation* cannot be substituted for *reparation* where reparation is due, because they satisfy two differing requirements of justice. In addition, practically speaking, since it is by demanding and giving justice where it is due that the members of a community continually reaffirm their belief in each other's equality, a stable and equitable society is not possible without reparation being given and demanded when it is due.

Consider now the assertion that the present generation of white Americans owe the present generation of black Americans reparation for the injustices of slavery inflicted on the ancestors of the black population by the ancestors of the white population. To begin, consider the very simplest instance of a case where reparation may be said to be due: Tom has an indisputable moral right to possession of a certain item, say a bicycle, and Dick steals the bicycle from Tom. Here, clearly, Dick owes Tom, at least the bicycle and a concession of error, in reparation. Now complicate the case slightly; Dick steals the bicycle from Tom and "gives" it to Harry. Here again, even if he is innocent of complicity in the theft, and does not know that his "gift" was stolen, Harry must return the bicycle to Tom with the acknowledgment that, though innocent or blameless, he did not rightfully possess the bicycle. Consider a final complication; Dick steals the bicycle from Tom and gives it to Harry; in the meantime Tom dies, but leaves a will clearly conferring his right to ownership of the bicycle to his son, Jim. Here again we should have little hesitation in saying that Harry must return the bicycle to Jim.

Now, though it involves complications, the case for reparation under consideration is essentially the same as the one last mentioned: the slaves had an indisputable moral right to the products of their labour; these products were stolen from them by the slave masters who ultimately passed them on to their descendants; the slaves presumably have conferred their rights of ownership to the products of their labour to their descendants; thus, the descendants of slave masters are in possession of wealth to which the descendants of slaves have rights; hence, the descendants of slave masters must return this wealth to the descendants of 214 slaves with a concession that they were not rightfully in possession of it.

It is not being claimed that the descendants of slaves must seek reparation from those among the white population who happen to be descendants of slave owners. This perhaps would be the case if slavery had produced for the slave owners merely specific hoards of gold, silver or diamonds, which could be passed on in a very concrete way from father to son. As a matter of fact, slavery produced not merely specific hoards, but wealth which has been passed down mainly to descendants of the white community to the relative exclusion of the descendants of slaves. Thus, it is the white community as a whole that prevents the descendants of slaves from exercising their rights of ownership, and the white community as a whole that must bear the cost of reparation.

The above statement contains two distinguishable arguments. In the first argument the assertion is that each white person, individually, owes reparation to the black community because membership in the white community serves to identify an individual as a recipient of benefits to which the black community has a rightful claim. In the second argument, the conclusion is that the white community as a whole, considered as a kind of corporation or company, owes reparation to the black community.

In the first of the arguments sketched above, individuals are held liable to make reparation even if they have been merely passive recipients of benefits; that is, even if they have not deliberately chosen to accept the benefits in question. This argument invites the objection that, for the most part, white people are simply not in a position to choose to receive or refuse benefits belonging to the descendants of slaves and are, therefore, not culpable or blameable and hence not liable to make reparation. But this objection misses the point. The argument under consideration simply does not depend on or imply the claim that white people are culpable or blameable; the argument is that merely by being white, an individual receives benefits to which others have at least partial rights. In such cases, whatever one's choice or moral culpability, reparation must be made. Consider an extreme case: Harry has an unexpected heart attack and is taken unconscious to the hospital. In the same hospital Dick has recently died. A heart surgeon transplants the heart from Dick's dead body to Harry without permission from Dick's family. If Harry recovers, he must make suitable reparation to Dick's family, conceding that he is not in rightful possession of Dick's heart even if he had no part in choosing to receive it.

The second of the arguments distinguished above concluded that for the purpose in question, the white community can be regarded as a corporation or company which, as a whole, owes reparation to the sons of slaves. Certainly the white community resembles a corporation or company in some striking ways; like such companies, the white community has interests distinct from, and opposed to, other groups in the same 215 society, and joint action is often taken by the members of the white community to protect and enhance their interests. Of course, there are differences; people are generally born into the white community and do not deliberately choose their membership in it; on the other hand, deliberate choice is often the standard procedure for gaining membership in a company. But this difference is unimportant; European immigrants often deliberately choose to become part of the white community in the United States for the obvious benefits this brings, and people often inherit shares and so, without deliberate choice, become members of a company. What is important here is not how deliberately one chooses to become part of a community or a company; what is relevant is that one chooses to continue to accept the benefits which circulate exclusively within the community, sees such benefits as belonging exclusively to the members of the community, identifies one's interests with those of the community, viewing them as opposed to those of others outside the community, and finally, takes joint action with other members of the community to protect such interests. In such a case, it seems not unfair to consider the present white population as members of a company that incurred debts before they were members of the company, and thus to ask them justly to bear the cost of such debts.

It may be objected that the case for reparation depends on the validity of inheritance; for, only if the sons of slaves inherit the rights of their ancestors can it be asserted that they have rights against the present white community. If the validity of inheritance is rejected, a somewhat different, but perhaps even stronger, argument for reparation can still be formulated. For if inheritance is rejected with the stipulation that the wealth of individuals be returned to the whole society at their deaths, then it is even clearer that the white community owes reparation to the black community. For the white community has appropriated, almost exclusively, the wealth from slavery in addition to the wealth from other sources; but such wealth belongs jointly to all members of the society, white as well as black; hence, it owes them reparation. The above formulation of the argument is entirely independent of the fact of slavery and extends the rights of the black community to its just portion of the total wealth of the society.

Selected Bibliography

Carmichael, Stokely, and Hamilton, Charles. *Black Power*. New York: Random House, 1967.

Dixon, Marlene. "Why Women's Liberation?", *Ramparts,* Vol. 8, No. 6 (1969), 59.

Lucas, J. R. " 'Because You Are a Woman,' " *Philosophy,* Vol. 48 (1971), 161.

Mill, John Stuart. *The Subjection of Women,* London: Longmans, 1869.

Melden, A. I. (ed.) *Human Rights.* Belmont: Calif. Wadsworth Publishing Co., 1970.

Nagel, Thomas. "Equal Treatment and Compensatory Justice," *Philosophy and Public Affairs,* Vol. 2, No. 4 (1973), 349.

Thomson, Judith Jarvis. "Preferential Hiring," *Philosophy and Public Affairs,* Vol. 2, No. 4 (1973), 364.

4 SEXUAL MORALITY

PETER A. BERTOCCI
The Human Venture in Sex, Love and Marriage

The Significance of Sexual Intercourse in Married Life

In trying to give Harry and Judith a reasonable answer [to the question of why it may be wrong for two persons who care for each other to have intercourse before marriage] we must assume that the basic motive behind their desire for premarital sexual intercourse is love. Judith and Harry are not in lust with each other, but in love with each other. The main motive is not exploitation, not the pleasure of satisfying sexual desire as such, but the desire to express in a physical way the unity that they feel spiritually. The sexual act would here symbolize the yearning of each person to unite himself more completely with the beloved; it becomes one of the best ways of saying, "I love you."

It is because we believe that this motive is psychologically and ethically sound that we wish to elaborate further what seems to be the profoundest meaning of the sexual act, before trying to show that sexual intercourse before marriage endangers that meaning. We cannot take the argument on its own ground without evaluating the place of sex in the marriage of lovers.

The act of sexual intercourse between a man and a woman gives pleasure at the purely biological level. As the expression of feelings that involve their whole psychophysical being,

Reprinted from Peter A. Bertocci, *The Human Venture in Sex, Love and Marriage*, pp. 61–71, 95–106, 110–115 (New York: Association Press, 1949), with the permission of the author.

especially when they are stirred to a high emotional pitch, it is highly satisfying. The psychological satisfaction is deepest when the couple experience orgasm together, when in these brief rhythmic moments of mutual physiological response, both persons reach the climax of their emotional expression at the same time. If human beings were simply physiological organisms, and if this act could be dissociated from other human needs, the physiological and psychological pleasure and satisfaction involved in it would justify it as an end in itself. *But because human beings are more than physiological reactions, because these responses mean more than they themselves as actions in intercourse are, sexual intercourse can seldom, if ever, be an isolated experience of satisfaction.* This physiological transaction can become a source either of much mental discontent, moral guilt, and aesthetic disgust, or of profound mental peace, moral satisfaction, and aesthetic delight, not to mention the possibilities of religious value.

Here, for human beings, is the crux of the sexual problem in life. Sex is a means of communicating a variety of meanings; it objectifies or symbolizes a variety of feelings and ideas that human beings have about themselves and others. It can mean simply, "I'm sexually hungry and I want satisfaction through you." It can mean, "I love you and I want to be identified as far as possible with you." Or it can mean, "We love each other. Life means so much to us that we want children to share its creative joy and values." There are other meanings, of course—as many meanings as the mates find possible in and through each other. These three stages need not exclude each other though the first may endanger the next two. But for two persons who love each other, and therefore find life's meaning heightened and focused in that love, there can hardly be conceived a more expressive symbol of the yearning for unity than a mutual, harmonious orgasm. Two persons find their deepest satisfaction not in mere self-satisfaction, but in making it possible for the loved one to express his feelings in and through his own contribution to a harmonious act.

The testimony of married persons who have found it possible so to discipline their reaction as to find mutuality in orgasm gives clear corroboration at this point. To feel that one's partner encourages and enjoys one's own activity and responses, to feel that one can meet the needs of the person one loves even as one expresses the intensity and meaning of one's own desires, is, indeed, a human experience worth cherishing. We cannot emphasize enough the qualitative enjoyment and meaning of this experience. What two lovers experience, especially in simultaneous orgasm, is not so much physiological simultaneity but the meanings that they, as two human beings dedicated to each other, so want to express. No wonder lovers who have experienced exhaustion in the psychological and physical release of their tension can continue to embrace each other 219 in the afterglow of mental peace, physiological relaxation, and grateful appreciation. How clearly this act can symbolize what the marriage of two loving persons means, the dedication of one's being to the growing happiness of another.

This is an experience that does work creatively in the lives of two persons, for it renews confidence and infuses new meaning. The amazing fact about it is that it can, on the same physiological base, go on being a source of renewal. Youth, middle age, and maturity find different levels of meaning and renewal thereby. This would hardly be so were it not that through sexual intercourse the lovers who are now parents (or the lovers who are now the center of responsibilities and joys in family and civic life, or the lovers who are now older physically but more mature as persons) go on using it to communicate meanings that never find adequate expression in words.

If what I have been saying is true, it is clear that both the harmony of sex experience and the expressive significance of that unity are such sources of strength and enjoyment in married life that they deserve the needed preparation and protection. Violins cannot create music if they are not tuned, or if the violinist cannot control his feelings, thoughts, and muscles to suit his meaning. If there is no "music" in the violinist, even the greatest skill in playing will not produce "music with a soul." To carry this figure further, violinists cannot create music when they are not playing the same score or when they have not been able to synchronize their playing in accordance with their respective parts in the musical whole. Harmony, physiological and spiritual, requires more than good will; it requires careful discriminating thought, sensitive and sincere feeling, and self-discipline that subordinates tensions for the sake of the whole.

It may seem that we are making too much of the unity of intercourse, but if that be an error it is one that needs underscoring since we are purposely insisting upon the quality of the experience. Sexual intercourse has its greatest value when the minds and actions of two persons communicate their meanings. From this viewpoint, it is unfortunate that so many persons, in and out of marriage, are forfeiting such a high quality of experience, frequently without realizing that they are doing so. They are expressing lust, decreasing sexual tension, experiencing different depths of pleasure. But they are usually sacrificing, or jeopardizing, richer values otherwise open to them.

Let us pause here and attempt to avoid misunderstanding.

We are not saying that young men and women, for whom sex has been simply a pleasurable outlet, or who have been unable, for differing reasons, to live controlled sexual lives, are inevitably barred from mutuality in orgasm (or that those who have remained virginal will by that very fact have guaranteed mutuality). But other things being equal, a personal history of relative promiscuity and a loss of self-confidence and adequate self-control are not conducive to achievement of mutuality. While it is important to realize that many other psychological factors will enter into the achievement of mutual orgasm at any one point in married life, we fly in the face of all we know about psychological habits and associations if we allow ourselves to think that a relatively undisciplined past, with all its associations and psychological effects upon the individual, will not become an obstacle—not necessarily insuperable to be sure—to mutuality.

To continue, part of our central thesis is that human beings have been and are, in fact, losing much of the joy possible in sex and love because they are thinking too much of sex expression and not enough about expressing values through sex and in love. We cannot be said to be educating persons with regard to sex until we are as much concerned about the objectives of complete sexual experience as we have been about removing inhibitions. Sex expression is not self-expression. And self-expression is not necessarily the expression of love. We have taken too little cognizance of the probable fact that multitudes of men and women are disappointed with their sexual experience; it becomes, like ordinary eating, a means of regularly satisfying an otherwise discomforting need. The less persons understand about the meaning that sex can have in their lives, the more likely are they to find the most direct means of expression.[1] The very fact that the physical pleasure of releasing tension is theirs blinds them to higher values that would both intensify the physiological pleasure and also lead to more complete fulfillment of their total being.

From this point of view of quality in sex experience, there is very little value in Kinsey's data with regard to the relation of premarital intercourse and sexual effectiveness in marriage. He says:

It is sometimes asserted that all persons who have premarital intercourse subsequently regret the experience, and that such regrets may constitute a major cloud on their lives. There are a few males whose histories seem to indicate that they have so reacted to their premarital experience, but a high proportion of the thousands of experienced males whom we have questioned on this point indicated that they did not regret having had such an experience, and that the premarital intercourse had not caused any trouble in their subsequent marital adjustments (p. 562).

As Kinsey realizes, even at this level of description one needs accurate data from the wives. But the ambiguous words in his statement are

[1] This statement finds support in Kinsey's statistics with regard to the differences both in freedom of sex expression and mode of sex expression in persons with little school education—and, one assumes, what that means to the development of human understanding.

221

"trouble" and "regret." If "no trouble" means simply that there were no special inhibitions, or feelings of guilt that hindered physiological reaction, or that no serious disunity between the partners was involved, the crux of the problem is not touched. Assuming—what we doubt can be assumed—that "experienced males" would admit that they had been deceived by their desires, what we need to know (and cannot find out probably from men habituated to satisfy desires conveniently) is the effect upon the quality of their marital relation, both sexually and as a whole. Did it make for greater loyalty, for deeper appreciation and respect, both of oneself, one's partner, and the act itself?

When Kinsey continues, "It is notable that most of the males who did regret the experience were individuals who had had very little premarital intercourse, amounting in most cases to not more than one or two experiences" (p. 563), is the conclusion to be drawn that if they had further indulged they would have ceased being disturbed? Or does this also suggest that some persons expected more from themselves and from the sexual experience, and that they realized how little sex as a merely biological or even sociable experience had to contribute to their lives? Obviously, there are no definite conclusions to be drawn from such data.

But Kinsey goes so far in trying to avoid any generalization condemning premarital experience that he makes "the significance of premarital intercourse" depend "upon the situations under which it is had" (p. 561), upon whether the experience is free from fear or "satisfying." This again begs the real question of the kind of fear and the quality of satisfaction. The whole problem is: Can a person outside of married love find the most that sex can bring to human life? Can experiences in which one's fundamental concern is the satisfaction of one's own desire become the psychological basis for an experience in which concern for another's complete well-being is symbolized in the sexual act? Can ego-centered habituation, in idea, in motive, in emotion, in action, be a help in establishing a relation in which another human being, a home, and children call for self-mastery?

A little reflection, then, will make clear the task before any two married persons. It will be evident that much discipline may be required if mutuality is to be realized at the psychophysiological level. Even assuming that past experience with sex has been without serious conflict, so that both persons are emotionally free and are ready to discover the full meaning of sex in their relations to each other, they cannot be sure that the experience of unity will readily be theirs. The sexual responsiveness of the male and female orgasm is by no means the same, and every couple has to work out the modes of mutual response suited to their own particular natures.

222 At this point of physiological unity one cannot dogmatize about the

prerequisites in terms of past sexual experience. As already suggested, one cannot universalize the statement that habits of response derived from premarital experience will interfere necessarily with present adjustment to one's partner. A person's attitude toward his or her past experience, the effect of it upon his emotional life, the attitude of the mate, the total import of the other values in a marriage are always probably more important than the mere fact of abstinence or nonabstinence. But even from the point of view of physiological unity, are not the probabilities on our side when we say that, other things being normal, the chances of harmonizing responses are much greater when two lovers come together who have a history of self-mastery and confidence with regard to sex? Will not "a past of pleasure" be a threat to the more important psychological, moral, aesthetic, and religious overtones—those which transform physical notes into a human symphony.

We need not here go into the different physical and psychological causes that might well lead to an initial disharmony and to a long struggle to achieve the kind of mental freedom and control necessary for increasing sexual harmony. Suffice it to say that one of the greatest misconceptions that young people bring to marriage is that there will be no sex problem in marriage. The fact is that marriage may create as many sex problems as it solves. Too many honeymoons have found two persons who loved each other not a little disturbed, and sometimes shocked, by inability to enjoy the kind of sexual harmony for which their spirits were prepared. To repeat, then, any couple that looks forward to married life needs to face honestly and resolutely the fact that the finest psychophysical expression of their love may have to await the patient discipline and understanding for which their particular response patterns call. Fortunately their meaning to each other, the unity they feel, can be expressed in other ways as they work for greater unity in the sexual satisfaction of their love.

One of the strongest reasons for urging that a person come through adolescence feeling that he is in control of sex (and not sex in control of him) should now be clear. For the less he can control his mind and body, the more difficult his readjustment to his beloved may be at the very time he is most anxious to succeed. The more he is conditioned to a certain form of sexual progression, the more habituated he has become to certain modes of response, the greater the variety of thoughts and associations that come crowding into his mind now that he is trying to meet the needs of his life partner, the harder it is to make the new adjustment that has to be made to his loved one. The person whose past experience with sex has been that of the hungry animal, or that of the egotistic philanderer who has thought of his partner essentially as a means to his enjoyment, will not have an easy time meeting a new situation in which his highest nature wants expression for the sake of his 223 beloved. From the point of view of married life as a whole, the person who has learned to think of human beings as "males" or "females" who can be "used" may indeed find and create more trouble than he can imagine.

It would be tragic to underemphasize the importance of such psychological influences. Let two persons bring wandering thoughts, feelings of insecurity and guilt, desires for self-aggrandizement, or any other expectations foreign to the unique problem of welding two lives together, and the marriage of their spirits will have this much more to overcome.

. . .

Are Not Our Sexual Standards Artificial?

We must now turn to another lingering doubt, which is related to what we have been saying about the conflict between the sex desire and the social code. For I am sure that someone will say: In other societies, where no one expects young people to abstain from the satisfaction of their sexual desires, and where the element of fear and social ostracism is reduced to a minimum, there are no bad results, and people seem to be healthier in their attitudes toward sex. May it not be, then, that in developing our social codes and laws we have created problems for young people that did not have to arise at all? Indeed, if a person just does not care about what society thinks, if he has no moral compunctions and, therefore, no resultant sense of guilt about his free sexual life, that person does not seem to suffer any of the disturbances associated with sexual repression.

And my reader might add: Are you sure that all the fuss you are making about sexual control, yes, even as a means to a fuller love relation, is worth the bother? Since sex is so recurrent in human life, would it not be better to remove the bars at this point and let individuals (and society) use the energy now spent in combatting "sexual license" for other desirable personal and social objectives? If we are actually pitting individuals against a drive that in their ripening years is a constant thorn in their sides, are we not really flagellating them unnecessarily? Why not make legal and acceptable what so many people are now doing covertly, and at the expense of an artificially created bad conscience?

Indeed, why not be sensible and scientific, and provide persons from adolescence on with knowledge of contraceptives and prophylactics so that they will be able to enjoy sexual relations with a minimum of fear and with a maximum of birth control? If, as they come into marriage, a couple did not expect premarital abstinence any more than they expect abstinence from other forms of social relations, it would not bother them, and marriage would not be undermined. After all, remember that a great 224 many people even now are breaking the social code, for they reject the moral conception on which it is based. They do not seem to be worse for it. Is it not our problem, then, really to recognize that our present moral and legal codes, developed in earlier stages of socio-economic-religious development, are no longer applicable and are, in fact, creating more problems today than they solve?

Thus many a thoughtful young person will argue. Remembering our own prolonged collegiate harangues and bull sessions, we can honestly say that this line of argument still strikes a sympathetic chord, especially when we note the great amount of time and energy young and old alike, in and out of family, spend in worrying about maintaining chastity. There are many difficult theoretical questions here, and we can no more than hint at an approach to them.

1. Let us not fool ourselves that we would minimize our social problems by making knowledge of prophylactics and contraceptives more available. Such knowledge and the medical attention necessary should be available as soon as possible, but not because in this way unwanted births might be decreased. There are no methods of contraception that are foolproof (aside from medical operations that keep sperm and ovum from making contact). Errors in adjustment and imperfection in the materials —let alone carelessness or even failure to use them—would certainly occur many times. Unless we were to make provision for an enormous program of legal abortions, a multitude of children would be born when neither father nor mother were mature enough or economically able to take care of their children.

Let us make no mistake about the choices before us. If our psychological and sociological investigations have told us much about the sex urge, they have also emphasized the need that infants and children have for feeling wanted and loved. The constant feeling of insecurity makes deeper inroads on healthy living than the frustration of sex as such. Parents must be psychologically and morally mature to help children meet their problems as they grow up. Our central obligation, therefore, is to preserve the kind of parental care that will enable children to feel at home in their world. To suppose that removal of social restraints regarding sexual control would take us nearer to this goal is to be blind to the many problems with which society would then be beset. Are we willing to have many more children born than can receive adequate care psychologically and morally? We might, indeed, decrease the number of sexual disturbances that are (supposedly) due to sexual inhibition, and increase the many other problems that occur when the life ventures of children and adults are rendered insecure and unstable.

Our choice is not between black and white, and any system will work hardship on many persons. But, surely, any suggestions that would tend to increase the number of inadequately cared-for children, let alone endanger the stability that monogamous marriage provides, cannot compare 225 even with our present imperfect system. A main reason why those who now indulge in premarital sex experience, or even extramarital sex experience, can enjoy the supposed benefits of their "freedom" is that there are enough other human beings left who, despite their imperfections, stand by the system that does give the social stability needed. Let the order of the day emphasize not control but convenience, not long-range planning but "doing what I want when I want it," and it will not take long for physical and social decay to set in. Would this be more "natural" than the kind of system we have? Can those who live by such parasitism honestly encourage others to join them as they "use" and endanger the lives of other persons in order to guarantee their own pleasures?

2. We might remind ourselves, before passing to the next point, that what recommends the idea of birth control is not that there may be a limitation in the number of children, but that birth of children can be controlled in a manner designed to ensure the most adequate care of the number of children a given family can absorb and support. We do not face the facts if we allow ourselves to forget that, the imperfections of contraceptives from the point of safety aside, they are aesthetically obnoxious, to say the least, to a large number of married people who use them only because they do want to limit their families or adequately space their children. The purpose of birth control is to help enrich the experience of sexual love by reducing the probability of pregnancy, and to increase the possibilities of health and education in a given family. The goal of birth control is to help improve the quality of adult life and the opportunities of children for sensitive nurture. To consider the use of contraceptives simply as a way of providing individuals with pleasure minus responsibility is to encourage the dilution of the meaning of sexual intercourse.

3. But these considerations are not so important as those pointed out earlier in discussing the sexual progression and the place of self-control in the complete enjoyment of sex experience itself. To express sex as sex with different "congenial" partners is to establish certain modes and tempos of response, many mental and emotional associations, that cannot be sloughed off at will. If we remember that sex itself is not the cause of love (though it is certainly a factor in love), but that love is a profound cause of sexual intimacy in human experience, we are confronted with another stubborn fact of our psychological nature that forces us to make a choice.

Let us assume that Dick or Jane have, as the supporter of sexual freedom would advocate, moved through their adolescence and early youth indulging their sexual urge discreetly and prudently. Since they have felt no rigorous moral compunctions or morbid sense of guilt, they are not vulnerable to mental disease, and, let us grant, they have enjoyed good, clean, fun on the sexual level. For they have experienced

226

the release of sexual tension when they were really bothered, and they have been fortunate enough to find suitable partners with whom they shared normal, companionable relations and friendships. Let us make their case even stronger by assuming that their attitudes throughout their varied experience were not dominated by an abnormal, aggressive desire for mastery.

With this psychological orientation to men and women and sex, let us suppose that Dick and Jane meet each other and fall in love. They now *fall in love,* but their past experience has been of *falling in lust.* They now no longer anticipate a good-for-a-while relationship, but a life-long partnership in which they may share as much of life's meaning as possible with each other and make each other the home base for all adventures in value. Two persons like these (whatever their past, I am assuming) want to be one; they want to feel unified in every way. For them the sexual experience, even if they had never had it before, would now be an opportunity demanded by the total impetus of their love and not merely their lust. This love dictates loyalty to each other, for it represents the fact that the other is valued above all others.

Is it now more serious psychologically and spiritually to disappoint the natural desires of sex than the natural desires of love for loyalty and concentrated devotion? What Dick and Jane want now supremely is love; and, speaking objectively, what they need is love if their lives are to have the quality and inspiration that love contributes to life. Yet the Dick-and-Jane-in-love are confronted by the Dick-and-Jane-in-lust, and the habits of the past—such as finding the attractive physical specimen to share the pleasure of lust, such as desiring sexual experience every so often and in a certain manner or mode—now assert themselves. Here, let us emphasize, *it is not society that is making artificial laws which cause conflict and make them unhappy; it is the psychological laws of their natures as human beings.* Lust and the habits of lust stand in conflict with love and the demands of love. The past of life, enhanced and strengthened by habit, stands in defiance of the development of life as a whole. Dick and Jane want each other completely, dependably, forever. They do not want to feel that the sexual habits of the past may break up something which they now so wholly approve. They dread the thought that their past may threaten the foundations of their happiness together as central units of a family. If Jane and Dick are honest with themselves and with each other, they may well pause and face the fact that, much as they wish to follow the high, broad avenue of growth, because of their past habits they are better fitted to travel the lower, narrower streets of sexual satisfaction.

Let us now assume that, having become engaged, they find it impossible because of established habits to refrain from sexual intercourse. But the sexual intercourse they now want is more than the satisfaction of a 227 strong urge. They want to express their love by the very actions which in the past have expressed lust. They want so much to have this experience say what they cannot say in words. They want everything to be perfect. But now past habits of response, and many past associations with this act, crowd in upon the activity of mind and body, barring the way to the kind of unity and satisfaction their love calls for. It is not society which is barring their way to joy and peace now, but their own past in conflict with the present. Society and its laws did not artificially create this situation. It is the psychological structure of Jane and Dick—the way their natures work out once they have made certain choices. The problem they have—the struggle between self-satisfying lust and other-regarding love—is one their natures would develop in *any* social situation (assuming the value of love). They may, indeed, after a kind of discipline they are not used to, be able to make their way to a harmonious unity of confident love, but the struggle before them is not artificially created by society.

It will not be forgotten, of course, that two other persons, Harry and Judith, despite their controlled psychological past, may have difficulty in achieving the kind of sexual unity that will adequately re-create their bodies and minds. But, we hold out much more hope for their achievement of this unity and for the prolongation and enrichment of this love than we do for Jane and Dick. And happily it cannot be asserted that Jane and Dick may not under the incentive and inspiration of their love find their way with patience, mutual forgiveness, and persistent self-discipline to the kind of unity, mutual confidence, and loyalty to which their love aspires. Nevertheless, the moral attitudes and psychological habits of Dick and Jane may well stand in the way of the present satisfaction of their love. These attitudes and habits may destroy more than one moment of peace and trust, especially when the other tensions of married partnership and home building come into their lives. Once more, then, we come back to a question we have been asking over and over in these pages: When we are honest with the facts of our lives, and when we consider what we desire from life as a whole, is the satisfaction of sex lust along the way worth it? Do we not, in fact, endanger or sacrifice our unique heritage of love for a mess of pottage by thinking that we have solved the sex problem by convenient expression?

In a society where people came together physically and separated whenever they pleased, one might be tempted to think that artificial frustrations would be avoided. But how sure could we be that both persons would find it convenient to separate at the same time? The one who gets caught by love suffers. In the midst of their enjoyment can they keep from being haunted by the knowledge that on their principle of action one or the other may change his mind when he pleases? These are not problems society's codes create. They are snares into which our human nature falls once we play fast and loose with it.

228

4. Before closing this section, we must dwell a little longer on another aspect of the suggestion that it is society which makes all the trouble by imposing unnatural standards of conduct on the young. When we talk this way, we seem to assume that our forebears had somehow discovered and forced upon their children a group of moral edicts that had no intimate relation to their needs. Now, it is certainly true that this attitude of the law enforcer has been present in a great deal of societal restriction on human beings. No doubt many laws have been enforced that took little or no account of the needs and desires of the persons who were expected to live by them. They do reflect a slave morality.

Some philosophical and theological theories of law easily lend themselves to manipulation of persons rather than to a regard for the growth of persons. Against them let us assert quite vigorously that human beings are not to be considered the playthings of the gods or, for that matter, of fate, let alone of society or state or church. But it is a great calamity that persons whom study should have at least rendered more cautious make the puerile assertion that the restrictions upon sexual behavior have been imposed only by the philosophical rationalizations of ascetic kill-joys who had little regard for the normal enjoyments of normal persons. It is true that sexual restraint has been advocated in the name of, and as the will of, God. But let it be remembered that God was usually considered not the torturer of little children, but the lover of men. If more of the truth be known, we suspect that the will of God was indeed called in to back up what was shrewdly observed to be a law of the human nature—which, incidentally, God had made that way! This is not the place to review and refute different theories, for the question is an involved one. But it seems fair to say that it is erroneous to maintain that the grounds of sexual control lie not in the nature of human experience and experiment, but in artificial restraints imposed without any realistic justification by society.

That there must be some control of sexual activity is patent in any reflective analysis of the problem of human beings as they come together. Different societies may exercise different controls in order to preserve their form of social organization. Sometimes the controls may be to encourage persons to have more sexual experience, more wives or husbands, and more children. However, we make serious mistakes in the study of values when we compare a mode of behavior in one society with a similar mode of behavior in another without carefully evaluating each mode in the light of the total pattern of values and customs in each society. The fact is that each society must pay in some way or other for the controls that it seeks to enforce on sex, or on property, education, or anything else, for that matter.

The real question, therefore, is: What form of society, what kind of institutions will help human beings in their situations to complete their lives and fulfill their potentialities in the richest possible manner and 229 with the minimum of fruitless frustration? One part of this large question seems clear, namely, that a monogamous home built about confident, controlled love is the best kind of insurance for the growth of human beings and the symphonic satisfaction of human drives.

We can imagine societies in which ideological, economic, and social problems would be such that the kind of love and home we have in mind is beyond present reach and grasp. Theirs, then, would have to be a different form of social code, and that code might work better for them without home-building possibilities than it would for us. But it does not mean that they too would not be better off if they could pay the price for the kind of human love and nurture that joins two lovers and their progeny in a common pursuit of creative living. The problem every person and every society has to face is: Do we want to protect the experience of love even more than the experience of sex? If we agree that the experience of love, given the structure of human beings, is endangered by the expression of sex as an end in itself, then we must organize our institutions and educational efforts to encourage love. And we must discipline sex for the sake of love. . . .

. . .

Is Sexual Guilt Not an Artificial Barrier?

If boy or girl were not taught to inhibit their sexual desires, and if as young people they felt no moral guilt or anxiety about it, would it have any bad effect on their lives? The answer is: If, indeed, they had no moral compunctions about free sexual expression, it would not produce mental disturbance, for no real conflict would be set up in their lives. But if these persons ever decided to move into the area of love, they might well expect conflict, and then other disturbances would have to be faced. No one could predict the outcome.

But when we say that some sexual promiscuity will not have a bad effect, I suspect we have in mind mental disorder rooted in the sex-conscience conflict. It is unfortunate that so many of us have got into the habit of thinking that if we do not develop a neurosis we are not being badly affected. But here we really misinterpret what our psychology does in fact teach us. As might be expected, we know the diseased extreme better than we understand what makes for the most effective and enduring health.

Does the fact that a person does not develop a neurosis, owing to the fact that he has no moral compunctions about premarital or extramarital sex-expression, mean that he is better off because he is expressing sex? Study that person's life carefully—his attitudes toward himself, his sense of responsibility for the needs of others—and you may well discover a

230 weakness of moral fiber, of capacity to get the most out of himself

despite hardship and sacrifice. What does such a person do in the presence of frustration now? What will he do if he ever undertakes a vocation and marriage, in which there will be great need for willingness to forego present personal pleasures for the sake of later satisfactions? The person who can pleasurably indulge in sexual intercourse owing to his freedom from moral guilt may escape a "complex" or specific mental disorder, but when the total quality of his life is analyzed, when his human sensitiveness and his capacity to forego self-indulgence for the sake of others is evaluated, the deficit in his personality may be more serious than he realizes.

One other fact of experience must be emphasized in relation to this question. I have listened frequently to young men and women, some of them engaged, who because of their thwarted desires for sexual intercourse have wished that they had never been brought up to think it's "bad." And some have concluded that "since we only think it's bad and it really isn't, there really is no good reason why we shouldn't express our desires." Many young people who have gone this way have discovered, to their dismay and undiminished sense of guilt, that their conscience would not keep quiet just because they told it that it was all wrong.

We cannot here discuss the whole problem of conscience, though we must protest the oversimplified and superficially "scientific" accounts of it given by those who reduce it merely to the watchdog voice of society in us. Whatever final theoretical position we take, the fact cannot be forgotten that it does no good to try to laugh off a "conscience," and it frequently does much harm. Laughing the conscience off is hardly the way to get rid of it, any more than laughing away sex or any other strong desire exiles it. It is not impossible to change the content of one's conscience so that it will take account of the present actualities of life as well as of the past. A person whose conscience tells him that every manifestation of sex is bad may be suffering from a distasteful emotional experience in childhood which he then illogically generalized. It will take him time and effort of thought and will to feel differently about that verdict and change his conscience at that point. During the interlude, when his conscience is changing, he will experience the uncertainty that goes with any new development. One does not, however, make a new conscience simply by breaking the old one. The redirection calls for painstaking insight and effort if it is going to represent a real, unified growth of the personality.

Let us apply this fact to the question before us. Too many young people are sure that, in view of the strength of their desire for each other, they can dismiss the conscientious scruples which have been exerting themselves, enter into sex experience, enjoy it thoroughly, and never feel any aftereffects. "After all," they may say, "this conscience about 231 sex is just a fairy tale I picked up in my childhood, like the idea of Santa Claus." But then they find that the experience does not take up the whole mind, that they did not enjoy it quite as much as they thought they would. Later they find that they do keep on feeling guilty about it. Both the possibility of premarital sex experience and the whole idea of sex experience now evoke guilt. Thus, when the sex experience is later to be used as an expression of marital love, it comes into mind with the guilt feeling attached, to destroy what might otherwise be a communication of undivided devotion and love.

This kind of effect was quite clear in the experience of Arthur and Ethel. Arthur had been brought up on the idea that sex should express love and that it should be a bond in married love only. The war came on when he was a sophomore in college and interrupted his life and the normal course of an excellent relation with Ethel. On one of his three-day leaves Ethel met him half-way across the country, so that they could be together longer. They had earlier discussed the possibility of sexual experience, and we suspect that under normal peacetime conditions they would have abstained from sexual intercourse despite their strong love for each other. Now, however, they convinced each other at their hotel that those compunctions they had been feeling about "going all the way" were silly residuals of childhood. They met each other on several other occasions and shared their love with each other.

The last time we saw Ethel she said that soon after Arthur had returned to college, his work (he had been a college leader and an excellent scholar) had gone to pieces, he had broken his engagement and had written her excoriating letters filled with bitterness and the feeling that she had allowed him to make a mess of his life. Anyway, he was no longer any good. We are afraid that Arthur's conscience is still barking, and that the guilt he has been feeling at this point is so heavy upon him that he has allowed it to seep into other areas of his life. And now Ethel, whose conscience "didn't feel too bad" earlier, is miserable, not only about the breaking of the engagement, but also about his attitude toward himself and toward her. This is only one instance of a truth we need to remember, that our conscience, whatever its ultimate nature, has a way of staying with us, and that we are being more than careless when we think we can change it *simply by breaking it*.

In a chapter in which we have been considering lingering doubts, we must not leave the impression of being satisfied with the present status of morality or custom on these problems. It has been our concern to suggest rather the direction in which we need to go in our thinking. What is really disturbing is the fact that so few people are getting from sex the profound, creative experience possible through it. People are cheating themselves of the deeper possibilities sex experience can open to them

232 *if* it symbolically binds together two personalities committed to each

other, to their God, their children, and their civil responsibilities. Comparatively speaking, persons are at present experiencing jazz when they might know the stirring themes of symphonies. Our task is not so much to control sex as it is to increase every opportunity for understanding and for growth of personality. Crusades against sex will not do what we really need to do—work with intelligent commitment to the kind of living in which love for others and respect for self are the magnetic poles.

From the cradle to the grave, literally, our task is to develop appreciation for the enriching responsibilities and activities of human experience and, within these, the meaning of sex and love. And we need, as part of this total conception, to change our attitude toward those who have failed to meet their social responsibilities from one of vindictive punishment to one of understanding redirection. Only thus may such persons re-enter, as far as possible for them, into their heritage of sex, love, and family. We do not protect society simply by penalizing its weaker members, especially when this frequently means hurting their children more than they need to be hurt. We help society—indeed, we prove that we have the highest and most stable type of society—when we can help those who fall by the way to rediscover their good potentialities and rebuild them.

POPE PAUL VI
from Humanae Vitae (1964)

CONJUGAL LOVE

Conjugal love reveals its true nature and nobility when it is considered in its supreme origin, God, Who is Love,[1] 'the Father, from whom every family in heaven and on earth is named'.[2]

Marriage is not, then, the effect of chance or the product of evolution of unconscious natural forces; it is the wise institution of the Creator to realize in mankind His design of love. By means of the reciprocal personal gift of self, proper and exclusive to them, husband and wife tend towards the communion of their beings in view of mutual personal perfection, to collaborate with God in the generation and education of new lives.

For baptized persons, moreover, marriage invests the dignity of a sacramental sign of grace, inasmuch as it represents the union of Christ and of the Church.

[1] Cf. I, Jn. 4, 8.
[2] Cf. Eph. 3, 15.

233

ITS CHARACTERISTICS

Under this light, there clearly appear the characteristic marks and demands of conjugal love, and it is of supreme importance to have an exact idea of these.

This love is first of all fully *human,* that is to say, of the senses and of the spirit at the same time. It is not, then, a simple transport of instinct and sentiment, but also, and principally, an act of the free will, intended to endure and to grow by means of the joys and sorrows of daily life, in such a way that husband and wife become one only heart and one only soul, and together attain their human perfection.

Then, this love is *total,* that is to say, it is a very special form of personal friendship, in which husband and wife generously share everything, without undue reservations or selfish calculations. Whoever truly loves his marriage partner loves not only for what he receives, but for the partner's self, rejoicing that he can enrich his partner with the gift of himself.

Again, this love is *faithful* and *exclusive* until death. Thus in fact do bride and groom conceive it to be on the day when they freely and in full awareness assume the duty of the marriage bond. A fidelity, this, which can sometimes be difficult, but is always possible, always noble and meritorious, as no one can deny. The example of so many married persons down through the centuries shows, not only that fidelity is according to the nature of marriage, but also that it is a source of profound and lasting happiness.

And finally, this love is *fecund,* for it is not exhausted by the communion between husband and wife, but is destined to continue, raising up new lives. 'Marriage and conjugal love are by their nature ordained toward the begetting and educating of children. Children are really the supreme gift of marriage and contribute very substantially to the welfare of their parents'.[3]

RESPONSIBLE PARENTHOOD

Hence conjugal love requires in husband and wife an awareness of their mission of 'responsible parenthood', which today is rightly much insisted upon, and which also must be exactly understood. Consequently it is to be considered under different aspects which are legitimate and connected with one another.

In relation to the biological processes, responsible parenthood means the knowledge and respect of their functions; human intellect discovers in the power of giving life biological laws which are part of the human person.[4]

[3] Cf. II Vat. Council, Pastoral Const. *Gaudium et Spes,* No. 50.

[4] Cf. St Thomas, *Summa Theologica,* I–II, Q. 94, Art. 2.

In relation to the tendencies of instinct or passion, responsible parenthood means that necessary dominion which reason and will must exercise over them.

In relation to physical, economic, psychological and social conditions, responsible parenthood is exercised, either by the deliberate and generous decision to raise a numerous family, or by the decision, made for grave motives and with due respect for the moral law, to avoid for the time being, or even for an indeterminate period, a new birth.

Responsible parenthood also and above all implies a more profound relationship to the objective moral order established by God, of which a right conscience is the faithful interpreter. The responsible exercise of parenthood implies, therefore, that husband and wife recognize fully their own duties towards God, towards themselves, towards the family and towards society, in a correct hierarchy of values.

In the task of transmitting life, therefore, they are not free to proceed completely at will, as if they could determine in a wholly autonomous way the honest path to follow; but they must conform their activity to the creative intention of God, expressed in the very nature of marriage and of its acts, and manifested by the constant teaching of the Church.[5]

RESPECT FOR THE NATURE AND PURPOSES OF THE MARRIAGE ACT
These acts, by which husband and wife are united in chaste intimacy, and by means of which human life is transmitted are, as the Council recalled, 'noble and worthy',[6] and they do not cease to be lawful if, for causes independent of the will of husband and wife, they are foreseen to be infecund, since they always remain ordained towards expressing and consolidating their union. In fact, as experience bears witness, not every conjugal act is followed by a new life. God has wisely disposed natural laws and rhythms of fecundity which, of themselves, cause a separation in the succession of births. None the less the Church, calling men back to the observance of the norms of the natural law, as interpreted by her constant doctrine, teaches that each and every marriage act (*quilibet matrimonii usus*) must remain open to the transmission of life.[7]

TWO INSEPARABLE ASPECTS: UNION AND PROCREATION
That teaching, often set forth by the Magisterium, is founded upon the inseparable connection, willed by God and unable to be broken by man on his own initiative, between the two meanings of the conjugal act: the unitive meaning and the procreative meaning. Indeed, by its intimate

[5] Cf. Pastoral Const. *Gaudium et Spes,* Nos. 50, 51.

[6] *Ibid.,* No. 49.

[7] Cf. Pius XI, Encyc. *Casti Connubii,* in AAS XXII (1930), p. 560; Pius XII, in AAS XLIII (1951), p. 843.

structure, the conjugal act, while most closely uniting husband and wife, capacitates them for the generation of new lives, according to laws inscribed in the very being of man and of woman. By safeguarding both these essential aspects, the unitive and the procreative, the conjugal act preserves in its fullness the sense of true mutual love and its ordination towards man's most high calling to parenthood. We believe that the men of our day are particularly capable of seizing the deeply reasonable and human character of this fundamental principle.

FAITHFULNESS TO GOD'S DESIGN

It is in fact justly observed that a conjugal act imposed upon one's partner without regard for his or her condition and lawful desires is not a true act of love, and therefore denies an exigency of right moral order in the relationships between husband and wife. Hence, one who reflects well must also recognize that a reciprocal act of love, which jeopardizes the disponibility to transmit life which God the Creator, according to particular laws, inserted therein, is in contradiction with the design constitutive of marriage, and with the will of the Author of life. To use this divine gift destroying, even if only partially, its meaning and its purpose is to contradict the nature both of man and woman and of their most intimate relationship, and therefore it is to contradict also the plan of God and His will. On the other hand, to make use of the gift of conjugal love while respecting the laws of the generative process means to acknowledge oneself not to be the arbiter of the sources of human life, but rather the minister of the design established by the Creator. In fact, just as man does not have unlimited dominion over his body in general, so also, with particular reason, he has no such dominion over his generative faculties as such, because of their intrinsic ordination towards raising up life, of which God is the principle. 'Human life is sacred', Pope John XXIII recalled; 'from its very inception it reveals the creating hand of God'.[8]

ILLICIT WAYS OF REGULATING BIRTH

In conformity with these landmarks in the human and Christian vision of marriage, We must once again declare that the direct interruption of the generative process already begun, and, above all, directly willed and procured abortion, even if for therapeutic reasons, are to be absolutely excluded as licit means of regulating birth.[9]

[8] Cf. John XXIII, Encyc. *Mater et Magista,* in AAS LIII (1961), p. 447.

[9] Cf. *Catechisms Romanus Concilii Tridentini,* Part II, Ch. VIII; Pius XI, Encyc. *Casti Connubii,* in AAS XXII (1930), pp. 562–564; Pius XII, *Discorsi e Radiomessaggi,* VI (1944), pp. 191–192; AAS XLIII (1951), pp. 842–843; pp. 857–859; John XXIII, Encyc. *Pacem in Terris,* Apr. 11, 1963, in AAS LV (1963), pp. 259–260; *Gaudium et Spes,* No. 51.

Equally to be excluded, as the teaching authority of the Church has frequently declared, is direct sterilization, whether perpetual or temporary, whether of the man or of the woman.[10] Similarly excluded is every action which, either in anticipation of the conjugal act, or in its accomplishment, or in the development of its natural consequences, proposes, whether as an end or as a means, to render procreation impossible.[11]

To justify conjugal acts made intentionally infecund, one cannot invoke as valid reasons the lesser evil, or the fact that such acts would constitute a whole together with the fecund acts already performed or to follow later, and hence would share in one and the same moral goodness. In truth, if it is sometimes licit to tolerate a lesser evil in order to avoid a greater evil or to promote a greater good,[12] it is not licit, even for the gravest reasons, to do evil so that good may follow therefrom;[13] that is, to make into the object of a positive act of the will something which is intrinsically disorder, and hence unworthy of the human person, even when the intention is to safeguard or promote individual, family or social well-being. Consequently it is an error to think that a conjugal act which is deliberately made infecund and so is intrinsically dishonest could be made honest and right by the ensemble of a fecund conjugal life.

LICITNESS OF THERAPEUTIC MEANS

The Church, on the contrary, does not at all consider illicit the use of those therapeutic means truly necessary to cure diseases of the organism, even if an impediment to procreation, which may be foreseen, should result therefrom, provided such impediment is not, for whatever motive, directly willed.[14]

LICITNESS OF RECOURSE TO INFECUND PERIODS

To this teaching of the Church on conjugal morals, the objection is made today, as We observed earlier (No. 3), that it is the prerogative of the human intellect to dominate the energies offered by irrational nature and to orientate them towards an end conformable to the good of man. Now, some may ask: In the present case, is it not reasonable in many circum-

[10] Cf. Pius XI, Encyc. *Casti Connubii,* in AAS XXII (1930), p. 565; Decree of the Holy Office, Feb. 22, 1940, in AAS L (1958), pp. 734–735.

[11] Cf. *Catechismus Romanus Concilii Tridentini,* Part II, Ch. VIII; Pius XI, Encyc. *Casti Connubii,* in AAS XXII (1930), pp. 559–561; Pius XII, AAS XLIII (1951), p. 843; AAS L (1958), pp. 734–735; John XXIII, Encyc. *Mater et Magistra,* in AAS LIII (1961), p. 447.

[12] Cf. Pius XII, Alloc. to the National Congress of the Union of Catholic Jurists, Dec. 6, 1953, in AAS XLV (1953), pp. 798–799.

[13] Cf. *Rom.,* 3, 8.

[14] Cf. Pius XII, Alloc. to Congress of the Italian Association of Urology, Oct. 8, 1953, in AAS XLV (1953), pp. 674–675; AAS L (1958), pp. 734–735.

stances to have recourse to artificial birth control if, thereby, we secure the harmony and peace of the family, and better conditions for the education of the children already born? To this question it is necessary to reply with clarity: The Church is the first to praise and recommend the intervention of intelligence in a function which so closely associates the rational creature with his Creator; but she affirms that this must be done with respect for the order established by God.

If, then, there are serious motives to space out births, which derive from the physical or psychological conditions of husband and wife, or from external conditions, the Church teaches that it is then licit to take into account the natural rhythms immanent in the generative functions, for the use of marriage in the infecund periods only, and in this way to regulate birth without offending the moral principles which have been recalled earlier.[15]

The Church is coherent with herself when she considers recourse to the infecund periods to be licit, while at the same time condemning, as being always illicit, the use of means directly contrary to fecundation, even if such use is inspired by reasons which may appear honest and serious. In reality, there are essential differences between the two cases: in the former, the married couple make legitimate use of a natural disposition; in the latter, they impede the development of natural processes. It is true that, in the one and the other case, the married couple are concordant in the positive will of avoiding children for plausible reasons, seeking the certainty that offspring will not arrive; but it is also true that only in the former case are they able to renounce the use of marriage in the fecund periods when, for just motives, procreation is not desirable, while making use of it during infecund periods to manifest their affection and to safeguard their mutual fidelity. By so doing, they give proof of a truly and integrally honest love.

GRAVE CONSEQUENCES OF METHODS OF ARTIFICIAL BIRTH CONTROL

Upright men can even better convince themselves of the solid grounds on which the teaching of the Church in this field is based, if they care to reflect upon the consequences of methods of artificial birth control. Let them consider, first of all, how wide and easy a road would thus be opened up towards conjugal infidelity and the general lowering of morality. Not much experience is needed in order to know human weakness, and to understand that men—especially the young, who are so vulnerable on this point—have need of encouragement to be faithful to the moral law, so that they must not be offered some easy means of eluding its observance. It is also to be feared that the man, growing used to the employment of anti-conceptive practices, may finally lose respect for the woman and, no

[15] Cf. Pius XII, AAS XLIII (1951), p. 846.

longer caring for her physical and psychological equilibrium, may come to the point of considering her as a mere instrument of selfish enjoyment, and no longer as his respected and beloved companion.

Let it be considered also that a dangerous weapon would thus be placed in the hands of those public Authorities who take no heed of moral exigencies. Who could blame a Government for applying to the solution of the problems of the community those means acknowledged to be licit for married couples in the solution of a family problem? Who will stop rulers from favouring, from even imposing upon their peoples, if they were to consider it necessary, the method of contraception which they judge to be most efficacious? In such a way men, wishing to avoid individual, family, or social difficulties encountered in the observance of the divine law, would reach the point of placing at the mercy of the intervention of public Authorities the most personal and most reserved sector of conjugal intimacy.

Consequently, if the mission of generating life is not to be exposed to the arbitrary will of men, one must necessarily recognize insurmountable limits to the possibility of man's domination over his own body and its functions; limits which no man, whether a private individual or one invested with authority, may licitly surpass. And such limits cannot be determined otherwise than by the respect due to the integrity of the human organism and its functions, according to the principles recalled earlier, and also according to the correct understanding of the 'principle of totality' illustrated by Our Predecessor Pope Pius XII.[16]

THE CHURCH GUARANTOR OF TRUE HUMAN VALUES

It can be foreseen that this teaching will perhaps not be easily received by all: too numerous are those voices—amplified by the modern means of propaganda—which are contrary to the voice of the Church. To tell the truth, the Church is not surprised to be made, like her divine Founder, a 'sign of contradiction';[17] yet she does not because of this cease to proclaim with humble firmness the entire moral law, both natural and evangelical. Of such laws the Church was not the author, nor consequently can she be their arbiter; she is only their depositary and their interpreter, without ever being able to declare to be licit that which is not so by reason of its intimate and unchangeable opposition to the true good of man.

In defending conjugal morals in their integral wholeness, the Church knows that she contributes towards the establishment of a truly human civilization; she engages man not to abdicate from his own responsibility in order to rely on technical means; by that very fact she defends the dignity of man and wife. Faithful to both the teaching and the example of the Saviour, she shows herself to be the sincere and disinterested friend of

[16] Cf. AAS XLV (1953), pp. 674–675; AAS XLVIII (1956), pp. 461–462.
[17] Cf. *Lk.*, 2, 34.

men, whom she wishes to help, even during their earthly sojourn, 'to share as sons in the life of the living God, the Father of al men.'[18]

RICHARD WASSERSTROM
Is Adultery Immoral?

Many discussions of the enforcement of morality by the law take as illustrative of the problem under consideration the regulation of various types of sexual behavior by the criminal law. It was, for example, the Wolfenden Report's recommendations concerning homosexuality and prostitution that led Lord Devlin to compose his now famous lecture, "The Enforcement of Morals." And that lecture in turn provoked important philosophical responses from H. L. A. Hart, Ronald Dworkin, and others.

Much, if not all, of the recent philosophical literature on the enforcement of morals appears to take for granted the immorality of the sexual behavior in question. The focus of discussion, at least, is whether such things as homosexuality, prostitution, and adultery ought to be made illegal even if they are immoral, and not whether they are immoral.

I propose in this paper to think about the latter, more neglected topic, that of sexual morality, and to do so in the following fashion. I shall consider just one kind of behavior that is often taken to be a case of sexual immorality—adultery. I am interested in pursuing at least two questions. First, I want to explore the question of in what respects adulterous behavior falls within the domain of morality at all. For this surely is one of the puzzles one encounters when considering the topic of sexual morality. It is often hard to see on what grounds much of the behavior is deemed to be either moral or immoral, for example, private homosexual behavior between consenting adults. I have purposely selected adultery because it seems a more plausible candidate for moral assessment than many other kinds of sexual behavior.

The second question I want to examine is that of what is to be said about adultery, without being especially concerned to stay within the area of morality. I shall endeavor, in other words, to identify and to assess a number of the major arguments that might be advanced against adultery. I believe that they are the chief arguments that would be given in support of the view that adultery is immoral, but I think they are worth considering even if some of them turn out to be nonmoral arguments and considerations.

A number of the issues involved seem to me to be complicated and

[18] Cf. Paul VI, Encyc. *Populorum Progessio*, March 26, 1967, No. 21.

difficult. In a number of places I have at best indicated where further philosophical exploration is required without having successfully conducted the exploration myself. The paper may very well be more useful as an illustration of how one might begin to think about the subject of sexual morality than as an elucidation of important truths about the topic.

Before I turn to the arguments themselves there are two preliminary points that require some clarification. Throughout the paper I shall refer to the immorality of such things as breaking a promise, deceiving someone, etc. In a very rough way, I mean by this that there is something morally wrong that is done in doing the action in question. I mean that the action is, in a strong sense, of *"prima facie"* prima facie wrong or unjustified. I do not mean that it may never be right or justifiable to do the action; just that the fact that it is an action of this description always does count against the rightness of the action. I leave entirely open the question of what it is that makes actions of this kind immoral in this sense of "immoral."

The second preliminary point concerns what is meant or implied by the concept of adultery. I mean by "adultery" any case of extramarital sex, and I want to explore the arguments for and against extramarital sex, undertaken in a variety of morally relevant situations. Someone might claim that the concept of adultery is conceptually connected with the concept of immorality, and that to characterize behavior as adulterous is already to characterize it as immoral or unjustified in the sense described above. There may be something to this. Hence the importance of making it clear that I want to talk about extramarital sexual relations. If they are always immoral, this is something that must be shown by argument. If the concept of adultery does in some sense entail or imply immorality, I want to ask whether that connection is a rationally based one. If not all cases of extramarital sex are immoral (again, in the sense described above), then the concept of adultery should either be weakened accordingly or restricted to those classes of extramarital sex for which the predication of immorality is warranted.

One argument for the immorality of adultery might go something like this: what makes adultery immoral is that it involves the breaking of a promise, and what makes adultery seriously wrong is that it involves the breaking of an important promise. For, so the argument might continue, one of the things the two parties promise each other when they get married is that they will abstain from sexual relationships with third persons. Because of this promise both spouses quite reasonably entertain the expectation that the other will behave in conformity with it. Hence, when one of the parties has sexual intercourse with a third person he or she breaks that promise about sexual relationships which was made when the marriage was entered into, and defeats the reasonable expectations of exclusivity entertained by the spouse.

241

In many cases the immorality involved in breaching the promise relating to extramarital sex may be a good deal more serious than that involved in the breach of other promises. This is so because adherence to this promise may be of much greater importance to the parties than is adherence to many of the other promises given or received by them in their lifetime. The breaking of this promise may be much more hurtful and painful than is typically the case.

Why is this so? To begin with, it may have been difficult for the non-adulterous spouse to have kept the promise. Hence that spouse may feel the unfairness of having restrained himself or herself in the absence of reciprocal restraint having been exercised by the adulterous spouse. In addition, the spouse may perceive the breaking of the promise as an indication of a kind of indifference on the part of the adulterous spouse. If you really cared about me and my feelings—the spouse might say—you would not have done this to me. And third, and related to the above, the spouse may see the act of sexual intercourse with another as a sign of affection for the other person and as an additional rejection of the non-adulterous spouse as the one who is loved by the adulterous spouse. It is not just that the adulterous spouse does not take the feelings of the spouse sufficiently into account, the adulterous spouse also indicates through the act of adultery affection for someone other than the spouse. I will return to these points later. For the present, it is sufficient to note that a set of arguments can be developed in support of the proposition that certain kinds of adultery are wrong just because they involve the breach of a serious promise which, among other things, leads to the intentional infliction of substantial pain by one spouse upon the other.

Another argument for the immorality of adultery focuses not on the existence of a promise of sexual exclusivity but on the connection between adultery and deception. According to this argument, adultery involves deception. And because deception is wrong, so is adultery.

Although it is certainly not obviously so, I shall simply assume in this paper that deception is always immoral. Thus the crucial issue for my purposes is the asserted connection between extramarital sex and deception. Is it plausible to maintain, as this argument does, that adultery always does involve deception and is on that basis to be condemned?

The most obvious person on whom deceptions might be practiced is the nonparticipating spouse; and the most obvious thing about which the nonparticipating spouse can be deceived is the existence of the adulterous act. One clear case of deception is that of lying. Instead of saying that the afternoon was spent in bed with A, the adulterous spouse asserts that it was spent in the library with B, or on the golf course with C.

There can also be deception even when no lies are told. Suppose, for instance, that a person has sexual intercourse with someone other than his or her spouse and just does not tell the spouse about it. Is that deception?

242

It may not be a case of lying if, for example, the spouse is never asked by the other about the situation. Still, we might say, it is surely deceptive because of the promises that were exchanged at marriage. As we saw earlier, these promises provide a foundation for the reasonable belief that neither spouse will engage in sexual relationships with any other persons. Hence the failure to bring the fact of extramarital sex to the attention of the other spouse deceives that spouse about the present state of the marital relationship.

Adultery, in other words, can involve both active and passive deception. An adulterous spouse may just keep silent or, as is often the fact, the spouse may engage in an increasingly complex way of life devoted to the concealment of the facts from the nonparticipating spouse. Lies, half-truths, clandestine meetings, and the like may become a central feature of the adulterous spouse's existence. These are things that can and do happen, and when they do they make the case against adultery an easy one. Still, neither active nor passive deception is inevitably a feature of an extramarital relationship.

It is possible, though, that a more subtle but pervasive kind of deceptiveness is a feature of adultery. It comes about because of the connection in our culture between sexual intimacy and certain feelings of love and affection. The point can be made indirectly at first by seeing that one way in which we can, in our culture, mark off our close friends from our mere acquaintances is through the kinds of intimacies that we are prepared to share with them. I may, for instance, be willing to reveal my very private thoughts and emotions to my closest friends or to my wife, but to no one else. My sharing of these intimate facts about myself is from one perspective a way of making a gift to those who mean the most to me. Revealing these things and sharing them with those who mean the most to me is one means by which I create, maintain, and confirm those interpersonal relationships that are of most importance to me.

Now in our culture, it might be claimed, sexual intimacy is one of the chief currencies through which gifts of this sort are exchanged. One way to tell someone—particularly someone of the opposite sex—that you have feelings of affection and love for them is by allowing to them or sharing with them sexual behaviors that one doesn't share with the rest of the world. This way of measuring affection was certainly very much a part of the culture in which I matured. It worked something like this. If you were a girl, you showed how much you liked someone by the degree of sexual intimacy you would allow. If you liked a boy only a little, you never did more than kiss—and even the kiss was not very passionate. If you liked the boy a lot and if your feeling was reciprocated, necking, and possibly petting, was permissible. If the attachment was still stronger and you thought it might even become a permanent relationship, the sexual activity was correspondingly more intense and more intimate, although 243 whether it would ever lead to sexual intercourse depended on whether the parties (and particularly the girl) accepted fully the prohibition on non-marital sex. The situation for the boy was related, but not exactly the same. The assumption was that males did not naturally link sex with affection in the way in which females did. However, since women did, males had to take this into account. That is to say, because a woman would permit sexual intimacies only if she had feelings of affection for the male and only if those feelings were reciprocated, the male had to have and express those feelings, too, before sexual intimacies of any sort would occur.

The result was that the importance of a correlation between sexual intimacy and feelings of love and affection was taught by the culture and assimilated by those growing up in the culture. The scale of possible positive feelings toward persons of the other sex ran from casual liking at the one end to the love that was deemed essential to and characteristic of marriage at the other. The scale of possible sexual behavior ran from brief, passionless kissing or hand-holding at the one end to sexual intercourse at the other. And the correlation between the two scales was quite precise. As a result, any act of sexual intimacy carried substantial meaning with it, and no act of sexual intimacy was simply a pleasurable set of bodily sensations. Many such acts were, of course, more pleasurable to the participants because they were a way of saying what the participants feelings were. And sometimes they were less pleasurable for the same reason. The point is, however, that in any event sexual activity was much more than mere bodily enjoyment. It was not like eating a good meal, listening to good music, lying in the sun, or getting a pleasant back rub. It was behavior that meant a great deal concerning one's feelings for persons of the opposite sex in whom one was most interested and with whom one was most involved. It was among the most authoritative ways in which one could communicate to another the nature and degree of one's affection.

If this sketch is even roughly right, then several things become somewhat clearer. To begin with, a possible rationale for many of the rules of conventional sexual morality can be developed. If, for example, sexual intercourse is associated with the kind of affection and commitment to another that is regarded as characteristic of the marriage relationship, then it is natural that sexual intercourse should be thought properly to take place between persons who are married to each other. And if it is thought that this kind of affection and commitment is only to be found within the marriage relationship, then it is not surprising that sexual intercourse should only be thought to be proper within marriage.

Related to what has just been said is the idea that sexual intercourse ought to be restricted to those who are married to each other as a means by which to confirm the very special feelings that the spouses have for each other. Because the culture teaches that sexual intercourse means that the strongest of all feelings for each other are shared by the lovers, it is natural that persons who are married to each other should be able to say this to each other in this way. Revealing and confirming verbally that these feelings are present is one thing that helps to sustain the relationship; engaging in sexual intercourse is another.

In addition, this account would help to provide a framework within which to make sense of the notion that some sex is better than other sex. As I indicated earlier, the fact that sexual intimacy can be meaningful in the sense described tends to make it also the case that sexual intercourse can sometimes be more enjoyable than at other times. On this view, sexual intercourse will typically be more enjoyable where the strong feelings of affection are present than it will be where it is merely "mechanical." This is so in part because people enjoy being loved, especially by those whom they love. Just as we like to hear words of affection, so we like to receive affectionate behavior. And the meaning enhances the independently pleasureable behavior.

More to the point, moreover, an additional rationale for the prohibition on extramarital sex can now be developed. For given this way of viewing the sexual world, extramarital sex will almost always involve deception of a deeper sort. If the adulterous spouse does not in fact have the appropriate feelings of affection for the extramarital partner, then the adulterous spouse is deceiving that person about the presence of such feelings. If, on the other hand, the adulterous spouse does have the corresponding feelings for the extramarital partner but not toward the nonparticipating spouse, the adulterous spouse is very probably deceiving the nonparticipating spouse about the presence of such feelings toward that spouse. Indeed, it might be argued, whenever there is no longer love between the two persons who are married to each other, there is deception just because being married implies both to the participants and to the world that such a bond exists. Deception is inevitable, the argument might conclude, because the feelings of affection that ought to accompany any act of sexual intercourse can only be held toward one other person at any given time in one's life. And if this is so, then the adulterous spouse always deceives either the partner in adultery or the nonparticipating spouse about the existence of such feelings. Thus extramarital sex involves deception of this sort and is for this reason immoral even if no deception vis-à-vis the occurrence of the act of adultery takes place.

What might be said in response to the foregoing arguments? The first thing that might be said is that the account of the connection between sexual intimacy and feelings of affection is inaccurate. Not inaccurate in the sense that no one thinks of things that way, but in the sense that there is substantially more divergence of opinion than that account suggests. For example, the view I have delineated may describe reasonably accu- 245 rately the concepts of the sexual world in which I grew up, but it does not capture the sexual *weltanschauung* of today's youth at all. Thus, whether or not adultery implies deception in respect to feelings depends very much on the persons who are involved and the way they look at the "meaning" of sexual intimacy.

Second, the argument leaves to be answered the question of whether it is desirable for sexual intimacy to carry the sorts of messages described above. For those persons for whom sex does have these implications, there are special feelings and sensibilities that must be taken into account. But it is another question entirely whether any valuable end—moral or otherwise—is served by investing sexual behavior with such significance. That is something that must be shown and not just assumed. It might, for instance, be the case that substantially more good than harm would come from a kind of demystification of sexual behavior: one that would encourage the enjoyment of sex more for its own sake and one that would reject the centrality both of the association of sex with love and of love with only one other person.

I regard these as two of the more difficult, unresolved issues that our culture faces today in respect to thinking sensibly about the attitudes toward sex and love that we should try to develop in ourselves and in our children. Much of the contemporary literature that advocates sexual liberation of one sort or another embraces one or the other of two different views about the relationship between sex and love.

One view holds that sex should be separated from love and affection. To be sure sex is probably better when the partners genuinely like and enjoy each other. But sex is basically an intensive, exciting sensuous activity that can be enjoyed in a variety of suitable settings with a variety of suitable partners. The situation in respect to sexual pleasure is no different from that of the person who knows and appreciates fine food and who can have a very satisfying meal in any number of good restaurants with any number of congenial companions. One question that must be settled here is whether sex can be so demystified; another, more important question is whether it would be desirable to do so. What would we gain and what might we lose if we all lived in a world in which an act of sexual intercourse was no more or less significant or enjoyable than having a delicious meal in a nice setting with a good friend? The answer to this question lies beyond the scope of this paper.

The second view seeks to drive the wedge in a different place. It is not the link between sex and love that needs to be broken; rather, on this view, it is the connection between love and exclusivity that ought to be severed. For a number of the reasons already given, it is desirable, so this argument goes, that sexual intimacy continue to be reserved to and shared with only those for whom one has very great affection. The mistake lies
246 in thinking that any "normal" adult will only have those feelings toward

one other adult during his or her lifetime—or even at any time in his or her life. It is the concept of adult love, not ideas about sex, that, on this view, needs demystification. What are thought to be both unrealistic and unfortunate are the notions of exclusivity and possessiveness that attach to the dominant conception of love between adults in our and other cultures. Parents of four, five, six, or even ten children can certainly claim and sometimes claim correctly that they love all of their children, that they love them all equally, and that it is simply untrue to their feelings to insist that the numbers involved diminish either the quantity or the quality of their love. If this is an idea that is readily understandable in the case of parents and children, there is no necessary reason why it is an impossible or undesirable ideal in the case of adults. To be sure, there is probably a limit to the number of intimate, "primary" relationships that any person can maintain at any given time without the quality of the relationship being affected. But one adult ought surely be able to love two, three, or even six other adults at any one time without that love being different in kind or degree from that of the traditional, monogomous, lifetime marriage. And as between the individuals in these relationships, whether within a marriage or without, sexual intimacy is fitting and good.

The issues raised by a position such as this one are also surely worth exploring in detail and with care. Is there something to be called "sexual love" which is different from parental love or the nonsexual love of close friends? Is there something about love in general that links it naturally and appropriately with feelings of exclusivity and possession? Or is there something about sexual love, whatever that may be, that makes these feelings especially fitting here? Once again the issues are conceptual, empirical, and normative all at once: What is love? How could it be different? Would it be a good thing or a bad thing if it were different?

Suppose, though, that having delineated these problems we were now to pass them by. Suppose, moreover, we were to be persuaded of the possibility and the desirability of weakening substantially either the links between sex and love or the links between sexual love and exclusivity. Would it not then be the case that adultery could be free from all of the morally objectionable features described so far? To be more specific, let us imagine that a husband and wife have what is today sometimes characterized as an "open marriage." Suppose, that is, that they have agreed in advance that extramarital sex is—under certain circumstances—acceptable behavior for each to engage in. Suppose, that as a result there is no impulse to deceive each other about the occurrence or nature of any such relationships, and that no deception in fact occurs. Suppose, too, that there is no deception in respect to the feelings involved between the adulterous spouse and the extramarital partner. And suppose, finally, that one or the other or both of the spouses then has sexual intercourse in circumstances consistent with these understandings. Under this description, so the agreement might 247 conclude, adultery is simply not immoral. At a minimum, adultery cannot very plausibly be condemned either on the ground that it involves deception or on the ground that it requires the breaking of a promise.

At least two responses are worth considering. One calls attention to the connection between marriage and adultery; the other looks to more instrumental arguments for the immorality of adultery. Both issues deserve further exploration.

One way to deal with the case of the "open marriage" is to question whether the two persons involved are still properly to be described as being married to each other. Part of the meaning of what it is for two persons to be married to each other, so this argument would go, is to have committed oneself to have sexual relationships only with one's spouse. Of course, it would be added, we know that that commitment is not always honored. We know that persons who are married to each other often do commit adultery. But there is a difference between being willing to make a commitment to marital fidelity, even though one may fail to honor that commitment, and not making the commitment at all. Whatever the relationship may be between the two individuals in the case described above, the absence of any commitment to sexual exclusivity requires the conclusion that their relationship is not a marital one. For a commitment to sexual exclusivity is a necessary although not a sufficient condition for the existence of a marriage.

Although there may be something to this suggestion, as it is stated it is too strong to be acceptable. To begin with, I think it is very doubtful that there are many, if any, *necessary* conditions for marriage; but even if there are, a commitment to sexual exclusivity is not such a condition.

To see that this is so, consider what might be taken to be some of the essential characteristics of a marriage. We might be tempted to propose that the concept of marriage requires the following: a formal ceremony of some sort in which mutual obligations are undertaken between two persons of the opposite sex; the capacity on the part of the persons involved to have sexual intercourse with each other; the willingness to have sexual intercourse only with each other; and feelings of love and affection between the two persons. The problem is that we can imagine relationships that are clearly marital and yet lack one or more of these features. For example, in our own society, it is possible for two persons to be married without going through a formal ceremony, as in the common-law marriages recognized in some jurisdictions. It is also possible for two persons to get married even though one or both lacks the capacity to engage in sexual intercourse. Thus, two very elderly persons who have neither the desire nor the ability to have intercourse can, nonetheless, get married, as can persons whose sexual organs have been injured so that intercourse is not possible. And we certainly know of marriages in which love was not present at the time of the marriage, as, for instance, in marriages of state and 248 marriages of convenience.

Counterexamples not satisfying the condition relating to the abstention from extramarital sex are even more easily produced. We certainly know of societies and cultures in which polygamy and polyandry are practiced, and we have no difficulty in recognizing these relationships as cases of marriages. It might be objected, though, that these are not counterexamples because they are plural marriages rather than marriages in which sex is permitted with someone other than with one of the persons to whom one is married. But we also know of societies in which it is permissible for married persons to have sexual relationships with persons to whom they were not married, for example, temple prostitutes, concubines, and homosexual lovers. And even if we knew of no such societies, the conceptual claim would still, I submit, not be well taken. For suppose all of the other indicia of marriage were present: suppose the two persons were of the opposite sex. Suppose they had the capacity and desire to have intercourse with each other, suppose they participated in a formal ceremony in which they understood themselves voluntarily to be entering into a relationship with each other in which substantial mutual commitments were assumed. If all these conditions were satisfied, we would not be in any doubt about whether or not the two persons were married even though they had not taken on a commitment of sexual exclusivity and even though they had expressly agreed that extramarital sexual intercourse was a permissible behavior for each to engage in.

A commitment to sexual exclusivity is neither a necessary nor a sufficient condition for the existence of a marriage. It does, nonetheless, have this much to do with the nature of marriage: like the other indicia enumerated above, its presence tends to establish the existence of a marriage. Thus, in the absence of a formal ceremony of any sort, an explicit commitment to sexual exclusivity would count in favor of regarding the two persons as married. The conceptual role of the commitment to sexual exclusivity can, perhaps, be brought out through the following example. Suppose we found a tribe which had a practice in which all the other indicia of marriage were present but in which the two parties were *prohibited* ever from having sexual intercourse with each other. Moreover, suppose that sexual intercourse with others was clearly permitted. In such a case we would, I think, reject the idea that the two were married to each other and we would describe their relationship in other terms, for example, as some kind of formalized, special friendship relation—a kind of heterosexual "blood-brother" bond.

Compare that case with the following. Suppose again that the tribe had a practice in which all of the other indicia of marriage were present, but instead of a prohibition on sexual intercourse between the persons in the relationship there was no rule at all. Sexual intercourse was permissible with the person with whom one had this ceremonial relationship, but it was no more or less permissible than with a number of other persons to whom one was not so related (for instance, all consenting adults of the 249 opposite sex). Although we might be in doubt as to whether we ought to describe the persons as married to each other, we would probably conclude that they were married and that they simply were members of a tribe whose views about sex were quite different from our own.

What all of this shows is that *a prohibition* on sexual intercourse between the two persons involved in a relationship is conceptually incompatible with the claim that the two of them are married. The *permissibility* of intramarital sex is a necessary part of the idea of marriage. But no such incompatibility follows simply from the added permissibility of extramarital sex.

These arguments do not, of course, exhaust the arguments for the prohibition on extramarital sexual relations. The remaining argument that I wish to consider—as I indicated earlier—is a more instrumental one. It seeks to justify the prohibition by virtue of the role that it plays in the development and maintenance of nuclear families. The argument, or set of arguments, might, I believe, go something like this.

Consider first a farfetched nonsexual example. Suppose a society were organized so that after some suitable age—say, 18, 19, or 20—persons were forbidden to eat anything but bread and water with anyone but their spouse. Persons might still choose in such a society not to get married. Good food just might not be very important to them because they have underdeveloped taste buds. Or good food might be bad for them because there is something wrong with their digestive system. Or good food might be important to them, but they might decide that the enjoyment of good food would get in the way of the attainment of other things that were more important. But most persons would, I think, be led to favor marriage in part because they preferred a richer, more varied, diet to one of bread and water. And they might remain married because the family was the only legitimate setting within which good food was obtainable. If it is important to have society organized so that persons will both get married and stay married, such an arrangement would be well suited to the preservation of the family, and the prohibitions relating to food consumption could be understood as fulfilling that function.

It is obvious that one of the more powerful human desires is the desire for sexual gratification. The desire is a natural one, like hunger and thirst, in the sense that it need not be learned in order to be present within us and operative upon us. But there is in addition much that we do learn about what the act of sexual intercourse is like. Once we experience sexual intercourse ourselves—and in particular once we experience orgasm—we discover that it is among the most intensive, short-term pleasures of the body.

Because this is so, it is easy to see how the prohibition upon extramarital sex helps to hold marriage together. At least during that period of life when the enjoyment of sexual intercourse is one of the desirable bodily 250 pleasures, persons will wish to enjoy those pleasures. If one consequence of being married is that one is prohibited from having sexual intercourse with anyone but one's spouse, then the spouses in a marriage are in a position to provide an important source of pleasure for each other that is unavailable to them elsewhere in the society.

The point emerges still more clearly if this rule of sexual morality is seen as of a piece with the other rules of sexual morality. When this prohibition is coupled, for example, with the prohibition on nonmarital sexual intercourse, we are presented with the inducement both to get married and to stay married. For if sexual intercourse is only legitimate within marriage, then persons seeking that gratification which is a feature of sexual intercourse are furnished explicit social directions for its attainment; namely marriage.

Nor, to continue the argument, is it necessary to focus exclusively on the bodily enjoyment that is involved. Orgasm may be a significant part of what there is to sexual intercourse, but it is not the whole of it. We need only recall the earlier discussion of the meaning that sexual intimacy has in our own culture to begin to see some of the more intricate ways in which sexual exclusivity may be connected with the establishment and maintenance of marriage as the primary heterosexual, love relationship. Adultery is wrong, in other words, because a prohibition on extramarital sex is a way to help maintain the institutions of marriage and the nuclear family.

Now I am frankly not sure what we are to say about an argument such as this one. What I am convinced of is that, like the arguments discussed earlier, this one also reveals something of the difficulty and complexity of the issues that are involved. So, what I want now to do—in the brief and final portion of this paper—is to try to delineate with reasonable precision what I take several of the fundamental, unresolved issues to be.

The first is whether this last argument is an argument for the *immorality* of extramarital sexual intercourse. What does seem clear is that there are differences between this argument and the ones considered earlier. The earlier arguments condemned adulterous behavior because it was behavior that involved breaking of a promise, taking unfair advantage, or deceiving another. To the degree to which the prohibition on extramarital sex can be supported by arguments which invoke considerations such as these, there is little question but that violations of the prohibition are properly regarded as immoral. And such a claim could be defended on one or both of two distinct grounds. The first is that things like promise-breaking and deception are just wrong. The second is that adultery involving promise-breaking or deception is wrong because it involves the straightforward infliction of harm on another human being—typically the nonadulterous spouse—who has a strong claim not to have that harm so inflicted.

The argument that connects the prohibition on extramarital sex with the maintenance and preservation of the institution of marriage is an argument for the instrumental value of the prohibition. To some degree this 251 counts, I think, against regarding all violations of the prohibition as obvious cases of immorality. This is so partly because hypothetical imperatives are less clearly within the domain of morality than are categorical ones, and even more because instrumental prohibitions are within the domain of morality only if the end they serve or the way they serve it is itself within the domain of morality.

What this should help us see, I think, is the fact that the argument that connects the prohibition on adultery with the preservation of marriage is at best seriously incomplete. Before we ought to be convinced by it, we ought to have reasons for believing that marriage is a morally desirable and just social institution. And this is not quite as easy or obvious a task as it may seem to be. For the concept of marriage is, as we have seen, both a loosely structured and a complicated one. There may be all sorts of intimate, interpersonal relationships which will resemble but not be identical with the typical marriage relationship presupposed by the traditional sexual morality. There may be a number of distinguishable sexual and loving arrangements which can all legitimately claim to be called *marriages*. The prohibitions of the traditional sexual morality may be effective ways to maintain some marriages and ineffective ways to promote and preserve others. The prohibitions of the traditional sexual morality may make good psychological sense if certain psychological theories are true, and they may be purveyors of immense psychological mischief if other psychological theories are true. The prohibitions of the traditional sexual morality may seem obviously correct if sexual intimacy carries the meaning that the dominant culture has often ascribed to it, and they may seem equally bizarre when sex is viewed through the perspective of the counter-culture. Irrespective of whether instrumental arguments of this sort are properly deemed moral arguments, they ought not to fully convince anyone until questions like these are answered.

RONALD ATKINSON
The Morality of
Homosexual Behavior

The Wolfenden Committee did not spend much time on the question of morality of homosexual behaviour. Possibly they felt that in any way to question its immorality would only arouse opposition to their recommenda-

Reprinted from Ronald Atkinson, *Sexual Morality*, copyright © 1965 by Ronald Atkinson. Reprinted by permission of the author, Harcourt Brace Jovanovich, Inc., and Hutchinson & Co., London.

tion concerning the attitude to be taken to it by the law. They are emphatic that, in staking a claim for a sphere of private morality and immorality beyond the reach of the law, they do not wish to be understood as condoning private immorality. Moreover, in so far as the concern is with *positive* morality, the received code of behaviour such as it is, there is no doubt at all that homosexual activity is immoral. But can one avoid asking the question whether positive morality is right on this matter? Suppose, as the Wolfenden Committee thought, that there may be homosexual acts which do no harm to non-consenting non-adults, and which, being private, are no affront to public decency—on what grounds could they be held to be morally wrong?

Not on utilitarian grounds, obviously; nor, leaving out of account the present state of the law and public opinion, on prudential grounds either. People do not choose to become homosexuals, they rather find that they are: and even if they should then want to change the direction of their sexual inclinations, which they may not, there would at present seem to be no certainty that this can be successfully accomplished. To deny one's sexual nature all physical expression, still ignoring the consequences homosexuals may suffer from law and public opinion, goes beyond, if not contrary to, the demands of prudence.

It may be that, in fact, many homosexual relationships present morally objectionable features: they may involve seduction, and exploitation of the young. But the evidence noticed above suggests that most do not, and that the risk of a homosexual who practices with fellow adults turning to boys is comparatively small. It is, moreover, relevant to the assessment of the moral importance of such risk as there is to point out that the harm done by seduction, or even assault, to young boys can easily be exaggerated— as can the damage done by heterosexual interference with small girls. In both cases the extreme reactions of parents, understandable though they may be, tend to increase the harm. And the likelihood of a boy being turned into a homosexual by seduction would not seem to be very great, as home influences are more important than outside encounters in determining one's sexual orientation. Most men who engage in homosexual activity in special circumstances—school, prison, the army—appear to abandon it when heterosexual opportunities become available. Some, much, even most homosexual activity may be morally exceptionable: so too is a good deal of heterosexual activity. In neither case is this necessarily so. Nor does it appear that homosexual relationships in themselves are necessarily more objectionable than heterosexual ones. I can see no good reason to doubt that it is possible for a homosexual to conduct his sexual life with prudence, beneficence, fairness and responsibility. If he does, there is no ground for moral complaint.

Another claim that is often made is that homosexual relationships are apt to be morally worthless or of little worth, to fall very far short of the ideal form of human relationship. (It is important to distinguish this com- 253 plaint from the previous one. *That* was to the effect that they offended against, so to say, 'basic morality': *this* is to the effect that they are not ideal. . . .) Homosexual relations seem normally to be of brief duration, and homosexual promiscuity to be common. They seem, that is to say, to resemble those heterosexual relationships which are held to be least worth while. This sort of contention has great rhetorical force. It purports to make a lavish concession, to allow, as, of course, many people do not, that homosexual relationships are to be judged on the *same footing* as heterosexual ones, and yet still contrives to find them objectionable. How far must we go along with it?

Two comments are in place. The first, and less important one, is that the unworthwhile features manifested by some homosexual relationships may largely be the result of the public attitude to them. The result of, and hence not the justification for, that attitude. Stable relationships are hardly possible when all homosexual associations are condemned out of hand. The more important point is that, low though casual sexual encounters may be on the heterosexual's scale of preference, they may still be the best or only form of sexual association available to the homosexuals involved. The basic morality of avoiding harm and unfairness to others we may reasonably demand of everybody: our ideals in so far as they go beyond this are for the guidance of our own, not other people's, conduct. In general we do not blame people, or hold them to be wicked or immoral, for not sharing our ideals; at worst we may hold them misguided or mistaken, or that they are 'missing something'. It is doubtful, in fact, whether even such mild criticisms or commiserations fit the case of the homosexual, who has not chosen his condition and probably cannot change it.

It may further be noted that from the point of view of the morality of personal relationships, which was considered in a different connexion above . . . , homosexual associations as such cannot be held to be immoral. The authors of the Quaker pamphlet recognise this with characteristic candour:

. . . we see no reason why the physical nature of a sexual act should be
the criterion by which the question whether it is moral should be decided. An
act which (for example) expresses true affection between two individuals
and gives pleasure to them both, does not seem to us to be sinful by
reason *alone* of the fact that it is homosexual. The same criteria seem to us
to apply whether a relationship is heterosexual or homosexual [p. 36].

I expressed some doubt above about the responsibility of viewing heterosexual associations exclusively from the agent-centred ethic of personal relationships. This seemed to me to take insufficient account of the possibility of children being conceived. This consideration does not arise where homosexual associations are concerned.

It is true, of course, that many people find the thought of homosexual practice deeply disgusting. It is sometimes suggested that this is the result

254

of over-compensation for their own latent homosexuality, but whatever the explanation of it, the fact remains. One cannot, however, allow any simple inference from the disgusting to the immoral. In fact, surely, in this case the movement of thought is the other way. Homosexual practices are felt to be peculiarly disgusting because they are held to be exceptionally sinful or immoral. They disgust because they are 'unnatural'.

No one who thinks like this will be induced to improve his view of homosexual activity by such claims as that made by Chesser (*Live and Let Live,* pp. 30–1) that the most abominated homosexual act, anal intercourse, is probably commoner among married than homosexual couples. The act is felt to be abominable whenever and between whomsoever it occurs. What puts homosexuals utterly beyond the pale is that *all* their physical sexual activities are necessarily unnatural in some degree, even if not in the very highest.

It is, as already suggested . . . , a matter of great difficulty to grasp the rationale of this way of thinking, to make sense of the notions of *nature* and *the natural* involved. As a beginning one has to suppose that the purpose or function of sex is mainly procreation. It would seem to follow that heterosexual intercourse which is intended to be fertile is the ideally natural sexual act. This is not, however, exactly the conclusion usually desired, for such intercourse clearly could take place outside marriage or even a loving relationship. Consequently sex has to be allowed a second, non-procreative, 'relational' or companionate purpose, which may then be held to be achievable only within marriage. Provided not too much is made of the relational purpose, provided that it is kept firmly subordinate to the procreational one, homosexual activity is still bound to come out as unnatural—it cannot fulfil procreational purposes at all. But, as we shall see in connexion with contraception in the next chapter, there are snags in emphasising the importance of the procreational purpose. Suppose we want to allow deliberately infertile heterosexual intercourse within marriage. Even in this case it is still possible to pay some regard to the claims of procreation by insisting that couples should not refuse to have children altogether, even though they may use contraceptives for a large proportion of their married life. This is a typically Anglican attitude, expressed for instance by Dr. D. S. Bailey in his 'Homosexuality and Christian Morals' (in Rees & Usill). From this point of view homosexual activity can still consistently be held to be unnatural. I do not, however, see how it can be by anyone prepared to allow permanently childless marriages, or intentionally infertile heterosexual relationships outside marriage.

It is, in my opinion, *possible* consistently to hold homosexual activity to be unnatural. Much care and ingenuity are, however, required, and I suspect that many people who do regard it as unnatural are, in fact, inconsistent at one point or another. Nor, rare though it is, is consistency enough. The *truth* of the premises concerning the purposes of sex, and the 255 relative importance of the purposes assigned, is crucial too. And yet, as observed above, it is very difficult to see how it is to be ascertained. They are not empirical premises, of which the truth could be assessed by some sort of morally neutral scientific enquiry—biological, psychological, sociological, or whatever it might be. The relevant form of enquiry is, perhaps, theological—but whether there is a subject-matter for theology is itself a controversial question. There is no ground, even in principle, for expecting reasonable men to agree on matters of theology, as there is on matters of biology, psychology and sociology. The credentials of theology as a subject are in dispute. And the propositions of natural theology are just as uncertain as those of revealed.

Accordingly, to the unbeliever, arguing to moral conclusions from theologically based premises about the nature or purpose of sex seems to be little more than a matter of arbitrarily selecting those premises which yield the moral conclusions desired. If you want to condemn contraception and homosexuality you have to emphasise the procreational purpose. If you want to permit contraception you must give greater weight to non-procreational purposes. To the believer, on the other hand, it does not seem like this at all. He must believe that questions about the nature and purpose of sex relate to matters of (non-empirical) fact. He will not see himself as arbitrarily choosing answers that are in line with moral judgments he has reached on other grounds, but rather, when he differs from his predecessors in moral theology, as correcting their mistakes of emphasis. These mistakes he may see as the result of prejudices resulting from local and temporary features of his predecessors' situation. If they attributed undue importance to procreation this will be because they did not write from the vantage point of a potentially over-populated world. The truth will never change, but our view of it does, perhaps getting nearer to it all the time.

I have myself no enthusiasm at all for appraising human conduct as natural or unnatural. I have, however, tried to draw attention to the *complexity* of the notion of the natural employed by moral theologians, mainly in order to show how different it is from that implicit in the popular condemnation of homosexual behaviour as unnatural. In the popular view the unnatural and the disgusting are closely connected, and judging something to be unnatural is felt to be the simple, direct, inevitable reaction of the 'healthy' mind to it. But there can be nothing simple in any notion of the natural which will admit of application over the whole range of sexual behaviour, which will serve as the key idea in a comprehensive sexual morality. Nor will there be any necessary connexion between the corresponding notion of the *un*natural and the disgusting.

Paris Adult Theatre I v. Slaton, 431, U.S. 49, 93 S.Ct. 2628 (1973)

The State of Georgia brought a civil action to enjoin the showing of two motion pictures, "It All Comes Out in the End" and "Magic Mirror," being shown at the Paris Adult Theatres I and II in Atlanta, Georgia. The State claimed that the films were obscene under the standards set forth in Georgia Code § 26–2101 (b) which defined obscene material as follows:

Material is obscene if considered as a whole, applying community standards, its predominant appeal is to prurient interest, that is, a shameful or morbid interest in nudity, sex or excretion, and utterly without redeeming social value and if, in addition, it goes substantially beyond customary limits of candor in describing or representing such matters. Undeveloped photographs, molds, printing plates and the like shall be deemed obscene notwithstanding that processing or other acts may be required to make the obscenity patent or to disseminate it.

The trial court denied injunctive relief, holding that even if the films were obscene, this commercial presentation could not be prohibited in the absence of proof that they were shown to minors or unconsenting adults.

The Supreme Court of Georgia reversed, holding that the films were obscene and that it was constitutionally irrelevant whether care was taken to avoid showing the movies to minors or unconsenting adults. What follows is Part II of the majority opinion by Chief Justice Burger of the Supreme Court of the United States together with Parts V and VI of the dissenting opinion of Mr. Justice Brennan.

Many of the case citations have been omitted, and the footnotes have been renumbered.

The Opinion of Mr. Chief Justice Burger

We categorically disapprove the theory, apparently adopted by the trial judge, that obscene, pornographic films acquire constitutional immunity from state regulation simply because they are exhibited for consenting adults only. This holding was properly rejected by the Georgia Supreme Court. Although we have often pointedly recognized the high importance of the state interest in regulating the exposure of obscene materials to juveniles and unconsenting adults, . . . this Court has never declared these to be the only legitimate state interests permitting regulation of obscene 257 material. The States have a long-recognized legitimate interest in regulating the use of obscene material in local commerce and in all places of public accommodation, as long as these regulations do not run afoul of specific constitutional prohibitions.... "In an unbroken series of cases extending over a long stretch of this Court's history, it has been accepted as a postulate that 'the primary requirements of decency may be enforced against obscene publications.' *Id*. [Near v. Minnesota ex rel. Olson, 283 U.S. 697 (1931)], at 716 [51 S.Ct. 625 at 631, 15 L.Ed. 1357]." Kingsley Books, Inc. v. Brown, *supra,* 354 U.S., at 440, 77 S.Ct., at 1327 (1957).

In particular, we hold that there are legitimate state interests at stake in stemming the tide of commercialized obscenity, even assuming it is feasible to enforce effective safeguards against exposure to juveniles and to the passerby.[1] Rights and interests "other than those of the advocates are involved." Cf. Breard v. Alexandria, 341 U.S. 622, 642, 71 S.Ct. 920, 932, 95 L.Ed. 1233 (1951). These include the interest of the public in the quality of life and the total community environment, the tone of commerce in the great city centers, and, possibly, the public safety itself. The Hill-Link Minority Report of the Commission on Obscenity and Pornography indicates that there is at least an arguable correlation between obscene material and crime.[2] Quite apart from sex crimes, however, there remains

[1] It is conceivable that an "adult" theatre can—if it really insists—prevent the exposure of its obscene wares to juveniles. An "adult" bookstore, dealing in obscene books, magazines, and pictures, cannot realistically make this claim. The Hill-Link Minority Report of the Commission on Obscenity and Pornography emphasizes evidence (the Abelson National Survey of Youth and Adults) that, although most pornography may be bought by elders, "the heavy users and most highly exposed people to pornography are adolescent females (among women) and adolescent and young males (among men)." The Report of the Commission on Obscenity (1970 ed.), 401. The legitimate interest in preventing exposure of juveniles to obscene materials cannot be fully served by simply barring juveniles from the immediate physical premises of "adult" book stores, when there is a flourishing "outside business" in these materials.

[2] The Report of the Commission on Obscenity and Pornography (1970 ed.), 390–412 (Hill-Link Minority Report). For a discussion of earlier studies indicating "a division of thought [among behavioral scientists] on the correlation between obscenity and socially deleterious behavior" and references to expert opinions that obscene material may induce crime and antisocial conduct, see Memoirs v. Massachusetts, *supra,* 383 U.S., at 451–453, 86 S.Ct., at 993–995 (1966) (Clark, J., dissenting). As Mr. Justice Clark emphasized:

"While erotic stimulation caused by pornography may be legally insignificant in itself, there are medical experts who believe that such stimulation frequently manifests itself in criminal sexual behavior or other antisocial conduct. For example, Dr. George W. Henry of Cornell University has expressed the opinion that obscenity, with its exaggerated and morbid emphasis on sex, particularly abnormal and perverted practices, and its unrealistic presentation of sexual behavior and attitudes, may induce antisocial conduct by the average person. A number of so-one problem of large proportions aptly described by Professor Bickel:

> It concerns the tone of the society, the mode, or to use terms that have
> perhaps greater currency, the style and quality of life, now and in the future.
> A man may be entitled to read an obscene book in his room, or expose
> himself indecently there. . . . We should protect his privacy. But if he demands
> a right to obtain the books and pictures he wants in the market and to
> foregather in public places—discreet, if you will, but accessible to all—with
> others who share his tastes, *then to grant him his right is to affect the*
> *world about the rest of us, and to impinge on other privacies.* Even supposing
> that each of us can, if he wishes, effectively avert the eye and stop the
> ear (which, in truth, we cannot), what is commonly read and seen and heard
> and done intrudes upon us all, want it or not.
> 22 The Public Interest 25, 25–26 (Winter, 1971).[3] (Emphasis supplied.)

As Chief Justice Warren stated there is a "right of the Nation and of the States to maintain a decent society . . . ," Jacobellis v. Ohio, 378 U.S. 184, 199, 84 S.Ct. 1676, 1684, 12 L.Ed.2d 793 (1964) (Warren, C. J., dissenting).[4] . . .

But, it is argued, there is no scientific data which conclusively demonstrates that exposure to obscene materials adversely affects men and women or their society. It is urged on behalf of the petitioner that, absent such a demonstration, any kind of state regulation is "impermissible." We reject this argument. It is not for us to resolve empirical uncertainties underlying state legislation, save in the exceptional case where that legislation plainly impinges upon rights protected by the Constitution itself. Mr. Justice Brennan, speaking for the Court in Ginsberg v. New York, 390 U.S. 629, 642, 88 S.Ct. 1274, 1282, 20 L.Ed.2d 195 (1968), said "We do not demand of legislatures 'scientifically certain criteria of legislation.' Noble State Bank v. Haskell, 219 U.S. 104, 110 [31 S.Ct. 186, 187] 55 L.Ed. 112." Al-

---

ciologists think that this material may have adverse effects upon individual mental health, with potentially disruptive consequences for the community.

"   . . .

"Congress and the legislatures of every State have enacted measures to restrict the distribution of erotic and pornographic material, justify these controls by reference to evidence that antisocial behavior may result in part from reading obscenity." [Footnotes omitted.] *Id.,* 383 U.S., at 452–453, 86 S.Ct., at 994–995.

[3] See also Berns, Pornography v. Democracy: The Case for Censorship, in 22 The Public Interest 3 (Winter, 1971); Van der Haag, Censorship: For and Against (H. H. Hart ed., 1971), 156–157.

[4] "In this and other cases in this area of the law, which are coming to us in ever-increasing numbers, we are faced with the resolution of rights basic both to individuals and to society as a whole. Specifically, we are called upon to reconcile the right of the Nation and of the States to maintain a decent society and, on the other hand, the right of individuals to express themselves freely in accordance with the guarantees of the First and Fourteenth Amendments." Jacobellis v. Ohio, *supra,* 378 U.S., at 199, 84 S.Ct., at 1684 (1964) (Warren, C. J., dissenting).

though there is no conclusive proof of a connection between antisocial behavior and obscene material, the legislature of Georgia could quite reasonably determine that such a connection does or might exist. In deciding *Roth,* this Court implicitly accepted that a legislature could legitimately act on such a conclusion to protect *"the social interest in order and morality."* Roth v. United States, *supra,* 354 U.S., at 485, 77 S.Ct., at 1309 (1957), quoting Chaplinsky v. New Hampshire, 315 U.S. 568, 572, 62 S.Ct. 766, 769, 86 L.Ed. 1031 (1942) (emphasis added in *Roth*).[5]

From the beginning of civilized societies, legislators and judges have acted on various unprovable assumptions. Such assumptions underlie much lawful state regulation of commercial and business affairs. . . . The same is true of the federal securities, antitrust laws and a host of other federal regulations. . . . On the basis of these assumptions both Congress and state legislatures have, for example, drastically restricted associational rights by adopting antitrust laws, and have strictly regulated public expression by issuers of and dealers in securities, profit sharing "coupons," and "trading stamps," commanding what they must and may not publish and announce. . . . Understandably those who entertain an absolutist view of the First Amendment find it uncomfortable to explain why rights of association, speech, and press should be severely restrained in the marketplace of goods and money, but not in the marketplace of pornography.

Likewise, when legislatures and administrators act to protect the physical environment from pollution and to preserve our resources of forests, streams and parks, they must act on such imponderables as the impact of a new highway near or through an existing park or wilderness area. . . . Thus the Federal-Aid Highway Act of 1968, 82 Stat. 823, 23 U.S.C. § 138, and the Department of Transportation Act of 1966, 82 Stat. 824, 49 U.S.C. § 1653(f), have been described by Mr. Justice Black as "a solemn determination of the highest law-making body of this Nation that beauty and health-giving facilities of our parks are not to be taken away for public roads without hearings, fact-findings, and policy determinations under the supervision of a Cabinet officer. . . ." *Citizens to Preserve Overton Park, supra,* 401 U.S., at 421, 91 S.Ct., at 826 (separate opinion joined by Brennan, J.) (1971). The fact that a congressional directive reflects unprovable assumptions about what is good for the people, including imponderable aesthetic assumptions, is not a sufficient reason to find that statute unconstitutional.

If we accept the unprovable assumption that a complete education re-

---

[5] *"It has been well observed that such* [lewd and obscene] *utterances are no essential part of any exposition of ideas, and are of such slight social value as a step to truth that any benefit that may be derived from them is clearly outweighed by the social interest in order and morality."* Roth v. United States, *supra,* 354 U.S., at 485, 77 S.Ct., at 1309 (1957), quoting Chaplinsky v. New Hampshire, 315 U.S., *supra,* at 572, 62 S.Ct., at 769 (1942) (emphasis added in *Roth*).

quires certain books, . . . and the well nigh universal belief that good books, plays, and art lift the spirit, improve the mind, enrich the human personality and develop character, can we then say that a state legislature may not act on the corollary assumption that commerce in obscene books, or public exhibitions focused on obscene conduct, have a tendency to exert a corrupting and debasing impact leading to antisocial behavior? "Many of these effects may be intangible and indistinct, but they are nonetheless real." *American Power & Light Co., supra,* 329 U.S., at 103, 67 S.Ct., at 141 (1946). Mr. Justice Cardozo said that all laws in Western civilization are "guided by a robust common sense. . . ." Steward Machine Co. v. Davis, 301 U.S. 548, 590, 57 S.Ct. 883, 892, 81 L.Ed. 1279 (1937). The sum of experience, including that of the past two decades, affords an ample basis for legislatures to conclude that a sensitive, key relationship of human existence, central to family life, community welfare, and the development of human personality, can be debased and distorted by crass commercial exploitation of sex. Nothing in the Constitution prohibits a State from reaching such a conclusion and acting on it legislatively simply because there is no conclusive evidence or empirical data.

It is argued that individual "free will" must govern, even in activities beyond the protection of the First Amendment and other constitutional guarantees of privacy, and that Government cannot legitimately impede an individual's desire to see or acquire obscene plays, movies, and books. We do indeed base our society on certain assumptions that people have the capacity for free choice. Most exercises of individual free choice— those in politics, religion, and expression of ideas—are explicitly protected by the Constitution. Totally unlimited play for free will, however, is not allowed in ours or any other society. We have just noted, for example, that neither the First Amendment nor "free will" precludes States from having "blue sky" laws to regulate what sellers of securities may write or publish about their wares. See p. 2637, *supra.* Such laws are to protect the weak, the uninformed, the unsuspecting, and the gullible from the exercise of their own volition. Nor do modern societies leave disposal of garbage and sewage up to the individual "free will," but impose regulation to protect both public health and the appearance of public places. States are told by some that they must await a "laissez faire" market solution to the obscenity-pornography problem, paradoxically "by people who have never otherwise had a kind word to say for laissez-faire," particularly in solving urban, commercial, and environmental pollution problems. See Kristol, On the Democratic Idea in America (1972 ed.) 37.

The States, of course, may follow such a "laissez faire" policy and drop all controls on commercialized obscenity, if that is what they prefer, just as they can ignore consumer protection in the market place, but nothing in the Constitution *compels* the States to do so with regard to matters falling within state jurisdiction. . . . "We do not sit as a super-legislature to deter- 261 mine the wisdom, need, and propriety of laws that touch economic problems, business affairs, or social conditions." Griswold v. Connecticut, 381 U.S. 479, 482, 85 S.Ct. 1678, 1680, 14 L.Ed.2d 510 (1965)....

It is asserted, however, that standards for evaluating state commercial regulations are inapposite in the present context, as state regulation of access by consenting adults to obscene material violates the constitutionally protected right to privacy enjoyed by petitioners' customers. Even assuming that petitioners have vicarious standing to assert potential customers' rights, it is unavailing to compare a theatre, open to the public for a fee, with the private home of Stanley v. Georgia, 394 U.S. 557, 568, 89 S.Ct. 1243, 1249, 22 L.Ed.2d 542 (1969), and the marital bedroom of Griswold v. Connecticut, 381 U.S. 479, 485–486, 85 S.Ct. 1678, 1682–1683, 14 L.Ed.2d 510 (1965). This Court, has, on numerous occasions, refused to hold that commercial ventures such as a motion-picture house are "private" for the purpose of civil rights litigation and civil rights statutes.... The Civil Rights Act of 1964 specifically defines motion-picture houses and theatres as places of "public accommodation" covered by the Act as operations affecting commerce. 42 U.S.C. § 2000a(b)(3), (c).

Our prior decisions recognizing a right to privacy guaranteed by the Fourteenth Amendment included "only those personal rights that can be deemed 'fundamental' or 'implicit in the concept of ordered liberty.' Palko v. Connecticut, 302 U.S. 319, 325, [58 S.Ct. 149, 152] 82 L.Ed. 288." Roe v. Wade, 410 U.S. 113, 152, 93 S.Ct. 705, 726, 35 L.Ed.2d 147 (1973). This privacy right encompasses and protects the personal intimacies of the home, the family, marriage, motherhood, procreation, and child rearing.... Nothing, however, in this Court's decisions intimates that there is any "fundamental" privacy right "implicit in the concept of ordered liberty" to watch obscene movies in places of public accommodation.

If obscene material unprotected by the First Amendment in itself carried with it a "penumbra" of constitutionally protected privacy, this Court would not have found it necessary to decide Stanley on the narrow basis of the "privacy of the home," which was hardly more than a reaffirmation that "a man's home is his castle." Stanley v. Georgia, supra, 394 U.S. 557, at 564, 89 S.Ct. 1243, at 1247, 22 L.Ed.2d 542 (1969).[6] Moreover, we have declined to equate the privacy of the home relied on in Stanley with

---

[6] The protection afforded by Stanley v. Georgia, supra, is restricted to a place, the home. In contrast, the constitutionally protected privacy of family, marriage, motherhood, procreation, and child rearing is not just concerned with a particular place, but with a protected intimate relationship. Such protected privacy extends to the doctor's office, the hospital, the hotel room, or as otherwise required to safeguard the right to intimacy involved. Cf. Roe v. Wade, supra, 410 U.S., at 152–154, 93 S.Ct., at 726–727 (1973); Griswold v. Connecticut, supra, 381 U.S., at 485–486, 85 S.Ct., at 1682–1683. Obviously, there is no necessary or legitimate expectation of privacy which would extend to marital intercourse on a street corner or a theatre stage.

a "zone" of "privacy" that follows a distributor or a consumer of obscene materials wherever he goes. . . . (1971). The idea of a "privacy" right and a place of public accommodation are, in this context, mutually exclusive. Conduct or depictions of conduct that the state police power can prohibit on a public street does not become automatically protected by the Constitution merely because the conduct is moved to a bar or a "live" theatre stage, any more than a "live" performance of a man and woman locked in a sexual embrace at high noon in Times Square is protected by the Constitution because they simultaneously engage in a valid political dialogue.

It is also argued that the State has no legitimate interest in "control [of] the moral content of a person's thoughts," Stanley v. Georgia, *supra*, 394 U.S., at 565, 89 S.Ct., at 1248 (1969), and we need not quarrel with this. But we reject the claim that the State of Georgia is here attempting to control the minds or thoughts of those who patronize theatres. Preventing unlimited display or distribution of obscene material, which by definition lacks any serious literary, artistic, political, or scientific value as communication, . . . is distinct from a control of reason and the intellect. . . . Where communication of ideas, protected by the First Amendment, is not involved, nor the particular privacy of the home protected by *Stanley,* nor any of the other "areas or zones" of constitutionally protected privacy, the mere fact that, as a consequence, some human "utterances" or "thoughts" may be incidentally affected does not bar the State from acting to protect legitimate state interests. . . . The fantasies of a drug addict are his own and beyond the reach of government, but government regulation of drug sales is not prohibited by the Constitution. . . .

Finally, petitioners argue that conduct which directly involves "consenting adults" only has, for that sole reason, a special claim to constitutional protection. Our Constitution establishes a broad range of conditions on the exercise of power by the States, but for us to say that our Constitution incorporates the proposition that conduct involving consenting adults only is always beyond state regulation,[7] that is a step we are unable to take.[8] Com-

[7] Cf. Mill, On Liberty (1955 ed.), 13.

[8] The state statute books are replete with constitutionally unchallenged laws against prostitution, suicide, voluntary self-mutilation, brutalizing "bare fist" prize fights, and duels, although these crimes may only directly involve "consenting adults." Statutes making bigamy a crime surely cut into an individual's freedom to associate, but few today seriously claim such statutes violate the First Amendment or any other constitutional provision. . . . Consider also the language of this Court in McLaughlin v. Florida, 379 U.S. 184, 196, 85 S.Ct. 283, 290, 13 L.Ed.2d 222 (1964), as to adultery, Southern Surety Co. v. Oklahoma, 241 U.S. 582, 586, 36 S.Ct. 692, 694, 60 L.Ed. 1187 (1916), as to fornication; Hoke v. United States, 227 U.S. 308, 320–322, 33 S.Ct. 281, 283–284, 57 L.Ed. 523 (1913), and Caminetti v. United States, 242 U.S. 470, 484–487, 491–492, 37 S.Ct. 192, 194–195, 196–197, 61 L.Ed. 442 (1917), as to "white slavery"; Murphy v. California, 225 U.S. 623, 629, 32 S.Ct. 697, 698, 56 L.Ed. 1229 (1912), as to billiard halls; and The Lottery Case, 188 U.S. 321, 355–356, 23 S.Ct. 321, 326–327, 47 L.Ed. 263

mercial exploitation of depictions, descriptions, or exhibitions of obscene conduct on commercial premises open to the adult public falls within a State's broad power to regulate commerce and protect the public environment. The issue in this context goes beyond whether someone, or even the majority, considers the conduct depicted as "wrong" or "sinful." The States have the power to make a morally neutral judgment that public exhibition of obscene material, or commerce in such material, has a tendency to injure the community as a whole, to endanger the public safety, or to jeopardize in Chief Justice Warren's words, the States' "right . . . to maintain a decent society." Jacobellis v. Ohio, *supra,* 378 U.S., at 199, 84 S.Ct., at 1684 (1964) (dissenting opinion).

To summarize, we have today reaffirmed the basic holding of United States v. Roth, *supra,* that obscene material has no protection under the First Amendment. . . . We have directed our holdings, not at thoughts or speech, but at depiction and description of specifically defined sexual conduct that States may regulate within limits designed to prevent infringement of First Amendment rights. We have also reaffirmed the holdings of United States v. Reidel, *supra,* and United States v. Thirty-Seven Photographs, *supra,* that commerce in obscene material is unprotected by any constitutional doctrine of privacy. . . . In this case we hold that the States have a legitimate interest in regulating commerce in obscene material and in regulating exhibition of obscene material in places of public accommodation, including so-called "adult" theatres from which minors are excluded. In light of these holdings, nothing precludes the State of Georgia from the regulation of the allegedly obscene materials exhibited in Paris Adult Theatre I or II, provided that the applicable Georgia law, as written or authoritatively interpreted by the Georgia courts, meets the First Amendment standards set forth in Miller v. California, *supra,* . . .

Vacated and remanded for further proceedings.

The Dissenting Opinion of Mr. Justice Brennan

Our experience since *Roth* requires us not only to abandon the effort to pick out obscene materials on a case-by-case basis, but also to reconsider a fundamental postulate of *Roth:* that there exists a definable class of sexually oriented expression that may be totally suppressed by the Federal

---

492 (1903), as to gambling. See also the summary of state statutes prohibiting bear baiting, cock-fighting, and other brutalizing animal "sports," in Stevens, Fighting and Baiting, Animals and Their Legal Rights (Leavitt ed., 1970 ed.), 112–127. As Professor Kristol has observed "Bearbaiting and cockfighting are prohibited only in part out of compassion for the suffering animals; the main reason they were abolished was because it was felt that they debased and brutalized the citizenry who flocked to witness such spectacles." On the Democratic Idea in America, *supra,* 33.

and State Governments. Assuming that such a class of expression does in fact exist, I am forced to conclude that the concept of "obscenity" cannot be defined with sufficient specificity and clarity to provide fair notice to persons who create and distribute sexually oriented materials, to prevent substantial erosion of protected speech as a by-product of the attempt to suppress unprotected speech, and to avoid very costly institutional harms. Given these inevitable side-effects of state efforts to suppress what is assumed to be *unprotected* speech, we must scrutinize with care the state interest that is asserted to justify the suppression. For in the absence of some very substantial interest in suppressing such speech, we can hardly condone the ill-effects that seem to flow inevitably from the effort.[9]

.   .   .

Obscenity laws have a long history in this country. Most of the States that had ratified the Constitution by 1792 punished the related crime of blasphemy or profanity despite the guarantees of free expression in their constitutions, and Massachusetts expressly prohibited the "composing, writing, printing or publishing of any filthy, obscene or profane song, pamphlet, libel or mock-sermon, in imitation of preaching, or any other part of divine worship." Province Laws, 1711–1712, ch. 6, § 19. In 1815 the first reported obscenity conviction was obtained under the common law of Pennsylvania. See Commonwealth v. Sharpless, 2 S. & R. 91. A conviction in Massachusetts under its common law and colonial statute followed six years later. See Commonwealth v. Holmes, 17 Mass. 336 (1821). In 1821 Vermont passed the first state law proscribing the publication or sale of "lewd or obscene" material, Laws of Vermont, 1824, ch. XXIII, No. 1, § 23, and federal legislation barring the importation of similar matter appeared in 1842. See Customs Law of 1842, § 28, 5 Stat. 566. Although the number of early obscenity laws was small and their enforcement exceedingly lax, the situation significantly changed after

---

[9] Cf. United States v. O'Brien, 391 U.S. 367, 376–377, 88 S.Ct. 1673, 1678–1679, 20 L.Ed.2d 672 (1968):

"This Court has held that when 'speech' and 'nonspeech' elements are combined in the same course of conduct, a sufficiently important governmental interest in regulating the nonspeech element can justify incidental limitations on First Amendment freedoms. To characterize the quality of the governmental interest which must appear, the Court has employed a variety of descriptive terms: compelling; substantial; subordinating; paramount; cogent; strong. Whatever imprecision inheres in these terms, we think it clear that a government regulation is sufficiently justified if it is within the constitutional power of the Government; if it furthers an important or substantial government interest; if the governmental interest is unrelated to the suppression of free expression; and if the incidental restriction on alleged First Amendment freedoms is no greater than is essential to the furtherance of that interest." (Footnotes omitted.) See also Speiser v. Randall, 357 U.S. 513, 78 S.Ct. 1332, 2 L.Ed.2d 1460 (1958).

about 1870 when Federal and State Governments, mainly as a result of the efforts of Anthony Comstock, took an active interest in the suppression of obscenity. By the end of the 19th Century at least 30 States had some type of general prohibition on the dissemination of obscene materials, and by the time of our decision in *Roth* no State was without some provision on the subject. The Federal Government meanwhile had enacted no fewer than 20 obscenity laws between 1842 and 1956. . . .

This history caused us to conclude in *Roth* "that the unconditional phrasing of the First Amendment [that "Congress shall make no law . . . abridging the freedom of speech, or of the press . . ."] was not intended to protect every utterance." 354 U.S., at 483, 77 S.Ct., at 1308. It also caused us to hold, as numerous prior decisions of this Court had assumed, see *id., at* 481, 77 S.Ct., at 1306, that obscenity could be denied the protection of the First Amendment and hence suppressed because it is a form of expression "utterly without redeeming social importance," *id.,* at 484, 77 S.Ct., at 1309, as "mirrored in the universal judgment that [it] should be restrained. . . ." *Id.,* at 485, 77 S.Ct., at 1309.

Because we assumed—incorrectly, as experience has proven—that obscenity could be separated from other sexually oriented expression without significant costs either to the First Amendment or to the judicial machinery charged with the task of safeguarding First Amendment freedoms, we had no occasion in *Roth* to probe the asserted state interest in curtailing unprotected, sexually oriented speech. Yet as we have increasingly come to appreciate the vagueness of the concept of obscenity, we have begun to recognize and articulate the state interests at stake. Significantly, in Redrup v. New York, *supra,* where we set aside findings of obscenity with regard to three sets of material, we pointed out that

[i]n none of the cases was there a claim that the statute in question reflected a specific and limited state concern for juveniles. See Prince v. Massachusetts, 321 U.S. 158 [64 S.Ct. 438] 88 L.Ed. 645; cf. Butler v. Michigan, 352 U.S. 380 [77 S.Ct. 524] 1 L.Ed.2d 412. In none was there any suggestion of an assault upon individual privacy by publication in a manner so obtrusive as to make it impossible for an unwilling individual to avoid exposure to it. Cf. Breard v. Alexandria, 341 U.S. 622 [71 S.Ct. 920] 95 L.Ed. 1233; Public Utilities Comm'n v. Pollak, 343 U.S. 451 [72 S.Ct. 813] 96 L.Ed. 1068. And in none was there evidence of the sort of 'pandering' which the Court found significant in Ginzburg v. United States, 383 U.S. 463 [86 S.Ct. 942] 16 L.Ed.2d 31." 386 U.S., at 769, 87 S.Ct., at 1415.

. . .

The opinions in *Redrup* and Stanley v. Georgia reflected our emerging view that the state interests in protecting children and in protecting uncon-
266 senting adults may stand on a different footing from the other asserted

state interests. It may well be, as one commentator has argued, that "exposure to [erotic material] is for some persons an intense emotional experience. A communication of this nature, imposed upon a person contrary to his wishes, has all the characteristics of a physical assault. . . . [And it] constitutes an invasion of his privacy. . . ."[10] Similarly, if children are "not possessed of that full capacity for individual choice which is the presupposition of the First Amendment guarantees," Ginsberg v. New York, 390 U.S., at 649–650, 88 S.Ct., at 1286 (Stewart, J., concurring), then the State may have a substantial interest in precluding the flow of obscene materials even to consenting juveniles. . . .

But whatever the strength of the state interests in protecting juveniles and unconsenting adults from exposure to sexually oriented materials, those interests cannot be asserted in defense of the holding of the Georgia Supreme Court in this case. That court assumed for the purposes of its decision that the films in issue were exhibited only to persons over the age of 21 who viewed them willingly and with prior knowledge of the nature of their contents. And on that assumption the state court held that the films could still be suppressed. The justification for the suppression must be found, therefore, in some independent interest in regulating the reading and viewing habits of consenting adults.

At the outset it should be noted that virtually all of the interests that might be asserted in defense of suppression, laying aside the special interests associated with distribution to juveniles and unconsenting adults, were also posited in Stanley v. Georgia, *supra,* where we held that the State could not make the "mere private possession of obscene material a crime." *Id.,* 394 U.S., at 568, 89 S.Ct., at 1249. That decision presages the conclusions I reach here today.

In *Stanley* we pointed out that "[t]here appears to be little empirical basis for" the assertion that "exposure to obscene materials may lead to deviant sexual behavior or crimes of sexual violence." *Id.,* at 566 and n. 9, 89 S.Ct., at 1249.[11] In any event, we added that "if the State is only con-

---

[10] T. Emerson, The System of Freedom of Expression 496 (1970).

[11] Indeed, since *Stanley* was decided, the President's Commission on Obscenity and Pornography has concluded:

"In sum, empirical research designed to clarify the question has found no evidence to date that exposure to explicit sexual materials plays a significant role in the causation of delinquent or criminal behavior among youth or adults. The Commission cannot conclude that exposure to erotic materials is a factor in the causation of sex crime or sex delinquency." Report of the Commission on Obscenity and Pornography 27 (1970) (footnote omitted).

To the contrary, the Commission found that "[o]n the positive side, explicit sexual materials are sought as a source of entertainment and information by substantial numbers of American adults. At times, these materials also appear to serve to increase and facilitate constructive communication about sexual matters within marriage." *Id.,* at 53.

cerned about printed or filmed materials inducing antisocial conduct, we believe that in the context of private consumption of ideas and information we should adhere to the view that '[a]mong free men, the deterrents ordinarily to be applied to prevent crime are education and punishment for violations of the law. . . .' Whitney v. California, 274 U.S. 357, 378 [, 47 S.Ct. 641, 649] 71 L.Ed. 1095 (1927) (Brandeis, J., concurring)." *Id.,* at 566–567, 89 S.Ct., at 1249.

Moreover, in *Stanley* we rejected as "wholly inconsistent with the philosophy of the First Amendment," *id.,* at 566, 89 S.Ct., at 1248, the notion that there is a legitimate state concern in the "control [of] the moral content of a person's thoughts," *id.,* at 565, 89 S.Ct., at 1248, and we held that a State "cannot constitutionally premise legislation on the desirability of controlling a person's private thoughts." *Id.,* at 566, 89 S.Ct., at 1249. That is not to say, of course, that a State must remain utterly indifferent to—and take no action bearing on—the morality of the community. The traditional description of state police power does embrace the regulation of morals as well as the health, safety, and general welfare of the citizenry. . . . And much legislation—compulsory public education laws, civil rights laws, even the abolition of capital punishment—are grounded at least in part on a concern with the morality of the community. But the State's interest in regulating morality by suppressing obscenity, while often asserted, remains essentially unfocused and ill-defined. And, since the attempt to curtail unprotected speech necessarily spills over into the area of protected speech, the effort to serve this speculative interest through the suppression of obscene material must tread heavily on rights protected by the First Amendment.

In Roe v. Wade, 410 U.S. 113, 93 S.Ct. 705, 35 L.Ed.2d 147 (1973), we held constitutionally invalid a state abortion law, even though we were aware of

the sensitive and emotional nature of the abortion controversy, of the vigorous opposing views, even among physicians, and of the deep and seemingly absolute convictions that the subject inspires. One's philosophy, one's experiences, one's exposure to the raw edges of human existence, one's religious training, one's attitudes toward life and family and their values, and the moral standards one establishes and seeks to observe, are all likely to influence and to color one's thinking and conclusions about abortion. 410 U.S., at 116, 93 S.Ct., at 708.

Like the proscription of abortions, the effort to suppress obscenity is predicated on unprovable, although strongly held, assumptions about human behavior, morality, sex, and religion.[12] The existence of these assumptions cannot validate a statute that substantially undermines the guarantees of

---

[12] See Henkin, Morals and the Constitution; The Sin of Obscenity, 63 Col.L.Rev. 391, 395 (1963).

the First Amendment, any more than the existence of similar assumptions on the issue of abortion can validate a statute that infringes the constitutionally protected privacy interests of a pregnant woman.

If, as the Court today assumes, "a state legislature may . . . act on the . . . assumption that . . . commerce in obscene books, or public exhibitions focused on obscene conduct, have a tendency to exert a corrupting and debasing impact leading to antisocial behavior," Paris Adult Theatre I v. Slaton, *ante,* at 2638, then it is hard to see how state-ordered regimentation of our minds can ever be forestalled. For if a State may, in an effort to maintain or create a particular moral tone, prescribe what its citizens cannot read or cannot see, then it would seem to follow that in pursuit of that same objective a State could decree that its citizens must read certain books or must view certain films. . . . However laudable its goal—and that is obviously a question on which reasonable minds may differ—the State cannot proceed by means that violate the Constitution. The precise point was established a half century ago in Meyer v. Nebraska, 262 U.S. 390, 43 S.Ct. 625, 67 L.Ed. 1042 (1923).

"That the State may do much, go very far, indeed, in order to improve the quality of its citizens, physically, mentally and morally, is clear; but the individual has certain fundamental rights which must be respected. The protection of the Constitution extends to all, to those who speak other languages as well as to those born with English on the tongue. Perhaps it would be highly advantageous if all had ready understanding of our ordinary speech, but this cannot be coerced by methods which conflict with the Constitution—a desirable end cannot be promoted by prohibited means.

"For the welfare of his Ideal Commonwealth, Plato suggested a law which should provide: 'That the wives of our guardians are to be common, and their children are to be common, and no parent is to know his own child, nor any child his parent. . . . The proper officers will take the offspring of the good parents to the pen or fold, and there they will deposit them with certain nurses who dwell in a separate quarter; but the offspring of the inferior, or of the better when they chance to be deformed, will be put away in some mysterious, unknown place, as they should be.' In order to submerge the individual and develop ideal citizens, Sparta assembled the males at seven into barracks and intrusted their subsequent education and training to official guardians. Although such measures have been deliberately approved by men of great genius, their ideas touching the relation between individual and State were wholly different from those upon which our institutions rest; and it hardly will be affirmed that any legislature could impose such restrictions upon the people of a State without doing violence to both letter and spirit of the Constitution." *Id.,* at 401–402, 43 S.Ct., at 627–628.

Recognizing these principles, we have held that so-called thematic ob- 269 scenity—obscenity which might persuade the viewer or reader to engage in "obscene" conduct—is not outside the protection of the First Amendment:

It is contended that the State's action was justified because the motion picture attractively portrays a relationship which is contrary to the moral standards, the religious precepts, and the legal code of its citizenry. This argument misconceives what it is that the Constitution protects. Its guarantee is not confined to the expression of ideas that are conventional or shared by a majority. It protects advocacy of the opinion that adultery may sometimes be proper, no less than advocacy of socialism or the single tax. And in the realm of ideas it protects expression which is eloquent no less than that which is unconvincing. Kingsley Int'l Pictures Corp. v. Regents, 360 U.S. 684, 688–689, 79 S.Ct. 1362, 1365, 3 L.Ed.2d 1512 (1959).

Even a legitimate, sharply focused state concern for the morality of the community cannot, in other words, justify an assault on the protections of the First Amendment. . . . Where the state interest in regulation of morality is vague and ill-defined, interference with the guarantees of the First Amendment is even more difficult to justify.[13]

In short, while I cannot say that the interests of the State—apart from the question of juveniles and unconsenting adults—are trivial or nonexistent, I am compelled to conclude that these interests cannot justify the substantial damage to constitutional rights and to this Nation's judicial machinery that inevitably results from state efforts to bar the distribution even of unprotected material to consenting adults. . . . I would hold, therefore, that at least in the absence of distribution to juveniles or obtrusive exposure to unconsenting adults, the First and Fourteenth Amendments prohibit the state and federal governments from attempting wholly to suppress sexually oriented materials on the basis of their allegedly "obscene" contents. Nothing in this approach precludes those governments from taking action to serve what may be strong and legitimate interests through regulation of the manner of distribution of sexually oriented material.

[13] "[I]n our system, undifferentiated fear or apprehension of disturbance is not enough to overcome the right to freedom of expression. Any departure from absolute regimentation may cause trouble. Any variation from the majority's opinion may inspire fear. Any word spoken, in class, in the lunchroom, or on the campus, that deviates from the views of another person may start an argument or cause a disturbance. But our Constitution says we must take this risk, Terminiello v. Chicago, 337 U.S. 1 [69 S.Ct. 894], 93 L.Ed. 1131 (1949); and our history says that it is this sort of hazardous freedom—this kind of openness—that is the basis of our national strength and of the independence and vigor of Americans who grow up and live in this relatively permissive, often disputatious, society." Tinker v. Des Moines Indep. Commun. School Dist., 393 U.S. 503, 508–509, 89 S.Ct. 733, 737–738, 21 L.Ed.2d 731 (1969). See also Cohen v. California, 403 U.S. 15, 23, 91 S.Ct. 1780, 1787, 29 L.Ed.2d 284 (1971).

Selected Bibliography

Leiser, Burton. *Liberty, Justice and Morals.* New York: Macmillan, 1973, chaps. 1, 2, 3, 4, and 6.

Nagel, Thomas. "Sexual Perversion," *The Journal of Philosophy,* Vol. 66 (1969), 5.

Ruddick, Sara. "On Sexual Morality," in James Rachel (ed.), *Moral Problems.* New York: Harper & Row, 1971, p. 85.

Russell, Bertrand. *Marriage and Morals.* New York: Liveright, 1929.

Wasserstrom, Richard, (ed.). *Morality and the Law.* Belmont, Calif.: Wadsworth Publishing Co., 1970.

Whitely, C. H., and W. M. Whitely. *Sex and Morals.* London: Batsford, 1967.

Wilson, John. *Logic and Sexual Morality.* Harmondsworth, Middlesex: Penguin Books, 1965.

5 PUNISHMENT

H. L. A. HART
Prolegomenon to the Principles of Punishment

Introductory

The main object of this paper is to provide a framework for the discussion of the mounting perplexities which now surround the institution of criminal punishment, and to show that any morally tolerable account of this institution must exhibit it as a compromise between radically distinct and partly conflicting principles.

General interest in the topic of punishment has never been greater than it is at present and I doubt if the public discussion of it has ever been more confused. The interest and the confusion are both in part due to relatively modern scepticism about two elements which have figured as essential parts of the traditionally opposed "theories" of punishment. On the one hand, the old Benthamite confidence in fear of the penalties threatened by the law as a powerful deterrent, has waned with the growing realisation that the part played by calculation of any sort in anti-social behaviour has been exaggerated. On the other hand a cloud of doubt has settled over the keystone of "Retributive" theory. Its advocates can no longer speak with the old confidence that statements of the form "This man who has broken the law could have kept it" had a univocal or agreed meaning; or where scepticism does not attach to the *meaning* of this form of statement, it has shaken the confi-

Reprinted from *Proceedings of the Aristotelian Society,* Vol. 60 (1959–60), 1–26, by permission of the author and by courtesy of the Editor of The Aristotelian Society. © 1959 The Aristotelian Society.

dence that we are generally able to distinguish the cases where this form of statement is true from those where it is not.[1]

Yet quite apart from the uncertainty engendered by these fundamental doubts, which seem to call in question the accounts given of the efficacy, and the morality of punishment by all the old competing theories, the public utterances of those who conceive themselves to be expounding, as plain men for other plain men, orthodox or common-sense principles, untouched by modern psychological doubts are uneasy. Their words often sound as if the authors had not fully grasped their meaning or did not intend the words to be taken quite literally. A glance at the parliamentary debates or the *Report of the Royal Commission on Capital Punishment* shows that many are now troubled by the suspicion that the view that there is just one supreme value or objective (*e.g.,* Deterrence, Retribution or Reform) in terms of which *all* questions about the justification of punishment are to be answered, is somehow wrong: yet, from what is said on such occasions no clear account of what the different values or objectives are, or how they fit together in the justification of punishment, can be extracted.[2]

No one expects judges or statesmen occupied in the business of sending people to the gallows or prison, or in making (or unmaking) laws which enable this to be done, to have much time for philosophical discussion of the principles which make it morally tolerable to do these things. A judicial bench is not and should not be a professorial chair. Yet what is said in public debates about punishment by those specially concerned with it as judges or legislators is important. Few are likely to be more circumspect, and if what they say seems, as it often does, unclear, one-sided and easily refutable by pointing to some aspect of things which they have overlooked, it is likely that in our inherited ways of talking or thinking about punishment there is some persistent drive towards an over-simplification of multiple issues which require separate consideration. To counter this drive what is most needed is *not* the simple admission that instead of a single value or aim (Deterrence, Retribution, Reform or any other) a plurality of different values and aims should be given as a conjunctive answer to some *single* question concerning the justification of punishment. What is

---

[1] See Barbara Wootton *Social Science and Social Pathology* for a clear and most comprehensive modern statement of these doubts.

[2] In the Lords' debate in July 1956 the Lord Chancellor agreed with Lord Denning that "the ultimate justification of any punishment is not that it is a deterrent but that it is the emphatic denunciation of the committing of a crime" yet also said that "the real crux of the question at issue is whether capital punishment is a uniquely effective deterrent." See 198 *H. L. Deb* (5th July) 576, 577, 596 (1956). In his article "An Approach to the Problems of Punishment" (*Philosophy,* 1958) Mr. S. L. Benn rightly observes of Lord Denning's view that denunciation does not imply the deliberate imposition of suffering which is the feature needing justification (325 n.l.).

needed is the realisation that different principles (each of which may in a sense be called a "justification") are relevant at different points in any morally acceptable account of punishment. What we should look for are answers to a number of different questions such as: What justifies the general practice of punishment? To whom may punishment be applied? How severely may we punish? In dealing with these and other questions concerning punishment we should bear in mind that in this, as in most other social institutions, the pursuit of one aim may be qualified by or provide an opportunity, not to be missed, for the pursuit of others. Till we have developed this sense of the complexity of punishment (and this prolegomenon aims only to do this) we shall be in no fit state to assess the extent to which the whole institution has been eroded by or needs to be adapted to new beliefs about the human mind.

II. Justifying Aims and Principles of Distribution

There is, I think, an analogy worth considering between the concept of Punishment and that of Property. In both cases we have to do with a social institution of which the centrally important form is a structure of *legal* rules, though it would be dogmatic to deny the names of Punishment or Property to the similar though more rudimentary rule-regulated practices within groups such as a family, or a school, or in customary societies whose customs may lack some of the standard or salient features of law (*e.g.*, legislation, organised sanctions, courts). In both cases we are confronted by a complex institution presenting different inter-related features calling for separate explanation; or, if the morality of the institution is challenged, for separate justification. In both cases failure to distinguish separate questions or attempting to answer them all by reference to a single principle ends in confusion. Thus in the case of Property we should distinguish between the question of the *definition* of Property, the question why and in what circumstance it is a *good* institution to maintain, and the questions in what ways individuals may become *entitled* to property and *how much* they should be allowed to acquire. These we may call questions of *Definition, General Justifying Aim,* and *Distribution* with the last subdivided into questions of *Title* and *Amount.* It is salutary to take some classical exposition of the idea of Property, say Locke's Chapter 'Of Property' in the *Second Treatise,*[3] and to observe how much darkness is spread by the use of a single notion (in this case "the labour of (a man's) body and the work of his hands") to answer all these different questions which press upon us when we reflect on the institution of Property. In the case of Punishment the beginning of wisdom (though by no means its end) is to distinguish similar questions and confront them separately.

274   [3] Chapter IV.

(a) DEFINITION

Here I shall simply draw upon the recent admirable work scattered through English philosophical[4] journals and add to it only an admonition of my own against the abuse of definition in the philosophical discussion of punishment. So with Mr. Benn and Professor Flew I shall define the standard or central case of 'punishment' in terms of five elements:

(i) It must involve pain or other consequences normally considered unpleasant.
(ii) It must be for an offence against legal rules.
(iii) It must be of an actual or supposed offender for his offence.
(iv) It must be intentionally administered by human beings other than the offender.
(v) It must be imposed and administered by an authority constituted by a legal system against which the offence is committed.

In calling this the standard or central case of punishment I shall relegate to the position of sub-standard or secondary cases the following among many other possibilities:

(*a*) Punishments for breaches of legal rules imposed or administered otherwise than by officials (decentralised sanctions).
(*b*) Punishments for breaches of non-legal rules or orders (punishments in a family or school).
(*c*) Vicarious or collective punishment of some member of a social group for actions done by others without the former's authorisation, encouragement, control or permission.
(*d*) Punishment of persons (otherwise than under (*c*)) who are neither in fact nor supposed to be offenders.

The chief importance of listing these sub-standard cases is to prevent the use of what I shall call the "definitional stop" in discussions of punishment. This is an abuse of definition especially tempting when use is made of conditions (ii) and (iii) of the standard case against the utilitarian claim that the practice of punishment is justified by the beneficial consequences resulting from the observance of the laws which it secures. Here the stock 'retributive' argument[5] is: If *this* is the justification of

[4] K. Baier "Is Punishment Retributive?" *Analysis,* March 16, p. 26 (1955). A. Flew "The Justification of Punishment," *Philosophy,* 1954, pp. 291–307. S. I. Benn, *op. cit.,* pp. 325–326.

[5] Ewing, *The Morality of Punishment,* D. J. B. Hawkins, *Punishment and Moral Responsibility* (The Kings Good Servant, p. 92), J. D. Mabbott, "Punishment." *Mind,* 1939, p. 153.

275

punishment, why not apply it when it pays to do so to those innocent of any crime chosen at random, or to the wife and children of the offender? And here the wrong reply is: That, by definition, would not be "punishment" and it is the justification of punishment which is in issue.[6] Not only will this definitional stop fail to satisfy the advocate of 'Retribution'; it would prevent us from investigating the very thing which modern scepticism most calls in question: namely the rational and moral status of our preference for a system of punishment under which measures painful to individuals are to be taken against them only when they have committed an offence. Why do we prefer this to other forms of social hygiene which we might employ instead to prevent anti-social behaviour and which we do employ in special circumstances sometimes with reluctance? No account of punishment can afford to dismiss this question with a definition.

(b) THE NATURE OF AN OFFENCE

Before we reach any question of justification we must identify a preliminary question to which the answer is so simple that the question may not appear worth asking; yet it is clear that some curious "theories" of punishment gain their only plausibility from ignoring it, and others from confusing it with other questions. This question is: Why are certain kinds of action forbidden by law and so made crimes or offences? The answer is: To announce to society that these actions are not to be done and to secure that fewer of them are done. These are the common immediate aims of making any conduct a criminal offence and until we have laws made with these primary aims we shall lack the notion of a 'crime' and so of a 'criminal'. Without recourse to the simple idea that the criminal law sets up, in its rules, standards of behaviour to encourage certain types of conduct and discourage others we cannot distinguish a punishment in the form of a fine from a tax on a course of conduct.[7] This indeed is one grave objection to those theories of law which in the interests of simplicity or uniformity obscure the distinction between primary laws setting standards for behaviour and secondary laws specifying what officials must or may do when they are broken. Such theories insist that all legal rules are "really" directions to officials to exact "sanctions" under

---

[6] Mr. Benn seemed to succumb at times to the temptation to give "The short answer to the critics of utilitarian theories of punishment—that they are theories of *punishment* not of any sort of technique involving suffering" (*op. cit.* p. 322). He has since told me that he does not now rely on the definitional stop.

[7] This generally clear distinction may be blurred. Taxes may be imposed to discourage the activities taxed though the law does not announce this as it does when it makes them criminal. Conversely fines payable for some criminal offences because of a depreciation of currency, became so small that they are cheerfully paid and offences are frequent. They are then felt to be mere taxes because the sense is lost that the rule is meant to be taken seriously as a standard of behaviour.

certain conditions, *e.g.,* if people kill.[8] Yet only if we keep alive the distinction (which such theories thus obscure) between the primary objective of the law in encouraging or discouraging certain kinds of behaviour and its merely ancillary sanction or remedial steps, can we give sense to the notion of a crime or offence.

It is important however to stress the fact that in thus identifying the immediate aims of the criminal law we have not reached the stage of justification. There are indeed many forms of undesirable behaviour which it would be foolish because ineffective or too costly to attempt to inhibit by use of the law and some of these may be better left to educators, trades unions, churches, marriage guidance councils or other non-legal agencies. Conversely there are some forms of conduct which we believe cannot be effectively inhibited without use of the law. But it is only too plain that in fact the law may make activities criminal which it is morally important to promote and the suppression of these may be quite unjustifiable. Yet confusion between the simple immediate aim of any criminal legislation and the justification of punishment seems to be the most charitable explanation of the claim that punishment is justified as an "emphatic denunciation by the community of a crime". Lord Denning's[9] dictum that this is the ultimate justification of punishment can be saved from Mr. Benn's criticism, noted above, only if it is treated as a blurred statement of the truth that the aim not of punishment, but of criminal legislation is indeed to denounce certain types of conduct as something not to be practised. Conversely the immediate aim of criminal legislation cannot be any of the things which are usually mentioned as justifying punishment: for until it is settled what conduct is to be legally denounced and discouraged we have not settled from what we are to *deter* people, or who are to be considered *criminals* from whom we are to exact *retribution,* or on whom we are to wreak *vengeance,* or whom we are to *reform.*

Even those who look upon human law as a mere instrument for enforcing "morality as such" (itself conceived as the law of God or Nature) and who at the stage of justifying punishment wish to appeal not to socially beneficial consequences but simply to the intrinsic value of inflicting suffering on wrongdoers who have disturbed by their offence the moral order, would not deny that the aim of criminal legislation is to set up types of behaviour (in this case conformity with a pre-existing moral law) as legal standards of behaviour and to secure conformity with them. No doubt in all communities certain moral offences, *e.g.,* killing, will always be selected for suppression as crimes and it is conceivable that

---

[8] *Cf.* Kelsen, *General Theory of Law and State,* 30–3, 33–34, 143–144 (1946). "Law is the primary norm which stipulates the sanction. . . ." (*id.* 61)

[9] In evidence to the Royal Commission on Capital Punishment, Cmd. 8932. §53 (1953). *Supra,* p. 3, n.2.

this may be done not to protect human beings from being killed but to save the potential murderer from sin; but it would be paradoxical to look upon the law as designed not to prevent murder at all (even conceived as sin rather than harm) but simply to extract the penalty from the murderer.

(c) GENERAL JUSTIFYING AIM

I shall not here criticise the intelligibility or consistency or adequacy of these theories that are united in denying that the practice of a system of punishment is justified by its beneficial consequences and claim instead that the main justification of the practice lies in the fact that when breach of the law involves moral guilt the application to the offender of the pain of punishment is itself a thing of value. A great variety of claims of this character designating 'Retribution' or 'Expiation' or 'Reproba- tion' as the justifying aim, fall in spite of differences under this rough general description. Though in fact I agree with Mr. Benn[10] in thinking that these all either avoid the question of justification altogether or are in spite of their protestations distinguished forms of Utilitarianism, I shall assume that Retribution, defined simply as the application of the pains of punishment to an offender who is morally guilty, may figure among the conceivable justifying aims of a system of punishment. Here I shall merely insist that it is one thing to use the word Retribution *at this point* in an account of the principle of punishment in order to designate the General Justifying Aim of the system, and quite another to use it to secure that to the question "To whom may punishment be applied?" (the question of Distribution) the answer given is "Only to an offender for an offence". Failure to distinguish Retribution as a Gen- eral Justifying Aim from retribution as the simple insistence that only those who have broken the law—and voluntarily broken it—may be punished may be traced in many writers even perhaps in Mr. J. D. Mab- bott's[11] otherwise most illuminating essay. We shall distinguish the latter from Retribution in General Aim as "retribution in Distribution". Much confusing shadow-fighting between Utilitarians and their opponents may be avoided if it is recognized that it is perfectly consistent to assert *both* that the General Justifying Aim of the practice of punishment is its beneficial consequences and that the pursuit of this general aim should be qualified or restricted out of deference to principles of Distribution which require that punishment should be only of an offender for an offence. Conversely it does not in the least follow from the admission of the latter principle of retribution in Distribution that the General Justi- fying Aim of punishment is Retribution though of course Retribution in General Aim entails retribution in Distribution.

[10] *Op. cit.,* pp. 326–335.

278 [11] *Op. cit.* It is not always quite clear what he considers a "retributive" theory to be.

We shall consider later the principles of justice lying at the root of retribution in Distribution. Meanwhile it is worth observing that both the most old fashioned Retributionist (in General Aim) and the most modern sceptic often make the same and, I think, wholly mistaken assumption that sense can only be made of the restrictive principle that punishment be applied only to an offender for an offence if the General Justifying Aim of the practice of punishment is Retribution. The sceptic consequently imputes to all systems of punishment (when they are restricted by the principle of retribution in Distribution) all the irrationality he finds in the idea of Retribution as a General Justifying Aim; conversely the advocates of the latter think the admission of retribution in Distribution is a refutation of the utilitarian claim that the social consequences of punishment are its Justifying Aim.

The most general lesson to be learnt from this extends beyond the topic of punishment. It is, that in relation to any social institution, after stating what general aim or value its maintenance fosters we should enquire whether there are any and if so what principles limiting the unqualified pursuit of that aim or value. Just because the pursuit of any single social aim always has its restrictive qualifier our main social institutions always possess a plurality of features which can only be understood as a compromise between partly discrepant principles. This is true even of relatively minor legal institutions like that of a contract. In general this is designed to enable individuals to give effect to their wishes to create structures of legal rights and duties and so to change, in certain ways their legal position. Yet at the same time there is need to protect those in good faith understand a verbal offer made to them to mean what it would ordinarily mean, accept it, and then act on the footing that a valid contract has been concluded. As against them, it would be unfair to allow the other party to say that the words he used in his verbal offer or the interpretation put on them did not express his real wishes or intention. Hence principles of "estoppel" or doctrines of the "objective sense" of a contract are introduced to prevent this and to qualify the principle that the law enforces contracts in order to give effect to the joint wishes of the contracting parties.

(d) DISTRIBUTION

This as in the case of property has two aspects (i) Liability (Who may be punished?) and (ii) Amount. In this section I shall chiefly be concerned with the first of these.[12]

From the foregoing discussions two things emerge. First, though we may be clear as to what value the practice of punishment is to promote we have still to answer as a question of Distribution "Who may be

---

[12] Amount is considered below in Section III (in connexion with Mitigation) and Section V.

punished?" Secondly, if in answer to this question we say "only an offender for an offence" this admission of retribution in Distribution is not a principle from which anything follows as to the severity or amount of punishment; in particular it neither licenses nor requires as Retribution in General Aim does more severe punishments than deterrence or other utilitarian criteria would require.

The root question to be considered is however why we attach the moral importance which we do to retribution in Distribution. Here I shall consider the efforts made to show that restriction of punishment to offenders is a simple consequence of whatever principles (Retributive or Utilitarian) constitute the Justifying Aim of punishment.

The standard example used by philosophers to bring out the importance of retribution in Distribution is that of a wholly innocent person who has not even unintentionally done anything which the law punishes if done intentionally. It is supposed that in order to avert some social catastrophe officials of the system fabricate evidence on which he is charged, tried, convicted and sent to prison or death. Or it is supposed that without resort to any fraud more persons may be deterred from crime if wives and children of offenders were punished vicariously for their crimes. In some forms this kind of thing may be ruled out by a consistent sufficiently comprehensive utilitarianism.[13] Certainly expedients involving fraud or faked charges might be very difficult to justify on utilitarian grounds. We can of course imagine that a Negro might be sent to prison or executed on a false charge of rape in order to avoid widespread lynching of many others; but a *system* which openly empowered authorities to do this kind of thing, even if it succeeded in averting specific evils like lynching, would awaken such apprehension and insecurity that any gain from the exercise of these powers would by any utilitarian calculation be offset by the misery caused by their existence. But official resort to this kind of fraud on a particular occasion in breach of the rules and the subsequent indemnification of the officials responsible might save many lives and so be thought to yield a clear surplus of value. Certainly vicarious punishment of an offender's family might do so and legal systems have occasionally though exceptionally resorted to this. An example of it is the Roman *Lex Quisquis* providing for the punishment of the children of those guilty of *majestas*.[14] In extreme cases many might still think it right to resort to these expedients but we should do so with the sense of sacrificing an important principle. We should be conscious of choosing the lesser of two evils, and this would be inexplicable if the principle sacrificed to utility were itself only a requirement of utility.

[13] See J. Rawls "Two Concepts of Rules", *Philosophical Review*, 1955, pp. 4–13.

[14] Constitution of emperors Arcadius and Honorius.

Similarly the moral importance of the restriction of punishment to the offender cannot be explained as merely a consequence of the principle that the General Justifying Aim is Retribution for immorality involved in breaking the law. Retribution in the Distribution of punishment has a value quite independent of Retribution as Justifying Aim. This is shown by the fact that we attach importance to the restrictive principle that only offenders may be punished even where breach of this law might not be thought immoral: indeed even where the laws themselves are hideously immoral as in Nazi Germany, *e.g.,* forbidding activities (helping the sick or destitute of some racial group) which might be thought morally obligatory, the absence of the principle restricting punishment to the offender would be a further *special* iniquity; whereas admission of this principle would represent some residual respect for justice though in the administration of morally bad laws.

III.   Justification, Excuse and Mitigation

What is morally at stake in the restrictive principle of Distribution cannot, however, be made clear by these external examples of its violation by faked charges or vicarious punishment. To make it clear we must allot to their place the appeals to matters of Justification, Excuse and Mitigation made in answer to the claim that someone should be punished. The first of these depends on the General Justifying Aim; the last two are different aspects of the principles of Distribution of punishment.

(a) JUSTIFICATION AND EXCUSE

English lawyers once distinguished between 'excusable' homicide (*e.g.,* accidental non-negligent killing) and 'justifiable' homicide (*e.g.,* killing in self-defence or the arrest of a felon) and different legal consequences once attached to these two forms of homicide. To the modern lawyer this distinction has no longer any legal importance: he would simply consider both kinds of homicide to be cases where some element, negative or positive, required in the full definition of criminal homicide (murder or manslaughter) was lacking. But the distinction between these two different ways in which actions may fail to constitute a criminal offence is still of great moral importance. Killing in self-defence is an exception to a general rule making killing punishable; it is admitted because the policy or aims which in general justify the punishment of killing (*e.g.,* protection of human life) do not include cases such as this. In the case of 'justification' what is done is regarded as something which the law does not condemn or even welcomes.[15] But where killing (*e.g.,* accidental) is excused, criminal responsibility is excluded on a

[15] In 1811 Mr. Purcell of Co. Cork, a septuagenarian, was knighted for killing four burglars with a carving knife. Kenny, *Outlines of Criminal Law,* 5th Ed., p. 103, n.3.   281

different footing. What has been done is something which is deplored, but the psychological state of the agent when he did it exemplified one or more of a variety of conditions which are held to rule out the public condemnation and punishment of individuals. This is a requirement of fairness or of justice to individuals independent of whatever the General Aim of punishment is, and remains a value whether the laws are good, morally indifferent or iniquitous.

The most prominent of these excusing conditions are those forms of lack of knowledge which make action unintentional: lack of muscular control which make it involuntary, subjection to gross forms of coercion by threats, and types of mental abnormality, which are believed to render the agent incapable of choice or of carrying out what he has chosen to do. Not all these excusing conditions are admitted by all legal systems for all offenders. Nearly all penal systems make some compromise at this point as we shall see with other principles; but most of them are admitted to some considerable extent in the case of the most serious crimes. Actions done under these excusing conditions are in the misleading terminology of Anglo-American law done without "mens rea";[16] and most people would say of them that they were 'not voluntary' or 'not wholly voluntary'.

(b) MITIGATION

Justification and Excuse though different from each other are alike in that if either is made out then conviction and punishment are excluded. In this they differ from the idea of Mitigation which presupposes that someone is convicted and liable to be punished and the question of the severity of his punishment is to be decided. It is therefore relevant to that aspect of Distribution which we have termed Amount. Certainly the severity of punishment is in part determined by the General Justifying Aim. A utilitarian will for example exclude in principle punishments the infliction of which is held to cause more suffering than the offence unchecked, and will hold that if one kind of crime causes greater suffering than another then a greater penalty may be used to repress it. He will also exclude degrees of severity which are useless in the sense that they do no more to secure or maintain a higher level of law-observance or any other valued result than less severe penalties. But in addition to restrictions on the severity of punishment which follow from the aim of punishing special limitations are imported by the idea of Mitigation. These, like the principle of Distribution restricting liability to punishment to offenders, have a status which is independent of the general Aim. The special features of Mitigation are that a good reason for administer-

---

[16] Misleading because it suggests moral guilt is a necessary condition of criminal responsibility.

ing a less severe penalty is made out if the situation or mental state of the convicted criminal is such that he was exposed to an unusual or specially great temptation, or his ability to control his actions is thought to have been impaired or weakened otherwise than by his own action, so that conformity to the law which he has broken was a matter of special difficulty for him as compared with normal persons normally placed.

The special features of the idea of Mitigation are however often concealed by the various legal techniques which make it necessary to distinguish between what may be termed 'informal' and 'formal' Mitigation. In the first case the law fixes a maximum penalty and leaves it to the judge to give such weight as he thinks proper in selecting the punishment to be applied to a particular offender to (among other considerations) mitigating factors. It is here that the barrister makes his 'plea in mitigation'. Sometimes however legal rules provide that the presence of a mitigating factor shall always remove the offence into a separate category carrying a lower maximum penalty. This is 'formal' mitigation and the most prominent example of it is Provocation which in English law is operative only in relation to homicide. It is not a matter of Justification or Excuse for it does not exclude conviction or punishment; but "reduces" the charges from murder to manslaughter and the possible maximum penalty from death to life imprisonment. It is worth stressing that not every provision reducing the maximum penalty can be thought of as "Mitigation": the very peculiar provisions of s. 5 of the Homicide Act 1957 which (*inter alia*) restricted the death penalty to types of murder not including, for example, murder by poisoning, did not in doing this recognise the use of poison as a "mitigating circumstance". Only a reduction of penalty made in view of the individual criminal's special difficulties in keeping the law which he has broken is so conceived.

Though the central cases are distinct enough the border lines between Justification, Excuse and Mitigation are not. There are many features of conduct which can be and are thought of in more than one of these ways. Thus, though little is heard of it, duress (coercion by threat of serious harm) is in English law in relation to some crimes an Excuse excluding responsibility. Where it is so treated the conception is that since *B* has committed a crime only because *A* has threatened him with gross violence or other harm, *B's* action is not the outcome of a 'free' or independent choice; *B* is merely an instrument of *A* who has 'made him do it'. Nonetheless *B* is not an instrument in the same sense that he would have been had he been pushed by *A* against a window and broken it: unless he is literally paralysed by fear of the threat, we may believe that *B* could have refused to comply. If he complies we may say '*coactus voluit*' and treat the situation not as one making it intolerable to punish at all, but as one calling for mitigation of the penalty as gross provocation does. On the other hand if the crime which *A* requires *B* to 283 commit is a petty one compared with the serious harm threatened (*e.g.,* death) by *A* there would be no absurdity in treating *A's* threat as a Justification for *B's* conduct though few legal systems overtly do this. If this line is taken coercion merges into the idea of "Necessity"[17] which appears on the margin of most systems of criminal law as an exculpating factor.

In view of the character of modern sceptical doubts about criminal punishment it is worth observing that even in English law the relevance of mental disease to criminal punishment is not always as a matter of Excuse though exclusive concentration on the M'Naghten rules relating to the criminal responsibility of the mentally diseased encourages the belief that it is. Even before the Homicide Act 1957 a statute[18] provided that if a mother murdered her child under the age of 12 months "while the balance of her mind was disturbed" by the processes of birth or lactation she should be guilty only of the felony of infanticide carrying a maximum penalty of life imprisonment. This is to treat mental abnormality as a matter of (formal) Mitigation. Similarly in other cases of homicide the M'Naghten rules relating to certain types of insanity as an Excuse no longer stand alone; now such abnormality of mind as "substantially impaired the mental responsibility"[19] of the accused is a matter of formal mitigation, which like provocation reduces the homicide to the category of manslaughter which does not carry the death penalty.

IV. The Rationale of Excuses

The admission of excusing conditions is a feature of the Distribution of punishment is required by distinct principles of Justice which restrict the extent to which general social aims may be pursued at the cost of individuals. The moral importance attached to these in punishment distinguishes it from other measures which pursue similar aims (*e.g.,* the protection of life, wealth or property) by methods which like punishment are also often unpleasant to the individuals to whom they are applied, *e.g.,* the detention of persons of hostile origin or association in war time, or of the insane, or the compulsory quarantine of persons suffering from infectious disease. To these we resort to avoid damage of a catastrophic character.

Every penal system in the name of some other social value compromises over the admission of excusing conditions and no system goes as far (particularly in cases of mental disease) as many would wish. But it is important (if we are to avoid a superficial but tempting answer to

---

[17] *i.e.,* when breaking the law is held justified as the lesser of two evils.

[18] Infanticide Act, 1938.

[19] Homicide Act, 1957, sec. 2.

modern scepticism about the meaning or truth of the statement that a criminal could have kept the law which he has broken) to see that our moral preference for a system which does recognise such excuses cannot, any more than our reluctance to engage in the cruder business of false charges or vicarious punishment, be explained by reference to the General Aim which we take to justify the practice of punishment. Here, too, even where the laws appear to us morally iniquitous or where we are uncertain as to their moral character so that breach of law does not entail moral guilt, punishment of those who break the law unintentionally would be an added wrong and refusal to do this some sign of grace.

Retributionists (in General Aim) have not paid much attention to the rationale of this aspect of punishment; they have usually (wrongly) assumed that it has no status except as a corollary of Retribution in General Aim. But Utilitarians have made strenuous, detailed efforts to show that the restriction on the use of punishment to those who have voluntarily broken the law is explicable on purely utilitarian lines. Bentham's efforts are the most complete, and their failure is an instructive warning to contemporaries.

Bentham's argument was a reply to Blackstone who in expounding the main excusing conditions recognised in the criminal law of his day,[20] claimed that "all the several pleas and excuses which protect the committer of a forbidden act from punishment which is otherwise annexed thereunto reduce to this single consideration: the want or defect of will" . . . . [and to the principle] "that to constitute a crime . . . . there must be first a vitious will". In the Principles of Morals and Legislation[21] under the heading "Cases unmeet for punishment" Bentham sets out a list of the main excusing conditions similar to Blackstone's; he then undertakes to show that the infliction of punishment on those who have done what the law forbids while in any of these conditions "must be inefficacious: it cannot act so as to prevent the mischief". All Blackstone's talk about want or defect of will or lack of a "vitious" will is he says "nothing to the purpose", except so far as it implies the reason (inefficacy of punishment) which he himself gives for recognising these excuses.

Bentham's argument is in fact a spectacular *non-sequitur*. He sets out to prove that to *punish* the mad, the infant child or those who break the law unintentionally or under duress or even under "necessity" must be inefficacious; but all that he proves (at the most) is the quite different proposition that the *threat* of punishment will be ineffective so far as the class of persons who suffer from these conditions are concerned. Plainly is it possible that the actual *infliction* of punishment on those persons, though (as Bentham says) the *threat* of punishment could not

---

[20] *Commentaries,* Book IV, Chap. 11.

[21] Chap. XIII.

have operated on them, may secure a higher measure of conformity to law on the part of normal persons than is secured by the admission of excusing conditions. If this is so and if Utilitarian principles only were at stake, we should, without any sense that we were sacrificing any principle of value or were choosing the lesser of two evils, drop from the law the restriction on punishment entailed by the admission of excuses; unless, of course, we believed that the terror or insecurity or misery produced by the operation of laws so Draconic was worse than the lower measure of obedience to law secured by the law which admits excuses.

This objection to Bentham's rationale of excuses is not merely a fanciful one. Any increase in the number of conditions required to establish criminal liability increases the opportunity for deceiving courts or juries by the pretence that some condition is not satisfied. When the condition is a psychological factor the chances of such pretence succeeding are considerable. Quite apart from the provision made for mental disease, the cases where an accused person pleads that he killed in his sleep or accidentally or in some temporary abnormal state of unconsciousness show that deception is certainly feasible. From the Utilitarian point of view this may lead to two sorts of 'losses'. The belief that such deception is feasible may embolden persons who would not otherwise risk punishment to take their chance of deceiving a jury in this way. Secondly, a murderer who actually succeeds in this deception will be left at large, though belonging to the class which the law is concerned to incapacitate. Developments in Anglo-American law since Bentham's day have given more concrete form to the objection to this argument. There are now offences (known as offences of "strict liability") where it is not necessary for conviction to show that the accused either intentionally did what the law forbids or could have avoided doing it by use of care: selling liquor to an intoxicated person, possessing an altered passport, selling adulterated milk[22] are examples out of a range of 'strict liability' offences where it is no defence that the accused did not offend intentionally, or through negligence, *e.g.*, that he was under some mistake against which he had no opportunity to guard. Two things should be noted about them. First, the justification of this form of criminal liability can only be that if proof of intention or lack of care were required guilty persons would escape. Secondly, 'strict liability' is generally viewed with great odium and admitted as an exception to the general rule with the sense that an important principle has been sacrificed to secure a higher measure of conformity and conviction of offenders. Thus Bentham's argument curiously ignores both the two possibilities which have been realised. First, actual punishment of those who act unintentionally or in some

[22] See Glanville Williams *The Criminal Law,* Chap. 7, p. 238, for a discussion of and protest against strict liability.

other normally excusing condition may have a utilitarian value in its effects on others; and secondly, that when because of this probability, strict liability is admitted and the normal excuses are excluded, this may be done with the sense that some other principle has been overriden.

On this issue modern extended forms of Utilitarianism fare no better than Bentham's whose main criterion here of 'effective' punishment was deterrence of the offender or of others by example. Sometimes the principle that punishment should be restricted to those who have voluntarily broken the law is defended not as a principle which is rational or morally important in itself but as something so engrained in popular conceptions of justice[23] in certain societies, including our own, that not to recognise it would lead to disturbances, or to the nullification of the criminal law since officials or juries might refuse to co-operate in such a system. Hence to punish in these circumstances would either be impracticable or would create more harm than could possibly be offset by any superior deterrent force gained by such a system. On this footing, a system should admit excuses much as, in order to prevent disorder or lynching, concessions might be made to popular demands for more savage punishment than could be defended on other grounds. Two objections confront this wider pragmatic form of Utilitarianism. The first is the factual observation that even if a system of strict liability for all or very serious crime would be unworkable, a system which admits it on its periphery for relatively minor offences is not only workable but an actuality which we have, though many object to it or admit it with reluctance. The second objection is simply that we do not dissociate ourselves from the principle that it is wrong to punish the hopelessly insane or those who act unintentionally, etc., by treating it as something merely embodied in popular *mores* to which concessions must be made sometimes. We condemn legal systems where they disregard this principle; whereas we try to educate people out of their preference for savage penalties even if we might in extreme cases of threatened disorder concede them.

It is therefore impossible to exhibit the principle by which punishment is excluded for those who act under the excusing conditions merely as a corollary of the general Aim—Retributive or Utilitarian—justifying the practice of punishment. Can anything positive be said about this principle except that it is one to which we attach moral importance as a restriction on the pursuit of any aim we have in punishing?

It is clear that like all principles of Justice it is concerned with the adjustment of claims between a multiplicity of persons. It incorporates the idea that each individual person is to be protected against the claim of the rest for the highest possible measure of security, happiness or welfare which could be got at his expense by condemning him for the

---

[23] Wechsler and Michael "A Rationale of the Law of Homicide" 37, *Columbia Law Review,* 701, esp. pp. 752–757, and Rawls *op cit.*

breach of the rules and punishing him. For this a moral licence is required in the form of proof that the person punished broke the law by an action which was the outcome of his free choice, and the recognition of excuses is the most we can do to ensure that the terms of the licence are observed. Here perhaps the elucidation of this restrictive principle should stop. Perhaps we (or I) ought simply to say that it is a requirement of Justice, and Justice simply consists of principles to be observed in adjusting the competing claims of human beings which (i) treat all alike as persons by attaching special significance to human voluntary action and (ii) forbid the use of one human being for the benefit of others except in return for his voluntary actions against them. I confess however to an itch to go further; though what I have to say may not add to these principles of Justice. There are, however, three points which even if they are restatements from different points of view of the principles already stated, may help us to identify what we now think of as values in the practice of punishment and what we may have to reconsider in the light of modern scepticism.

(*a*) We may look upon the principle that punishment must be reserved for voluntary offences from two different points of view. The first is that of the rest of society considered as *harmed* by the offence (either because one of its members has been injured or because the authority of the law essential to its existence has been challenged or both). The principle then appears as one securing that the suffering involved in punishment is a return for the harm done to others: this is valued, not as the Aim of punishment, but as the only fair terms on which the General Aim (protection of society, maintenance of respect for law, etc.) may be pursued.

(*b*) The second point of view is that of society concerned not as harmed by the crime but as *offering* individuals including the criminal the protection of the laws on terms which are fair, because they not only consist of a framework of reciprocal rights and duties, but because within their framework each individual is given a *fair* opportunity to choose between keeping the law required for society's protection or paying the penalty. From the first point of view the actual punishment of a criminal appears not merely as something useful to society (General Aim) but as justly extracted from the criminal as a return for harm done; from the second it appears as a price justly extracted because the criminal had a fair opportunity beforehand to avoid liability to pay.

(*c*) Criminal punishment as an attempt to secure desired behaviour differs from the manipulative techniques of the Brave New World (conditioning propaganda, etc.) or the simple incapacitation of those with anti-social tendencies by taking a risk. It defers action till harm has been done; its primary operation consists simply in announcing certain standards of behaviour and attaching penalties for deviation, making it less eligible, and then leaving individuals to choose. This is a method of social control which maximises individual freedom within the coercive framework of law in a number of different ways, or perhaps, different senses. First, the individual has an option between obeying or paying. The worse the laws are, the more valuable the possibility of exercising this choice becomes in enabling an individual to decide how he shall live. Secondly, this system not only enables individuals to exercise this choice but increases the power of individuals to identify beforehand periods when the law's punishments will not interfere with them and to plan their lives accordingly. This very obvious point is often overshadowed by the other merits of restricting punishment to offences voluntarily committed, but is worth separate attention. Where punishment is not so restricted individuals will be liable to have their plans frustrated by punishments for what they do unintentionally, in ignorance, by accident or mistake. Such a system of strict liability for all offences, it is logically possible,[24] would not only vastly increase the number of punishments, but would diminish the individual's power to identify beforehand particular periods during which he will be free from them. This is so because we can have very little grounds for confidence that during a particular period we will not do something unintentionally, accidentally, etc.; whereas from their own knowledge of themselves many can say with justified confidence that for some period ahead they are not likely to engage intentionally in crime and can plan their lives from point to point in confidence that they will be left free during that period. Of course the confidence justified does not amount to certainty though drawn from knowledge of ourselves. My confidence that I will not during the next 12 months intentionally engage in any crime and will be free from punishment, may turn out to be misplaced; but it is both greater and better justified than my belief that I will not do unintentionally any of the things which our system punishes if done intentionally.

V. Reform and the Individualization of Punishment

The idea of Mitigation incorporates the conviction that though the amount or severity of punishment is primarily to be determined by reference to the General Aim, yet Justice requires that those who have special difficulties to face in keeping the law which they have broken should be punished less. Principles of Justice however are also widely taken to bear on the amount of punishment in at least two further ways. The first is the somewhat hazy requirement that 'like cases be treated alike'. This is certainly felt to be infringed at least when the ground for different punishment for those guilty of the same crime is neither some

[24] Some crimes, *e.g.*, demanding money by menaces, cannot (logically) be committed unintentionally.

personal characteristic of the offender connected with the commission of the crime nor the effect of punishment on him. If because at a given time a certain offence is specially prevalent a Judge passes a heavier sentence than on previous offenders ("as a warning") some sacrifice of justice to the safety of society is involved though it is often acceptable to many as the lesser of two evils.

The further principle that different kinds of offence of different gravity (however that is assessed) should not be punished with equal severity is one which like other principles of Distribution may qualify the pursuit of our General Aim and is not deducible from it. Long sentences of imprisonment might effectually stamp out car parking offences, yet we think it wrong to employ them; *not* because there is for each crime a penalty 'naturally' fitted to its degree of iniquity (as some Retributionists in General Aim might think); nor because we are convinced that the misery caused by such sentences (which might indeed be slight because they would need to be rarely applied) would be greater than that caused by the offences unchecked (as a Utilitarian might argue). The guiding principle is that of a proportion within a system of penalties between those imposed for different offences where these have a distinct place in a commonsense scale of gravity. This scale itself no doubt consists of very broad judgments both of relative moral iniquity and harmfulness of different types of offence: it draws rough distinctions like that between parking offences and homicide, or between 'mercy killing' and murder for gain, but cannot cope with any precise assessment of an individual's wickedness in committing a crime (Who can?) Yet maintenance of proportion of this kind may be important: for where the legal gradation of crimes expressed in the relative severity of penalties diverges sharply from this rough scale, there is a risk of either confusing common morality or flouting it and bringing the law into contempt.

The ideals of Reform and Individualization of punishment (*e.g.,* corrective training, preventive detention) which have been increasingly accepted in English penal practice since 1900 plainly run counter to the second if not to both of these principles of Justice or proportion. Some fear, and others hope, that the further intrusion of these ideals will end with the substitution of "treatment" by experts for judicial punishment. It is, however, important to see precisely what the relation of Reform to punishment is because its advocates too often mis-state it. 'Reform' as an objective is no doubt very vague; it now embraces any strengthening of the offender's disposition and capacity to keep within the law which is intentionally brought about by human effort otherwise than through fear of punishment. Reforming methods include the inducement of states of repentance or recognition of moral guilt or greater awareness of the character and demands of society, the provision of education in a broad sense, vocational training and psychological treatment. Many seeing the futility and indeed harmful character of much traditional punishment speak as if Reform could and should be the General Aim of the whole practice of punishment or the dominant objective of the criminal law:

The corrective theory based upon a conception of multiple causation and curative rehabilitative treatment should clearly predominate in legislation and in judicial and administrative practices.[25]

Of course this is a possible ideal but is not an ideal for punishment. Reform can only have a place within a system of punishment as an exploitation of the opportunities presented by the conviction or compulsory detention of offenders. It is not an alternative General Justifying Aim of the practice of punishment but something the pursuit of which within a system of punishment qualifies or displaces altogether recourse to principles of justice or proportion in determining the amount of punishment. This is where both Reform and individualized punishment have run counter to the customary morality of punishment.

There is indeed a paradox in asserting that Reform should "predominate" in a system of Criminal Law, as if the main purpose of providing punishment for murder was to reform the murderer not to prevent murder; and the paradox is greater where the legal offence is not a serious moral one: *e.g.,* infringing a state monopoly of transport. The objection to assigning to Reform this place in punishment is not merely that punishment entails suffering and Reform does not; but that Reform is essentially a remedial step for which *ex hypothesi* there is an opportunity only at the point where the criminal law has failed in its primary task of securing society from the evil which breach of the law involves. Society is divisible at any moment into two classes (i) those who have actually broken a given law and (ii) those who have not yet broken it but may. To take Reform as the dominant objective would be to forgo the hope of influencing the second and—in relation to the more serious offences—numerically much greater class. We should thus subordinate the prevention of first offences to the prevention of recidivism.

Consideration of what conditions or beliefs would make this appear a reasonable policy brings us to the topic to which this paper is a mere prolegomenon: modern sceptical doubt about the whole institution of punishment. If we believed that nothing was achieved by announcing penalties or by the example of their infliction either because those who do not commit crimes would not commit them in any event or because the penalties announced or inflicted on others are not among the factors which influence them in keeping the law then some dramatic change concentrating wholly on actual offenders would be necessary. Just because at

[25] Hall and Gluck *Cases on Criminal Law and is Enforcement,* 8 (1951).

present we do not entirely believe this we have a dilemma and an uneasy compromise. Penalties which we believe are required as a threat to maintain conformity to law at its maximum may convert the offender to whom they are applied into a hardened enemy of society; while the use of measures of Reform may lower the efficacy and example of punishment on others. At present we compromise on this relatively new aspect of punishment as we do over its main elements. What makes this compromise seem tolerable is the belief that the influence which the threat and example of punishment exerts is often independent of the severity of the punishment and is due more to the disgrace attached to conviction for crime and to the deprivation of freedom which many reforming measures at present used, would in any case involve.

BARBARA WOOTTON
The Problem of the Mentally Abnormal Offender

The problem of the mentally abnormal offender raises in a particularly acute form the question of the primary function of the courts. If that function is conceived as punitive, mental abnormality must be related to guilt; for a severely subnormal offender must be less blameworthy, and ought therefore to incur a less severe punishment, than one of greater intelligence who has committed an otherwise similar crime, even though he may well be a worse risk for the future. But from the preventive standpoint it is this future risk which matters, and the important question to be asked is not: does his abnormality mitigate or even obliterate his guilt? but, rather, is he a suitable subject for medical, in preference to any other, type of treatment? In short, the punitive and the preventive are respectively concerned the one with culpability and the other with treatability.

In keeping with its traditional obsession with the concept of guilt, English criminal law has, at least until lately, been chiefly concerned with the effect of mental disorder upon culpability. In recent years, however, the idea that an offender's mental state might also have a bearing on his treatability has begun to creep into the picture—with the result that the two concepts now lie somewhat uneasily side by side in what has become a very complex pattern.

Reprinted from Barbara Wootton, *Crime and the Criminal Law* (London: Sweet & Maxwell Ltd, 1963), pp. 58–66, 78–84, with the permission of the author and the publisher. Some footnotes omitted; original footnote numbering retained.

Under the present law there are at least six distinct legal formulae under which an accused person's mental state may be put in issue in a criminal case. First, he may be found unfit to plead, in which case of course no trial takes place at all, unless and until he is thought to have sufficiently recovered. Second, on a charge of murder (and theoretically in other cases also) a defendant may be found to be insane within the terms of the M'Naughten Rules, by the illogical verdict of guilty but insane which, to be consistent with the normal use of the term guilt, ought to be revised to read—as it once did—"not guilty on the ground of insanity." Third, a person accused of murder can plead diminished responsibility under section 2 of the Homicide Act, in which case, if this defence succeeds, a verdict of manslaughter will be substituted for one of murder.

Up to this point it is, I think, indisputable that it is the relation between the accused's mental state and his culpability or punishability which is in issue. Obviously a man who cannot be tried cannot be punished. Again, one who is insane may have to be deprived of his liberty in the interests of the public safety, but, since an insane person is not held to be blameworthy in the same way as one who is in full possession of his faculties, the institution to which he is committed must be of a medical not a penal character; and for the same reason, he must not be hung if found guilty on a capital charge. So also under the Homicide Act a defence of diminished responsibility opens the door to milder punishments than the sentences of death and life imprisonment which automatically follow the respective verdicts of capital and non-capital murder; and the fact that diminished responsibility is conceived in terms of reduced culpability, and not as indicative of the need for medical treatment, is further illustrated by the fact that in less than half the cases in which this defence has succeeded since the courts have had power to make hospital orders under the Mental Health Act, have such orders actually been made.[1] In the great majority of all the successful cases under section 2 of the Homicide Act a sentence of imprisonment has been imposed, the duration of this ranging from life to a matter of not more than a few months. Moreover, the Court of Criminal Appeal has indicated[2] approval of such sentences on the ground that a verdict of manslaughter based on diminished responsibility implies that a "residue of responsibility" rests on the accused person and that this "residue of criminal intent" may be such as to deserve punishment—a judgment which surely presents a sentencing judge with a problem of nice mathematical calculation as to the appropriate measure of punishment.

Under the Mental Health Act of 1959, however, the notion of reduced culpability begins to be complicated by the alternative criterion of treatability. Section 60 of that Act provides the fourth and fifth of my six

[1] House of Lords Debates, May 1, 1963, col. 174.

[2] R. v. *James* [1961] Crim.L.R. 842.

formulae. Under the first subsection of this section an offender who is convicted at a higher court (or at a magistrates' court if his offence is one which carries liability to imprisonment) may be compulsorily detained in hospital, or made subject to a guardianship order, if the court is satisfied, on the evidence of two doctors (one of whom must have special experience in the diagnosis or treatment of mental disorders) that this is in all the circumstances the most appropriate way of dealing with him. In the making of such orders emphasis is clearly on the future, not on the past: the governing consideration is not whether the offender deserves to be punished, but whether in fact medical treatment is likely to succeed. No sooner have we said this, however, than the old concept of culpability rears its head again. For a hospital order made by a higher court may be accompanied by a restriction order of either specified or indefinite duration, during the currency of which the patient may only be discharged on the order of the Home Secretary; and a magistrates' court also, although it has no similar power itself to make a restriction order, may commit an offender to sessions to be dealt with, if it is of the opinion that, having regard to the nature of the offence, the antecedents of the offender and the risk of his committing further offences if set at liberty, a hospital order should be accompanied by a restriction order.

The restriction order is thus professedly designed as a protection to the public; but a punitive element also, I think, still lingers in it. For if the sole object was the protection of the public against the premature discharge of a mentally disordered dangerous offender, it could hardly be argued that the court's prediction of the safe moment for release, perhaps years ahead, is likely to be more reliable than the judgment at the appropriate time of the hospital authorities who will have had the patient continuously under their surveillance.[3] If their purpose is purely protective all orders ought surely to be of indefinite duration, and the fact that this is not so suggests that they are still tainted with the tariff notion of sentencing—that is to say, with the idea that a given offence "rates" a certain period of loss of liberty. Certainly, on any other interpretation the judges who have imposed restriction orders on offenders to run for ten or more years must credit themselves with truly remarkable powers of medical prognosis. In fairness, however, it should be said that the practice of imposing indefinite rather than fixed term orders now seems to be growing.

So, too, with the fifth of my formulae, which is to be found in a later subsection of section 60 of the same Act. Under this, an offender who

---

[3] One curious feature of this provision is the fact that a hospital order can apparently be made on a diagnosis of mental disorder, even if the disorder has no connection with the offence. See the Court of Criminal Appeal's judgment in the unsuccessful appeal of *R. v. Hatt* ([1962] Crim.L.R. 647) in which the appellant claimed that his predilection for unnecessary surgical operations had no connection with his no less fervent passion for making off with other people's cars.

is charged before a magistrates' court with an offence for which he could be imprisoned, may be made the subject of a hospital or guardianship order *without being convicted,* provided that the court is satisfied that he did the act or made the omission of which he is accused. This power, however (which is itself an extended version of section 24 of the Criminal Justice Act, 1948, and has indeed a longer statutory history), may only be exercised if the accused is diagnosed as suffering from either mental illness or severe subnormality. It is not available in the case of persons suffering from either of the two other forms of mental disorder recognised by the Act, namely psychopathy, or simple, as distinct from severe, subnormality. And why not? One can only presume that the reason for this restriction is the fear that in cases in which only moderate mental disorder is diagnosed, or in which the diagnosis is particularly difficult and a mistake might easily be made, an offender might escape the punishment that he deserved. Even though no hospital or guardianship order can be made unless the court is of opinion that this is the "most suitable" method of disposing of the case, safeguards against the risk that this method might be used for the offender who really deserved to be punished are still written into the law.

One curious ambiguity in this provision, however, deserves notice at this stage. Before a hospital order is made the court must be satisfied that the accused "did the act, or made the omission with which he is charged." Yet what, one may ask, is the meaning, in this context, of "the act"? Except in the case of crimes of absolute liability, a criminal charge does not relate to a purely physical action. It relates to a physical action accompanied by a guilty mind or malicious intention. If then a person is so mentally disordered as to be incapable of forming such an intention, is he not strictly incapable of performing the act with which he is charged? The point seems to have been raised when the 1948 Criminal Justice Bill was in Committee in the House of Commons, but it was not pursued.[4] Such an interpretation would, of course, make nonsense of the section, and one must presume, therefore, that the words "the act" must be construed to refer solely to the prohibited physical action, irrespective of the actor's state of mind. But in that case the effect of this subsection would seem to be to transfer every type of crime, in the case of persons of severely disordered mentality, to the category of offences of absolute liability. In practice little use appears to be made of this provision (and in my experience few magistrates are aware of its existence); but there would seem to be an important principle here, potentially capable, as I hope to suggest later, of wider application.

The last of my six formulae, which, however, antedates all the others, stands in a category by itself. It is to be found in section 4 of the Criminal Justice Act of 1948, under which a court may make mental treat-

[4] House of Commons Standing Committee A, February 12, 1948, col. 1054.

ment (residential or non-residential) a condition of a probation order, provided that the offender's mental condition is "such as requires and as may be susceptible to treatment," but is not such as to justify his being in the language of that day certified as "of unsound mind" or "mentally defective." Such a provision represents a very whole-hearted step in the direction of accepting the criterion of treatability. For, although those to whom this section may be applied must be deemed to be guilty —in the sense that they have been convicted of offences involving *mens rea*—the only question to be decided is that of their likely response to medical or other treatment. Moreover, apart from the exclusion of insanity or mental defect, no restriction is placed on the range of diagnostic categories who may be required to submit to mental treatment under this section, although as always in the case of a probation order imposed on adults, the order cannot be made without the probationer's own consent. Nor is any reference anywhere made or even implied as to the effect of their mental condition upon their culpability. It is of interest, too, that, in practice, the use of these provisions has not been confined to what are often regarded as "pathological" crimes. Dr. Grünhut who made a study of cases to which the section was applied in 1953[5] found that out of a total of 636 probationers, 275 had committed offences against property, 216 sexual offences, ninety-seven offences of violence (other than sexual) and forty-eight other types of offence. Some of the property crimes had, it is true, "an apparently pathological background," but no less than 48 per cent. were classified as "normal" acquisitive thefts.

All these modifications in the criminal process in the case of the mentally abnormal offender thus tend (with the possible exception of the 1948 Act) to treat such abnormality as in greater or less degree exculpatory. Their purpose is not just to secure that medical treatment should be provided for any offender likely to benefit from this, but rather to guard against the risk that the mentally disordered will be unjustly punished. Their concern with treatability, where it occurs, is in effect consequential rather than primary: the question—can the doctors help him? follows, if at all, upon a negative answer to the question: is he really to blame?

Nowhere is this more conspicuous than in section 2 of the Homicide Act; and it was indeed from a study of the operation of that section that I was led nearly four years ago to the conclusion that this was the wrong approach; that any attempt to distinguish between wickedness and mental abnormality was doomed to failure; and that the only solution for the future was to allow the concept of responsibility to "wither away" and to concentrate instead on the problem of the choice of treatment, without attempting to assess the effect of mental peculiarities or degrees

[5] Grünhut, M., *Probation and Mental Treatment* (to be published in the Library of Criminology).

of culpability. That opinion was based on a study of the files of some seventy-three cases in which a defence of diminished responsibility had been raised,[6] which were kindly made available by the Home Office. To these have since been added the records of another 126 cases, the two series together covering the five and a half years from the time that the Act came into force down to mid-September 1962.

.   .   .

I have dealt at some length with our experience of diminished responsibility cases under the Homicide Act because taken together, the three facts, first, that under this Act questions of responsibility have to be decided before and not after conviction; second, that these questions fall to be decided by juries; and, third, that the charges involved are of the utmost gravity, have caused the relationship of responsibility to culpability to be explored with exceptional thoroughness in this particular context. But the principles involved are by no means restricted to the narrow field of charges of homicide. They have a far wider applicability, and are indeed implicit also in section 60 of the Mental Health Act. Unfortunately, up till now, and pending completion of the researches upon which I understand that Mr. Nigel Walker and his colleagues at Oxford are engaged, little is known of the working of this section. But it seems inevitable that if in any case a convicted person wished (as might well happen) to challenge the diagnosis of mental disorder which must precede the making of a hospital order, he would quickly be plunged into arguments about subnormality and psychopathy closely parallel to those which occupy so many hours of diminished responsibility trials.

At the same time the proposal that we should bypass, or disregard, the concept of responsibility is only too easily misunderstood; and I propose, therefore, to devote the remainder of this lecture to an attempt to meet some of the criticisms which have been brought against this proposal, to clarify just what it does or does not mean in the present context and to examine its likely implications.

First, it is to be observed that the term "responsibility" is here used in a restricted sense, much narrower than that which it often carries in ordinary speech. The measure of a person's responsibility for his actions is perhaps best defined in the words that I used earlier in terms of his capacity to act otherwise than as he did. A person may be described as totally irresponsible if he is wholly incapable of controlling his actions, and as being in a state of diminished responsibility if it is abnormally difficult for him to control them. Responsibility in this restricted sense is not to be confused with the sense in which a man is often said to

[6] Wootton, Barbara, "Diminished Responsibility: A Layman's View" (1960) 76 *Law Quarterly Review* 224.

be responsible for an action if he has in fact committed it. The questions: who broke the window? and could the man who broke the window have prevented himself from doing so? are obviously quite distinct. To dismiss the second as unanswerable in no way diminishes the importance of finding an answer to the first. Hence the primary job of the courts in determining by whom a forbidden act has actually been committed is wholly unaffected by any proposal to disregard the question of responsibility in the narrower sense. Indeed the only problem that arises here is linguistic, inasmuch as one is accustomed to say that X was "responsible" for breaking the window when the intention is to convey no more than that he did actually break it. Another word is needed here (and I must confess that I have not succeeded in finding one) to describe "responsibility" for doing an action as distinct from the capacity to refrain from doing it. "Accountable" has sometimes been suggested, but its usage in this sense is often awkward. "Instrumental" is perhaps better, though one could still wish for an adjective such perhaps as "agential" derived from the word "agent." However, all that matters is to keep firmly in mind that responsibility in the present context has nothing to do with the authorship of an act, only with the state of mind of its author.

In the second place, to discard the notion of responsibility does not mean that the mental condition of an offender ceases to have any importance, or that psychiatric considerations become irrelevant. The difference is that they become relevant, not to the question of determining the measure of his culpability, but to the choice of the treatment most likely to be effective in discouraging him from offending again; and even if these two aspects of the matter may be related, this is not to be dismissed as a distinction without a difference. The psychiatrist to whom it falls to advise as to the probable response of an offender to medical treatment no doubt has his own opinion as to the man's responsibility or capacity for self-control; and doubtless also those opinions are a factor in his judgment as to the outlook for medical treatment, or as to the probability that the offence will be repeated. But these are, and must remain, matters of opinion, "incapable," in Lord Parker's words, "of scientific proof." Opinions as to treatability, on the other hand, as well as predictions as to the likelihood of further offences can be put to the test of experience and so proved right or wrong. And by systematic observation of that experience, it is reasonable to expect that a body of knowledge will in time be built up, upon which it will be possible to draw, in the attempt to choose the most promising treatment in future cases.

Next, it must be emphasised that nothing in what has been said involves acceptance of a deterministic view of human behaviour. It is an indisputable fact of experience that human beings do respond predictably to various stimuli—whether because they choose to or because they can do no other it is not necessary to inquire. There are cases in which medical treatment works: there are cases in which it fails. Equally there are

298

cases in which deterrent penalties appear to deter those upon whom they are imposed from committing further offences; and there are cases in which they do not. Once the criminal law is conceived as an instrument of crime prevention, it is these facts which demand attention, and from which we can learn to improve the efficiency of that instrument; and the question whether on any occasion a man could or could not have acted otherwise than as he did can be left on one side or answered either way, as may be preferred. It is no longer relevant.

Failure to appreciate this has, I think, led to conflicts between psychiatry and the law being often fought on the wrong ground. Even so radical a criminologist as Dr. Sheldon Glueck seems to see the issue as one between "those who stress the prime social need of blameworthiness and retributive punishment as the core-concept in crime and justice and those who, under the impact of psychiatric, psycho-analytic, sociological, and anthropological views insist that man's choices are the product of forces largely beyond his conscious control . . ."[14] Indeed Dr. Glueck's discussion of the relation of psychiatry to law is chiefly devoted to an analysis of the exculpatory effect of psychiatric knowledge, and to the changes that have been, or should be, made in the assessment of guilt as the result of the growth of this knowledge. In consequence much intellectual ingenuity is wasted in refining the criteria by which the wicked may be distinguished from the weak-minded. For surely to argue thus is to argue from the wrong premises: the real difference between the psychiatric and the legal approach has nothing to do with free will and determinism. It has to do with their conceptions of the objectives of the criminal process, with the question whether the aim of that process is punitive or preventive, whether what matters is to punish the wrongdoer or to set him on the road to virtue; and, in order to take a stand on that issue, neither party need be a determinist.

So much for what disregard of responsibility does not mean. What, in a more positive sense, is it likely to involve? Here, I think, one of the most important consequences must be to obscure the present rigid distinction between the penal and the medical institution. As things are, the supposedly fully responsible are consigned to the former: only the wholly or partially irresponsible are eligible for the latter. Once it is admitted that we have no reliable criterion by which to distinguish between those two categories, strict segregation of each into a distinct set of institutions becomes absurd and impracticable. For purposes of convenience offenders for whom medical treatment is indicated will doubtless tend to be allocated to one building, and those for whom medicine has nothing to offer to another; but the formal distinction between prison and hospital will become blurred, and, one may reasonably expect, eventually obliterated altogether. Both will be simply "places of safety" in which offenders receive the treatment which experience suggests is most likely to evoke the desired response.

[14] Glueck, Sheldon, *Law and Psychiatry* (Tavistock Publications) 1962, p. 6.

Does this mean that the distinction between doctors and prison officers must also become blurred? Up to a point it clearly does. At the very least it would seem that some fundamental implications for the medical profession must be involved when the doctor becomes part of the machinery of law enforcement. Not only is the normal doctor-patient relationship profoundly disturbed, but far-reaching questions also arise as to the nature of the condition which the doctor is called upon to treat. If a tendency to break the law is not in itself to be classified as a disease, which does he seek to cure—the criminality or the illness? To the medical profession these questions, which I have discussed at length elsewhere,[15] must be of primary concern. But for present purposes it may be more relevant to notice how, as so often happens in this country, changes not yet officially recognised in theory are already creeping in by the back door. Already the long-awaited institution at Grendon Underwood is administered as an integral part of the prison system; yet the régime is frankly medical. Its purpose has been described by the Prison Commission's Director of Medical Services as the investigation and treatment of mental disorder generally recognised as calling for a psychiatric approach; the investigation of the mental condition of offenders whose offences in themselves suggest mental instability; and an exploration of the problem of the treatment of the psychopath. Recommendations for admission are to come from prison medical officers, and the prison itself is under the charge of a medical superintendent with wide experience in psychiatry.[16]

Grendon Underwood is (unless one should include Broadmoor which has, of course, a much narrower scope) the first genuinely hybrid institution. Interchange between medical and penal institutions is, however, further facilitated by the power of the Home Secretary to transfer to hospital persons whom, on appropriate medical evidence, he finds to be suffering from mental disorder of a nature or degree to warrant their detention in a hospital for medical treatment. Such transfers have the same effect as does a hospital order, and they may be (and usually are) also accompanied by an order restricting discharge. It is, moreover, of some interest that transfers are sometimes made quite soon after the court has passed sentence. Out of six cases convicted under section 2 of the Homicide Act in which transfers under section 72 were effected, three were removed to hospital less than three months after sentence. Although it is, of course, always possible that the prisoner had been mentally normal at the time of his offence and had only suffered a mental breakdown later, transfer after a relatively short period does indicate at least a possibility that in the judgment of the Home Secretary some mental abnormality may have been

[15] Wootton, Barbara, "The Law, The Doctor and The Deviant," *British Medical Journal,* July 27, 1963.

[16] Snell, H. K. (Director of Medical Services, Prison Commission), "H.M. Prison Grendon," *British Medical Journal,* September 22, 1962.

already present either at the time of sentence or even when the crime was committed.

The courts, however, seem to be somewhat jealous of the exercise of this power, which virtually allows the Home Secretary to treat as sick persons whom they have sentenced to imprisonment and presumably regard as wicked. Indeed it seems that, if a diagnosis of mental disorder is to be made, the courts hold that it is, generally speaking, their business, and not the Home Secretary's, to make it. So at least it would appear from the judgments of the Court of Criminal Appeal in the cases of Constance Ann James[17] and Philip Morris,[18] both of whom had been found guilty of manslaughter on grounds of diminished responsibility and had been sentenced to imprisonment. In the former case, in which the evidence as to the accused's mental condition was unchallenged, the trial judge apparently had misgivings about the public safety and in particular the safety of the convicted woman's younger child whose brother she had killed. He therefore passed a sentence of three years' imprisonment, leaving it, as he said, to the appropriate authorities to make further inquiries so that the Secretary of State might, if he thought fit, transfer the prisoner to hospital under section 72 of the Mental Health Act. The appeal was allowed, on the ground that there was obviously no need for punishment, and that there were reasonable hopes that the disorder from which the woman suffered would prove curable. In the circumstances, though reluctant to interfere with the discretion of the sentencing court, the Court of Criminal Appeal substituted a hospital order accompanied by an indefinite restriction.

In Philip Morris' case, in which, however, the appellant was unsuccessful, the matter was put even more clearly. Again the trial judge had refused to make a hospital order on grounds of the public safety and, failing any vacancy in a secure hospital, had passed a sentence of life imprisonment. But on this the Court of Criminal Appeal commented as follows: "Although the discretion . . . is very wide indeed, the basic principle must be that in the ordinary case where punishment as such is not intended, and where the sole object of the sentence is that a man should receive mental treatment, and be at large as soon as he can safely be discharged, a proper exercise of the discretion demands that steps should be taken to exercise the powers under section 60 and that the matter should not be left to be dealt with by the Secretary of State under section 72."

These difficulties are, one may hope, of a transitional nature. They would certainly not arise if all sentences involving loss of liberty were indeterminate in respect of the type of institution in which the offender is to be detained: still less if rigid distinctions between medical and penal institutions were no longer maintained. The elimination of those distinctions, moreover, though unthinkable in a primarily punitive system which must

[17] R. v. *James* [1961] Crim.L.R. 842.

[18] R. v. *Morris* (1961) 45 Cr.App.R. 233.

at all times segregate the blameworthy from the blameless, is wholly in keeping with a criminal law which is preventive rather than punitive in intention.

In this lecture and in that which preceded it I have tried to signpost the road towards such a conception of the law, and to indicate certain landmarks which suggest that this is the road along which we are, if hesitantly, already treading. At first blush it might seem that strict liability and mental abnormality have not much in common; but both present a challenge to traditional views as to the point at which, and the purpose for which, considerations of guilty intent become relevant; and both illustrate the contemporary tendency to use the criminal law to protect the community against damage, no matter what might be the state of mind of those by whom that damage is done. In this context, perhaps, the little-noticed provisions of section 60 (2) of the Mental Health Act, with its distinction between the forbidden act and the conviction, along with the liberal implications of section 4 of the Criminal Justice Act, with its emphasis on treatability rather than culpability, are to be seen as the writing on the wall. And perhaps, too, it is significant that Dr. Glueck, notwithstanding his immediate preoccupation with definitions of responsibility, lets fall, almost as if with a sigh, the forecast that some day it may be possible "to limit criminal law to matters of behavior alone," and that in his concluding lecture he foresees the "twilight of futile blameworthiness."[19] That day may be still a long way off: but at least it seems to be nearer than it was.

HERBERT MORRIS
Persons and Punishment

They acted and looked . . . at us, and around in our house, in a way that had about it the feeling—at least for me—that we were not people. In their eyesight we were just things, that was all.

[*Malcolm X*]

We have no right to treat a man like a dog.

[*Governor Maddox of Georgia*]

Alfredo Traps in Durrenmatt's tale discovers that he has brought off, all by himself, a murder involving considerable ingenuity. The mock prosecutor in the tale demands the death penalty "as reward for a crime that

[19] Glueck, Sheldon, *Law and Psychiatry* (Tavistock Publications) 1962, pp. 33, 147.

Reprinted from *The Monist*, Vol. 52, No. 4 (October 1968), 475–501, La Salle, Illinois, with the permission of the publisher and the author.

merits admiration, astonishment, and respect." Traps is deeply moved; indeed, he is exhilarated, and the whole of his life becomes more heroic, and, ironically, more precious. His defense attorney proceeds to argue that Traps was not only innocent but incapable of guilt, "a victim of the age." This defense Traps disavows with indignation and anger. He makes claim to the murder as his and demands the prescribed punishment—death.

The themes to be found in this macabre tale do not often find their way into philosophical discussions of punishment. These discussions deal with large and significant questions of whether or not we ever have the right to punish, and if we do, under what conditions, to what degree, and in what manner. There is a tradition, of course, not notable for its present vitality, that is closely linked with motifs in Durrenmatt's tale of crime and punishment. Its adherents have urged that justice requires a person be punished if he is guilty. Sometimes—though rarely—these philosophers have expressed themselves in terms of the criminal's *right to be punished*. Reaction to the claim that there is such a right has been astonishment combined, perhaps, with a touch of contempt for the perversity of the suggestion. A strange right that no one would ever wish to claim! With that flourish the subject is buried and the right disposed of. In this paper the subject is resurrected.

My aim is to argue for four propositions concerning rights that will certainly strike some as not only false but preposterous: first, that we have a right to punishment; second, that this right derives from a fundamental human right to be treated as a person; third, that this fundamental right is a natural, inalienable, and absolute right; and, fourth, that the denial of this right implies the denial of all moral rights and duties. Showing the truth of one, let alone all, of these large and questionable claims, is a tall order. The attempt or, more properly speaking, the first steps in an attempt, follow.

1. When someone claims that there is a right to be free, we can easily imagine situations in which the right is infringed and easily imagine situations in which there is a point to asserting or claiming the right. With the right to be punished, matters are otherwise. The immeditae reaction to the claim that there is such a right is puzzlement. And the reasons for this are apparent. People do not normally value pain and suffering. Punishment is associated with pain and suffering. When we think about punishment we naturally think of the strong desire most persons have to avoid it, to accept, for example, acquittal of a criminal charge with relief and eagerly, if convicted, to hope for pardon or probation. Adding, of course, to the paradoxical character of the claim of such a right is difficulty in imagining circumstances in which it would be denied one. When would one rightly demand punishment and meet with any threat of the claim being denied?

So our first task is to see when the claim of such a right would have a point. I want to approach this task by setting out two complex types of 303 institutions both of which are designed to maintain some degree of social control. In the one a central concept is punishment for wrongdoing and in the other the central concepts are control of dangerous individuals and treatment of disease.

Let us first turn attention to the institutions in which punishment is involved. The institutions I describe will resemble those we ordinarily think of as institutions of punishment; they will have, however, additional features we associate with a system of just punishment.

Let us suppose that men are constituted roughly as they now are, with a rough equivalence in strength and abilities, a capacity to be injured by each other and to make judgments that such injury is undesirable, a limited strength of will, and a capacity to reason and to conform conduct to rules. Applying to the conduct of these men are a group of rules, ones I shall label 'primary', which closely resemble the core rules of our criminal law, rules that prohibit violence and deception and compliance with which provides benefits for all persons. These benefits consist in noninterference by others with what each person values, such matters as continuance of life and bodily security. The rules define a sphere for each person, then, which is immune from interference by others. Making possible this mutual benefit is the assumption by individuals of a burden. The burden consists in the exercise of self-restraint by individuals over inclinations that would, if satisfied, directly interfere or create a substantial risk of interference with others in proscribed ways. If a person fails to exercise self-restraint even though he might have and gives in to such inclinations, he renounces a burden which others have voluntarily assumed and thus gains an advantage which others, who have restrained themselves, do not possess. This system, then, is one in which the rules establish a mutuality of benefit and burden and in which the benefits of noninterference are conditional upon the assumption of burdens.

Connecting punishment with the violation of these primary rules, and making public the provision for punishment, is both reasonable and just. First, it is only reasonable that those who voluntarily comply with the rules be provided some assurance that they will not be assuming burdens which others are unprepared to assume. Their disposition to comply voluntarily will diminish as they learn that others are with impunity renouncing burdens they are assuming. Second, fairness dictates that a system in which benefits and burdens are equally distributed have a mechanism designed to prevent a maldistribution in the benefits and burdens. Thus, sanctions are attached to noncompliance with the primary rules so as to induce compliance with the primary rules among those who may be disinclined to obey. In this way the likelihood of an unfair distribution is diminished.

Third, it is just to punish those who have violated the rules and caused the unfair distribution of benefits and burdens. A person who violates the rules has something others have—the benefits of the system—but by re-
304

nouncing what others have assumed, the burdens of self-restraint, he has acquired an unfair advantage. Matters are not even until this advantage is in some way erased. Another way of putting it is that he owes something to others, for he has something that does not rightfully belong to him. Justice—that is punishing such individuals—restores the equilibrium of benefits and burdens by taking from the individual what he owes, that is, exacting the debt. It is important to see that the equilibrium may be restored in another way. Forgiveness—with its legal analogue of a pardon—while not the righting of an unfair distribution by making one pay his debt is, nevertheless, a restoring of the equilibrium by forgiving the debt. Forgiveness may be viewed, at least in some types of cases, as a gift after the fact, erasing a debt, which had the gift been given before the fact, would not have created a debt. But the practice of pardoning has to proceed sensitively, for it may endanger in a way the practice of justice does not, the maintenance of an equilibrium of benefits and burdens. If all are indiscriminately pardoned less incentive is provided individuals to restrain their inclinations, thus increasing the incidence of persons taking what they do not deserve.

There are also in this system we are considering a variety of operative principles compliance with which provides some guarantee that the system of punishment does not itself promote an unfair distribution of benefits and burdens. For one thing, provision is made for a variety of defenses, each one of which can be said to have as its object diminishing the chances of forcibly depriving a person of benefits others have if that person has not derived an unfair advantage. A person has not derived an unfair advantage if he could not have restrained himself or if it is unreasonable to expect him to behave otherwise than he did. Sometimes the rules preclude punishment of classes of persons such as children. Sometimes they provide a defense if on a particular occasion a person lacked the capacity to conform his conduct to the rules. Thus, someone who in an epileptic seizure strikes another is excused. Punishment in these cases would be punishment of the innocent, punishment of those who do not voluntarily renounce a burden others have assumed. Punishment in such cases, then, would not equalize but rather cause an unfair distribution in benefits and burdens.

Along with principles providing defenses there are requirements that the rules be prospective and relatively clear so that persons have a fair opportunity to comply with the rules. There are, also, rules governing, among other matters, the burden of proof, who shall bear it and what it shall be, the prohibition on double jeopardy, and the privilege against self-incrimination. Justice requires conviction of the guilty, and requires their punishment, but in setting out to fulfill the demands of justice we may, of course, because we are not omniscient, cause injustice by convicting and punishing the innocent. The resolution arrived at in the system I am describing consists in weighing as the greater evil the punishment of the 305 innocent. The primary function of the system of rules was to provide individuals with a sphere of interest immune from interference. Given this goal, it is determined to be a greater evil for society to interfere unjustifiably with an individual by depriving him of good than for the society to fail to punish those that have unjustifiably interfered.

Finally, because the primary rules are designed to benefit all and because the punishments prescribed for their violation are publicized and the defenses respected, there is some plausibility in the exaggerated claim that in choosing to do an act violative of the rules an individual has chosen to be punished. This way of putting matters brings to our attention the extent to which, when the system is as I have described it, the criminal "has brought the punishment upon himself" in contrast to those cases where it would be misleading to say "he has brought it upon himself," cases, for example, where one does not know the rules or is punished in the absence of fault.

To summarize, then: first, there is a group of rules guiding the behavior of individuals in the community which establish spheres of interest immune from interference by others; second, provision is made for what is generally regarded as a deprivation of some thing of value if the rules are violated; third, the deprivations visited upon any person are justified by that person's having violated the rules; fourth, the deprivation, in this just system of punishment, is linked to rules that fairly distribute benefits and burdens and to procedures that strike some balance between not punishing the guilty and punishing the innocent, a class defined as those who have not voluntarily done acts violative of the law, in which it is evident that the evil of punishing the innocent is regarded as greater than the nonpunishment of the guilty.

At the core of many actual legal systems one finds, of course, rules and procedures of the kind I have sketched. It is obvious, though, that any ongoing legal system differs in significant respects from what I have presented here, containing 'pockets of injustice'.

I want now to sketch an extreme version of a set of institutions of a fundamentally different kind, institutions proceeding on a conception of man which appears to be basically at odds with that operative within a system of punishment.

Rules are promulgated in this system that prohibit certain types of injuries and harms.

In this world we are now to imagine when an individual harms another his conduct is to be regarded as a symptom of some pathological condition in the way a running nose is a symptom of a cold. Actions diverging from some conception of the normal are viewed as manifestations of a disease in the way in which we might today regard the arm and leg movements of an epileptic during a seizure. Actions conforming to what is normal are assimilated to the normal and healthy functioning of bodily organs. What a person does, then, is assimilated, on this conception, to what we believe today, or at least most of us believe today, a person undergoes. We draw a distinction between the operation of the kidney and raising an arm on request. This distinction between mere events or happenings and human actions is erased in our imagined system.[1]

There is, however, bound to be something strange in this erasing of a recognized distinction, for, as with metaphysical suggestions generally, and I take this to be one, the distinction may be reintroduced but given a different description, for example, 'happenings with X type of causes' and 'happenings with Y type of causes'. Responses of different kinds, today legitimated by our distinction between happenings and actions may be legitimated by this new manner of description. And so there may be isomorphism between a system recognizing the distinction and one erasing it. Still, when this distinction is erased certain tendencies of thought and re-

---

[1] "When a man is suffering from an infectious disease, he is a danger to the community, and it is necessary to restrict his liberty of movement. But no one associates any idea of guilt with such a situation. On the contrary, he is an object of commiseration to his friends. Such steps as science recommends are taken to cure him of his disease, and he submits as a rule without reluctance to the curtailment of liberty involved meanwhile. The same method in spirit ought to be shown in the treatment of what is called 'crime.' "

Bertrand Russell, *Roads to Freedom* (London: George Allen and Unwin Ltd., 1918), p. 135.

"We do not hold people responsible for their reflexes—for example, for coughing in church. We hold them responsible for their operant behavior—for example, for whispering in church or remaining in church while coughing. But there are variables which are responsible for whispering as well as coughing, and these may be just as inexorable. When we recognize this, we are likely to drop the notion of responsibility altogether and with it the doctrine of free will as an inner causal agent."

B. F. Skinner, *Science and Human Behavior* (1953), pp. 115–6.

"Basically, criminality is but a symptom of insanity, using the term in its widest generic sense to express unacceptable social behavior based on unconscious motivation flowing from a disturbed instinctive and emotional life, whether this appears in frank psychoses, or in less obvious form in neuroses and unrecognized psychoses. . . . If criminals are products of early environmental influences in the same sense that psychotics and neurotics are, then it should be possible to reach them psychotherapeutically."

Benjamin Karpman, "Criminal Psychodynamics," *Journal of Criminal Law and Criminology,* 47 (1956), p. 9.

"We, the agents of society, must move to end the game of tit-for-tat and blow-for-blow in which the offender has foolishly and futilely engaged himself and us. We are not driven, as he is, to wild and impulsive actions. With knowledge comes power, and with power there is no need for the frightened vengeance of the old penology. In its place should go a quiet, dignified, therapeutic program for the rehabilitation of the disorganized one, if possible, the protection of society during the treatment period, and his guided return to useful citizenship, as soon as this can be effected."

Karl Menninger, "Therapy, Not Punishment," *Harper's Magazine* (August 1959), pp. 63–64.

sponses might naturally arise that would tend to affect unfavorably values respected by a system of punishment.

Let us elaborate on this assimilation of conduct of a certain kind to symptoms of a disease. First, there is something abnormal in both the case of conduct, such as killing another, and a symptom of a disease such as an irregular heart beat. Second, there are causes for this abnormality in action such that once we know of them we can explain the abnormality as we now can explain the symptoms of many physical diseases. The abnormality is looked upon as a happening with a causal explanation rather than an action for which there were reasons. Third, the causes that account for the abnormality interfere with the normal functioning of the body, or, in the case of killing with what is regarded as a normal functioning of an individual. Fourth, the abnormality is in some way a part of the individual, necessarily involving his body. A well going dry might satisfy our three foregoing conditions of disease symptoms, but it is hardly a disease or the symptom of one. Finally, and most obscure, the abnormality arises in some way from within the individual. If Jones is hit with a mallet by Smith, Jones may reel about and fall on James who may be injured. But this abnormal conduct of Jones is not regarded as a symptom of disease. Smith, not Jones, is suffering from some pathological condition.

With this view of man the institutions of social control respond, not with punishment, but with either preventive detention, in case of 'carriers', or therapy in the case of those manifesting pathological symptoms. The logic of sickness implies the logic of therapy. And therapy and punishment differ widely in their implications. In bringing out some of these differences I want again to draw attention to the important fact that while the distinctions we now draw are erased in the therapy world, they may, in fact, be reintroduced but under different descriptions. To the extent they are, we really have a punishment system combined with a therapy system. I am concerned now, however, with what the implications would be were the world indeed one of therapy and not a disguised world of punishment and therapy, for I want to suggest tendencies of thought that arise when one is immersed in the ideology of disease and therapy.

First, punishment is the imposition upon a person who is believed to be at fault of something commonly believed to be a deprivation where that deprivation is justified by the person's guilty behavior. It is associated with resentment, for the guilty are those who have done what they had no right to do by failing to exercise restraint when they might have and where others have. Therapy is not a response to a person who is at fault. We respond to an individual, not because of what he has done, but because of some condition from which he is suffering. If he is no longer suffering from the condition, treatment no longer has a point. Punishment, then, focuses on the past; therapy on the present. Therapy is normally associated with compassion for what one undergoes, not resentment for what one has

308   illegitimately done.

Second, with therapy, unlike punishment, we do not seek to deprive the person of something acknowledged as a good, but seek rather to help and to benefit the individual who is suffering by ministering to his illness in the hope that the person can be cured. The good we attempt to do is not a reward for desert. The individual suffering has not merited by his disease the good we seek to bestow upon him but has, because he is a creature that has the capacity to feel pain, a claim upon our sympathies and help.

Third, we saw with punishment that its justification was related to maintaining and restoring a fair distribution of benefits and burdens. Infliction of the prescribed punishment carries the implication, then, that one has 'paid one's debt' to society, for the punishment is the taking from the person of something commonly recognized as valuable. It is this conception of 'a debt owed' that may permit, as I suggested earlier, under certain conditions, the nonpunishment of the guilty, for operative within a system of punishment may be a concept analogous to forgiveness, namely pardoning. Who it is that we may pardon and under what conditions—contrition with its elements of self-punishment no doubt plays a role—I shall not go into though it is clearly a matter of the greatest practical and theoretical interest. What is clear is that the conceptions of 'paying a debt' or 'having a debt forgiven' or pardoning have no place in a system of therapy.

Fourth, with punishment there is an attempt at some equivalence between the advantage gained by the wrongdoer—partly based upon the seriousness of the interest invaded, partly on the state of mind with which the wrongful act was performed—and the punishment meted out. Thus, we can understand a prohibition on 'cruel and unusual punishments' so that disproportionate pain and suffering are avoided. With therapy attempts at proportionality make no sense. It is perfectly plausible giving someone who kills a pill and treating for a lifetime within an institution one who has broken a dish and manifested accident proneness. We have the concept of 'painful treatment'. We do not have the concept of 'cruel treatment'. Because treatment is regarded as a benefit, though it may involve pain, it is natural that less restraint is exercised in bestowing it, than in inflicting punishment. Further, protests with respect to treatment are likely to be assimilated to the complaints of one whose leg must be amputated in order for him to live, and, thus, largely disregarded. To be sure, there is operative in the therapy world some conception of the "cure being worse than the disease," but if the disease is manifested in conduct harmful to others, and if being a normal operating human being is valued highly, there will naturally be considerable pressure to find the cure acceptable.

Fifth, the rules in our system of punishment governing conduct of individuals were rules violation of which involved either direct interference with others or the creation of a substantial risk of such interference. One could imagine adding to this system of primary rules other rules proscribing preparation to do acts violative of the primary rules and even rules 309 proscribing thoughts. Objection to such suggestions would have many sources but a principal one would consist in its involving the infliction of punishment on too great a number of persons who would not, because of a change of mind, have violated the primary rules. Though we are interested in diminishing violations of the primary rules, we are not prepared to punish too many individuals who would never have violated the rules in order to achieve this aim. In a system motivated solely by a preventive and curative ideology there would be less reason to wait until symptoms manifest themselves in socially harmful conduct. It is understandable that we should wish at the earliest possible stage to arrest the development of the disease. In the punishment system, because we are dealing with deprivations, it is understandable that we should forbear from imposing them until we are quite sure of guilt. In the therapy system, dealing as it does with benefits, there is less reason for forbearance from treatment at an early stage.

Sixth, a variety of procedural safeguards we associate with punishment have less significance in a therapy system. To the degree objections to double jeopardy and self-incrimination are based on a wish to decrease the chances of the innocent being convicted and punished, a therapy system, unconcerned with this problem, would disregard such safeguards. When one is out to help people there is also little sense in urging that the burden of proof be on those providing the help. And there is less point to imposing the burden of proving that the conduct was pathological beyond a reasonable doubt. Further, a jury system which, within a system of justice, serves to make accommodations to the individual situation and to introduce a human element, would play no role or a minor one in a world where expertise is required in making determinations of disease and treatment.

In our system of punishment an attempt was made to maximize each individual's freedom of choice by first of all delimiting by rules certain spheres of conduct immune from interference by others. The punishment associated with these primary rules paid deference to an individual's free choice by connecting punishment to a freely chosen act violative of the rules, thus giving some plausibility to the claim, as we saw, that what a person received by way of punishment he himself had chosen. With the world of disease and therapy all this changes and the individual's free choice ceases to be a determinative factor in how others respond to him. All those principles of our own legal system that minimize the chances of punishment of those who have not chosen to do acts violative of the rules tend to lose their point in the therapy system, for how we respond in a therapy system to a person is not conditioned upon what he has chosen but rather on what symptoms he has manifested or may manifest and what the best therapy for the disease is that is suggested by the symptoms.

310   Now, it is clear I think, that were we confronted with the alternatives

I have sketched, between a system of just punishment and a thoroughgoing system of treatment, a system, that is, that did not reintroduce concepts appropriate to punishment, we could see the point in claiming that a person has a right to be punished, meaning by this that a person had a right to all those institutions and practices linked to punishment. For these would provide him with, among other things, a far greater ability to predict what would happen to him on the occurrence of certain events than the therapy system. There is the inestimable value to each of us of having the responses of others to us determined over a wide range of our lives by what we choose rather than what they choose. A person has a right to institutions that respect his choices. Our punishment system does; our therapy system does not.

Apart from those aspects of our therapy model which would relate to serious limitations on personal liberty, there are clearly objections of a more profound kind to the mode of thinking I have associated with the therapy model.

First, human beings pride themselves in having capacities that animals do not. A common way, for example, of arousing shame in a child is to compare the child's conduct to that of an animal. In a system where all actions are assimilated to happenings we are assimilated to creatures—indeed, it is more extreme than this—whom we have always thought possessed of less than we. Fundamental to our practice of praise and order of attainment is that one who can do more—one who is capable of more and one who does more is more worthy of respect and admiration. And we have thought of ourselves as capable where animals are not of making, of creating, among other things, ourselves. The conception of man I have outlined would provide us with a status that today, when our conduct is assimilated to it in moral criticism, we consider properly evocative of shame.

Second, if all human conduct is viewed as something men undergo, thrown into question would be the appropriateness of that extensive range of peculiarly human satisfactions that derive from a sense of achievement. For these satisfactions we shall have to substitute those mild satisfactions attendant upon a healthy well-functioning body. Contentment is our lot if we are fortunate; intense satisfaction at achievement is entirely inappropriate.

Third, in the therapy world nothing is earned and what we receive comes to us through compassion, or through a desire to control us. Resentment is out of place. We can take credit for nothing but must always regard ourselves—if there are selves left to regard once actions disappear —as fortunate recipients of benefits or unfortunate carriers of disease who must be controlled. We know that within our own world human beings who have been so regarded and who come to accept this view of themselves come to look upon themselves as worthless. When what we do is 311 met with resentment, we are indirectly paid something of a compliment.

Fourth, attention should also be drawn to a peculiar evil that may be attendant upon regarding a man's actions as symptoms of disease. The logic of cure will push us toward forms of therapy that inevitably involve changes in the person made against his will. The evil in this would be most apparent in those cases where the agent, whose action is determined to be a manifestation of some disease, does not regard his action in this way. He believes that what he has done is, in fact, 'right' but his conception of 'normality' is not the therapeutically accepted one. When we treat an illness we normally treat a condition that the person is not responsible for. He is 'suffering' from some disease and we treat the condition, relieving the person of something preventing his normal functioning. When we begin treating persons for actions that have been chosen, we do not lift from the person something that is interfering with his normal functioning but we change the person so that he functions in a way regarded as normal by the current therapeutic community. We have to change him and his judgments of value. In doing this we display a lack of respect for the moral status of individuals, that is, a lack of respect for the reasoning and choices of individuals. They are but animals who must be conditioned. I think we can understand and, indeed, sympathize with a man's preferring death to being forcibly turned into what he is not.

Finally, perhaps most frightening of all would be the derogation in status of all protests to treatment. If someone believes that he has done something right, and if he protests being treated and changed, the protest will itself be regarded as a sign of some pathological condition, for who would not wish to be cured of an affliction? What this leads to are questions of an important kind about the effect of this conception of man upon what we now understand by reasoning. Here what a person takes to be a reasoned defense of an act is treated, as the action was, on the model of a happening of a pathological kind. Not just a person's acts are taken from him but also his attempt at a reasoned justification for the acts. In a system of punishment a person who has committed a crime may argue that what he did was right. We make him pay the price and we respect his right to retain the judgment he has made. A conception of pathology precludes this form of respect.

It might be objected to the foregoing that all I have shown—if that—is that if the only alternatives open to us are a *just* system of punishment or the mad world of being treated like sick or healthy animals, we do in fact have a right to a system of punishment of this kind. But this hardly shows that we have a right *simpliciter* to punishment as we do, say, to be free. Indeed, it does not even show a right to a just system of punishment, for surely we can, without too much difficulty, imagine situations in which the alternatives to punishment are not this mad world but a world in which
312 we are still treated as persons and there is, for example, not the pain and

suffering attendant upon punishment. One such world is one in which there are rules but responses to their violation is not the deprivation of some good but forgiveness. Still another type of world would be one in which violation of the rules were responded to by merely comparing the conduct of the person to something commonly regarded as low or filthy, and thus, producing by this mode of moral criticism, feelings of shame rather than feelings of guilt.

I am prepared to allow that these objections have a point. While granting force to the above objections I want to offer a few additional comments with respect to each of them. First, any existent legal system permits the punishment of individuals under circumstances where the conditions I have set forth for a just system have not been satisfied. A glaring example of this would be criminal strict liability which is to be found in our own legal system. Nevertheless, I think it would be difficult to present any system we should regard as a system of punishment that would not still have a great advantage over our imagined therapy system. The system of punishment we imagine may more and more approximate a system of sheer terror in which human beings are treated as animals to be intimidated and prodded. To the degree that the system is of this character it is, in my judgment, not simply an unjust system but one that diverges from what we normally understand by a system of punishment. At least some deference to the choice of individuals is built into the idea of punishment. So there would be some truth in saying we have a right to any system of punishment if the only alternative to it was therapy.

Second, people may imagine systems in which there are rules and in which the response to their violation is not punishment but pardoning, the legal analogue of forgiveness. Surely this is a system to which we would claim a right as against one in which we are made to suffer for violating the rules. There are several comments that need to be made about this. It may be, of course, that a high incidence of pardoning would increase the incidence of rule violations. Further, the difficulty with suggesting pardoning as a general response is that pardoning presupposes the very responses that it is suggested it supplant. A system of deprivations, or a practice of deprivations on the happening of certain actions, underlies the practice of pardoning and forgiving, for it is only where we possess the idea of a wrong to be made up or of a debt owed to others, ideas we acquire within a world in which there have been deprivations for wrong acts, that we have the idea of pardoning for the wrong or forgiving the debt.

Finally, if we look at the responses I suggested would give rise to feelings of shame, we may rightly be troubled with the appropriateness of this response in any community in which each person assumes burdens so that each may derive benefits. In such situations might it not be that individuals have a right to a system of punishment so that each person could be assured that inequities in the distribution of benefits and burdens are unlikely 313 to occur and if they do, procedures exist for correcting them? Further, it may well be that, everything considered, we should prefer the pain and suffering of a system of punishment to a world in which we only experience shame on the doing of wrong acts, for with guilt there are relatively simple ways of ridding ourselves of the feeling we have, that is, gaining forgiveness or taking the punishment, but with shame we have to bear it until we no longer are the person who has behaved in the shameful way. Thus, I suggest that we have, wherever there is a distribution of benefits and burdens of the kind I have described, a right to a system of punishment.

I want also to make clear in concluding this section that I have argued, though very indirectly, not just for a right to a system of punishment, but for a right to be punished once there is in existence such a system. Thus, a man has the right to be punished rather than treated if he is guilty of some offense. And, indeed, one can imagine a case in which, even in the face of an offer of a pardon, a man claims and ought to have acknowledged his right to be punished.

2. The primary reason for preferring the system of punishment as against the system of therapy might have been expressed in terms of the one system treating one as a person and the other not. In invoking the right to be punished, one justifies one's claim by reference to a more fundamental right. I want now to turn attention to this fundamental right and attempt to shed light—it will have to be little, for the topic is immense—on what is meant by 'treating an individual as a person'.

When we talk of not treating a human being as a person or 'showing no respect for one as a person' what we imply by our words is a contrast between the manner in which one acceptably responds to human beings and the manner in which one acceptably responds to animals and inanimate objects. When we treat a human being merely as an animal or some inanimate object our responses to the human being are determined, not by his choices, but ours in disregard of or with indifference to his. And when we 'look upon' a person as less than a person or not a person, we consider the person as incapable of rational choice. In cases of not treating a human being as a person we interfere with a person in such a way that what is done, even if the person is involved in the doing, is done not by the person but by the user of the person. In extreme cases there may even be an elision of a causal chain so that we might say that X killed Z even though Y's hand was the hand that held the weapon, for Y's hand may have been entirely in X's control. The one agent is in some way treating the other as a mere link in a causal chain. There is, of course, a wide range of cases in which a person is used to accomplish the aim of another and in which the person used is less than fully free. A person may be grabbed against his will and used as a shield. A person may be drugged or hypnotized and then employed for certain ends. A person may be deceived into doing other than he intends doing. A person may be ordered

314

to do something and threatened with harm if he does not and coerced into doing what he does not want to. There is still another range of cases in which individuals are not used, but in which decisions by others are made that affect them in circumstances where they have the capacity for choice and where they are not being treated as persons.

But it is particularly important to look at coercion, for I have claimed that a just system of punishment treats human beings as persons; and it is not immediately apparent how ordering someone to do something and threatening harm differs essentially from having rules supported by threats of harm in case of noncompliance.

There are affinities between coercion and other cases of not treating someone as a person, for it is not the coerced person's choices but the coercer's that are responsible for what is done. But unlike other indisputable cases of not treating one as a person, for example using someone as a shield, there is some choice involved in coercion. And if this is so, why does the coercer stand in any different relation to the coerced person than the criminal law stands to individuals in society?

Suppose the person who is threatened disregards the order and gets the threatened harm. Now suppose he is told, "Well, you did after all bring it upon yourself." There is clearly something strange in this. It is the person doing the threatening and not the person threatened who is responsible. But our reaction to punishment, at least in a system that resembles the one I have described, is precisely that the person violating the rules brought it upon himself. What lies behind these different reactions?

There exist situations in the law, of course, which resemble coercion situations. There are occasions when in the law a person might justifiably say "I am not being treated as a person but being used" and where he might properly react to the punishment as something "he was hardly responsible for." But it is possible to have a system in which it would be misleading to say, over a wide range of cases of punishment for noncompliance, that we are using persons. The clearest case in which it would be inappropriate to so regard punishment would be one in which there were explicit agreement in advance that punishment should follow on the voluntary doing of certain acts. Even if one does not have such conditions satisfied, and obviously such explicit agreements are not characteristic, one can see significant differences between our system of just punishment and a coercion situation.

First, unlike the case with one person coercing another 'to do his will', the rules in our system apply to all, with the benefits and burdens equally distributed. About such a system it cannot be said that some are being subordinated to others or are being used by others or gotten to do things by others. To the extent that the rules are thought to be to the advantage of only some or to the extent there is a maldistribution of benefits and burdens, the difference between coercion and law disappears. 315

Second, it might be argued that at least any person inclined to act in a manner violative of the rules stands to all others as the person coerced stands to his coercer, and that he, at least, is a person disadvantaged as others are not. It is important here, I think, that he is part of a system in which it is commonly agreed that forbearance from the acts proscribed by the rules provides advantages for all. This system is the accepted setting; it is the norm. Thus, in any coercive situation, it is the coercer who deviates from the norm, with the responsibility of the person he is attempting to coerce, defeated. In a just punishment situation, it is the person deviating from the norm, indeed he might be a coercer, who is responsible, for it is the norm to restrain oneself from acts of that kind. A voluntary agent diverging in his conduct from what is expected or what the norm is, on general causal principles, regarded as the cause of what results from his conduct.

There is, then, some plausibility in the claim that, in a system of punishment of the kind I have sketched, a person chooses the punishment that is meted out to him. If, then, we can say in such a system that the rules provide none with advantages that others do not have, and further, that what happens to a person is conditioned by that person's choice and not that of others, then we can say that it is a system responding to one as a person.

We treat a human being as a person provided: first, we permit the person to make the choices that will determine what happens to him and second, when our responses to the person are responses respecting the person's choices. When we respond to a person's illness by treating the illness it is neither a case of treating or not treating the individual as a person. When we give a person a gift we are neither treating or not treating him as a person, unless, of course, he does not wish it, chooses not to have it, but we compel him to accept it.

3. This right to be treated as a person is a fundamental human right belonging to all human beings by virtue of their being human. It is also a natural, inalienable, and absolute right. I want now to defend these claims so reminiscent of an era of philosophical thinking about rights that many consider to have been seriously confused.

If the right is one that we possess by virtue of being human beings, we are immediately confronted with an apparent dilemma. If, to treat another as a person requires that we provide him with reasons for acting and avoid force or deception, how can we justify the force and deception we exercise with respect to children and the mentally ill? If they, too, have a right to be treated as persons are we not constantly infringing their rights? One way out of this is simply to restrict the right to those who satisfy the conditions of being a person. Infants and the insane, it might be argued, do not meet these conditions, and they would not then have the right. Another approach would be to describe the right they possess as a prima facie right to be treated as a person. This right might then be outweighed by other

316

considerations. This approach generally seems to me, as I shall later argue, inadequate.

I prefer this tack. Children possess the right to be treated as persons but they possess this right as an individual might be said in the law of property to possess a future interest. There are advantages in talking of individuals as having a right though complete enjoyment of it is postponed. Brought to our attention, if we ascribe to them the right, is the legitimacy of their complaint if they are not provided with opportunities and conditions assuring their full enjoyment of the right when they acquire the characteristics of persons. More than this, all persons are charged with the sensitive task of not denying them the right to be a person and to be treated as a person by failing to provide the conditions for their becoming individuals who are able freely and in an informed way to choose and who are prepared themselves to assume responsibility for their choices. There is an obligation imposed upon us all, unlike that we have with respect to animals, to respond to children in such a way as to maximize the chances of their becoming persons. This may well impose upon us the obligation to treat them as persons from a very early age, that is, to respect their choices and to place upon them the responsibility for the choices to be made. There is no need to say that there is a close connection between how we respond to them and what they become. It also imposes upon us all the duty to display constantly the qualities of a person, for what they become they will largely become because of what they learn from us is acceptable behavior.

In claiming that the right is a right that human beings have by virtue of being human, there are several other features of the right, that should be noted, perhaps better conveyed by labelling them 'natural'. First, it is a right we have apart from any voluntary agreement into which we have entered. Second, it is not a right that derives from some defined position or status. Third, it is equally apparent that one has the right regardless of the society or community of which one is a member. Finally, it is a right linked to certain features of a class of beings. Were we fundamentally different than we now are, we would not have it. But it is more than that, for the right is linked to a feature of human beings which, were that feature absent—the capacity to reason and to choose on the basis of reasons—, profound conceptual changes would be involved in the thought about human beings. It is a right, then, connected with a feature of men that sets men apart from other natural phenomena.

The right to be treated as a person is inalienable. To say of a right that it is inalienable draws attention not to limitations placed on what others may do with respect to the possessor of the right but rather to limitations placed on the dispositive capacities of the possessor of the right. Something is to be gained in keeping the issues of alienability and absoluteness separate.

317

There are a variety of locutions qualifying what possessors of rights may and may not do. For example, on this issue of alienability, it would be worthwhile to look at, among other things, what is involved in abandoning, abdicating, conveying, giving up, granting, relinquishing, surrendering, transferring, and waiving one's rights. And with respect to each of these concepts we should also have to be sensitive to the variety of uses of the term 'rights'. What it is, for example, to waive a Hohfeldian 'right' in his strict sense will differ from what it is to waive a right in his 'privilege' sense.

Let us look at only two concepts very briefly, those of transferring and waiving rights. The clearest case of transferring rights is that of transferring rights with respect to specific objects. I own a watch and owning it I have a complicated relationship, captured in this area rather well I think by Hohfeld's four basic legal relationships, to all persons in the world with respect to the watch. We crudely capture these complex relationships by talking of my 'property rights' in or with respect to the watch. If I sell the watch, thus exercising a capacity provided by the rules of property, I have transferred rights in or with respect to the watch to someone else, the buyer, and the buyer now stands, as I formerly did, to all persons in the world in a series of complex relationships with respect to the watch.

While still the owner, I may have given to another permission to use it for several days. Had there not been the permission and had the person taken the watch, we should have spoken of interfering with or violating or, possibly, infringing my property rights. Or, to take a situation in which transferring rights is inappropriate, I may say to another "go ahead and slap me—you have my permission." In these types of situations philosophers and others have spoken of 'surrendering' rights or, alternatively and, I believe, less strangely, of 'waiving one's rights'. And recently, of course, the whole topic of 'waiving one's right to remain silent' in the context of police interrogation of suspects has been a subject of extensive litigation and discussion.

I confess to feeling that matters are not entirely perspicuous with respect to what is involved in 'waiving' or 'surrendering' rights. In conveying to another permission to take a watch or slap one, one makes legally permissible what otherwise would not have been. But in saying those words that constitute permission to take one's watch one is, of course, exercising precisely one of those capacities that leads us to say he has, while others have not, property rights with respect to the watch. Has one then waived his right in Hohfeld's strict sense in which the correlative is the duty to forbear on the part of others?

We may wish to distinguish here waiving the right to have others forbear to which there is a corresponding duty on their part to forbear, from
318 placing oneself in a position where one has no legitimate right to com-

plain. If I say the magic words "take the watch for a couple of days" or "go ahead and slap me," have I waived my right not to have my property taken or a right not to be struck or have I, rather, in saying what I have, simply stepped into a relation in which the rights no longer apply with respect to a specified other person? These observations find support in the following considerations. The right is that which gives rise, when infringed, to a legitimate claim against another person. What this suggests is that the right is that sphere interference with which entitles us to complain or gives us a right to complain. From this it seems to follow that a right to bodily security should be more precisely described as 'a right that others not interfere without permission.' And there is the corresponding duty not to interfere unless provided permission. Thus when we talk of waiving our rights or 'giving up our rights' in such cases we are not waiving or giving up our right to property nor our right to bodily security, for we still, of course, possess the right not to have our watch taken without permission. We have rather placed ourselves in a position where we do not possess the capacity, sometimes called a right, to complain if the person takes the watch or slaps us.

There is another type of situation in which we may speak of waiving our rights. If someone without permission slaps me, there is an infringement of my right to bodily security. If I now acquiesce or go further and say "forget it" or "you are forgiven," we might say that I had waived my right to complain. But here, too, I feel uncomfortable about what is involved. For I do have the right to complain (a right without a corresponding duty) in the event I am slapped and I have that right whether I wish it or not. If I say to another after the slap, "you are forgiven" what I do is not waive the right to complain but rather make illegitimate my subsequent exercise of that right.

Now, if we turn to the right to be treated as a person, the claim that I made was that it was inalienable, and what I meant to convey by that word of respectable age is that (a) it is a right that cannot be transferred to another in the way one's right with respect to objects can be transferred and (b) that it cannot be waived in the ways in which people talk of waiving rights to property or waiving, within certain limitations, one's right to bodily security.

While the rules of the law of property are such that persons may, satisfying certain procedures, transfer rights, the right to be treated as a person logically cannot be transferred anymore than one person can transfer to another his right to life or privacy. What, indeed, would it be like for another to have our right to be treated as a person? We can understand transferring a right with respect to certain objects. The new owner stands where the old owner stood. But with a right to be treated as a person what could this mean? My having the right meant that my choices were respected. Now if I transfer it to another this will mean 319 that he will possess the right that my choices be respected? This is non-sense. It is only each person himself that can have his choices respected. It is no more possible to transfer this right than it is to transfer one's right to life.

Nor can the right be waived. It cannot be waived because any agreement to being treated as an animal or an instrument does not provide others with the moral permission to so treat us. One can volunteer to be a shield, but then it is one's choice on a particular occasion to be a shield. If without our permission, without our choosing it, someone used us as a shield, we may, I should suppose, forgive the person for treating us as an object. But we do not thereby waive our right to be treated as a person, for that is a right that has been infringed and what we have at most done is put ourselves in a position where it is inappropriate any longer to exercise the right to complain.

This is the right, then, such that the moral rules defining relationships among persons preclude anyone from morally giving others legitimate permissions or rights with respect to one by doing or saying certain things. One stands, then, with respect to one's person as the nonowner of goods stands to those goods. The nonowner cannot, given the rule-defined relationships, convey to others rights and privileges that only the owner possesses. Just as there are agreements nonenforceable because void is contrary to public policy, so there are permissions our moral outlook regards as without moral force. With respect to being treated as a person, one is 'disabled' from modifying relations of others to one.

The right is absolute. This claim is bound to raise eyebrows. I have an innocuous point in mind in making this claim.

In discussing alienability we focused on incapacities with respect to disposing of rights. Here what I want to bring out is a sense in which a right exists despite considerations for refusing to accord the person his rights. As with the topic of alienability there are a host of concepts that deserve a close look in this area. Among them are according, acknowledging, annulling, asserting, claiming, denying, destroying, exercising, infringing, insisting upon, interfering with, possessing, recognizing and violating.

The claim that rights are absolute has been construed to mean that 'assertions of rights cannot, for any reason under any circumstances be denied'. When there are considerations which warrant refusing to accord persons their rights, there are two prevalent views as to how this should be described: there is, first, the view that the person does not have the right, and second, the view that he has rights but of a prima facie kind and that these have been outweighed or overcome by the other considerations. "We can conceive times when such rights must give way, and, therefore, they are only prima facie and not absolute rights." (Brandt)

320   Perhaps there are cases in which a person claims a right to do a cer-

tain thing, say with his property, and argues that his property rights are absolute, meaning by this he has a right to do whatever he wishes with his property. Here, no doubt, it has to be explained to the person that the right he claims he has, he does not in fact possess. In such a case the person does not have and never did have, given a certain description of the right, a right that was prima facie or otherwise, to do what he claimed he had the right to do. If the assertion that a right is absolute implies that we have a right to do whatever we wish to do, it is an absurd claim and as such should not really ever have been attributed to political theorists arguing for absolute rights. But, of course, the claim that we have a prima facie right to do whatever we wish to do is equally absurd. The right is not prima facie either, for who would claim, thinking of the right to be free, that one has a prima facie right to kill others, if one wishes, unless there are moral considerations weighing against it?

There are, however, other situations in which it is accepted by all that a person possesses rights of a certain kind, and the difficulty we face is that of according the person the right he is claiming when this will promote more evil than good. The just act is to give the man his due and giving a man what it is his right to have is giving him his due. But it is a mistake to suppose that justice is the only dimension of morality. It may be justifiable not to accord to a man his rights. But it is no less a wrong to him, no less an infringement. It is seriously misleading to turn all justifiable infringements into noninfringements by saying that the right is only prima facie, as if we have, in concluding that we should not accord a man his rights, made out a case that he had none. To use the language of 'prima facie rights' misleads, for it suggests that a presumption of the existence of a right has been overcome in these cases where all that can be said is that the presumption in favor of according a man his rights has been overcome. If we begin to think the right itself is prima facie, we shall, in cases in which we are justified in not according it, fail sufficiently to bring out that we have interfered where justice says we should not. Our moral framework is unnecessarily and undesirably impoverished by the theory that there are such rights.

When I claim, then, that the right to be treated as a person is absolute what I claim is that given that one is a person, one always has the right so to be treated, and that while there may possibly be occasions morally requiring not according a person this right, this fact makes it no less true that the right exists and would be infringed if the person were not accorded it.

4. Having said something about the nature of this fundamental right I want now, in conclusion, to suggest that the denial of this right entails the denial of all moral rights and duties. This requires bringing out what is surely intuitively clear that any framework of rights and duties presupposes individuals that have the capacity to choose on the basis of reasons 321

presented to them, and that what makes legitimate actions within such a system are the free choices of individuals. There is, in other words, a distribution of benefits and burdens in accord with a respect for the freedom of choice and freedom of action of all. I think that the best way to make this point may be to sketch some of the features of a world in which rights and duties are possessed.

First, rights exist only when there is some conception of some things valued and others not. Secondly, and implied in the first point, is the fact that there are dispositions to defend the valued commodities. Third, the valued commodities may be interfered with by others in this world. A group of animals might be said to satisfy these first three conditions. Fourth, rights exist when there are recognized rules establishing the legitimacy of some acts and ruling out others. Mistakes in the claim of right are possible. Rights imply the concepts of interference and infringement, concepts the elucidation of which requires the concept of a rule applying to the conduct of persons. Fifth, to possess a right is to possess something that constitutes a legitimate restraint on the freedom of action of others. It is clear, for example, that if individuals were incapable of controlling their actions we would have no notion of a legitimate claim that they do so. If, for example, we were all disposed to object or disposed to complain, as the elephant seal is disposed to object when his territory is invaded, then the objection would operate in a causal way, or approximating a causal way, in getting the behavior of noninterference. In a system of rights, on the other hand, there is a point to appealing to the rules in legitimating one's complaint. Implied, then, in any conception of rights are the existence of individuals capable of choosing and capable of choosing on the basis of considerations with respect to rules. The distribution of freedom throughout such a system is determined by the free choice of individuals. Thus any denial of the right to be treated as a person would be a denial undercutting the whole system, for the system rests on the assumption that spheres of legitimate and illegitimate conduct are to be delimited with regard to the choices made by persons.

This conclusion stimulates one final reflection on the therapy world we imagined.

The denial of this fundamental right will also carry with it, ironically, the denial of the right to treatment to those who are ill. In the world as we now understand it, there are those who do wrong and who have a right to be responded to as persons who have done wrong. And there are those who have not done wrong but who are suffering from illnesses that in a variety of ways interfere with their capacity to live their lives as complete persons. These persons who are ill have a claim upon our compassion. But more than this they have, as animals do not, a right to be treated as persons. When an individual is ill he is entitled to that assistance which will make it possible for him to resume his functioning as a person. If it is an injustice to punish an innocent person, it is no less an injustice, and a far more significant one in our day, to fail to promote as best we can through adequate facilities and medical care the treatment of those who are ill. Those human beings who fill our mental institutions are entitled to more than they do in fact receive; they should be viewed as possessing the right to be treated as a person so that our responses to them may increase the likelihood that they will enjoy fully the right to be so treated. Like the child the mentally ill person has a future interest we cannot rightly deny him. Society is today sensitive to the infringement of justice in punishing the innocent; elaborate rules exist to avoid this evil. Society should be no less sensitive to the injustice of failing to bring back to the community of persons those whom it is possible to bring back.

JEFFRIE G. MURPHY
Marxism and Retribution

Punishment in general has been defended as a means either of ameliorating or of intimidating. Now what right have you to punish me for the amelioration or intimidation of others? And besides there is history—there is such a thing as statistics—which prove with the most complete evidence that since Cain the world has been neither intimidated nor ameliorated by punishment. Quite the contrary. From the point of view of abstract right, there is only one theory of punishment which recognizes human dignity in the abstract, and that is the theory of Kant, especially in the more rigid formula given to it by Hegel. Hegel says: "Punishment is the right of the criminal. It is an act of his own will. The violation of right has been proclaimed by the criminal as his own right. His crime is the negation of right. Punishment is the negation of this negation, and consequently an affirmation of right, solicited and forced upon the criminal by himself."

Reprinted from *Philosophy and Public Affairs*, Vol. 2, No. 3 (1973), 217–243. Copyright © 1973 by Princeton University Press. Reprinted by permission of the author and the publisher.

An earlier version of this essay was delivered to the Third Annual Colloquium in Philosophy ("The Philosophy of Punishment") at the University of Dayton in October, 1972. I am grateful to the Department of Philosophy at the University of Dayton for inviting me to participate and to a number of persons at the Colloquium for the useful discussion on my paper at the time. I am also grateful to Anthony D. Woozley of the University of Virginia and to two of my colleagues, Robert M. Harnish and Francis V. Raab, for helping me to clarify the expression of my views. 323

*There is no doubt something specious in this formula, inasmuch as
Hegel, instead of looking upon the criminal as the mere object, the slave
of justice, elevates him to the position of a free and self-determined
being. Looking, however, more closely into the matter, we discover that
German idealism here, as in most other instances, has but given a
transcendental sanction to the rules of existing society. Is it not a delusion
to substitute for the individual with his real motives, with multi-
farious social circumstances pressing upon him, the abstraction of "free
will"—one among the many qualities of man for man himself? . . .
Is there not a necessity for deeply reflecting upon an alteration of the
system that breeds these crimes, instead of glorifying the hangman
who executes a lot of criminals to make room only for the supply of
new ones?*

Karl Marx, *"Capital Punishment,"*
New York Daily Tribune, *18 February 1853*[1]

Philosophers have written at great length about the moral problems involved in punishing the innocent—particularly as these problems raise
obstacles to an acceptance of the moral theory of Utilitarianism. Punishment of an innocent man in order to bring about good social consequences
is, at the very least, not always clearly wrong on utilitarian principles.
This being so, utilitarian principles are then to be condemned by any
morality that may be called Kantian in character. For punishing an innocent man, in Kantian language, involves using that man as a mere means
or instrument to some social good and is thus not to treat him as an
end in himself, in accord with his dignity or worth as a person.

The Kantian position on the issue of punishing the innocent, and the
many ways in which the utilitarian might try to accommodate that posi-

---

[1] In a sense, my paper may be viewed as an elaborate commentary on this one passage, excerpted from a discussion generally concerned with the efficacy of capital
punishment in eliminating crime. For in this passage, Marx (to the surprise of many
I should think) expresses a certain admiration for the classical retributive theory of
punishment. Also (again surprisingly) he expresses this admiration in a kind of language he normally avoids—i.e., the moral language of rights and justice. He then,
of course, goes on to reject the applicability of that theory. But the question that
initially perplexed me is the following: what is the explanation of Marx's ambivalence concerning the retributive theory; why is he both attracted and repelled by it?
(This ambivalence is not shared, for example, by utilitarians—who feel nothing but
repulsion when the retributive theory is even mentioned.) Now except for some very
brief passages in *The Holy Family*, Marx himself has nothing more to say on the
topic of punishment beyond what is contained in this brief *Daily Tribune* article.
Thus my essay is in no sense an exercise in textual scholarship (there are not enough
texts) but is rather an attempt to construct an assessment of punishment, Marxist at
least in spirit, that might account for the ambivalence found in the quoted passage.
My main outside help comes, not from Marx himself, but from the writings of the
Marxist criminologist Willem Bonger.

tion, constitute extremely well-worn ground in contemporary moral and legal philosophy.[2] I do not propose to wear the ground further by adding additional comments on the issue here. What I do want to point out, however, is something which seems to me quite obvious but which philosophical commentators on punishment have almost universally failed to see—namely, that problems of the very same kind and seriousness arise for the utilitarian theory with respect to the punishment of the guilty. For a utilitarian theory of punishment (Bentham's is a paradigm) must involve justifying punishment in terms of its social results—e.g., deterrence, incapacitation, and rehabilitation. And thus even a guilty man is, on this theory, being punished because of the instrumental value the action of punishment will have in the future. He is being used as a means to some future good—e.g., the deterrence of others. Thus those of a Kantian persuasion, who see the importance of worrying about the treatment of persons as mere means, must, it would seem, object just as strenuously to the punishment of the guilty on utilitarian grounds as to the punishment of the innocent. Indeed the former worry, in some respects, seems more serious. For a utilitarian can perhaps refine his theory in such a way that it does not commit him to the punishment of the innocent. However, if he is to approve of punishment at all, he must approve of punishing the guilty in at least some cases. This makes the worry about punishing the guilty formidable indeed, and it is odd that this has gone generally unnoticed.[3] It has generally been assumed that if the utilitarian theory can just avoid entailing the permissibility of punishing the innocent, then all objections of a Kantian character to the theory will have been met. This seems to me simply not to be the case.

What the utilitarian theory really cannot capture, I would suggest, is the notion of persons having rights. And it is just this notion that is central to any Kantian outlook on morality. Any Kantian can certainly agree that punishing persons (guilty or innocent) may have either good or bad or indifferent consequences and that insofar as the consequences (whether in a particular case or for an institution) are good, this is something in favor of punishment. But the Kantian will maintain that this consequential outlook, important as it may be, leaves out of consideration entirely that which is most morally crucial—namely, the question of rights. Even if punishment of a person would have good consequences, what gives us (i.e., society) the moral right to inflict it? If we have such a right, what is its origin or derivation? What social circumstances must be present for it to be applicable? What does this right to punish tell

[2] Many of the leading articles on this topic have been reprinted in *The Philosophy of Punishment*, ed. H. B. Acton (London, 1969). Those papers not included are cited in Acton's excellent bibliography.

[3] One writer who has noticed this is Richard Wasserstrom. See his "Why Punish the Guilty?" *Princeton University Magazine* 20 (1964), pp. 14–19.

us about the status of the person to be punished—e.g., how are we to analyze his rights, the sense in which he must deserve to be punished, his obligations in the matter? It is this family of questions which any Kantian must regard as morally central and which the utilitarian cannot easily accommodate into his theory. And it is surely this aspect of Kant's and Hegel's retributivism, this seeing of rights as basic, which appeals to Marx in the quoted passage. As Marx himself puts it: "What right have you to punish me for the amelioration or intimidation of others?" And he further praises Hegel for seeing that punishment, if justified, must involve respecting the rights of the person to be punished.[4] Thus Marx, like Kant, seems prepared to draw the important distinction between (a) what it would be good to do on grounds of utility and (b) what we have a right to do. Since we do not always have the right to do what it would be good to do, this distinction is of the greatest moral importance; and missing the distinction is the Achilles heel of all forms of Utilitarianism. For consider the following example: A Jehovah's Witness needs a blood transfusion in order to live; but, because of his (we can agree absurd) religious belief that such transfusions are against God's commands, he instructs his doctor not to give him one. Here is a case where it would seem to be good or for the best to give the transfusion and yet, at the very least, it is highly doubtful that the doctor has a right to give it. This kind of distinction is elementary, and any theory which misses it is morally degenerate.[5]

To move specifically to the topic of punishment: How exactly does retributivism (of a Kantian or Hegelian variety) respect the rights of persons? Is Marx really correct on this? I believe that he is. I believe

[4] Marx normally avoids the language of rights and justice because he regards such language to be corrupted by bourgeois ideology. However, if we think very broadly of what an appeal to rights involves—namely, a protest against unjustified coercion—there is no reason why Marx may not legitimately avail himself on occasion of this way of speaking. For there is surely at least some moral overlap between Marx's protests against exploitation and the evils of a division of labor, for example, and the claims that people have a right not to be used solely for the benefit of others and a right to self-determination.

[5] I do not mean to suggest that under no conceivable circumstances would the doctor be justified in giving the transfusion even though, in one clear sense, he had no right to do it. If, for example, the Jehovah's Witness was a key man whose survival was necessary to prevent the outbreak of a destructive war, we might well regard the transfusion as on the whole justified. However, even in such a case, a morally sensitive man would have to regretfully realize that he was sacrificing an important principle. Such a realization would be impossible (because inconsistent) for a utilitarian, for his theory admits only one principle—namely, do that which on the whole maximizes utility. An occupational disease of utilitarians is a blindness to the possibility of genuine moral dilemmas—i.e., a blindness to the possibility that important moral principles can conflict in ways that are not obviously resolvable by a rational decision procedure.

that retributivism can be formulated in such a way that it is the only morally defensible theory of punishment. I also believe that arguments, which may be regarded as Marxist at least in spirit, can be formulated which show that social conditions as they obtain in most societies make this form of retributivism largely inapplicable within those societies. As Marx says, in those societies retributivism functions merely to provide a "transcendental sanction" for the status quo. If this is so, then the only morally defensible theory of punishment is largely inapplicable in modern societies. The consequence: modern societies largely lack the moral right to punish.[6] The upshot is that a Kantian moral theory (which in general seems to me correct) and a Marxist analysis of society (which, if properly qualified, also seems to me correct) produces a radical and not merely reformist attack not merely on the scope and manner of punishment in our society but on the institution of punishment itself. Institutions of punishment constitute what Bernard Harrison has called structural injustices[7] and are, in the absence of a major social change, to be resisted by all who take human rights to be morally serious—i.e., regard them as genuine action guides and not merely as rhetorical devices which allow people to morally sanctify institutions which in fact can only be defended on grounds of social expediency.

Stating all of this is one thing and proving it, of course, is another. Whether I can ever do this is doubtful. That I cannot do it in one brief article is certain. I cannot, for example, here defend in detail my belief that a generally Kantian outlook on moral matters is correct.[8] Thus I shall content myself for the present with attempting to render at least plausible two major claims involved in the view that I have outlined thus far: (1) that a retributive theory, in spite of the bad press that it has received, is a morally credible theory of punishment—that it can be, H. L. A. Hart to the contrary,[9] a reasonable general justifying aim of punishment; and (2) that a Marxist analysis of a society can undercut the practical applicability of that theory.

The Right of the State to Punish

It is strong evidence of the influence of a utilitarian outlook in moral and legal matters that discussions of punishment no longer involve a consideration of the right of anyone to inflict it. Yet in the eighteenth

[6] I qualify my thesis by the word "largely" to show at this point my realization, explored in more detail later, that no single theory can account for all criminal behavior.

[7] Bernard Harrison, "Violence and the Rule of Law," in *Violence,* ed. Jerome A. Shaffer (New York, 1971), pp. 139–176.

[8] I have made a start toward such a defense in my "The Killing of the Innocent," forthcoming in *The Monist* 57, no. 4 (October 1973).

[9] H. L. A. Hart, "Prolegomenon to the Principles of Punishment," from *Punishment and Responsibility* (Oxford, 1968), pp. 1–27.

and nineteenth centuries, this tended to be regarded as the central aspect of the problem meriting philosophical consideration. Kant, Hegel, Bosanquet, Green—all tended to entitle their chapters on punishment along the lines explicitly used by Green: "The Right of the State to Punish."[10] This is not just a matter of terminology but reflects, I think, something of deeper philosophical substance. These theorists, unlike the utilitarian, did not view man as primarily a maximizer of personal satisfactions— a maximizer of individual utilities. They were inclined, in various ways, to adopt a different model of man—man as a free or spontaneous creator, man as autonomous. (Marx, it may be noted, is much more in line with this tradition than with the utilitarian outlook.)[11] This being so, these theorists were inclined to view punishment (a certain kind of coercion by the state) as not merely a causal contributor to pain and suffering, but rather as presenting at least a prima facie challenge to the values of autonomy and personal dignity and self-realization—the very values which, in their view, the state existed to nurture. The problem as they saw it, therefore, was that of reconciling punishment as state coercion with the value of individual autonomy. (This is an instance of the more general problem which Robert Paul Wolff has called the central problem of political philosophy—namely, how is individual moral autonomy to be reconciled with legitimate political authority?)[12] This kind of problem, which I am inclined to agree is quite basic, cannot even be formulated intelligibly from a utilitarian perspective. Thus the utilitarian cannot even see the relevance of Marx's charge: Even if punishment has wonderful social consequences, what gives anyone the right to inflict it on me?

Now one fairly typical way in which others acquire rights over us is by our own consent. If a neighbor locks up my liquor cabinet to protect me against my tendencies to drink too heavily, I might well regard this as a presumptuous interference with my own freedom, no matter how good the result intended or accomplished. He had no right to do it and indeed violated my rights in doing it. If, on the other hand, I had asked him to do this or had given my free consent to his suggestion that he do it, the same sort of objection on my part would be quite out of order. I had given him the right to do it, and he had the right to do it. In doing it, he violated no rights of mine—even if, at the time of his doing it, I did not desire or want the action to be performed. Here then we seem to have a case where my autonomy may be regarded as intact

10 Thomas Hill Green, *Lectures on the Principles of Political Obligation* (1885), (Ann Arbor, 1967), pp. 180–205.

11 For an elaboration of this point, see Steven Lukes, "Alienation and Anomie," in *Philosophy, Politics and Society* (Third Series), ed. Peter Laslett and W. G. Runciman (Oxford, 1967), pp. 134–156.

12 Robert Paul Wolff, *In Defense of Anarchism* (New York, 1970).

even though a desire of mine is thwarted. For there is a sense in which the thwarting of the desire can be imputed to me (my choice or decision) and not to the arbitrary intervention of another.

How does this apply to our problem? The answer, I think, is obvious. What is needed, in order to reconcile my undesired suffering of punishment at the hands of the state with my autonomy (and thus with the state's right to punish me), is a political theory which makes the state's decision to punish me in some sense my own decision. If I have willed my own punishment (consented to it, agreed to it) then—even if at the time I happen not to desire it—it can be said that my autonomy and dignity remain intact. Theories of the General Will and Social Contract theories are two such theories which attempt this reconciliation of autonomy with legitimate state authority (including the right or authority of the state to punish). Since Kant's theory happens to incorporate elements of both, it will be useful to take it for our sample.

Moral Rights and the Retributive Theory of Punishment

To justify government or the state is necessarily to justify at least some coercion.[13] This poses a problem for someone, like Kant, who maintains that human freedom is the ultimate or most sacred moral value. Kant's own attempt to justify the state, expressed in his doctrine of the *moral title* (*Befugnis*),[14] involves an argument that coercion is justified only in so far as it is used to prevent invasions against freedom. Freedom itself is the only value which can be used to limit freedom, for the appeal to any other value (e.g., utility) would undermine the ultimate status of the value of freedom. Thus Kant attempts to establish the claim that some forms of coercion (as opposed to violence) are morally permissible because, contrary to appearance, they are really consistent with rational freedom. The argument, in broad outline, goes in the following way. Coercion may keep people from doing what they desire or want to do on a particular occasion and is thus prima facie wrong. However, such

[13] In this section, I have adapted some of my previously published material: *Kant: The Philosophy of Right* (London, 1970), pp. 109–112 and 140–144; "Three Mistakes About Retributivism," *Analysis* (April 1971): 166–169; and "Kant's Theory of Criminal Punishment," in *Proceedings of the Third International Kant Congress,* ed. Lewis White Beck (Dordrecht, 1972), pp. 434–441. I am perfectly aware that Kant's views on the issues to be considered here are often obscure and inconsistent— e.g., the analysis of "willing one's own punishment" which I shall later quote from Kant occurs in a passage the primary purpose of which is to argue that the idea of "willing one's own punishment" makes no sense! My present objective, however, is not to attempt accurate Kant scholarship. My goal is rather to build upon some remarks of Kant's which I find philosophically suggestive.

[14] Immanuel Kant, *The Metaphysical Elements of Justice* (1797), trans. John Ladd (Indianapolis, 1965), pp. 35ff.

coercion can be shown to be morally justified (and thus not absolutely wrong) if it can be established that the coercion is such that it could have been rationally willed even by the person whose desire is interfered with:

Accordingly, when it is said that a creditor has a right to demand from his debtor the payment of a debt, this does not mean that he can *persuade* the debtor that his own reason itself obligates him to this performance; on the contrary, to say that he has such a right means only that the use of coercion to make anyone do this is entirely compatible with everyone's freedom, *including the freedom of the debtor,* in accordance with universal laws.[15]

Like Rousseau, Kant thinks that it is only in a context governed by social practice (particularly civil government and its Rule of Law) that this can make sense. Laws may require of a person some action that he does not desire to perform. This is not a violent invasion of his freedom, however, if it can be shown that in some antecedent position of choice (what John Rawls calls "the original position"),[16] he would have been rational to adopt a Rule of Law (and thus run the risk of having some of his desires thwarted) rather than some other alternative arrangement like the classical State of Nature. This is, indeed, the only sense that Kant is able to make of classical Social Contract theories. Such theories are to be viewed, not as historical fantasies, but as ideal models of rational decision. For what these theories actually claim is that the only coercive institutions that are morally justified are those which a group of rational beings could agree to adopt in a position of having to pick social institutions to govern their relations:

The contract, which is called *contractus originarius,* or *pactum sociale . . .* need not be assumed to be a fact, indeed it is not [even possible as such. To suppose that would be like insisting] that before anyone would be bound to respect such a civic constitution, it be proved first of all from history that a people, whose rights and obligations we have entered into as their descendants, had *once upon a time* executed such an act and had left a reliable document or instrument, either orally or in writing, concerning this contract. Instead, this contract is a *mere idea* of reason which has undoubted practical reality; namely, to oblige every legislator to give us laws in such a manner that the laws *could* have originated from the united will of the entire people and to regard every subject in so far as he is a citizen as though he had consented to such [an expression of the general] will. This is the testing stone of the rightness of every publicly-known law, for if a law were such that it was impossible for an entire people to give consent to it (as for example a law that

[15] *Ibid.,* p. 37.

[16] John Rawls, "Justice as Fairness," *The Philosophical Review* 67 (1958): 164–194; and *A Theory of Justice* (Cambridge, Mass., 1971), especially pp. 17–22.

a certain class of subjects, by inheritance, should have the privilege of the *status of lords*), then such a law is unjust. On the other hand, if there is a mere *possibility* that a people might consent to a (certain) law, then it is a duty to consider that the law is just even though at the moment the people might be in such a position or have a point of view that would result in their refusing to give their consent to it if asked.[17]

The problem of organizing a state, however hard it may seem, can be solved even for a race of devils, if only they are intelligent. The problem is: "Given a multiple of rational beings requiring universal laws for their preservation, but each of whom is secretly inclined to exempt himself from them, to establish a constitution in such a way that, although their private intentions conflict, they check each other, with the result that their public conduct is the same as if they had no such intentions."[18]

Though Kant's doctrine is superficially similar to Mill's later self-protection principle, the substance is really quite different. For though Kant in some general sense argues that coercion is justified only to prevent harm to others, he understands by "harm" only certain invasions of freedom and not simply disutility. Also, his defense of the principle is not grounded, as is Mill's, on its utility. Rather it is to be regarded as a principle of justice, by which Kant means a principle that rational beings could adopt in a situation of mutual choice:

The concept [of justice] applies only to the relationship of a will to another person's will, not to his wishes or desires (or even just his needs) which are the concern of acts of benevolence and charity. . . . In applying the concept of justice we take into consideration only the form of the relationship between the wills insofar as they are regarded as free, and whether the action of one of them can be conjoined with the freedom of the other in accordance with universal law. Justice is therefore the aggregate of those conditions under which the will of one person can be conjoined with the will of another in accordance with a universal law of freedom.[19]

How does this bear specifically on punishment? Kant, as everyone knows, defends a strong form of a retributive theory of punishment. He holds that guilt merits, and is a sufficient condition for, the infliction of punishment. And this claim has been universally condemned—particularly by utilitarians—as primitive, unenlightened and barbaric.

But why is it so condemned? Typically, the charge is that infliction

---

[17] Immanuel Kant, "Concerning the Common Saying: This May be True in Theory but Does Not Apply in Practice (1793)," in *The Philosophy of Kant,* ed. and trans. Carl J. Friedrich (New York, 1949), pp. 421–422.

[18] Immanuel Kant, *Perpetual Peace* (1795), trans. Lewis White Beck in the Kant anthology *On History* (Indianapolis 1963), p. 112.

[19] Immanuel Kant, *The Metaphysical Elements of Justice,* p. 34.

of punishment on such grounds is nothing but pointless vengeance. But what is meant by the claim that the infliction is "pointless"? If "pointless" is tacitly being analyzed as "disutilitarian," then the whole question is simply being begged. You cannot refute a retributive theory merely by noting that it is a retributive theory and not a utilitarian theory. This is to confuse redescription with refutation and involves an argument whose circularity is not even complicated enough to be interesting.

Why, then, might someone claim that guilt merits punishment? Such a claim might be made for either of two very different reasons. (1) Someone (e.g., a Moral Sense theorist) might maintain that the claim is a primitive and unanalyzable proposition that is morally ultimate—that we can just intuit the "fittingness" of guilt and punishment. (2) It might be maintained that the retributivist claim is demanded by a general theory of political obligation which is more plausible than any alternative theory. Such a theory will typically provide a technical analysis of such concepts as crime and punishment and will thus not regard the retributivist claim as an indisputable primitive. It will be argued for as a kind of theorem within the system.

Kant's theory is of the second sort. He does not opt for retributivism as a bit of intuitive moral knowledge. Rather he offers a theory of punishment that is based on his general view that political obligation is to be analyzed, quasi-contractually, in terms of reciprocity. If the law is to remain just, it is important to guarantee that those who disobey it will not gain an unfair advantage over those who do obey voluntarily. It is important that no man profit from his own criminal wrongdoing, and a certain kind of "profit" (i.e., not bearing the burden of self-restraint) is intrinsic to criminal wrongdoing. Criminal punishment, then, has as its object the restoration of a proper balance between benefit and obedience. The criminal himself has no complaint, because he has rationally consented to or willed his own punishment. That is, those very rules which he has broken work, when they are obeyed by others, to his own advantage as a citizen. He would have chosen such rules for himself and others in the original position of choice. And, since he derives and voluntarily accepts benefits from their operation, he owes his own obedience as a debt to his fellow-citizens for their sacrifices in maintaining them. If he chooses not to sacrifice by exercising self-restraint and obedience, this is tantamount to his choosing to sacrifice in another way—namely, by paying the prescribed penalty:

A trangression of the public law that makes him who commits it unfit to be a citizen is called . . . a crime. . . .

What kind of what degree of punishment does public legal justice adopt as its principle and standard? None other than the principle of equality (illustrated by the pointer of the scales of justice), that is, the principle of not treating one side more favorably than the other. Accordingly, any undeserved evil that you inflict on someone else among the people is one you do to yourself. If you vilify him, you vilify yourself; if you steal from him, you steal from yourself; if you kill him, you kill yourself. . . .

To say, "I will to be punished if I murder someone" can mean nothing more than, "I submit myself along with everyone else to those laws which, if there are any criminals among the people, will naturally include penal laws."[20]

This analysis of punishment regards it as a debt owed to the law-abiding members of one's community; and, once paid, it allows reentry into the community of good citizens on equal status.

Now some of the foregoing no doubt sounds implausible or even obscurantist. Since criminals typically desire not to be punished, what can it really mean to say that they have, as rational men, really willed their own punishment? Or that, as Hegel says, they have a right to it? Perhaps a comparison of the traditional retributivist views with those of a contemporary Kantian—John Rawls—will help to make the points clearer.[21] Rawls (like Kant) does not regard the idea of the social contract as an historical fact. It is rather a model of rational decision. Respecting a man's autonomy, at least on one view, is not respecting what he now happens, however uncritically, to desire; rather it is to respect what he desires (or would desire) as a rational man. (On Rawls's view, for example, rational men are said to be unmoved by feelings of envy; and thus it is not regarded as unjust to a person or a violation of his rights, if he is placed in a situation where he will envy another's advantage or position. A rational man would object, and thus would never consent to, a practice where another might derive a benefit from a position at his expense. He would not, however, envy the position *simpliciter,* would not regard the position as itself a benefit.) Now on Kant's (and also, I think, on Rawls's) view, a man is genuinely free or autonomous only in so far as he is rational. Thus it is man's rational will that is to be respected.

Now this idea of treating people, not as they in fact say that they want to be treated, but rather in terms of how you think they would, if rational, will to be treated, has obviously dangerous (indeed Fascistic) implications. Surely we want to avoid cramming indignities down the

---

[20] *Ibid.,* pp. 99, 101, and 105, in the order quoted.

[21] In addition to the works on justice by Rawls previously cited, the reader should consult the following for Rawls's application of his general theory to the problem of political obligation: John Rawls, "Legal Obligation and the Duty of Fair Play," in *Law and Philosophy,* ed. Sidney Hook (New York, 1964), pp. 3–18. This has been reprinted in my anthology *Civil Disobedience and Violence* (Belmont, Cal., 1971), pp. 39–52. For a direct application of a similar theory to the problem of punishment, see Herbert Morris, "Persons and Punishment," *The Monist* 52, no. 4 (October 1968): 475–501.

throats of people with the offhand observation that, no matter how much they scream, they are really rationally willing every bit of it. It would be particularly ironic for such arbitrary repression to come under the mask of respecting autonomy. And yet, most of us would agree, the general principle (though subject to abuse) also has important applications—for example, preventing the suicide of a person who, in a state of psychotic depression, wants to kill himself. What we need, then, to make the general view work, is a check on its arbitrary application; and a start toward providing such a check would be in the formulation of a public, objective theory of rationality and rational willing. It is just this, according to both Kant and Rawls, which the social contract theory can provide. On this theory, a man may be said to rationally will X if, and only if, X is called for by a rule that the man would necessarily have adopted in the original position of choice—i.e., in a position of coming together with others to pick rules for the regulation of their mutual affairs. This avoids arbitrariness because, according to Kant and Rawls at any rate, the question of whether such a rule would be picked in such a position is objectively determinable given certain (in their view) noncontroversial assumptions about human nature and rational calculation. Thus I can be said to will my own punishment if, in an antecedent position of choice, I and my fellows would have chosen institutions of punishment as the most rational means of dealing with those who might break the other generally beneficial social rules that had been adopted.

Let us take an analogous example: I may not, in our actual society, desire to treat a certain person fairly—e.g., I may not desire to honor a contract I have made with him because so doing would adversely affect my own self-interest. However, if I am forced to honor the contract by the state, I cannot charge (1) that the state has no right to do this, or (2) that my rights or dignity are being violated by my being coerced into doing it. Indeed, it can be said that I rationally will it since, in the original position, I would have chosen rules of justice (rather than rules of utility) and the principle, "contracts are to be honored," follows from the rules of justice.

Coercion and autonomy are thus reconciled, at least apparently. To use Marx's language, we may say (as Marx did in the quoted passage) that one virtue of the retributive theory, at least as expounded by Kant and Hegel on lines of the General Will and Social Contract theory, is that it manifests at least a formal or abstract respect for rights, dignity, and autonomy. For it at least recognizes the importance of attempting to construe state coercion in such a way that it is a product of each man's rational will. Utilitarian deterrence theory does not even satisfy this formal demand.

The question of primary interest to Marx, of course, is whether this formal respect also involves a material respect; i.e., does the theory have application in concrete fact in the actual social world in which we live? Marx is confident that it does not, and it is to this sort of consideration that I shall now pass.

Alienation and Punishment

What can the philosopher learn from Marx? This question is a part of a more general question: What can philosophy learn from social science? Philosophers, it may be thought, are concerned to offer a priori theories, theories about how certain concepts are to be analyzed and their application justified. And what can the mundane facts that are the object of behavioral science have to do with exalted theories of this sort?

The answer, I think, is that philosophical theories, though not themselves empirical, often have such a character that their intelligibility depends upon certain empirical presuppositions. For example, our moral language presupposes, as Hart has argued,[22] that we are vulnerable creatures—creatures who can harm and be harmed by each other. Also, as I have argued elsewhere,[23] our moral language presupposes that we all share certain psychological characteristics—e.g., sympathy, a sense of justice, and the capacity to feel guilt, shame, regret, and remorse. If these facts were radically different (if, as Hart imagines for example, we all developed crustaceanlike exoskeletons and thus could not harm each other), the old moral language, and the moral theories which employ it, would lack application to the world in which we live. To use a crude example, moral prohibitions against killing presuppose that it is in fact possible for us to kill each other.

Now one of Marx's most important contributions to social philosophy, in my judgment, is simply his insight that philosophical theories are in peril if they are constructed in disregard of the nature of the empirical world to which they are supposed to apply.[24] A theory may be formally correct (i.e., coherent, or true for some possible world) but materially incorrect (i.e., inapplicable to the actual world in which we live). This insight, then, establishes the relevance of empirical research to philosophical theory and is a part, I think, of what Marx meant by "the union of ·

[22] H. L. A. Hart, *The Concept of Law* (Oxford, 1961), pp. 189–195.

[23] Jeffrie G. Murphy, "Moral Death: A Kantian Essay on Psychopathy," *Ethics* 82, no. 4 (July 1972): 284–298.

[24] Banal as this point may seem, it could be persuasively argued that all Enlightenment political theory (e.g., that of Hobbes, Locke and Kant) is built upon ignoring it. For example, once we have substantial empirical evidence concerning how democracies really work in fact, how sympathetic can we really be to classical theories for the justification of democracy? For more on this, see C. B. Macpherson, "The Maximization of Democracy," in *Philosophy, Politics and Society* (Third Series), ed. Peter Laslett and W. G. Runciman (Oxford, 1967), pp. 83–103. This article is also relevant to the point raised in note 11 above.

theory and practice." Specifically relevant to the argument I want to develop are the following two related points:

(1) The theories of moral, social, political and legal philosophy presuppose certain empirical propositions about man and society. If these propositions are false, then the theory (even if coherent or formally correct) is materially defective and practically inapplicable. (For example, if persons tempted to engage in criminal conduct do not in fact tend to calculate carefully the consequences of their actions, this renders much of deterrence theory suspect.)

(2) Philosophical theories may put forth as a necessary truth that which is in fact merely an historically conditioned contingency. (For example, Hobbes argued that all men are necessarily selfish and competitive. It is possible, as many Marxists have argued, that Hobbes was really doing nothing more than elevating to the status of a necessary truth the contingent fact that the people around him in the capitalistic society in which he lived were in fact selfish and competitive.)[25]

In outline, then, I want to argue the following: that when Marx challenges the material adequacy of the retributive theory of punishment, he is suggesting (a) that it presupposes a certain view of man and society that is false and (b) that key concepts involved in the support of the theory (e.g., the concept of "rationality" in Social Contract theory) are given analyses which, though they purport to be necessary truths, are in fact mere reflections of certain historical circumstances.

In trying to develop this case, I shall draw primarily upon Willem Bonger's *Criminality and Economic Conditions* (1916), one of the few sustained Marxist analyses of crime and punishment.[26] Though I shall not have time here to qualify my support of Bonger in certain necessary ways, let me make clear that I am perfectly aware that his analysis is not the whole story. (No monolithic theory of anything so diverse as criminal behavior could be the whole story.) However, I am convinced that he has discovered part of the story. And my point is simply that insofar as Bonger's Marxist analysis is correct, then to that same degree is the retributive theory of punishment inapplicable in modern societies. (Let me emphasize again exactly how this objection to retributivism differs from those traditionally offered. Traditionally, retributivism has been

---

[25] This point is well developed in C. B. Macpherson, *The Political Theory of Possessive Individualism* (Oxford, 1962). In a sense, this point affects even the formal correctness of a theory. For it demonstrates an empirical source of corruption in the analyses of the very concepts in the theory.

[26] The writings of Willem Adriaan Bonger (1876–1940), a Dutch criminologist, have fallen into totally unjustified neglect in recent years. Anticipating contemporary sociological theories of crime, he was insisting that criminal behavior is in the province of normal psychology (though abnormal society) at a time when most other writers were viewing criminality as a symptom of psychopathology. His major works are: *Criminality and Economic Conditions* (Boston, 1916); *An Introduction to Criminology* (London, 1936); and *Race and Crime* (New York, 1943).

rejected because it conflicts with the moral theory of its opponent, usually a utilitarian. This is not the kind of objection I want to develop. Indeed, with Marx, I have argued that the retributive theory of punishment grows out of the moral theory—Kantianism—which seems to me generally correct. The objection I want to pursue concerns the empirical falsity of the factual presuppositions of the theory. If the empirical presuppositions of the theory are false, this does indeed render its application immoral. But the immorality consists, not in a conflict with some other moral theory, but immorality in terms of a moral theory that is at least close in spirit to the very moral theory which generates retributivism itself— i.e., a theory of justice.)[27]

To return to Bonger. Put bluntly, his theory is as follows. Criminality has two primary sources: (1) need and deprivation on the part of disadvantaged members of society, and (2) motives of greed and selfishness that are generated and reinforced in competitive capitalistic societies. Thus criminality is economically based—either directly in the case of crimes from need, or indirectly in the case of crimes growing out of motives or psychological states that are encouraged and developed in capitalistic society. In Marx's own language, such an economic system alienates men from themselves and from each other. It alienates men from themselves by creating motives and needs that are not "truly human." It alienates men from their fellows by encouraging a kind of competitiveness that forms an obstacle to the development of genuine communities to replace mere social aggregates.[28] And in Bonger's thought, the concept of community is central. He argues that moral relations and moral restraint are possible only in genuine communities characterized by bonds of sympathetic identification and mutual aid resting upon a perception of common humanity. All this he includes under the general rubric of reciprocity.[29]

[27] I say "at least in spirit" to avoid begging the controversial question of whether Marx can be said to embrace a theory of justice. Though (as I suggested in note 4) much of Marx's own evaluative rhetoric seems to overlap more traditional appeals to rights and justice (and a total lack of sympathy with anything like Utilitarianism), it must be admitted that he also frequently ridicules at least the terms "rights" and "justice" because of their apparent entrenchment in bourgeois ethics. For an interesting discussion of this issue, see Allen W. Wood, "The Marxian Critique of Justice," *Philosophy & Public Affairs* 1, no. 3 (Spring 1972): 244–282.

[28] The importance of community is also, I think, recognized in Gabriel de Tarde's notion of "social similarity" as a condition of criminal responsibility. See his *Penal Philosophy* (Boston, 1912). I have drawn on de Tarde's general account in my "Moral Death: A Kantian Essay on Psychopathy."

[29] By "reciprocity" Bonger intends something which includes, but is much richer than, a notion of "fair trading or bargaining" that might initially be read into the term. He also has in mind such things as sympathetic identification with others and tendencies to provide mutual aid. Thus, for Bonger, reciprocity and egoism have a strong tendency to conflict. I mention this lest Bonger's notion of reciprocity be too quickly identified with the more restricted notion found in, for example, Kant and Rawls.

In the absence of reciprocity in this rich sense, moral relations among men will break down and criminality will increase.[30] Within bourgeois society, then, crimes are to be regarded as normal, and not psychopathological, acts. That is, they grow out of need, greed, indifference to others, and sometimes even a sense of indignation—all, alas, perfectly typical human motives.

To appreciate the force of Bonger's analysis, it is necessary to read his books and grasp the richness and detail of the evidence he provides for his claims. Here I can but quote a few passages at random to give the reader a tantalizing sample in the hope that he will be encouraged to read further into Bonger's own text:

The abnormal element in crime is a social, not a biological, element. With the exception of a few special cases, crime lies within the boundaries of normal psychology and physiology. . . .

We clearly see that [the egoistic tendencies of the present economic system and of its consequences] are very strong. Because of these tendencies the social instinct of man is not greatly developed; they have weakened the moral force in man which combats the inclination towards egoistic acts, and hence toward the crimes which are one form of these acts. . . . Compassion for the misfortunes of others inevitably becomes blunted, and a great part of morality consequently disappears. . . .

As a consequence of the present environment, man has become very egoistic and hence more *capable of crime,* than if the environment had developed the germs of altruism. . . .

There can be no doubt that one of the factors of criminality among the bourgeoisie is bad [moral] education. . . . The children—speaking of course in a general way—are brought up with the idea that they must succeed, no matter how; the aim of life is presented to them as getting money and shining in the world. . . .

Poverty (taken in the sense of absolute want) kills the social sentiments in man, destroys in fact all relations between men. He who is abandoned by all can no longer have any feeling for those who have left him to his fate. . . .

[Upon perception that the system tends to legalize the egoistic actions of the bourgeoisie and to penalize those of the proletariat], the oppressed resort

---

[30] It is interesting how greatly Bonger's analysis differs from classical deterrence theory—e.g., that of Bentham. Bentham, who views men as machines driven by desires to attain pleasure and avoid pain, tends to regard terror as the primary restraint against crime. Bonger believes that, at least in a healthy society, moral motives would function as a major restraint against crime. When an environment that destroys moral motivation is created, even terror (as statistics tend to confirm) will not eradicate crime.

to means which they would otherwise scorn. As we have seen above, the basis of the social feeling is reciprocity. As soon as this is trodden under foot by the ruling class the social sentiments of the oppressed become weak towards them. . . .[31]

The essence of this theory has been summed up by Austin J. Turk. "Criminal behavior," he says, "is almost entirely attributable to the combination of egoism and an environment in which opportunities are not equitably distributed."[32]

No doubt this claim will strike many as extreme and intemperate—a sample of the old-fashioned Marxist rhetoric that sophisticated intellectuals have outgrown. Those who are inclined to react in this way might consider just one sobering fact: of the 1.3 million criminal offenders handled each day by some agency of the United States correctional system, the vast majority (80 percent on some estimates) are members of the lowest 15-percent income level—that percent which is below the "poverty level" as defined by the Social Security Administration.[33] Unless one wants to embrace the belief that all these people are poor because they are bad, it might be well to reconsider Bonger's suggestion that many of them are

[31] *Introduction to Criminology,* pp. 75–76, and *Criminality and Economic Conditions,* pp. 532, 402, 483–484, 436, and 407, in the order quoted. Bonger explicitly attacks Hobbes: "The adherents of [Hobbes's theory] have studied principally men who live under capitalism, or under civilization; their correct conclusion has been that egoism is the predominant characteristic of these men, and they have adopted the simplest explanation of the phenomenon and say that this trait is inborn." If Hobbists can cite Freud for modern support, Bonger can cite Darwin. For, as Darwin had argued in the *Descent of Man,* men would not have survived as a species if they had not initially had considerably greater social sentiments than Hobbes allows them.

[32] Austin J. Turk, in the Introduction to his abridged edition of Bonger's *Criminality and Economic Conditions* (Bloomington, 1969), p. 14.

[33] Statistical data on characteristics of offenders in America are drawn primarily from surveys by the Bureau of Census and the National Council on Crime and Delinquency. While there is of course wide disagreement on how such data are to be interpreted, there is no serious disagreement concerning at least the general accuracy of statistics like the one I have cited. Even government publications openly acknowledge a high correlation between crime and socioeconomic disadvantages: "From arrest records, probation reports, and prison statistics a 'portrait' of the offender emerges that progressively highlights the disadvantaged character of his life. The offender at the end of the road in prison is likely to be a member of the lowest social and economic groups in the country, poorly educated and perhaps unemployed. . . . Material failure, then, in a culture firmly oriented toward material success, is the most common denominator of offenders" (*The Challenge of Crime in a Free Society, A Report by the President's Commission on Law Enforcement and Administration of Justice,* U.S. Government Printing Office, Washington, D.C., 1967, pp. 44 and 160). The Marxist implications of this admission have not gone unnoticed by prisoners. See Samuel Jorden, "Prison Reform: In Whose Interest?" *Criminal Law Bulletin* 7, no. 9 (November 1971): 779–787.

"bad" because they are poor.[34] At any rate, let us suppose for purposes of discussion that Bonger's picture of the relation between crime and economic conditions is generally accurate. At what points will this challenge the credentials of the contractarian retributive theory as outlined above? I should like to organize my answer to this question around three basic topics:

1. Rational choice. The model of rational choice found in Social Contract theory is egoistic—rational institutions are those that would be agreed to by calculating egoists ("devils" in Kant's more colorful terminology). The obvious question that would be raised by any Marxist is: Why give egoism this special status such that it is built, a priori, into the analysis of the concept of rationality? Is this not simply to regard as necessary that which may be only contingently found in the society around us? Starting from such an analysis, a certain result is inevitable—namely, a transcendental sanction for the status quo. Start with a bourgeois model of rationality and you will, of course, wind up defending a bourgeois theory of consent, a bourgeois theory of justice, and a bourgeois theory of punishment.

Though I cannot explore the point in detail here, it seems to me that this Marxist claim may cause some serious problems for Rawls's well-known theory of justice, a theory which I have already used to unpack some of the evaluative support for the retributive theory of punishment. One cannot help suspecting that there is a certain sterility in Rawls's entire project of providing a rational proof for the preferability of a certain conception of justice over all possible alternative evaluative principles, for the description which he gives of the rational contractors in the original position is such as to guarantee that they will come up with his two principles. This would be acceptable if the analysis of rationality presupposed were intuitively obvious or argued for on independent grounds. But it is not. Why, to take just one example, is a desire for wealth a rational trait whereas envy is not? One cannot help feeling that the desired result dictates the premises.[35]

---

[34] There are, of course, other factors which enter into an explanation of this statistic. One of them is the fact that economically disadvantaged guilty persons are more likely to wind up arrested or in prison (and thus be reflected in this statistic) than are economically advantaged guilty persons. Thus economic conditions enter into the explanation, not just of criminal behavior, but of society's response to criminal behavior. For a general discussion on the many ways in which crime and poverty are related, see Patricia M. Wald, "Poverty and Criminal Justice," *Task Force Report: The Courts*, U.S. Government Printing Office, Washington, D.C., 1967, pp. 139–151.

[35] The idea that the principles of justice could be proved as a kind of theorem (Rawls's claim in "Justice as Fairness") seems to be absent, if I understand the work correctly, in Rawls's recent *A Theory of Justice*. In this book, Rawls seems to be content with something less than a decision procedure. He is no longer trying to

2. Justice, benefits, and community. The retributive theory claims to be grounded on justice; but is it just to punish people who act out of those very motives that society encourages and reinforces? If Bonger is correct, much criminality is motivated by greed, selfishness, and indifference to one's fellows; but does not the whole society encourage motives of greed and selfishness ("making it," "getting ahead"), and does not the competitive nature of the society alienate men from each other and thereby encourage indifference—even, perhaps, what psychiatrists call psychopathy? The moral problem here is similar to one that arises with respect to some war crimes. When you have trained a man to believe that the enemy is not a genuine human person (but only a gook, or a chink), it does not seem quite fair to punish the man if, in a war situation, he kills indiscriminately. For the psychological trait you have conditioned him to have, like greed, is not one that invites fine moral and legal distinctions. There is something perverse in applying principles that presuppose a sense of community in a society which is structured to destroy genuine community.[36]

Related to this is the whole allocation of benefits in contemporary society. The retributive theory really presupposes what might be called a "gentlemen's club" picture of the relation between man and society—i.e., men are viewed as being part of a community of shared values and rules. The rules benefit all concerned and, as a kind of debt for the benefits derived, each man owes obedience to the rules. In the absence of such

---

pull his theory of justice up by its own bootstraps, but now seems concerned simply to *exhibit* a certain elaborate conception of justice in the belief that it will do a good job of systematizing and ordering most of our considered and reflective intuitions about moral matters. To this, of course, the Marxist will want to say something like the following: "The considered and reflective intuitions current in our society are a product of bourgeois culture, and thus any theory based upon them begs the question against us and in favor of the status quo." I am not sure that this charge cannot be answered, but I am sure that it deserves an answer. Someday Rawls may be remembered, to paraphrase Georg Lukács's description of Thomas Mann, as the last and greatest philosopher of bourgeois liberalism. The virtue of this description is that it perceives the limitations of his outlook in a way consistent with acknowledging his indisputable genius. (None of my remarks here, I should point out, are to be interpreted as denying that our civilization derived major moral benefits from the tradition of bourgeois liberalism. Just because the freedoms and procedures we associate with bourgeois liberalism—speech, press, assembly, due process of law, etc.—are not the only important freedoms and procedures, we are not to conclude with some witless radicals that these freedoms are not terribly important and that the victories of bourgeois revolutions are not worth preserving. My point is much more modest and noncontroversial—namely, that even bourgeois liberalism requires a critique. It is not self-justifying and, in certain very important respects, is not justified at all.)

[36] Kant has some doubts about punishing bastard infanticide and dueling on similar grounds. Given the stigma that Kant's society attached to illegitimacy and the halo that the same society placed around military honor, it did not seem totally fair to punish those whose criminality in part grew out of such approved motives. See *Metaphysical Elements of Justice,* pp. 106–107.

obedience, he deserves punishment in the sense that he owes payment for the benefits. For, as rational man, he can see that the rules benefit everyone (himself included) and that he would have selected them in the original position of choice.

Now this may not be too far off for certain kinds of criminals—e.g., business executives guilty of tax fraud. (Though even here we might regard their motives of greed to be a function of societal reinforcement.) But to think that it applies to the typical criminal, from the poorer classes, is to live in a world of social and political fantasy. Criminals typically are not members of a shared community of values with their jailers; they suffer from what Marx calls alienation. And they certainly would be hard-pressed to name the benefits for which they are supposed to owe obedience. If justice, as both Kant and Rawls suggest, is based on reciprocity, it is hard to see what these persons are supposed to reciprocate for. Bonger addresses this point in a passage quoted earlier (p. 236): "The oppressed resort to means which they would otherwise scorn. . . . The basis of social feelings is reciprocity. As soon as this is trodden under foot by the ruling class, the social sentiments of the oppressed become weak towards them."

3. Voluntary acceptance. Central to the Social Contract idea is the claim that we owe allegiance to the law because the benefits we have derived have been voluntarily accepted. This is one place where our autonomy is supposed to come in. That is, having benefited from the Rule of Law when it was possible to leave, I have in a sense consented to it and to its consequences—even my own punishment if I violate the rules. To see how silly the factual presuppositions of this account are, we can do no better than quote a famous passage from David Hume's essay "Of the Original Contract":

Can we seriously say that a poor peasant or artisan has a free choice to
leave his country—when he knows no foreign language or manners, and
lives from day to day by the small wages which he acquires? We may as
well assert that a man, by remaining in a vessel, freely consents to the
dominion of the master, though he was carried on board while asleep,
and must leap into the ocean and perish the moment he leaves her.

A banal empirical observation, one may say. But it is through ignoring such banalities that philosophers generate theories which allow them to spread iniquity in the ignorant belief that they are spreading righteousness.

It does, then, seem as if there may be some truth in Marx's claim that the retributive theory, though formally correct, is materially inadequate. At root, the retributive theory fails to acknowledge that criminality is, to a large extent, a phenomenon of economic class. To acknowledge this is 342 to challenge the empirical presupposition of the retributive theory—the presupposition that all men, including criminals, are voluntary participants in a reciprocal system of benefits and that the justice of this arrangement can be derived from some eternal and ahistorical concept of rationality.

The upshot of all this seems rather upsetting, as indeed it is. How can it be the case that everything we are ordinarily inclined to say about punishment (in terms of utility and retribution) can be quite beside the point? To anyone with ordinary language sympathies (one who is inclined to maintain that what is correct to say is a function of what we do say), this will seem madness. Marx will agree that there is madness, all right, but in his view the madness will lie in what we do say—what we say only because of our massive (and often self-deceiving and self-serving) factual ignorance or indifference to the circumstances of the social world in which we live. Just as our whole way of talking about mental phenomena hardened before we knew any neurophysiology—and this leads us astray, so Marx would argue that our whole way of talking about moral and political phenomena hardened before we knew any of the relevant empirical facts about man and society—and this, too, leads us astray. We all suffer from what might be called the *embourgeoisment* of language, and thus part of any revolution will be a linguistic or conceptual revolution. We have grown accustomed to modifying our language or conceptual structures under the impact of empirical discoveries in physics. There is no reason why discoveries in sociology, economics, or psychology could not and should not have the same effect on entrenched patterns of thought and speech. It is important to remember, as Russell remarked, that our language sometimes enshrines the metaphysics of the Stone Age.

Consider one example: a man has been convicted of armed robbery. On investigation, we learn that he is an impoverished black whose whole life has been one of frustrating alienation from the prevailing socio-economic structure—no job, no transportation if he could get a job, substandard education for his children, terrible housing and inadequate health care for his whole family, condescending-tardy-inadequate welfare payments, harassment by the police but no real protection by them against the dangers in his community, and near total exclusion from the political process. Learning all this, would we still want to talk—as many do—of his suffering punishment under the rubric of "paying a debt to society"? Surely not. Debt for what? I do not, of course, pretend that all criminals can be so described. But I do think that this is a closer picture of the typical criminal than the picture that is presupposed in the retributive theory —i.e., the picture of an evil person who, of his own free will, intentionally acts against those just rules of society which he knows, as a rational man, benefit everyone including himself.

But what practical help does all this offer, one may ask. How should we design our punitive practices in the society in which we now live? This   343 is the question we want to ask, and it does not seem to help simply to say that our society is built on deception and inequity. How can Marx help us with our real practical problem? The answer, I think, is that he cannot and obviously does not desire to do so. For Marx would say that we have not focused (as all piecemeal reform fails to focus) on what is truly the real problem. And this is changing the basic social relations. Marx is the last person from whom we can expect advice on how to make our intellectual and moral peace with bourgeois society. And this is surely his attraction and his value.

What does Bonger offer? He suggests, near the end of his book, that in a properly designed society all criminality would be a problem "for the physician rather than the judge." But this surely will not do. The therapeutic state, where prisons are called hospitals and jailers are called psychiatrists, simply raises again all the old problems about the justification of coercion and its reconciliation with autonomy that we faced in worrying about punishment. The only difference is that our coercive practices are now surrounded with a benevolent rhetoric which makes it even harder to raise the important issues. Thus the move to therapy, in my judgment, is only an illusory solution—alienation remains and the problem of reconciling coercion with autonomy remains unsolved. Indeed, if the alternative is having our personalities involuntarily restructured by some state psychiatrist, we might well want to claim the "right to be punished" that Hegel spoke of.[37]

Perhaps, then, we may really be forced seriously to consider a radical proposal. If we think that institutions of punishment are necessary and desirable, and if we are morally sensitive enough to want to be sure that we have the moral right to punish before we inflict it, then we had better first make sure that we have restructured society in such a way that criminals genuinely do correspond to the only model that will render punishment permissible—i.e., make sure that they are autonomous and that they do benefit in the requisite sense. Of course, if we did this then—if Marx and Bonger are right—crime itself and the need to punish would radically decrease if not disappear entirely.

Selected Bibliography

Acton, H. B. (ed.). *The Philosophy of Punishment*. London: Macmillan, 1969.
Ezorsky, Gertrude (ed.). *Philosophical Perspectives on Punishment*. Albany: State University of New York Press, 1972.

[37] This point is pursued in Herbert Morris, "Persons and Punishment." Bonger did not appreciate that "mental illness," like criminality, may also be a phenomenon of social class. On this, see August B. Hollingshead and Frederick C. Redlich, *Social Class and Mental Illness* (New York, 1958). On the general issue of punishment versus therapy, see my *Punishment and Rehabilitation* (Belmont, Cal., 1973).

Gerber, Rudolph J., and Patrick D. McAnany (eds.). *Contemporary Punishment: Views, Explanations and Justifications.* Notre Dame, Ind.: University of Notre Dame Press, 1972.

Hart, H. L. A. *Punishment and Responsibility: Essays in the Philosophy of Law.* Oxford: Oxford University Press, 1968.

Honderich, Ted. *Punishment: The Supposed Justifications.* New York: Harcourt, Brace & World, 1969.

Murphy, Jeffrie (ed.). *Punishment and Rehabilitation.* Belmont, Calif.: Wadsworth Publishing Co., 1973.

Pincoffs, Ed. *The Rationale of Legal Punishment.* New York: Humanities Press, 1966.

Wasserstrom, Richard. "H. L. A. Hart and the Doctrines of *Mens Rea* and Criminal Responsibility," *Chicago Law Review,* Vol. 35, p. 92 (1967).

6 THE OBLIGATION TO OBEY THE LAW

JOHN RAWLS
The Justification of Civil Disobedience

Introduction

I should like to discuss briefly, and in an informal way, the grounds of civil disobedience in a constitutional democracy. Thus, I shall limit my remarks to the conditions under which we may, by civil disobedience, properly oppose legally established democratic authority; I am not concerned with the situation under other kinds of government nor, except incidentally, with other forms of resistance. My thought is that in a reasonably just (though of course not perfectly just) democratic regime, civil disobedience, when it is justified, is normally to be understood as a political action which addresses the sense of justice of the majority in order to urge reconsideration of the measures protested and to warn that in the firm opinion of the dissenters the conditions of social cooperation are not being honored. This characterization of civil disobedience is intended to apply to dissent on fundamental questions of internal policy, a limitation which I shall follow to simplify our questions.

The Social Contract Doctrine

It is obvious that the justification of civil disobedience depends upon the theory of political obligation in general, and so we may appropriately begin with a few comments on this question. The two chief virtues of social institutions are justice and efficiency, where by the efficiency of institutions I understand their effectiveness for certain social conditions and ends the fulfillment of which is to everyone's advantage. We should comply with and do our part in just and efficient social arrangements for at least two reasons: first of all, we have a natural duty not to oppose the establishment of just and efficient institutions (when they do not yet exist) and to uphold and comply with them (when they do exist); and second, assuming that we have knowingly accepted the benefits of these institutions and plan to continue to do so, and that we have encouraged and expected others to do their part, we also have an obligation to do our share when, as the arrangement requires, it comes our turn. Thus, we often have both a natural duty as well as an obligation to support just and efficient institutions, the obligation arising from our voluntary acts while the duty does not.

Now all this is perhaps obvious enough, but it does not take us very far. Any more particular conclusions depend upon the conception of justice which is the basis of a theory of political obligation. I believe that the appropriate conception, at least for an account of political obligation in a constitutional democracy, is that of the social contract theory from which so much of our political thought derives. If we are careful to interpret it in a suitably general way, I hold that this doctrine provides a satisfactory basis for political theory, indeed even for ethical theory itself, but this is beyond our present concern.[1] The interpretation I suggest is the following: that the principles to which social arrangements must conform, and in particular the principles of justice, are those which free and rational men would agree to in an original position of equal liberty; and similarly, the principles which govern men's relations to institutions and define their natural duties and obligations are the principles to which they would consent when so situated. It should be noted straightway that in this interpretation of the contract theory the principles of justice are understood as the outcome of a hypothetical agreement. They are principles which would be agreed to if the situation of the original position were to arise. There is no mention of an actual agreement nor need such an agreement ever be made. Social arrangements are just or unjust according to whether they accord with the principles for assigning and securing fundamental rights and liberties which would be chosen in the original position. This position is, to be sure, the analytic analogue of the traditional notion of the state of nature, but it must not be mistaken for a historical occasion. Rather it is a hypothetical situation which embodies the basic ideas of the contract doctrine;

[1] By the social contract theory I have in mind the doctrine found in Locke, Rousseau, and Kant. I have attempted to give an interpretation of this view in: "Justice as Fairness," *Philosophical Review* (April, 1958): "Justice and Constitutional Liberty," *Nomos*, VI (1963); "The Sense of Justice," *Philosophical Review* (July 1963).

the description of this situation enables us to work out which principles would be adopted. I must now say something about these matters.

The contract doctrine has always supposed that the persons in the original position have equal powers and rights, that is, that they are symmetrically situated with respect to any arrangements for reaching agreement, and that coalitions and the like are excluded. But it is an essential element (which has not been sufficiently observed although it is implicit in Kant's version of the theory) that there are very strong restrictions on what the contracting parties are presumed to know. In particular, I interpret the theory to hold that the parties do not know their position in society, past, present, or future; nor do they know which institutions exist. Again, they do not know their own place in the distribution of natural talents and abilities, whether they are intelligent or strong, man or woman, and so on. Finally, they do not know their own particular interests and preferences or the system of ends which they wish to advance: they do not know their conception of the good. In all these respects the parties are confronted with a veil of ignorance which prevents any one from being able to take advantage of his good fortune or particular interests or from being disadvantaged by them. What the parties do know (or assume) is that Hume's circumstances of justice obtain: namely, that the bounty of nature is not so generous as to render cooperative schemes superfluous nor so harsh as to make them impossible. Moreover, they assume that the extent of their altruism is limited and that, in general, they do not take an interest in one another's interests. Thus, given the special features of the original position, each man tries to do the best he can for himself by insisting on principles calculated to protest and advance his system of ends whatever it turns out to be.

I believe that as a consequence of the peculiar nature of the original position there would be an agreement on the following two principles for assigning rights and duties and for regulating distributive shares as these are determined by the fundamental institutions of society: first, each person is to have an equal right to the most extensive liberty compatible with a like liberty for all; second, social and economic inequalities (as defined by the institutional structure or fostered by it) are to be arranged so that they are both to everyone's advantage and attached to positions and offices open to all. In view of the content of these two principles and their application to the main institutions of society, and therefore to the social system as a whole, we may regard them as the two principles of justice. Basic social arrangements are just insofar as they conform to these principles, and we can, if we like, discuss questions of justice directly by reference to them. But a deeper understanding of the justification of civil disobedience requires, I think, an account of the derivation of these principles provided by the doctrine of the social contract. Part of our task is to show why this is so.

The Grounds of Compliance with an Unjust Law

If we assume that in the original position men would agree both to the principle of doing their part when they have accepted and plan to continue to accept the benefits of just institutions (the principle of fairness), and also to the principle of not preventing the establishment of just institutions and of upholding and complying with them when they do exist, then the contract doctrine easily accounts for our having to conform to just institutions. But how does it account for the fact that we are normally required to comply with unjust laws as well? The injustice of a law is not a sufficient ground for not complying with it any more than the legal validity of legislation is always sufficient to require obedience to it. Sometimes one hears these extremes asserted, but I think that we need not take them seriously.

An answer to our question can be given by elaborating the social contract theory in the following way. I interpret it to hold that one is to envisage a series of agreements as follows: first, men are to agree upon the principles of justice in the original position. Then they are to move to a constitutional convention in which they choose a constitution that satisfies the principles of justice already chosen. Finally they assume the role of a legislative body and guided by the principles of justice enact laws subject to the constraints and procedures of the just constitution. The decisions reached in any stage are binding in all subsequent stages. Now whereas in the original position the contracting parties have no knowledge of their society or of their own position in it, in both a constitutional convention and a legislature, they do know certain general facts about their institutions, for example, the statistics regarding employment and output required for fiscal and economic policy. But no one knows particular facts about his own social class or his place in the distribution of natural assets. On each occasion the contracting parties have the knowledge required to make their agreement rational from the appropriate point of view, but not so much as to make them prejudiced. They are unable to tailor principles and legislation to take advantage of their social or natural position; a veil of ignorance prevents their knowing what this position is. With this series of agreements in mind, we can characterize just laws and policies as those which would be enacted were this whole process correctly carried out.

In choosing a constitution the aim is to find among the just constitutions the one which is most likely, given the general facts about the society in question, to lead to just and effective legislation. The principles of justice provide a criterion for the laws desired; the problem is to find a set of political procedures that will give this outcome. I shall assume that, at least under the normal conditions of a modern state, the best constitution is some form of democratic regime affirming equal political liberty and using some sort of majority (or other plurality) rule. Thus it follows that on the 349 contract theory a constitutional democracy of some sort is required by the principles of justice. At the same time it is essential to observe that the constitutional process is always a case of what we may call imperfect procedural justice: that is, there is no feasible political procedure which guarantees that the enacted legislation is just even though we have (let us suppose) a standard for just legislation. In simple cases, such as games of fair division, there are procedures which always lead to the right outcome (assume that equal shares is fair and let the man who cuts the cake take the last piece). These situations are those of perfect procedural justice. In other cases it does not matter what the outcome is as long as the fair procedure is followed: fairness of the process is transferred to the result (fair gambling is an instance of this). These situations are those of pure procedural justice. The constitutional process, like a criminal trial, resembles neither of these; the result matters and we have a standard for it. The difficulty is that we cannot frame a procedure which guarantees that only just and effective legislation is enacted. Thus even under a just constitution unjust laws may be passed and unjust policies enforced. Some form of the majority principle is necessary but the majority may be mistaken, more or less willfully, in what it legislates. In agreeing to a democratic constitution (as an instance of imperfect procedural justice) one accepts at the same time the principle of majority rule. Assuming that the constitution is just and that we have accepted and plan to continue to accept its benefits, we then have both an obligation and a natural duty (and in any case the duty) to comply with what the majority enacts even though it may be unjust. In this way we become bound to follow unjust laws, not always, of course, but provided the injustice does not exceed certain limits. We recognize that we must run the risk of suffering from the defects of one another's sense of justice; this burden we are prepared to carry as long as it is more or less evenly distributed or does not weigh too heavily. Justice binds us to a just constitution and to the unjust laws which may be enacted under it in precisely the same way that it binds us to any other social arrangement. Once we take the sequence of stages into account, there is nothing unusual in our being required to comply with unjust laws.

It should be observed that the majority principle has a secondary place as a rule of procedure which is perhaps the most efficient one under usual circumstances for working a democratic constitution. The basis for it rests essentially upon the principles of justice and therefore we may, when conditions allow, appeal to these principles against unjust legislation. The justice of the constitution does not insure the justice of laws enacted under it; and while we often have both an obligation and a duty to comply with what the majority legislates (as long as it does not exceed certain limits), there is, of course, no corresponding obligation or duty to regard what the majority enacts as itself just. The right to make law does not guarantee that the decision is rightly made; and while the citizen submits in his conduct to the judgment of democratic authority, he does not submit his judgment to it.[2] And if in his judgment the enactments of the majority exceed certain bounds of injustice, the citizen may consider civil disobedience. For we are not required to accept the majority's acts unconditionally and to acquiesce in the denial of our and others' liberties; rather we submit our conduct to democratic authority to the extent necessary to share the burden of working a constitutional regime, distorted as it must inevitably be by men's lack of wisdom and the defects of their sense of justice.

The Place of Civil Disobedience in a Constitutional Democracy

We are now in a position to say a few things about civil disobedience. I shall understand it to be a public, nonviolent, and conscientious act contrary to law usually done with the intent to bring about a change in the policies or laws of the government.[3] Civil disobedience is a political act in the sense that it is an act justified by moral principles which define a conception of civil society and the public good. It rests, then, on political conviction as opposed to a search for self or group interest; and in the case of a constitutional democracy, we may assume that this conviction involves the conception of justice (say that expressed by the contract doctrine) which underlies the constitution itself. That is, in a viable democratic regime there is a common conception of justice by reference to which its citizens regulate their political affairs and interpret the constitution. Civil disobedience is a public act which the dissenter believes to be justified by this conception of justice and for this reason it may be understood as addressing the sense of justice of the majority in order to urge reconsideration of the measures protested and to warn that, in the sincere opinion of the dissenters, the conditions of social cooperation are not being honored. For the principles of justice express precisely such conditions, and their persistent and deliberate violation in regard to basic liberties over any extended period of time cuts the ties of community and invites either submission or forceful resistance. By engaging in civil disobedience a minority leads the majority to consider whether it wants to have its acts taken in this way, or whether, in view of the common sense of justice, it wishes to acknowledge the claims of the minority.

Civil disobedience is also civil in another sense. Not only is it the outcome of a sincere conviction based on principles which regulate civic life, but it is public and nonviolent, that is, it is done in a situation where arrest and punishment are expected and accepted without resistance. In this way

[2] On this point see A. E. Murphy's review of Yves Simon's *The Philosophy of Democratic Government* (1951) in the *Philosophical Review* (April, 1952).

[3] Here I follow H. A. Bedau's definition of civil disobedience. See his "On Civil Disobedience," *Journal of Philosophy* (October, 1961).

it manifests a respect for legal procedures. Civil disobedience expresses disobedience to law within the limits of fidelity to law, and this feature of it helps to establish in the eyes of the majority that it is indeed conscientious and sincere, that it really is meant to address their sense of justice.[4] Being completely open about one's acts and being willing to accept the legal consequences of one's conduct is a bond given to make good one's sincerity, for that one's deeds are conscientious is not easy to demonstrate to another or even before oneself. No doubt it is possible to imagine a legal system in which conscientious belief that the law is unjust is accepted as a defense for noncompliance, and men of great honesty who are confident in one another might make such a system work. But as things are such a scheme would be unstable; we must pay a price in order to establish that we believe our actions have a moral basis in the convictions of the community.

The nonviolent nature of civil disobedience refers to the fact that it is intended to address the sense of justice of the majority and as such it is a form of speech, an expression of conviction. To engage in violent acts likely to injure and to hurt is incompatible with civil disobedience as a mode of address. Indeed, an interference with the basic rights of others tends to obscure the civilly disobedient quality of one's act. Civil disobedience is nonviolent in the further sense that the legal penalty for one's action is accepted and that resistance is not (at least for the moment) contemplated. Nonviolence in this sense is to be distinguished from nonviolence as a religious or pacifist principle. While those engaging in civil disobedience have often held some such principle, there is no necessary connection between it and civil disobedience. For on the interpretation suggested, civil disobedience in a democratic society is best understood as an appeal to the principles of justice, the fundamental conditions of willing social cooperation among free men, which in the view of the community as a whole are expressed in the constitution and guide its interpretation. Being an appeal to the moral basis of public life, civil disobedience is a political and not primarily a religious act. It addresses itself to the common principles of justice which men can require one another to follow and not to the aspirations of love which they cannot. Moreover by taking part in civilly disobedient acts one does not foreswear indefinitely the idea of forceful resistance; for if the appeal against injustice is repeatedly denied, then the majority has declared its intention to invite submission or resistance and the latter may conceivably be justified even in a democratic regime. We are not required to acquiesce in the crushing of fundamental liberties by democratic majorities which have shown themselves blind to the principles of justice upon which justification of the constitution depends.

[4] For a fuller discussion of this point to which I am indebted, see Charles Fried, "Moral Causation," *Harvard Law Review* (1964).

The Justification of Civil Disobedience

So far we have said nothing about the justification of civil disobedience, that is, the conditions under which civil disobedience may be engaged in consistent with the principles of justice that support a democratic regime. Our task is to see how the characterization of civil disobedience as addressed to the sense of justice of the majority (or to the citizens as a body) determines when such action is justified.

First of all, we may suppose that the normal political appeals to the majority have already been made in good faith and have been rejected, and that the standard means of redress have been tried. Thus, for example, existing political parties are indifferent to the claims of the minority and attempts to repeal the laws protested have been met with further repression since legal institutions are in the control of the majority. While civil disobedience should be recognized, I think, as a form of political action within the limits of fidelity to the rule of law, at the same time it is a rather desperate act just within these limits, and therefore it should, in general, be undertaken as a last resort when standard democratic processes have failed. In this sense it is not a normal political action. When it is justified there has been a serious breakdown; not only is there grave injustice in the law but a refusal more or less deliberate to correct it.

Second, since civil disobedience is a political act addressed to the sense of justice of the majority, it should usually be limited to substantial and clear violations of justice and preferably to those which, if rectified, will establish a basis for doing away with remaining injustices. For this reason there is a presumption in favor of restricting civil disobedience to violations of the first principle of justice, the principle of equal liberty, and to barriers which contravene the second principle, the principle of open offices which protects equality of opportunity. It is not, of course, always easy to tell whether these principles are satisfied. But if we think of them as guaranteeing the fundamental equal political and civil liberties (including freedom of conscience and liberty of thought) and equality of opportunity, then it is often relatively clear whether their principles are being honored. After all, the equal liberties are defined by the visible structure of social institutions; they are to be incorporated into the recognized practice, if not the letter, of social arrangements. When minorities are denied the right to vote or to hold certain political offices, when certain religious groups are repressed and others denied equality of opportunity in the economy, this is often obvious and there is no doubt that justice is not being given. However, the first part of the second principle which requires that inequalities be to everyone's advantage is a much more imprecise and controversial matter. Not only is there a problem of assigning it a determinate and precise sense, but even if we do so and agree on what it should be, there is often a wide variety of reasonable opinion as to whether the principle is 353 satisfied. The reason for this is that the principle applies primarily to fundamental economic and social policies. The choice of these depends upon theoretical and speculative beliefs as well as upon a wealth of concrete information, and all of this mixed with judgment and plain hunch, not to mention in actual cases prejudice and self-interest. Thus unless the laws of taxation are clearly designed to attack a basic equal liberty, they should not be protested by civil disobedience; the appeal to justice is not sufficiently clear and its resolution is best left to the political process. But violations of the equal liberties that define the common status of citizenship are another matter. The deliberate denial of these more or less over any extended period of time in the face of normal political protest is, in general, an appropriate object of civil disobedience. We may think of the social system as divided roughly into two parts, one which incorporates the fundamental equal liberties (including equality of opportunity) and another which embodies social and economic policies properly aimed at promoting the advantage of everyone. As a rule civil disobedience is best limited to the former where the appeal to justice is not only more definite and precise, but where, if it is effective, it tends to correct the injustices in the latter.

Third, civil disobedience should be restricted to those cases where the dissenter is willing to affirm that everyone else similarly subjected to the same degree of injustice has the right to protest in a similar way. That is, we must be prepared to authorize others to dissent in similar situations and in the same way, and to accept the consequences of their doing so. Thus, we may hold, for example, that the widespread disposition to disobey civilly clear violations of fundamental liberties more or less deliberate over an extended period of time would raise the degree of justice throughout society and would insure men's self-esteem as well as their respect for one another. Indeed, I believe this to be true, though certainly it is partly a matter of conjecture. As the contract doctrine emphasizes, since the principles of justice are principles which we would agree to in an original position of equality when we do not know our social position and the like, the refusal to grant justice is either the denial of the other as an equal (as one in regard to whom we are prepared to constrain our actions by principles which we would consent to) or the manifestation of a willingness to take advantage of natural contingencies and social fortune at his expense. In either case, injustice invites submission or resistance; but submission arouses the contempt of the oppressor and confirms him in his intention. If straightway, after a decent period of time to make reasonable political appeals in the normal way, men were in general to dissent by civil disobedience from infractions of the fundamental equal liberties, these liberties would, I believe, be more rather than less secure. Legitimate civil disobedience properly exercised is a stabilizing device in a constitutional regime, tending to make it more firmly just.

354

Sometimes, however, there may be a complication in connection with this third condition. It is possible, although perhaps unlikely, that there are so many persons or groups with a sound case for resorting to civil disobedience (as judged by the foregoing criteria) that disorder would follow if they all did so. There might be serious injury to the just constitution. Or again, a group might be so large that some extra precaution is necessary in the extent to which its members organize and engage in civil disobedience. Theoretically the case is one in which a number of persons or groups are equally entitled to and all want to resort to civil disobedience, yet if they all do this, grave consequences for everyone may result. The question, then, is who among them may exercise their right, and it falls under the general problem of fairness. I cannot discuss the complexities of the matter here. Often a lottery or a rationing system can be set up to handle the case; but unfortunately the circumstances of civil disobedience rule out this solution. It suffices to note that a problem of fairness may arise and that those who contemplate civil disobedience should take into account. They may have to reach an understanding as to who can exercise their right in the immediate situation and to recognize the need for special constraint.

The final condition, of a different nature, is the following. We have been considering when one has a right to engage in civil disobedience, and our conclusion is that one has this right should three conditions hold: when one is subject to injustice more or less deliberate over an extended period of time in the face of normal political protests; where the injustice is a clear violation of the liberties of equal citizenship; and provided that the general disposition to protest similarly in similar cases would have acceptable consequences. These conditions are not, I think, exhaustive but they seem to cover the more obvious points; yet even when they are satisfied and one has the right to engage in civil disobedience, there is still the different question of whether one should exercise this right, that is, whether by doing so one is likely to further one's ends. Having established one's right to protest one is then free to consider these tactical questions. We may be acting within our rights but still foolishly if our action only serves to provoke the harsh retaliation of the majority; and it is likely to do so if the majority lacks a sense of justice, or if the action is poorly timed or not well designed to make the appeal to the sense of justice effective. It is easy to think of instances of this sort, and in each case these practical questions have to be faced. From the standpoint of the theory of political obligation we can only say that the exercise of the right should be rational and reasonably designed to advance the protester's aims, and that weighing tactical questions presupposes that one has already established one's right, since tactical advantages in themselves do not support it.

Conclusion: Several Objections Considered

In a reasonably affluent democratic society justice becomes the first virtue of institutions. Social arrangements irrespective of their efficiency must be reformed if they are significantly unjust. No increase in efficiency in the form of greater advantages for many justifies the loss of liberty of a few. That we believe this is shown by the fact that in a democracy the fundamental liberties of citizenship are not understood as the outcome of political bargaining nor are they subject to the calculus of social interests. Rather these liberties are fixed points which serve to limit political transactions and which determine the scope of calculations of social advantage. It is this fundamental place of the equal liberties which makes their systematic violation over any extended period of time a proper object of civil disobedience. For to deny men these rights is to infringe the conditions of social cooperation among free and rational persons, a fact which is evident to the citizens of a constitutional regime since it follows from the principles of justice which underlie their institutions. The justification of civil disobedience rests on the priority of justice and the equal liberties which it guarantees.

It is natural to object to this view of civil disobedience that it relies too heavily upon the existence of a sense of justice. Some may hold that the feeling for justice is not a vital political force, and that what moves men are various other interests, the desire for wealth, power, prestige, and so on. Now this is a large question the answer to which is highly conjectural and each tends to have his own opinion. But there are two remarks which may clarify what I have said: first, I have assumed that there is in a constitutional regime a common sense of justice the principles of which are recognized to support the constitution and to guide its interpretation. In any given situation particular men may be tempted to violate these principles, but the collective force in their behalf is usually effective since they are seen as the necessary terms of cooperation among free men; and presumably the citizens of a democracy (or sufficiently many of them) want to see justice done. Where these assumptions fail, the justifying conditions for civil disobedience (the first three) are not affected, but the rationality of engaging in it certainly is. In this case, unless the costs of repressing civil dissent injures the economic self-interest (or whatever) of the majority, protest may simply make the position of the minority worse. No doubt as a tactical matter civil disobedience is more effective when its appeal coincides with other interests, but a constitutional regime is not viable in the long run without an attachment to the principles of justice of the sort which we have assumed.

Then, further, there may be a misapprehension about the manner in which a sense of justice manifests itself. There is a tendency to think that 356 it is shown by professions of the relevant principles together with action of an altruistic nature requiring a considerable degree of self-sacrifice. But these conditions are obviously too strong, for the majority's sense of justice may show itself simply in its being unable to undertake the measures required to suppress the minority and to punish as the law requires the various acts of civil disobedience. The sense of justice undermines the will to uphold unjust institutions and so a majority despite its superior power may give way. It is unprepared to force the minority to be subject to injustice. Thus, although the majority's action is reluctant and grudging, the role of the sense of justice is nevertheless essential, for without it the majority would have been willing to enforce the law and to defend its position. Once we see the sense of justice as working in this negative way to make established injustices indefensible, then it is recognized as a central element of democratic politics.

Finally, it may be objected against this account that it does not settle the question of who is to say when the situation is such as to justify civil disobedience. And because it does not answer this question, it invites anarchy by encouraging every man to decide the matter for himself. Now the reply to this is that each man must indeed settle this question for himself, although he may, of course, decide wrongly. This is true on any theory of political duty and obligation, at least on any theory compatible with the principles of a democratic constitution. The citizen is responsible for what he does. If we usually think that we should comply with the law, this is because our political principles normally lead to this conclusion. There is a presumption in favor of compliance in the absence of good reasons to the contrary. But because each man is responsible and must decide for himself as best he can whether the circumstances justify civil disobedience, it does not follow that he may decide as he pleases. It is not by looking to our personal interests or to political allegiances narrowly construed, that we should make up our mind. The citizen must decide on the basis of the principles of justice that underlie and guide the interpretation of the constitution and in the light of his sincere conviction as to how these principles should be applied in the circumstances. If he concludes that conditions obtain which justify civil disobedience and conducts himself accordingly, he has acted conscientiously and perhaps mistakenly, but not in any case at his convenience.

In a democratic society each man must act as he thinks the principles of political right require him to. We are to follow our understanding of these principles, and we cannot do otherwise. There can be no morally binding legal interpretation of these principles, not even by a supreme court or legislature. Nor is there any infallible procedure for determining what or who is right. In our system the Supreme Court, Congress, and the President often put forward rival interpretations of the Constitution. Although the Court has the final say in settling any particular case, it is not immune from powerful political influence that may change its reading of 357 the law of the land. The Court presents its point of view by reason and argument; its conception of the Constitution must, if it is to endure, persuade men of its soundness. The final court of appeal is not the Court, or Congress, or the President, but the electorate as a whole.[5] The civilly disobedient appeal in effect to this body. There is no danger of anarchy as long as there is a sufficient working agreement in men's conceptions of political justice and what it requires. That men can achieve such an understanding when the essential political liberties are maintained is the assumption implicit in democratic institutions. There is no way to avoid entirely the risk of devisive strife. But if legitimate civil disobedience seems to threaten civil peace, the responsibility falls not so much on those who protest as upon those whose abuse of authority and power justifies such opposition.

RICHARD WASSERSTROM
The Obligation to Obey the Law

I

The question of what is the nature and extent of one's obligation to obey the law is one of those relatively rare philosophic questions which can never produce doubts about the importance of theory for practice. To ask under what circumstances, if any, one is justified in disobeying the law, is to direct attention to problems which all would acknowledge to be substantial. Concrete, truly problematic situations are as old as civil society.

The general question was posed—though surely not for the first time—well over two thousand years ago in Athens when Crito revealed to Socrates that Socrates' escape from prison could be easily and successfully accomplished. The issue was made a compelling one—though once again

---

[5] For a presentation of this view to which I am indebted, see A. M. Bickel, *The Least Dangerous Branch* (Indianapolis, 1962), especially Chapters 5 and 6.

Reprinted from *UCLA Law Review*, Vol. 10 (1963), 780–807. © 1963 The Regents of the University of California. All Rights Reserved. Reprinted by permission of the publisher.
This is an expanded and substantially revised version of a paper, "Disobeying the Law," which was presented at the December, 1961, meeting of the Eastern Division of the American Philosophical Society and which was published in 58 J. Philosophy 641 (1961).

surely not for the first time—by Crito's insistence that escape was not only possible but also *desirable,* and that disobedience to law was in *this* case at least, surely justified. And the problem received at the hand of Socrates —here perhaps for the first time—a sustained theoretical analysis and resolution.

Just as the question of what is the nature and extent of one's obligation to obey the law demanded attention then—as it has throughout man's life in the body politic—it is no less with us today in equally vexing and perplexing forms. Freedom rides and sit-ins have raised the question of whether the immorality of segregation may justify disobeying the law. The all too awesome horrors of a nuclear war have seemed to some to require responsive action, including, if need be, deliberate but peaceful trespasses upon government-owned atomic testing grounds. And the rightness of disobedience to law in the face of court-ordered school integration has been insisted upon by the citizens of several states and acted upon by the governor of at least one.[1]

The problem is one of present concern and the questions it necessarily raises are real. But even if the exigencies of contemporary life were not such as to make this topic a compelling one, it is one which would still be peculiarly ripe for critical inquiry. In part this is so because despite their significance many of the central issues have been relatively neglected by legal or political philosophers and critics. Many of the important questions which bear upon the nature and extent of one's obligation to obey the law have been dealt with summarily and uncritically; distinguishable issues have been indiscriminately blurred and debatable conclusions gratuitously assumed.

More important is the fact that historically the topic has generally been examined from only one very special aspect of the problem. Those philosophers who have seriously considered questions relating to one's obligation to obey the law have considered them only in the context of revolution. They have identified the conditions under which one would, if ever, be justified in disobeying the law with the conditions under which revolution would, if ever, be justified; and they have, perhaps not surprisingly, tended thereby to conclude that one would be justified in disobeying the law if, and only if, revolution itself would in that case be justified.[2]

To view the problem in a setting of obedience or revolution is surely to misconstrue it. It is to neglect, among other things, something that is obvi-

---

[1] This is to say nothing of the stronger claim, involved in many of the war crimes prosecutions, that one does have a duty to disobey the law and, therefore, that one can be properly punished for having obeyed the law.

[2] See, *e.g.,* AUSTIN, THE PROVINCE OF JURISPRUDENCE DETERMINED 53–55 (1954); HUME, A TREASURE OF HUMAN NATURE, bk. III, §§ 9, 10; LOCKE, THE SECOND TREATISE OF GOVERNMENT, chs. 18, 19.

ously true—that most people who disobey the law are not revolutionaries and that most acts of disobedience of the law are not acts of revolution. Many who disobey the law are, of course, ordinary criminals: burglars, kidnappers, embezzlers, and the like. But even of those who disobey the law under a claim of justification, most are neither advocates nor practitioners of revolution.[3]

If the traditional, philosophical treatment of this subject is unduly simplistic and restrictive, contemporary legal thought is seldom more instructive. It is distressing, for one thing, that those whose daily intellectual concern is the legal system have said so little on this subject. And it is disturbing that many of those who have said anything at all appear so readily to embrace the view that justified disobedience of the law is a rare, if not impossible, occurrence. What is so disturbing is not the fact that this view is held—although I think it a mistaken one—but rather that such a conclusion is so summarily reached or assumed.[4]

I must make it clear at the outset that it is not my purpose to devote the remainder of this article to a documentation of the claims just made concerning either historical or contemporary thought. I do not wish to demonstrate that people in fact do believe what they appear to believe about the possibility of justified disobedience to law. Nor do I wish to show why it is that people have come to believe what they appear to be-

[3] A subject which has surely not received the philosophical attention it deserves is that of the nature of revolution. What, for instance, are the characteristics of a revolution? Must the procedures by which laws are made or the criteria of validity be altered? Or is it sufficient that the people who occupy certain crucial offices be removed in a manner inconsistent with existing rules? Must force or resistance accompany whatever changes or alterations are made? Whatever the answers may be to questions such as these, it is, I think, plain that particular laws may be disobeyed under a claim of justification without any of these features being present. One can *argue* that for one reason or another, any act of disobedience must necessarily lead to revolution or the overthrow of the government. But then this is an argument which must be demonstrated.

[4] Professor Henry Hart, for example, in his extremely stimulating analysis of the aims of the criminal law seems to hold such a view. Professor Hart believes, that the criminal law ought only be concerned with that conduct which is morally blameworthy. From this he infers that no real problem can ever be presented by laws which make knowledge of the illegality of an action one of the elements of the offense. And this is so because the "knowing or reckless disregard of legal obligation affords an independent basis of blameworthiness *justifying the actor's condemnation as a criminal,* even when his conduct was not intrinsically antisocial." Hart, *The Aims of the Criminal Law,* 23 LAW & CONTEMP. PROB. 401, 418 (1958). (Emphasis added.) Some such view can also be plausibly attributed to, among others, Professor Lon Fuller, see text at section II, and Professor Herbert Wechsler, see text at section IV. Of course, all of these scholars, or any other person holding such a view, might well insist that the position is tenable only if an important qualification is made, namely, that the legal system in question be that of an essentially democratic society. For a discussion of this more restricted claim, see text at section IV.

lieve. Rather, in very general terms I am concerned here with *arguments*—with those arguments which have been or which might be given in support of the claim that because one does have an obligation to obey the law, one ought not ever disobey the law.

To describe the focus of the article in this manner is, however, to leave several crucial matters highly ambiguous. And thus, before the arguments can be considered properly, the following matters must be clarified.

A. There are several different views which could be held concerning the nature of the stringency of one's obligation to obey the law. One such view, and the one which I shall be most concerned to show to be false, can be characterized as holding that one has an *absolute* obligation to obey the law. I take this to mean that a person is never justified in disobeying the law; to know that a proposed action is illegal is to know all one needs to know in order to conclude that the action ought not to be done;[5] to cite the illegality of an action is to give a sufficient reason for not having done it. A view such as this is far from uncommon. President Kennedy expressed the thoughts of many quite reflective people when he said not too long ago:

... [O]ur nation is founded on the principle that observance of the law is the eternal safeguard of liberty and defiance of the law is the surest road to tyranny.

The law which we obey includes the final rulings of the courts as well as the enactments of our legislative bodies. Even among law-abiding men few laws are universally loved.

But they are universally respected and not resisted.

Americans are free, in short, to disagree with the law, but not to disobey it. For in a government of laws and not of men, no man, however prominent or powerful, and no mob, however unruly or boisterous, is entitled to defy a court of law.

If this country should ever reach the point where any man or group of men, by force or threat of force, could long deny the commands of our court and our Constitution, then no law would stand free from doubt, no judge would be sure of his writ and no citizen would be safe from his neighbors.[6]

A more moderate or weaker view would be that which holds that, while one does have an obligation to obey the law, the obligation is a prima facie

---

[5] Because I am concerned with the question of whether one is ever *morally justified* in acting illegally, I purposely make the actor's knowledge of the illegality of the action part of the description of the act. I am not concerned with the question of whether ignorance of the illegality of the action ought to excuse one from moral blame.

[6] N.Y. Times, Oct. 1, 1962, p. 22, col. 6. The same qualification must be made here as was made in note 4 *supra*—President Kennedy may well have meant his remarks to be applicable only to the legal system which is a part of the set of political institutions of the United States.

rather than absolute one. If one knows that a proposed course of conduct is illegal then one has a good—but not necessarily a sufficient—reason for refraining from engaging in that course of conduct. Under this view, a person may be justified in disobeying the law, but an act which is in disobedience of the law does have to be justified, whereas an act in obedience of the law does not have to be justified.

It is important to observe that there is an ambiguity in this notion of a prima facie obligation. For the claim that one has a prima facie obligation to obey the law can come to one of two different things. On the one hand, the claim can be this: the fact that an action is an act of disobedience is something which always does count against the performance of the action. If one has a prima facie obligation to obey the law, one always has that obligation—although, of course, it may be overridden by other obligations in any particular case. Thus the fact that an action is illegal is a relevant consideration in every case and it is a consideration which must be outweighed by other considerations before the performance of an illegal action can be justified.

On the other hand, the claim can be weaker still. The assertion of a prima facie obligation to obey the law can be nothing more than the claim that as a matter of fact it is *generally* right or obligatory to obey the law. As a rule the fact that an action is illegal is a relevant circumstance. But in any particular case, after deliberation, it might very well turn out that the illegality of the action was not truly relevant. For in any particular case the circumstances might be such that there simply was nothing in the fact of illegality which required overriding—*e.g.,* there were no bad consequences at all which would flow from disobeying the law in this case.

The distinction can be made more vivid in the following fashion. One person, A, might hold the view that any action in disobedience of the law is intrinsically bad. Some other person, B, might hold the view that no action is intrinsically bad unless it has the property, P, and that not all actions in disobedience of the law have that property. Now for A, the fact of disobedience is *always* a relevant consideration,[7] for B, the fact of disobedience may always be initially relevant because of the existence of some well-established hypothesis which asserts that the occurrence of any action of disobedience is correlated highly with the occurrence of P. But if in any particular case disobedience does not turn out to have the property, P, then, upon reflection, it can be concluded by B that the fact that disobedience is involved is not a reason which weighs against the performance of the act in question. To understand B's position it is necessary to distinguish the relevance of *considering* the fact of disobedi-

---

[7] To repeat, though, it surely is not necessarily conclusive, or sufficient, since an action in obedience to the law may under some other description be worse, or less justifiable, than disobedience.

ence from the relevance of the fact of disobedience. The former must always be relevant, the latter is not.

Thus there are at least three different positions which might be taken concerning the character of the obligation to obey the law or the rightness of disobedience to the law. They are: (1) One has an absolute obligation to obey the law; disobedience is never justified. (2) One has an obligation to obey the law but this obligation can be overridden by conflicting obligations; disobedience can be justified, but only by the presence of outweighing circumstances. (3) One does not have a special obligation to obey the law, but it is in fact usually obligatory, on other grounds, to do so; disobedience to law often does turn out to be unjustified.

B. It must also be made clear that when I talk about the obligation to obey the law or the possibility of actions which are both illegal and justified, I am concerned solely with *moral obligations* and *morally justified* actions. I shall be concerned solely with arguments which seek to demonstrate that there is some sort of a connection between the legality or illegality of an action and its morality or immorality. Concentration on this general topic necessarily renders a number of interesting problems irrelevant. Thus, I am not at all concerned with the question of why, in fact, so many people do obey the law. Nor, concomitantly, am I concerned with the nonmoral reasons which might and do justify obedience to law—of these, the most pertinent, is the fact that highly unpleasant consequences of one form or another are typically inflicted upon those who disobey the law. Finally there are many actions which are immoral irrespective of whether they also happen to be illegal. And I am not, except in one very special sense, concerned with this fact either. I am not concerned with the fact that the immorality of the action itself may be a sufficient reason for condemning it regardless of its possible illegality.

C. My last preliminary clarification relates to the fact that there is a variety of kinds of legal rules or laws and that there is a variety of ways in which actions can be related to these rules. This is an important point because many moral philosophers, in particular, have tended to assimilate all legal rules to the model of a typical law or legal order which is enforced through the direct threat of the infliction by the government of severe sanctions, and have thereby tended to assume that all laws and all legal obligations can be broken or disobeyed only in the manner in which penal laws can be broken or disobeyed. That this assimilation is a mistake can be demonstrated quite readily. There are many laws that, unlike the typical penal law, do not require or prohibit the performance of any acts at all. They cannot, therefore, be disobeyed. There are laws, for example, that make testamentary dispositions of property ineffective, unenforceable, or invalid, if the written instrument was not witnessed by 363 the requisite number of disinterested witnesses. Yet a law of this kind obviously does not impose an obligation upon anyone to make a will. Nor, more significantly, could a person who executed a will without the requisite number of witnesses be said to have disobeyed the law. Such a person has simply failed to execute a valid will.[8]

The foregoing observations are relevant largely because it is important to realize that to talk about disobeying the law or about one's obligation to obey the law is usually to refer to a rather special kind of activity, namely, that which is exemplified by, among other things, actions in violation or disobedience of a penal law. It is this special type of activity which alone is the concern of this article.

II

One kind of argument in support of the proposition that one cannot be justified in disobeying the law is that which asserts the existence of some sort of *logical* or conceptual relationship between disobeying the law and acting immorally.[9] If the notion of illegality entails that of immorality then one is never justified in acting illegally just because part of the meaning of *illegal* is *immoral;* just because describing an action as illegal is—among other things—to describe it as unjustified.[10]

---

[8] See HART, THE CONCEPT OF LAW 27–48 (1961), particularly for the clearest and fullest extant philosophical analysis of the important distinguishing characteristics of different kinds of legal rules.

In this connection a stronger point than the one made above can be made. It is that there are many laws which, if they can be disobeyed at all, cannot be disobeyed in the way in which the typical criminal law can be disobeyed. For there are many laws that either impose or permit one to impose upon oneself any number of different legal obligations. And with many of these legal obligations, regardless of how created, it seems correct to say that one can breach or fail to perform them without thereby acting illegally or in disobedience of the law. One's obligation to obey the law may not, therefore, be coextensive with one's legal obligations. In the typical case of a breach of contract, for example, the failure to perform one's contractual obligations is clearly a breach of a legal obligation. Yet one can breach a contract and, hence, a legal obligation without necessarily acting illegally. This last assertion is open to question. And arguments for its correctness would not here be germane. It is sufficient to recognize only that failing to honor or perform some types of legal obligations may be a quite different kind of activity from violating or disobeying a law or order which is backed up, in some very direct fashion, by a governmentally threatened severe sanction.

[9] It is worth emphasizing that I am not at all interested in the claim—which in many ways is an odd one to belabor—that there is a logical relationship between disobeying the law and acting illegally. See, *e.g.,* Carnes, *Why Should I Obey the Law?,* 71 ETHICS 14 (1960).

[10] Professor Fuller may hold to some version of this view in his article, *Positivism and Fidelity to Law—A Reply to Professor Hart,* 71 HARV. L. REV. 630, 656 (1958), where, after characterizing the position of legal positivism as one which

A claim such as this is extremely difficult to evaluate. For one has great difficulty in knowing what is to count as truly relevant—let alone decisive—evidence of its correctness. There is, nevertheless, a supporting argument of sorts which can be made. It might go something like this:

It is a fact which is surely worth noticing that people generally justify action that *seems to be* illegal by claiming that the action *is not really* illegal. Typically an actor who is accused of having done something illegal will not defend himself by pointing out that, while illegal, his conduct was nevertheless morally justified. Instead, he will endeavor to show in one way or another that it is really inaccurate to call his conduct illegal at all. Now it looks as though this phenomenon can be readily accounted for. People try to resist the accusation of illegality, it might be argued, for the simple reason that they wish to avoid being punished. But what is interesting and persuasive is the fact that people try just as hard to evade a charge of illegality even in those situations where the threat of punishment is simply not an important or even relevant consideration.

The cases of the recent sit-ins or freedom rides are apt. To be sure, the claim was that the preservation of segregated lunch-counters, waiting rooms, and the like was morally indefensible. But an important justification for the rightness of the actions employed in integrating these facilities in the fashion selected rested upon the insistence that the perpetuation of segregation in these circumstances was itself illegal. One primary claim for the rightness of freedom rides was that these were not instances of disobeying the law. They were instead attempts to invoke judicial and executive protection of legal, indeed constitutional, rights. While there were some, no doubt, who might have insisted upon the rightness of sit-ins even if they were clearly illegal, most people were confident of the blamelessness of the participants just because it was plain that their actions were not, in the last analysis, illegal. Were it evident that sit-ins

---

says that "On the one hand, we have an amoral datum called law, which has the peculiar quality of creating a moral duty to obey it. On the other hand, we have a moral duty to do what we think is right and decent." Professor Fuller goes on to criticize this bifurcation of law and morality on the grounds that "The 'dilemma' it states has the verbal formulation of a problem, but the problem it states makes no sense. It is like saying I have to choose between giving food to a starving man and being mimsey with the borogroves. I do not think it unfair to the positivistic philosophy to say that it never gives any coherent meaning to the moral obligation of fidelity to law."

Others who at least suggest adherence to such a position are: BAIER, THE MORAL POINT OF VIEW 134 (1958); NOWELL-SMITH, ETHICS 236–37 (1959); and WELDON, THE VOCABULARY OF POLITICS 57, 62, 66–67 (1953). And there are surely passages in Hobbes that could also be read in this way. See, *e.g.,* HOBBES, LEVIATHAN, chs. XIII, XVIII. The claim that *illegal* entails *immoral* is closely related to, but surely distinguishable from, the position that Professor Fuller, among many others, may also hold, namely, that there are certain minimum "moral" requirements that must be met before any rule can be a law.

were truly illegal many might hold a different view about the rightness of sitting-in as a means to bring about integrated facilities.

Language commonly invoked in the course of disputes between nations furnishes another equally graphic illustration of the same point. In the continuing controversy over the status of Berlin, for instance, both the United States and Russia have relied upon claims of legality and have been sensitive to charges of illegality, to an appreciably greater extent than one would otherwise have supposed. And much the same can be said of the more recent dispute between India and China. Now if nations which have little to fear in the way of the imposition of sanctions for acting illegally are nevertheless extraordinarily sensitive to charges of illegal conduct, this also may be taken as evidence of the fact that *illegality* implies *immorality*.

Wholly apt, too, was the controversy over the Eichmann trial. To some, the fact that the seizure and trial of Eichmann by Israel was illegal was sufficient to cast grave doubts upon the justifiability of the proceedings. To others, the charge of illegality made it necessary to demonstrate that nothing really illegal had occurred. What is significant about all this is the fact that all of the disputants implicitly acknowledged that illegality was something which did have to be worried about.

Such in brief is the argument which might be advanced and the "evidence" which might be adduced to support it. I think that such an argument is not persuasive, and I can best show this to be so in the following fashion.

Consider the case of a law that makes it a felony to perform an abortion upon a woman unless the abortion is necessary to preserve *her* life. Suppose a teenager, the daughter of a local minister, has been raped on her way home from school by an escapee from a state institution for mental defectives. Suppose further that the girl has become pregnant and has been brought to a reputable doctor who is asked to perform an abortion. And suppose, finally, that the doctor concludes after examining the girl that her life will not be endangered by giving birth to the child.[11] An abortion under these circumstances is, it seems fair to say, illegal.[12] Yet, we would surely find both intelligible and appealing the doctor's claim that he was nonetheless justified in disobeying the law by performing an abortion on the girl. I at least can see nothing logically odd or inconsistent about recognizing both that there is a law prohibiting this conduct and that further questions concerning the rightness of obedience

---

[11] These facts are taken from Packer & Gampell, *Therapeutic Abortion: A Problem in Law and Medicine*, 11 STAN. L. REV. 417 (1959), where they are introduced in a different context.

[12] Such would seem to be the case in California, for example, where CAL. PEN. CODE § 274 makes the performance of an abortion a felony unless the abortion is necessary to preserve the life of the pregnant woman.

would be relevant and, perhaps, decisive. Thus I can see nothing logically odd about describing this as a case in which the performance of the abortion could be both illegal and morally justified.[13]

There is, no doubt, a heroic defense which can be made to the above. It would consist of the insistence that the activity just described simply cannot be both illegal and justified. Two alternatives are possible. First, one might argue that the commission of the abortion would indeed have been justified if it were not proscribed by the law. But since it is so prohibited, the abortion is wrong. Now if this is a point about the appropriateness of kinds of reasons, I can only note that referring the action to a valid law does not seem to preclude asking meaningful questions about the obligatoriness of the action. If this is a point about language or concepts it does seem to be perfectly intelligible to say that the conduct is both illegal and morally justified. And if this is, instead, an *argument* for the immorality of ever disobeying a valid law, then it surely requires appreciable substantiation and not mere assertion.

Second, one might take a different line and agree that other questions can be asked about the conduct, but that is because the commission of the abortion under these circumstances simply cannot be illegal. The difficulty here, however, is that it is hard to understand what is now meant by *illegal*. Of course, I am not claiming that in the case as I have described it, it is clear that the performance of the abortion must be illegal. It might not be. But it might be. Were we to satisfy all the usual tests that we do invoke when we determine that a given course of conduct is illegal, and were someone still to maintain that because the performance of the abortion is here morally justified it cannot be illegal, then the burden is on the proponent of this view to make clear how we are to decide when conduct is illegal. And it would further be incumbent upon him to demonstrate what seems to be highly dubious, namely, that greater clarity and insight could somehow be attained through a radical change in our present terminology. It appears to be a virtually conclusive refutation to observe that there has never been a legal system whose criteria of validity—no matter how sophisticated, how rational and how well defined—themselves guaranteed that morally justified action would never be illegal.

Thus an argument as strong as any of the above must fail. There is,

---

[13] I am supposing, of course, that one would regard the performance of the abortion—in the absence of the relevant penal law—as clearly morally justified. If one disagrees with this assessment of the morality of the case, then some other example ought to be substituted. One likely candidate, drawn from our own history, is that of the inherent rightness in refusing to return an escaped Negro slave to his "owner." If one believes that refusing to do so would be clearly justifiable, then consider whether the existence of the fugitive slave laws necessarily rendered a continued refusal unjustified.

of course, a weaker version which may be more appealing. If it is true that there is something disturbing about justifying actions that are conceded to be illegal, then one way to account for this is to insist that there is a logical connection between the concepts involved, but it is something less than the kind of implication already discussed. Perhaps it is correct that *illegal* does not entail *immoral; illegal* might nevertheless entail *prima facie immoral*. The evidence adduced tends to show that among one's moral obligations is the prima facie duty to obey the law.[14]

Once again, it is somewhat difficult to know precisely what to make of such a claim. It is hard to see how one would decide what was to count as evidence or whether the evidence was persuasive. At a minimum, it is not difficult to imagine several equally plausible alternative explanations of the disturbing character of accusations of illegal activity. In addition, to know only that one has a prima facie duty to obey the law is not to know a great deal. In particular, one does not know how or when that obligation can be overridden. And, of course, even if it is correct that acting illegally logically implies acting prima facie immorally, this in no way shows that people may not often be morally justified in acting illegally. At most, it demands that they have some good reason for acting illegally; at best, it requires what has already been hypothesized, namely, that the action in question, while illegal, be morally justified.

Thus, it is clear that if the case against ever acting illegally is to be made out, conceptual analysis alone cannot do it. Indeed, arguments of quite another sort must be forthcoming. And it is to these that I now turn.

III

One such argument, and the most common argument advanced, goes something like this: The reason why one ought never to disobey the law is simply that the consequences would be disastrous if everybody disobeyed the law. The reason why disobedience is never right becomes apparent once we ask the question "But what if everyone did that?"

Consider again the case of the doctor who has to decide whether he is justified in performing an illegal abortion. If he only has a prima facie duty to obey the law it looks as though he might justifiably decide that in this case his prima facie obligation is overridden by more stringent conflicting obligations. Or, if he is simply a utilitarian, it appears that he might rightly conclude that the consequences of disobeying the abortion law would be on the whole and in the long run less deleterious than

---

[14] Sir W. David Ross, for example, suggests that the obligation to obey the law is a prima facie obligation which is a compound of three more simple prima facie duties. ROSS, THE RIGHT AND THE GOOD 27–28 (1930).

those of obeying. But this is simply a mistake. The doctor would inevitably be neglecting the most crucial factor of all, namely, that in performing the abortion he was disobeying the law. And imagine what would happen if everyone went around disobeying the law. The alternatives are obeying the law and general disobedience. The choice is between any social order and chaos. As President Kennedy correctly observed, if any law is disobeyed, then no law can be free from doubt, no citizen safe from his neighbor.

Such an argument, while perhaps overdrawn, is by no means uncommon.[15] Yet, as it stands, it is an essentially confused one. Its respective claims, if they are to be fairly evaluated, must be delineated with some care.

At a minimum, the foregoing attack upon the possibility of justified disobedience might be either one or both of two radically different kinds of objection. The first, which relates to the consequences of an act of disobedience, is essentially a *causal* argument. The second questions the *principle* that any proponent of justified disobedience invokes. As to the causal argument, it is always relevant to point out that any act of disobedience may have certain consequences simply because it is an act of disobedience. Once the occurrence of the act is known, for example, expenditure of the state's resources may become necessary. The time and energy of the police will probably be turned to the task of discovering who it was who did the illegal act and of gathering evidence relevant to the offense. And other resources might be expended in the prosecution and adjudication of the case against the perpetrator of the illegal act. Illustrations of this sort could be multiplied, no doubt, but I do not think either that considerations of this sort are very persuasive or that they have been uppermost in the minds of those who make the argument now under examination. Indeed, if the argument is a causal one at all, it consists largely of the claim that any act of disobedience will itself cause, to some degree or other, general disobedience of all laws; it will cause or help to cause the overthrow or dissolution of the state. And while it is possible to assert that any act of disobedience will tend to further social disintegration or revolution, it is much more difficult to see why this must be so.

The most plausible argument would locate this causal efficacy in the

[15] Socrates, for instance, supposes that were he to escape he might properly be asked: "[W]hat are you about? Are you going by an act of yours to overturn us —the laws and the whole state, as far as in you lies? Do you imagine that a state can subsist and not be overthrown, in which the decisions of law have no power, but are set aside and overthrown by individuals?" PLATO, CRITO. Analogous arguments can be found in, for example: AUSTIN, THE PROVINCE OF JURISPRUDENCE DETERMINED 52–53 (1954); HOBBES, LEVIATHAN, ch. XV; HUME, A TREATISE OF HUMAN NATURE, bk. III, pt. II, 3, 6, 8, 9; TOULMIN, AN EXAMINATION OF THE PLACE OF REASON IN ETHICS 151 (1950).

kind of example set by any act of disobedience. But how plausible is this argument? It is undeniable, of course, that the kind of example that will be set is surely a relevant factor. Yet, there is nothing that precludes any proponent of justified disobedience from taking this into account. If, for example, others will somehow infer from the doctor's disobedience of the abortion law that they are justified in disobeying *any* law under *any* circumstances, then the doctor ought to consider this fact. This is a consequence—albeit a lamentable one—of his act of disobedience. Similarly, if others will extract the proper criterion from the act of disobedience, but will be apt to misapply it in practice, then this too ought to give the doctor pause. It, too, is a consequence of acting.[16] But if the argument is that disobedience would be wrong even if no bad example were set and no other deleterious consequences likely, then the argument must be directed against the principle the doctor appeals to in disobeying the law, and not against the consequences of his disobedience at all.

As to the attack upon a principle of justified disobedience, as a principle, the response "But what if everyone disobeyed the law?" does appear to be a good way to point up both the inherent inconsistency of almost any principle of justified disobedience and the manifest undesirability of adopting such a principle. Even if one need not worry about what others will be led to do by one's disobedience, there is surely something amiss if one cannot consistently defend his right to do what one is claiming he is right in doing.

In large measure, such an objection is unreal. The appeal to "But what if everyone did that?" loses much, if not all, of its persuasiveness once we become clearer about what precisely the "did that" refers to. If the question "But what if everyone did that?" is simply another way of asking "But what if everybody disobeyed the law?" or "But what if people generally disobeyed the laws?" then the question is surely quasi-rhetorical. To urge general or indiscriminate disobedience to laws is to invoke a principle that, if coherent, is manifestly indefensible. It is equally plain, however, that with few exceptions such a principle has never been seriously espoused. Anyone who claims that there are actions that are both illegal and justified surely need not be thereby asserting that it is right generally to disobey all laws or even any particular law. It is surely not inconsistent to assert both that indiscriminate disobedience is indefensible and that discriminate disobedience is morally right and proper conduct. Nor, analogously, is it at all evident that a person who claims to be justified in performing an illegal action is thereby committed to or giving endorsement to the principle that the entire legal system ought to be overthrown or renounced. At a minimum, therefore, the appeal to "But what if everyone did that?" cannot by itself support the

[16] For a very special and related version of this argument, see text at section V.

claim that one has an absolute obligation to obey the law—that disobeying the law can never be truly justified.

There is, however, a distinguishable but related claim which merits very careful attention—if for no other reason than the fact that it is so widely invoked today by moral philosophers. The claim is simply this: While it may very well be true that there are situations in which a person will be justified in disobeying the law, it is surely not true that disobedience can ever be justified solely on the grounds that the consequences of disobeying the particular law were in that case on the whole less deleterious than those of obedience.[17]

This claim is particularly relevant at this juncture because one of the arguments most often given to substantiate it consists of the purported demonstration of the fact that any principle which contained a proviso permitting a general appeal to consequences must itself be incoherent. One of the most complete statements of the argument is found in Marcus Singer's provocative book, *Generalization in Ethics*:

Suppose, . . . that I am contemplating evading the payment of income taxes. I might reason that I need the money more than the government does, that the amount I have to pay is so small in comparison with the total amount to be collected that the government will never miss it. Now I surely know perfectly well that if I evade the payment of taxes this will not cause others to do so as well. For one thing, I am certainly not so foolish as to publicize my action. But even if I were, and the fact became known, this would still not cause others to do the same, unless it also became known that I was being allowed to get away with it. In the latter case the practice might tend to become widespread, but this would be a consequence, not of my action, but of the failure of the government to take action against me. Thus there is no question of my act being wrong because it would set a bad example. It would set no such example, and to suppose that it must, because it would be wrong, is simply a confusion. . . . Given all this, then if the reasons mentioned would justify me in evading the payment of taxes, they would justify everyone whatsoever in doing the same thing. For everyone can argue in the same way— everyone can argue that if he breaks the law this will not cause others to do

---

[17] This is a particular illustration of the more general claim that for one reason or another utilitarianism cannot be a defensible or intelligible moral theory when construed as permitting one's moral obligation to do any particular action to be overridden by a direct appeal to the consequences of performing that particular action. For recent statements of the claim see, *e.g.*, NOWELL-SMITH, *op. cit. supra* note 10; Rawls, *Two Concepts of Rules*, 64 PHILOSOPHICAL REV. 3 (1955), in OLAFSON, SOCIETY, LAW, AND MORALITY 420 (1961); SINGER, GENERALIZATION IN ETHICS 61–138, 178–216 (1961); TOULMIN, *op. cit. supra* note 15, at 144–65; Harrison, *Utilitarianism, Universalisation, and Our Duty To Be Just*, 53 ARISTOTELIAN SOC'Y PROCEEDINGS 105 (1952–53).

For some criticisms of this restriction on utilitarianism see, *e.g.*, WASSERSTROM, THE JUDICIAL DECISION 118–37 (1961). But see Hart, *Book Review*, 14 STAN. L. REV. 919, 924–26 (1962).

the same. The supposition that this is a justification, therefore, leads to a contradiction.

I conclude from this that, just as the reply "Not everyone will do it" is irrelevant to the generalization argument, so is the fact that one knows or believes that not everyone will do the same; and that, in particular, the characteristic of knowing or believing that one's act will remain exceptional cannot be used to define a class of exceptions to the rule. One's knowledge or belief that not everyone will act in the same way in similar circumstances cannot therefore be regarded as part of the circumstances of one's action. One's belief that not everyone will do the same does not make one's circumstances relevantly different from the circumstances of others, or relevantly different from those in which the act is wrong. Indeed, on the supposition that it does, one's circumstances could never be specified, for the specification would involve an infinite regress.[18]

Singer's argument is open to at least two different interpretations. One quite weak interpretation is this: A person cannot be morally justified in acting as he does unless he is prepared to acknowledge that everyone else in the identical circumstances would also be right in acting the same way. If the person insists that he is justified in performing a certain action because the consequences of acting in that way are more desirable than those of acting in any alternative fashion, then he must be prepared to acknowledge that anyone else would also be justified in doing that action whenever the consequences of doing that action were more desirable than those of acting in any alternative fashion. To take Singer's own example: A person, A, could not be morally justified in evading the payment of his taxes on the grounds that the consequences of nonpayment were *in his case* more beneficial, all things considered, than those of payment, unless A were prepared to acknowledge that any other person, X, would also be justified in evading his, *i.e.*, X's taxes, if it is the case that the consequences of X's nonpayment would in X's case be more beneficial, all things considered, than those of payment. If this is Singer's point, it is, for reasons already elaborated, unobjectionable.[19]

But Singer seems to want to make a stronger point as well. He seems to believe that even a willingness to generalize in this fashion could not justify acting in this way. In part his argument appears to be that this

---

[18] SINGER, *op. cit. supra* note 17, at 149–50.

[19] Neither Singer nor I have adequately refuted the confirmed ethical egoist who insists that he is prepared to generalize but only in the sense that X's nonpayment is justified if, and only if, the consequences of X's nonpayment would in X's case be more beneficial to A than those of payment. This is a problem which surely requires more careful attention than it typically receives. It will not do simply to insist that the egoist does not understand ordinary moral discourse. Instead, what must be demonstrated are the respects in which the egoist's position is an inherently unjust one. But to make this showing is beyond the scope of this article.

somehow will permit everyone to justify nonpayment of taxes; and in part his argument appears to be that there is a logical absurdity involved in attempting to make the likelihood of other people's behavior part of the specification of the relevant consequences of a particular act. Both of these points are wrong. To begin with, on a common sense level it is surely true that the effect which one's action will have on other people's behavior is a relevant consideration. For as was pointed out earlier, if *A* determines that other people will be, or may be, led to evade *their* taxes even when the consequences of nonpayment will in their cases be less beneficial than those of payment, then this is a consequence of *A*'s action which he must take into account and attempt to balance against the benefits which would accrue to society from his nonpayment. Conversely, if for one reason or another *A* can determine that his act of nonpayment will not have this consequence, this, too, must be relevant. In this sense, at least, other people's prospective behavior is a relevant consideration.

More importantly, perhaps, it is surely a mistake—although a very prevalent one in recent moral philosophy—to suppose that permitting a general appeal to consequences would enable everyone to argue convincingly that he is justified in evading his taxes. Even if I adopt the principle that everyone is justified in evading his taxes whenever the consequences of evasion are on the whole less deleterious than those of payment, this in no way entails that I or anyone else will always, or ever, be justified in evading my taxes. It surely need not turn out to be the case—even if no one else will evade his taxes—that the consequences will on the whole be beneficial if I succeed in evading mine. It might surely be the case that I will spend the money saved improvidently or foolishly; it might very well be true that the government will make much better use of the money. Indeed, the crucial condition which must not be ignored and which Singer does ignore is the condition which stipulates that the avoidance of one's taxes in fact be optimific, that is, more desirable than any other course of conduct.

The general point is simply that it is an empirical question—at least in theory—what the consequences of any action will be. And it would surely be a mistake for me or anyone else to suppose that that action whose consequences are most pleasing to me—in either the short or long run—will in fact be identical with that action whose consequences are on the whole most beneficial to society. Where the demands of self-interest are strong, as in the case of the performance of an unpleasant task like paying taxes, there are particular reasons for being skeptical of one's conclusion that the consequences of nonpayment would in one's own case truly be beneficial. But once again there is no reason why there might not be cases in which evasion of taxes would be truly justified, nor is there any reason why someone could not consistently and 373 defensibly endorse nonpayment whenever these circumstances were in fact present.

There is one final point which Singer's discussion suggests and which does appear to create something of a puzzle. Suppose that I believe that I am justified in deliberately trespassing on an atomic test site, and thereby disobeying the law, because I conclude that this is the best way to call attention to the possible consequences of continued atmospheric testing or nuclear war. I conclude that the consequences of trespassing will on the whole be more beneficial than any alternative action I can take. But suppose I also concede—what very well may be the case— that if everyone were to trespass, even for this same reason and in the same way, the consequences would be extremely deleterious. Does it follow that there is something logically incoherent about my principle of action? It looks as though there is, for it appears that I am here denying others the right to do precisely what I claim I am right in doing. I seem to be claiming, in effect, that it is right for me to trespass on government property in order to protest atomic testing only if it is the case that others, even under identical circumstances, will not trespass. Thus, it might be argued, I appear to be unwilling or unable to generalize my principle of conduct.

This argument is unsound, for there is a perfectly good sense in which I am acting on a principle which is coherent and which is open to anyone to adopt. It is simply the principle that one is justified in trespassing on government property whenever—among other things—it happens to be the case that one can say accurately that others will not in fact act on that same principle. Whether anyone else will at any given time act on any particular principle is an empirical question. It is, to repeat what has already been said, one of the possible circumstances which can be part of the description of a class of situations. There is, in short, nothing logically self-contradictory or absurd about making the likelihood of even identical action one of the relevant justifying considerations. And there is, therefore, no reason why the justifiability of any particular act of disobedience cannot depend, among other things, upon the probable conduct of others.

IV

It would not be at all surprising if at this stage one were to feel considerable dissatisfaction with the entire cast of the discussion so far. In particular, one might well believe that the proverbial dead horse has received still another flaying for the simple reason that no one has ever seriously argued that people are never justified in disobeying the law. One might insist, for instance, that neither Socrates nor President Kennedy were talking about all law in all legal systems everywhere. And one might urge, instead, that their claims concerning the unjustifiability of any act of disobedience rest covertly, if not overtly, on the assumption that the disobedience in question was to take place in a society in which the lawmaking procedures and other political institutions were those which are characteristic of an essentially democratic, or free, society. This is, of course, an important and plausible restriction upon the original claim, and the arguments which might support it must now be considered.

While there are several things about a liberal, democratic or free society which might be thought to preclude the possibility of justified disobedience, it is evident that the presence of all the important constitutive institutions *cannot* guarantee that unjust or immoral laws will not be enacted. For the strictest adherence to principles of representative government, majority rule, frequent and open elections and, indeed, the realization of all of the other characteristics of such a society, in no way can insure that laws of manifest immorality will not be passed and enforced. And if even the ideal democratic society might enact unjust laws, no existing society can plausibly claim as much. Thus, if the case against the possibility of justified disobedience is to depend upon the democratic nature of the society in question, the case cannot rest simply on the claim that the only actions which will be made illegal are those which are already immoral.

What then are the arguments which might plausibly be advanced? One very common argument goes like this: It is, of course, true that even democratically selected and democratically constituted legislatures can and do make mistakes. Nevertheless, a person is never justified in disobeying the law as long as there exist alternative, "peaceful" procedures by which to bring about the amendment or repeal of undesirable or oppressive laws. The genuine possibility that rational persuasion and argument can bring a majority to favor any one of a variety of competing views, both requires that disapproval always be permitted and forbids that disobedience ever be allowed. This is so for several reasons.

First, it is clearly unfair and obviously inequitable to accept the results of any social decision-procedure only in those cases in which the decision reached was one of which one approves, and to refuse to accept those decisions which are not personally satisfying. If there is one thing which participation, and especially voluntary participation, in a decision-procedure entails, it is that all of the participants must abide by the decision regardless of what it happens to be. If the decision-procedure is that of majority rule, then this means that any person must abide by those decisions in which he was in a minority just as much as it means that he can insist that members of the minority abide when he is a member of the majority.

As familiar as the argument is, its plausibility is far from assured. On one reading, at least, it appears to be one version of the universalization 375 argument. As such, it goes like this. Imagine any person, *A*, who has voted with the majority to pass a law making a particular kind of conduct illegal. *A* surely would not and could not acknowledge the right of any person voting with the minority justifiably to disobey that law. But, if *A* will not and cannot recognize a right of justified disobedience here, then *A* certainly cannot consistently or fairly claim any right of justified disobedience on his part in those cases in which he, *A*, happened to end up being in a minority. Thus, justified disobedience can never be defensible.

This argument is fallacious. For a person who would insist that justified disobedience was possible even after majoritarian decision-making could very plausibly and consistently acknowledge the right of any person to disobey the law under appropriate circumstances regardless of how that person had voted on any particular law. Consider, once again, the case already put of the doctor and the pregnant girl. The doctor can surely be consistent in claiming both that circumstances make the performance of the illegal abortion justified and that any comparable action would also be right irrespective of how the actor, or the doctor, or anyone else, happened to have voted on the abortion law, or any other law. The point is simply that there is no reason why any person cannot consistently: (1) hold the view that majority decision-making is the best of all forms of decision-making; (2) participate voluntarily in the decision-making process; and (3) believe that it is right for *anyone* to disobey majority decisions whenever the relevant moral circumstances obtain, *e.g.,* whenever the consequence of obedience to that law at that time would on the whole be more deleterious than those of obedience.

But this may be deemed too facile an answer; it also may be thought to miss the point. For it might be argued that there is a serious logical inconsistency of a different sort which must arise whenever a voluntary participant in a social decision-procedure claims that not all the decisions reached in accordance with that procedure need be obeyed. Take the case of majority rule. It is inconsistent for anyone voluntarily to participate in the decision-process and yet at the same time to reserve the right to refuse to abide by the decision reached in any particular case. The problem is not an inability to universalize a principle of action. The problem is rather that of making any sense at all out of the notion of having a majority decide anything—of having a procedure by which to make group decisions. The problem is, in addition, that of making any sense at all out of the fact of voluntary participation in the decision-procedure—in knowing what this participation can come to if it does not mean that every participant is bound by all of the decisions which are reached. What can their participation mean if it is not an implicit promise to abide by all decisions reached? And even if the point is not a logical one, it is surely a practical one. What good could there possibly be to a scheme, an institutional means for making social decisions, which did not bind even the participants to anything?

The answer to this argument—or set of arguments—is wholly analogous to that which has been given earlier. But because of the importance and prevalence of the argument some repetition is in order.

One can simply assert that the notion of any social decision-making procedure is intelligible only if it entails that all participants always abide by all of the decisions which are made, no matter what those decisions are. Concomitantly, one can simply insist that any voluntary participant in the decision-process must be consenting or promising to abide by all decisions which are reached. But one cannot give as a plausible reason for this assertion the fact that the notion of group decision-making becomes incoherent if anything less in the way of adherence is required of all participants. And one cannot cite as a plausible reason for this assertion the fact that the notion of voluntary participation loses all meaning if anything less than a promise of absolute obedience is inferred.

It is true that the notion of a group decision-making procedure would be a meaningless notion if there were no respects in which a group decision was in any way binding upon each of the participants. Decisions which in no way bind anyone to do anything are simply not decisions. And it is also true that voluntary participation is an idle, if not a vicious, act if it does not commit each participant to something. If any voluntary participant properly can wholly ignore the decisions which are reached, then something is surely amiss.

But to say all this is not to say very much. Group decision-making can have a point just because it does preclude any participant from taking some actions which in the absence of the decision, he might have been justified in performing. And voluntary participation can still constitute a promise of sorts that one will not perform actions which, in the absence of voluntary participation, might have been justifiable. If the fact of participation in a set of liberal political institutions does constitute a promise of sorts, it can surely be a promise that the participant will not disobey a law just because obedience would be inconvenient or deleterious to him. And if this is the scope of the promise, then the fact of voluntary participation does make a difference. For in the absence of the participation in the decision to make this conduct illegal, inconvenience to the actor might well have been a good reason for acting in a certain way. Thus, participation can create new obligations to behave in certain ways without constituting a promise not to disobey the law under any circumstances. And if this is the case, adherence to a principle of justified disobedience is not inconsistent with voluntary participation in the decision-making process.

Indeed, a strong point can be made. The notion of making laws 377 through voluntary participation in democratic institutions is not even inconsistent with the insistence that disobedience is justified whenever the consequences of disobedience are on the whole more beneficial than those of obedience. This is so because a promise can be a meaningful promise even if an appeal to the consequences of performing the promise can count as a sufficient reason for not performing the promise.[20]

[20] The point here is analogous to that made in the discussion of Singer's argument. Moral philosophers have often argued that one cannot appeal simply to the consequences of performing or not performing a particular promise as a reason for not performing that promise. And the reason why this is so is that the notion of having promised to do something would be unintelligible if the promisor could always, when the time came for performance, be excused if it were the case that the consequences of nonperformance were more beneficial than those of performance. This would make promising unintelligible, so the argument goes, because promising entails or means obligating oneself to do something. But if the appeal to consequences is what is to be determinative of one's obligations, then the promise becomes a wholly superfluous, meaningless act. Rawls, for instance, puts the point this way: "Various defenses for not keeping one's promise are allowed, but among them there isn't the one that, on general utilitarian grounds, the promisor (truly) thought his action best on the whole, even though there may be the defense that the consequences of keeping one's promise would have been *extremely* severe. While there are too many complexities here to consider all the necessary details, one can see that the general defense isn't allowed if one asks the following question: what would one say of someone who, when asked why he broke his promise, replied simply that breaking it was best on the whole? Assuming that his reply is sincere, and that his belief was reasonable (i.e., one need not consider the possibility that he was mistaken), I think that one would question whether or not he knows what it means to say 'I promise' (in the appropriate circumstances). It would be said of someone who used this excuse without further explanation that he didn't understand what defenses the practice, which defines a promise, allows to him. If a child were to use this excuse one would correct him; for it is part of the way one is taught the concept of a promise to be corrected if one uses this excuse. The point of having the practice would be lost if the practice did allow this excuse." Rawls, *supra* note 17, at 17, in OLAFSON, *op. cit. supra* note 17, at 429–30.

Now I am not concerned to dispute Rawls' remark if taken as descriptive of our institution of promising. For what I am here concerned with is the claim, implicit throughout, that promising would be a meaningless or pointless activity if the excuse were permitted. I should say though that the passage quoted from Rawls is not, I think, central to his main argument. I think I can show this to be a mistake through the following two examples.

(1) *A* has promised *B* that he will mow *B*'s lawn for *B* on Sunday. On Sunday, *A* is feeling lazy and so he refuses to mow the lawn.

(2) *A* is sitting home on Sunday, feeling lazy, when *B* calls him up and asks him to come over and mow *B*'s lawn. *A* refuses to mow the lawn.

Ceteris paribus, it would be the case that *A* is wrong in refusing to mow *B*'s lawn in example (1) but not blamable for refusing to mow *B*'s lawn in example (2). Why is this so? Because *A*'s promise to mow *B*'s lawn creates an obligation which in the absence of such a promise is nonexistent. If this is so, then permitting the general utilitarian defense does not make a promise a meaningless gesture. This is so because there are many situations in which, in the absence of having promised to do so, we are not, for example, obligated to inconvenience ourselves

And if this is the case for promises generally, it can be no less the case for the supposed promise to obey the law.

Finally, even if it were correct that voluntary participation implied a promise to obey, and even if it were the case that the promise must be a promise not to disobey on consequential grounds, all of this would still not justify the conclusion that one ought never to disobey the law. It would, instead, only demonstrate that disobeying the law must be prima facie wrong, that everyone has a prima facie obligation to obey the law. This is so just because it is sometimes right even to break one's own promises. And if this, too, is a characteristic of promises generally, it is, again, no less a characteristic of the promise to obey the law.

The notions of promise, consent, or voluntary participation do not, however, exhaust the possible sources of the obligation to obey the laws of a democracy. In particular, there is another set of arguments which remains to be considered. It is that which locates the rightness of obedience in the way in which any act of disobedience improperly distributes certain burdens and benefits among the citizenry. Professor Wechsler, for example, sees any act of disobedience to the laws of the United States as "the ultimate negation of all neutral principles, to take the benefits accorded by the constitutional system, including the national market and common defense, while denying it allegiance when a special burden is imposed. That certainly is the antithesis of law."[21]

On the surface, at least, Professor Wechsler's claim seems overly simple; it appears to be the blanket assertion that the receipt by any citizen, through continued, voluntary presence of benefits of this character necessarily implies that no act of disobedience could be justified. To disobey any law after having voluntarily received these benefits would be, he seems to suggest, so unjust that there could never be overriding considerations. This surely is both to claim too much for the benefits of personal and commercial security and to say too little for the character of all types of disobedience. For even if the receipt of benefits such as these did simply impose an obligation to obey the law, it is implausible to suppose that the obligation thereby imposed would be one that stringent.

But there is a more involved aspect of Professor Wechsler's thesis—particularly in his insistence that disobedience of the law, where benefits of this kind have been received, is the negation of all neutral principles. I am not at all certain that I understand precisely what this means, but there are at least two possible interpretations: (1) Unless everyone al-

---

simply for another's convenience. Personal inconvenience then might be one excuse which must be inconsistent with the practice of promising, even if the general appeal to consequences is not. Thus, promising would and could have a real point even if the general appeal to consequences were a good defense.

[21] Wechsler, *Toward Neutral Principles of Constitutional Law,* 73 HARV. L. REV. 1, 35 (1959).

ways obeyed the law no one would receive these obviously valuable benefits. (2) Since the benefits one receives depend upon the prevalence of conditions of uniform obedience, it follows that no one who willingly receives these benefits can justly claim them without himself obeying. The first has already been sufficiently considered.[22] The second, while not unfamiliar, merits some further attention.

In somewhat expanded form, the argument is simply this. What makes it possible for any particular person to receive and enjoy the benefits of general, personal and economic security is the fact that everyone else obeys the law. Now, if injustice is to be avoided, it is surely the case that any other person is equally entitled to these same benefits. But he will have this security only if everyone else obeys the law. Hence the receipt of benefits at others' expense requires repayment in kind. And this means universal obedience to the law.[23]

There are two features of this argument which are puzzling. First, it is far from clear that the benefits of security received by anyone necessarily depend upon absolute obedience on the part of everyone else. It just might be the case that an even greater quantum of security would

---

[22] See text at section III.

[23] For a somewhat related characterization of the source of the obligation to obey the law, see Hart, *Are There Any Natural Rights?*, 64 PHILOSOPHICAL REV. 175, 185 (1955), in OLAFSON, LAW, SOCIETY, AND MORALITY 173, 180–81 (1961): "A third very important source of special rights and obligations which we recognize in many spheres of life is what may be termed mutuality of restrictions. . . . In its bare schematic outline it is this: when a number of persons conduct any joint enterprise according to rules and thus restrict their liberty, those who have submitted to these restrictions when required have a right to a similar submission from those who have benefited by their submission. The rules may provide that officials should have authority to enforce obedience and make further rules, and this will create a structure of legal rights and duties, but the moral obligation to obey the rules in such circumstances is *due to* the co-operating members of the society, and they have the correlative moral right to obedience. In social situations of this sort (of which political society is the most complex example) the obligation to obey the rules is something distinct from whatever other moral obligations there may be for obedience in terms of good consequences (*e.g.*, the prevention of suffering); the obligation is due to the co-operating members of the society as such and not because they are human beings on whom it would be wrong to inflict suffering."

I would point out only two things. First, as Professor Hart himself asserts—in a passage not quoted—the existence of this right in no way implies that one is never justified in disobeying the law. The right which any participating member has in others' obedience can justifiably be infringed in appropriate circumstances. Second, and here perhaps Professor Hart disagrees for reasons already elaborated, there is no reason that I can see why an appeal to the consequences of disobeying a particular law cannot be a sufficient justification for infringing upon that right. It is surely conceivable, at least, that this is all the submission to rules which anyone ought to have given, and hence all the submission which anyone is entitled to expect from others.

have accrued from something less than total obedience. But even if I am wrong here, there is a more important point at issue. For reasons already discussed, it is undeniable that even in a democracy a price would be paid for universal obedience—the price that might have to be paid, for instance, were the doctor to refuse to perform the abortion because it was illegal. If this is so, then the fact that a person received benefits from everyone else's obedience does not necessarily entail that it is unjust for him to fail to reciprocate in kind. The benefit of general security might not have been worth the cost. A greater degree of flexibility on the part of others, a general course of obedience except where disobedience was justified, might have yielded a greater benefit. People may, in short, have done more or less than they should have. And if they did, the fact that anyone or everyone benefitted to some degree in no way requires that injustice can only be avoided through like and reciprocal conduct. If it is better, in at least some circumstances, to disobey a law than to obey it, there is surely nothing unjust about increasing the beneficial consequences to all through acts of *discriminate* disobedience.

If the argument based upon the effect of receipt of certain benefits is therefore not very persuasive, neither in most cases is the argument which is derived from the way in which any act of disobedience is thought to distribute burdens unfairly among the citizenry. The argument can be put very briefly: If there is one thing which any act of disobedience inevitably does, it is to increase the burdens which fall on all the law-abiding citizens. If someone disobeys the law even for what seems to be the best of reasons, he inevitably makes it harder—in some quite concrete sense—on everyone else. Hence, at a minimum this is a good reason not to disobey the law, and perhaps a sufficient reason as well.

This argument is appealing because there is at least one kind of case it fits very well. It is the case of taxation. For suppose the following, only somewhat unreal, conditions: that the government is determined to raise a specified sum of money through taxation, and that, in the long, if not the short, run it will do so by adjusting the tax rate to whatever percentage is necessary to produce the desired governmental income. Under such circumstances it could plausibly be argued that one of the truly inevitable results of a successfully executed decision to evade the payment of one's taxes—a decision made, moreover, on ostensibly justifiable grounds—is that every other member of society will thereby be required to pay a greater tax than would otherwise have been the case. Thus in some reasonably direct and obvious fashion any act of disobedience—particularly if undetected—does add to the burdens of everyone else. And surely this is to make out at least a strong case of prima facie injustice.

Now, for reasons already elaborated, it would be improper to conclude that evasion of one's taxes could never be justified. But the argument is persuasive in its insistence that it does provide a very good 381 reason why evasion always must be justified and why it will seldom be justifiable. But even this feature of disobedience is not present in many cases. Tax evasion, as opposed to other kinds of potentially justified disobedience, is a special, far from typical case. And what is peculiar to it is precisely the fact that any act of disobedience to the tax laws arguably shifts or increases the burden upon others. Such is simply not true of most types of acts of disobedience because most laws do not prohibit or require actions which affect the distribution of resources in any very direct fashion.

Thus, if we take once again the case of the doctor who has decided that he is justified in performing an illegal abortion on the pregnant girl, it is extremely difficult, if not impossible, to locate the analogue of the shifting of burdens involved in tax evasion. How does the performance of the abortion thereby increase the "costs" to anyone else? The only suggestion which seems at all plausible is that which was noted earlier in a somewhat different context. Someone might argue that it is the occurrence of illegal actions which increase the cost of maintaining a police force, a judiciary and suitable correctional institutions. This cost is a burden which is borne by the citizenry as a whole. And hence, the doctor's illegal acts increase their burdens—albeit very slightly. The difficulty here is threefold. First, if the doctor's act is performed in secret and if it remains undetected, then it is hard to see how there is any shift of economic burden at all. Second, given the fact that police forces, courts and prisons will always be necessary as long as unjustified acts of disobedience are a feature of social existence, it is by no means apparent that the additional cost is anything but truly de minimus.[24] And third, the added costs, if any, are in the doctor's case assumed by the doctor *qua* member of the citizenry. He is not avoiding a burden; at most he adds something to everyone's—including his own—existing financial obligations. Thus, in cases such as these, it is not at all evident that disobedience need even be prima facie unjust and hence unjustified.

V

There is one final argument which requires brief elucidation and analysis. It is in certain respects a peculiarly instructive one both in its own right and in respect to the thesis of this article.

It may be true that on some particular occasions the consequences of disobeying a law will in fact be less deleterious on the whole than those of obeying it—even in a democracy. It may even be true that on some particular occasions disobeying a law will be just whereas obeying it

---

[24] Curiously, perhaps, given a legal system in which laws are in general good and hence in which the possibility of justified disobedience is rare, the special or added cost of an occasional act of justified disobedience is diminished still further.

would be unjust. Nevertheless, the reason why a person is never justified in disobeying a law—in a democracy—is simply this: The chances are so slight that he will disobey only those laws in only those cases in which he is in fact justified in doing so, that the consequences will on the whole be less deleterious if he never disobeys any law. Furthermore, since anyone must concede the right to everyone to disobey the law when the circumstances so demand it, the situation is made still worse. For once we entrust this right to everyone we can be sure that many laws will be disobeyed in a multitude of cases in which there was no real justification for disobedience. Thus, given what we know of the possibilities of human error and the actualities of human frailty, and given the tendency of democratic societies to make illegal only those actions which would, even in the absence of a law, be unjustified, we can confidently conclude that the consequences will on the whole and in the long run be best if no one ever takes it upon himself to "second-guess" the laws and to conclude that in his case his disobedience is justified.[25]

The argument is, in part, not very different from those previously considered. And thus, what is to be said about it is not very different either. Nonetheless, upon pain of being overly repetitive, I would insist that there is a weak sense in which the argument is quite persuasive and a strong sense in which it is not. For the argument makes, on one reading, too strong an empirical claim—the claim that the consequences will in the long run always in fact be better if no one in a democracy ever tries to decide when he is justified in disobeying the law. As it stands, there is no reason to believe that the claim is or must be true, that the consequences will always be better. Indeed, it is very hard to see why, despite the hypothesis, someone might still not be justified in some particular case in disobeying a law. Yet, viewed as a weaker claim, as a summary rule, it does embody a good deal that is worth remembering. It can, on this level, be understood to be a persuasive reminder of much that is relevant to disobedience: that in a democracy the chances of having to live under bad laws are reduced; that in a democracy there are typically less costly means available by which to bring about changes in the law; that in a democracy—as in life in general—a justified action may always be both inaptly and ineptly emulated; and that in a democracy—as in life in general—people often do make mistakes as to which of their own actions are truly justified. These are some of the lessons of human experience which are easy to forget and painful to relearn.

But there are other lessons, and they are worth remembering too. What is especially troubling about the claim that disobedience of the law is never justified, what is even disturbing about the claim that disobedience of the law is never justified in a democratic or liberal society, is the

---

[25] For fuller analyses and assessments of this argument in different contexts see, e.g., Rawls, *supra* note 17; WASSERSTROM, *op. cit. supra* note 17, at 118–71.

facility with which its acceptance can lead to the neglect of important moral issues. If no one is justified in disobeying the Supreme Court's decision in *Brown v. Board of Educ.*[26] this is so because, among other things, there is much that is wrong with segregation. If there was much that was peculiarly wrong in Mississippi this fall, this was due to the fact, among other facts, that a mob howled and a governor raged when a court held that a person whose skin was black could go to a white university. Disobeying the law is often—even usually—wrong; but this is so largely because the illegal is usually restricted to the immoral and because morally right conduct is still less often illegal. But we must always be sensitive to the fact that this has not always been the case, is not now always the case and need not always be the case in the future. And undue concentration upon what is wrong with disobeying the law rather than upon the wrong which the law seeks to prevent can seriously weaken and misdirect that awareness.

M. B. E. SMITH
Is There a Prima Facie Obligation to Obey the Law?

It isn't a question of whether it was legal or illegal. That isn't enough. The question is, was it morally wrong?
—Richard Nixon, "Checkers Speech" 1952.

Many political philosophers have thought it obvious that there is a prima facie obligation to obey the law; and so, in discussing this obligation, they have thought their task to be more that of explaining its basis than of arguing for its existence. John Rawls has, for example, written:

I shall assume, as requiring no argument, that there is, at least in a society such as ours, a moral obligation to obey the law, although it may, of course, be overriden in certain cases by other more stringent obligations.[1]

---

26 347 U.S. 483 (1954).

Reprinted by permission of the author, The Yale Law Journal Company and Fred B. Rothman & Company from *The Yale Law Journal*, Vol. 82 (1973), 950–976.

I wish to thank Judith Jarvis Thomson, Hugo A. Bedau, Gerald Barnes, Murray Kiteley, Robert Ackermann, and Stanley Rothman, for their criticism of earlier drafts of this article.

1 Rawls, *Legal Obligation and the Duty of Fair Play,* in LAW AND PHILOSOPHY 3 (S. Hook ed. 1964).

As against this, I suggest that it is not at all obvious that there is such an obligation, that this is something that must be shown, rather than so blithely assumed. Indeed, were he uninfluenced by conventional wisdom, a reflective man might on first considering the question be inclined to deny any such obligation: As H. A. Prichard once remarked, "the mere receipt of an order backed by force seems, if anything, to give rise to the duty of resisting, rather than obeying."[2]

I shall argue that, although those subject to a government often have a prima facie obligation to obey particular laws (*e.g.*, when disobedience has seriously untoward consequences or involves an act that is *mala in se*), they have no prima facie obligation to obey all its laws. I do not hope to prove this contention beyond a reasonable doubt: My goal is rather the more modest one of showing that it is a reasonable position to maintain by first criticizing arguments that purport to establish the obligation and then presenting some positive argument against it.

First, however, I must explain how I use the phrase "prima facie obligation." I shall say that a person S has a prima facie obligation to do an act X if, and only if, there is a moral reason for S to do X which is such that, unless he has a moral reason not to do X at least as strong as his reason to do X, S's failure to do X is wrong.[3] In this discussion it will also be convenient to distinguish two kinds of prima facie obligation via the difference between the two kinds of statement which ascribe them. A specific statement asserts that some particular person has a prima facie obligation to perform some particular act. In contrast, a generic statement (*e.g.*, "Parents have a prima facie obligation to care for their infant children") asserts that everyone who meets a certain description has a prima facie obligation to perform a certain kind of act whenever he has an opportunity to do so. I shall therefore say that a person S has a *specific* prima facie obligation to do X if, and only if, the specific statement "S has a prima facie obligation to do X" is true; and that he has a *generic* prima facie obligation to do X if, and only if, S meets some description D and the generic statement "Those who are D have a prima facie obligation to do X" is true.[4]

[2] H. A. PRICHARD, *Green's Principles of Political Obligation*, in MORAL OBLIGATION 54 (1949).

[3] The distinction between prima facie and absolute obligation was first made by W.D. ROSS in THE RIGHT AND THE GOOD ch. 2 (1930). My account of prima facie obligation differs somewhat from Ross; but I believe it adequately captures current philosophical usage. As for absolute obligation, I shall not often speak of it; but when I do, what I shall mean by "S has an absolute obligation to do X" is that "S's failure to do X is wrong."

[4] My motive for distinguishing generic and specific prima facie obligations is simply convenience, and not because I think it provides a perspicuous way of classifying prima facie obligations. As a classification it is obviously defective: The two kinds of obligation overlap, since in a trivial sense every specific obligation can be construed as a generic one; and there are some prima facie obligations (*e.g.*, the obligation to keep one's promise), that fit neither definition.

Now, the question of whether there is a prima facie obligation to obey the law is clearly about a generic obligation. Everyone, even the anarchist, would agree that in many circumstances individuals have specific prima facie obligations to obey specific laws. Since it is clear that there is in most circumstances a specific prima facie obligation to refrain from murder, rape, or breach of contract, it is plain that in these circumstances each of us has a specific prima facie obligation not to violate laws which prohibit these acts. Again, disobeying the law often has seriously untoward consequences; and, when this is so, virtually everyone would agree that there is a specific prima facie obligation to obey. Therefore, the interesting question about our obligation vis-à-vis the law is not "Do individual citizens ever have specific prima facie obligations to obey particular laws?," but rather "Is the moral relation of any government to its citizens such that they have a prima facie obligation to do certain things merely because they are legally required to do so?" This is, of course, equivalent to asking "Is there a generic prima facie obligation to obey the law?" Hereafter, when I use the phrase "the prima facie obligation to obey the law" I shall be referring to a generic obligation.

One final point in clarification: As used here, the phrase "prima facie" bears a different meaning than it does when used in legal writing. In legal materials, the phrase frequently refers to evidence sufficiently persuasive so as to require rebuttal. Hence, were a lawyer to ask "Is there a prima facie obligation to obey the law?," a reasonable interpretation of his question might be "May a reasonable man take mere illegality to be sufficient evidence that an act is morally wrong, so long as there is no specific evidence tending to show it is right?" Let us call this the "lawyer's question." Now, the question of primary concern in this inquiry is "Is there any society in which mere illegality is a moral reason for an act's being wrong?" The difference between these questions is that, were there a prima facie obligation to obey the law in the lawyer's sense, mere illegality would, in the absence of specific evidence to the contrary, be evidence of wrongdoing, but it would not necessarily be relevant to a determination of whether lawbreaking is wrong where there is reason to think such conduct justified or even absolutely obligatory. In contrast, if there is a prima facie obligation to obey the law in the sense in which I am using the phrase, the mere illegality of an act is always relevant to the determination of its moral character, despite whatever other reasons are present.[5] Hence, there may be a prima facie obligation to obey the

---

[5] An example may help to make the point clear. If I promise that I will meet someone at a certain time, I have a prima facie obligation to keep my promise. Now, were this merely a prima facie obligation in the lawyer's sense, without evidence to the contrary the fact that I had promised would be sufficient to hold that a breach of my promise was wrong, yet it would not be evidence of wrongdoing were there reason to believe the breach was justified or even obligatory. But,

law in the lawyer's sense and yet be no such obligation in the sense of the phrase used here. Near the end of this article I shall return briefly to the lawyer's question; for the present, I raise it only that it may not be confused with the question I wish to examine.

I

The arguments I shall examine fall into three groups: First, those which rest on the benefits each individual receives from government; second, those relying on implicit consent or promise; third, those which appeal to utility or the general good. I shall consider each group in turn.

Of those in the first group, I shall begin with the argument from gratitude. Although they differ greatly in the amount of benefits they provide, virtually all governments do confer substantial benefits on their subjects. Now, it is often claimed that, when a person accepts benefits from another, he thereby incurs a debt of gratitude towards his benefactor. Thus, if it be maintained that obedience to the law is the best way of showing gratitude towards one's government, it may with some plausibility be concluded that each person who has received benefits from his government has a prima facie obligation to obey the law.

On reflection, however, this argument is unconvincing. First, it may reasonably be doubted whether most citizens have an obligation to act gratefully towards their government. Ordinarily, if someone confers benefits on me without any consideration of whether I want them, and if he does this in order to advance some purpose other than promotion of my particular welfare, I have no obligation to be grateful towards him. Yet the most important benefits of government are not accepted by its citizens, but are rather enjoyed regardless of whether they are wanted. Moreover, a government typically confers these benefits, not to advance the interests of particular citizens, but rather as a consequence of advancing some purpose of its own. At times, its motives are wholly admirable, as when it seeks to promote the general welfare; at others, they are less so, as when it seeks to stay in power by catering to the demands of some powerful faction. But, such motives are irrelevant: Whenever government forces benefits on me for reasons other than my particular welfare, I clearly am under no obligation to be grateful to it.

---

in fact, this is not what we think of promising. We think that if someone promises to do a thing there is a strong moral reason for him to do it and that, although this reason may sometimes be opposed by stronger reasons to the contrary, its weight does not disappear. In such cases, my promise is yet relevant to what I am absolutely obligated to do, although it is not always determinative. But, even when this reason is outweighed, it still discloses its existence by imposing fresh prima facie obligations (*e.g.*, to tell the person I promised why I broke it). Hence, there is a prima facie obligation to keep one's promise in the sense in which I here use the phrase.

Second, even assuming *arguendo* that each citizen has an obligation to be grateful to his government, the argument still falters. It is perhaps true that cheerful and willing obedience is the best way to show one's gratitude towards government, in that it makes one's gratitude unmistakable. But, when a person owes a debt of gratitude towards another, he does not necessarily acquire a prima facie obligation to display his gratitude in the most convincing manner: A person with demanding, domineering parents might best display his gratitude towards them by catering to their every whim, but he surely has no prima facie obligation to do so. Without undertaking a lengthy case-by-case examination, one cannot delimit the prima facie obligation of acting gratefully, for its existence and extent depends on such factors as the nature of the benefits received, the manner in which they are conferred, the motives of the benefactor, and so forth. But, even without such an examination, it is clear that the mere fact that a person has conferred on me even the most momentous benefits does not establish his right to dictate all of my behavior; nor does it establish that I always have an obligation to consider his wishes when I am deciding what I shall do. If, then, we have a prima facie obligation to act gratefully towards government, we undoubtedly have an obligation to promote its interests when this does not involve great sacrifice on our part and to respect some of its wishes concerning that part of our behavior which does not directly affect its interests. But, our having this obligation to be grateful surely does not establish that we have a prima facie obligation to obey the law.

A more interesting argument from the benefits individuals receive from government is the argument from fair play. It differs from the argument from gratitude in contending that the prima facia obligation to obey the law is owed, not to one's government but rather to one's fellow citizens. Versions of this argument have been offered by H. L. A. Hart and John Rawls.

According to Hart, the mere existence of cooperative enterprise gives rise to a certain prima facie obligation. He argues that:

> when a number of persons conduct any joint enterprise according to rules and thus restrict their liberty, those who have submitted to these restrictions when required have a right to a similar submission from those who have benefitted by their submission. The rules may provide that officials should have authority to enforce obedience and make further rules, and this will create a structure of legal rights and duties, but the moral obligation to obey the rules in such circumstances is *due to* the cooperating members of the society, and they have the correlative moral right to obedience.[6]

[6] Hart, *Are There Any Natural Rights?*, 64 PHIL. REV. 185 (1955). I must note that Hart does not use the phrase "prima facie obligation," maintaining that his argument establishes an obligation *sans phrase* to comply with the rules of cooperative enterprises. However, since his use of "obligation" seems much the same as my use of "prima facie obligation," I shall ignore his terminological scruples.

Rawls' account of this obligation in his essay, *Legal Obligations and the Duty of Fair Play*,[7] is rather more complex. Unlike Hart, he sets certain requirements on the kinds of cooperative enterprises that give rise to the obligation: First, that success of the enterprise depends on near-universal obedience to its rules, but not on universal cooperation; second, that obedience to its rules involves some sacrifice, in that obeying the rules restricts one's liberty; and finally, that the enterprise conform to the principles of justice.[8] Rawls also offers an explanation of the obligation: He argues that, if a person benefits from participating in such an enterprise and if he intends to continue receiving its benefits, he acts unfairly when he refuses to obey its rules. With Hart, however, Rawls claims that this obligation is owed not to the enterprise itself, nor to its officials, but rather to those members whose obedience has made the benefits possible. Hart and Rawls also agree that this obligation of fair play—"fair play" is Rawls' term—is a fundamental obligation, not derived from utility or from mutual promise or consent.[9] Finally, both Hart and Rawls conceive of legal systems, at least those in democratic societies, as complex practices of the kind which give rise to the obligation of fair play; and they conclude that those who benefit from such legal systems have a prima facie obligation to obey their laws.

These arguments deserve great respect. Hart and Rawls appear to have isolated a kind of prima facie obligation overlooked by other philosophers and have thereby made a significant contribution to moral theory. However, the significance of their discovery to jurisprudence is less clear. Although Hart and Rawls have discovered the obligation of fair play, they do not properly appreciate its limits. Once these limits are understood, it is clear that the prima facie obligation to obey the law cannot be derived from the duty of fair play.

The obligation of fair play seems to arise most clearly within small, voluntary cooperative enterprises. Let us suppose that a number of persons have gone off into the wilderness to carve out a new society, and that they have adopted certain rules to govern their communal life. Their enterprise

---

[7] Rawls, *supra* note 1. The same argument appears, although in less detail, in Rawls, *Justice as Fairness*, 67 PHIL. REV. 164 (1958), and Rawls, *The Justification of Civil Disobedience*, in CIVIL DISOBEDIENCE: THEORY AND PRACTICE (H.A. Bedau ed. 1969).

[8] Rawls, *Legal Obligation and the Duty of Fair Play*, in LAW AND PHILOSOPHY 10 (S. Hook ed. 1964). According to Rawls, the principles of justice are

that everyone have an equal right to the most extensive liberty compatible with a like liberty for all; . . . [and] that inequalities are arbitrary unless it is reasonable to expect that they will work out for everyone's advantage and provided that the positions and offices to which they attached or from which they may be gained are open to all.

Id. at 11.

[9] *Id.* at 13; Hart, *supra* note 6, at 185.

meets Rawls' requirements on success, sacrifice, and justice. We can now examine the moral situation of the members of that community in a number of circumstances, taking seriously Hart's insistence that cooperating members have a right to the obedience of others and Rawls' explanation of this right and its correlative obligation on grounds of fairness.

Let us take two members of the community, A and B. B, we may suppose, has never disobeyed the rules, and A has benefitted from B's previous submission. Has B a right to A's obedience? It would seem necessary to know the consequences of A's obedience. If, in obeying the rules, A will confer on B a benefit roughly equal to those he has received from B, it would be plainly unfair for A to withhold it from B; and so, in this instance, B's right to A's obedience is clear. Similarly, if, in disobeying the rule, A will harm the community, B's right to A's obedience is again clear. This is because in harming the community A will harm B indirectly, by threatening the existence or efficient functioning of an institution on which B's vital interests depend. Since A has benefitted from B's previous submission to the rules, it is unfair for A to do something which will lessen B's chances of receiving like benefits in the future. However, if A's compliance with some particular rule does not benefit B and if his disobedience will not harm the community, it is difficult to see how fairness to B could dictate that A must comply. Surely, the fact that A has benefitted from B's submission does not give B the right to insist that A obey when B's interests are unaffected. A may in this situation have an obligation to obey, perhaps because he has promised or because his disobedience would be unfair to some other member; but, if he does disobey, he has surely not been unfair to B.

We may generalize from these examples. Considerations of fairness apparently do show that, when cooperation is perfect and when each member has benefitted from the submission of every other, each member of an enterprise has a prima facie obligation to obey its rules when obedience benefits some other member or when disobedience harms the enterprise. For, if in either circumstance a member disobeys, he is unfair to at least one other member and is perhaps unfair to them all. However, if a member disobeys when his obedience would have benefitted no other member and when his disobedience does no harm, his moral situation is surely different. If his disobedience is then unfair, it must be unfair to the group but not to any particular member. But this, I take it, is impossible: Although the moral properties of a group are not always a simple function of the moral properties of its members, it is evident that one cannot be unfair to a group without being unfair to any of its members. It would seem, then, that even when cooperation is perfect, considerations of fairness do not establish that members of a cooperative enterprise have a simple obligation to obey all of its rules, but have rather the more complex obligation to obey when 390 obedience benefits some other member or when disobedience harms the enterprise. This does not, it is worth noting, reduce the obligation of fair play to a kind of utilitarian obligation, for it may well be that fair play will dictate in certain circumstances that a man obey when disobedience would have better consequences. My point is merely that the obligation of fair play governs a man's actions only when some benefit or harm turns on whether he obeys. Surely, this is as should be, for questions of fairness typically arise from situations in which burdens or benefits are distributed or in which some harm is done.

The obligation of fair play is therefore much more complex than Hart or Rawls seem to have imagined. Indeed, the obligation is even more complex than the above discussion suggests, for the assumption of perfect cooperation is obviously unrealistic. When that assumption is abandoned, the effect of previous disobedience considered, and the inevitable disparity among the various members' sacrifice in obeying the rules taken into account, the scope of the obligation is still further limited; we shall then find that it requires different things of different members, depending on their previous pattern of compliance and the amount of sacrifice they have made.[10] These complications need not detain us, however, for they do not affect the fact that fairness requires obedience only in situations where non-compliance would withhold benefits from someone or harm the enterprise. Now it must be conceded that all of this makes little difference when we confine our attention to small, voluntary, cooperative enterprises. Virtually any disobedience may be expected to harm such enterprises to some extent, by diminishing the confidence of other members in its probable success and therefore reducing their incentive to work diligently towards it. Moreover, since they are typically governed by a relatively small number of rules, none of which ordinarily require behavior that is useless to other members, we may expect that when a member disobeys he will probably withhold a benefit from some other member and that he has in the past

---

[10] Those intrigued by the mention of these additional factors may be interested to know that, when imperfect cooperation is taken into account, it can be shown that considerations of fairness establish no more than: (1) that a member A of a co-operative enterprise has a prima facie obligation to obey when his obedience will benefit some other member B from whose submission A has previously benefitted and it is not the case that B has withheld from A more significant benefits than A withholds from $B;$ and (2) that A has a prima facie obligation to obey when his disobedience harms the enterprise and there is some other member B from whose submission A has previously benefitted and B has by his disobedience harmed the enterprise less than the harm which would be done by $A's$ disobedience.

As for the effect of disparity in sacrifice, it was only recently suggested to me that this factor must be taken into account, and I have not yet attempted to determine its effects precisely. A moment's reflection discloses, however, that this additional factor would make the obligation still more complex. Were anyone to attempt a precise specification of the citizen's obligations vis-à-vis the laws of his government, he would have to master these complexities; but my task is not so ambitious.

benefitted significantly from that member's obedience. We may therefore expect that virtually every time the rules of a small, voluntary enterprise call on a member to obey he will have a specific prima facie obligation to do so because of his obligation of fair play.

In the case of legal systems, however, the complexity of the obligation makes a great deal of difference. Although their success may depend on the "habit of obedience" of a majority of their subjects, all legal systems are designed to cope with a substantial amount of disobedience.[11] Hence, individual acts of disobedience to the law only rarely have an untoward effect on legal systems. What is more, because laws must necessarily be designed to cover large numbers of cases, obedience to the law often benefits no one. Perhaps the best illustration is obedience of the traffic code: Very often I benefit no one when I stop at a red light or observe the speed limit. Finally, virtually every legal system contains a number of pointless or even positively harmful laws, obedience to which either benefits no one or, worse still, causes harm. Laws prohibiting homosexual activity or the dissemination of birth control information are surely in this category. Hence, even if legal systems are the kind of cooperative enterprise that gives rise to the obligation of fair play, in a great many instances that obligation will not require that we obey specific laws. If, then, there is a generic prima facie obligation to obey the laws of any legal system, it cannot rest on the obligation of fair play. The plausibility of supposing that it does depends on an unwarranted extrapolation from what is largely true of our obligations within small, cooperative enterprises to what must always be true of our obligations within legal systems.

In his recent book, Rawls has abandoned the argument from fair play as proof that the entire citizenry of even just governments has a prima facie obligation to obey the law. He now distinguishes between obligations (*e.g.,* to be fair or to keep promises) and natural duties (*e.g.,* to avoid injury to others). Obligations, according to Rawls, are incurred only by one's voluntary acts, whereas this is not true of natural duties.[12] In his book, he retains the obligation of fair play (now "fairness"); but he now thinks that this obligation applies only to those citizens of just governments who hold office or who have advanced their interests through the government. He excludes the bulk of the citizenry from having a prima facie obligation to obey the law on the ground that, for most persons, receiving benefits from government is nothing they do voluntarily, but is rather something that

---

[11] Indeed, it seems strange that Rawls should have attempted to base the prima facie obligation to obey the law on fair play, since he maintains that this latter obligation is incurred within cooperative enterprises that depend on near-universal cooperation. Rawls, *Legal Obligation and the Duty of Fair Play,* in LAW AND PHILOSOPHY 10 (S. Hook ed. 1964).

[12] J. RAWLS, A THEORY OF JUSTICE 108 (1971).

merely happens to them.[13] He does not, however, take this to imply that most citizens of a reasonably just government are morally free to disobey the law: He maintains that everyone who is treated by such a government with reasonable justice has a natural duty to obey all laws that are not grossly unjust, on the ground that everyone has a natural duty to uphold and to comply with just institutions.[14]

It is tempting to criticize Rawls' present position in much the same way that I criticized his earlier one. One might argue that, while it is true that officeholders and those who have profited by invoking the rules of a just government must in fairness comply with its laws when disobedience will result in harm to that government or when it withholds a benefit from some person who has a right to it, it is simply false that fairness dictates obedience when disobedience does no harm or withholds no benefit. One might further argue that the utility of a just government is such that one has a prima facie duty to obey when disobedience is harmful to it, but that, so long as disobedience does no harm, the government's character is irrelevant to the question of whether one has a prima facie obligation to obey. These criticisms would, I think, show that if we are to base our normative ethics on an appeal to intuitively reasonable principles of duty and obligation, Rawls' present position is no more satisfying than is his earlier one. However, although certainly relevant to an assessment of Rawls' present position, these arguments cannot be regarded as decisive, for in his book Rawls does not rely on a bare appeal to moral intuition. He does not disregard the evidence of intuition, and he is glad to enlist its aid when he can; but, in putting forward particular principles of duty and obligation, he is more concerned with showing that they follow from his general theory of justice. Hence, to refute Rawls' present position, one would have to set out his elaborate theory and then show either that it is mistaken or that the particular claims he makes on its basis do not follow from it. Such a task is beyond the scope of this article; and I shall therefore be content to observe that Rawls' present position lacks intuitive support and, hence, that it rests solely on a controversial ethical theory and a complicated argument based upon it, neither of which have as yet emerged unscathed from the fire of critical scrutiny. His view deserves great respect and demands extended discussion, but it is not one which we must now accept, on pain of being unreasonable.

II

The second group of arguments are those from implicit consent or promise. Recognizing that among the clearest cases of prima facie obligation are those in which a person voluntarily assumes the obligation, some philoso-

[13] *Id.* at 336, 344.

[14] *Id.* at 334–37, 350–62.

phers have attempted to found the citizen's obligation to obey the law upon his consent or promise to do so. There is, of course, a substantial difficulty in any such attempt, *viz.*, the brute fact that many persons have never so agreed. To accommodate this fact, some philosophers have invoked the concept of implicit promise or consent. In the *Second Treatise,* Locke argued that mere residence in a country, whether for an hour or a lifetime, constitutes implicit consent to its law.[15] Plato[16] and W. D. Ross[17] made the similar argument that residence in a country and appeal to the protection of its laws constitutes an implicit promise to obey.

Nevertheless, it is clear that residence and use of the protection of the law do not constitute any usual kind of consent to a government nor any usual kind of promise to obey its laws. The phrases "implicit consent" and "implicit promise" are somewhat difficult to understand, for they are not commonly used; nor do Locke, Plato, or Ross define them. Still, a natural way of understanding them is to assume that they refer to acts which differ from explicit consent or promise only in that, in the latter cases, the person has said "I consent . . ." or "I promise . . . ," whereas in the former, he has not uttered such words but has rather performed some act which counts as giving consent or making a promise. Now, as recent investigation in the philosophy of language has shown, certain speech acts are performed only when someone utters certain words (or performs some other conventional act) with the intention that others will take what he did as being an instance of the particular act in question.[18] And it is certain that, in their ordinary usage, "consenting" and "promising" refer to speech acts of this kind. If I say to someone, "I promise to give you fifty dollars," but it is clear from the context that I do not intend that others will take my utterance as a promise, no one would consider me as having promised. Bringing this observation to bear on the present argument, it is perhaps possible that some people reside in a country and appeal to the protection of its laws with the intention that others will take their residence and appeal as consent to the laws or as a promise to obey; but this is surely true only of a very small number, consisting entirely of those enamoured with social contract theory.[19]

It may be argued, however, that my criticism rests on an unduly narrow reading of the words "consent" and "promise." Hence, it may be supposed that, if I am to refute the implicit consent or promise arguments, I must show that there is no other sense of the words "consent" or "promise" in

[15] J. LOCKE, TWO TREATISES OF GOVERNMENT Bk. II, ¶ 119 (1690).

[16] I PLATO, DIALOGUES 435 (B. Jowett transl. 1892).

[17] Ross, *supra* note 3, at 27.

[18] *Cf.* Strawson, *Intention and Convention in Speech Acts,* 73 PHIL. REV. 439, 448–49, 457–59 (1964).

[19] A similar argument could also be made utilizing the analysis of promising in J. SEARLE, SPEECH ACTS: AN ESSAY IN THE PHILOSOPHY OF LANGUAGE 60 (1969).

which it is true that citizens, merely by living in a state and going about their usual business, thereby consent or promise to obey the law. This objection is difficult to meet, for I know of no way to show that there is no sense of either word that is suitable for contractarian purposes. However, I can show that two recent attempts, by John Plamenatz and Alan Gewirth, to refurbish the implicit consent argument along this line have been unsuccessful.[20] I shall not quarrel with their analyses of "consent," though I am suspicious of them; rather, I shall argue that given their definitions of "consent" the fact that a man consents to government does not establish that he has a prima facie obligation to obey the law.

Plamenatz claims that there are two kinds of consent. The first, which is common-garden variety consent, he terms "direct." He concedes that few citizens directly consent to their government.[21] He suggests, however, that there is another kind of consent, which he calls "indirect," and that, in democratic societies, consent in this sense is widespread and establishes a prima facie obligation to obey the law. Indirect consent occurs whenever a person freely votes or abstains from voting.[22] Voting establishes a prima facie obligation of obedience because:

Even if you dislike the system and wish to change it, you put yourself by your vote under a [prima facie] obligation to obey whatever government comes legally to power. . . . For the purpose of an election is to give authority to the people who win it and, if you vote knowing what you are doing and without being compelled to do it, you voluntarily take part in a process which gives authority to these people.[23]

Plamenatz does not explain why abstention results in a prima facie obligation, but perhaps his idea is that, if a person abstains, he in effect acknowledges the authority of whoever happens to win.

The key premise then in the argument is that "the purpose of an election is to give authority to the people who win it," and it is clear that Plamenatz

---

[20] Another recent tacit consent theory is found in J. TUSSMAN, OBLIGATION AND THE BODY POLITIC (1960). I shall not discuss this theory, however, because it has already received adequate criticism in Pitkin, *Obligation and Consent I,* 59 AM. POL. SCI. REV. 990 (1965). Nor shall I discuss Pitkin's own "hypothetical consent" theory that obedience is owed to those governments to which one ought to consent, because in her discussion of how political obligation is justified she does not appeal to the concept of hypothetical consent. She takes the problem of justifying political obligation to be the question "Why am I ever obligated to obey even legitimate authority?" She gives the question short shrift, however, replying that it is simply part of the meaning of the phrase "legitimate authority" that those subject to legitimate authority have a prima facie obligation to obey it. *See* Pitkin, *Obligation and Consent II,* 60 AM. POL. SCI. REV. 39, 45–49 (1966).

[21] J. PLAMENATZ, MAN AND SOCIETY 228, 238–39 (1963).

[22] *Id.* at 239–40.

[23] *Id.*

believes that this implies that elections do give authority to their winners. In assessing the truth of these contentions, it is, of course, vital to know what Plamenatz means by "authority." Unfortunately, he does not enlighten us, and we must therefore speculate as to his meaning. To begin, the word "authority," when used without qualification, is often held to mean the same as "legitimate authority." Since prima facie obligation is the weakest kind of obligation, part of what we mean when we ascribe authority to some government is that those subject to it have at least a prima facie obligation to obey. However, if this is what Plamenatz means by "authority," his argument simply begs the question: For, in order to be justified in asserting that the purpose of an election is to confer authority and that elections succeed in doing this, he must first show that everyone subject to an elected government has a prima facie obligation to obey its law, both those eligible to vote and those ineligible.

It is possible, however, that Plamenatz is using "authority" in some weaker sense, one that does not entail that everyone subject to it has a prima facie obligation to obey. If this is so, his premises will perhaps pass, but he must then show that those who are eligible to take part in conferring authority have a prima facie obligation to obey it. However, it is difficult to see how this can be done. First, as Plamenatz recognizes, voting is not necessarily consenting in the "direct" or usual sense, and merely being eligible to vote is even more clearly not consenting. Hence, the alleged prima facie obligation of obedience incurred by those eligible to vote is not in consequence of their direct consent. Second, Plamenatz cannot appeal to "common moral sentiment" to bolster his argument: This is because if we really believed that those eligible to vote have a prima facie obligation to obey, an obligation not incurred by the ineligible, we should then believe that the eligible have a stronger obligation than those who are ineligible. But, as far as I can tell, we do not ordinarily think that this is true. Finally, Plamenatz cannot rely on a purely conceptual argument to make his point. It is by no means an analytic truth that those subject to elected governments have a prima facie obligation to obey the law.[24] The

---

[24] A defender of Plamenatz, John Jenkins, appears to hold that something like this is an analytic truth, maintaining that:

> if a person supposes that he has no obligation to a successful candidate because that candidate happens not to be the person for whom he cast his vote, then there is an excellent case for saying that the man has failed to understand the nature of the electoral process.

Jenkins, *Political Consent*, 20 PHIL. Q. (1970).

This seems a silly claim. Many who voted for George McGovern believe themselves to be under no obligation to Richard Nixon. Some are highly educated and close observers of the political scene. Were such a person to explain his belief that he is not obligated to Nixon solely on the ground that he did not vote for him, we might think him mistaken or wish that he had chosen a better reason, but we should have no reason at all to think that he fails to understand "the nature of the electoral process."

radical who says, "The present government of the United States was freely elected, but because it exploits people its citizens have no obligation to obey it," has perhaps said something false, but he has not contradicted himself. Plamenatz's argument is therefore either question-begging or inconclusive, depending on what he means by "authority."

Gewirth's argument is similar to Plamenatz's in that he also holds that a person's vote establishes his prima facie obligation of obedience. He argues that men consent to government when "certain institutional arrangements exist in the community as a whole," including "the maintenance of a method which leaves open to every sane, noncriminal adult the opportunity to discuss, criticize, and vote for or against the government."[25] He holds that the existence of such consent "justifies" government and establishes the subject's prima facie obligation to obey because:

The method of consent combines and safeguards the joint values of freedom and order as no other method does. It provides a choice in the power of government which protects the rights of the electorate more effectively than does any other method. It does more justice to man's potential rationality than does any other method, for it gives all men the opportunity to participate in a reasoned discussion of the problem of society and to make their discussion effective in terms of political control.[26]

As it stands, Gewirth's argument is incomplete. He makes certain claims about the benefits of government by consent which are open to reasonable doubt. Some communists, for example, would hold that Gewirth's method of consent has led to exploitation, and that human rights and freedom are better protected by the rule of the party. This aside, Gewirth's argument still needs strengthening. The fact that certain benefits are given only by government with a method of consent establishes only that such a government is better than one which lacks such a method. But, to show that one government is better than another, or even to show that it is the best possible government, does not prove that its subjects have a prima facie obligation to obey its laws: There is a prior question, which remains to be settled, as to whether there can be a prima facie obligation to obey any government. Gewirth does not carry the argument farther in his discussion of "consent," but earlier in his paper he hints as to how he would meet this objection. He argues that "government as such" is justified, or made legitimate, by its being necessary to avoid certain evils.[27] Indeed, although

[25] Earlier in his discussion Gewirth distinguishes three senses of "consent": an "occurrence" sense, a "dispositional" sense, and an "opportunity" sense. *Id.* at 131. It is only the last that will concern us here, since he admits that the prima facie obligation to obey the law cannot be shown by relying on the occurrence or dispositional senses. Gewirth, *Political Justice,* in SOCIAL JUSTICE 138 (R. Brandt ed. 1962).

[26] *Id.* at 139.

[27] *Id.* at 135.

he does not explicitly so state, he seems to think that utilitarian considerations demonstrate that there is a prima facie obligation to obey any government that protects its subjects from these evils, but that there is an additional prima facie obligation to obey a government with a method of consent because of the more extensive benefits it offers. In the next section, I shall discuss whether a direct appeal to utility can establish a prima facie obligation to obey the law.

III

I shall consider three utilitarian arguments: the first appealing to a weak form of act-utilitarianism, the second and third to rule-utilitarian theories. To my knowledge, the first argument has never been explicitly advanced. It is nevertheless worth considering, both because it possesses a certain plausibility and because it has often been hinted at when philosophers, lawyers, and political theorists have attempted to derive an obligation to obey the law from the premise that government is necessary to protect society from great evil. The argument runs as follows:

There is obviously a prima facie obligation to perform acts which have good consequences. Now, government is absolutely necessary for securing the general good: The alternative is the state of nature in which everyone is miserable, in which life is "solitary, poor, nasty, brutish and short." But, no government can long stand in the face of widespread disobedience, and government can therefore promote the general good only so long as its laws are obeyed. Therefore, obedience to the law supports the continued existence of government and, hence, always has good consequences. From this it follows that there is a prima facie obligation to obey the law.

On even brief scrutiny, however, this argument quickly disintegrates. The first thing to be noticed is that its principle of prima facie obligation is ambiguous. It may be interpreted as postulating either (a) an obligation to perform those acts which have any good consequences, or (b) an obligation to perform optimific acts (*i.e.*, those whose consequences are better than their alternatives). Now, (a) and (b) are in fact very different principles. The former is obviously absurd. It implies, for example, that I have a prima facie obligation to kill whomever I meet, since this would have the good consequence of helping to reduce overpopulation. Thus, the only weak act-utilitarian principle with any plausibility is (b). But, regardless of whether (b) is acceptable—and some philosophers would not accept it[28]—the conclusion that there is a prima facie obligation to obey the law, cannot be derived from it, inasmuch as there are obvious and familiar

---

[28] For example, some philosophers would hold that there is a prima facie obligation to refrain from acts which have undesirable consequences, but not that there is an obligation to perform the one act which has the best consequences. *See, e.g.,*

M.G. SINGER, GENERALIZATION IN ETHICS, ch. 7 (1961).

cases in which breach of a particular law has better consequences than obedience. The only conclusion to be derived from (b) is that there is a specific prima facie obligation to obey the law whenever obedience is optimific. But no generic prima facie obligation to obey can be derived from weak act-utilitarianism.[29]

The second utilitarian argument appeals not to the untoward consequences of individual disobedience, but rather to those of general disobedience. Perhaps the most common challenge to those who defend certain instances of civil disobedience is "What would happen if everyone disobeyed the law?" One of the arguments implicit in this question is the generalization argument, which may be expanded as follows:

No one can have a right to do something unless everyone has a right to do it. Similarly, an act cannot be morally indifferent unless it would be morally indifferent if everyone did it. But, everyone's breaking the law is not a matter of moral indifference; for no government can survive in such a circumstance and, as we have already agreed, government is necessary for securing and maintaining the general good. Hence, since the consequences of general disobedience would be disastrous, each person subject to law has a prima facie obligation to obey it.

In assessing this argument, we must first recognize that the generalization argument is a moral criterion to be applied with care, as virtually everyone who has discussed it has recognized.[30] If we simply note that if everyone committed a certain act there would be disastrous consequences and thereupon conclude that there is a prima facie obligation not to commit acts of that kind, we will be saddled with absurdities. We will have to maintain, for example, that there is a prima facie obligation not to eat dinner at five o'clock, for if everyone did so, certain essential services could not be maintained. And, for similar reasons, we will have to maintain that there is a prima facie obligation not to produce food. Now, those who believe that the generalization argument is valid argue that such absurdities arise when the criterion is applied to acts which are either too generally described or described in terms of morally irrelevant features. They would

[29] For purposes of clarification, I should emphasize that I am here concerned with act utilitarianism as a theory of prima facie, not absolute, obligation. There is no incongruity here. The consequences of acts count as having great moral significance on virtually every moral theory; and so, one need not be a strict act utilitarian in order to maintain the principle that there is a prima facie obligation to act optimifically. Indeed, for a strict act utilitarian such as Bentham, it is pointless to worry about whether there is a prima facie obligation to obey the law: He would hold that there is an absolute obligation to obey the law when, and only when, obedience is optimific, and would there end the discussion. At most, an act utilitarian would hold that the rule "Obey the law" is a useful rule of thumb, to be followed only when the consequences of obedience or disobedience are difficult to discern.

[30] SINGER, *supra* note 28, at ch. 4.

argue that the generalization argument appears to go awry when applied to these examples because the description "producing food" is too general to give the argument purchase and because the temporal specification in "eating dinner at five o'clock" is morally irrelevant.[31]

However, such a restriction on the generalization argument is fatal to its use in proving a prima facie obligation to obey the law. This is because a person who denies any such obligation is surely entitled to protest that the description "breaking the law" is overly general, on the ground that it refers to acts of radically different moral import.[32] Breaking the law perhaps always has some bad consequences; but sometimes the good done by it balances the bad or even outweighs it. And, once we take these differences in consequences into account, we find that utilitarian generalization, like weak act-utilitarianism, can only establish a specific prima facie obligation to obey the law when obedience is optimific. Were everyone to break the law when obedience is optimific, the consequences would undoubtedly be disastrous; but it is by no means clear that it would be disastrous if everyone broke the law when obedience is not optimific. Since no one knows, with respect to any society, how often obedience is not optimific, no one can be certain as to the consequences of everyone acting in this way. Indeed, for all we know, if everyone broke the law when obedience was not optimific the good done by separate acts of lawbreaking might more than compensate for any public disorder which might result. In sum, even if the generalization argument is regarded as an acceptable principle of prima facie obligation, the most it demonstrates is that there is a specific prima facie obligation to obey the law whenever the consequences of obedience are optimific.

Some readers—especially those unfamiliar with the recent literature on utilitarianism[33]—may suspect that this last argument involves sleight of hand. They may object:

[31] I have borrowed these cases and this strategy for handling them from Singer, *Id.* at 71–83.

[32] According to Singer, a mark of a description's being overly general is that the generalization argument is "invertible" with respect to it, *i.e.,* the consequences of everyone's doing the act (given that description) is disastrous and the consequences of everyone's failing to do it is also disastrous, *Id.* at 76–77. It is relevant to note that the generalization argument is plainly invertible with respect to the description "breaking the law." Sometimes breaking the law is the only way to avoid a great evil; and so, if everyone were always to obey the law, such evils could never be avoided.

[33] That the generalization argument and weak act utilitarianism offer the same advice on the topic of obedience to the law should surprise no one familiar with D. LYONS, FORMS AND LIMITS OF UTILITARIANISM (1965). Lyons there shows that act utilitarianism and the generalization argument are extensionally equivalent. There is, it should be noted, a substantial difference between Lyons' argument for equivalence and the argument I have here offered. Lyons argues for equivalence on a priori grounds, whereas I have relied on the empirical impossibility of determin-

In your discussion of the generalization argument, you argued that we have no way of knowing the consequences if everyone disobeyed when obedience was not optimific. But, your argument rests on the premise that the act-utilitarian formula can be perfectly applied, whereas this is in fact impossible: The consequences of many acts are difficult or impossible to foretell; and so, were we all to attempt to be act utilitarians, we would either make horrendous mistakes or be paralyzed into inaction. In constructing a rule-utilitarian theory of prima facie obligations, we should therefore concentrate not on the consequences of everyone following certain rules, but rather on the consequences of everyone trying to follow them. And, it seems reasonable to believe that, on such a theory, the rule "Obey the law" would receive utilitarian blessing.

As it stands, this objection is overdrawn. My argument does not presuppose that persons can generally succeed in applying the act-utilitarian formula: I merely speculated on the consequences of everyone behaving in a certain way; and I made no assumption as to what made them act that way. Moreover, the objection severely overestimates the difficulty in being a confirmed act-utilitarian. Still, the objection makes one substantial point that deserves further attention. Rule-utilitarian theories which focus on the consequences of everyone accepting (although not always following) a certain set of rules do differ markedly from the generalization argument; and so the question remains as to whether such a theory could establish a prima facie obligation to obey the law. I shall therefore discuss whether the most carefully developed such theory, that given by R. B. Brandt,[34] does just this.

In Brandt's theory, one's obligations are (within certain limits) relative to his society and are determined by the set of rules whose acceptance in that society would have better consequences than would acceptance of any other set.[35] According to this theory, then, there can be a generic prima

---

ing the consequences of everyone disobeying the law when obedience is not optimific.

[34] Brandt, *Toward a Credible Formal Utilitarianism*, in MORALITY AND THE LANGUAGE OF CONDUCT 107 (H.N. Costenada & G. Nakhnikian eds. 1963). In the following I shall not be attacking a position Brandt holds, but only an argument that might be offered on the basis of his theory. In fact, in *Utility and the Obligation to Obey the Law*, in LAW AND PHILOSOPHY 43, 47–49 (S. Hook ed. 1964) Brandt expresses doubt as to whether there is such an obligation.

[35] According to Brandt's theory, there is an absolute obligation to perform an act if it conforms with that learnable set of rules the recognition of which as morally binding—roughly at the time of the act—by everyone in the society of the agent, except for the retention by individuals of already formed and decided moral convictions, would maximize intrinsic value.
Brandt, *Toward a Credible Formal Utilitarianism*, in MORALITY AND THE LANGUAGE OF CONDUCT 107, 139 (H.N. Castenada & G. Nakhnikian eds. 1963). He distinguishes three levels of rules, the first stating prima facie obligations and the latter two dealing with cases in which lower-level rules conflict. At every level, 401

facie obligation to obey the law—within a given society if, and only if, general acceptance of the rule "Obey the law," as a rule of prima facie obligation, would have better consequences than were no rule accepted with respect to obeying the law, as well as better consequences than were some alternative rule accepted (*e.g.,* "Obey the law when obedience to the law is optimific," or "Obey the law so long as it is just"). Now, to many it may seem obvious that the ideal set of rules for any society will contain the rule "Obey the law," on the ground that, were its members not generally convinced of at least a prima facie obligation to obey, disobedience would be widespread, resulting in a great many crimes against person and property. But, there are two reasons to doubt such a gloomy forecast. First, we must surely suppose that in this hypothetical society the laws are still backed by sanctions, thereby giving its members a strong incentive to obey its laws. Second, we must also assume that the members of that society accept other moral rules (*e.g.,* "Do not harm others," "Keep promises," "Tell the truth") which will give them a moral incentive to obey the law in most circumstances. It is, in short, a mistake to believe that unless people are convinced that they have a generic prima facie obligation to obey the law, they cannot be convinced that in most circumstances they have a specific prima facie obligation to obey particular laws. We may therefore expect that, even though members of our hypothetical society do not accept a moral rule about obedience to the law per se, they will still feel a prima facie obligation to act in accordance with the law, save when disobedience does no harm. There is, then, no reason to think that an orgy of lawbreaking would ensue were no rule about obedience to the law generally recognized; nor, I think, is there any good reason to believe that acceptance of the rule "Obey the law" would in any society have better consequences than were no such rule recognized And, if this is so, there is surely no reason to think that recognition of this rule would have better consequences than recognition of some alternative rule. In sum, Brandt's theory requires that we be able to determine the truth-value of a large number of counter-factual propositions about what would happen were entire societies persuaded of the truth of certain moral rules. But, even if we assume—and it is hardly clear that we should[36]—that we can reliably determine the truth-value of such counter-factuals through "common sense" and our knowledge of human nature, Brandt's form of rule

---

however, those in the favored set of rules are those whose recognition would have the best consequences, *i.e.,* consequences better than were any alternative rule accepted, as well as better than were no such rule accepted. *Id.* at 118–19.

[36] As an illustration of the difficulty, Brandt suggests that the first-level rule "Keep your promises" is neither the one that we accept nor the rule about promising that would maximize utility. *Id.* at 131–32. I think he is right to say that it is not the rule we accept, but how does he know that some more complex rule maximizes utility?

utilitarianism gives no support for the proof of a prima facie obligation to obey the law.

IV

In the foregoing discussion, I have played the skeptic, contending that no argument has as yet succeeded in establishing a prima facie obligation to obey the law. I want now to examine this supposed obligation directly. I shall assume *arguendo* that such an obligation exists in order to inquire as to how it compares in moral weight with other prima facie obligations. As we shall see, this question is relevant to whether we should hold that such an obligation exists.

To discuss this question, I must, of course, first specify some test for determining the weight of a prima facie obligation. It will be recalled that I defined "prima facie obligation" in terms of wrongdoing: To say that a person S has a prima facie obligation to do an act X is to say that S has a moral reason to do X which is such that, unless he has a reason not to do X that is at least as strong, S's failure to do X is wrong. Now, we are accustomed, in our reflective moral practice, to distinguish degrees of wrongdoing. And so, by appealing to this notion, we can formulate two principles that may reasonably be held to govern the weight of prima facie obligations: First, that a prima facie obligation is a serious one if, and only if, an act which violates that obligation and fulfils no other is seriously wrong; and, second, that a prima facie obligation is a serious one if, and only if, violation of it will make considerably worse an act which on other grounds is already wrong.[37] These principles, which constitute tests for determining an obligation's weight, are closely related, and application of either to a given prima facie obligation is a sufficient measure; but I shall apply both to the presumed prima facie obligation to obey the law in order to make my argument more persuasive.

First, however, we should convince ourselves of the reliability of these tests by applying them to some clear cases. I suppose it will be granted that we all have a prima facie obligation not to kill (except perhaps in

[37] The second principle may be thought objectionable on the ground that it trivializes obviously weighty prima facie obligations. It may perhaps be held that, were a man to kill a thousand persons, his act would not have been much worse had he killed but one more. The principle therefore seems to imply that the prima facie obligation not to kill that one person is trivial. The objection is plausible, but misguided. Surely there is a substantial moral difference between killing a thousand persons and killing a thousand-and-one—exactly the difference between killing one person and killing none. To deny this is to imply that the thousand-and-first person's life has little moral significance. At first glance, however, we may be inclined to take the difference to be trivial, because both acts are so monstrous that we should rarely see any point in distinguishing between them. That this objection might be raised against the principle was pointed out to me by Anne Bowen. 403

self-defense), and that this obligation is most weighty. Our first test corroborates this, for, if a person kills another when he is not defending himself and if he has no specific prima facie obligation to kill that person, his act is seriously wrong. By contrast, our prima facie obligation to observe rules of etiquette—if indeed there is any such obligation—is clearly trifling. This is borne out by our test, for if I belch audibly in the company of those who think such behavior rude, my wrongdoing is at most trivial. The same results are obtained under our second test. If I attempt to extort money from someone my act is much worse if I kill one of his children and threaten the rest than if I merely threatened them all; and so the obligation not to kill again counts as substantial. Similarly, the prima facie obligation to observe the rules of etiquette is again trivial, for if I am rude during the extortion my act is hardly worse than it would have been had I been polite.

By neither of these tests, however, does the prima facie obligation to obey the law count as substantial. As for the first test, let us assume that while driving home at two o'clock in the morning I run a stop sign. There is no danger, for I can see clearly that there was no one approaching the intersection, nor is there any impressionable youth nearby to be inspired to a life of crime by my flouting of the traffic code. Finally, we may assume that I nevertheless had no specific prima facie obligation to run the stop sign. If, then, my prima facie obligation to obey the law is of substantial moral weight, my action must have been a fairly serious instance of wrongdoing. But clearly it was not. If it was wrong at all—and to me this seems dubious—it was at most a mere peccadillo. As for the second test, we may observe that acts which are otherwise wrong are not made more so—if they are made worse at all—by being illegal.[38] If I defraud someone my act is hardly worse morally by being illegal than it would have been were it protected by some legal loophole. Thus, if there is a prima facie obligation to obey the law, it is at most of trifling weight.

This being so, I suggest that considerations of simplicity indicate that we should ignore the supposed prima facie obligation to obey the law and refuse to count an act wrong merely because it violates some law. There is certainly nothing to be lost by doing this, for we shall not thereby recommend or tolerate any conduct that is seriously wrong, nor shall we fail to recommend any course of action that is seriously obligatory. Yet, there is much to be gained, for in refusing to let trivialities occupy our attention,

---

[38] I have taken this point from 1 W. BLACKSTONE, COMMENTARIES 54:
Neither do divine or natural *duties* (such as, for instance, the worship of God, the maintenance of children, and the like) receive any stronger sanction from being also declared to be duties by the law of the land. The case is the same as to crimes and misdemeanors, that are forbidden by the superior laws, and therefore styled *mala in se,* such as murder, theft, and perjury; which contract no additional turpitude from being declared unlawful by the inferior legislature.

we shall not be diverted from the important questions to be asked about illegal conduct, *viz.,* "What kind of act was it?," "What were its consequences?," "Did the agent intend its consequences?," and so forth. Morality is, after all, a serious business; and we are surely right not to squander our moral attention and concern on matters of little moral significance.

To illustrate what can be gained, let us consider briefly the issue of civil disobedience. Most philosophers who have written on the subject have argued that, at least in democratic societies, there is always a strong moral reason to obey the law. They have therefore held that civil disobedience is a tactic to be employed only when all legal means of changing an unjust law have failed, and that the person who engages in it must willingly accept punishment as a mark of respect for the law and recognition of the seriousness of lawbreaking. However, once we abandon the notion that civil disobedience is morally significant per se, we shall judge it in the same way we judge most other kinds of acts, that is, on the basis of their character and consequences. Indeed, we can then treat civil disobedience just as we regard many other species of illegal conduct. If breaking the law involves an act which is *mala in se* or if it has untoward consequences, we are ordinarily prepared to condemn it and to think that the malefactor ought to accept punishment. But if lawbreaking does not involve an act that is *mala in se* and if it has no harmful consequences, we do not ordinarily condemn it, nor do we think that its perpetrator must accept punishment, unless evading punishment itself has untoward consequences. If we adopt this view of civil disobedience, we shall have done much to escape the air of mystery that hovers about most discussions of it.

Of course, this is not to say it will be easy to determine when civil disobedience is justified. Some have maintained that the civil disobedience of the last decade has led to increasing violation of laws which safeguard people and property.[39] If this is true, each instance of disobedience which has contributed to this condition has a share in the evil of the result. Others maintain that such disobedience has had wholly good consequences, that it has helped to remedy existing injustice and to restrain government from fresh injustice.[40] Still others think its consequences are mixed. Which position is correct is difficult to determine. I myself am inclined to believe that, although the consequences have been mixed, the good far outweigh the bad; but I would be hard pressed to prove it. What is clear, however, is that either abandoning or retaining the supposed prima facie obligation to obey the law will not help settle these questions about consequences. But, if we do abandon it, we shall then at least be able to focus on these questions without having to worry about a prima facie obligation of trivial

[39] C. WHITTAKER, *First Lecture,* in LAW, ORDER AND CIVIL DISOBEDIENCE (1967).

[40] *See* H. ZINN, DISOBEDIENCE AND DEMOCRACY (1968).

weight that must nevertheless somehow be taken into account. Finally, if we abandon the prima facie obligation to obey the law, we shall perhaps look more closely at the character of acts performed in the course of civil disobedience, and this may, in turn, lead to fruitful moral speculation. For example, we shall be able to distinguish between acts which cannot conceivably violate the obligation of fair play (*e.g.,* burning one's draft card) and acts which may do so (*e.g.,* tax refusal or evasion of military service). This in turn may provide an incentive to reflect further on the obligation of fair play, to ask, for example, whether Rawls is right in his present contention that a person can incur the obligation of fair play only so long as his acceptance of the benefits of a cooperative enterprise is wholly voluntary.

V

It is now time to take stock. I initially suggested that it is by no means obvious that there is any prima facie obligation to obey the law. In the foregoing, I have rejected a number of arguments that purport to establish its existence. The only plausible argument I have not rejected is the one of Rawls that purports to prove that there is a natural duty to obey the laws of reasonably just governments. However, I did note that his position lacks intuitive support and rests on a controversial ethical theory which has not yet withstood the test of critical scrutiny. Finally, I have shown that even if such an obligation is assumed, it is of trivial weight and that there are substantial advantages in ignoring it. I suggest that all of this makes it reasonable to maintain that there is in no society a prima facie obligation to obey the law.

Before I conclude my discussion, however, I want to tie up one loose thread. Near the beginning of my argument I distinguished the question to be discussed from that which I called the lawyer's question, "May a reasonable man take mere illegality to be sufficient evidence that an act is morally wrong, so long as he lacks specific evidence that tends to show that it is right?" Since I have raised the question, I believe that, for the sake of completeness, I should consider it, if only briefly. To begin, it seems very doubtful that there is, in the lawyer's sense, a prima facie obligation to obey the law. It is undoubtedly true that most instances of lawbreaking are wrong, but it is also true that many are not: This is because there are, as Lord Devlin once remarked, "many fussy regulations whose breach it would be pedantic to call immoral,"[41] and because some breaches of even non-fussy regulations are justified. Now, unless—as in a court of law—there is some pressing need to reach a finding, the mere fact that most *A*s are also *B* does not, in the absence of evidence that a particular *A* is not *B,* warrant an inference that the *A* in question is also a *B:* In order for this inference to be reasonable, one must know that virtually

[41] P. DEVLIN, THE ENFORCEMENT OF MORALS 27 (1965).

all *A*s are *B*s. Since, then, it rarely happens that there is a pressing need to reach a moral finding, and since to know merely that an act is illegal is not to know very much of moral significance about it, it seems clear that, if his only information about an act was that it was illegal, a reasonable man would withhold judgment until he learned more about it. Indeed, this is not only what the fictitious reasonable man would do, it is what we should expect the ordinary person to do. Suppose we were to ask a large number of people: "Jones has broken a law; but I won't tell you whether what he did is a serious crime or merely violation of a parking regulation, nor whether he had good reason for his actions. Would you, merely on the strength of what I have just told you, be willing to say that what he did was morally wrong?" I have conducted only an informal poll; but, on its basis, I would wager that the great majority would answer "I can't yet say—you must tell me more about what Jones did."

More importantly, it appears to make little difference what answer we give to the lawyer's question. While an affirmative answer establishes a rule of inference that an illegal act is wrong in the absence of specific information tending to show it to be right, it is a rule that would in fact virtually never be applied in any reasonable determination of whether an illegal act is wrong. If, on the one hand, we have specific information about an illegal act which tends to show it to be right, then the rule is irrelevant to our determination of the act's moral character. Should we be inclined, in this instance, to hold the act wrong we must have specific information which tends to show this; and it is clear that our conclusions about its moral character must be based on this specific information, and not on the supposed reasonableness of holding illegal conduct wrong in the absence of specific information tending to show it is right. On the other hand, if we have specific information tending to show that an illegal act is wrong and no information tending to show it is right, the rule is applicable but otiose: Since we have ample specific reason to condemn the act, the rule is superfluous to our judgment. It would seem, then, that the rule is relevant only when we have no specific information about the illegal conduct's rightness or wrongness; and this, I suggest, is something that virtually never occurs. When we are prompted to make a moral judgment about an illegal act, we virtually always know something of its character or at least its consequences; and it is these that we consider important in determining the rightness or wrongness of lawbreaking. In short, it seems to make little difference what answer we give to the lawyer's question; I raise it here only that it may hereafter be ignored.

In conclusion, it is, I think, important to recognize that there is nothing startling in what I am recommending, nothing that in any way outrages common sense. Even the most conscientious men at times violate trivial and pointless laws for some slight gain in convenience and, when they do so, they do not feel shame or remorse. Similarly, when they observe other 407 men behaving in a like fashion, they do not think of passing moral censure. For most people, violation of the law becomes a matter for moral concern only when it involves an act which is believed to be wrong on grounds apart from its illegality. Hence, anyone who believes that the purpose of normative ethics is to organize and clarify our reflective moral practice should be skeptical of any argument purporting to show that there is a prima facie obligation to obey the law. It is necessary to state this point with care: I am not contending that reflective and conscientious citizens would, if asked, deny that there is a prima facie obligation to obey the law. Indeed, I am willing to concede that many more would affirm its existence than deny it. But, this is in no way inconsistent with my present point. We often find that reflective people will accept general statements which are belied by their actual linguistic practice. That they also accept moral generalizations that are belied by their actual reflective moral practice should occasion no surprise.

This last point may, however, be challenged on the ground that it implies that there is in our reflective moral practice no distinction between raw power and legitimate authority. As I noted above, the concept of legitimate authority is often analyzed in terms of the right to command, where "right" is used in the strict sense as implying some correlative obligation of obedience. Given this definition, if it is true that the principle "There is a prima facie obligation to obey the law" is not observed in our reflective moral practice, it follows that we do not really distinguish between governments which possess legitimate authority (e.g., that of the United States) and those which do not (e.g., the Nazi occupation government of France). And this, it may justly be held, is absurd. What I take this argument to show, however, is not that the principle is enshrined in our reflective morality, but rather that what we ordinarily mean when we ascribe legitimate authority to some government is not captured by the usual analysis of "legitimate authority." It is a mistake to believe that, unless we employ the concept of authority as it is usually analyzed, we cannot satisfactorily distinguish between the moral relation of the government of the United States vis-à-vis Americans and the moral relation of the Nazi occupation government vis-à-vis Frenchmen. One way of doing this, for example, is to define "legitimate authority" in terms of "the right to command and to enforce obedience," where "right" is used in the sense of "what is morally permissible." Thus, according to this analysis of the notion, the government of the United States counts as having legitimate authority over its subjects because within certain limits there is nothing wrong in its issuing commands to them and enforcing their obedience, whereas the Nazi occupation government lacked such authority because its issuing commands to Frenchmen was morally impermissible. It is not my intention to proffer this as an adequate analysis of the notion of legiti-
408 mate authority or to suggest that it captures what we ordinarily mean

when we ascribe such authority to some government. These are difficult matters, and I do not wish to address myself to them here. My point is rather that the questions "What governments enjoy legitimate authority?" and "Have the citizens of any government a prima facie obligation to obey the law?" both can be, and should be, kept separate.

Selected Bibliography

Bedau, Hugo (ed.). *Civil Disobedience: Theory and Practice.* New York: Pegasus, 1969.

Dworkin, Ronald. "A Theory of Civil Disobedience," in Kiefer and Munitz (eds.), *Ethics and Social Justice.* New York: New York University Press, 1968.

The Monist, "Legal Obligation and Civil Disobedience," Vol. 54, No. 4 (October 1970).

Murphy, Jeffrie (ed.). *Civil Disobedience and Violence.* Belmont, Calif.: Wadsworth Publishing Co., 1971.

Pennock, Roland J., and John W. Chapman (eds.). *Political and Legal Obligation* (Nomos XII). New York: Atherton Press, 1970.

Pitkin, Hannah. "Obligation and Consent," *American Political Science Review,* Vol. 5 (1965), 990.

Walzer, Michael. "The Obligation to Disobey," *Ethics,* Vol. 77 1967, 163.

VIOLENCE, NONVIOLENCE, AND WAR

7

NEWTON GARVER
What Violence Is

I

Most people deplore violence, many people embrace violence
(perhaps reluctantly) and a few people renounce violence.
But through all these postures there runs a certain obscurity:
it is never entirely clear just what violence is.

Those who deplore violence loudest and most publicly are
usually identified with the status quo—school principals, businessmen, politicians, ministers. What they deplore is generally
overt attacks on property or against the "good order of society." They rarely see violence in defense of the status quo
in the same light as violence directed against it. At the time
of the Watts riots in 1965 President Johnson urged Negroes to
realize that nothing of any value can be won through violent
means—an idea which may be true but which Johnson himself
did not apply to the escalation of the Vietnam war he was
simultaneously embarking upon, and which it never would
have occurred to him to apply to the actions of the Los
Angeles Police Department. But the President is not the only
one who deplores violence while at the same time perpetrating
it, and a little more clarity about what exactly we deplore
might help all around.

Those who renounce violence are equally hard to follow.
Tolstoy, Gandhi, and Muste stand out among the advocates of
nonviolence of the past century, and as one reads them it becomes clear that they do not all renounce exactly the same

Reprinted from *The Nation* (June 24, 1968), 817–822, with the permission of the author and the publisher. The article has been revised
by the author for inclusion in this volume.

thing. There is much that is concrete and detailed in the writings of these men, but nonetheless it is not easy to avoid the impression that "non-violence" is really just morality itself rather than a specific commitment to eschew a certain well-defined sort of behavior.

Those who embrace violence are in a much better position, for they stand ready to embrace whatever is "inevitable" or "necessary" in the circumstances, and hence the question of just where violence begins or leaves off does not arise for them. But if we want to know about the nature and varieties of violence, it does not help to be told that violence is unavoidable or that it is a necessary means to some end. There is a question about understanding violence before we come to adopt a posture toward it, and it is to that question we now turn.

II

What I want to do is to present a kind of typology of violence. I want, that is, to try to make clear what some of the different types and kinds and forms of violence are, and thereby to give a perspective of the richness of this topic. Unfortunately, I can't begin saying what the types of violence are without saying first what it is I'm giving you a typology of. So let's begin with a definition of violence.

What is violence? That is a typical philosophical question. The psychiatrists and the sociologists are interested in the questions: why is there violence? what causes violence? That's not my concern—at least not my professional concern nor my concern here. What I'm interested in is the old-fashioned philosophical question: What is the nature or essence of violence?

We can make a good start etymologically. The word 'violence' comes, of course, from the French, prior to that from the Latin, and you can find Greek roots if you're up to it—which I'm not. The Latin root of the word 'violence' is a combination of two Latin words—the word '*vis*' (force) and the past participle '*latus*' of the word '*fero*' (to carry). The Latin word '*violare*' is itself a combination of these two words, and its present participle '*violans*' is a plausible source for the word 'violence' —so that the word 'violence', in its etymological origin, has the sense of *to carry force at or toward*. A second feature of the etymology is that the word 'violation' comes from this very same source as the word 'violence', which suggests to us the interesting idea that violence is somehow a violation of something: that carrying force against something constitutes in one way or another a violation of it.

In human affairs the idea of violence is much more closely connected with the idea of violation than it is with the idea of force. It is clear that force is often used on another person's body and there is no violence done. For example, if a man is drowning—thrashing around and 411 is apparently unable to save himself—and you use the standard Red Cross life-saving techniques, you will use force against his body although certainly you won't be doing any violence to him. You will, in fact, be saving his life instead. Similarly, surgeons and dentists use force on our bodies without doing violence to us. To think so rigidly of force and violence being identical with one another that you call these actions acts of violence is to have lost sight entirely of the significance of the concept.

What is fundamental about violence in human affairs is that a person is violated. Now that is a tough notion to explain. It is easy enough to understand how you can violate a moral rule or a parking regulation, but what in the world does it mean to talk about "violating a person"? That, I think, is a very important question, and can give a fresh perspective on what it means to be human. If it rings true to talk about violating a person, that just is because a person has certain rights which are undeniably, indissolubly, connected with his being a person. The very idea of natural rights is controversial since it is redolent of Scholasticism, but I find myself forced to accept natural rights in order to understand the moral dimension of violence.

One of the most fundamental rights a person has is a right to his body —to determine what his body does and what is done to his body—because without his body he wouldn't be a person anymore. The most common way a person ceases to exist is that his body stops functioning—a point which appeals especially forcefully if you think of a person as a living, growing thing rather than as something static or as a substance in the traditional sense. Apart from a body what is essential to one's being a person is dignity in something like the existentialist sense, or in other words what Kant called "autonomy." The dignity of a person does not consist in his remaining prim and unruffled, but rather in his making his own decisions. In this respect what is fundamental about a person is radically different from what is fundamental, for example, about a dog. I have a dog. I don't expect him to make decisions: When I tell him to sit or to stay I expect him just to do it, not to decide. And, indeed, the way I have treated my dog, which seems to be a good way to treat a dog, is to train him to respond in a more or less mechanical way to certain commands. Such treatment, it seems to me, gives a dog a rather good place in life, at least as we have arranged it. However, to treat a human being that way is an affront to his dignity as a human being, just because it is essential to a human being that he have a kind of dignity or autonomy.

The right to one's body and the right to autonomy are undoubtedly the most fundamental natural rights of persons, but there are subsidiary ones that deserve mention as part of the background for our discussion of violence. One of these stems from the right to autonomy. It is characteristic of human action to be purposive and to have results and conse-

412

quences, and freedom therefore is normally conceived as involving not only the right to decide what to do but also the right to dispose of or cope with the consequences of one's action. One aspect of this right is the right to the product of one's labor, which has played an important role in the theory of both capitalism and communism, as the basis for the theory of property on the one hand and the theory of exploitation on the other. It is one of the ironies of intellectual history that the right of persons to the product of their labor constitutes the basis for both Locke's defense of private property and Marx's attack on it. If we follow this line of thought to the extent that we consider one's property as an extension of his person, the scope of the concept of violence becomes greatly enlarged, perhaps in harmony with popular thought on the subject, at least on the part of propertied persons; but one should always bear in mind that a person can reconcile himself much more readily to loss of property than he can to loss of life.

If we say that the results of what a person does belongs to him, we should have in mind not only this kind of labor theory of value but also the more or less natural and expectable consequences of a person's action. One of Jean-Paul Sartre's most interesting plays, *Altona,* develops this theme. In this play Sartre depicts a young man who does things that would normally have very serious consequences, probably his death. At one time he defies the Nazis, at another time the American Military Government that is occupying the country. On both occasions his father intervenes and cuts him off from the normal, expected consequences of his actions, consequences which anybody else would have suffered. Sartre shows what an awful impact it has upon this man, as a person, to have the consequences of his actions cut off in this way. In the end this victim of paternalism is one of Sartre's rather hideous characters, sequestered in a room in the center of his father's grand mansion having hallucinations of crabs and visions of expiation.

So violence in human affairs comes down to violating persons. It occurs in a variety of guises, and can usefully be classified into four different kinds based on two criteria, whether the violence is personal or institutionalized and whether the violence is overt or a kind of covert or quiet violence.

III

Overt physical assault of one person on the body of another is the most obvious form of violence. Mugging, rape and murder are the flagrant "crimes of violence," and when people speak of the danger of violence in the streets it is usually visions of these flagrant cases that float before their minds. I share the general concern over the rising rate of these crimes, but at the same time I deplore the tendency to cast our image of 413 violence just in the mold of these flagrant cases. These are cases where an attack on a human body is also clearly an attack on a person and clearly illegal. We must not tie these characteristics in too tight a package, for some acts of violence are intended as a defense of law or a benefit to the person whose body is beaten—e.g. ordinary police activity (not "police brutality")[1] and the corporal punishment of children by parents and teachers. The humbler cases are violence too: although the fact that policemen, teachers, and parents have socially defined roles which they invoke when they resort to violence indicates that these cases have institutional aspects that overshadow the purely personal ones, these institutional overtones cannot erase the violence done.[2] Whenever you do something to another person's body without his consent you are attacking not just a physical entity—you are attacking a person. You are doing something by force, so the violence in this case is something that is easily visible, has long been recognized as violence, and is a case of overt, personal violence.

In war, what one group tries to do to another group is what happens to individuals in cases of mugging and murder, but it is more difficult to assign moral responsibility for the violence done. The soldiers involved in a war are responsible for acts of violence against "the enemy," at least in the logical sense that the violence would not have occurred if the soldiers had refused to act. The Nuremberg trials after World War II attempted to establish that individual soldiers are also responsible morally and legally, but this attempt overlooked the extent to which the institutionalization of violence changes its moral dimension. On the one hand an individual soldier is not acting on his own initiative and responsibility, and with the enormous difficulty in obtaining reliable information and making a timely confrontation of government claims, not even U.S. Senators, let alone soldiers and private citizens, are in a good position to make the necessary judgments about the justice of a military engagement. On the other hand a group does not have a soul and cannot act except through the agency of individual men. Thus there is a real difficulty in assigning responsibility for such institutional violence. The other side of the violence, its object, is equally ambiguous, for "the enemy" are being attacked as an organized political force rather than as individuals, and yet since a group does not have a body any more than it has a soul "the enemy" is attacked by attacking the bodies of individual men (and

---

[1] A persuasive account of the extent to which law itself can be a form of violence, rather than an alternative to it, is to be found in E. Z. Friedenberg's essay "A Violent Country" in the *New York Review*, October 20, 1966.

[2] Of course not all cases are so clear: I leave to the reader to ponder whether all sex acts are acts of violence, or just how to distinguish in practical terms those that are from those that are not.

women and children). Warfare, therefore, because it is an institutionalized form of violence, differs from murder in certain fundamental respects.

Riots are another form of institutionalized violence, although their warlike character was not widely recognized until the publication of the report of the President's National Advisory Commission on Civil Disorders. In a riot, as in a war, there are many instances of personal violence, and some persons maintain that the civil disorders are basically massive crime waves. But there is also much of a warlike character. One of the characteristics of the Watts riots, as any will know who have read Robert Conot's *The Rivers of Blood, Years of Darkness,* is that in that riot the people who were supposed to be controlling the situation, the Los Angeles police and their various reinforcements, simply did not know basic facts about the community. In particular they did not know who was the person who could exercise a sort of leadership if the group were left alone and that person's hand was strengthened. One incident illustrates the sort of thing that happened. A Negro policeman was sent in plain clothes into the riot area and told to call back into the precinct whenever there was anything to report. He was told, furthermore, not to identify himself as a policeman under any conditions for fear of jeopardizing himself. At one point, he tried to intervene when some cops were picking on just altogether the wrong person and he ended up getting cursed and having his head bashed in by one of his fellow members of the Los Angeles police force. In effect, the Los Angeles police and their various allies conducted what amounted to a kind of war campaign. They acted like an army going out to occupy a foreign territory where they didn't know the people and didn't speak the language. The result was that their actions had the effect of breaking down whatever social structure there might have been. And the breakdown of the social structure then had the effect of releasing more and more overt violence. The military flavor of our urban disturbances increased over the years, and 1967 saw the appearance not only of machine guns and automatic rifles but also of tanks and armored personnel carriers in Newark and Detroit, in what the Kerner Commission characterized as "indiscriminate and excessive use of force." For that reason urban disorders are really quite different from a normal criminal situation where police act against individual miscreants.

Since these overt forms of violence are, on the whole, fairly easily recognized, let us go on to consider the other forms of violence, the quiet forms which do not necessarily involve any overt physical assault on anybody's person or property. There are both personal and institutional forms of quiet violence, and I would like to begin with a case of what we might call psychological violence, where individuals are involved as individuals and there are not social institutions responsible for the violation of persons that takes place. Consider the following news item: 415

PHOENIX, Ariz., Feb. 6 (AP)—Linda Marie Ault killed herself, policemen said today, rather than make her dog Beauty pay for her night with a married man.

The police quoted her parents, Mr. and Mrs. Joseph Ault, as giving this account:

Linda failed to return home from a dance in Tempe Friday night. On Saturday she admitted she had spent the night with an Air Force lieutenant.

The Aults decided on a punishment that would "wake Linda up." They ordered her to shoot the dog she had owned about two years.

On Sunday, the Aults and Linda took the dog into the desert near their home. They had the girl dig a shallow grave. Then Mrs. Ault grasped the dog between her hands, and Mr. Ault gave his daughter a .22-caliber pistol and told her to shoot the dog.

Instead, the girl put the pistol to her right temple and shot herself.

The police said there were no charges that could be filed against the parents except possibly cruelty to animals.[3]

Obviously, the reason there can be no charges is that the parents did no physical damage to Linda. But I think your reaction might be the same as mine—that they really did terrible violence to the girl by the way they behaved in this situation. Of course one must agree that Linda did violence to herself, but that is not the whole account of the violence in this case. The parents did far more violence to the girl than the lieutenant, and the father recognized that when he said to a detective, "I killed her. I killed her. It's just like I killed her myself." If we fail to recognize that there is really a kind of psychological violence that can be perpetrated on people, a real violation of their autonomy, their dignity, their right to determine things for themselves, their right to be humans rather than dogs, then we fail to realize the full dimension of what it is to do violence to one another.

One of the most obvious transition cases between overt personal violence and quiet personal violence is the case of a threat. Suppose that a robber comes into a bank with a pistol, threatens to shoot one of the tellers, and walks out with money or a hostage or both. This is a case of armed robbery, and we rightly lump it together with cases of mugging and assault, morally and legally speaking, even if everybody emerges from the situation without any bruises or wounds. The reason is that there is a clear threat to do overt physical violence. By means of such a threat a person very often accomplishes what he might otherwise accomplish by actual overt violence. In this case the robber not only gets as much loot but he also accomplishes pretty much the same thing with respect to degrading the persons he is dealing with. A person who is threatened with being shot and then does something which he certainly would never otherwise do is degraded by losing his own autonomy as a person. We recognize that in law and morals: if a person who is threat-ened with a revolver takes money out of a safe and hands it to the rob-ber we don't say that the person who has taken the money out of the safe has stolen it. We say that that person acted under compulsion, and hence the responsibility for what is done does not lie with him but with the person who threatened him.

It is very clear, and very important, that in cases where there is a threat of overt physical violence that we acknowledge that a person acting under that sort of a threat loses his autonomy. Of course, he needn't surrender his autonomy: he could just refuse to hand over the loot. There can be a great deal of dignity in such a refusal, and one of the messages of Sartre's moral philosophy, his existentialism, is that whenever you act other than with full responsibility yourself for your own actions that you are acting in bad faith. That is a very demanding philosophy; but it is one which puts a great deal of emphasis upon autonomy and dignity in human action and is not to be lightly dismissed. Nevertheless we do not expect that people will act with such uncompromising strength and dig-nity. To recognize that people can be broken down by threats and other psychological pressures, as well as by physical attack, and that to have acted under threat or duress is as good an excuse before the law as physical restraint—these recognitions constitute acknowledgement of the pertinence of the concept of psychological violence.

Psychological violence often involves manipulating people. It often in-volves degrading people. It often involves a kind of terrorism one way or another. Perhaps these forms that involve manipulation, degradation and terror are best presented in George Orwell's book *1984*. In that book the hero is deathly afraid of being bitten by a rat. He never is bitten by the rat, but he is threatened with the rat and the threat is such as to break down his character in an extraordinary way. Here we have what might be called the phenomenology of psychological violence.

Apart from these cases of terror and manipulation and degradation there are certain other forms of psychological violence. One of the most insidious is what might be called the "Freudian rebuff."[4] The Freudian rebuff works something like this. A person makes a comment on the Viet-nam war or on civil rights or on some other current topic. The person he is talking to then says, "Well, you're just saying that because of your Oedipal relations with your father." The original speaker naturally ob-jects, "Don't be silly. Of course I had a father and all that. But look at the facts." And then he starts bringing out the journals and newspapers and presents facts and statistics from them. "You must have a terrible Oedipal complex; you're getting so excited about this." And the person then

---

[4] Of course this is an aspect of cocktail-party Freudianism rather than of psycho-analytic theory, and what Freud invented was not this little ploy but the concepts that were later distorted into it.

says, "Look, I've had some fights with my father, but I'm not hung-up on him, I just have normal spats and affection. I've read the paper and I have an independent interest in the civil rights question. It has nothing to do with my relations with my father." To which the response is, "Well, your denial just proves how deep your Oedipal complex is."

This type of Freudian rebuff has the effect of what John Henry Newman[5] called "poisoning the wells." It gives its victim just no ground to stand on. If he tries to stand on facts and statistics, they are discounted and his involvement is attributed to Freudian factors. If he tries to prove that he doesn't have the kind of psychological aberration in question, his very attempt to prove that he doesn't have it is taken to be evidence that he does. He can't get out of the predicament. It is like a quagmire in which the victim sinks deeper no matter which way he moves. So long as the proffered definition of the situation is imposed on him, a person has no way to turn: there is no possible sort of response that can extricate him from that charge laid upon him. To structure a situation against a person in such a manner does violence to him by depriving him of his dignity: no matter what he does there is no way at all, so long as he accepts the problem in the terms in which it is presented, for him to make a response that will allow him to emerge with honor.

Although this sort of cocktail-party Freudianism is not very serious in casual conversations, where the definition of the situation can be challenged or the whole matter just shrugged off, it must be kept in mind that there are many forms of this ploy and that sometimes the whole life and character of a person may be involved. A classic literary and religious version is the dispute between Charles Kingsley and John Henry Newman in the 19th century, in which Kingsley challenged Newman's integrity and ended up losing his stature as a Protestant spokesman, and which is written up in fascinating detail in Newman's *Apologia*. A political variation is the Marxian rebuff where, of course, it is because of your class standing that you have such and such a view, and if you deny that the class standing is influencing you in that way your very denial shows how imbued you are with the class ideology. Between parent and child as well as between husband and wife there are variations of this ploy which turn around the identification (by one insistent party) of love with some particular action or other, so that the other party must either surrender his autonomy or acknowledge his faithlessness.

The cases where this sort of psychological violence are damaging are those where the person structuring the situation is in some position of special authority. Another form particularly virulent in urban schools— and probably suburban schools too—is the teacher's rebuff. An imagina-

---

[5] In his famous debate with Charles Kingsley. See his *Apologia Pro Vita Sua*, conveniently available in a paperback edition (Garden City, N.Y.: Doubleday, 1956).

tive child does something out of the ordinary, and the teacher's response is that he is a discipline problem. It now becomes impossible for the child to get out of being a problem. If he tries to do something creative he will be getting out of line and thereby "confirm" that he is a discipline problem. If he stays in line he will be a scholastic problem, thereby "confirming" that he did not have potential for anything but mischief. The result is a kind of stunted person typical of schools in large urban areas.

This last variation of the psychological rebuff brings us to the fourth general category of violence, institutionalized quiet violence. The schools are an institution, and teachers are hired not so much to act on their own in the classroom as to fulfil a predetermined role. Violence done by the teacher in the classroom may therefore not be personal but institutional, done while acting as a faithful agent of the educational system. The idea of such institutional violence is a very important one.

A clearer example of quiet institutional violence might be a well-established system of slavery or colonial oppression, or the life of contemporary American ghettos. Once established such a system may require relatively little overt violence to maintain it. It is legendary that Southerners used to boast, "We understand our nigras. They are happy here and wouldn't want any other kind of life"—and there is no reason to doubt that many a Southerner, raised in the system and sheltered from the recurrent lynchings, believed it quite sincerely. In that sort of situation it is possible for an institution to go along placidly, as we might say, with no overt disturbances and yet for that institution to be one which is terribly brutal, which does great harm to its victims, and which at the same time brutalizes people who are on top, since they lose a certain measure of their human sensitivity.[6]

There is more violence in the black ghettos than there is anywhere else in America—even when they are quiet. At the time of the Harlem riots in 1964 the Negro psychologist, Kenneth Clark, said that there was more ordinary, day-to-day violence in the life of the ghettos than there was in any day of those disturbances. I'm not sure exactly what he meant. The urban ghettos are places where there is a great deal of overt violence, much of it a kind of reaction to the frustrations of ghetto life. Fanon describes the similar phenomenon of the growth of violence within the oppressed community in the colonial situation in Algeria.[7] When people are suppressed by a colonial regime, when they lack the oppor-

---

[6] Compare Simone Weil: "Thus violence obliterates anybody who feels its touch. It comes to seem just as external to its employer as to its victim. And from this springs the idea of a destiny before which executioner and victim stand equally innocent, before which conquered and conqueror are brothers in the same distress." *The Iliad, or the Poem of Force* (Pendel Hill; Wallingford, Pa., n.d.), p. 19.

[7] Frantz Fanon, *The Wretched of the Earth* (New York: Grove Press, 1966).

tunities which they see other people, white people, around them enjoying, then they become frustrated and have great propensities to violence. The safest target for such angry, frustrated people are their own kind. The Algerians did their first violence to other Algerians, in part because it wasn't safe to do it to a Frenchman. And the same is largely true of the situation that has developed in our urban ghettos. It isn't safe for a person living in the ghettos, if he is feeling frustrated and at the point of explosion, to explode against somebody outside the ghetto; but he can do it to his kids, his wife, his brother and his neighbor, and society will tend to look the other way. So there is a good deal of overt violence in the black ghettos. Perhaps, that is what Clark meant.

But we also have to recognize that there is sometimes a kind of quiet violence in the very operation of the system. Bernard Lafayette, who has worked in urban areas for both the American Friends Service Committee and the Southern Christian Leadership Conference, speaks angrily of the violence of the status quo: "The real issue is that part of the 'good order of society' is the routine oppression and racism committed against millions of Americans every day. That is where the real violence is."[8] The fact is that there is a black ghetto in most American cities which operates very like any system of slavery. Relatively little violence is needed to keep the institution going and yet the institution entails a real violation of the human beings involved, because they are systematically denied the options which are obviously open to the vast majority of the members of the society in which they live. A systematic denial of options is one way to deprive men of autonomy. If I systematically deprive a person of the options that are normal in our society, then he is no longer in a position to decide for himself what to do. Any institution which systematically robs certain people of rightful options generally available to others does violence to those people.

Perhaps denying options would not do violence to people if each individual person was an island unto himself and individuality were the full truth about human life. But it is not. We are social beings. Our whole sense of what we are is dependent on the fact that we live in society and have open to us socially determined options. I am now writing. As I write I make many choices about what to say, some having to do with whole paragraphs, some with single words, and some with punctuation. These choices are dependent upon a social institution language. Unless I knew the language, and unless there were a society of language speakers, I would have no options at all about what to say. The options opened to us by language are very important, but language is only one part of our society. There are many sorts of options which are open to us and important to us as individuals. It is how we act, how we choose with

8 In *Soul Force*, February 15, 1968.

respect to socially defined options, that constitutes what we really are as human beings.

What access we have to socially defined options is much more important than which language or which system of property rights we inherit at birth. By suppressing options you deprive a person of the opportunity to be somebody because you deprive him of choices. The institutional form of quiet violence operates when people are deprived of choices in a systematic way by the very manner in which transactions normally take place, without any individual act being violent in itself or any individual decision being responsible for the system. It is as real, and as overwhelming, as the thief with a knife.

These, then, are the main types of violence that I see. By recognizing those types of violence we begin to get the whole question of violence into a much richer perspective than when we hear the Chief of Police deplore violence. Such a richer perspective is vitally necessary, because we cannot do anything about the violence in our society unless we can see it, and most of us do not see it very well. Conceptions and perceptions are closely dependent on one another, and perhaps having a better idea of what violence is will enable us to recognize more readily the many sorts of violence that surround our lives.

IV

In concluding I want to make four points. The first is that the concept of violence is a moral concept, but not one of absolute condemnation. Very often psychologists and sociologists and other scientists and students of animal behavior avoid the word 'violence' just because it does have a moral connotation. The word 'aggression' is sometimes used instead because it lacks the moral connotations of the term 'violence'. It is important to recognize that these moral elements come in through the fact that an act of violence is a violation of a person. It is also important to recognize that the normal pattern of moral discourse allows for excuses and rationalization. We don't expect people never to do anything which is at all wrong: we allow for excuses.[9]

When a person commits an act of violence he is not necessarily to be condemned, though he does have some explaining to do. The fact that we would require an excuse from him, or some justification of his behavior, indicates that a person's doing an act of violence puts the burden of proof on him; but it doesn't suffice to show that the case has gone against him yet.

The second thing I want to say is that it is entirely clear to me that

[9] The late Professor John L. Austin called the attention of moral philosophers to the importance of excuses in moral discourse. See "A Plea for Excuses," *Philosophical Papers* (London: Oxford University Press, 1961).

there are degrees of violence. All these various forms of violence are indeed violence, but if I simply say of an act or an institution that it is violent I have not yet said enough to give a clear evaluation of that act. I must also take account of how *much* violence it does to persons affected. Unfortunately this is easier said than done. It might at first be thought that overt violence is always worse than quiet violence, but that rule does not hold generally except in the case of murder; in fact physical injury often heals more readily than psychological damage. It is more plausible to argue that institutional violence is always of greater magnitude than personal violence, but that obviously depends on the degree of violence on each side—which means that we must be able to judge the degree of violence in an act or an institution independent of the kind of violence involved. We need a scale for measuring degrees of violence, and we don't have one. Still there are degrees of violence, and it is possible to achieve considerable intersubjective agreement about comparisons of pairs of cases.

My third dictum is that it is not "just a matter of semantics," but a matter with considerable social consequences, whether a particular act or institution is classified as violent. What is at stake is where the "burden of proof" lies in moral and political controversies. If proofs were as decisive in public affairs as they are in logic these stakes would be insignificant; but they are vastly more elusive,[10] and therefore to shift the burden of proof often constitutes a decisive political advantage. An earlier, substantially identical, version of this essay was widely read and often used to effect such a shift in the burden of proof: because black violence and New Left violence could be seen, in terms of this essay, as responses to institutional violence rather than just as attacks on neutral (or good) institutions, their partisans claimed to be relieved of the onus of having initiated violence; sometimes this defense was phrased in terms of "making visible the violence that was there all along." What is at issue is condemnation and justification, not just a choice of words.

Nonviolence, finally, however admirable as personal commitment, is not a viable social goal, and is probably harmful as a slogan for social policy. It does make sense for an individual to commit himself not voluntarily to do violence or to profit from violence. But societies, unlike persons, are not actors; they are the stages where actors perform. So such a commitment makes no sense for a society. And to interpret nonviolence

---

[10] This is partly because "violence," like "democracy" and "reasonable man" and other basic terms of our political vocabulary, is what W. B. Gallie has called an "essentially contestable concept," meaning that one essential feature of its use is that there are no fixed criteria for its application, so that disputes are not just about whether "the criteria" are met but also about what criteria are "really" appropriate. See his essay in M. Black (ed.), *The Importance of Language* (Englewood Cliffs, N.J.: Prentice-Hall, 1962).

on the social level as a program for the "complete elimination of violence" simply distracts attention and energy from the sensible and laudable goal of containing and defusing social violence. Here three goals make sense. One is the obvious goal of reducing the level and degree of violence—of all forms, not just overt violence. A second is finding techniques for breaking the chain of violence and counterviolence. The last is the more ambitious and admittedly utopian goal of Camus:

People like myself want not a world in which murder no longer exists (we are not so crazy as that!) but rather one in which murder is no longer legitimate.[11]

J. GLENN GRAY
The Enduring Appeals of Battle

Millions of men in our day—like millions before us—have learned to live in war's strange element and have discovered in it a powerful fascination. The emotional environment of warfare has always been compelling; it has drawn most men under its spell. Reflection and calm reasoning are alien to it. I wrote in my war journal that I was obsessed with "the tyranny of the present"; the past and the future did not concern me. It was hard for me to think, to be alone. When the signs of peace were visible, I wrote, in some regret: "The purgative force of danger which makes men coarser but perhaps more human will soon be lost and the first months of peace will make some of us yearn for the old days of conflict."

Beyond doubt there are many who simply endure war, hating every moment. Though they may enjoy garrison life or military maneuvers, they experience nothing but distaste and horror for combat itself. Still, those who complain the most may not be immune from war's appeals. Soldiers complain as an inherited right and traditional duty, and few wish to admit to a taste for war. Yet many men both hate and love combat. They know why they hate it; it is harder to know and to be articulate about why they love it. The novice may be eager at times to describe his emotions in combat, but it is the battle-hardened veterans to whom battle has offered the deeper appeals. For some of them the war years are what Dixon Wecter has well called "the one great lyric passage in their lives."

[11] A. Camus: *Neither Victims Nor Executioners* (Chicago: World Without War Publications, 1972), p. 25.

Reprinted from J. Glenn Gray, *The Warriors* (New York: Harcourt, Brace & World, 1959), pp. 28–34, 39–58, with the permission of the author.

What are these secret attractions of war, the ones that have persisted in the West despite revolutionary changes in the methods of warfare? I believe that they are: the delight in seeing, the delight in comradeship, the delight in destruction. Some fighters know one appeal and not the others, some experience all three, and some may, of course, feel other appeals that I do not know. These three had reality for me, and I have found them also throughout the literature of war.

War as a spectacle, as something to see, ought never to be underestimated. There is in all of us what the Bible calls "the lust of the eye," a phrase at once precise and of the widest connotation. It is precise because human beings possess as a primitive urge this love of watching. We fear we will miss something worth seeing. This passion to see surely precedes in most of us the urge to participate in or to aid. Anyone who has watched people crowding around the scene of an accident on the highway realizes that the lust of the eye is real. Anyone who has watched the faces of people at a fire knows it is real. Seeing sometimes absorbs us utterly; it is as though the human being became one great eye. The eye is lustful because it requires the novel, the unusual, the spectator. It cannot satiate itself on the familiar, the routine, the everyday.

This lust may stoop to mindless curiosity, a primordial impulse. Its typical response is an open-minded gaping at a parade or at the explosion of a hydrogen bomb. How many men in each generation have been drawn into the twilight of confused and murderous battle "to see what it is like"? This appeal of war is usually described as the desire to escape the monotony of civilian life and the cramping restrictions of an unadventurous existence. People are often bored with a day that does not offer variety, distraction, threat, and insecurity. They crave the satisfaction of the astonishing. Although war notoriously offers monotony and boredom enough, it also offers the outlandish, the exotic, and the strange. It offers the opportunity of gaping at other lands and other peoples, at curious implements of war, at groups of others like themselves marching in order, and at the captured enemy in a cage.

However, sensuous curiosity is only one level of seeing. The word "see," with its many derivatives, like "insight" and "vision," has an imaginative and intellectual connotation which is far more expansive than the physical. Frequently we are unable to separate these levels of seeing, to distinguish the outer from the inner eye. This is probably no accident. The human being is, after all, a unity, and the sensuous, imaginative, and intellectual elements of his nature can fuse when he is absorbed. Mindless curiosity is not separated as much as we like to believe from what art lovers call the disinterested contemplation of beauty. The delight in battle as a mere spectacle may progress almost insensibly to an aesthetic contemplation or to a more dominantly intellectual contemplation of its awfulness. From the simplest soldier who gazes openmouthed at the panorama of battle in his portion of the field to the trained artist observing the scene, there is, I believe, only a difference of degree. The "seeing" both are engaged in is for them an end in itself before it becomes a spur to action. The dominant motive in both cases appears to be neither the desire for knowledge, though there is much that is instructive in the scene, nor the need to act, though that, too, will become imperative. Their "seeing" is for the sake of seeing, the lust of the eye, where the eye stands for the whole human being, for man the observer.

There is a popular conviction that war and battle are the sphere of ugliness, and, since aesthetic delight is associated with the beautiful, it may be concluded that war is the natural enemy of the aesthetic. I fear that this is in large part an illusion. It is, first of all, wrong to believe that only beauty can give us aesthetic delight; the ugly can please us too, as every artist knows. And furthermore, beauty in various guises is hardly foreign to scenes of battle. While it is undeniable that the disorder and distortion and the violation of nature that conflict brings are ugly beyond compare, there are also color and movement, variety, panoramic sweep, and sometimes even momentary proportion and harmony. If we think of beauty and ugliness without their usual moral overtones, there is often a weird but genuine beauty in the sight of massed men and weapons in combat. Reputedly, it was the sight of advancing columns of men under fire that impelled General Robert E. Lee to remark to one of his staff: "It is well that war is so terrible—we would grow too fond of it."

Of course, it is said that modern battles lack all the color and magnificence of spectacle common to earlier wars. John Neff, in his valuable study entitled *War and Human Progress,* makes much of the decline in our century of the power and authority of what he calls "the claims of delight." In earlier times men at war, he points out, were much more dominated by artistic considerations in the construction of their weapons. They insisted on the decorative and beautiful in cannons, ships, and small arms, even at the obvious expense of the practical and militarily effective. Then, artists of great skill and fame worked on weapons of war, and gunsmiths took great pride in the beauty of their products. The claims of beauty, Neff believes, have had to give way more and more to materialistic and pragmatic aims in this century of total warfare. When I remember some of the hideous implements of battle in World War II, it is hard indeed not to agree with him. Standardization and automatization of weapons have frequently stripped them of any pretense to beauty.

This, though, is only one aspect of battle and of modern war. What has been lost in one realm is compensated for in another. War is now fought in the air as well as on land and sea, and the expanse of vision and spectacle afforded by combat planes is hard to exaggerate. Because these powerful new weapons usually remove those who use them further from the gruesome consequences of their firing, they afford more opportunity 425 for aesthetic satisfaction. Combat in the skies is seldom devoid of the form, grace, and harmony that ground fighting lacks. There are spectacular sweep and drama, a colorfulness and a precision about such combat which earlier centuries knew only in a few great sea battles. It is true that the roar of fighting planes can be unpleasant in its assault upon the ears, and their dives upon their victims for strafing or bombing can be terror-inspiring. But the combatant who is relieved from participation and given the spectator's role can nearly sate the eye with all the elements of fearful beauty.

I remember most vividly my feelings while watching from a landing boat, on the morning of August 25, 1944, the simultaneous bombardment of the French Riviera by our planes and by our fleet of warships. We had come relatively close to the targets under the cover of darkness. As dawn broke and the outline of the coast appeared, thousands of us watched motionless and silent, conscious that we would be called upon to act only after the barrage and bombing were over. Then we saw the planes, appearing from nowhere, and in perfect alignment over their targets. Suddenly, fire and smoke issued from huge cannon on our ships, and the invasion had begun. Our eyes followed the planes as they dived into the melee of smoke and flame and dust and emerged farther down the coast to circle for another run. The assault of bomb and shell on the line of coast was so furious that I half expected a large part of the mainland to become somehow detached and fall into the sea.

When I could forget the havoc and terror that was being created by those shells and bombs among the half-awake inhabitants of the villages, the scene was beyond all question magnificent. I found it easily possible, indeed a temptation hard to resist, to gaze upon the scene spellbound, completely absorbed, indifferent to what the immediate future might bring. Others appeared to manifest a similar intense concentration on the spectacle. Many former soldiers must be able to recall some similar experience. However incomprehensible such scenes may be, and however little anyone would want to see them enacted a second time, few of us can deny, if we are honest, a satisfaction in having seen them. As far as I am concerned, at least part of that satisfaction can be ascribed to delight in aesthetic contemplation.

As I reflect further, it becomes clear, however, that the term "beauty," used in any ordinary sense, is not the major appeal in such spectacles. Instead, it is the fascination that manifestations of power and magnitude hold for the human spirit. Some scenes of battle, much like storms over the ocean or sunsets on the desert or the night sky seen through a telescope, are able to overawe the single individual and hold him in a spell. He is lost in their majesty. His ego temporarily deserts him, and he is absorbed into what he sees. An awareness of power that far surpasses his limited imagination transports him into a state of mind unknown in his everyday experiences. Fleeting as these rapt moments may be, they are, for the majority of men, an escape from themselves that is very different from the escapes induced by sexual love or alcohol. This raptness is a joining and not a losing, a deprivation of self in exchange for a union with objects that were hitherto foreign. Yes, the chief aesthetic appeal of war surely lies in this feeling of the sublime, to which we, children of nature, are directed whether we desire it or not. Astonishment and wonder and awe appear to be part of our deepest being, and war offers them an exercise field par excellence.

.   .   .

Another appeal of war, the communal experience we call comradeship, is thought, on the other hand, to be especially moral and the one genuine advantage of battle that peace can seldom offer. Whether this is true or not deserves to be investigated. The term "comradeship" covers a large number of relationships, from the most personal to the anonymous and general, and here I will consider only some essentials of military comradeship. What calls it into being in battle, what strengthens or weakens it, what is its essential attraction?

The feeling of belonging together that men in battle often find a cementing force needs first to be awakened by an external reason for fighting, but the feeling is by no means dependent on this reason. The cause that calls comradeship into being may be the defense of one's country, the propagation of the one true religious faith, or a passionate political ideology; it may be the maintenance of honor or the recovery of a Helen of Troy. So long as there is a cause, the hoped-for objective may be relatively unimportant in itself. When, through military reverses or the fatiguing and often horrible experiences of combat, the original purpose becomes obscured, the fighter is often sustained solely by the determination not to let down his comrades.

Numberless soldiers have died, more or less willingly, not for country or honor or religious faith or for any other abstract good, but because they realized that by fleeing their post and rescuing themselves, they would expose their companions to greater danger. Such loyalty to the group is the essence of fighting morale. The commander who can preserve and strengthen it knows that all other psychological or physical factors are little in comparison. The feeling of loyalty, it is clear, is the result, and not the cause, of comradeship. Comrades are loyal to each other spontaneously and without any need for reasons. Men may learn to be loyal out of fear or from rational conviction, loyal even to those they dislike. But such loyalty is rarely reliable with great masses of men unless it has some cement in spontaneous liking and the feeling of belonging.

Though comradeship is dependent on being together physically in time   427 and space, it is not a herding animal instinct. Little can be learned, I am convinced, from attempting to compare animal and human forms of association. In extreme danger and need, there is undeniably a minimal satisfaction in having others of your own species in your vicinity. The proverb that "misery loves company" is not without basis, particularly in situations where defense and aggression are involved. But it is equally true that men can live in the same room and share the same suffering without any sense of belonging together. They can live past each other and be irresponsible toward each other, even when their welfare is clearly dependent on co-operation.

German soldiers who endured Russian prisoner-of-war camps in the decade after World War II have described convincingly how the Communist system succeeded in destroying any sense of comradeship among prisoners simply by making the results of individual labor the basis of food allotments. Under a system like this, men can not only eat their fill but also enjoy superfluity without any concern for a mate who may slowly be starving to death. This lamentable fact about human nature has too often been observed to require much further confirmation. The physical proximity of men can do no more than create the minimal conditions of comradeship. It no more explains the communal appeal of war than it explains why people love cities.

What then are the important components of comradeship, if physical presence is only a minimal condition? The one that occurs immediately is organization for a common goal. Even a very loose type of organization can induce many people to moderate their self-assertiveness and accommodate themselves to the direction of a superpersonal will. Everyone is aware of the vast difference between a number of men as a chance collection of individuals and the same number as an organized group or community. A community has purpose and plan, and there is in us an almost instinctive recognition of the connection between unity and strength.

Those who stand in disorganized masses against smaller groups of the organized are always aware of the tremendous odds against them. The sight of huge crowds of prisoners of war being herded toward collection centers by a few guards with rifles slung over their backs is one filled with pathos. It is not the absence of weapons that makes these prisoners helpless before their guards. It is the absence of a common will, the failing assurance that others will act in concert with you against the conquerors.

But organization is of many kinds, and the military kind is special in aiming at common and concrete goals. The organization of a civilian community, a city, for example, is not without goals, but they are rarely concrete, and many members are hardly aware of their existence. If a 428 civilian community has goals with more reality and power to endure than military goals, as I believe it does, its goals are, nevertheless, unable to generate the degree of loyalty that a military organization can.

In war it is a commonplace of command that the goals of the fighting forces need to be clear and to be known. Naturally, the over-all goal is to win the war and then go home. But in any given action, the goal is to overcome the attacking enemy or, if you are the attacker, to win the stated objective. Any fighting unit must have a limited and specific objective, and the more defined and bounded it is, the greater the willingness, as a rule, on the part of soldiers to abandon their natural desire for self-preservation. Officers soon learn to dread hazy and ill-defined orders from above. If the goal is physical, a piece of earth to take or defend, a machine-gun nest to destroy, a strong point to annihilate, officers are much more likely to evoke the sense of comradeship. They realize that comradeship at first develops through the consciousness of an obstacle to be overcome through common effort. A fighting unit with morale is one in which many are of like mind and determination, unconsciously agreed on the suppression of individual desires in the interest of a shared purpose.

Organization for a common and concrete goal in peacetime organizations does not evoke anything like the degree of comradeship commonly known in war. Evidently, the presence of danger is distinctive and important. Men then are organized for a goal whose realization involves the real possibility of death or injury. How does danger break down the barriers of the self and give man an experience of community? The answer to this question is the key to one of the oldest and most enduring incitements to battle.

Danger provides a certain spice to experience; this is common knowledge. It quickens the pulse and makes us more aware of being alive by calling attention to our physical selves. The thrill of the chase in hunting, of riding a horse very fast, or of driving an automobile recklessly is of this sort. But the excitement created in us by such activities has little communal significance. Its origin appears to be sexual, if we understand sex in the wide sense given to it by Freud. The increased vitality we feel where danger is incidental is due to awareness of mastery over the environment. It is an individualist, not a communal, drive.

The excitement and thrill of battle, on the other hand, are of a different sort, for there danger is central and not incidental. There is little of the play element about combat, however much there may have been in training for it. Instead, for most soldiers there is the hovering inescapable sense of irreversibility. "This is for keeps," as soldier slang is likely to put it. This profound earnestness is by no means devoid of lightheartedness, as seen in teasing and horseplay, but men are conscious that they are on a one-way street, so to speak, and what they do or fail to do can be of great consequence. Those who enter into battle, as distinguished 429 from those who only hover on its fringes, do not fight as duelists fight. Almost automatically, they fight as a unit, a group. Training can help a great deal in bringing this about more quickly and easily in an early stage. But training can only help to make actual what is inherent. As any commander knows, an hour or two of combat can do more to weld a unit together than can months of intensive training.

Many veterans who are honest with themselves will admit, I believe, that the experience of communal effort in battle, even under the altered conditions of modern war, has been a high point in their lives. Despite the horror, the weariness, the grime, and the hatred, participation with others in the chances of battle had its unforgettable side, which they would not want to have missed. For anyone who has not experienced it himself, the feeling is hard to comprehend, and, for the participant, hard to explain to anyone else. Probably the feeling of liberation is nearly basic. It is this feeling that explains the curious combination of earnestness and lightheartedness so often noted in men in battle.

Many of us can experience freedom as a thrilling reality, something both serious and joyous, only when we are acting in unison with others for a concrete goal that costs something absolute for its attainment. Individual freedom to do what we will with our lives and our talents, the freedom of self-determination, appears to us most of the time as frivolous or burdensome. Such freedom leaves us empty and alone, feeling undirected and insignificant. Only comparatively few of us know how to make this individual freedom productive and joyous. But communal freedom can pervade nearly everyone and carry everything before it. This elemental fact about freedom the opponents of democracy have learned well, and it constitutes for them a large initial advantage.

The lightheartedness that communal participation brings has little of the sensuous or merely pleasant about it, just as the earnestness has little of the calculating or rational. Both derive instead from a consciousness of power that is supra-individual. We feel earnest and gay at such moments because we are liberated from our individual impotence and are drunk with the power that union with our fellows brings. In moments like these many have a vague awareness of how isolated and separate their lives have hitherto been and how much they have missed by living in the narrow circle of family or a few friends. With the boundaries of the self expanded, they sense a kinship never known before. Their "I" passes insensibly into a "we," "my" becomes "our," and individual fate loses its central importance.

At its height, this sense of comradeship is an ecstasy not unlike the aesthetic ecstasy previously described, though occasioned by different forces. In most of us there is a genuine longing for community with our human species, and at the same time an awkwardness and helplessness about finding the way to achieve it. Some extreme experience—mortal

430

danger or the threat of destruction—is necessary to bring us fully together with our comrades or with nature. This is a great pity, for there are surely alternative ways more creative and less dreadful, if men would only seek them out. Until now, war has appealed because we discover some of the mysteries of communal joy in its forbidden depths. Comradeship reaches its peak in battle.

The secret of comradeship has not been exhausted, however, in the feeling of freedom and power instilled in us by communal effort in combat. There is something more and equally important. The sense of power and liberation that comes over men at such moments stems from a source beyond the union of men. I believe it is nothing less than the assurance of immortality that makes self-sacrifice at these moments so relatively easy. Men are true comrades only when each is ready to give up his life for the other, without reflection and without thought of personal loss. Who can doubt that every war, the two world wars no less than former ones, has produced true comradeship like this?

Such sacrifice seems hard and heroic to those who have never felt communal ecstasy. In fact, it is not nearly so difficult as many less absolute acts in peacetime and in civilian life, for death becomes in a measure unreal and unbelievable to one who is sharing his life with his companions. Immortality is not something remote and otherworldly, possibly or probably true and real; on the contrary, it becomes a present and self-evident fact.

Nothing is further from the truth than the insistence of certain existentialist philosophers that each person must die his own death and experience it unsharably. If that were so, how many lives would have been spared on the battlefield! But in fact, death for men united with each other can be shared as few other of life's great moments can be. To be sure, it is not death as we know it usually in civilian life. In the German language men never die in battle. They *fall*. The term is exact for the expression of self-sacrifice when it is motivated by the feeling of comradeship. I may fall, but I do not die, for that which is real in me goes forward and lives on in the comrades for whom I gave up my physical life.

Let me not be misunderstood. It is unquestionably true that thousands of soldiers die in battle, miserable, alone, and embittered, without any conviction of self-sacrifice and without any other satisfactions. I suspect the percentage of such soldiers has increased markedly in recent wars. But for those who in every battle are seized by the passion for self-sacrifice, dying has lost its terrors because its reality has vanished.

There must be a similarity between this willingness of soldier-comrades for self-sacrifice and the willingness of saints and martyrs to die for their religious faith. It is probably no accident that the religions of the West have not cast away their military terminology or even their militant char- 431 acter—"Onward, Christian soldiers! Marching as to war . . ." nor that our wars are defended in terms of devotion and salvation. The true believer must be ready to give up his life for the faith. And if he is a genuine saint he will regard this sacrifice as no loss, for the self has become indestructible in being united with a supreme reality. There are, of course, important differences. The reality for which the martyr sacrifices himself is not visible and intimate like the soldier's. The martyr usually dies alone, scorned by the multitude. In this sense his lot is infinitely harder. It is hardly surprising that few men are capable of dying joyfully as martyrs whereas thousands are capable of self-sacrifice in wartime. Nevertheless, a basic point of resemblance remains, namely, that death has lost not only its sting but its reality, too, for the self that dies is little in comparison with that which survives and triumphs.

This is the mystical element of war that has been mentioned by nearly all serious writers on the subject. William James spoke of it as a sacrament, and once remarked that "society would rot without the mystical blood payment." And G. F. Nicolai, in his book *The Biology of War,* is persuaded that "the boundless capacity for self-sacrifice" is what is intoxicating and great about war. It is this that occasions frequent doubt in lovers of peace whether men will ever give up warfare, and, at times, the vagrant question whether it is desirable that they should. This capacity for self-sacrifice is what all defenders of war (in our day grown few) use as their final argument for the necessity and ultimate morality of war. Since men can only be brought by such extreme means to a recognition of their true nature and their essential relationships, these defenders tell us, it is folly to seek to abolish war, because it would be to abolish death itself.

Many humanists and humanitarians, on the other hand, attack the impulse to self-sacrifice as the very core of moral evil. It offends their whole rational image of the distinctively human. And the more forthright do not hesitate to express their abhorrence for the Christian faith insofar as it is founded on the theme of self-sacrifice. Readers of Rebecca West's *Black Lamb and Grey Falcon* will not easily forget the bitterness with which she deals with the notion of sacrifice and her rejection of Saint Paul, Saint Augustine, and Luther for burdening the Christian faith with "this ugly theme."

Her reflections, after witnessing a rather gruesome ceremony in the backwaters of Yugoslavia in which black lambs are sacrificed in the belief that they will heal the local peasants of sundry diseases, conclude as follows:

I knew this rock well. I had lived under the shadow of it all my life. All our Western thought is founded on this repulsive pretence that pain is the proper price of any good thing. Here it could be seen how the meaning of the Crucifixion had been hidden from us, though it was written clear. A supremely good man was born on earth, a man who was without cruelty, who could have taught mankind to live in perpetual happiness; and because we are infatuated with this idea of sacrifice, of shedding innocent blood to secure innocent advantages, we found nothing better to do with this passport to deliverance than to destroy him.

It is true that we in the West are frequently infatuated with the idea of sacrifice, particularly self-sacrifice. Why are some people so strongly repelled and others again and again attracted by the impulse to self-sacrifice? Or why do both attraction and repulsion have place in the same breast at different moments? As moralists, we are repelled, I suspect, because the impulse to sacrifice is not subject to rational judgment and control. It takes hold of us and forces us against our will, later claiming justification from some higher authority than the human. As often as not, it puts itself at the service of an evil cause, perhaps more frequently than in the service of the good. The mysterious power that such leaders as Napoleon, Hitler, and Stalin had in their being that enabled them to create a love for self-sacrifice perplexes us endlessly. We cannot condemn it with full conviction, since it seems likely that both leaders and led were in large degree powerless to prevent the impulses that dominated them.

Yet such power is appalling beyond measure and from a rational viewpoint deserving of the deepest condemnation. The limits of free will and morality are transgressed, and man is forced to seek religious and metaphysical justification for self-sacrifice, even when committed in an evil cause. As in the aesthetic appeal of war, when we reach the impulse of the sublime, so in the communal appeal of comradeship, when we reach the impulse to self-sacrifice, we are confronted with contradictions that are deeply embedded in our culture, if not in human nature itself. What our moral self tells us is abhorrent, our religious self and our aesthetic self yearn for as the ultimate good. This is part of the riddle of war.

If we are truly wise, perhaps we should not want to alter these capacities of our human nature, even though we suffer from them immeasurably and may yet succumb to their threat. For the willingness to sacrifice self, like the attraction of the sublime, is what makes possible the higher reaches of the spirit into the realms of poetry, philosophy, and genuine religion. They prevent our best men from losing interest in and hope for our species. They stand in the way of discouragement and cynicism. As moralists, we can condemn Saint Paul and Saint Augustine for their mystical conviction that without sacrifice no purgation from sin is possible. But we should be cautious in so doing, for they were convinced that without the supra-moral act, we human beings are not able to lead even a normally moral existence. Though they were not disposed to believe that God was without moral qualities, they were quite certain that there was more in His universe than the determinations of good and evil. 433

For them the "I am" preceded logically and in time the "I ought." And vast numbers of people have agreed with them that the religious order is superior to the moral, though they continue to be confused about how the two are related.

Are we not right in honoring the fighter's impulse to sacrifice himself for a comrade, even though it be done, as it so frequently is, in an evil cause? I think so. It is some kind of world historical pathos that the striving for union and for immortality must again and again be consummated while men are in the service of destruction. I do not doubt for a moment that wars are made many times more deadly because of this striving and this impulse. Yet I would not want to be without the assurance their existence gives me that our species has a different destiny than is granted to other animals. Though we often sink below them, we can at moments rise above them, too.

If the lust of the eye and the yearning for communion with our fellows were the only appeals of combat, we might be confident that they would be ultimately capable of satisfaction in other ways. But my own observation and the history of warfare both convince me that there is a third impulse to battle much more sinister than these. Anyone who has watched men on the battlefield at work with artillery, or looked into the eyes of veteran killers fresh from slaughter, or studied the descriptions of bombardiers' feelings while smashing their targets, finds hard to escape the conclusion that there is a delight in destruction. A walk across any battlefield shortly after the guns have fallen silent is convincing enough. A sensitive person is sure to be oppressed by a spirit of evil there, a radical evil which suddenly makes the medieval images of hell and the thousand devils of that imagination believable. This evil appears to surpass mere human malice and to demand explanation in cosmological and religious terms.

Men who have lived in the zone of combat long enough to be veterans are sometimes possessed by a fury that makes them capable of anything. Blinded by the rage to destroy and supremely careless of consequences, they storm against the enemy until they are either victorious, dead, or utterly exhausted. It is as if they are seized by a demon and are no longer in control of themselves. From the Homeric account of the sacking of Troy to the conquest of Dienbienphu, Western literature is filled with descriptions of soldiers as berserkers and mad destroyers.

Perhaps the following account from the diary of Ernst Juenger in World War I may stand for many because it is so concise and exactly drawn. It describes the beginning of the last German offensive in the West.

The great moment had come. The curtain of fire lifted from the front trenches. We stood up.

With a mixture of feelings, evoked by bloodthirstiness, rage, and intoxication, we moved in step, ponderously but irresistibly toward the enemy lines. I was well ahead of the company, followed by Vinke and a one-year veteran named Haake. My right hand embraced the shaft of my pistol, my left a riding stick of bamboo cane. I was boiling with a mad rage, which had taken hold of me and all the others in an incomprehensible fashion. The overwhelming wish to kill gave wings to my feet. Rage pressed bitter tears from my eyes.

The monstrous desire for annihilation, which hovered over the battlefield, thickened the brains of the men and submerged them in a red fog. We called to each other in sobs and stammered disconnected sentences. A neutral observer might have perhaps believed that we were seized by an excess of happiness.

Happiness is doubtless the wrong word for the satisfaction that men experience when they are possessed by the lust to destroy and to kill their kind. Most men would never admit that they enjoy killing, and there are a great many who do not. On the other hand, thousands of youths who never suspected the presence of such an impulse in themselves have learned in military life the mad excitement of destroying. The appetite is one that requires cultivation in the environment of disorder and deprivation common to life at the front. It usually marks the great difference between green troops and veterans. Generals often name it "the will to close with the enemy." This innocent-sounding phrase conceals the very substance of the delight in destruction slumbering in most of us. When soldiers step over the line that separates self-defense from fighting for its own sake, as it is so easy for them to do, they experience something that stirs deep chords in their being. The soldier-killer is learning to serve a different deity, and his concern is with death and not life, destruction and not construction.

Of the many writers who are preoccupied today with man's urge toward destruction, Ernest Hemingway stands out as one who has succeeded in incorporating the spirit of violence in his men and women. In his *For Whom the Bell Tolls,* he has his hero say at one point: "Stop making dubious literature about the Berbers and the old Iberians and admit that you have liked to kill as all who are soldiers by choice have enjoyed it at some time whether they lie about it or not." And his old colonel in the more recent book *Across the River and into the Trees* is as profound a portrait of the soldier-killer as we have seen in recent literature. The colonel is so far aware of this impulse to destruction in himself that he tries to counterbalance it by the contrary appeal, namely, Eros, in the form of the young and beautiful countess. This latter book has been harshly criticized from an artistic point of view, and not many have seen, I believe, how well Hemingway grasps the two primordial forces that are in conflict within the colonel, as within many a professional warrior, conflicts that can be resolved in a fashion only by death.

Sigmund Freud has labeled these forces in human nature the Eros drive or instinct, the impulse within us that strives for closer union with others and seeks to preserve and conserve, and the Thanatos (death) drive or instinct, the impulse that works for the dissolution of everything 435 living or united. Freud felt that these two are in eternal conflict within man, and he became, consequently, pessimistic about ever eradicating war as an institution. Men are in one part of their being in love with death, and periods of war in human society represent the dominance of this impulsion.

Of course, this idea of an independent destructive force in life is age-old. The early Greek philosopher Empedocles gave imaginative form to a cosmology in which two universal principles explain the universe. Empedocles taught that the universe is in ceaseless change, in generation and decay, because Love and Strife are ever at work in the animate and the inanimate. Love unites all forms of life, for a period holding the upper hand, and Strife tears them apart and breaks down what previously belonged together. The original components are not annihilated, but simply dispersed in various forms by Strife. They are able to form new unions once more, and the endless process of composition and decomposition continues. Empedocles conceived both forces as of equal strength, both eternal, and both mixed equally in all things. In this imaginative version of the world process, he sees, also, a necessary relationship between these cosmological powers, an insight that is sounder and more fruitful than most modern conceptions.

We are tempted under the influence of Darwinian thought to explain away man's delight in destruction as a regressive impulse, a return to primitivism and to animal nature. We picture, sometimes with the help of Freudians, all our cultural institutions as a kind of mask covering up the animalistic instincts that lie beneath the surface of all behavior. Such a view tends to explain all phenomena of human destructiveness, from the boyish pleasure in the tinkle of broken glass to the sadistic orgies of concentration camps, as a reassertion of man's animal nature under the veneer of culture. Man when he destroys is an animal; when he conserves he is distinctively human.

I cannot escape the conviction that this is an illusion, and a dangerous one. When man is at his destructive work, he is on a different plane from the animal altogether. And destructive urges are as capable of being found in highly cultivated natures as in the simpler ones, if not more so. The satisfaction in destroying seems to me peculiarly human, or, more exactly put, devilish in a way animals can never be. We sense in it always the Mephistophelean cry that all created things deserve to be destroyed. Sometimes there is no more concrete motive for destroying than this one, just as there is no expressible motive for creating. I described this kind of wanton behavior in my journal one night.

It was an unforgivable spectacle. They shamed us as Americans, as colleagues and junior officers, they shamed us before our hired people. Our President lay
on his bier in Washington, boys from our Division lay wounded and dying on

the battlefields round about, and these lordly colonels drank themselves sense-less and wantonly destroyed property with their pistols. It was a commentary on the war, on the ueslessness of fighting for ideals, on the depravity of the military life.

Indeed, there are many important similarities, I feel, between the creative and destructive urges in most of us. Surely the immediate sense of release that is the satisfaction in accomplishment and mastery is not very different in the two impulses. One may become a master in one field as in the other, and there are perhaps as many levels of accomplishment. Few men ever reach superlatives in the realm of destruction; most of us remain, as in the domain of creation, moderately capable.

But artistry in destruction is qualitatively different in its effects upon the individual, in a way that minimizes similarities. It loosens one by one our ties with others and leaves us in the end isolated and alone. Destruction is an artistry directed not toward perfection and fulfillment, but toward chaos and moral anarchy. Its delights may be deep and within the reach of more men than are the joys of creation, but their capacity to reproduce and to endure is very limited. Just as creation raises us above the level of the animal, destruction forces us below it by eliminating communication. As creativity can unite us with our natural and human environment, destruction isolates us from both. That is why destruction in retrospect usually appears so repellent in its inmost nature.

If we ask what the points of similarity are between the appeal of destruction and the two appeals of war I have already examined, I think it is not difficult to recognize that the delight in destroying has, like the others, an ecstatic character. But in one sense only. Men feel overpowered by it, seized from without, and relatively helpless to change or control it. Nevertheless, it is an ecstasy without a union, for comradeship among killers is terribly difficult, and the kinship with nature that aesthetic vision often affords is closed to them. Nor is the breaking down of the barriers of self a quality of the appeal of destroying. On the contrary, I think that destruction is ultimately an individual matter, a function of the person and not the group. This is not to deny, of course, that men go berserk in groups and kill more easily together than when alone. Yet the satisfaction it brings appears to lie, not in losing themselves and their egos, but precisely in greater consciousness of themselves. If they hold together as partners in destruction, it is not so much from a feeling of belonging as from fear of retaliation when alone.

The willingness to sacrifice self for comrades is no longer characteristic of soldiers who have become killers for pleasure. War henceforth becomes for them increasingly what the philosopher Hobbes thought to be the primal condition of all human life, a war of every man against every man. That soldier-killers seldom reach this stage must be attributed to the 437 presence of other impulses in their nature and to the episodical character of battle and combat. I can hardly doubt that the delight in destruction leads in this direction.

This is not the only melancholy consequence of this impulse, for its very nature is to be totalitarian and exclusive. Unlike other delights, it becomes, relatively soon in most men, a consuming lust which swallows up other pleasures. It tends to turn men inward upon themselves and make them inaccessible to more normal satisfactions. Because they rarely can feel remorse, they experience no purgation and cannot grow. The utter absence of love in this inverted kind of creation makes the delight essentially sterile. Though there may be a fierce pride in the numbers destroyed and in their reputation for proficiency, soldier-killers usually experience an ineffable sameness and boredom in their lives. The restlessness of such men in rest areas behind the front is notorious.

How deeply is this impulse to destroy rooted and persistent in human nature? Are the imaginative visions of Empedocles and Freud true in conceiving that the destructive elements in man and nature is as strong and recurrent as the conserving, erotic element? Or can our delight in destruction be channeled into other activities than the traditional one of warfare? We are not far advanced on the way to these answers. We do not know whether a peaceful society can be made attractive enough to wean men away from the appeals of battle. Today we are seeking to make war so horrible that men will be frightened away from it. But this is hardly likely to be more fruitful in the future than it has been in the past. More productive will certainly be our efforts to eliminate the social, economic, and political injustices that are always the immediate occasion of hostilities. Even then, we shall be confronted with the spiritual emptiness and inner hunger that impel many men toward combat. Our society has not begun to wrestle with this problem of how to provide fulfillment to human life, to which war is so often an illusory path.

The weather has been unspeakably bad also, and what with the dawning realization that the war may continue through the winter, it has been sufficient to lower my previous high spirits. Perhaps "high spirits" is not the proper term for the nervous excitement and tension of this war front. I experience so much as in a dream or as on a stage, and at times I can step aside, as one does in a dream, and say: Is this really I? "Sad and laughable and strange" is the best combination of adjectives to describe these twilight days of our old world— the words that Plato used to describe his great myth at the end of The Republic. I would say, first strange, then sad, then laughable—but the laugh is not the same as the laugh of one in love when his beloved has delighted him with some idiosyncrasy of love. It is the laugh of the fallen angels who have renounced heaven but find hell hard to endure. (War journal, October 2, 1944)

JAN NAVERSON
Pacifism: A Philosophical Analysis

Several different doctrines have been called "pacifism," and it is impossible
to say anything cogent about it without saying which of them one has in
mind. I must begin by making it clear, then, that I am limiting the discussion of pacifism to a rather narrow band of doctrines, further distinctions
among which will be brought out below. By "pacifism," I do *not* mean the
theory that violence is evil. With appropriate restrictions, this is a view
that every person with any pretensions to morality doubtless holds: Nobody thinks that we have a right to inflict pain wantonly on other people.
The pacifist goes a very long step further. *His* belief is not only that violence is evil but also that it is morally wrong to use force to resist, punish,
or prevent violence. This further step makes pacifism a radical moral
doctrine. What I shall try to establish below is that it is in fact, more than
merely radical—it is actually incoherent because self-contradictory in its
fundamental intent. I shall also suggest that several moral attitudes and
psychological views which have tended to be associated with pacifism as I
have defined it do not have any necessary connection with that doctrine.
Most proponents of pacifism, I shall argue, have tended to confuse these
different doctrines, and that confusion is probably what accounts for such
popularity as pacifism has had.

It is next in order to point out that the pacifistic attitude is a matter of
degree, and this in two respects. In the first place, there is the question:
How much violence should not be resisted, and what degree of force is
one not entitled to use in resisting, punishing, or preventing it? Answers
to this question will make a lot of difference. For example, everyone would
agree that there are limits to the kind and degree of force with which a
particular degree of violence is to be met: we do not have a right to kill
someone for rapping us on the ribs, for example, and yet there is no
tendency toward pacifism in this. We might go further and maintain, for
example, that capital punishment, even for the crime of murder, is unjustified without doing so on pacifist grounds. Again, the pacifist should say
just what sort of a reaction constitutes a forcible or violent one. If somebody attacks me with his fists and I pin his arms to his body with wrestling
holds which restrict him but cause him no pain, is that all right in the
pacifist's book? And again, many non-pacifists could consistently maintain

Reprinted from *Ethics*, Vol. 75 (1965), 259–271. Copyright 1965 by The University of Chicago Press. Reprinted with the permission of the author and the publisher.

that we should avoid, to the extent that it is possible, inflicting a like pain on those who attempt to inflict pain on us. It is unnecessary to be a pacifist merely in order to deny the moral soundness of the principle, "an eye for an eye and a tooth for a tooth." We need a clarification, then, from the pacifist as to just how far he is and is not willing to go. But this need should already make us pause, for surely the pacifist cannot draw these lines in a merely arbitrary manner. It is his reasons for drawing the ones he does that count, and these are what I propose to discuss below.

The second matter of degree in respect of which the pacifist must specify his doctrine concerns the question: Who ought not to resist violence with force? For example, there are pacifists who would only claim that they themselves ought not to. Others would say that only pacifists ought not to, or that all persons of a certain type, where the type is not specified in terms of belief or non-belief in pacifism, ought not to resist violence with force. And, finally, there are those who hold that everyone ought not to do so. We shall see that considerations about this second variable doom some forms of pacifism to contradiction.

My general program will be to show that (1) only the doctrine that everyone ought not to resist violence with force is of philosophical interest among those doctrines known as "pacifism"; (2) that doctrine, if advanced as a moral doctrine, is logically untenable; and (3) the reasons for the popularity of pacifism rest on failure to see exactly what the doctrine is. The things which pacifism wishes to accomplish, insofar as they are worth accomplishing, can be managed on the basis of quite ordinary and conservative moral principles.

Let us begin by being precise about the kind of moral force the principle of pacifism is intended to have. One good way to do this is to consider what it is intended to deny. What would non-pacifists, which I suppose includes most people, say of a man who followed Christ's suggestion and, when unaccountably slapped, simply turned the other cheek? They might say that such a man is either a fool or a saint. Or they might say, "It's all very well for him to do that, but it's not for me"; or they might simply shrug their shoulders and say, "Well, it takes all kinds, doesn't it?" But they would *not* say that a man who did that ought to be punished in some way; they would not even say that he had done anything wrong. In fact, as I have mentioned, they would more likely than not find something admirable about it. The point, then, is this: The non-pacifist does *not* say that it is your *duty* to resist violence with force. The non-pacifist is merely saying that there's nothing wrong with doing so, that one has every right to do so if he is so inclined. Whether we wish to add that a person would be foolish or silly to do so is quite another question, one on which the non-pacifist does not *need* to take any particular position.

Consequently, a genuine pacifist cannot merely say that we may, if we wish, prefer not to resist violence with force. Nor can he merely say that there is something admirable or saintly about not doing so, for, as pointed out above, the non-pacifist could perfectly well agree with that. He must say, instead, that, for whatever class of people he thinks it applies to, there is something positively wrong about meeting violence with force. He must say that, insofar as the people to whom his principle applies resort to force, they are committing a breach of moral duty—a very serious thing to say. Just how serious, we shall ere long see.

Next, we must understand what the implications of holding pacifism as a moral principle are, and the first such implication requiring our attention concerns the matter of the size of the class of people to which it is supposed to apply. It will be of interest to discuss two of the four possibilities previously listed, I think. The first is that in which the pacifist says that only pacifists have the duty of pacifism. Let us see what this amounts to.

If we say that the principle of pacifism is the principle that all and only pacifists have a duty of not opposing violence with force, we get into a very odd situation. For suppose we ask ourselves, "Very well, which people are the pacifists then?" The answer will have to be "All those people who believe that pacifists have the duty not to meet violence with force." But surely one could believe that a certain class of people, whom we shall call "pacifists," have the duty not to meet violence with force without believing that one ought not, oneself, to meet violence with force. That is to say, the "principle" that pacifists ought to avoid meeting violence with force, is circular: It presupposes that one already knows who the pacifists are. Yet this is precisely what that statement of the principle is supposed to answer! We are supposed to be able to say that anybody who believes that principle is a pacifist; yet, as we have seen, a person could very well believe that a certain class of people called "pacifists" ought not to meet violence with force without believing that he himself ought not to meet violence with force. Thus everyone could be a "pacifist" in the sense of believing that statement and yet no one believe that he *himself* (or anyone in particular) ought to avoid meeting violence with force. Consequently, pacifism cannot be specified in that way. A pacifist must be a person who believes either that he himself (at least) ought not to meet force with force or that some larger class of persons, perhaps everyone, ought not to meet force with force. He would then be believing something definite, and we are then in a position to ask why.

Incidentally, it is worth mentioning that when people say things such as "Only pacifists have the duty of pacifism," "Only Catholics have the duties of Catholicism," and, in general, "Only X-ists have the duties of X-ism" they probably are falling into a trap which catches a good many people. It is, namely, the mistake of supposing that what it *is* to have a certain duty is to *believe* that you have a certain duty. The untenability of this is parallel to the untenability of the previously mentioned attempt to say what pacifism is. For, if having a duty is believing that you have a certain 441 duty, the question arises, "*What* does such a person believe?" The answer that must be given if we follow this analysis would then be, "He believes that he believes that he has a certain duty"; and so on, ad infinitum.

On the other hand, one might believe that having a duty does not consist in believing that one has and yet believe that only those people really have the duty who believe that they have it. But in that case, we would, being conscientious, perhaps want to ask the question, "Well, *ought* I to believe that I have that duty, or oughtn't I?" If you say that the answer is "Yes," the reason cannot be that you already do believe it, for you are asking whether you *should*. On the other hand, the answer "No" or "It doesn't make any difference—it's up to you," implies that there is really no reason for doing the thing in question at all. In short, asking whether I ought to believe that I have a duty to do *x,* is equivalent to asking whether I should *do x*. A person might very well believe that he ought to do *x* but be wrong. It might be the case that he really ought *not* to do *x;* in that case the fact that he believes he ought to do *x,* far from being a reason why he ought to do it, is a reason for us to point out his error. It also, of course, presupposes that he has some reason other than his belief for thinking it is his duty to do *x*.

Having cleared this red herring out of the way, we must consider the view of those who believe that they themselves have a duty of pacifism and ask ourselves the question: What general kind of reason must a person have for supposing a certain type of act to be *his* duty, in a moral sense? Now, one answer he might give is that pacifism as such is a duty, that is, that meeting violence with force is, as such, wrong. In that case, however, what he thinks is not merely that *he* has this duty, but that *everyone* has this duty.

Now he might object, "Well, but no; I don't mean that everyone has it. For instance, if a man is defending, not himself, but *other* people, such as his wife and children, then he has a right to meet violence with force." Now this, of course, would be a very important qualification to his principle and one of a kind which we will be discussing in a moment. Meanwhile, however, we may point out that he evidently still thinks that, if it weren't for certain more important duties, everyone would have a duty to avoid meeting violence with force. In other words, he then believes that, other things being equal, one ought not to meet violence with force. He believes, to put it yet another way, that if one does meet violence with force, one must have a special excuse or justification of a moral kind; then he may want to give some account of just which excuses and justifications would do. Nevertheless, he is now holding a general principle.

Suppose, however, he holds that no one *else* has this duty of pacifism, that only he himself ought not to meet force with force, although it is quite all right for others to do so. Now if this is what our man feels, we may continue to call him a "pacifist," in a somewhat attenuated sense, but he

442

is then no longer holding pacifism as a *moral* principle or, indeed, as a principle at all.[1] For now his disinclination for violence is essentially just a matter of taste. I like pistachio ice cream, but I wouldn't dream of saying that other people have a duty to eat it; similarly, this man just doesn't *like* to meet force with force, although he wouldn't dream of insisting that others act as he does. And this is a secondary sense of "pacifism," first, because pacifism has always been advocated on moral grounds and, second, because non-pacifists can easily have this same feeling. A person might very well feel squeamish, for example, about using force, even in self-defense, or he might not be able to bring himself to use it even if he wants to. But none of these has anything to do with asserting pacifism to be a duty. Moreover, a mere attitude could hardly license a man to refuse military service if it were required of him, or to join ban-the-bomb crusades, and so forth. (I fear, however, that such attitudes have sometimes caused people to do those things.)

And, in turn, it is similarly impossible to claim that your support of pacifism is a moral one if your position is that a certain selection of people, but no one else, ought not to meet force with force, even though you are unprepared to offer any reason whatever for this selection. Suppose, for example, that you hold that only the Arapahoes, or only the Chinese, or only people more than six feet high have this "duty." If such were the case, and no reasons offered at all, we could only conclude that you had a very peculiar attitude toward the Arapahoes, or whatever, but we would hardly want to say that you had a moral principle. Your "principle" amounts to saying that these particular individuals happen to have the duty of pacifism just because they are the individuals they are, and this, as Bentham would say, is the "negation of all principles." Of course, if you meant that somehow the property of being over six feet tall *makes* it your duty not to use violence, then you have a principle, all right, but a very queer one indeed unless you can give some further reasons. Again, it would not be possible to distinguish this from a sheer attitude.

Pacifism, then, must be the principle that the use of force to meet force is wrong *as such,* that is, that nobody may do so unless he has a special justification.

There is another way in which one might advocate a sort of "pacifism," however, which we must also dispose of before getting to the main point. One might argue that pacifism is desirable as a tactic: that, as a matter of fact, some good end, such as the reduction of violence itself, is to be achieved by "turning the other cheek." For example, if it were the case that turning the other cheek caused the offender to break down and repent, then that would be a very good reason for behaving "pacifistically."

---

[1] Compare, for example, K. Baier, *The Moral Point of View* (Cornell, 1958), p. 191.

If unilateral disarmamant causes the other side to disarm, then certainly unilateral disarmament would be a desirable policy. But note that its desirability, if this is the argument, is due to the fact that peace is desirable, a moral position which anybody can take, pacifist or no, plus the purely contingent fact that this policy causes the other side to disarm, that is, it brings about peace.

And, of course, that's the catch. If one attempts to support pacifism because of its probable effects, then one's position depends on what the effects are. Determining what they are is a purely empirical matter, and, consequently, one could not possibly be a pacifist as a matter of pure principle if his reasons for supporting pacifism are merely tactical. One must, in this case, submit one's opinions to the governance of fact.

It is not part of my intention to discuss matters of fact, as such, but it is worthwhile to point out that the general history of the human race certainly offers no support for the supposition that turning the other cheek always produces good effects on the aggressor. Some aggressors, such as the Nazis, were apparently just "egged on" by the "pacifist" attitude of their victims. Some of the S.S. men apparently became curious to see just how much torture the victim would put up with before he began to resist. Furthermore, there is the possibility that, while pacifism might work against some people (one might cite the British, against whom pacifism in India was apparently rather successful—but the British are comparatively nice people), it might fail against others (e.g., the Nazis).

A further point about holding pacifism to be desirable as a tactic is that this could not easily support the position that pacifism is a *duty*. The question whether we have no *right* to fight back can hardly be settled by noting that not to fight back might cause the aggressor to stop fighting. To prove that a policy is a desirable one because it works is not to prove that it is *obligatory* to follow it. We surely need considerations a good deal less tenuous than this to prove such a momentous contention as that we have no *right* to resist.

It appears, then, that to hold the pacifist position as a genuine, full-blooded moral principle is to hold that nobody has a right to fight back when attacked, that fighting back is inherently evil, as such. It means that we are all mistaken in supposing that we have a right of self-protection. And, of course, this is an extreme and extraordinary position in any case. It appears to mean, for instance, that we have no right to punish criminals, that all of our machinery of criminal justice is, in fact, unjust. Robbers, murderers, rapists, and miscellaneous delinquents ought, on this theory, to be let loose.

Now, the pacifist's first move, upon hearing this, will be to claim that he has been misrepresented. He might say that it is only one's *self* that one has no right to defend, and that one may legitimately fight in order 444 to defend other people. This qualification cannot be made by those pacifists who qualify as conscientious objectors, however, for the latter are refusing to defend their fellow citizens and not merely themselves. But this is comparatively trivial when we contemplate the next objection to this amended version of the theory. Let us now ask ourselves what it is about attacks on *other* people which could possibly justify *us* in defending them, while we are not justified in defending ourselves? It cannot be the mere fact that they are other people than ourselves, for, of course, everyone is a different person from everyone else, and if such a consideration could ever of itself justify anything at all it could also justify anything whatever. That mere difference of person, as such, is of no moral importance, is a presupposition of anything that can possibly pretend to be a moral theory.

Instead of such idle nonsense, then, the pacifist would have to mention some specific characteristic which every *other* person has which we lack and which justifies us in defending them. But this, alas, is impossible, for, while there may be some interesting difference between *me,* on the one hand, and everyone else, on the other, the pacifist is not merely addressing himself to me. On the contrary, as we have seen, he has to address himself to everyone. He is claiming that each person has no right to defend himself, although he does have a right to defend other people. And, therefore, what is needed is a characteristic which distinguishes *each* person from everyone else, and not just *me* from everyone else—which is plainly self-contradictory.

If the reader does not yet see why the "characteristic" of being identical with oneself cannot be used to support a moral theory, let him reflect that the proposition "Everyone is identical with himself" is a trivial truth—as clear an example of an analytic proposition as there could possibly be. But a statement of moral principle is not a trivial truth; it is a substantive moral assertion. But non-tautologous statements, as everyone knows, cannot logically be derived from tautologies, and, consequently, the fact that everyone is identical with himself cannot possibly be used to prove a moral position.

Again, then, the pacifist must retreat in order to avoid talking idle nonsense. His next move, now, might be to say that we have a right to defend all those who are not able to defend themselves. Big, grown-up men who are able to defend themselves ought not to do so, but they ought to defend mere helpless children who are unable to defend themselves.

This last, very queer theory could give rise to some amusing logical gymnastics. For instance, what about groups of people? If a group of people who cannot defend themselves singly can defend themselves together, then when it has grown to that size ought it to stop defending itself? If so, then every time a person *can* defend someone else, he would form with the person being defended a "defensive unit" which was able to defend itself, and thus would by his very presence debar himself from making the defense. At this rate, no one will ever get defended, it seems: The defense- 445 less people by definition cannot defend themselves, while those who can defend them would enable the group consisting of the defenders and the defended to defend themselves, and hence they would be obliged not to do so.

Such reflections, however, are merely curious shadows of a much more fundamental and serious logical problem. This arises when we begin to ask: But why should even defenseless people be defended? If resisting violence is inherently evil, then how can it suddenly become permissible when we use it on behalf of other people? The fact that they are defenseless cannot possibly account for this, for it follows from the theory in question, that everyone ought to put himself in the position of people who are defenseless by refusing to defend himself. This type of pacifist, in short, is using the very characteristic (namely, being in a state of not defending oneself) which he wishes to encourage in others as a reason for denying it in the case of those who already have it (namely, the defenseless). This is indeed self-contradictory.

To attempt to be consistent, at least, the pacifist is forced to accept the characterization of him at which we tentatively arrived. He must indeed say that no one ought ever to be defended against attack. The right of self-defense can be denied coherently only if the right of defense, in general, is denied. This in itself is an important conclusion.

It must be borne in mind, by the way, that I have not said anything to take exception to the man who simply does not wish to defend himself. So long as he does not attempt to make his pacifism into a principle, one cannot accuse him of any inconsistency, however much one might wish to say that he is foolish or eccentric. It is solely with moral principles that I am concerned here.

We now come to the last and most fundamental problem of all. If we ask ourselves what the point of pacifism is, what gets it going, so to speak, the answer is, of course, obvious enough: opposition to violence. The pacifist is generally thought of as the man who is so much opposed to violence that he will not even use it to defend himself or anyone else. And it is precisely this characterization which I wish to show is far from being plausible, morally inconsistent.

To begin with, we may note something which at first glance may seem merely to be a matter of fact, albeit one which should worry the pacifist, in our latest characterization of him. I refer to the commonplace observation that, generally speaking, we measure a man's degree of opposition to something by the amount of effort he is willing to put forth against it. A man could hardly be said to be dead set against something if he is not willing to lift a finger to keep it from going on. A person who claims to be completely opposed to something yet does nothing to prevent it would ordinarily be said to be a hypocrite.

446   As facts, however, we cannot make too much of these. The pacifist could

claim to be willing to go to any length, short of violence, to prevent violence. He might, for instance, stand out in the cold all day long handing out leaflets (as I have known some to do), and this would surely argue for the sincerity of his beliefs.

But would it really?

Let us ask ourselves, one final time, what we are claiming when we claim that violence is morally wrong and unjust. We are, in the first place, claiming that a person *has no right* to indulge in it, as such (meaning that he has no right to indulge in it, *unless* he has an overriding justification). But what do we mean when we say that he has no right to indulge in it? Violence, of the type we are considering, is a two-termed affair: one does violence *to* somebody, one cannot simply "do violence." It might be oneself, of course, but we are not primarily interested in those cases, for what makes it wrong to commit violence is that it harms the people to whom it is done. To say that it is wrong is to say that those to whom it is done have a right *not* to have it done to them. (This must again be qualified by pointing out that this is so only if they have done nothing to merit having that right abridged.)

Yet what could that right to their own security, which people have, possibly consist in, if not a right at least to defend themselves from whatever violence might be offered them? But lest the reader think that this is a gratuitous assumption, note carefully the reason why having a right involves having a right to be defended from breaches of that right. It is because the prevention of infractions of that right is precisely what one has a right to when one has a right at all. A right just *is* a status justifying preventive action. To say that you have a right to X but that no one has any justification whatever for preventing people from depriving you of it, is self-contradictory. If you claim a right to X, then to describe some action as an act of depriving you of X, is logically to imply that its absence is one of the things that you have a right to.

Thus far it does not follow logically that we have a right to use force in our own or anyone's defense. What does follow logically is that one has a right to whatever may be necessary to prevent infringements of his right. One might at first suppose that the universe *could* be so constructed that it is never necessary to use force to prevent people who are bent on getting something from getting it.

Yet even this is not so, for when we speak of "force" in the sense in which pacifism is concerned with it, we do not mean merely physical "force." To call an action a use of force is not merely to make a reference to the laws of mechanics. On the contrary, it is to describe whatever is being done as being a means to the infliction on somebody of something (ordinarily physical) which he does not want done to him; and the same is true for "force" in the sense in which it applies to war, assault and battery, and the like.

447

The proper contrary of "force" in this connection is "rational persuasion." Naturally, one way there *might* be of getting somebody not to do something he has no right to do is to convince him he ought not to do it or that it is not in his interest to do it. But it is inconsistent, I suggest, to argue that rational persuasion is the only morally permissible method of preventing violence. A pragmatic reason for this is easy enough to point to: Violent people are too busy being violent to be reasonable. We cannot engage in rational persuasion unless the enemy is willing to sit down and talk; but what if he isn't? One cannot contend that every human being can be persuaded to sit down and talk before he strikes, for this is not something we can determine just by reasoning: it is a question of observation, certainly. But these points are not strictly relevant anyway, for our question is not the empirical question of whether there is some handy way which can always be used to get a person to sit down and discuss moral philosophy when he is about to murder you. Our question is: *If* force is the only way to prevent violence in a given case, is its use justified *in that case?* This is a purely moral question which we can discuss without any special reference to matters of fact. And, moreover, it is precisely this question which we should have to discuss with the would-be violator. The point is that if a person can be rationally persuaded that he ought not to engage in violence, then precisely what he would be rationally persuaded of if we were to succeed would be the proposition that the use of force is justifiable to prevent him from doing so. For note that if we were to argue that only rational persuasion is permissible as a means of preventing him, we would have to face the question: Do we mean *attempted* rational persuasion, or *successful* rational persuasion, that is, rational persuasion which really does succeed in preventing him from acting? Attempted rational persuasion might fail (if only because the opponent is unreasonable), and then what? To argue that we have a right to use rational persuasion which also succeeds (i.e., we have a right to its success as well as to its use) is to imply that we have a right to prevent him from performing the act. But this, in turn, means that, if attempts at rational persuasion fail, we have a right to the use of force. Thus what we have a right to, if we ever have a *right* to anything, is not merely the use of rational persuasion to keep people from depriving you of the thing to which you have the right. We do indeed have a right to that, but we also have a right to anything else that might be necessary (other things being equal) to prevent the deprivation from occurring. And it is a logical truth, not merely a contingent one, that what *might* be necessary is *force.* (If merely saying something could miraculously deprive someone of the ability to carry through a course of action, then those speech-acts would be called a type of force, if a very mysterious one. And we could properly begin to oppose their use for precisely the same reasons as we now oppose violence.)

448 What this all adds up to, then, is that *if* we have any rights at all, we

have a right to use force to prevent the deprivation of the thing to which we are said to have a right. But the pacifist, of *all* people, is the one most concerned to insist that we do have some rights, namely, the right not to have violence done to us. This is logically implied in asserting it to be a duty on everyone's part to avoid violence. And this is why the pacifist's position is self-contradictory. In saying that violence is wrong, one is at the same time saying that people have a right to its prevention, by force if necessary. Whether and to what extent it may be necessary is a question of fact, but, since it is a question of fact only, the *moral* right to use force on some possible occasions is established.

We now have an answer to the question. How much force does a given threat of violence justify for preventive purposes? The answer, in a word, is "Enough." That the answer is this simple may at first sight seem implausible. One might suppose that some elaborate equation between the aggressive and the preventive force is needed: the punishment be proportionate to the crime. But this is a misunderstanding. In the first place, prevention and punishment are not the same, even if punishment is thought to be directed mainly toward prevention. The punishment of a particular crime logically cannot prevent *that* instance of the crime, since it presupposes that it has already been performed; and punishment need not involve the use of any violence at all, although law-enforcement officers in some places have a nasty tendency to assume the contrary. But preventive force is another matter. If a man threatens to kill me, it is desirable, of course, for me to try to prevent this by the use of the least amount of force sufficient to do the job. But I am justified even in killing him *if* necessary. This much, I suppose, is obvious to most people. But suppose his threat is much smaller: suppose that he is merely pestering me, which is a very mild form of aggression indeed. Would I be justified in killing him to prevent this, under any circumstances whatever?

Suppose that I call the police and they take out a warrant against him, and suppose that when the police come, he puts up a struggle. He pulls a knife or a gun, let us say, and the police shoot him in the ensuing battle. Has my right to the prevention of his annoying me extended to killing him? Well, not exactly, since the immediate threat in response to which he is killed is a threat to the lives of the policemen. Yet my annoyer may never have contemplated real violence. It is an unfortunate case of unpremeditated escalation. But this is precisely what makes the contention that one is justified in using enough force to do the job, whatever amount that may be, to prevent action which violates a right less alarming than at first sight it seems. For it is difficult to envisage a reason why extreme force is needed to prevent mild threats from realization except by way of escalation, and escalation automatically justifies increased use of preventive force.

The existence of laws, police, courts, and more or less civilized modes   449 of behavior on the part of most of the populace naturally affects the answer to the question of how much force is necessary. One of the purposes of a legal system of justice is surely to make the use of force by individuals very much less necessary than it would otherwise be. If we try to think back to a "state of nature" situation, we shall have much less difficulty envisaging the need for large amounts of force to prevent small threats of violence. Here Hobbes's contention that in such a state every man has a right to the life of every other becomes understandable. He was, I suggest, relying on the same principle as I have argued for here: that one has a right to use as much force as necessary to defend one's rights, which include the right of safety of person.

I have said that the duty to avoid violence is only a duty, other things being equal. We might arrive at the same conclusion as we have above by asking the question: Which "other things" might count as being *un*equal? The answer to this is that whatever else they may be, the purpose of preventing violence from being done is necessarily one of these justifying conditions. That the use of force is never justified to prevent initial violence being done to one logically implies that there is nothing wrong with initial violence. We cannot characterize it as being wrong if preventive violence is not simultaneously being characterized as justifiable.

We often think of pacifists as being gentle and idealistic souls, which in its way is true enough. What I have been concerned to show is that they are also confused. If they attempt to formulate their position using our standard concepts of rights, their position involves a contradiction: Violence is wrong, *and* it is wrong to resist it. But the right to resist is precisely what having a right of safety of person is, if it is anything at all.

Could the position be reformulated with a less "committal" concept of rights? I do not think so. It has been suggested[2] that the pacifist need not talk in terms of this "kind" of rights. He can affirm, according to this suggestion, simply that neither the aggressors nor the defenders "have" rights to what they do, that to affirm their not having them is simply to be against the use of force, without this entailing the readiness to use force if necessary to protect the said rights. But this will not do, I believe. For I have not maintained that having a right, or believing that one has a right, entails a *readiness* to defend that right. One has a perfect right not to resist violence to oneself if one is so inclined. But our question has been whether self-defense is justifiable, and not whether one's belief that violence is wrong entails a willingness or readiness to use it. My contention has been that such a belief does entail the justifiability of using it. If one came upon a community in which no sort of violence was ever resisted and it was claimed in that community that the non-resistance was a matter of conscience, we should have to conclude, I think, not that this was a community of saints, but rather that this community lacked the concept of

[2] I owe this suggestion to my colleague, Leslie Armour.

justice—or perhaps that their nervous systems were oddly different from ours.

The true test of the pacifist comes, of course, when he is called upon to assist in the protection of the safety of other persons and not just of himself. For while he is, as I have said, surely entitled to be pacific about his own person if he is so inclined, he is not entitled to be so about the safety of others. It is here that the test of principles comes out. People have a tendency to brand conscientious objectors as cowards or traitors, but this is not quite fair. They are acting as if they were cowards or traitors, but claiming to do so on principle. It is not surprising if a community should fail to understand such "principles," for the test of adherence to a principle is willingness to act on it, and the appropriate action, if one believes a certain thing to be grossly wrong, is to take steps to prevent or resist it. Thus people who assess conscientious objection as cowardice or worse are taking an understandable step: from an intuitive feeling that the pacifist does not really believe what he is saying they infer that his actions (or inaction) must be due to cowardice. What I am suggesting is that this is not correct: The actions are due, not to cowardice, but to confusion.

I have not addressed myself specifically to the question whether, for instance, conscription is morally justifiable, given that the war effort on behalf of which it is invoked is genuinely justifiable. Now, war efforts very often aren't justifiable (indeed, since at least one of the parties to each war must be an aggressor, a minimum of 50 per cent of war efforts must be unjustifiable); but if they ever are, is it then justifiable to conscript soldiers? In closing, I would suggest an answer which may seem surprising in view of my arguments a few pages back. My answer is that it is, but that in the case of conscientious objectors, the only justifiable means of getting them to comply is rational persuasion.

The reason is that, in showing that self-defense is morally justifiable, one has not simultaneously shown that the defense of other people is morally *obligatory*. The kinds of arguments needed to show that an act is obligatory are quite different from those which merely show that it is justified. And, since what has been shown is that self-defense is justifiable and not obligatory, the only conclusion that can be immediately inferred from this is that defense of others is also justifiable and not obligatory. Would it be possible to show that the defense of others (at least in some circumstances) is obligatory and not merely justifiable, without at the same time showing that self-defense is obligatory and not merely justifiable?

The only thing I can suggest here is that the answer requires us to speculate about the obligations of living in a community. If a community expects its members to assist in the common defense when necessary, it can make this clear to people and give them their choice either to be prepared to meet this obligation or to live somewhere else. But a community of pacifists would also be quite conceivable, a community in which no citizen could expect the others to defend him as a part of their community re- 451 sponsibilities. One might not care to live in such a community, but then, a pacifist might not care to live in our sort. When the community is a whole nation of present-day size, it is much more difficult to put the issue clearly to each citizen in advance. But the upshot of it is that (1) the issue depends upon what sort of community we conceive ourselves to have; (2) we do not have clearly formed views on this point; (3) there is no basic moral duty to defend others; (4) we therefore have no direct right to force people to become soldiers in time of justified wars; (5) but we do have a right to deny many basic community services to people who will not assist us in time of need by contributing the force of their arms; and so (6) the only thing to do is to try to argue conscientious objectors into assistance, pointing to all of the above factors and leaving them their choice.

Too much can easily be made of the issue of conscription *versus* voluntary service in time of war. (In time of peace, we have another issue altogether; my arguments here apply only when there is clear justification for defensive measures.) It must be remembered that there is a limit to what law can do in "requiring" compliance, and the pacifist is precisely the person who cannot be reached by the ordinary methods of the law, since he has made up his mind not to be moved by force. The philosophical difference lies, not in the question of whether compliance is ultimately voluntary, since with all laws it to some extent must be, but in the moral status which military service is presumed to have. The draft is morally justifiable if the defense of persons is considered a basic obligation of the citizen. In contemporary communities, it seems to me that there is good reason for giving it that status.

Many questions remain to be discussed, but I hope to have exposed the most fundamental issues surrounding this question and to have shown that the pacifist's central position is untenable.

TOM REGAN
A Defense of Pacifism

The title of this paper is misleading. I do not intend to defend pacifism against those who would contend that it is false. In point of fact, I agree that pacifism is false, and profoundly so, if any moral belief is. Yet paci-

This material is here reprinted from Volume 2, Number 1 of the *Canadian Journal of Philosophy* (1972), 73–86. Reprinted with the permission of the author and the Canadian Association for Publishing in Philosophy.

A somewhat shorter version of this paper was presented at the sixty-third annual

fism's critics sometimes believe it is false for inadequate reasons, and it is important to make the inadequacy of these reasons apparent whenever possible. Otherwise pacifism's apologists are apt to suppose that they have overcome their critic's strongest objections, when, in fact, in exposing the inadequacy of the grounds of certain objections, they have succeeded only in meeting the weaker ones. What I intend to defend, then, is not the truth of pacifism, but the very different claim that pacifism is not *necessarily* false. This objection to pacifism, which, if sound, would silence the debate over its possible merits, and which, therefore, if sound, would be a strong objection indeed, is set forth by Jan Narveson in his paper on pacifism.[1] I hope to show that this objection is unfounded, and I shall, accordingly, direct my argument principally against Narveson's. And yet it is with a certain degree of reluctance that I do so, since Narveson, himself, suggests that "most people" whose opinion he has solicited would agree with me that pacifism, although false, is not necessarily so.[2] One runs a risk, in such a situation, of pouring old wine into new bottles. Still, the only published critique of his view to which Narveson has replied—namely, a short note by M. Jay Whitman[3]—has met with what, for reasons I shall indicate directly, I take to be an incisive rejoiner. And the only other published critique of his analysis, with which I am familiar, fails, I think,[4] to make

meeting of the Southern Society for Philosophy and Psychology, held on April 8–10, 1971, at the University of Georgia, Athens, Georgia. I want to acknowledge the helpful criticisms of an earlier draft by my colleagues, Paul A. Bredenberg and A. Donald VanDeVeer.

[1] Narveson, Jan. "Pacifism: A Philosophical Analysis," *Ethics,* Vol. 75 (1965), pp. 259–271. Reprinted in *War and Morality,* edited by Richard A. Wasserstrom, Wadsworth Publishing Company, Inc.: Belmont, California, 1970, pp. 63–77. Page references are to the Wasserstrom edition.

[2] Narveson, Jan. "Is Pacifism Consistent?," *Ethics,* Vol. 78 (1968), p. 148.

[3] Whitman, M. J. "Is Pacifism Self-Contradictory?," *Ethics,* Vol. 76 (1966), pp. 307–08.

[4] Miller, Ronald B. "Violence, Force and Coercion," in *Violence,* "Award Winning Essays in the Council for Philosophical Studies Competition." Edited by Jerome A. Shaffer, David McKay Company, Inc.: New York, 1971, pp. 11–44, especially pp. 41–44. Miller attempts to show that Narveson's objections against pacifism can be raised against "*any* moral principle that asserts that an action is wrong," (p. 143). According to Miller, since it is true, not only in the case of pacifism, as Narveson argues, but in any case in which an act is declared wrong, that "it is always logically possible that in order to prevent any given wrongful act we may have to do that act itself" (p. 44), it follows that Narveson's line of argument, when generalized, shows not that pacifism alone is self-contradictory, but that "*any* moral principle that asserts that an action is wrong is self-contradictory." And this, Miller concludes, is "patently absurd." (*Ibid*).

Miller's argument will not stand careful examination. Narveson's argument does not lead to the conclusion that "*any* moral principle that asserts that an action is wrong is self-contradictory." When Miller's interpretation of Narveson's argument is applied to principles of *prima facie* duty, for example, these principles do not

a reasonable case against it. Perhaps it is not altogether unfitting, therefore, to speak out in print for the otherwise silent majority.

In his paper Narveson argues that pacifism, when understood as a "moral doctrine"—that is, when understood as setting forth a principle of obligation binding on all rational, free beings, and not as the expression of, say, a mere strategy for social change or a passionate dislike of violence —when understood in this way, Narveson argues pacifism can be shown to be logically untenable because self-contradictory. He holds this position for what appear to be two different but related reasons; first, because he thinks the pacifist, in order to be consistent with his assumptions, must admit that there are cases where the use of force would be justified, an admission which, Narveson argues, is inconsistent with the pacifist's absolute prohibition against the use of force; and, second, because he thinks the pacifist is inconsistent in affirming, on the one hand, our right not to have others inflict harm or suffering on us by the use of force, while denying,

---

emerge as self-contradictory, despite the fact that it is "logically possible that in order to prevent any given (*prima facie*) wrongful act we may have to do that act itself." Our *prima facie* duty not to lie, for example, may always be overridden, but the assertion expressing this duty is not self-contradictory simply because it is conceivable that in order to prevent future lies, we may have to tell one now. Miller, therefore, is rash to suppose that Narveson's argument has the consequences he attributes to it.

In response to this, Miller might say that what he means by "any moral principle" is "any *absolute* moral principle. . ."—i.e., "any principle declaring of an identifiable action that it is always, without exception wrong." But this, even if it is what Miller means, exposes his argument to two further objections. For now Miller's claim that the belief that all such principles are self-contradictory is "patently absurd" is gratuitous and question-begging. What we want to know is *if* there are such principles that are not self-contradictory, especially since, as Miller concedes, "it is always logically possible that in order to prevent a given wrongful act that we may have to do that act itself." The question is, "in such a case, ought we to do the wrongful act?" And what we want is some well thought out answer to this question, not a begging leave of it. My argument in the sequel, I think, goes some way toward satisfying this demand.

However, even if it is "patently absurd" to believe that *all* principles that assert that a given action is wrong are self-contradictory, Miller fails to show that Narveson is guilty of this particular absurdity. At the very most Narveson's analysis can be generalized to apply, not to all moral principles of the type in question, but to those only according to which (a) a given action, A, is declared to be absolutely wrong, and (b) actions of type A are thought to be wrong because of the consequences of performing them—namely, because they lead to greater evil, and, in particular, to greater A-ing, in the future, than would result from not A-ing. Now, it is consistent with the belief that not all absolute moral prohibitions are self-contradictory, that all absolute moral prohibitions satisfying conditions (a) and (b) are. Accordingly, even if we were to concede the former belief to Miller, nothing whatever would follow concerning the "absurdity" of the latter one. And since it is this latter belief which Narveson's argument against pacifism, when generalized, can be argued to imply, conceding Miller the former belief could go no way toward exposing the "absurdity" of Narveson's analysis.

on the other, our right to use force to resist such attacks. In what follows I shall concern myself almost exclusively with the former of Narveson's arguments and try to show that it is unsuccessful. I do not consider his second argument in detail because I think that, if pacifism can be defended against the first line of argument, it can also be defended against the second. If, that is, the pacifist's fundamental moral outlook can be shown to be logically consistent, then I believe his account of human rights, as these are qualified by this moral outlook, also can be shown to be logically consistent.

I

Before the consistency of pacifism can be determined, the position, itself, must be characterized, at least in some general way. For present purposes, Narveson's characterization can be accepted, although it is not exhaustive; there are, that is, recognizable versions of pacifism which his characterization fails to take into account. In large measure this is due to Narveson's tendency to treat the concepts of force and violence interchangeably, so that he is led to suppose that anyone who prohibits the use of force must also prohibit the use of violence, and vice versa. In fact, however, these two concepts are logically distinct,[5] and it is both conceivable and has actually been the case that recognized pacifists consistently have spoken out against the use of violence while at the same time sanctioning certain uses of force. According to Narveson's characterization, however, the pacifist is categorically opposed, not only to violence, but also to the use of force, both when force is used to attack harmless, undefended or innocent persons, as well as when it is used by any such person when attacked by another. As such, the pacifist is not opposed merely to the *aggressive* use of force or violence. He must be understood as opposing their *defensive* use as well. As Narveson writes:

. . . [T]o hold the pacifist position as a genuine, full-blooded moral principle is to hold that nobody has a right to fight back when attacked, that fighting back is inherently evil, as such.[6]

Pacifism, then, as Narveson understands it, and as I shall defend it, can be characterized as the view that no one is ever justified in using force or,

[5] Cf., e.g., Miller's essay, as well as Robert Audi's "On the Meaning and Justification of Violence," also in Shaffer's *Violence, op. cit.* One might choose, of course, to limit the usage of "pacifism" so that it applies only to those who oppose violence, but not to those who oppose both violence and force; or to those only who oppose a particular form of violence—namely, war; etc. Ordinary usage provides no sharp guidelines, but Narveson seems to me to have captured adequately one way in which the term 'pacifism' is ordinarily used.

[6] Narveson (in Wasserstrom), *op. cit.,* p. 69.

455

alternatively, that the use of force is always wrong. If my defense of what might aptly be termed "extreme pacifism" is sound, then defenses similar to mine of less extreme forms can easily be constructed.

Now, Narveson rightly points out that this concept of "using force" is very vague, and it may be that any attempt to make it very precise will have an air of arbitrariness about it. How this concept should be analysed, however, is not a question that must be settled prior to defending pacifism against Narveson's attack, since his attack is meant to apply to pacifism, no matter how the concept of "the use of force" is understood. I propose, therefore, to treat the concept at an intuitive level. Pushing, punching, kicking, scratching, tackling and biting people involve the use of physical force. As such, and with Narveson's own understanding of pacifism serving as a precedent, I shall assume that a pacifist would hold that we ought never to do them, whether we do them to someone who has not attacked us, or in self-defense against someone who has. (I believe, in fact, that a pacifist could consistently distinguish between those cases of, say, pushing he denounces, and those he does not; but to explore this problem would be to take me well outside the limited objectives of this paper.)

A further question, by way of clarification, concerns how the pacifist's prohibition against the use of force might fit into a more general moral outlook. Here I shall follow some of the suggestions of Whitman. The pacifist's prohibition against the use of force, he suggests,[7] has the status of a "priority rule"; that is, this prohibition, in the eyes of the pacifist, must always take priority over any rule of *prima facie* obligation, in the sense that if or as this prohibition conflicts with any other rule, the rule against the use of force must always be honored at the expense of the other(s). Furthermore, by characterizing the prohibition against the use of force as a "priority *rule*," Whitman implies, what Narveson accepts, that this prohibition need not be thought of as occupying the status of the supreme or fundamental moral principle within the structure of the pacifist's thought. What is fundamental, Whitman suggests, is the principle, "One ought never to do evil . . . or, if we must choose between evils, never to choose the greater."[8] Thus, in saying that the rule against the use of force has the status of a priority rule, in the sense indicated above, one is saying, what both Whitman and Narveson accept, that, for the pacifist, *the greatest evil* is to use force, either aggressively or defensively. In summary, therefore, the relevant features of the pacifist's outlook, are the following.

There is:

1. A supreme principle: "Never do what is evil or, if we must choose between evils, never choose the greater."
2. A priority rule, or a rule which (a) specifies which among those things

---

[7] Whitman, *op. cit.,* p. 307.

[8] *Ibid.*

that are evil is the greatest; (b) declares that, as such, and in view of the supreme moral principle, no person can be justified in doing it (the greatest evil); so that (c) when this rule conflicts with any other rule or rules concerning what is evil, the priority rule always is to take precedence. For the pacifist, this is the rule: "One ought never to use force."

and

3. A set of other rules, which we might call "secondary rules," which specify those things other than the use of force which are evil and which constitute a subclass of our *prima facie* obligations.

II

Narveson's argument against pacifism consists essentially in his pointing out that it is conceivable that the pacifist's priority-rule can come into conflict with the pacifist's supreme principle; it consists, that is to say, in his arguing that it is conceivable that, in order to avoid doing the greatest evil, we might have to choose to use force. The question then becomes: "Which will the pacifist give up: his supreme principle or his priority-rule? He cannot have both." In summarizing this argument in his reply to Whitman, Narveson writes:

> . . . [A]s I was trying to make clear in my paper . . ., no use of a priority rule *as such* can escape the kind of contradiction I was claiming the pacifist is committed to. It seems to me logically true, on any moral theory whatever, that the lesser evil must be preferred to the greater. If the use of force by me, now, is necessary to avoid the use of *more* physical force (by others, perhaps) later, then to say that physical force is the supreme (kind of) evil is precisely to say that under these circumstances I am committed to the use of physical force.[9]

Now, in response to this line of argument, a pacifist might maintain that the use of force never does, as a matter of fact, lead to a reduction of evil, including a reduction of force. Whitman, in fact, openly espouses just this interpretation. "[T]he use of force," he writes,[10] "is (for the pacifist) itself a substantive evil and inevitably leads to greater substantive evil than any other immoral act." But this reply, Narveson argues, is not adequate. Whether the use of force in any given case will lead to a reduction of evil is a *factual* question, and one, therefore, that cannot be settled *a priori*. "It cannot be maintained," he writes,

> that it is logically impossible for a given violent act to prevent more violence. . . . And the question I was discussing . . . is what the pacifist would say to the

[9] Narveson, *Ethics*, Vol. 78 (1968), p. 148.

[10] Whitman, *op. cit.*, p. 307.

question whether he would agree that the use of force would be justified *if* it were necessary to prevent what the pacifist himself regards as the greatest of evils. Whitman doesn't seem to have addressed himself to this crucial question.[11]

I believe Narveson's reply is sound. Whitman does not address himself to this "crucial question," and, by failing to do so, he fails to make it clear whether the pacifist can answer it without making an exception to either his supreme principle or his priority rule. I want to argue that he can.

Central to Narveson's argument is the claim that "the lesser evil must be preferred to the greater." Now, these expressions, "greater and lesser evil," are ambiguous, and Narveson uses them in at least two distinguishable ways. (I shall shortly distinguish a third.) There is, first, a *quantitative* sense. Sometimes when people speak about evil they speak about *how much* of it there is, and how one amount is greater (exceeds) the other (the lesser). It is in its quantitative sense that Narveson asks whether force might not be necessary to prevent *more* (a greater quantity or amount of) force or evil in the future. Second, there is a *qualitative* sense, in which to speak of one evil as being greater or lesser than another is not to say that the quantity of evil is greater or lesser in amount, but, instead, that it is inherently or intrinsically more or less evil. It is in this sense that philosophers have distinguished between kinds of evil and ranked them as greater or less, considered as kinds of evil; and it is in this sense that Narveson understands the pacifist's contention that physical force is the supreme (kind of) evil.

With these distinctions in mind, we can, I think, reformulate Narveson's argument with some gain in precision. When reformulated, it reads:

1. The lesser evil must be preferred to the greater.
2. Therefore, a lesser quantity of qualitatively equivalent evils must be preferred to a greater quantity of qualitatively equivalent evils.
3. The use of force is a substantive evil.
4. Therefore, a lesser quantity of force must be preferred to a greater quantity of force.
5. If any given action, A, is necessary to bring about a lesser rather than a greater quantity of qualitatively equivalent evil, then one's obligation is to do A.
6. Therefore, if any given action, F, is necessary to bring about a lesser rather than a greater quantity of force, then one's obligation is to do F.
7. Therefore, if the use of force is necessary to bring about a lesser rather than a greater quantity of force, then one's obligation is to use force.

Thus, if the pacifist accepts (1), as he does; and if he views the use of force as a substantive ("the greatest") evil, as he does; then he must con-

11 Narveson, *Ethics,* Vol. 78 (1968), p. 149.

cede that there are conceivable situations in which force should be used. He must, therefore, qualify his priority rule, and the only way he could escape this conclusion is by qualifying his supreme principle.

I find this argument unconvincing. Narveson assumes, without argument, that the pacifist must accept premise (2) above—the premise, namely, "A lesser quantity of qualitatively equivalent evils must be preferred to a greater quantity of qualitatively equivalent evils." And he assumes that the pacifist must accept this because he assumes that the pacifist would accept both the claim, (1) "The lesser evil must be preferred to the greater," *and* the claim, (2) "A lesser quantity of qualitatively equivalent evils *is a lesser evil than* a greater quantity of qualitatively equivalent evils." It is this latter assumption of Narveson's I want to question.

To do this, a third sense of "greater or lesser evil" needs to be distinguished. It is what I shall call its "resultant sense." It is distinct from, but related to both its quantitative and qualitative senses. It is in this sense that we would speak of various combinations of qualitatively equivalent or non-equivalent evils, combined in various quantities, *qua* combinations, as being greater or lesser evils. For example, even if we were to agree that a certain evil, P, was qualitatively greater than another evil, Q, we might want to ask which would be the greater resultant evil—a given quantity, M, of Q or a lesser quantity, M minus N, of P. And which would be the greater resultant evil would not be *simply* a matter of determining which was lesser in the quantitative or qualitative sense of "lesser evil."

One sense, then, in which the claim, "The lesser evil must be preferred to the greater," can be understood, is in its resultant sense—i.e., "The lesser resultant evil must be preferred to the greater resultant evil." And it is in this sense that we must understand Narveson's second premise (above). What he assumes, on the part of the pacifist, in other words, is, "A lesser quantity of qualitatively equivalent evils is a *lesser resultant evil than* a greater quantity of qualitatively equivalent evils." And the question to be raised is, "Why should it be thought that the pacifist *must* accept this? Why *must* he have just this view of resultant evils?" Narveson gives no reason for believing that he must, and I, myself, cannot think of any, except, perhaps, the initial intuitive plausibility of this interpretation, together with the fact that many pacifists would seem, as a matter of fact, to believe something like this. In fact, however, I believe there is an alternative to this interpretation available to the pacifist, one that indicates that *how* one brings about force or evil in the future makes a decisive difference to the greatness of the resultant evil in any given case. This would be

(2′) The resultant evil of a given combination, X, is greater than the resultant evil of any other combination, Y, if X is *caused by force,* while Y is not.

As (2′) makes clear, *that* a given combination of evils (or goods!) was 459 caused by force, is a sufficient condition of its being resultantly a greater evil than any other combination not caused by force. Or, to put this same point differently, (2') involves the supposition that in calling the use of force the greatest evil, the pacifist may mean that it, unlike any other evil, is *irredeemably* evil—an evil, that is, that makes *any* combination of which it is the cause resultantly a greater evil than any other combination of evils that might be brought into existence by any other means. As such, then, no future state of affairs that could be achieved by the use of force could be morally preferable to any other state of affairs, achieved by other means, no matter how evil the latter might be. It is a greater evil to use force than to make additional force possible by refusing to use it, which is to say, no one ought ever to use force. And this, once again, is precisely what the pacifist is presumed to maintain.

For the pacifist to conceive of the use of force as an irredeemable evil, is, I believe, sufficient as a response to Narveson's recurrent objection. "I agree entirely," he writes,

with the pacifist who would maintain that violence is never justified merely in order to bring about good. But is it ever justified in order to avoid evil, namely, the evil of more violence? Given that it is violence as such, rather than violence as employed by the pacifist himself, which is being held to be supremely evil, then *it would seem* that the only way to avoid inconsistency here would be to deny that the quantity of violence prevented by a given act of violence was ever greater than the quantity of violence inherent in the act aimed at preventing it.[12]

Granted, this may *seem* to be "the only way to avoid inconsistency"; nevertheless, it is not. For if *how* future evil is avoided can make a decisive difference to how great is the resultant evil involved in avoiding it, then the greater resultant evil is not always simply a question of how much of what kind of evil is caused or avoided.

By viewing the use of force as an irredeemable evil, moreover, the pacifist has a basis for disputing Narveson's second line of argument— namely, that he (the pacifist) is inconsistent in affirming, on the one hand, our right not to have others use force against us, while denying, on the other, our right to fight back if attacked. What the pacifist could concede to Narveson is his claim that "a right just is a status justifying preventive action,"[13] so that it would be, as Narveson contends, selfcontradictory to say "You have a right to X, but you are never justified in preventing people from depriving you of it." What does not follow from this, however, is that we are justified in using force against those who use force against us. The pacifist could insist that we would be justified in using our ability to persuade people, by rational, nonviolent means, to

---

[12] *Ibid.* (my italics).

[13] Narveson (in Wasserstrom), *op. cit.*, p. 72.

desist from attacking us; he could insist, that is, that we *are* justified in using *some* means to prevent people from violating our right not to have them use force against us. But he could consistently deny that this right entitles us to make use of means involving force to remedy infringements upon it. For what means we would be justified in using would be a function of what, in general, we would be justified in doing. And if to use force is always an irredeemable evil, then it remains an irredeemable evil when resorted to in the name of defending our rights. As such, therefore, no person could be justified in resorting to it.

III

Now, this defense of pacifism is, I think, consistent with the most general claims made about it, both by Narveson and Whitman. Verbally, at least, the same supreme principle is recognized, as is the same priority-rule. Where my interpretation of pacifism differs from theirs is in the content given to the supreme principle and to the priority-rule. They interpret "greater" or "greatest evil" in one way; I interpret them in another. And perhaps their interpretation is closer to what actual pacifists believe than is mine. Perhaps no self-avowed pacifist believes that the use of force is an irredeemable evil. The issue is unclear at best. But before turning to this question, two possible objections of Narveson's can be anticipated and rejected. The first concedes that the position I have defended *is* a recognizable, legitimate version of pacifism but argues that it is, nonetheless, susceptible to the same line of argument Narveson advances against the version of pacifism he examines. The second is to the effect that the position I have defended is not a pacifistic one, which, if true, would put an end to the need to search for any further reason for rejecting my defense of it. I shall consider each objection briefly before articulating the consequences of my analysis.

"Your defense is vulnerable for the same old reason," Narveson might contend. "Rather than asking, as I did, whether the *consequences* of not using force might be worse than the consequences of using it, we can ask of your pacifist whether it is not possible that he might have to choose between just two alternatives, A and B, the latter of which would involve in its performance the use of *more* force than the former. This is a conceivable state of affairs, and the question then is: 'Which ought to be done —A or B?' Surely any morally sensitive pacifist would agree that A ought to be done. And just as surely this puts him on record as sanctioning the use of force in conceivable circumstances. Once again, therefore, the pacifist, to be consistent, must concede that the prohibition against the use of force is not absolute. Your defense, accordingly, is no defense at all."

This line of argument, given Narveson's predilections, is natural enough. 461

It calls forth various responses, two of which deserve mention. First, it is worth noting that this argument is impotent to demonstrate, even assuming that the pacifist could choose only between A and B, that he must, to be consistent, choose A. A pacifist *could* believe that the wrongness involved in using force is not proportionate to the *amount* of force used. A pacifist *could* believe, in other words, that no act of using force is more or less wrong than any other. Accordingly, even assuming that a pacifist could choose only between A and B, it would not follow that he *must* choose A. One might profoundly hope that he would, indeed, but that is a different matter.

More fundamental as a response, however, is the following. The state of affairs alleged to be "conceivable" in the above simply is not. That B might involve the use of more force than A is, of course, conceivable, but is not the point at issue. What is at issue is the conceivability of a situation in which an agent *can choose only between* doing an action of type A or one of type B. Any conceivable state of affairs in which a person can choose between actions of these types must also include in it the possibility of the agent's *choosing to do neither*. And because it must include this possibility, it becomes quite academic to pursue the question of which one, A or B, a pacifist would sanction choosing. The short answer, given my interpretation, is: "Neither."

Granted this, Narveson might still go on to suggest the following kind of case. "It is conceivable," he could maintain, "that your pacifist might have to choose between doing some action, C, which would involve his using a modest amount of force, or not doing C, which would give rise to someone else's using a vast amount of force. A desert island case where, say, the pacifist has the choice of either breaking a small child's arm or, choosing not to do this, of seeing his captor, a mad tyrant, destroy the pacifist's homeland, is a graphic if fantastic example of the type of case I have in mind. Now, surely any morally sensitive person would opt for C. And just as surely any morally sensitive pacifist who would do so would be on record as having sanctioned the use of force in conceivable circumstances. There is no saving pacifism, therefore, from the kind of latent inconsistency I claimed is indigenous to it."

I do not believe this argument fares any better than the former one. If we postpone, for the moment, any discussion of the "moral sensitivity" of the pacifist, as I have defended him, and concentrate on the alleged inconsistency of his position, I believe we shall see that the "desert island" argument confuses the questions, "Morally speaking, what do we think the pacifist (or anyone else) ought to choose in such cases?," and "Logically speaking, what can the pacifist claim ought to be chosen?" *If* the pacifist believes that the use of force is an irredeemable evil, then, not only is it consistent with his position, it is required by it, that he choose not to do actions of type C; for the description of actions of this type, *ex hypothesi,* includes the expression "involves the use of force," whereas the choice not to do actions of type C, since it is the choice *not* to do some action, cannot itself be described as "a choice to do an action," let alone an action that could be described as "involving the use of force." That we might have well grounded moral objections to someone who would advocate such inaction in such circumstances is logically distinct from, and should not be confused with, the fact that a pacifist could consistently advocate it. The only merit the present argument has over the previous one, therefore, is that the state of affairs it hypothesizes is conceivable. But this is a necessary and not a sufficient condition of mounting a successful attack against the pacifist.

There is, then, no reason to believe that pacifism, as I have defended it, is vulnerable to the type of argument Narveson raises against pacifism, as he understands it. Yet this very fact suggests a second line of criticism he might well develop—namely, that the view I have set forth is *not* pacifism. How much this issue, if it were raised, would turn out to be merely verbal, it is difficult to say. However, it does seem to me that what *grounds* one might have for opposing absolutely the use of force is a distinct question from whether one does oppose it, and it does seem to me that what is definite of pacifism is that it is the absolute opposition to the use of force, and not that pacifism necessarily involves such opposition for one or another type reason. To limit the usage of 'pacifist' to those who oppose force on the grounds that it leads to evil consequences, therefore, seems to me to confuse the conceptual question, "What is pacifism?," with the factual question, "How is it always (or most often) defended?" Thus, even if no self-avowed pacifist would accept my defense of the consistency of his position, it would not follow that my defense could not be a defense of pacifism; for it might be that no self-avowed pacifist would be satisfied with the grounds that my defense requires him to accept,[14] and not that we are looking for grounds for two quite different moral positions. Part of the problem one encounters in discussing pacifism, as Narveson would agree, is to discover just what it is that a pacifist does believe and why, and part of this consists, I think, in finding out how a pacifist could answer Narveson's question

If force is the only way to prevent violence in a given case, is its use justified *in that case?*[15]

I do not know how every self-avowed pacifist would answer this question, but I do believe a person could answer this question negatively, which

---

[14] This is somewhat misleading. The point is that a pacifist needn't have grounds for his belief, in the sense that he must infer his opposition to the use of force from the presumed truth of some other proposition. It is open to him to claim to intuit its truth, rather than to infer it. In the jargon of moral theory, pacifism can be either "teleological" or "deontological."

[15] Narveson (in Wasserstrom), *op. cit.*, p. 73.

is the answer the pacifist's priority rule seems to require, without thereby making an exception to the pacifist's supreme principle. *If* he believes that the use of force is an irredeemable evil, in the sense that to use it is a sufficient condition of producing a greater resultant evil than any that could result from not using force, *then* a person could consistently maintain *both* that one ought always to do the lesser rather than the greater evil *and* that one ought never to use force, not even when using it would reduce the amount of force in the future. Such a person, I believe, satisfies the conditions for the application of the term "pacifist," whether or not anyone who claims to be one would also happen to accept my account of why he might and how he can consistently believe what he does. For my thesis concerns not simply how pacifists have, as a matter of fact, attempted to defend their belief, an issue which is, as I mentioned earlier, unclear at best, and one which, in the case of celebrated pacifists such as Ghandi, say, calls for extended and careful elucidation,[16] rather than perfunctory pronouncements; my thesis concerns, instead, how pacifism *can* be defended. At the very most, therefore, Narveson's argument could show that it is inconsistent to ground pacifism on considerations of negative utility—i.e., on the grounds that using force leads to more evil than abstaining from doing so—*and,* at the same time, to believe that, should the use of force lead to a reduction of evil, we ought not to use it.[17] Even if we were to grant this much to Narveson, however, it would not follow that *pacifism* is therefore self-contradictory. For the concept is broader than any particular basis that might be invoked to justify the pacifist's belief.

Two consequences of my defense deserve mention. First, no pacifist who would accept it can indulge in the practice of appealing to the presumed evil consequences of the use of force as *grounds* for why force should not be used. For if the use of force is thought to be an irredeemable evil, then it is an irredeemable evil no matter what are its consequences; and if it is an irredeemable evil, no matter what are its consequences, then what its consequences are, either in a particular case,

[16] In this connection, see Arne Naess' "A Systematization of Ghandian Ethics of Conflict Resolution," in *Conflict Resolution,* Volume II, Number 2, 1958, pp. 140–155.

[17] Even this is to concede to Narveson more than his argument shows. The question he discusses is whether any person could ever be justified in using force. To argue that a person could be because it is conceivable that the use of force might reduce evil is surely inadequate. What is required in addition to this is an argument to show that people sometimes *can know,* as a matter of fact, that the use of force will reduce evil. Narveson does not even begin to argue for this position, and yet a pacifist could agree that, conceivably, the use of force could reduce evil, and yet deny that we can ever know, in advance, that it will. Such a pacifist could, it would seem, consistently maintain that no person ought ever to use force. A full scale inquiry into the credentials of pacifism would require a careful examination of this alternative.

in most cases or, following Whitman, "inevitably," is logically irrelevant to the prohibition against using it. To accept my defense, on the one hand, and, on the other, to attempt to justify the prohibition against using force by appealing to the consequences that allegedly flow from its use, *is* inconsistent.

Secondly, and paradoxically, my defense of pacifism, if sound, and if it represents what one needs to believe in order to avoid Narveson's charge of inconsistency, confirms the view of "the majority" to whom Narveson makes reference, who believe that pacifism is "bizarre and vaguely ludicrous, but nevertheless not unintelligible."[18] To regard the use of force as irredeemably evil does, I believe, save pacifism from the charge of inconsistency. But any view that would require that we judge, say, a woman who uses what physical power she has to attempt to free herself from an aspiring rapist, as having done, not, what might sometimes be the case, a foolish thing, but instead, and necessarily, an irredeemably evil act, must, I believe, shock and offend the moral sensibilities of rational men. There is, to be sure, a certain antiseptic cleanness involved in dismissing a moral position on purely logical grounds: such a procedure does not require us to stain our analytical hands with the guts of a moral judgment. It remains true, nonetheless, that the strongest objections to an extreme pacifism of the kind discussed are moral, not logical ones. A person committed to an extreme pacifism, though he need make no logical mistake, yet lacks a fully developed moral sensitivity to the vagaries and complexities of human existence. To regard the pacifist's belief as "bizarre and vaguely ludicrous" is, perhaps, to put it mildly.

R. B. BRANDT
Utilitarianism and the Rules of War

The topic of the present symposium is roughly the moral proscriptions and prescriptions that should govern the treatment by a belligerent, and in particular by its armed forces, of the nationals of an enemy, both combatants and noncombatants. In addressing myself to it, the central question I shall try to answer is: What, from a moral point of view, ought to be the rules of war? But this question, taken as an indication of what I shall be discussing, is both too broad and too narrow. Too

---

[18] Narveson, *Ethics,* Vol. 78 (1968), p. 148.

Reprinted from *Philosophy and Public Affairs,* Vol. 1, No. 2 (Winter 1972), 145–165. Copyright © 1971 by Princeton University Press. Reprinted by permission of the author and the publisher.

broad because the rules of war include many topics like the rights and duties of neutral countries and the proprieties pertaining to an armistice. And too narrow because a full view of the topic requires me to consider, as I shall, such questions as: Is it ever morally right for a person to infringe "ideal" rules of war?

I shall aim to illuminate our topic by discussing it from the point of view of a rule-ultilitarianism of the "contractual" variety (to use a term employed by John Rawls in his book *A Theory of Justice*).[1] What this point of view is has of course to be explained, as do the special problems raised by the fact that the rules are to apply to nations at war. I believe it will become clear that the rule-utilitarian viewpoint is a very helpful one for thinking of rules of warfare, and I believe reflection on its implications will confirm us both in conclusions about certain normative rules and in a conviction that a contractual utilitarian view of such matters is essentially sound. Needless to say, I shall be led to express some disagreement with Professor Nagel.[2]

I shall take Nagel to be defending, first, the general view that certain kinds of action are, from a moral point of view, absolutely out of bounds, no matter what the circumstances; and second, a specific prohibition that applies this principle to the area of our interest. (His first thesis makes it proper to call his view "absolutist," in the sense that some general moral prohibitions do not have prima facie force only but are binding without exception, indefeasible.) Now Nagel is tentative in his espousal of these two theses, and sometimes contends only that we have some moral intuitions of this sort and that a study of these will show "the complexity, and perhaps the incoherence" of our moral ideas. Indeed, he says he is offering only a "somewhat qualified defense of absolutism," and concedes that in extreme circumstances there may be exceptions to his absolutist principles after all. Where Nagel is committed definitely is to a criticism of utilitarianism; he speaks scathingly of "the abyss of utilitarian apologetics for large-scale murder." In view of Nagel's tentativeness, I think it fair to disassociate him from the positive view I wish to criticize, although I am *calling* it Nagel's "absolutism." This positive view is, however, the only definite proposal he puts forward, and if I am to consider critically any positive antiutilitarian view in connection with Nagel's essay, it has to be this one. At any rate, this view is one that somebody *might* hold, and is well worth discussing.

The first point I wish to make is that a rule-utilitarian may quite well agree with Nagel that certain kinds of action are morally out of bounds absolutely and no matter what the circumstances. Take, for instance, some of the rules of warfare recognized by the United States Army:

[1] Cambridge, Mass., 1971.

[2] *Editor's Note:* Thomas Nagel, "War and Massacre," *Philosophy and Public Affairs,* Vol. 1, No. 2 (1971), 123.

It is especially forbidden . . . to declare that no quarter will be given. . . . It is especially forbidden . . . to kill or wound an enemy who, having laid down his arms, or having no longer means of defense, has surrendered at discretion. . . .

It is especially forbidden . . . to employ arms, projectiles, or material calculated to cause unnecessary suffering. . . .

The pillage of a town or place, even when taken by assault, is prohibited. . . .

A commander may not put his prisoners to death because their presence retards his movements or diminishes his power of resistance by necessitating a large guard, or by reason of their consuming supplies, or because it appears certain that they will regain their liberty through the impending success of their forces. It is likewise unlawful for a commander to kill his prisoners on grounds of self-preservation, even in the case of airborne or commando operations, although the circumstances of the operation may make necessary rigorous supervision of and restraint upon the movement of prisoners of war.[3]

A rule-utilitarian is certainly in a position to say that utilitarian considerations cannot morally justify a departure from these rules; in that sense they are absolute. But he will of course also say that the moral justification of these rules lies in the fact that their acceptance and enforcement will make an important contribution to long-range utility. The rule-utilitarian, then, may take a two-level view: that in justifying the rules, utilitarian considerations are in order and nothing else is; whereas in making decisions about what to do in concrete circumstances, the rules are absolutely binding. In the rule-utilitarian view, immediate expediency is not a moral justification for infringing the rules.[4]

It is not clear that Nagel recognizes this sort of absolutism about "ideal" rules of war as a possible utilitarian view, but he seems to disagree with it when he claims that some moral prohibitions are entirely independent of utilitarian considerations.

What absolute rule, then, does Nagel propose? I shall formulate and criticize his proposal in a moment. But first we should note that his rule

[3] Department of the Army Field Manual PM 27–10, *The Law of Land Warfare* (Department of the Army, July 1956), pp. 17, 18, 21, 35. The Manual specifically states that the rules of war may not be disregarded on grounds of "military necessity" (p. 4), since considerations of military necessity were fully taken into account in framing the rules. (All page numbers in the text refer to this publication, hereafter called the Army Manual.)

Other valuable discussions of contemporary rules of warfare are to be found in L. Oppenheim, *International Law*, ed. H. Lauterpacht, 7th edn. (New York, 1952) and in Marjorie M. Whiteman, *Digest of International Law*, esp. Vol. X (U.S. Department of State, 1963).

[4] It is conceivable that ideal rules of war would include one rule to the effect that anything is allowable, if necessary to prevent absolute catastrophe. As Oppenheim remarks, it may be that if the basic values of society are threatened nations are possibly released from all the restrictions in order to do what "they deem to be decisive for the ultimate vindication of the law of nations" (*International Law*, p. 351).

is intended to be restricted in scope; it applies only to what "we deliberately do to people." This is an important restriction. Suppose bombers are dispatched to destroy a munitions factory—surely a legitimate military target in a night raid; in fact and predictably, and from a military point of view incidentally, the bombs kill five thousand people. Is this a case of "deliberately doing" something to these people? Nagel's view here seems obscure. He rejects the law of double effect and says he prefers to "stay with the original, unanalyzed distinction between what one does to people and what merely happens to them as a result of what one does." He concedes that this distinction "needs clarification." Indeed it does. Without more clarification, Nagel is hardly giving an explicit theory. I note that the U.S. Army Manual appears to reject this distinction, and in a paragraph declaring the limitations on strategic bombing states that "loss of life and damage to property must not be out of proportion to the military advantage to be gained" (p. 19).

The absolutist principle that Nagel espouses as the basic restriction on legitimate targets and weapons is this: "hostility or aggression should be directed at its true object. This means both that it should be directed at the person or persons who provoke it and that it should aim more specifically at what is provocative about them. The second condition will determine what form the hostility may appropriately take." Now, while I find this principle reasonably clear in its application to simple two-person cases discussed by him, I find it difficult to apply in the identification of morally acceptable military operations. With some trepidation I suggest that Nagel intends it to be construed to assert something like the following for the case of military operations: "Persons may be attacked 'deliberately' only if their presence or their position prevents overpowering the military forces of the enemy in some way; and they may be attacked only in a manner that is reasonably related to the objective of disarming or disabling them." If this is what he has in mind it is still rather vague, since it does not make clear whether attacks on munitions factories are legitimate, or whether attacks on persons involved in supporting services, say, the provisioning of the army, are acceptable.

It is worth noting that a principle resembling this one might have a utilitarian justification of the kind alluded to above. But the principle standing by itself does not seem to me self-evident; nor does another principle Nagel asserts, that "the maintenance of a direct interpersonal response to the people one deals with is a requirement which no advantages can justify one in abandoning."

II. Morally Justifiable Rules as Rules Impartially Preferable

I shall now proceed to a positive account of the rules of war and of their justification. We shall have to consider several distinct questions, but the central question will be: Which of the possible rules of war are morally justifiable?

But first, what do I mean by "rules of war" or by talk of the "authoritative status" of rules of war? What I have in mind is, roughly, rules with the status that the articles of the Hague and Geneva Conventions have or have had. That is, certain rules pertaining to war are stated in formal treaties. These rules are seriously taught, as being legally binding, to officers and to some extent to enlisted men; they are recognized as legally binding restrictions on the decisions of the general staff; members of the army know that actions forbidden by these rules are contrary both to international law and to their own army's manual of rules for proper conduct; these rules are enforced seriously by the courts, either military or international; and so on. Proscriptions or prescriptions with this status I call "rules of war"; and in speaking of a rule having "authoritative status" I have this kind of force in mind. The U.S. Army Manual lists such rules; and digests of international law such as those by Whiteman and Oppenheim contain information on what such rules are and have been.

I have said that I shall offer a utilitarian answer to the question which rules of war (in the above sense) are morally justifiable. But I have also said that I shall be offering what I (following Rawls) call a *contractual* utilitarian answer. What I mean by that (the term "contractual" may be a bit misleading) is this. I accept the utilitarian answer to the question which rules of war are morally justifiable because utilitarian rules of war are the ones *rational, impartial persons would choose* (the ones they would be willing to put themselves under a contract to obey). The more basic question is, then: Which rules of war would people universally prefer to have accorded authoritative status among nations if the people deciding were rational, believed they might be involved in a war at some time, and were impartial in the sense that they were choosing behind a veil of ignorance? (It is understood that their ignorance is to be such as to prevent them from making a choice that would give them or their nation a special advantage; it would, for instance, prevent them from knowing what weaponry their country would possess were it to be at war, and from knowing whether, were war to occur, they would be on the front lines, in a factory, or in the general staff office.) In other words, the more fundamental question is: What rules would rational, impartial people, who expected their country at some time to be at war, want to have as the authoritative rules of war—particularly with respect to the permitted targets and method of attack? I suggest that the rules of war which rational, impartial persons would choose are the rules that would maximize long-range expectable utility for nations at war. In saying this I am offering a contractual utilitarian answer to the question what rules of war are morally justifiable. I am saying, then: (1) that rational, impartial persons would choose certain rules of war; (2) that I take as a basic premise ("analytic" in some sense, if you like) that a rule of war is morally justified if and only if it would be chosen by rational, impartial 469 persons; and (3) that the rules rational, impartial persons would choose are ones which will maximize expectable long-range utility for nations at war.[5]

Nagel objects to utilitarianism and hence presumably would object to (3), but he might be agreeable to both (1) and (2). At least he seems close to these principles, since he seems to hold that an action is justified if one can justify to its victim what is being done to him. For instance, he implies that if you were to say to a prisoner, "You understand, I have to pull out your fingernails because it is absolutely essential that we have the name of your confederates" and the prisoner agreed to this as following from principles he accepts, then the torture would be justified. Nagel rather assumes that the prisoner would not agree, in an appropriate sense. In this connection we must be clearly aware of an important distinction. A judge who sentences a criminal might also be unable to persuade the criminal to want the sentence to be carried out; and if persuading him to want this were necessary for a moral justification of the criminal law, then the system of criminal justice would also be morally objectionable. We must distinguish between persuading a person to whom something horrible is about to be done to want that thing to happen or to consent to its happening at that very time and something quite different—getting him to accept, when he is rational and choosing in ignorance of his own future prospects, some general principles from which it would follow that this horrible thing should or might be done to a person in his present circumstances. I think Nagel must mean, or ought to mean, that a set of rules of war must be such as to command the assent of rational people choosing behind a veil of ignorance, *not* that a person must be got to assent at the time to his fingernails being pulled out in order to get information, if that act is to be justified. It may be, however, that Nagel does not agree with this distinction, since he hints at the end of his discussion that something more may be required for moral justification than I have suggested, without indicating what the addition might be.

We should notice that the question which rules of war would be preferred by rational persons choosing behind a veil of ignorance is roughly the question that bodies like the Hague Conventions tried to answer. For there were the representatives of various nations, gathered together, say, in 1907, many or all of them making the assumption that their nations would at some time be at war. And, presumably in the light of calculated national self-interest and the principles of common humanity, they decided which rules they were prepared to commit themselves to follow, in advance of knowing how the fortunes of war might strike them in par-

---

[5] This summary statement needs much explanation, e.g., regarding the meaning of "rational." It is only a close approximation to the view I would defend, since I think it is better to substitute a more complex notion for that of impartiality or a veil of ignorance.

ticular. The questions the signatories to the Hague Conventions actually did ask themselves are at least very close to the questions I think we must answer in order to know which rules of war are morally justified.

III. The Rational, Impartial Choice: Utilitarian Rules

I wish now to explain in a few words why I think rational, impartial persons would choose rules of war that would maximize expectable utility. Then—and this will occupy almost all of the present section—I shall classify the rules of war into several types, and try to show that representative rules of each type would be utility-maximizing and therefore chosen. I shall hope (although I shall not say anything explicitly about this) that the ideal rules of war, identified in this way, will coincide with the reflective intuitions of the reader. If so, I assume that this fact will commend to him the whole of what I am arguing.

I have suggested that rational persons, choosing behind a veil of ignorance but believing that their country may well be involved in a war at some time, would prefer rules of war that would maximize expectable utility, *in the circumstance that two nations are at war*. Why would they prefer such rules? About this I shall say only that if they are self-interested they will choose rules which will maximize expectable utility generally, for then their chance of coming out best will be greatest (and they do not know how especially to favor themselves); and that if they are altruistic they will again choose that set of rules, for they will want to choose rules which will maximize expectable utility generally. The rules of war, then, subject to the restriction that the rules of war may not prevent a belligerent from using all the power necessary to overcome the enemy, will be ones whose authorization will serve to maximize welfare.

It is worth noting that a preamble to the U.S. Army Manual offers an at least partially utilitarian theory of the rules of war (I say "at least partially" because of doubts about the interpretation of clause *b*). This preamble states that the law of land warfare "is inspired by the desire to diminish the evils of war by: *a*. Protecting both combatants and noncombatants from unnecessary suffering; *b*. Safeguarding certain fundamental human rights of persons who fall into the hands of the enemy, particularly prisoners of war, the wounded and sick, and civilians; and *c*. Facilitating the restoration of peace" (p. 3).

Which rules, then, would maximize expectable utility for nations at war? (I shall later discuss briefly whether the ideal rules would altogether forbid war as an instrument of national policy.)

First, however, we must understand why the above-mentioned restriction, guaranteeing that the rules of war will not prevent a belligerent from using all the force necessary to overcome the enemy, must be placed 471 on the utility-maximizing rules of war. The reason for this restriction is to be found in the nature of a serious war. There are, of course, many different kinds of war. Wars differ in magnitude, in the technologies they employ, in the degree to which they mobilize resources, in the type of issue the belligerents believe to be at stake, and in many other ways as well. The difference between the Trojan War and World War II is obviously enormous. The former was a simple, small-scale affair, and the issues at stake might well have been settled by a duel between Paris and Menelaus, or Hector and Achilles, and the belligerents might not have been seriously dissatisfied with the outcome. In the case of World War II, the British thought that Hitler's Germany and its policies threatened the very basis of civilized society. The destruction of Hitler's power seemed so important to the British that they were willing to stake their existence as a nation on bringing it about. Wars have been fought for many lesser reasons: to spread a political or religious creed, to acquire territory or wealth, to obtain an outlet to the sea, or to become established as a world power. Wars may be fought with mercenaries, or primarily by the contribution of equipment and munitions; such wars make relatively little difference to the domestic life of a belligerent.

It is possible that the rules which would maximize expectable utility might vary from one type of war to another. I shall ignore this possibility for the most part, and merely note that practical difficulties are involved in equipping military handbooks with different sets of rules and establishing judicial bodies to identify the proper classification of a given war. I shall take the position of Britain in World War II as typical of that of a belligerent in a serious war.

The position of a nation in a serious war is such, then, that it considers overpowering the enemy to be absolutely vital to its interests (and possibly to those of civilized society generally)—so vital, indeed, that it is willing to risk its very existence to that end. It is doubtful that both sides can be well justified in such an appraisal of the state of affairs. But we may assume that in fact they do make this appraisal. In this situation, we must simply take as a fact that neither side will consent to or follow rules of war which seriously impair the possibility of bringing the war to a victorious conclusion. This fact accounts for the restriction within which I suggested a choice of the rules of war must take place. We may notice that the recognized rules of war do observe this limitation: they are framed in such a way as not to place any serious obstacle in the way of a nation's using any available force, if necessary, to destroy the ability of another to resist. As Oppenheim has observed, one of the assumptions underlying the recognized rules of war is that "a belligerent is justified in applying any amount and any kind of force which is necessary for . . . the overpowering of the opponent."[6] This limitation, however,

[6] *International Law*, p. 226.

leaves a good deal of room for rules of war which will maximize expectable long-range utility for all parties.

This restriction, incidentally, itself manifests utilitarian considerations, for a nation is limited to the use of means *necessary* to overcome an opponent. Clearly it is contrary to the general utility that any amount or manner of force be employed when it is *not* necessary for victory.

It will be convenient to divide the rules restricting military operation, especially the targets and weapons of attack, into three types. (I do not claim that these are exhaustive.)

1. *Humanitarian Restrictions of No Cost to Military Operation.* There are some things that troops may be tempted to do which are at best of negligible utility to their nation but which cause serious loss to enemy civilians, although not affecting the enemy's power to win the war. Such behavior will naturally be forbidden by rules designed to maximize expectable utility within the understood restriction. Consider, for example, rules against the murder or ill-treatment of prisoners of war. A rule forbidding wanton murder of prisoners hardly needs discussion. Such murder does not advance the war effort of the captors; indeed, news of its occurrence only stiffens resistance and invites retaliation. Moreover, there is an advantage in returning troops having been encouraged to respect the lives of others. A strict prohibition of wanton murder of prisoners therefore has the clear support of utilitarian considerations. Much the same may be said for a rule forbidding ill-treatment of prisoners. There can, of course, be disagreement about what constitutes ill-treatment—for instance, whether a prisoner is entitled to a diet of the quality to which he is accustomed if it is more expensive than that available to troops of the captor army. It is clear, however, that in a war between affluent nations prisoners can generally be well-housed and well-fed and receive adequate medical care without cost to the war effort of the captors. And if they receive such treatment, of course the captives gain. Thus a policy of good treatment of prisoners may be expected to make many nationals of both sides better off, and at a cost which in no way impairs the ability of either to wage the war.

Again, much the same may be said of the treatment of civilians and of civilian property in occupied territories. There is no military advantage, at least for an affluent nation, in the plunder of private or public property. And the rape of women or the ill-treatment of populations of occupied countries serves no military purpose. On the contrary, such behavior arouses hatred and resentment and constitutes a military liability. So utility is maximized, within our indicated basic limitations, by a strict rule calling for good treatment of the civilian population of an occupied territory. And the same can be said more generally for the condemnation of the wanton destruction of cities, towns, or villages, or devastation not 473 justified by military necessity, set forth in the Charter of the Nuremberg Tribunal.

Obviously these rules, which the maximization of expectable utility calls for, are rules that command our intuitive assent.

2. *Humanitarian Restrictions Possibly Costly to Military Victory*. Let us turn now to rules pertaining to actions in somewhat more complex situations. There are some actions which fall into neither of the classes so far discussed. They are not actions which must be permitted because they are judged necessary or sufficient for victory, and hence actions on which no party to a major war would accept restrictions. Nor are they actions which morally justified rules of war definitely prohibit, as being actions which cause injury to enemy nationals but serve no military purpose. It is this large class of actions neither clearly permitted nor definitely prohibited, for reasons already discussed, that I wish now to consider. I want to ask which rules of war are morally justified, because utility-maximizing, for actions of this kind. In what follows I shall be distinguishing several kinds of action and suggesting appropriate rules for them. The first type is this: doing something which will result in widespread destruction of civilian life and property and at the same time will add (possibly by that very destruction) to the *probability* of victory but will not definitely decide the war. Some uses of atomic weapons, and area bombing of the kind practiced at Hamburg, illustrate this sort of case.

A proper (not ideally precise) rule for such operations might be: substantial destruction of lives and property of enemy civilians is permissible only when there is good evidence that it will significantly enhance the prospect of victory. Application of the terms "good evidence" and "significantly enhance" requires judgment, but the rule could be a useful guideline all the same. For instance, we now know that the destruction of Hamburg did not significantly enhance the prospect of victory; in fact, it worked in the wrong direction, since it both outraged the population and freed workers formerly in non-war-supporting industries to be moved into industry directly contributing to the German war effort. The generals surely did not have good evidence that this bombing would significantly enhance the prospect of victory.

This rule is one which parties to a war might be expected to accept in advance, since following it could be expected to minimize the human cost of war on both sides, and since it does not involve a significant compromise of the goal of victory. The proposed rule, incidentally, has some similarities to the accepted rule cited above from the U.S. Army Manual, that "loss of life and damage to property must not be out of proportion to the military advantage to be gained."

This rule, which I am suggesting only for wars like World War II, 474 where the stakes are very high, may become clearer if seen in the perspective of a more general rule that would also be suitable for wars in which the stakes are much lower. I pointed out above that what is at stake in a war may be no more than a tiny strip of land or national prestige. (The utility of these, may, however, be considered very great by a nation.) Now, it is clear that a risk of defeat which may properly be taken when the stakes are small may not be a proper risk when the stakes are virtually infinite; and a risk that could not properly be run when the stakes are enormous might quite properly be run when the stakes are small. So if the above-suggested rule is plausible for serious wars, in which the stakes are great, a somewhat different rule will be plausible in the case of wars of lesser importance—one that will require more in the way of "good evidence" and will require that the actions more "significantly enhance" the prospect of victory than is necessary when the stakes are much higher. These thoughts suggest the following general principle, applicable to all types of war: a military action (e.g., a bombing raid) is permissible only if the utility (broadly conceived, so that the maintenance of treaty obligations of international law could count as a utility) of victory to all concerned, multiplied by the increase in its probability if the action is executed, on the evidence (when the evidence is reasonably solid, considering the stakes), is greater than the possible disutility of the action to both sides multiplied by its probability. The rule for serious wars suggested above could then be regarded as a special case, one in which the utility of victory is virtually set at infinity —so that the only question is whether there is reasonably solid evidence that the action will increase the probability of victory. The more general rule obviously involves difficult judgments; there is a question, therefore, as to how it could be applied. It is conceivable that tough-minded civilian review boards would be beneficial, but we can hardly expect very reliable judgments even from them.[7]

These rules are at least very different from a blanket permission for

---

[7] If we assume that both sides in a major struggle somehow manage to be persuaded that their cause is just, we shall have to expect that each will assign a net positive utility to its being the victor. For this reason it makes very little difference whether the more general principle uses the concept of the utility of victory by one side for everyone concerned, or the utility for that side only.

One might propose that the general restriction on rules of war, to the effect that in a serious war the use of any force necessary or sufficient for victory must be permitted, might be derived from the above principle if the utility of victory is set virtually at infinity and the probability of a certain action affecting the outcome is set near one. I believe this is correct, if we assume, as just suggested, that each side in a serious war will set a very high positive utility on *its* being the victor, despite the fact that both sides cannot possibly be correct in such an assessment. The reason for this principle as stated in the text, however, seems to me more realistic and simple. There is no reason, as far as I can see, why *both* lines of reasoning may not be used in support of the claim that the principle (or restriction) in question is a part of a morally justifiable system of rules of war.

anything the military thinks might conceivably improve the chances of victory, irrespective of any human cost to the enemy. In practice, it must be expected that each party to a war is likely to estimate the stakes of victory quite high, so that the rule which has the best chance of being respected is probably the first one mentioned, and not any modification of it that would be suggested to an impartial observer by the second, more general principle.

The reader may have been struck by the fact that these suggested rules are essentially institutionalized applications of a kind of act-utilitarian principle for certain contexts. This may seem inconsistent with the notion of a system of absolute rules themselves justified by long-range utilitarian considerations. But there is nothing inconsistent in the suggestion that some of the "absolute" rules should require that in certain situations an action be undertaken if and only if it will maximize expectable utility.

It may be objected that the rules suggested are far too imprecise to be of practical utility. To this I would reply that there is no reason why judgment may not be required in staff decisions about major operations. Furthermore, the U.S. Army Manual already contains several rules the application of which requires judgment. For example:

Absolute good faith with the enemy must be observed as a rule of conduct. . . . In general, a belligerent may resort to those measures for mystifying or misleading the enemy against which the enemy ought to take measures to protect himself.

The measure of permissible devastation is found in the strict necessities of war. Devastation as an end in itself or as a separate measure of war is not sanctioned by the law of war. There must be some reasonably close connection between the destruction of property and the overcoming of the enemy's army. . . .

The punishment imposed for a violation of the law of war must be proportionate to the gravity of the offense. The death penalty may be imposed for grave breaches of the law. . . . Punishments should be deterrent . . . (pp. 22, 23–24, 182).

It has sometimes been argued, for instance by Winston Churchill, that obliteration bombing is justified as retaliation. It has been said that since the Germans destroyed Amsterdam and Coventry, the British had a right to destroy Hamburg. And it is true that the Hague Conventions are sometimes regarded as a contract, breach of which by one side releases the other from its obligations. It is also true that a government which has itself ordered obliteration bombing is hardly in a position to complain if the same tactic is employed by the enemy. But maximizing utility permits obliteration bombing only as a measure of deterrence or deterrent reprisal. This rule, incidentally, is recognized by the Army Man-

476

ual as a principle governing all reprisals: "Reprisals are acts of retaliation . . . for the purpose of enforcing future compliance with the recognized rules of civilized warfare. . . . Other means of securing compliance with the law of war should normally be exhausted before resort is had to reprisals. . . . Even when appeal to the enemy for redress has failed, it may be a matter of policy to consider, before resorting to reprisals, whether the opposing forces are not more likely to be influenced by a steady adherence to the law of war on the part of the adversary" (p. 177). Purposes of retaliation, then, do not permit bombing in contravention of the suggested general principles.

Special notice should be taken that widespread civilian bombing might be defended by arguing that a significant deterioration in civilian morale could bring an end to a war by producing internal revolution. Our principle does not exclude the possibility of such reasoning, in the presence of serious evidence about civilian morale, when the stakes of victory are high. But we know enough about how bombing affects civilian morale to know that such bombing could be justified only rarely, if at all. The U.S. Army seems to go further than this; its rule asserts that any attack on civilians "for the sole purpose of terrorizing the civilian population is also forbidden."[8] It may be, however, that in actual practice this rule is interpreted in such a way that it is identical with the less stringent rule which is as much as utilitarian considerations can justify; if not, I fear we have to say that at this point the Army's theory has gone somewhat too far.

3. *Acceptance of military losses for humanitarian reasons.* Let us now turn to some rules which have to do with what we might call the *economics* of warfare, when the ultimate outcome is not involved, either because the outcome is already clear or because the action is fairly local and its outcome will not have significant repercussions. What damage may one inflict on the enemy in order to cut one's own losses? For instance, may one destroy a city in order to relieve a besieged platoon, or in order to avoid prolonging a war with consequent casualties? (The use of atom bombs in Japan may be an instance of this type of situation.) It is convenient to deal with two types of cases separately.

First, when may one inflict large losses on the enemy in order to avoid smaller losses for oneself, given that the issue of the war is not in doubt? A complicating fact is that when the issue is no longer in doubt it would seem that the enemy ought to concede, thereby avoiding losses to both sides. Why fight on when victory is impossible? (Perhaps to get better terms of peace.) But suppose the prospective loser is recalcitrant. May the prospective victor then unleash any horrors whatever in order to terminate the war quickly or reduce his losses? It is clear that the superior

[8] Whiteman, *Digest of International Law,* X, 135.

power should show utmost patience and not make the terms of peace so severe as to encourage further resistance. On the other hand, long-range utility is not served if the rules of war are framed in such a way as to provide an umbrella for the indefinite continuation of a struggle by an inferior power. So it must be possible to inflict losses heavy enough to produce capitulation but not so heavy as to be out of proportion to the estimated cost of further struggle to both sides. This condition is especially important in view of the fact that in practice there will almost always be other pressures that can be brought to bear. The application of such a rule requires difficult judgments, but some such rule appears called for by long-range utilitarian considerations.

The second question is: Should there be restrictions on the treatment of an enemy in the case of local actions which could hardly affect the outcome of the war, when these may cause significant losses? Rules of this sort are in fact already in force. For instance, as mentioned above, the Army Manual forbids killing of prisoners when their presence retards one's movements, reduces the number of men available for combat, uses up the food supply, and in general is inimical to the integrity of one's troops. Again, the Second Hague Convention forbids forcing civilians in occupied territory to give information about the enemy, and it forbids reprisals against the general civilian population "on account of the acts of individuals for which they cannot be regarded as jointly and severally responsible."[9] The taking of hostages is prohibited (Army Manual, p. 107).

All these rules prescribe that a belligerent be prepared to accept certain military disadvantages for the sake of the lives and welfare of civilians and prisoners. The disadvantages in question are not, however, losses that could be so serious as to affect the outcome of a war. Furthermore, the military gains and losses are ones which are likely to be evenly distributed, so that neither side stands to gain a long-term advantage if the rules are observed by both. So, without affecting the outcome of the war and without giving either side an unfair advantage, a considerable benefit can come to both belligerents in the form of the welfare of their imprisoned and occupied populations. Thus the long-run advantage of both parties is most probably served if they accept forms of self-restraint which can work out to be costly in occasional instances. Such rules will naturally be accepted by rational, impartial people in view of their long-range benefits.

IV. Rules of War and Morality

I have been arguing that there is a set of rules governing the conduct of warfare which rational, impartial persons who believed that their country

478   [9] Article L.

might from time to time be engaged in a war would prefer to any alternative sets of rules and to the absence of rules. I have also suggested, although without argument, that it is proper to say of such a set of rules that it is morally justified (and of course I think that such a set ought to be formally recognized and given authoritative status). There is thus a fairly close parallel with the prohibitions (and justifications and recognized excuses) of the criminal law: certain of these would be preferred to alternative sets and to an absence of legal prohibitions by rational, impartial persons; the prohibitions that would be so preferred may (I think) be said to be morally justified; and such rules ought to be adopted as the law of the land. I do not say the parallel is exact.

It may be suggested that there will be a considerable discrepancy between what is permitted by such "morally justifiable" rules of war and what it is morally permissible for a person to do in time of war. (Nagel mentions dropping the bomb on Hiroshima, attacks on trucks bringing up food, and the use of flamethrowers in any situation whatever as examples of actions not morally permissible; but it is not clear that he would say these would be permitted by morally justifiable rules of war, or even that he recognizes a distinction between what is morally permissible and what is permitted by morally justifiable rules of war.) Moreover, it might be thought that such "morally justifiable" rules of war could not be derived from justified moral principles. It might be asked, too, what the moral standing of these "morally justified" rules of war is, in view of the fact that the rules of war actually accepted and in force may, at least in some particulars, be rather different. These are difficult questions, about which I wish to say something.

It is obvious that there may well be discrepancies between what a person morally may do in wartime and what is permitted by morally justified rules of war, just as there are discrepancies between what is morally permitted and what is permitted by morally justifiable rules of the criminal law. For one thing, the rules of war, like the criminal law, must be formulated in such a way that it is decidable whether a person has violated them; it must be possible to produce evidence that determines the question and removes it from the realm of speculation. More important, just as there are subtle interpersonal relations—such as justice and self-restraint in a family—which it is undesirable for the criminal law to attempt to regulate but which may be matters of moral obligation, so there may well be moral obligations controlling relations between members of belligerent armies which the rules of war cannot reach. For instance, one might be morally obligated to go to some trouble or even take a certain risk in order to give aid to a wounded enemy, but the rules of war could hardly prescribe doing so. I am unable to think of a case in which moral principles require a person to do what is forbidden by morally justifiable rules of war; I suppose this is possible. But it 479 is easy to think of cases in which moral principles forbid a person to injure an enemy, or require him to aid an enemy, when morally justifiable rules of war do not prescribe accordingly and when the military law even forbids the morally required behavior. (Consider, for instance, the fact that, according to the Manual, the U.S. Army permits severe punishment for anyone who "without proper authority, knowingly harbors or protects or gives intelligence to, or communicates or corresponds with or holds any intercourse with the enemy, either directly or indirectly . . ." [p. 33].)

The possible contrast between morally justifiable rules of war and what is morally permitted will seem quite clear to persons with firm moral intuitions. It may be helpful, however, to draw the contrast by indicating what it would be, at least for one kind of rule-utilitarian theory of moral principles. A rule-utilitarian theory of morality might say that what is morally permissible is any action that would not be forbidden by the kind of conscience which would maximize long-range expectable utility were it built into people as an internal regulator of their relations with other sentient beings, as contrasted with other kinds of conscience or not having a conscience at all. Then justifiable rules of war (with the standing described above) would be one thing; what is morally permissible, in view of ideal rules of conscience, might be another. Rational, impartial persons, understanding that their country may be involved in a war, might want one set of rules as rules of war, whereas rational, impartial persons choosing among types of conscience might want a different and discrepant set of rules as rules of conscience. In the same way there may be a discrepancy between a morally justified system of criminal law and morally justified rules of conscience. And just as, consequently, there may occasionally be a situation in which it is one's moral duty to violate the criminal law, so there may occasionally be a situation in which it is one's moral duty to violate morally justifiable rules of war.

It might be asked whether a person who subscribed to sound moral principles would, if given the choice, opt for a system of rules of war; and if so, whether he would opt for a set that would maximize expectable utility for the situation of nations at war. I suggest that he would do so; that such a person would realize that international law, like the criminal law, has its place in human society, that not all decisions can simply be left to the moral intuitions of the agent, and that the rules of war and military justice are bound to be somewhat crude. He would opt for that type of system which will do the most good, given that nations will sometimes go to war. I am, however, only *suggesting* that he would; in order to show that he would one would have to identify the sound moral principles which would be relevant to such a decision.

Another question that might be raised is whether a person should follow the actual military rules of his country or the morally justifiable ones 480 (in the sense explained above). This question can obviously be taken in either of two ways. If the question is which rules are legally binding, of course the actual rules of war recognized at present are legally binding on him. But the question might be: Is a person morally bound to follow the "ideal" rules of war, as compared with the actual ones (or the legal orders of his officer), if they come into conflict? Here two possible situations must be distinguished. It is logically possible that a morally justifiable set of rules of war would permit damage to the enemy more severe than would the actual rules of war; in that case, assuming the actual rules of war have the status of an obligation fixed by a treaty, the moral obligation would seem to be to follow the provisions of the treaty (subject to the usual difficulties about older treaties not contemplating contemporary situations). Suppose, however, that a superior officer commands one to do something that is permitted by the actual rules of war (that is, not explicitly forbidden) but which clearly would be forbidden by morally justifiable rules of war. The question is then whether a moral person would refuse to do what is permitted by an unjust institution but would be forbidden by a just one. It would have to be argued in detail that sound moral principles would not permit a person to do what would be permitted only by an unjust institution. I shall not attempt to argue the matter, but only suggest that sound moral principles would *not* permit obedience to an order forbidden by morally justifiable rules of war. It is quite possible, incidentally, contrary to what I have just said about the legal issues, that a court-martial would not succeed in convicting a person who refused an order of this sort and defended his action along these lines.

There is space only to advert to the larger issue of the moral justification for nations being belligerents at all. Presumably, just as there are morally justified rules of war, in the sense of rules which rational, impartial persons would choose on the assumption their country might be involved in a war, so there are morally justified rules about engaging in a war at all, in the sense of rules governing the behavior of nations which rational, impartial persons would subscribe to if they believed that they would live in a world in which the chosen rules might obtain. Not only are there such morally justified rules regarding belligerency, but almost every nation is in fact signatory to a treaty abjuring war as an instrument of policy. Moreover, it has been declared criminal by the Treaty of London for a person to plan, prepare, initiate, or wage a war of aggression or a war in violation of international treaties, agreements, or assurances. So there is basis both in morally justified principles of international law and in actual international law for questioning the position of a belligerent. Presumably the relation between these and the moral obligations of citizens and government officials is complex, rather parallel to that just described for the case of rules of war.

RICHARD WASSERSTROM
The Laws of War

Many persons who consider the variety of moral and legal problems that arise in respect to war come away convinced that the firmest area for judgment is that of how persons ought to behave in time of war. Such persons feel a confidence about dealing with questions of how war ought to be conducted that is absent when other issues about war are raised. They are, for example, more comfortable with the rules relating to how soldiers ought to behave vis-a-vis enemy soldiers and enemy civilians— the laws of war—than they are with the principles relating to when war is permissible and when it is not. Thus, most commentators and critics are uneasy about the applicability to the American scene of that part of Nuremberg that deals with crimes against peace and crimes against humanity. But they have no comparable uneasiness about insisting that persons who commit war crimes, violations of the laws of war, be held responsible for their actions.

I propose to consider several features of this view—and I do think it a widely held one—which accepts the moral significance and urges the primacy of the laws of war. I am not interested in providing a genetic account of why this view gets held. I am, rather, concerned to explicate at least one version of this view and to explore the grounds upon which such a view might rest. And I want also to show why such a position is a mistaken one: mistaken in the sense that this conception of the laws of war is a morally unattractive one and one which has no special claim upon our attention or our energies.

There are two general, quite distinct arguments for this notion of the primacy of the laws of war. One is that the laws of war are important and deserving of genuine respect and rigorous enforcement because they reflect, embody and give effect to fundamental moral distinctions and considerations. The other is that, considered simply as laws and conventions, they merit this dominant role because general adherence to them has important, desirable effects. The former of these arguments emphasizes the contents of the laws of war and the connection they have with more basic moral ideals. The latter argument emphasizes the beneficial consequences that flow from their presence and acceptance.

The arguments are clearly not mutually exclusive; indeed, they are related to each other in several important respects. Nonetheless, it is useful

Reprinted from *The Monist,* Vol. 56, No. 1 (January 1972), 1–19, La Salle, Illinois, with the permission of the publisher.

to distinguish sharply between them for purposes of analysis and to examine the strengths and weaknesses of each in turn. Before I do so, however, it is necessary to explicate more fully the nature of the laws of war with which I shall be concerned. This is so because it is important to see that I am concerned with a particular view of the character of the laws of war and the related notion of a war crime.[1] I believe it to be the case that this account constitutes an accurate description of the existing laws of war and the dominant conception of a war crime. That is to say, I think it is what many if not most lawyers, commentators, military tribunals, and courts have in mind when they talk about the laws of war and the responsibility of individuals for the commission of war crimes. In this sense at least, the sketch I am about to give constitutes an actual, and not merely a possible, conception of the laws of war. If I am right, the criticisms that I make have substantial practical importance. But I may of course be wrong; I may have misstated the actual laws of war and the rules for their applicability. To the degree that I have done so, my criticism will, perhaps, less forcefully apply to the real world, but not thereby to the conception of the laws of war I delineate below.

I

The system I am concerned to describe and discuss has the following features. There are, to begin with, a number of formal agreements, conventions, and treaties among countries that prescribe how countries (chiefly through their armies) are to behave in time of war. And there are, as well, generally accepted, "common law" rules and practices which also regulate behavior in warfare. Together they comprise the substantive laws of war. For the most part, the laws of war deal with two sorts of things: how classes of persons are to be treated in war, e.g. prisoners of war, and what sorts of weapons and methods of attack are impermissible, e.g. the use of poison gas. Some of the laws of war—particularly those embodied in formal documents—are narrow in scope and specific in formulation. Thus, Article 4 of the Annex to the Hague Convention on Land Warfare, 1907 provided in part that all the personal belongings of prisoners of war, "except arms, horses, and military papers," remain their property. Others are a good deal more general and vague. For example, Article 23(e) of the same Annex to Hague Convention prohibits resort to ". . . arms, projectiles, or material calculated to cause unnecessary suffering." Similarly, Article 3 of the Geneva Conventions on the Law of War, 1949 provides in part that "Persons taking no active part in the hostilities . . . shall in all

---

[1] For my purpose I treat the laws of war and war crimes as identical phenomena. I recognize that for other purposes and in other contexts this would be a mistake. See, e.g., Richard Falk, Gabriel Kolko, and Robert Lifton, eds., *Crimes of War* (New York, 1971), p. 33.

circumstances be treated humanely. . . ." And at Nuremberg, war crimes were defined as follows:

> . . . violations of the laws or customs of war. Such violations shall include but not be limited to, murder, ill-treatment or deportation to slave-labour or for any other purpose of civilian population of or in occupied territory, murder or ill-treatment of prisoners of war or persons on the seas, killing of hostages, plunder of public property, wanton destruction of cities, towns or villages, or devastation not justified by military necessity.[2]

The most important feature of this conception of the laws of war is that the laws of war are to be understood as in fact prohibiting only violence and suffering that are not connected in any direct or important way with the waging of war. As one commentator has put it, the laws of war have as their objective that ". . . the ravages of war should be mitigated as far as possible by prohibiting needless cruelties, and other acts that spread death and destruction and are not reasonably related to the conduct of hostilities."[3]

This is reflected by the language of many of the laws themselves. But it is demonstrated far more forcefully by the way, even relatively unambiguous and absolute prohibitions, are to be interpreted. The former characteristic is illustrated by that part of the Nuremberg definition of war crimes which prohibits the ". . . *wanton* destruction of cities, towns or villages." The latter characteristic is illustrated by the following commentary upon Article 23(c) of the Hague Convention quoted above. That article, it will be recalled, prohibits the resort to arms calculated to cause unnecessary suffering. But "unnecessary suffering" means suffering that is not reasonably related to any military advantage to be derived from its infliction. "The legality of hand grenades, flame-throwers, napalm, and incendiary bombs in contemporary warfare is a vivid reminder that suffering caused by weapons with sufficiently large destructive potentialities is not 'unnecessary' in the meaning of this rule."[4]

Another way to make the same point is to indicate the way in which the doctrine of "military necessity" places a central role in this conception of the laws of war. It, too, is explicitly written into a number of the laws of war as providing a specific exception. Thus, to quote a portion of the Nuremberg definition once again, what is prohibited is ". . . devastation not justified by military necessity."

The doctrine of military necessity is, moreover, more firmly and centrally embedded in this conception of the laws of war than illustrations of the preceding type would suggest. The doctrine does not merely create an

---

[2] *The Charter of the International Military Tribunal,* Article Six (b).

[3] Telford Taylor, *Nuremberg and Vietnam: An American Tragedy* (New York, 1970), p. 20.

[4] Georg Schwarzenberger, *The Legality of Nuclear Weapons* (London, 1958), p. 44.

explicit exception, i.e. as in "devastation not justified by military necessity." Instead, it functions as a general justification for the violation of most, if not all, of even the specific prohibitions which constitute a portion of the laws of war. Thus, according to one exposition of the laws of war, the flat prohibition against the killing of enemy combatants who have surrendered is to be understood to permit the killing of such persons where that is required by "military necessity." There may well be times in any war when it is permissible to kill combatants who have laid down their arms and tried to surrender.

Small detachments on special missions, or accidentally cut off from their main force, may take prisoners under such circumstances that men cannot be spared to guard them or take them to the rear, and that to take them along would greatly endanger the success of the mission or the safety of the unit. The prisoners will be killed by operation of the principle of military necessity, and no military or other court has been called upon, so far as I am aware, to declare such killings a war crime.[5]

Or, consider another case where, according to Taylor, the doctrine of military necessity makes ostensibly impermissible conduct permissible. In 1930, a number of nations signed the London Naval Treaty. That treaty required that no ship sink a merchant vessel "without having first placed

---

[5] Taylor, p. 36. There is an ambiguity in this quotation that should be noted. Taylor may not mean that the laws of war permit an exception in this kind of case. He may mean only that the law is uncertain, that he knows of no court decision which authoritatively declares this to be either a war crime or a permitted exception. It is sufficient for my purposes if he means the weaker claim, that it is an open question.

A more serious objection to my assertion that I am accurately characterizing the existing laws of war would call attention to the following quotation from the *U.S. Army Field Manual, The Law of Land Warfare*, Chap. I, sec. I.3:

"The law of war places limits on the exercise of a belligerent's power in the interests mentioned in paragraph 2 and requires that belligerents refrain from employing any kind or degree of violence which is not actually necessary for military purposes and that they conduct hostilities with regard for the principles of humanity and chivalry.

"The prohibitory effect of the law of war is not minimized by 'military necessity' which has been defined as that principle which justifies those measures not forbidden by international law which are indispensable for securing the complete submission of the enemy as soon as possible. Military necessity has generally been rejected as a defence for acts forbidden by the customary and conventional laws of war inasmuch as the latter have been developed and framed with consideration for the concept of military necessity."

I leave it to the reader to decide exactly what this means. It seems to anticipate, on the one hand, that the laws of war and the doctrine of military necessity can conflict. It seems to suppose, on the other hand, that substantial conflicts will not arise either because the laws of war prohibit militarily unnecessary violence or because they were formulated with considerations of military necessity in mind. In substance, the view expressed in the quotation is not inconsistent with the conception I am delineating.

passengers, crew and ship's papers in a place of safety." The provisions of this treaty were regularly violated in the Second World War. Nonetheless these violations were not war crimes punished at Nuremberg. This is so, says Taylor, for two reasons. First, the doctrine of military necessity makes the treaty unworkable. If submarines are to be effective instrumentations of war, they cannot surface before they attack merchant ships, nor can they stand around waiting to pick up survivors. The answer is not that it is wrong to use submarines. Rather it is that in the interest of military necessity the prohibitions of the treaty cease to be prohibitions. And second, even if considerations of military necessity were not decisive here, violations of the London treaty would still not have been war crimes because the treaty was violated by both sides during the Second World War. And nothing is properly a war crime, says Taylor (at least in the absence of a genuine international tribunal) if both sides engage in the conduct in question.

As long as enforcement of the laws of war is left to the belligerents themselves, whether during the course of hostilities or by the victors at the conclusion, the scope of their application must be limited by the extent to which they have been observed by the enforcing party. To punish the foe—especially the vanquished foe—for conduct in which the enforcing nation has engaged, would be so grossly inequitable as to discredit the laws of themselves.[6]

Finally, the question of the legality of aerial warfare is especially instructive and important. Once more I take Telford Taylor's analysis to be illustrative of the conception I have been trying to delineate. The bombing of cities was, he observes, not punished at Nuremberg and is not a war crime. Why not? For the two reasons he has already given. Since it was engaged in by the Allies—and on a much more intensive level than by the Germans or the Japanese—it would have been improper to punish the Germans and the Japanese for what we also did. But more importantly the bombing of cities with almost any kind of bomb imaginable is perfectly proper because bombing is an important instrument of the war.

There is nothing illegal about bombing population centers; there is nothing impermissible about using anti-personnel bombs. To begin with, it is not a war crime because aerial bombardments were not punished at Nuremberg. Nor, more importantly, should they be proscribed. For bombs are important weapons of war. But what about the fact that they appear to violate the general prohibition against the killing of non-combatants?

[6] Taylor, p. 39. Once again, there is an ambiguity here. Taylor may mean that it is procedurally unfair to punish the loser but not the victor for the same act. He may also mean, though, that there is a principle at work which legitimizes a practice which was previously proscribed on the ground that the practice has now become widespread. He does not distinguish these two positions in his book and he seems to me to hold both.

They certainly do end up killing lots of civilians, Taylor concedes. But that just cannot be helped because a bomb is, unfortunately, the kind of weapon that cannot discriminate between combatants and non-combatants. What is more, bombing is an inherently inaccurate undertaking. The pilots of fast moving planes—no matter how carefully they try to annihilate only enemy soldiers—will invariably miss lots of times. And if there are civilians nearby, they will, regrettably, be wiped out instead.

The general test for the impermissibility of bombing is, says Taylor, clear enough. Bombing is a war crime if and only if there is no proportioned relationship between the military objective sought to be achieved by the bombing and the degree of destruction caused by it.

This collection of specific prohibitions, accepted conventions, and general excusing and justifying conditions is the conception of the laws of war with which I am concerned. I want now to examine the deficiencies of such a view and to indicate the respects in which I find unconvincing the two general arguments mentioned at the beginning of the paper.

II

I indicated at the outset that one argument for the importance and value of the laws of war is that they in some sense reflect, embody or give effect to fundamental moral distinctions and considerations. I can help to make clear the character of my criticism of this argument in the following fashion. There are at least three grounds upon which we might criticize any particular criminal code. We might criticize it on the ground that it contained a particular criminal law that ought not to be there because the behavior it proscribed was behavior that it was not morally wrong for people to engage in.[7]

So, we might criticize our criminal code because it punishes the use of marijuana even though there is nothing wrong with using marijuana. Or, we might criticize a criminal code because it is *incomplete*. It proscribes a number of things that ought to be proscribed and regards them with the appropriate degree of seriousness, but it omits to punish something that ought, *ceteris paribus*, to be included in the criminal law. So, we might criticize our criminal code because it fails to make criminal the commission of acts of deliberate racial discrimination.

Compare both of these cases with a criminal code that made criminal only various thefts. Such a code would be incomplete in a different way from the code that just omitted to prohibit racial discrimination. It would be systematically incomplete in the sense that it omitted to forbid many

---

[7] I recognize that this is vague. For my purposes it does not matter. It does not matter, that is, whether the law is criticized because the behavior is not immoral, or because the behavior is immoral but not harmful, or because the behavior is harmful but not sufficiently so to justify the use of the criminal law, etc.

types of behavior that any decent criminal code ought to prohibit. It would, I think, be appropriate to describe such a code as a morally incoherent one and to regard this incoherence, by itself, as a very serious defect. The code would be incoherent in that it could not be rendered intelligible either in terms of the moral principles that ought to underlie any criminal code or even in terms of the moral principles that justified making theft illegal.[8] One could not, we might say, make moral sense out of a scheme that regarded as most seriously wrong (and hence a fit subject for the criminal law) a variety of harmful acts against property, but which permitted, and treated as in this sense legitimate, all acts of violence against persons. It would be proper to regard such a code as odious, it should be noted, even though one thought that thefts were, on the whole, among the sorts of things that should be prohibited by the criminal law.

As I hope the following discussion makes clear, it is this last kind of criticism that I am making of the conception of the laws of war set out above. So conceived, the laws of war possess the kind of incompleteness and incoherence that would be present in a criminal code that punished only theft.

The chief defense to the accusation that the laws of war are in this sense incomplete and incoherent would, I think, rest on the claim that the laws of war are complete and coherent—the difference is that they set a lower standard for behavior than that set by the typical criminal code. Even in war, so the argument would go, morality has some place; there are some things that on moral grounds ought not be permitted even in time of war. Admittedly, the argument might continue, the place to draw the line between what is permissible and impermissible is different, is "lower," in time of war than in time of peace, but the guiding moral principles and criteria remain the same. The laws of war can quite plausibly be seen as coherently reflecting, even if imperfectly, this lower but still intelligible morality of war. Thus, the argument might conclude the laws of war are not like a criminal code that only punishes theft. Rather, they are like a criminal code that only punishes intentional homicides, rapes, and serious assaults and thefts.

Although I do not argue the point at length in this paper, I accept the idea that even in war morality has some place. What I do challenge, therefore, is the claim that the laws of war as I have sketched them can be plausibly understood as reflecting or embodying in any coherent fashion this lower, but still intelligible morality of war.

Consider first the less permissive (and hence morally more attractive)

---

8 Of course, there is still a fourth possible code. It would make illegal only those things that it is morally right and permissible to do, or that ought, on other grounds, never be made illegal. Such a code would certainly be the very worst of all. I am not claiming, it should be emphasized, that the laws of war are like this fourth possible case.

conception of the laws of war, the conception that does not always permit military necessity to be an exception or an excuse. It cannot be plausibly claimed, I submit, that this scheme of what in war is permissible and impermissible reflects simply a lowering of our basic moral expectations or standards. The most serious problem, I think, is that the distinction between combatants and non-combatants is not respected by the laws of war —particularly as they relate to aerial warfare and the use of weapons of mass destruction. This constitutes a deviation in kind and not merely a diminution of standards in respect to our fundamental moral notions. This is so because the failure meaningfully to distinguish between combatants and non-combatants obliterates all concern for two basic considerations: the degree of choice that persons had in getting into the position in which they now find themselves, and the likelihood that they are or are about to be in a position to inflict harm on anyone else. The distinction between combatants and non-combatants is admittedly a crude one. Some non-combatants are able in reasonably direct ways to inflict harm on others, e.g. workers in a munitions factory. And some non-combatants may very well have knowingly and freely put themselves in such a position. Concomitantly, many combatants may have been able to exercise very little choice in respect to the assumption of the role of a combatant, e.g. soldiers who are drafted into an army under circumstances where the penalties for refusing to accept induction are very severe. Difficulties such as these might make it plausible to argue that the laws of war cannot reasonably be expected to capture perfectly these distinctions. That is to say, it would, I think, be intelligible to argue that it is unreasonable to expect anyone to be able to distinguish the conscripts from the volunteers in the opponent's army. It would, perhaps, even be plausible to argue (although less convincingly, I think) that civilians who are engaged in activities that are directly connected with the prosecution of the war can reasonably be expected to understand that they will be subject to attack. If the laws of war even preserved a distinction between soldiers, munitions workers, and the like on the one hand and children, the aged, and the infirm on the other, one might maintain that the laws of war did succeed in retaining— at a low level and in an imprecise way—a distinction of fundamental moral importance. But, as we have seen, the laws of war that relate to aerial warfare and the use of weapons of mass destruction do not endeavor to preserve a distinction of even this crudity.

A similar point can be made about those laws of war that deal primarily with combatants. Here, though, there is a bit more that can be said on behalf of the rationality of some of the relevant laws of war. The strongest case is that for the special, relatively unequivocal prohibitions against the mistreatment of prisoners of war and the infliction of damage upon hospitals and medical personnel. Someone might object that these make no sense, that there is no difference between attacking a wounded soldier in a hospital and attacking an unwounded soldier with a weapon against which he is defenseless, e.g. strafing or bombing infantrymen armed with rifles. Similarly, it might be objected that there is no coherent principle that distinguishes the wrongness of killing (generally) prisoners of war and the permissibility of killing enemy soldiers who are asleep.

Such an objection would be too strong, for there does seem to be a morally relevant distinction between these two kinds of cases. It is the distinction between those who have obviously been rendered incapable of fighting back (the wounded and the prisoners of war) and those who only may be incapable of fighting back.

It would be wrong, however, to make too much of this point. In the first place, for the reasons suggested earlier, distinctions among combatants are morally less significant than the distinction between combatants and non-combatants. And in the second place, the principle justifying this distinction among combatants is a pretty crude and not wholly attractive one. In particular, it does not very convincingly, I think, establish the obvious appropriateness of using deadly force against combatants who pose no direct threat and who are defenseless against the force used.[9]

Be that as it may, this is the strongest case for these particular laws of war. There are others for which no comparable rationale can be urged. Thus, it cannot be argued successfully that the laws of war concerning combatants can be generally understood to be a reflection or embodiment of a lower, but coherent set of standards relating to how combatants ought to behave toward one another. More specifically, it cannot be maintained, as persons sometimes seek to maintain, that the laws of war relating to which weapons are permissible and which are impermissible possess a similar coherence. Someone might argue, for example, that there are some ways of killing a person that are worse, more inhumane and savage than other ways. War both permits and requires that combatants kill one another in a variety of circumstances in which, in any other context, it would be impermissible to do so. Nonetheless, so the argument might continue, the laws of war do record and give effect to this perception that some techniques of killing are so abhorrent that they ought not be employed even in war.

Once again, my response is not a direct challenge to the claim that it may be possible to distinguish on some such ground among methods of killing. Indeed, were such a distinction to be preserved by the laws of war,

[9] It is, for example, legitimate to bomb the barracks of soldiers who are not at the front lines, to ambush unsuspecting (and possibly even unarmed) enemy soldiers, and to use all sorts of weapons against which the particular combatants may be completely defenseless. At some stage it just ceases to be very satisfactory to insist that this is unobjectionable because the combatants could defend themselves if they chose and because they chose to be combatants in the first place. For both claims about the combatants may in fact be false and known to be such.

important and desirable alterations in the nature of war would almost surely have to take place. What I am concerned to deny is that the laws of war that deal with weapons can be plausibly viewed as reflecting distinctions of genuine moral significance. Since it is permissible to kill an enemy combatant with an anti-personnel bomb, a nuclear weapon, or even a flame-thrower, it just cannot be plausibly maintained that it is a war crime to kill a combatant with poison gas because it is morally worse to use poison gas than to invoke the former methods of human destruction.

It must be observed that so far I have been concerned with that morally more attractive view of the laws of war which does not permit a general exception to all of the laws on grounds of military necessity. Once such a general exception is permitted, whatever plausibility and coherence there is to this conception of the laws of war is diminished virtually to the vanishing point. That this is so can be shown in the following fashion.

To begin with, it is important to notice that the doctrine of "military necessity" is employed in an ambiguous and misleading fashion. "Necessity" leads us naturally to think of various sorts of extreme circumstances which excuse, if they do not justify, otherwise impermissible behavior. Thus, the exception to the rule about taking prisoners is, perhaps, a case where necessitarian language does fit: if the prisoners are taken by the patrol deep in enemy territory the captors will themselves almost surely be captured or killed. They cannot, in such circumstances, be held to the rule against killing prisoners because it is "necessary" that the prisoners be killed.

Now, one may not be convinced that necessitarian language is appropriately invoked even in this case. But what should nonetheless be apparent is the inappropriateness of describing the doctrine that justifies aerial warfare, submarine warfare, or the use of flame-throwers as one of military *necessity*. Necessity has nothing whatsoever to do with the legitimacy of the aerial bombardment of cities or the use of other weapons of mass destruction. To talk of military necessity in respect to such practices is to surround the practice with an aura of justification that is in no way deserved. The appeal to the doctrine of military necessity is in fact an appeal to a doctrine of military utility. The laws of war really prohibit (with only a few minor exceptions) some wrongful practices that also lack significant military value. The laws of war permit and treat as legitimate almost any practice, provided only that there is an important military advantage to be secured.

The more that *this* doctrine of military necessity permeates the conception of the laws of war, the less intelligible and attractive is the claim that the laws of war are a coherent, complete, or admirable code of behavior— even for the jungle of warfare. Given the pervasiveness of this doctrine of military utility, the laws of war are reducible in large measure to the principle that in war it is still wrong to kill (or maim or torture) another per- 491 son for no reason at all, or for reasons wholly unrelated to the outcome of the war. But the laws of war also tell us what it is permissible and legitimate to do in time of war. Here the governing principle is that it is legitimate, appropriate (and sometimes obligatory) to do almost anything to anybody, provided only that what is done is reasonably related to an important military objective. It is, in short, to permit almost all possible moral claims to be overridden by considerations of military utility. Whatever else one may wish to claim for the preservation of such a system of the laws of war, one cannot, therefore, claim that they deserve either preservation or respect because of the connection these laws maintain with the idea of morality.

Finally, it should be noted, too, that the case is hardly improved by the condition that a practice which is otherwise prohibited ceases to be so, if the practice was engaged in by both sides. As I indicated earlier, this may not be the way to interpret the argument for not punishing the Germans for, say, engaging in unrestricted submarine warfare. But if part of the idea of a war crime is, as some of the literature surely suggests it is, that an offense ceases to be an offense once the practice becomes uniform, then this, too, must count against the possibility of making the case for this conception of the laws of war rest on moral grounds.

III

As I indicated at the outset, there is another way to approach the laws of war and to argue for their worth and significance. This route emphasizes the beneficial consequences of having and enforcing the laws of war, and is relatively unconcerned with the "intrinsic" morality of the rules. The arguments in support of such a view go something like this.

Despite some real fuzziness about the edges, (or even closer to the center) many of the laws of war are reasonably precise. A number of the laws of war are written down and embodied in rather specific conventions and agreements. It is relatively easy, therefore, to tell, at least in a good many cases, what is a war crime and what is not. It is certainly simpler to decide, for example, what constitutes a war crime than it is to determine whether a crime against peace or humanity has been committed. And the fact that the laws of war are more readily ascertainable has certain important consequences of its own.

To begin with, there is first the intellectual confidence that comes from dealing with rules that are written down and that are reasonably specific and precise. More to the point, it is this feature which makes it quite fair to hold persons responsible for violations of the laws of war. The laws of war can be ascertained in advance by the individuals concerned, they can be applied impartially by an appropriate tribunal, and they can be independently "verified" by disinterested observers. They are, in sum, more like typical criminal laws than any of the other rules or principles that relate to war.

A second argument for the primacy of the laws of war also concerns their enforcibility.

It goes like this. It is certainly not wholly unrealistic to imagine the laws of war being enforced, even while a war is going on. More importantly it is not wholly unrealistic to imagine the laws of war being enforced by a country against members of its own armed forces, as well as against members of the opposing army. Such has indeed been the case in the United States as well as in other countries. Once again, the contrast with crimes against peace is striking. It is quite unlikely that the perpetrators of crime against peace, who will be the leaders of the enemy, will ever be caught until the war is over. It is surely unlikely, therefore, that the existence of rules making the waging of aggressive war a crime will ever deter leaders from embarking on aggressive war. If they win, they have nothing to fear. If they lose, they expect to die whether they are guilty or not.

The case is more bleak still where the perpetrators of crimes against peace are the leaders of one's own country. While one can in theory imagine the courts of a country holding the leaders of the country liable for waging aggressive war, this is a theoretical but not a practical possibility. While a war is going on the one thing that national institutions are most unlikely to do is to subject the conduct of the leaders of the nation to cool, critical scrutiny. The leaders of a country are hardly likely to be deterred by the prospect that the courts of their own country will convict them of having committed crimes against peace.

The situation in respect to crimes against war is markedly different in both cases. Soldiers fighting on the opposing side do run a real risk of being caught while the war is on. If they know that they may be captured, and if they also know that they may be punished for any war crimes they have committed, this can have a significant effect on the way they behave toward their opponents. Similarly, the knowledge that they may be punished by their own side for misbehavior toward the enemy can influence the way soldiers in the army go about fighting the war. Hence there is a genuine prospect that the members of both armies will behave differently just because there are laws of war than they would have were there no such laws.

What all of this shows is that the laws of war will influence the behavior of persons in time of war. There are additional arguments, connected with those that have just been presented, to show that the behavior will be affected in ways that are both desirable and important.

The first such argument is that, despite all of their imperfections, the laws of war do represent the consensus that does at present exist about how persons ought to behave in time of war. The fact that the laws of war are embodied in conventions and treaties, most of which have been ex- 493 plicitly ratified by almost all the countries of the world, means that we are dealing with conduct about whose character there can be relatively little genuine disagreement. To be sure, the conventions may not go as far or be as precise as we might like. The laws of war may be unambitious in scope and even incoherent in the sense described earlier. Nonetheless, they do constitute those rules and standards about which there is universal agreement concerning what may not be done, even in time of war. And the fact that all nations have consented to these laws and agreed upon them gives them an authority that is almost wholly lacking anywhere else in the area of morality and war.

Closely related to, but distinguishable from, the above is the claim that past experience provides independent evidence of the importance and efficacy of having laws of war. They have worked to save human life. If we look at wars that have been fought, we see that the laws of war have had this effect. Perhaps this was because the participants were deterred by the threat of punishment. Perhaps this was because the laws of war embody standards of behavior that men, even in time of war, thought it worth respecting. Perhaps this was because countries recognized a crude kind of self-interest in adhering to the conventions as a means of securing adherence by the other side. It does not matter very much why the laws of war were respected to the degree that they were—and they were respected to some extent in the total wars of the Twentieth Century. What matters is that they were respected. Telford Taylor has put the matter this way:

Violated or ignored as they often are, enough of the rules are observed enough of the time so that mankind is very much better off with them than without them. The rules for the treatment of civilian populations in occupied countries are not as susceptible to technological change as rules regarding the use of weapons in combat. If it were not regarded as wrong to bomb military hospitals, they would be bombed all of the time instead of some of the time.

It is only necessary to consider the rules on taking prisoners in the setting of the Second World War to realize the enormous saving of life for which they have been responsible. Millions of French, British, German and Italian soldiers captured in Western Europe and Africa were treated in general compliance with the Hague and Geneva requirements, and returned home at the end of the war. German and Russian prisoners taken in the eastern front did not fare nearly so well and died in captivity by the millions, but many survived. Today there is surely much to criticize about the handling of prisoners on both sides of the Vietnam war, but at least many of them are alive, and that is because the belligerents are reluctant to flout the laws of war too openly.[10]

The final argument for the preservation of the laws of war concerns the effect of the laws—or their absence—upon the moral sensibilities of individuals. Were we to do away with the laws of war, were we to concede

[10] Taylor, p. 40.

that in time of war anything and everything is permissible, the effect upon the capacity of persons generally to respond in accordance with the dictates of morality would be diminished rather than enhanced. This, too, is one of Telford Taylor's main theses. "All in all," he argues, "this has been a pretty bloody century and people do not seem to shock very easily, as much of the popular reaction to the report of Son My made depressingly plain. The kind of world in which all efforts to mitigate the horrors of war are abandoned would hardly be a world sensitive to the consequences [of total war]."[11]

The consequences for military sensibilities are at least as important, Taylor continues, as are the consequences for civilian sensibilities. The existence of the laws of war and the insistence upon their importance prevent combatants from becoming completely dehumanized and wholly vicious by their participation in war. The laws of war, Taylor asserts, are

... necessary to diminish the corrosive effect of mortal combat on the participants. War does not confer a license to kill for personal reasons—to gratify perverse impulses, or to put out of the way anyone who appears obnoxious, or to whose welfare the soldier is indifferent. War is not a license at all, but an obligation to kill for reasons of state; it does not countenance the infliction of suffering for its own sake or for revenge.

Unless troops are trained and required to draw the distinction between military and nonmilitary killings, and to retain such respect for the value of life that unnecessary death and destruction will continue to repel them, they may lose the sense for that distinction for the rest of their lives. The consequence would be that many returning soldiers would be potential murderers.[12]

It should not be difficult to foresee the sorts of objections that I believe can most tellingly be raised against these arguments. I will state them very briefly.

It is, to begin with, far less obvious than the argument would have it that the laws of war possess the kind of specificity we typically require of an ordinary criminal law. In particular, the pervasive character of the doctrine of military "necessity" comes close to leaving as unambiguously criminal only senseless or gratuitous acts of violence against the enemy.

Similarly, the fact that countries have been able to agree upon certain conventions does not seem to me to be a matter of particular significance. At the very least, it is certainly a mistake to infer from this fact of agreement that we have somehow succeeded in identifying those types of behavior that really matter the most. Indeed, it is at least as likely as not, that agreement was forthcoming just because the issues thereby regulated were not of great moment. And it is surely far more likely than not that

11 Taylor, p. 39.

12 Taylor, pp. 40–41.

agreement was forthcoming just because it was perceived that adherence to these laws would not affect very much the way wars got fought.

This leads me to what seem to me to be the two most significant criticisms that can be made against the assertion that beneficial consequences of various sorts flow from respecting and enforcing the laws of war. There is first the claim that adherence to the laws of war teaches important moral lessons (or prevents soldiers from becoming totally corrupt). Just what sort of things about killing do the laws of war (in theory, let alone in practice) teach soldiers; will someone who has mastered the distinctions established by the laws of war thereby be less a potential murderer? It is difficult to see that getting straight about the laws of war will permit someone to learn important moral lessons and to maintain a decent respect for the value of human life. It is difficult to be at all confident that soldiers who have mastered the distinctions established by the laws of war will be for that reason turned away from the path of murder. This is so just because the laws of war possess the kind of incompleteness and incoherence I described earlier. We can, of course, teach soldiers to obey the laws of war, whatever their content may happen to be. But we must not confuse that truth with the question of whether we will have, through that exercise, taught them to behave in morally responsible ways.[13]

The issue is made more doubtful, still, because the laws of war inescapably permit as well as prohibit; they make some conduct criminal and other conduct legitimate. The evidence is hardly all in, either from the Twentieth Century in general or Vietnam in particular. It will probably never be in. But it surely appears to be at least as likely as not that the laws of war—if they have taught anything at all—have taught soldiers and civilians alike that it is permissible and lawful to kill and maim and destroy, provided only that it will help to win the war. And I do think this constitutes morally retrograde movement.

But this still leaves unanswered what may appear to be the most important argument of all, the argument put forward by Telford Taylor and others that the laws of war are important and deserving of respect because they work. Isn't it sufficient that even somewhat irrational, incoherent and incomplete rules have the consequences of saving lives? Even if it is permissible to kill women and children whenever military necessity requires it, isn't it important to save the lives of those women and children whose deaths are not necessitated by military considerations?

The argument is both sound and deceptive. Of course it is better to save some lives rather than none at all. If adhering to the laws of war as we now have them will save the lives of persons (and especially "innocent"

---

13 Unless, of course, one holds the view that teaching persons to obey orders, or even laws, whatever they may happen to be is an important constituent of the curriculum of moral education. It is not a view I hold.

persons) in time of war, that is a good reason (but not a decisive one) for maintaining these laws of war. If punishing soldiers (like Lieutenant Calley) for war crimes will keep other soldiers from gratuitously killing women and children, among others, in Vietnam, that is a good reason for punishing persons for the commission of these war crimes.

But to concede this is not to put an end to the matter at hand. For reasons I have tried to make plain there are costs as well as gains from concentrating our attention upon the laws of war and their enforcement. There is to put it simply a risk to human life that is quite substantial. The risk is that we inevitably and necessarily legitimate behavior that is morally indefensible, that is, truly criminal. The cost—and it is a cost in human life—is, for example, that the sanitized war in Vietnam that would result from a scrupulous adherence to the laws of war will increase still further our tolerance for and acceptance of the horror, the slaughter, and the brutality that is the essence of Twentieth Century war. There is something genuinely odious about a code of behavior that says: if there is a conflict between the attainment of an important military objective and one or more of the prohibitions of the laws of war, it is the prohibitions that quite properly are to give way. And there is something dangerous about a point of view that accepts such a system and directs us to concentrate our energies and our respect upon its enforcement. The corrosive effect of living in a world in which we embrace such a code and insist upon its value seems to me appreciably more dangerous than the effect of a refusal to accord a position of primacy to the sometimes bizarre, often morally incoherent laws of war.

The answer is not, of course, to throw out the laws of war with a view toward inculcating in us all the belief that in war anything goes. But neither is it an acceptable answer to take as given the nature of modern war and modern weapons and to conform, as best one can, the laws of war to their requirements. This, it seems to me, is the fatal flaw in the conception of the laws of war with which I have been concerned. The beginning of a morally defensible position is surely to be found in a different conception of the laws of war. A conception sufficiently ambitious that it refuses to regard as immutable the character of contemporary warfare and weaponry, and that requires instead, that war itself change so as to conform to the demands of morality.

Selected Bibliography

Ginzberg, Robert (ed.). *The Critique of War*. Chicago: Henry Regnery, 1969.

Honderich, Ted. "Democratic Violence," *Philosophy and Public Affairs*, Vol. 2, No. 2 (1973), 190.

Merleau-Ponty, Maurice. *Humanism and Terror*. Boston: Beacon Press, 1969.

Levinson, Sanford. "Responsibility for Crimes of War," *Philosophy and Public Affairs,* Vol. 2, No. 3 (1973), 244.

Murphy, Jeffrie (ed.). *Civil Disobedience and Violence*. Belmont, Calif.: Wadsworth Publishing Co., 1971.

Nagel, Thomas. "War and Massacre," *Philosophy and Public Affairs,* Vol. 1, No. 2 (1972), 123.

Shaffer, Jerome (ed.). *Essays on Violence*. New York: David McKay, 1971.

Wasserstrom, Richard. "On the Morality of War: A Preliminary Inquiry," *Stanford Law Review,* Vol. 21, No. 6 (1969), 1627.

Wasserstrom, Richard (ed.). *War and Morality*. Belmont, Calif.: Wadsworth Publishing Co., 1969.

Wasserstrom, Richard. "The Relevance of Nuremberg," *Philosophy and Public Affairs,* Vol. 1, No. 1 (1972), 22.

Wasserstrom, Richard. "The Responsibility of Individuals for War Crimes," in Virgina Held, Sidney Morgenbesser, and Thomas Nagel (eds.), *Philosophy, Morality and International Affairs,* New York: Oxford University Press, 1974.

Wells, Donald. "How Much Can 'The Just War' Justify?", *The Journal of Philosophy,* Vol. 66, No. 23 (1969), 619.

Wells, Donald. *The War Myth*. New York: Pegasus, 1967.

Wolff, Robert Paul. "On Violence," *The Journal of Philosophy,* Vol. 66, No. 19 (1969), 601.